# NAVAL SEAMEN'S WOMEN IN NINETEENTH-CENTURY BRITAIN

# Naval Seamen's Women in Nineteenth-Century Britain

*Melanie Holihead*

THE BOYDELL PRESS

© Melanie Holihead 2024

*All Rights Reserved.* Except as permitted under current legislation
no part of this work may be photocopied, stored in a retrieval system,
published, performed in public, adapted, broadcast,
transmitted, recorded or reproduced in any form or by any means,
without the prior permission of the copyright owner

The right of Melanie Holihead to be identified as
the author of this work has been asserted in accordance with
sections 77 and 78 of the Copyright, Designs and Patents Act 1988

First published 2024
The Boydell Press, Woodbridge

ISBN 978 1 83765 011 8

The Boydell Press is an imprint of Boydell & Brewer Ltd
PO Box 9, Woodbridge, Suffolk IP12 3DF, UK
and of Boydell & Brewer Inc.
668 Mt Hope Avenue, Rochester, NY 14620–2731, USA
website: www.boydellandbrewer.com

A CIP catalogue record for this book is available
from the British Library

The publisher has no responsibility for the continued existence or accuracy of URLs
for external or third-party internet websites referred to in this book, and does not
guarantee that any content on such websites is, or will remain, accurate or appropriate

*To Phoebe*

# CONTENTS

| | |
|---|---|
| *List of Illustrations* | viii |
| *Foreword by N.A.M. Rodger* | xii |
| *Preface* | xiv |
| *Acknowledgements* | xviii |
| *List of Abbreviations* | xx |
| *Terms Used* | xxii |
| *Weights, Measures and Currency* | xxiv |
| Introduction | 1 |
| 1 The Naval Context | 15 |
| 2 Naval Women | 44 |
| 3 Place and Birthplace | 67 |
| 4 Marriage | 74 |
| 5 Children | 99 |
| 6 Household Structure | 114 |
| 7 Home Environment | 134 |
| 8 Work | 144 |
| 9 Making Ends Meet | 157 |
| 10 Parish Relief and Prostitution | 178 |
| 11 Crime | 201 |
| 12 Marital Violence | 217 |
| 13 Marital Complexities | 232 |
| 14 Farewells, Returns, and Between | 254 |
| 15 Death | 275 |
| Conclusion | 300 |
| *Bibliography* | 305 |
| *Index* | 325 |

# ILLUSTRATIONS

## FIGURES

| | | |
|---|---|---|
| 1 | Seamen's declarations in ship's allotment register. National Archives (TNA) Kew, Navy Board, and Admiralty, Accountant General's Department: Registers of Allotments and Allotment Declarations, ADM 27 (1792–1852): ADM 27/110/105-6. Reproduced under licence by kind permission of The National Archives, Kew | 7 |
| 2 | Allotment pay bill. TNA, Navy Board, and Admiralty, Accountant General's Department: Registers of Allotments and Allotment Declarations, ADM 27/109/543. Reproduced under licence by kind permission of The National Archives, Kew | 32 |
| 3 | Number of allottees receiving multiple payments in different capacities (n=112). Total allotments per person shown in brackets | 47 |
| 4 | Distribution of allotments per men's rating category (n=1,328) | 49 |
| 5 | Wives' ages per husbands' status (n=808) | 49 |
| 6 | Birthplaces of allottee wives born outside Portsea Island (n=429) | 68 |
| 7 | Brides' fathers' occupations per parish marriage records, 1850–51 | 77 |
| 8 | Grooms' fathers' occupations per parish marriage records, 1850–51 | 79 |
| 9 | Naval grooms' age at marriage, 1815–51 (n=342) | 86 |
| 10 | Naval brides' age at marriage, 1815–51 (n=342) | 86 |
| 11 | Naval brides' age at first marriage (n=176) | 94 |
| 12 | Naval family size, per 1851 Portsea Island census (n=586) | 102 |
| 13 | Mean average number of naval and civilian couples' children; per 1851 Portsea Island census, and Robert Woods, *The Demography of Victorian England and Wales* (2000), p. 116 | 103 |

| | | |
|---|---|---|
| 14 | Comparative size of naval and civilian families, per 1861 Portsea Island census | 105 |
| 15 | Naval wives' estimated age at birth of first surviving child (n=85) | 113 |
| 16 | Relationships of householders to co-resident (accommodated) married allottees (n=153) | 122 |
| 17 | Genogram of Spratt household. Genogram model based upon that used by Laslett (Peter Laslett, 'Introduction', in Peter Laslett and Richard Wall (eds), *Household and Family in Past Time* (Cambridge, 1972), 1–89, at p. 42). Reproduced, with alterations as described in Chapter Six, by permission of the Licensor through PLSClear | 126 |
| 18 | Genogram of Oliver/Allen household. Genogram model based upon that used by Laslett (Peter Laslett, 'Introduction', in Peter Laslett and Richard Wall (eds), *Household and Family in Past Time* (Cambridge, 1972), 1–89, at p. 42). Reproduced, with alterations as described in Chapter Six, by permission of the Licensor through PLSClear | 128 |
| 19 | Genogram of Davey/Leese/Plummer/Matthias household. Genogram model based upon that used by Laslett (Peter Laslett, 'Introduction', in Peter Laslett and Richard Wall (eds), *Household and Family in Past Time* (Cambridge, 1972), 1–89, at p. 42). Reproduced, with alterations as described in Chapter Six, by permission of the Licensor through PLSClear | 130 |
| 20 | Hobbs Court, Portsea; covered alley entrance arrowed. Portsmouth History Centre (PHC), Portsmouth, Ordnance Survey, 1:500 scale map of Portsea, showing Hobbs Court and Dean Street, PHC 114A/OS2/23, Hampshire Sheet LXXXIII.7.25 (C10) (1864). Detail; arrow and house numbers added. Reproduced, with these alterations, by kind permission of Portsmouth Library & Archive Service, Portsmouth City Council. All rights reserved | 135 |
| 21 | Havant Street, Portsea. Peter N. Rogers, *Portsmouth & Southsea* (Stroud, 1996), p. 32 (n.d.). Attempts to identify and locate the current copyright holder for this image have been unsuccessful | 137 |

## Illustrations

22 Occupancy of Havant Street per allotment declarations and 1851 Portsea Island census. Portsmouth History Centre (PHC), Portsmouth, Ordnance Survey, 1:500 scale map of Portsea, showing Havant Street (upper part), PHC 114A/OS2/15/1, Hampshire Sheet LXXXIII.7.19 (B9) (1864), and Portsmouth, Portsmouth History Centre (PHC), Ordnance Survey, 1:500 scale map of Portsea, showing Havant Street (lower part), PHC 114A/OS2/21/2, Hampshire Sheet LXXXIII.7.24 (B10) (1864); 1851 census: HO107/1658, fol. 226, pp. 1–24. Map images cropped, conjoined horizontally, symbols added. Reproduced, with these alterations, by kind permission of Portsmouth Library & Archive Service, Portsmouth City Council. All rights reserved 140

23 Naval wives' monthly rent, as percentage of husbands' pay per *Navy List* 1851 (n=157). Joseph Allen, *The New Navy List* (Whitehall, 1851), pp. 199–210 (selected text) 141

24 Occupations of female allottees, per 1851 Portsea Island census (n=1,549) 148

25 Age-distribution of allottees having occupations stated in 1851 Portsea Island census (n=417) 149

26 Charges against female defendants, Portsea Island courts 1848–52 (n=876) 203

27 Genogram of Greenleaf family. Genogram model based upon that used by Laslett (Peter Laslett, 'Introduction', in Peter Laslett and Richard Wall (eds), *Household and Family in Past Time* (Cambridge, 1972), 1–89, at p. 42). Reproduced, with alterations as described in Chapter Six, by permission of the Licensor through PLSClear 247

28 '"Home Again": a Sketch on the Deck of the *Discovery* at Portsmouth'. Godefroy Durand (*The Graphic*, 11 Nov. 1876), p. 476. Image © Illustrated London News/Mary Evans Picture Library. Reproduced by kind permission of the Mary Evans Picture Library 270

29 Allottee wives' age at death (n=190) 283

*Illustrations*

## TABLES

| 1 | Ship's company pay scales, per *Navy List* 1851 (extract) | 20 |
| 2 | Portsea Island allotments by category (n=2,300) | 44 |
| 3 | Mean age at first marriages | 88 |
| 4 | Notional weekly budget for £1 6s 6d average monthly allotment | 164 |

The author and publisher are grateful to all the institutions and individuals listed for permission to reproduce the materials in which they hold copyright. Every effort has been made to trace the copyright holders; apologies are offered for any omission, and the publisher will be pleased to add any necessary acknowledgement in subsequent editions.

# FOREWORD BY N.A.M. RODGER

Over the course of the last half-century, historians have greatly extended their coverage of naval social history. Within living memory, the view presented by authors writing in English was predominantly seen from the quarterdeck, if not indeed from the gentleman's club. The larger part of it was exclusively a story of officers' lives. The social history of the lower deck was not altogether forgotten, but the tone and attitude of the books of Michael Lewis, the best-known writer on British naval social history in the 1950s and 60s, were redolent of the Edwardian schoolmaster which he had been. His willingness to give some attention to the lives of common seamen distinguished him from his contemporaries, most of whom were only interested in officers, but he never used documents and scarcely attracted the attention of serious scholars. For Lewis and his contemporaries, indeed for most writers until recent years, it was obvious that all forms of naval history concerned officers and men, but not women. Historians were aware, of course, that naval men had wives and mothers, to say nothing of sisters, cousins and aunts, but their proper sphere was comic opera, not serious history. Only slowly did naval historians of the post-war era begin to take account of the social reality that their favourite service was the seagoing part of a social structure which in many dimensions involved and depended on women and children. The notable services rendered during the Second World War by the Women's Royal Naval Service could no longer be overlooked – especially as so many post-war naval officers married former Wrens and incorporated women into their personal naval careers in a way which would have been unthinkable to the Victorians.

There are still not a few people in the Navy, and even some historians, who grew up in a naval family while their father was away at sea. In the twenty-first century, however, it is still with a slight shock that one encounters a serious historical study based on extensive documentary research and devoted entirely to the ratings of the mid-Victorian Royal Navy. The documentary sources Melanie Holihead has used are so little known that many readers will probably be surprised to discover that the eighteenth- and nineteenth-century Navy was a pioneer in allowing naval ratings to 'allot' up to half their pay to their dependants at home. Painstaking analysis of these records has allowed Dr Holihead to dissect the home and family

*Foreword by N.A.M. Rodger*

lives of mid-Victorian sailors and their womenfolk in astonishing detail. In place of the handful of dubious anecdotes which sufficed until recently to entertain naval writers, we now have under high magnification the real story of the fortunes and misfortunes of hundreds of naval families, most of them headed for long periods by women alone while their husbands were at sea. As she explains, they had to learn – in many cases from their mothers or mothers-in-law who had been naval wives before them – 'how to cope with long separations; to raise a family without husbandly help; to effect domestic repairs unaided; to make decisions and undertake domestic tasks normally the province of husbands; to manage a household alone; to exercise authority over one's children; to budget on an allotment income that would never be more than half of a husband's already modest wage; and how to argue their corner when criticised for doing all that, and more.' It is a fascinating and moving study, and the social history of the Royal Navy will never be the same again.

N.A.M. Rodger
All Souls College, Oxford

# PREFACE

> It is only very recently that historians have realised that the experience of those wives who stayed at home ... is an integral and essential part of the ... story, as vital to our understanding of this vast panorama as the exploits of [their] men.[1]

With these words, Philip Payton's Foreword acknowledges the importance of Lesley Trotter's study of the stay-at-home wives of many thousands of Cornishmen who emigrated in the second half of the nineteenth century. Payton's words have a resonance beyond Cornwall, beyond Cornish wives. They may equally be applied to the subjects of this book, a community of nineteenth-century women who stayed at home while their husbands pursued a living. The near 1,600 individuals on whom this study is based were sisters, mothers and wives of lower-deck (non-officer) seamen of the Royal Navy, and foster-mothers of seamen's motherless children. Residents of a major naval port town, they stand proxy for countless thousands of other such women whose homes lay anywhere from Cape Cornwall to Cape Wrath. Irrespective of location, what they had in common was kinship with, and financial dependence on, a Royal Navy seaman of the mid-nineteenth century.

The British naval seaman is familiar to us from learned articles and books, popular fiction, television documentaries, drama series and films. Through these media we learn of the world he inhabited, the natural and man-made dangers he faced, his pay, uniforms, grievances, courage, trades and drinking habits. But as Nicholas Rodger observed, little attempt has been made to establish what life was like for

> ... the female half of the naval community as a whole: not the minority of women who went to sea, but the wives and mothers who stayed at home, bringing up small children, earning their living as best they might while their menfolk were at sea, enduring years of absence and uncertainty.[2]

---

[1] Philip Payton, 'Foreword', in Lesley Trotter (ed.), *The Married Widows of Cornwall: the Story of the Wives Left Behind by Emigration* (Cornwall, 2018), i–vii, at p. ii.

[2] N.A.M. Rodger, *The Command of the Ocean: a naval history of Britain, 1649–1815* (London, 2004), p. 407.

This book fills something of what Rodger termed 'an enormous void of ignorance' in naval social history.[3] The 'something' it delivers is an evidence-based insight into the lives, backgrounds and social conditions of a community of women who lived and worked and '[earned] their living as best they might' in the Royal Navy's premier port town of Portsmouth. These were real women, identifiable in their thousands via admiralty records, and locatable in the mid-century census. They endured environmental conditions no different from those endured by their civilian neighbours, and faced the same social restrictions and gendered expectations as other working-class women. Their connection with the Royal Navy, however, set them apart – from their non-naval working-class neighbours, and from the rest of society.

The book provides evidence of the women's origins, family backgrounds and everyday existence. It explores the challenges they faced while trying, over months and years, to survive in a world slow to appreciate the sacrifices they made, the support they provided to their men and, by proxy, to the Royal Navy. It identifies what set them apart from the rest of society, from neighbours with civilian husbands, even from neighbours whose husbands were serving in different Royal Navy ships, on different commissions in different oceans. It considers why popular assumptions, prejudices and pejorative imagery persisted within the wider community, and why the truer, more representative features of the women's lives were distorted or ignored, leaving the women themselves all but lost to history.

What emerges is a rounded, evidence-based picture of a familiar yet misinterpreted archetype. Some of the findings are unsurprising, some startling; all are concrete, and in that respect fresh. Seamen's women emerge as for the most part poor, living among other low earners and paupers. Their built environment was shoddy, overcrowded, disease-ridden and filthy, their port town community notorious for brawling, drunkenness and violence. To the reader familiar with urban and maritime history, none of that is news. What is new is evidence of seamen's women's place in those communities, and their participation in port town life.

The women were to be found in many a location, port town or other. In character and behaviour, however, they were uncommon. To survive without male protection they had to be resourceful, if not tough. It is arguable that naval seamen's women were tougher and more resourceful than their civilian peers, for when ships were at sea they had no seaman-husband, -son or -brother to speak for them, to plead with rent collectors, pawnbrokers or bailiffs, to discipline challenging children, to lug heavy loads from front step to scullery, repel importunate advances, or bolster

---

[3] *Ibid.*

their confidence, provide physical comfort, and keep their spirits up. The wives became, to borrow from Trotter, 'married widows'.[4] Unlike true widows, however, they could be regarded not as victims of cruel circumstance but of their own making, in that they had chosen to marry men whose livelihood took them away for months and years at a time. If sympathy for their lot were lacking, the lack lay in a perception that in choosing naval marriage seamen's women brought difficulties upon themselves. To borrow a phrase familiar in naval circles, 'If you can't take a joke, then you shouldn't have joined.'[5]

Their toughness sometimes got them into trouble with the law. We find them charged with offensive language, indecent behaviour, assaulting each other, stealing. Their disreputable conduct was described with glee by journalists who knew the tastes of a readership willing to have its prejudices confirmed via a drip-feed of mockery and disapproval which merely reinforced the popular image of Jack Tar's raucous, roistering Nancy. But the Nancies of cartoon and popular song do not represent the many thousand ordinary Marys and Sarahs and Elizas who, like the women featuring here, trudged along muddy unmetalled urban streets to collect their men's 'half-pay', and strove to eke it out from month to month. The picture revealed here is truer to life than cartoon, shanty and ballad would have us believe.

'[I]t is the business of the historian to plunge into the deep waters of the past and to bring up vanished lives.'[6] This book plunges into the past to bring up the vanished lives of a shoreside naval community. It is baffling that these lives were lost from sight for so long, for seamen's women were capable of affecting naval manpower and performance. When, as many did, they suffered poverty to the extent of facing admission to the workhouse, their men were prepared to abandon sea service in favour of better and more regularly paid employment on shore. The too-rapid turnover of valuable seamen, and the difficulty in recruiting replacements, were problems which in wartime necessitated the Royal Navy's taking politically unpopular measures. But recruitment and retention problems did not disappear when peace was declared and impressment suspended, for seamen's women continued to suffer poverty, and seamen continued to abandon sea service for employment on shore. If the Navy were not to

---

[4] Lesley Trotter, *The Married Widows of Cornwall: the story of the wives left behind by emigration* (Cornwall, 2018), *passim*.

[5] Rick Jolly and Tugg Willson, *Jackspeak: a guide to British naval slang and usage* (Torpoint, 2000), p. 244.

[6] N.A.M. Rodger, 'I want to be an Admiral', *London Review of Books*: 42:15 (2020), <https://www.lrb.co.uk/the-paper/v42/n15/n.a.m.-rodger/i-want-to-be-an-admiral> [accessed 22 April 2024].

continue to lose mature, experienced, skilled men it must do more than acknowledge seamen's women's circumstances and needs, and the part wives played in naval manning: it must take action. To reduce the impact of prolonged breadwinner absence upon naval families (and by extension upon the Navy itself), one of the largest government bodies of the day was thus moved to create the means by which seamen's women could receive financial support in their men's absence at sea. This, for its time, was an extraordinary development.

The book examines the documentary product of that corporate development, and uses it to bring the seaman's woman up from the deep waters of the past. By way of government-issued statistics and previous historical studies, secondary sources provide national, military, environmental, legal and social context against which new material is considered. This approach sets named individuals, their actions and major life events against a backdrop broad enough to encompass sea service and events in naval history, close enough to show the gas lamp on the street corner, the distance between front step and communal privy. The correlating of original admiralty records, census returns and parish records reveals trends and patterns previously hidden. As the focus narrows, named individuals appear, their reconstructed stories illustrating the challenges and choices confronting seamen's women in the port towns of nineteenth-century England.

Why should these women matter to the reader? At one level they matter because service in the Royal Navy features in many a family tree, to the extent where there are books written specifically to help the family historian trace his or her naval ancestor.[7] To be descended from a naval seaman necessarily involves a naval seaman's woman, and in these pages the reader may discern what life was like for female antecedents related to lower-deck men serving in Victoria's Navy. For this book to matter, however, it is not necessary for the reader to be a seafarer's descendant, or to have a particular interest in the Royal Navy. It is enough simply to be curious about a community of remarkable and remarkably ordinary people of whom too little notice has been taken, and whose story deserves to be told. They, as much as their men, are part of naval history.

---

[7] For example, Randolph Cock and N.A.M. Rodger, *A Guide to the Naval Records in the National Archives of the UK* (London, 2008), N.A.M. Rodger, *Naval Records for Genealogists* (Richmond, 1998), and Bruno Pappalardo, *Tracing Your Naval Ancestors* (Kew, Surrey, 2002).

# ACKNOWLEDGEMENTS

Many people were involved in the creation of this book. Chief among them is Professor N.A.M. (Nicholas) Rodger, historian of the Royal Navy. It was he who, when I told him I wanted to study lower-deck seamen's wives but had been unable to find secondary sources from which to embark upon the subject, encouraged me to go for it. I was right (he said, in answer to my question) in thinking that little had been written about naval seamen's women, but I was wrong (he said) to think that this meant it was a topic no self-respecting historian would touch. It is because of his support, guidance, kindness, forbearance and immense patience that I was able to fulfil my aim. To him my heartfelt and abiding thanks.

Thanks are due to the staff of the National Archives at Kew, especially those who helped me navigate the complex sub-categories of admiralty records. I'm grateful, too, to Katy Ball and the staff of Portsmouth City Museum, and to Dr John Stedman and the staff of Portsmouth History Centre (PHC). In visit after visit the PHC team unearthed for me obscure court records, steered me through parish registers, and on their own initiative brought out archival holdings they thought I might find useful. (They were right. I did.) For advice, insights and local knowledge, sincere thanks go to Portsmouth historian Ray Riley. Also in Portsmouth, Heather Jones of the National Museum of the Royal Navy located personal correspondence which shed fresh light upon how men at sea maintained relationships with shoreside relatives, a rare and precious resource in its own way every bit as valuable as the much larger wealth of civil and parish material.

In Oxford, the libraries of Corpus Christi and All Souls provided space, silence, books and pamphlets; warm thanks to Librarians Joanna Snelling and Gaye Morgan and their teams. When I could no longer use institutional routes to access certain material online, kind fellow Corpuscle Alexander Dymond did so on my behalf. Other Corpuscles also deserve mention. President, professors, porters, chaplain, archivist, academic registrar, accommodation officers, scouts: all in their way have sustained me. With great speed and kindness Cheryl Fury, Professor of History at the University of New Brunswick (St John), Canada, accessed journal articles otherwise beyond my reach. In her role of discussant in the European Social Science History Conference, and in correspondence arising from it,

## Acknowledgements

Dr Beatrice Moring of the University of Helsinki was generous with her time and wisdom, directing me to sources upon and providing insights into the complexities of household structure. Professors Jane Humphries of the University of Oxford and Brad Beaven of the University of Portsmouth challenged some of my thinking, set me on to material which in turn brought fresh insight and understanding, and urged me to persevere with my work. This monograph owes much to their encouragement.

Local historian, genealogist and friend Linda Rollitt provided valuable commentary on an earlier incarnation of this study, as did the late Dr Les Prince, former tutor, polymath, friend. Linda also joined in the hunt for some elusive individuals, shining lights into the recesses of parish records and wisely preventing me from reaching overenthusiastic conclusions. My sisters Angela Green and Fi Ballard provided accommodation, company, encouragement and wine on my many research trips to Portsmouth, enabling me to decompress after hours crouched over microfiche and card index; and my niece-in-law Leri Williams kindly helped solve a mapping problem. When I needed the opinion of individuals coming from a non-naval, non-historian perspective, Margaret Meikle and Dick Hobbs rose to the occasion. Meanwhile, Boydell and Brewer's Peter Sowden has shown immense restraint through the many (too many) months it has taken me to finish the script. He it was who had the insight to discern, from my technologically challenged presentation to the New Researchers in Maritime History conference in Bristol, the makings of a monograph that would break new ground. I thank him for his patience and encouragement. Boydell and Brewer's choice of independent copy editor was Georgina Asfaw, of www.gasfaweditorial.com. It is thanks to the sharpness of her eye, mind and visual memory that a variety of errors, gaps, inconsistencies and other clangers – all of them of my own making – were spotted in time to be resolved. If any others escaped her attention, the responsibility is mine alone.

Beyond all these, however, it is to my husband Phil and daughter Phoebe that I am most grateful. Phil has supported me through years of study and writing, minding home and dogs during my absence at conferences and on research forays, reading draft chapters, listening to my lunchtime descriptions of genealogical discoveries and marital complexities, and to his credit neither rolling his eyes nor allowing them to glaze over; at least, not too much. Phoebe has cheered me on from keyboard and Sheldonian gallery, across oceans and continents, keeping up my spirits and commitment during Covid-enforced separation, and never losing faith that the book would, one day, emerge into the light. She has, above all, believed in her mamma. Without these two, it would have been a harder, lonelier and less rewarding journey.

# ABBREVIATIONS

| | |
|---|---|
| **AB** | Able seaman |
| **ADM** | Prefix of admiralty records series held in the National Archives |
| **BNA** | British Newspaper Archive |
| **CDA(s)** | Contagious Diseases Act(s) |
| **CHU** | Prefix of Portsea Island parish church records, per the Portsmouth History Centre (PHC) index system |
| **GCB(s)** | Good Conduct Badge(s) |
| **GRO** | General Register Office |
| *H/Tel* | *Hampshire Telegraph* |
| **HMS** | Her Majesty's Ship (pl. HM Ships) |
| **HC** | House of Commons |
| **Mne** | Marine |
| **NMRN** | National Museum of the Royal Navy, Portsmouth |
| **PHC** | Portsmouth History Centre, Portsmouth |
| **PLU(s)** | Poor Law Union(s) |
| **PO(s)** | Petty Officer(s) |
| **PRB(s)** | Poor Rate Book(s) |
| **Pte** | Private |
| **QRs** | Queen's Regulations for the Government of Her Majesty's Naval Service, and Admiralty Instructions |
| **RM(s)** | Royal Marine(s) |

*Abbreviations*

**RMA**   Royal Marine Artillery

**RN**    Royal Navy

**TNA**   The National Archives, Kew

**WO(s)** Warrant officer(s)

# TERMS USED

The 'seamen's women' of the title refers primarily to wives, but includes other female relatives and non-relatives of lower-deck Royal Navy men. Individuals named in seamen's allotment declarations are referred to as 'allottees'. Some readers may regard 'allottee(s)' as anachronistic, others as a chilly administrative term which reduces dependants to mere recipients of coin. Not a Royal Navy term, it is used here to distinguish between recipients of financial support and the unknowable number of dependants *not* in receipt of seamen's wages. An alternative to 'seamen's women', the term 'naval women' refers to the female side of the naval community on shore, relatives who remained at home during their men's absence at sea. It neither implies naval service nor includes the dwindling minority of women who were smuggled, or smuggled themselves, on board Royal Navy ships. 'Civilian' is used to denote men not engaged in naval service, and land-based individuals (notably women) having no known relationship with serving or superannuated seamen.

'Portsea Island' means the land mass known nowadays as Portsmouth. Here, 'Portsmouth' primarily refers to the ancient gated town and parish of Portsmouth township, at the south-west corner of the island; but 'Portsmouth' is occasionally used as shorthand for the naval port and port town community. 'Portsea' means the historical and modern-day district north of Portsmouth town, close by the dockyard.

'Sailor' and 'seaman' had different meanings in naval terminology, but are used interchangeably here. 'Rating' refers to the lower-deck man, 'rate' to his designation, position on pay-scale, etc. In naval parlance the role and rank of paymaster and purser is conventionally given as 'pusser', his clerk as 'pusser's clerk'; the convention is observed.[1]

Abbreviations used in ships' muster books include:

- D: Discharged (left the ship per due formalities)
- DSQ: Discharged to Sick Quarters (hospital)
- Inv: Invalided
- R: Run (deserted)

---

[1] Jolly and Willson, *Jackspeak*, pp. 346–8.

## Terms Used

- Rq: Suspected Deserter (straggler)
- DD: Discharged Dead (died in service)

References to the National Archives' holdings of admiralty documents begin with the class code ADM. Prime source for this study, ships' allotment registers for 1795–1852 are catalogued under ADM 27. Individual allotment citations are given as ADM 27, followed by volume number, (right-hand) page number and the man's pay or muster number, thus 'ADM 27/110/275/42'. Original allotment registers are available for examination at the National Archives at Kew, but many have now been digitised via the search engine FindMyPast.com.[2] For the 1851 census, examined online via genealogy search engines, householders' returns are cited here by archive reference, piece number, folio and page, thus 'HO107/1657, fol. 424, p. 46'; unless otherwise stated, all refer to the registration district of Portsea Island. Citations for civil registrations of births, marriages and deaths in England and Wales refer to the year and quarter of the event, with relevant register volume and page numbers, thus 'E&W Births [or Deaths, or Marriages]: Q1/1847, vol. 2B, p. 495'; again, unless otherwise specified, all refer to the Portsea Island registration district. Where additional information has been obtained from a civil registration certificate, this is indicated.

Portsmouth History Centre's referencing system gives each Portsea Island parish church its own reference code beginning 'CHU', additional letters and numerals denoting baptism, marriage or burial records. Parish records cited in footnotes thus contain information sufficient to locate any certificate via on-site searches of PHC's indexes and microfiche holdings. The CHU church codes and suffixes, together with page and register entry numbers, are also locatable online, but only from the results of searches using data on individuals, e.g. names, place and year of birth, marriage or death, etc., and by examining both the digitised images and their transcriptions.

Other parish records are locatable online, but appear listed under 'England Marriages 1538–1973, parish marriages', followed by place and date of marriage. FindMyPast lists them as 'Record Set: Hampshire Marriages. Category: Birth, Marriage, Death & Parish Records; Subcategory: Parish Marriages'. As with Portsmouth History Centre's 'CHU' codes (see above), for online searches of England Marriages 1538–1973 it is necessary to search using data on individuals, e.g. names, place and year of birth, marriage or death, etc.

---

[2] FindMyPast.com, 'British Royal Navy Allotment Declarations, 1795–1852' (FindMyPast.com in association with The National Archives (TNA) Kew), <https://search.findmypast.com/search-world-records/british-royal-navy-allotment-declarations-1795-1852> [accessed 22 April 2024].

# WEIGHTS, MEASURES AND CURRENCY

All units of weight, volume, measurement and currency are given in the imperial form used in mid-nineteenth century Britain, thus:

**Pint**  unit of volume, equivalent to 568 millilitres. There were eight pints to the British gallon.

**Gallon**  unit of volume, equivalent to 4.55 litres.

**Inch**  unit of length, commonly expressed as 1in, and equivalent to 25.4 millimetres. There were twelve inches to the foot.

**Foot/feet**  unit of length, commonly expressed as 1ft, and equivalent to 0.305 metres. There were three feet to the yard.

**Yard**  unit of length, commonly expressed as 1yd, and equivalent to 0.914 metres. There were 1760 yards to the mile.

**Mile**  unit of length, equivalent to 1.609 kilometres.

**Ounce**  unit of weight, commonly expressed as 1oz, and equivalent to 28 grams. There were sixteen ounces to the pound weight.

**Pound**  unit of weight, commonly expressed as 1lb, and equivalent to 0.4535 kilograms.

**Farthing**  unit of currency, commonly expressed as ¼d. There were four farthings to the penny.

**Halfpenny**  unit of currency, commonly expressed as ½d. There were two halfpennies to the penny.

**Penny**  unit of currency, commonly expressed as 1d. There were twelve pennies to the shilling.

**Shilling**  unit of currency, commonly expressed as 1s (or 1/-). There were twenty shillings to the pound.

**Half-crown**   unit of currency to the value of two shillings and six pence, commonly expressed as 2s 6d or 2/6. There were eight half-crowns to the pound.

**Pound**   unit of currency, commonly expressed as £1.

**Guinea**   unit of currency to the value of one pound and one shilling, commonly expressed as 1gn, or £1. 1s.

## LANGUAGE

Quotations transcribed from seamen's original correspondence retain the writers' spelling and capitalisation. While still conveying his authorial tone and attitude, the extract quoted from Lasseter (p. 152) censors a term now deemed offensive.[1]

---

[1] W.L. Lasseter, 'The Portsmouth Corset Industry: its origins and growth', *Port of Portsmouth Chamber of Commerce Journal*, 1:12 (1947), 23–9, at p. 23.

# INTRODUCTION

My Dear Wife and Child, I Received your kind letter This morning and you are Determined to come down to Me Nothing will pleas me Better to have you with Me My dear Sarah I Will Send you Five Shilngs So you will be able to come Down and i will get our Ship's Cook to look out for A Room for us as he Live hear he his a Respectible Man … I think you better come down Monday Twelve o clock Boat and I Will Be Thare to meat You Pleas god … Dear Sarah you must Have a understanding at the Dock yard about your Alotment because it his Made out for you to Draw It at Chatham dock yard The First of Janwary … Peck up and come down For i ham as uncomfortable By myself as you are … In march I shall Be Paid up and then that Will find us on our leags [legs] the money that i send you in the name of Sarah Simpson god bless you And my dear Child and one And All god Love you x[1]

This rare example of correspondence between nineteenth-century Royal Navy sailors and their dependants on shore captures the preoccupations of a lower-deck seaman. His naval service has absented him from his wife. He longs to see her, has persuaded a respectable shipmate to find somewhere for them to stay when she visits the port where his ship will call, and looks forward to the day when the arrears of pay due him will set him on his financial feet again. Meanwhile he urges her to follow the correct procedure ('you must Have a understanding at the Dock yard about your Alotment') to collect that portion of his wages he has made available to her via the Navy's allotment system.

The letter is significant not only in its being one of very few surviving examples of contact between nineteenth-century naval seamen and their families, and its all too rare conveying of the relationship between shipboard man and wife at home.[2] It is significant, too, for its recognition of a naval wife's determination and resourcefulness, and for its reference to allotments, a support system unique to the Royal Navy.

---

[1] National Museum of the Royal Navy (NMRN) Portsmouth, William Simpson, letter to wife, NMRN 627/86/9 (19 December 1856).
[2] Oliver Walton, 'Social History of the Royal Navy, c.1856–1900: corporation and community' (University of Exeter, unpublished PhD thesis, 2004), p. 173.

If, as Walton suggests, 'beyond the officer corps we have hitherto had little idea of who was in the navy', we have had even less idea who comprised the naval community on shore.[3] Least of all do we know about the wives and other female dependants of lower-deck men; yet numbered in hundreds of thousands, these nineteenth-century naval dependants constituted a major subset of the population.[4] On this basis alone they deserve attention, but few studies so much as acknowledge their existence. Lean pickings are partly attributable to the omission of seamen from most histories of the working class generally, and to the (perceived or assumed) sheer ordinariness of seamen's women, for 'the exceptional was newsworthy ... the commonplace went unrecorded'.[5] This neglect is not due to lack of interest in the lower-deck man. Alongside studies of naval manning, sea warfare and technological development there are specialist studies concerned with sailors' social origins, health, training, literacy and their recognisable communities within port towns.[6] There is ample evidence of interest in the Navy man, yet little in his women.

The neglect is surprising, for the condition of sailors' families was intimately connected to naval manning. The eighteenth and nineteenth centuries saw naval dependants facing destitution. In order to provide for them, mature and experienced lower-deck men abandoned sea service in search of better and more regularly paid work on shore, or transferred to the merchant marine where wages were higher, conditions safer.[7] Needing to retain these valuable workers, the Royal Navy took the extraordinary

---

[3] *Ibid.*

[4] *Ibid.*, p. 33.

[5] David M. Williams, 'Henry Mayhew and the British Seaman', in Stephen Fisher (ed.), *Lisbon as a Port Town, the British Seaman and Other Maritime Themes* (Exeter, 1988), 111–27; quote: Rodger, *Command of the Ocean*, p. 212.

[6] Oliver Walton, '"A Great Improvement in the Sailor's Feeling towards the Naval Service": recruiting seamen for the Royal Navy, 1815–1853', *Journal for Maritime Research*, 12 (2010), 27–57; John Winton, 'Life and Education in a Technologically Evolving Navy, 1815–1925', in J.R. Hill (ed.), *The Oxford Illustrated History of the Royal Navy* (Oxford, 1995), 250–79; Michael Lewis, *The Navy in Transition, 1814–1864: a social history* (London, 1965); Virginia Preston, 'Constructing Communities: living and working in the Royal Navy, c.1830–1860' (University of Greenwich, unpublished PhD thesis, 2008); Lesley A. Hall, 'What Shall We Do with the Poxy Sailor? The problem of venereal diseases in the British mercantile marine, 1860–1950', *Journal of Maritime Research*, 6:1 (2004), 113–44; Brian Lavery, *Able Seamen: the lower deck of the Royal Navy from 1850 to the present day* (London, 2011); Louise Moon, '"Sailorhoods": sailortown and sailors in the port of Portsmouth circa 1850–1900' (University of Portsmouth, unpublished PhD thesis, 2015).

[7] Walton, 'Social History', p. 36; Stephen F. Gradish, *The Manning of the British Navy during the Seven Years' War* (London, 1980), p. 46.

step of creating a remittance system through which dependants might be supported. It is upon the Navy's allotment system, which succeeded remittances, that this book is founded.

The premise underpinning remittances and allotments held that men would be less inclined to abandon sea service if they knew that during ships' absences their families could access a regular source of income on shore.[8] In ingenuity, political boldness and sheer scale, the two systems had, for their time, no equal. From remittances' shaky start in 1728 there evolved a bureaucratic structure which by 1858 saw more than 17,000 allotments in force across the United Kingdom, supporting many tens of thousands of dependants in port towns, inland cities, remote islands and rural communities, two-thirds of them located in the Royal Navy's major port towns of Portsmouth, Devonport, Chatham and Sheerness.[9] Taking Portsmouth as an exemplar, this study focuses upon one naval community in one of those port towns.

Just as one naval community was chosen for examination, so a specific study period was selected. Three features determined the mid-century period it covers. First, there was the introduction in 1853 of Continuous Service, a development bringing about significant improvements in Royal Navy sailors' occupational security, pay, career prospects and pension rights, and enhancing the financial security and well-being of seamen's dependants.[10] Secondly, the mid-century years spanned the first of the 'mature' Victorian censuses.[11] The 1851 census made available data on allottees' places of birth, residence, occupation and household composition, material which could be compared where necessary with records from the previous 'rather *ad hoc*' national census of 1841 with its 'somewhat idiosyncratic …

---

[8] N.A.M. Rodger, *The Wooden World: an anatomy of the Georgian Navy* (Annapolis, Md., 1986), pp. 131–2, 134–5; Margaret Hunt, 'Women and the Fiscal-imperial State in the late Seventeenth and early Eighteenth Centuries', in Kathleen Wilson (ed.), *A New Imperial History: culture, identity, and modernity in Britain and the Empire, 1660–1840* (Cambridge, 2004), 29–47, at p. 34; Melissa Reibe, 'Public Perceptions of Sailors' Wives in Eighteenth-Century England' (University of Missouri-Kansas City, unpublished MA thesis, 2011), p. 30.

[9] National Archives (TNA) Kew, Admiralty: Miscellanea: History of the Allotment System in the Navy ('Pitcairn Report'), ADM 7/719 (1858), p. 33; Walton, 'Social History', pp. 88–91; House of Commons Paper no. 295, Navy: 'Return of the Number of Seamen, and Petty Officers of the Royal Navy and Marines, who allot a Portion of their Pay for the Support of their Families and Others; and showing the Place of Residence of such Persons', XXXIX, 13, 1857–58, pp. 13–15.

[10] *Naval Enlistment Act*, 16 & 17 Vict., c. 69 (1853).

[11] Edward Higgs, *Making Sense of the Census Revisited: census records for England and Wales 1801–1901, a handbook for historical researchers* (London, 2005), p. 11.

returns'.[12] An unavoidable end-point to the study was then imposed by the petering-out, from 1852 onward, of surviving allotment records.

The conjunction of these three factors nailed the study period to a narrow range of years uncoloured not only by the effects of Continuous Service, but by the impact of the Contagious Diseases Acts (CDAs) of the 1860s, implementation of which in garrison towns such as Plymouth and Portsmouth subjected working-class women's conduct, appearance, their very presence in public, to heightened levels of scrutiny and suspicion. Properly to cover CDA implementation would require discussion of military fitness levels and physical health, political motive, practical application and above all the social consequences for naval women locally. To address these would be to unbalance the book, giving the topic of prostitution a disproportionate level of attention within a study seeking to present it as one aspect of a rounded picture.

Just as Portsmouth stands proxy for other naval port towns, so in some respects the mid-nineteenth century stands proxy for previous years, for in focusing on the early 1850s the study captures a snapshot of a naval community as had existed for many decades. Throughout the eighteenth and nineteenth centuries, naval women endured their husbands' long absences, managed households unaided, brought up children without the presence of a father figure, and had little choice but to accept poor housing, poor sanitation and overcrowding. Daily life in naval communities changed little. Houses still crumbled here, sprang up overnight there. Pubs, brothels, and beerhouses still offered entertainment to men on runs-ashore, providing profit for brewer, landlord and pimp, and opportunities for women in need of company or cash.[13] Naval outfitters and tailors still needed needlewomen to sew men's shirts and apply gold lace to officers' uniforms. Privies were still shared, still foul, water still purchased by the bucketful from hand pumps, and streetlights (where they existed) were still dim. Dress apart, the Georgian-era naval wife would recognise much about her Victorian peer, her environment, and the privations of daily living.

Not for decades after Trafalgar and Waterloo, however, did nineteenth-century naval women suffer, as their predecessors had suffered, the strain and anxiety of war. For the naval community, war meant not only sustained fear (of invasion, and of the death, injury in battle or capture of husbands, sons, fathers and brothers); it also meant the terrible reality of men returning disabled, traumatised by conflict and unfit to support their families. It brought grief to bereaved neighbours and friends, and sent the

---

[12] *Ibid.*, p. 13.
[13] 'Run-ashore: a social visit, with various shipmates, to a series of pubs or clubs': Jolly and Willson, *Jackspeak*, p. 373.

*Introduction*

cost of necessities spiralling, all of which effects 'bore with terrible force upon women, children and other "non-combatants".'[14] For our mid-century naval women the nearest equivalent to wartime was the prolonged absence of men on vessels engaged in discovery service, a term covering the Navy's exploring and mapping of uncharted shores, or – as witness the Franklin expedition, one of whose members relates to this study – the seeking of new navigable passages in dangerous conditions. Discovery service did not mean armed conflict and the fear of invasion; it did, however, send vessels beyond the usual sea areas frequented by Royal Navy and merchant ships, disconnecting them from communication with home, and placing them out of reach of help in time of distress. Pending her husband's safe return, to the seaman's wife 'discovery service' meant widowhood in all but name.

## PURPOSE

After such long years of neglect, it would do seamen's women a disservice if this book only set out the bare bones of their social condition and circumstances, leaving the reader none the wiser as to what those bare bones signify. Statistics (abstracted from data drawn from primary sources, and provided by contemporary government reports) answer the question 'What?', but not the 'So what?' To answer the latter requires not production of new evidence but evaluation of that evidence, weighing up what has been discovered and comparing it with local and national scenarios. The twofold purpose of the book, therefore, is to set out the 'What?' of seamen's women's lives – unearthing material to show where their families originated, who they married, where and how they lived, and with whom, and the social and environmental challenges they faced – and, by setting this fresh evidence against what is known about their civilian neighbours and other women in nineteenth-century Britain, to answer the evaluative 'So what?'

This latter question demands we compare the women with others at local and/or national level, and consider what the results imply. For example, how much younger or older were they than other first-time brides in England and Wales, and what does their marital age signify in terms of their ability to fulfil the role of seaman's wife? How much poorer or better-off were they than their civilian peers? How did their employment, their household structures, their family backgrounds differ from those of women unrelated to lower-deck seamen, with what consequences to household income? With differences identified it becomes possible to explore their underpinnings by asking such questions as: what explains the relatively limited range of seamen's women's occupations, their relatively unusual household

---

[14] Hunt, 'Women and the Fiscal-imperial State', p. 29.

structures and family sizes? Were unorthodoxies forced upon them by tight budgets or lack of alternatives, or willingly adopted for the implicit benefits they offered the woman striving to manage alone? For some of these 'So what?' questions there is an obvious, rational explanation; for others, without the words of the women themselves, there can only be speculation, a weighing-up of alternatives, a pointing to the likeliest of answers given the wider circumstances.

The answering of the 'What? question relies on original, primary source material which this study has mined for fresh evidence; the 'So what?' question turns us to the work of other historians, other writers and government statistics.

## PRIMARY SOURCES

Trusted and valued by men and dependants alike, the Royal Navy's allotment system survived into the 1980s when electronic banking rendered it redundant; even then, within the naval community its passing was lamented.[15] The Navy's investment in the construct, and men's usage of it, are proof of its importance; yet beyond Rodger's description of remittances' inception, historians have given only brief nods to remittances or allotments. Allotments kept the wolf from many a naval woman's door. Allotment records enable naval women's history to be explored.

Prime original source, then, was the National Archives' collection of ships' allotment registers.[16] In order to allow dependants on shore regular access to part of their pay, men serving on ships at sea were required to make oral declarations to that effect. Recorded in registers, and confirmed by the men via signature or mark, these declarations were returned to Whitehall via other, homeward-bound vessels. Once processed by admiralty clerks (the landward part of the process is described in Chapter One), the registers were collated in bound volumes. Now held as National Archives' series ADM 27, with some volumes digitised for online access, they contain allotments declared on board HM Ships in commission between 1795 and 1852.[17]

Ships' allotment registers recorded seamen's names, their 'quality' (substantive or acting rate and trade), muster number and relationship to the intended recipient. If the recipient were a wife, date and place of the

---

[15] House of Commons Debate, Ministry of Defence: Royal Navy Ratings (Allotments), 13, cc311-2W, 23 November 1981.

[16] Bruno Pappalardo, 'A Lot to be Excited About - Admiralty Allotment Registers' (The National Archives, 2019) <https://blog.nationalarchives.gov.uk/lot-excited-admiralty-allotment-registers/> [accessed 22 April 2024].

[17] ADM 27; FindMyPast.com, 'FMP: Allotment Registers online' [accessed 22 April 2024].

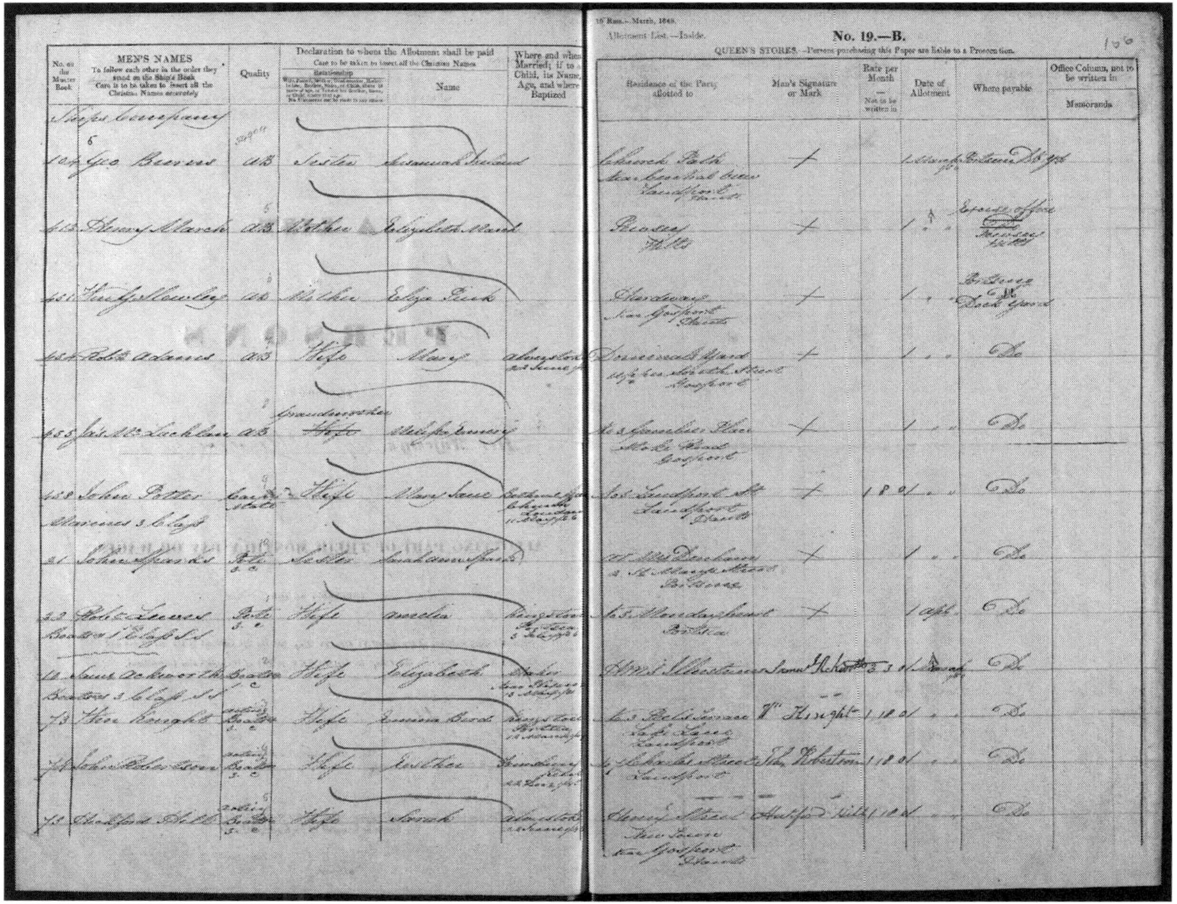

**Fig. 1** Seamen's declarations in ship's allotment register. National Archives (TNA) Kew, Navy Board, and Admiralty, Accountant General's Department: Registers of Allotments and Allotment Declarations, ADM 27 (1792–1852): ADM 27/110/105-6. Reproduced under licence by kind permission of The National Archives, Kew.

couple's marriage were required; when the declaration favoured a 'trustee' (foster carer), the entrusted children's names, ages and baptism locations were required. Warning pussers that it was 'Not to be written in', there was also a column in which Whitehall-based admiralty clerks could record the amount allotted, though this was not routinely done. In Fig. 1, which shows a register for HMS *Illustrious*, amounts are visible in the middle column on the right-hand page. Allotment declaration data thus facilitate analysis of kinship, household economies and structures at a level of depth and detail rarely available to social and demographic historians.

Pay numbers and 'quality' helped identify men entered in ships' muster and description books.[18] Muster books yielded data of individuals' on-board expenditure, and the date and circumstances of their leaving the ship, whether by being routinely paid off at the end of the ship's commission, transferred to another vessel, invalided to hospital, having deserted or being 'discharged dead' (died during the ship's commission). Description books provided men's places of birth and usual residence, civil status, the trade to which they had been brought up, their physical attributes, length of service and previous ships. It was not unknown for men to lie about their origins, abilities and marital status when being entered in a ship's books, as witness two individuals of whom we shall hear more later: marine private third class Robert Lewis, who on joining *Illustrious* declared himself single despite being two years married to his wife Amelia (*q.v.*); and AB Eli Bone, HMS *Resolute*, who asserted that he had been 'brought up to sea' when he had been raised the son of an agricultural labourer, in an isolated Hampshire village ten miles from the coast.[19] That said, the ancillary information contained in muster and description books enabled allottees' circumstances to be seen in a wider context, for example by clarifying whether a man had been long in the Navy when he married, whether he imposed financial strain on his family by being fined for straggling (returning late on board) or were judged to be of good character.[20] Accident and tragedy are detectable in mass entries of 'DD' or 'DSQ' (for vessels suffering major incident or disease), while disproportionately high numbers of sailors recorded as 'R' or 'Rq' raise the possibility of a vessel's being an 'unhappy ship' (see p. 265).

---

[18] National Archives (TNA) Kew, Admiralty: Ships' Musters (Series III), ADM 38 (1793–1878); National Archives (TNA) Kew, Admiralty: Royal Marines: Description Books, Woolwich Division, ADM 158 (1750–1940).

[19] ADM 38/8325/2; CHU3/1D/44, p. 103 n. 206; ADM 38/8862/47; CHU39A/1A/5, p. 27 n. 215; Melanie Holihead, 'Portsea Poll, Poor Poll? The social condition of wives and families receiving allotments of pay from Royal Navy sailors in mid-nineteenth century Portsea Town' (University of Oxford, unpublished MSc dissertation, 2011), pp. 73–4. '*Q.v.*': *quod vide*, ('which see'), indicating the named individual or issue is referenced elsewhere in the text.

[20] Walton, 'Social History', pp. 85–7.

*Introduction*

A longitudinal view of some men's careers is revealed in their service records.[21] Applying solely to men who signed up for Continuous Service, but listing all previous service per date, ship and rate, these records reveal individuals' health, conduct, invalidity, advancement and merit, issues affecting the financial security and welfare of families at home. Ships' logs yielded details of vessels' movements and shipboard life, while Queen's Regulations set an administrative and disciplinary framework against which men's day to day work could be considered.[22] Surgeons' logs proved a source of useful additional detail, particularly for ships bound for distant stations or on dangerous commissions; but not all ships had surgeons, and not all logs have survived.[23] To be approved by admiralty inspectors, seamen's wills had to meet certain legal criteria, hence their formulaic structure and tone; variations in terminology, however, conveyed differing degrees of affection on the part of testators, while names and addresses of executrices and beneficiaries were often accompanied by explanatory remarks as to the nature of relationship with the testator, or past shared experiences.[24] Belatedly commissioned by the Accountant General of the Royal Navy, an unpublished internal history summarised the allotment system's development and key features.[25] A Royal Commission took evidence of the system's workings; statistical reports informed Parliament of the scale of its operation; and newspapers and periodicals reported with relish attempted infringements and abuses.[26] To one degree or another, a range of sources provided a wealth of information relating to seamen's women. Central to them, however, were allotment registers.

---

[21] National Archives (TNA) Kew, Admiralty: Royal Navy, Royal Marines, Coastguard and Related Services: Officers' and Ratings' Service Records (Series II), ADM 29 (1802–1919); National Archives (TNA) Kew, Admiralty: Royal Navy Continuous Service Engagement Books, ADM 139 (1853–72).

[22] National Archives (TNA) Kew, Admiralty: Supplementary Logs and Journals of Ships on Exploration, ADM 55 (1757–1904); Royal Navy, *The Queen's Regulations for the Government of Her Majesty's Naval Service* (Whitehall, 1844).

[23] National Archives (TNA) Kew, Admiralty and Predecessors: Office of the Director General of the Medical Department of the Navy and Predecessors: Medical Journals, ADM 101 (1785–1963).

[24] National Archives (TNA) Kew, Navy Board, Navy Pay Office and Admiralty, Accountant General's Department: Seamen's Wills, ADM 48 (1786–1882).

[25] Pitcairn, *Report*.

[26] Earl Hardwicke, *et al.*, *Report of the Commissioners appointed to Inquire into the Best Means of Manning the Navy* (London: HMSO, 1859); House of Commons: Report of the Commissioners appointed to Inquire into the Best Means of Manning the Navy, 1859, [Command Paper] 2469; House of Commons Paper no. 295, XXXIX, 13, 1857–58, pp. 13–15; *Hampshire Telegraph, and Sussex Chronicle,* Portsmouth police court reports, 1845–65, *passim*, via British Newspaper Archive, <https://www.britishnewspaperarchive.co.uk> [accessed 22 April 2024].

Allottees' names and addresses, as cited by sailors, enabled census records for Portsea Island to be searched for women's census entries.[27] Inconsistent transcription by online genealogy search engines hid some individuals from all but serendipitous discovery. There was inconsistency, too, in census officials' counting or delineating of dwellings and households, their difficulties compounded by districts' numbering systems: some streets had even numbers on one side of the street, odd on the other, while elsewhere the house-numbers ran consecutively up one way before doubling back on the opposite side.[28] These practices made it difficult to pinpoint allottees' residences on maps, a cause for frustration when examining issues such as proximity of naval households and women's kin.

Civil birth, marriage and death registers, and data extracted from certificates purchased from the General Register Office, informed the construction of genograms and helped verify or disprove suspected kinship networks.[29] Parish baptismal, marriage and burial registers, particularly for events occurring prior to the introduction in 1837 of civil registration, were accessed initially on microfiche at Portsmouth History Centre (PHC), subsequently online once the collection had been digitised.[30] PHC's collection of slum inspection reports revealed domestic detail such as room sizes, WC provision and the physical condition of some of the very dwellings in which allottees had lived.[31] Portsea Island Poor Law Union data on the administration of in- and out-relief proved limited. Pre-1879 workhouse admission and discharge registers had been lost to wartime damage, while Poor Law Guardians' minute books were primarily concerned with business and budgetary matters, making little mention of individual applications for relief.[32] PHC's Local Studies Collection furnished maps, most valuable of which were the Ordnance Survey's 1:500-scale town plans. These were detailed enough to show the size and proximity of domestic dwellings, and facilities such as public houses, pawnbrokers, street lighting, doorsteps, water supplies, factories and barracks.

---

[27] Ancestry.co.uk, <http://www.ancestry.co.uk/> [accessed 10 April 2024]; FindMyPast.com, <http://www.findmypast.co.uk/> [accessed 10 April 2024].

[28] Higgs, *Census Revisited*, p. 62; WEA, *Gateway to Queen Street* (Portsmouth, 1982), p. 9; WEA, *Memories of Portsea* (Portsmouth, 2007), p. 4.

[29] www.gov.uk, 'Order a Birth, Death, Marriage or Civil Partnership Certificate' (HM Government, 2023) <https://www.gov.uk/order-copy-birth-death-marriage-certificate> [accessed 22 April 2024].

[30] Via <https://www.findmypast.co.uk> [accessed 13 June 2023].

[31] Portsmouth History Centre (PHC) Portsmouth, Slum Inspection Reports, PHC PMRS/DV/9B/1 (1929).

[32] Portsmouth History Centre (PHC) Portsmouth, Portsea Island Poor Law Union, Minute Books of Board of Guardians, BG/M/1/3 (1851–55).

*Introduction*

Where naval couples' correspondence has survived it tends to be as letters from (well-known, officer cadre) husbands rather than wives and families.[33] Little remains by way of letters between lower-deck sailors and their wives, denying us 'the genuine voice of the literate working woman'.[34] Many working-class women could at the very least sign their names, and the popularity of penny weekly magazines suggests they were not necessarily illiterate; but the cost of paper and postage, and the hours it took for servantless women to tend to children and fulfil essential domestic tasks, made for infrequent correspondence.[35] Having servants to do domestic work, officers' wives had more time to sit and write. They were more likely, too, to own their own furniture – a desk at which to write, a drawer in which to lock precious letters. Better preserved, in warmer dwellings, their husbands' correspondence was less likely to suffer the destructive effects of damp, mould and vermin. It was also less likely to be folded to make a taper, or crumpled as a firelighter when there was no money for kindling. There was less likelihood, too, of officers' wives' having to do a moonlight flit to cheaper accommodation, a domestic disruption in which personal items were easily lost.

A few precious letters have survived. The National Museum of the Royal Navy holds papers relating to the career of one John Ford, ordinary seaman and later chief boatswain, 1838–62.[36] As well as letters written to his future wife, and to his daughter, they include his service certificate and official documents relating to pension, prize money and allotment of wages. Robert Mackenzie, too, wrote tenderly to his wife and child, as did son-in-law Bill Simpson to Mackenzie's daughter.[37] The women's words, alas, have not survived.

---

[33] Helen Doe, 'Those They Left Behind: navy wives and widows during the French wars', *Trafalgar Chronicle* (2015), 188–200, at pp. 188–9; Walton, 'Social History', p. 173.
[34] Helen Watt and Anne Hawkins, *Letters of Seamen in the Wars with France, 1793–1815* (Woodbridge, 2016), p. 15; Margarette Lincoln, *Naval Wives and Mistresses* (Stroud, 2011), pp. 30–1; David Lewis, 'Married to the Navy: the lives of naval officers' wives, 1870–1914' (Thames Polytechnic, unpublished master's degree dissertation, 1988), p. 5; Walton, 'Social History', p. 173; Doe, 'Those They Left Behind', p. 8.
[35] Sally Mitchell, 'The Forgotten Women of the Period: penny weekly family magazines of the 1840s and 1850s', in Martha Vicinus (ed.), *A Widening Sphere: changing roles of Victorian women* (Indiana, 1977), 29–51, at p. 29; Lincoln, *Naval Wives*, pp. 30–1, 137; Joan Perkin, *Women and Marriage in Nineteenth-century England* (London, 1989), p. 148; Patricia Lin, 'Caring for the Nation's Families: British Soldiers' and Sailors' Families and the State, 1793–1815', in Alan I. Forrest, Karen Hagemann and Jane Rendall (eds), *Soldiers, Citizens and Civilians: experiences and perceptions of the revolutionary and Napoleonic Wars, 1790–1820* (Basingstoke, 2009), 99–136, at p. 99.
[36] National Museum of the Royal Navy (NMRN) Portsmouth: 353/85 (10–21).
[37] National Museum of the Royal Navy (NMRN) Portsmouth: 627/86 (7–12, 28, 29).

## SECONDARY SOURCES

Authorial interest in 'wives at sea' is out of proportion with the actuality. By the mid-nineteenth century the practice of allowing women on board Royal Navy vessels was in decline, its demise hastened in part by changes in ship design affording less space for wives or stowaways.[38] What has been written about 'naval women' must therefore be viewed with caution, not least because the term has become associated with women who went to sea. Rowbotham asserts that since naval wives had no official status on board, they were neither shown in muster books nor victualled.[39] But women do from time to time appear in muster books, hiding in plain sight among men listed under 'SLWV' (Supplementary List for Wages and Victuals). How many were wives of ships' officers and crew, how many travelling as soldiers' dependants in troopships, or evacuees being transported to safety or home to England, are questions ripe for further research. Concerned primarily with naval officers, Padfield mentions sailors' wives, but statements such as 'a few sailors were married, though these were older men ... some of whom seem to have taken wives to sea with them' lack scale and citation.[40] Lavery's *Royal Tars* refers to the wives of six men in every hundred being allowed to accompany them on board Royal Navy ships in the 1790s, HMS *Goliath* accommodating up to one hundred women for a 570-strong crew; there is no mention of the unnumbered majority of wives who remained on shore.[41] Two points should be made. First, none of these writers sets out to explore sailors' lives beyond the shipboard experience, hence the indifferent treatment of wives' lives on shore. Secondly, as noted earlier, there is little original source material specifically relating to the vast majority of wives who did *not* go to sea, and even less by way of pre-existing research to which these writers could have turned for material representing that greater population of naval women.

Sailors' autobiographies and memoirs were often written long after retirement, with one eye on sales. Their focus was the authors' sea service, references to women usually comprising unsubstantiated nudge-and-wink anecdote rather than personal reminiscence or verifiable fact. This may explain their being plundered in the lighter-weight naval histories, as

---

[38] Walton, 'Social History', p. 168.
[39] W.B. Rowbotham, 'Soldiers' and Seamen's Wives and Children in HM Ships', *The Mariner's Mirror*, 47: 1 (1961), 42–8, at p. 44.
[40] Peter Padfield, *Rule Britannia: the Victorian and Edwardian Navy* (London, 2002), p. 24.
[41] Brian Lavery, *Royal Tars: the lower deck of the Royal Navy, 875–1850* (London, 2010), pp. 272–3, 304.

*Introduction*

Baynham does with Jack Nastyface's stories, Winton with Baynham's.[42] Less concerned to entertain is McKee's examination of autobiographical records created by social historians who tracked down and interviewed Royal Navy sailors serving in the first half of the twentieth century.[43] The interviewees' reflections yielded telling insights upon seamen's attitudes toward prostitutes, naval marriage, household management and domestic authority; but the result was an imbalanced collection, for 'no-one was interested in finding and speaking with the women of Chatham, Portsmouth and Plymouth ... [and] history is left with only half the story.'[44]

While admiring their fortitude, the book does not whitewash its subjects. The chapters that follow tell of child brides, unlawful marriages, out-of-wedlock conceptions, poxed and demented husbands, intra-family violence, extra-marital affairs, shipwreck, bereavement, grinding poverty, lasting friendship, the spectre – for some, the reality – of the workhouse. From explaining, in Chapter One, the women's association with the Royal Navy, the book takes the reader by stages from birth, marriage and family, to economic and social survival strategies, marital challenges, longevity and death. Chapter Two deconstructs the study cohort of nearly 1,600 individuals, Chapter Three the women's origins and migrations. Chapter Four examines evidence of the influence of paternal occupation upon the women's choice of husband, considering how naval brides' nuptiality compared with that of their non-naval peers at local and national levels. Chapter Five considers the factors which, along with would-be fathers' absence at sea, determined the size of naval families. Many naval households did not consist solely of wife and child(ren), hence Chapter Six's examination of living arrangements adopted in seamen's absence. Chapter Seven looks outward to the physical environment in which the women lived. Chapter Eight considers where they worked, in what trade, with what materials, at what risk to health, for what reward. Paid work notwithstanding they were hard pressed to make ends meet, hence Chapter Nine, drawing upon secondary sources to construct a notional household budget, concludes that if she were not to fall into debt, and from debt to destitution, many a wife would need income additional to an allotted portion of her seaman-husband's wage. Pursuing this argument, Chapter Ten looks at

---

[42] Henry Baynham, *From the Lower Deck: The Old Navy, 1780–1840* (London, 1969), pp. 68–9, 77; William Robinson, *Jack Nastyface: memoirs of an English seaman* (London, 2002), p. 89; John Winton, *Hurrah for the Life of a Sailor!: life on the lower-deck of the Victorian Navy* (London, 1977), p. 59; Henry D. Capper, *Aft – from the Hawsehole: Sixty-two Years of Sailors' Evolution* (London, 1927).

[43] Christopher McKee, *Sober Men and True: sailor lives in the Royal Navy, 1900–1945* (London, 2002).

[44] *Ibid.*, p. 186.

the women's reliance on parish relief, and at their hitherto presumed but unproven involvement in prostitution. Underpinning the lack of proof is the fact that prostitution itself was not a crime; but no evidence has been found to support certain writers' assumptions that many if not most naval wives resorted to the sex trade during their husbands' absence. It does, however, propose that within the naval community, and possibly within certain elements of local society, there existed unwritten, transactional constructs which both allowed the women to engage in the sex trade and protected them from judicial consequences, thereby creating a prostitutional iceberg of which only a trace remains visible.

Prostitution might not be a crime, but there were penalties for prostitution-associated behaviour. Most were less severe than penalties imposed for assault, theft or personation, offences featuring in Chapter Eleven's examination of the crimes committed by naval women. From offending to suffering: Chapter Twelve looks at seamen's wives as victims of domestic abuse. A different form of strife is the focus of Chapter Thirteen, which explores the challenges and complexities facing women whose marriages proved less happy than they had hoped. To escape, some were prepared to break social convention, even to break the law. In doing so they created complicated family networks, and situations of tension and risk, and contributed to their own unsavoury reputation.

All naval marriages endured long separations arising from the absence of ships on commission, and all naval marriages ended with a bereavement – of the seaman-husband, of his stay-at-home wife. Chapter Fourteen looks at the dangers and risks seamen encountered during their long absences, and what these meant for wives and families at home. Chapter Fifteen goes further. Avoiding too-easy assumptions that seamen's women met their end diseased, drunk or drowned, it shows them dying of conditions associated with poverty, unremitting hard physical work and stress; yet amid the pitifully early demise of some individuals there are also lives of extraordinary length, with women born under Victoria's predecessor surviving beyond the First World War. These contrasts are echoed in the modest respectability of some seamen's women, the roistering, brawling, snook-cocking criminality of others. The very phrase 'naval seamen's women' both incorporates and masks a broad range of types, none of which is typical of her kind, yet any of which constituted part of an extraordinary community. These women were real people, living individuals. They were remarkable, important and deserve their place in history.

*1*

# THE NAVAL CONTEXT

Just as the life and health of a farmer's wife were affected by her husband's occupation, so the lives and wellbeing of naval wives, mothers, sisters and daughters were intimately connected to and affected by their men's naval service. Issues such as long absences, shared risk, hard physical work and vulnerability to the weather changed little over centuries; others, such as technological developments, shifting international relations and changes in government policy, altered the tenor both of naval service and of naval family life on shore. Technological advances aside, a sailor of Nelson's Navy would recognise much about the mid-nineteenth-century, pre-Continuous Service Royal Navy; and the older naval wife who had managed alone throughout her man's absences at war would recognise in the lives of her younger peers her own experiences from decades past. Setting the wider naval context, this chapter considers things directly affecting dependants at home: the ships in which men served; the allotment system through which men could provide financial support; and seamen's pay, image and reputation.

## HM SHIPS

The allotments of pay underpinning this study were declared by lower-deck men serving in flagships, guard ships, wooden paddle sloops, frigates, brigantines and first rate ships of the line – at 125 in number, a solid cross-section of the fleet, comprising over one-third of the mid-nineteenth century Navy's 354 vessels.[1] These ships were deployed in a variety of locations, from home ports in southern England to the Cove of Cork, the

---

[1] Joseph Allen, *The New Navy List* (Whitehall, 1850), *passim*; J.J. Colledge, *Ships of the Royal Navy: an Historical Index* (Newton Abbot, 1969), *passim*; J.J. Colledge, *Ships of the Royal Navy: the Complete Record of all Fighting Ships of the Royal Navy from the Fifteenth Century to the Present* (London, 1987), *passim*; Conrad Dixon, *Ships of the Victorian Navy* (Southampton, 1987), *passim*.

Mediterranean, West Indies, West Africa, South America, Australia and the Pacific. They might be away for a few weeks at a time, or for two or more years, ships assigned to overseas stations generally spending about three years there.[2] Some remained closer to home. HMS *Excellent*, a gunnery training ship since 1830, was stationed in Portsmouth Harbour, as were guard ships *Britannia* and *Blenheim*, and HMS *Victory*, formerly flagship to the port admiral, now a harbour-based training ship for naval apprentices. Launched in 1765, *Victory* was the oldest of the study's 125 vessels, fifty-five of which were built in the years 1840–50.[3] Thirteen others had seen service during the Napoleonic Wars, some having undergone conversion to screw propulsion, the rest now in varying degrees of obsolescence.[4]

Fifty-eight per cent of the study's gross total of 2,300 allotment declarations were made by men serving in steamships. Steam engines at this stage were still fairly crude and inefficient, using vast quantities of coal which was not readily available in those parts of the world where British ships were deployed.[5] As well as giving them access to coal supplies, steamships' more frequent visits to ports enabled them to take on fresh food, lack of which was a particular problem for vessels serving in inclement conditions in remote waters.[6] 'Remote' embraced distant but well mapped and frequently traversed oceans; it also included uncharted seas where ships on discovery service were deployed. Men on discovery service vessels enjoyed double pay, but with extra money came greater privation, and greater risk of injury, disease, environment-related health conditions and death. Less arduous commissions might afford more chance of home leave, more frequent contact with ships bringing or taking home mail, and opportunities for leave in exotic and interesting ports; but whether serving in a small tender in Portsmouth Harbour or a discovery vessel trapped in Arctic ice, all on board faced occupational hazards, the effect of which was felt far beyond the wooden or iron-clad walls within which men served.

---

[2] Winton, 'Life and Education in a Technologically Evolving Navy', p. 254; Winton, *Hurrah!*, p. 14; Geoffrey Osborn, *Naval Officers' Letters: a study of letters sent to and from British Royal Navy officers serving abroad in the Victorian era* (Bristol, 1995), p. 74; Thomas Holman, *Life in the Royal Navy, by 'a ranker'* (Portsmouth, 1891), pp. 109–10; Mary A. Conley, *From Jack Tar to Union Jack: Representing Naval Manhood in the British Empire, 1870–1918* (Manchester, 2009), p. 21; Andrew Lambert, 'The Shield of Empire, 1815–1895', in J.R. Hill (ed.), *The Oxford Illustrated History of the Royal Navy* (Oxford, 1995), 161–99, at p. 171.

[3] Holman, *Life in the Royal Navy*, p. 2; Lavery, *Able Seamen*, pp. 15, 17; Walton, '"Great Improvement"', p. 37.

[4] Walton, 'Social History', p. 39.

[5] Colin White, *Victoria's Navy: the end of the sailing Navy* (Havant, 1981), p. 28.

[6] Preston, 'Constructing Communities', p. 191.

## ROYAL NAVY MEN

The mid-century Royal Navy bore on its books approximately 33,000 of the 38,000 men it was authorised to employ. The number of seamen 'borne for wages' included fictitious individuals whose wages were used to pay for a range of expenses such as pilots' fees or pensions to the relicts of officers killed in combat. Those 'borne for wages' therefore exceeded the 29,000 actually mustered, hence the 1,547 seamen whose allottees form the nett cohort of this study comprise approximately 5 per cent of the Navy's active and available manpower.[7]

Ships' books capture the broad range of traditional and modern trades on which the service depended. Some had their civilian analogues in HM dockyards, for 'sailors who learned skills on ship during wartime could move into the dockyard, building or refitting ships laid up "in ordinary", during the peace.'[8] Beyond the dockyard walls, in hotels and clubs, music halls, naval outfitters' shops and breweries, worked the civilian equivalents of naval cooks, coopers, tailors, painters, musicians and stewards. A man with experience of one commonplace shoreside occupation might thus join the Navy, maintain his skills on board, and provided he were not disabled in service could be hopeful of resuming his shoreside trade upon being discharged, or between ships' commissions.[9] Other 'qualities' were more narrowly associated with maritime and military life. For gunners, engineers, stokers, coxswains, boatswains and seamen whose rates ranged from ordinary to able, third class to first, there were fewer shoreside equivalents, fewer opportunities. There was no guarantee of finding seagoing employment either, for as a witness to the 1859 Royal Commission on naval manning observed, 'all the occupations of the community are open to soldiers ... but ... such a mass of [seamen] could not find a place suddenly in the merchant service.'[10] Two branches – seamen (boatswains and gunners) and carpenters – offered the possibility of advancement to warrant rank. Each warrant officer (WO) had his own group of men. For example, depending on the

---

[7] Gradish, *Manning of the British Navy*, p. 51 fn 2; Lavery, *Able Seamen*, p. 15; Eugene L. Rasor, *Reform in the Royal Navy: a social history of the lower deck, 1850 to 1880* (Hamden, Conn., 1976), p. 105 fn 67; Christopher Lloyd, *The British Seaman 1200–1860: a social survey* (London, 1968), pp. 228–9 table 3.

[8] Lavery, *Able Seamen*, p. 107; Alison Light, *Common People: the history of an English family* (London, 2014), p. 195. 'When ships paid off into the Ordinary (the dockyard reserve) [they] lay at their moorings stripped to a gantline ... with a force of shipkeepers ... to maintain them': Rodger, *Wooden World*, p. 21.

[9] Jennine Hurl-Eamon, 'The Fiction of Female Dependence and the Makeshift Economy of Soldiers, Sailors and their Wives in Eighteenth-century London', *Labor History*, 49: 4 (2008), 481–501, at p. 492.

[10] Hardwicke, *Report*, p. 154 s. 2679.

size of the ship and its complement, subordinate to the carpenter there might be a carpenter's mate, caulker, shipwright and men of the carpenter's crew, while the carpenter himself might himself be rated first, second or third class, gradations similarly applying to gunners and boatswains. In this study, 195 (12.6 per cent) of the men were listed as gunners, boatswains or carpenters *tout court*, or first, second or third class.

Warrant officers were men of no small significance. The attaining of a warrant 'symbolised an important division which was both social and professional', for although WOs were without pretensions to gentility, their standing and seniority as experienced and highly-respected men distinguished them from the rest of the ship's company.[11] As for men with neither warrant nor specific trade, it was reckoned that 'one year at sea would make an ordinary, and two years an able seaman.'[12] Most of those styled 'ordinary seaman' bore the title without further qualification, but some were rated first or second class, and paid accordingly. At this mid-century point, 'marines' served either in the Royal Marine Light Infantry (RMLI) or the Royal Marine Artillery (RMA); in allotment declarations, census returns and service records, however, most were recorded simply as marine, private, corporal or sergeant. Cooks might be trained, but many were simply aged petty officers working their retirement, as was the case with James Matthias, bigamous husband of Rosalinda (*q.v.*), whom we shall meet in later chapters.[13] Whereas 'ship's cook' denoted a man of some seniority serving the ship in general and earning as much as a leading stoker (see Table 1), officers' cooks were untrained domestics from the main group of ratings, dedicated respectively to wardroom, gun room, 'sub[ordinate] officers', midshipmen.[14] Nicknamed 'crushers', ship's corporals were responsible for enforcing everyday rules; according to one boatswain, they were 'not generally seamen; some have been bandsmen, some are servants.'[15]

Some titles indicated the bearing of a specific responsibility: a coxswain had charge of the ship's pinnace, cutter or launch, whereas the captain's coxswain, in addition to serving as his personal assistant, had charge of the captain's barge. There were also captains of the hold, forecastle, main top, after guard, mizzen top and mast. The first three of these 'captain' roles were skilled, ergo substantive posts, the latter three non-substantive (impermanent) posts held by some petty officers second-class. On transferring to another vessel, a man who had previously been 'captain of' mast,

[11] Rodger, *Wooden World*, pp. 19, 22.
[12] Ibid., p. 26.
[13] ADM 27/92/264/18.
[14] Lavery, *Able Seamen*, p. 107. The term 'sub[ordinate]-officers' is found in allotment registers and some ships' muster books, but is little used elsewhere.
[15] Hardwicke, *Report*, p. 204 ss. 3169–70.

mizzen top or after guard would very likely revert to his former rate, losing his additional pay and the 'social capital' of his rate, both of which losses would be felt by his dependants at home.[16] This touches upon a key aspect of mid-century naval service affecting more men than the 'captains of' parts of ship, for no pre-Continuous Service seaman had security of employment. Only commissioned and warrant officers had any permanent connection with the Royal Navy; a lower-deck man would simply join a ship fitting out for its next deployment.[17] His employment ended with the fulfilling of the ship's commission, at which point, had he not transferred to another vessel, deserted, been invalided, died or been killed, he would be marked in the ship's muster book as 'D' ('Discharged'), and 'Paid Off'.[18]

## SEAMEN'S PAY

From Tudor times seamen's pay had been calculated on a per diem basis, expressed in lunar terms and tabulated as thirty-one-day months. How often the individual was actually paid was a different matter. When his ship was ready for sea he was awarded an advance, but this might be disbursed up to six months after he had joined the vessel.[19] He was paid in arrears not only because of the service's budgetary complications, but also to discourage desertion, for deserters forfeited any unpaid wages.[20] Compared with many civilian occupations, his wage was poor. The nett sum he received varied according to the vessel in which he served (first, second, third rate, etc.), its location, the nature of its commission, and the man's trade, rate or class, pitched according to skill levels and length of service. Wages could be supplemented by sea pay, by allowances for the tools of a man's trade,

---

[16] Walton, 'Social History', p. 46; White, *Victoria's Navy*, p. 68.
[17] Rodger, *Wooden World*, p. 113; Daniel A. Baugh, 'The Eighteenth-Century Navy as a National Institution, 1690–1815', in J.R. Hill (ed.), *The Oxford Illustrated History of the Royal Navy* (Oxford, 1995), 120–60, at p. 146; Walton, '"Great Improvement"', p. 28.
[18] Holman, *Life in the Royal Navy*, pp. 70–2; Lewis, *Navy in Transition*, p. 217; ADM 38.
[19] Oliver Walton, 'New Kinds of Discipline: the Royal Navy in the second half of the nineteenth century', in Richard Harding, Helen Doe and Michael Duffy (eds), *Naval Leadership and Management, 1650–1950: essays in honour of Michael Duffy* (Woodbridge, 2012), 143–55, at p. 148.
[20] Alan Ramsay Skelley, *The Victorian Army at Home: the recruitment and terms and conditions of the British Regular, 1859–1899* (London, 1977), p. 251; J.D. Davies, 'A Permanent National Maritime Fighting Force, 1642–1869', in J.R. Hill (ed.), *The Oxford Illustrated History of the Royal Navy* (Oxford, 1995), 56–79, at p. 64; Winton, 'Life and Education in a Technologically Evolving Navy', p. 253; Cheryl A. Fury, 'Seamen's Wives and Widows', in Cheryl A. Fury (ed.), *The Social History of English Seamen, 1485–1649* (London, 2012), 253–76, at p. 257.

additional duties undertaken, his drawing extra pay in lieu of rum allowance, or, in the case of stokers, by the ship's being under full steam in the tropics.[21] He could, after five years' service, and if he behaved himself, earn up to three good conduct badges (GCBs), each badge adding one penny per day to his pay; after ten years' service and further good behaviour, his second GCB would earn him twopence per day, his third bringing him threepence after fifteen years.[22] The actuality was thus more complex than is suggested by pay scales published in the *Navy List* (Table 1), to the extent where 'not one man in twenty knows what he's going to receive when paid.'[23]

Table 1   Ship's company pay scales, per *Navy List* 1851 (extract).

| Ship's Company | Per Year | Per 31-Day Month | Per Day |
|---|---|---|---|
| Gunner 1st class | £88 4s 2d on Harbour Service Pay | £7 9s 10d on Harbour Service Pay | £0 4s 10d on Harbour Service Pay |
| Boatswain 1st class Carpenter 1st class | £94 5s 10d on Sea Pay | £8 0s 2d on Sea Pay | £0 5s 2d on Sea Pay |
| Tool Money to Carpenter on Sea Pay | £4 11s 3d | £0 7s 9d | £0 0s 3d |
| Gunner 2nd class Boatswain 2nd class Carpenter 2nd class | £59 6s 3d on Harbour Service Pay | £5 0s 9d on Harbour Service Pay | £0 3s 2d on Harbour Service Pay |
|  | £74 10s 5d on Sea Pay | £6 6s 7d on Sea Pay | £0 4s 1d on Sea Pay |
| Gunner 3rd class Boatswain 3rd class Carpenter 3rd class | £48 13s 4d on Harbour Service Pay | £4 2s 8d on Harbour Service Pay | £0 2s 8d on Harbour Service Pay |
|  | £63 17s 6d on Sea Pay | £5 8s 6d on Sea Pay | £0 3s 6d on Sea Pay |

[21] Walton, '"Great Improvement"', pp. 32, 35, 42; Lavery, *Able Seamen*, p. 66; Henry Baynham, *Before the Mast: Naval Ratings of the Nineteenth Century* (London, 1971), p. 119; White, *Victoria's Navy*, p. 77; James Woods, *Our Fighting Seamen, by Lionel Yexley* (London, 1911), pp. 9–10; Walton, 'Social History', pp. 41–2, 49, 60–1.

[22] Hardwicke, *Report*, p. 18 s. 194. The holding of GCBs had the additional benefit of protecting men from corporal punishment, though through no fault of his own a man could lose both badge and bonus on account of a punitive captain.

[23] Walton, 'Social History', pp. 81–2; Royal Navy, *The Queen's Regulations for the Government of Her Majesty's Naval Service*, Chapter X; Robinson, *Jack Nastyface*, p. 96.

| | | | |
|---|---|---|---|
| Ship's Cook<br>Leading stoker*<br>Chief Boatswain's Mate<br>Carpenter's Mate, in vessels where no Carpenter is borne<br>Seaman's Schoolmaster<br>Master at Arms<br>Sailmaker<br>Ropemaker<br>Caulker†<br>Blacksmith | £36 10s 0d<br>In 1st, 2nd & 3rd-rate ships<br>£34 19s 7d in all other ships | £3 2s 0d<br>In 1st, 2nd & 3rd-rate ships<br>£2 19s 5d in all other ships | £0 2s 0d<br>In 1st, 2nd & 3rd-rate ships<br>£0 1s 11d in all other ships |
| Stoker/Coal Trimmer*<br>Ship's Corporal<br>Captain's Coxswain<br>Quartermaster<br>Gunner's Mate<br>Boatswain's Mate<br>Coxswain of the Launch<br>Captain of the Forecastle/Hold/Maintop/Foretop/Afterguard | £31 18s 9d | £2 14s 3d | £0 1s 9d |
| Sailmaker's Mate<br>Caulker's Mate†<br>Armourer<br>Cooper | £30 8s 4d | £2 11s 8d | £0 1s 8d |
| Yeoman of the Signals<br>Coxswain of the Barge/Cutter/Pinnace<br>Captain of the Mizzen Top/Mast<br>Paymaster & Purser's Steward<br>Musician | £28 17s 11d | £2 9s 1d | £0 1s 7d |

*(Table 1 continued)*

| Ship's Company | Per Year | Per 31-Day Month | Per Day |
|---|---|---|---|
| Painter | £25 17s 1d | £2 3s 11d | £0 1s 5d |
| Sailmaker's Crew | £4 11s 3d | £0 7s 9d | £0 0s 3d |
| Cooper's Crew | | | |
| Carpenter's Crew | | | |
| Tool Money to Carpenter's Crew | | | |
| Able Seaman | £24 6s 8d | £2 1s 4d | £0 1s 4d |
| Sick Berth Attendant | | | |
| Bandsman | | | |
| Officers' Cook/Steward/Domestic | | | |
| Ordinary Seaman 2nd Class | £16 14s 7d | £1 8s 5d | £0 0s 11d |
| Paymaster & Purser's Steward's Mate | | | |

† Caulker and Caulker's Mate eligible for Tool Money, if employed in the Carpenter's Crew and in possession of Carpenter's Tools.

* Stokers: while in the tropics and while steam is up, half-pay allowed in addition.

Source: Allen, *Navy List* 1851, pp. 199–210 (selected text). Given fluctuations in costs and values, conversion of historical sums into twenty-first century equivalents is generally unhelpful. For an approximate equivalent sum, the following online tool may be useful: Bank of England, 'Inflation Calculator' (Bank of England, 1209–2021) <https://www.bankofengland.co.uk/monetary-policy/inflation/inflation-calculator> [accessed 30 March 2024].

Over one hundred different job titles are discernible among allotment declarations made during the study period by 1,547 men naming Portsea Island-resident dependants. For seventy-two trades a basic annual wage is known from published pay scales, but pay actually received varied for reasons described above. Other job titles include five species of cook and steward (captain's, gun room, midshipmen's, sub[ordinate] officers' and wardroom), and two rarities, the keeper of apartments and the trimmer of lamps of HM Yacht *Victoria and Albert*.[24] The latter two do not feature in the *Navy List* of the day, and since naval pay books have not survived

---

[24] ADM 27/113/59A/11; ADM 27/113/62/62.

beyond 1832 it is impossible to know which pay scale these men occupied, let alone the nett amount received once deductions had been made.[25] In general terms, however, these more unusual jobs are unlikely to have netted much less than the annual wage of £16 14s 7d for ordinary seamen second class or pussers' stewards' mates, but nothing approaching the maximum of £94 5s 10d paid to warrant officer gunners, carpenters and boatswains first class, with sea pay.

## SHORE LEAVE AND ACCOMMODATION

From 1846 officers had been empowered to grant ships' companies four to six weeks' paid leave at the end of a commission, extended to eight weeks from 1850.[26] When his paid leave ended, unless he found work on shore, a man had no further income until he joined ship again. Many men immediately (re-)entered a ship, but in doing so they forfeited time ashore with their families.[27] Not all were faced with choosing between family and income maintenance. Since 1828, when their ranks were made substantive, petty officers (POs) had enjoyed the right to sign on to the port flagship and take leave between commissions; that men below PO were not trusted with occasional liberty was the cause of much resentment.[28] Only HMS *Excellent*, moored in the northern reaches of Portsmouth Harbour, granted its trainee gunners daily leave five times per week, from early evening until the following morning.[29] The steadier sort might even be allowed to live on shore, for 'an old man-o'-war's man with family living in a house on shore ... [is] a man to be trusted ... [he] goes chiefly out of the dockyard to his home when his work is done.'[30] In addition to spousal comforts there was a financial inducement for his doing so, because every day lived on shore earned him 1s 7d in compensation for the victuals he would have received had he remained on board.[31] As Chapter Nine will show, his wife's (estimated) weekly food expenditure was in the region of 3s 4d, so the 1s 7d 'compensation' – nearly half her week's food budget – was a substantial income-boost, though how much of it actually arrived in her hand is

---

[25] National Archives (TNA) Kew, Navy Board: Navy Pay Office: Ships' Pay Books (Series III), ADM 35 (1777–1832).
[26] Lavery, *Royal Tars*, p. 217; Walton, '"Great Improvement"', p. 42.
[27] Hardwicke, *Report*, p. 13 s. 90.
[28] White, *Victoria's Navy*, p. 68; Winton, *Hurrah!*, p. 71; Rodger, *Command of the Ocean*, p. 499.
[29] Holman, *Life in the Royal Navy*, p. 83; James Woods, *The Inner Life of the Navy, by Lionel Yexley* (London, 1908), p. 137.
[30] Hardwicke, *Report*, p. 62 s. 804; Winton, *Hurrah!*, p. 71.
[31] Woods, *Inner Life of the Navy*, pp. 126–7.

debatable. Were his ship on harbour duties, however, even the steadier sort might prefer to be at sea, most men considering lower-paid harbour duty a waste of time.[32]

While a ship was being refitted its marines were billeted in local barracks, its sailors on hulks moored in the harbour. Barracks and hulks were unpopular, hulks particularly so.[33] Their ship might be alongside the quay, or lying at anchor within sight of land, but unless despatched ashore on errand, between watches men remained on board the hulk. For the 'newly raised' man with no home to go to or money for shoreside accommodation, the hulk was where he ate, abluted and slept, in spartan conditions. For the seaman and his wife there was no service-provided accommodation, married quarters not being introduced until the twentieth century.[34] There were no barracks for unmarried sailors either, but there was one institutional alternative. Situated on Queen Street, Portsea, within a hundred yards of the dockyard's main gate, the first Sailors' Home opened in 1851, providing clean, affordable, safe accommodation for the serving seaman.[35] It was much appreciated: within its first year alone over 9,000 beds were occupied, a further 1,000 sailors sleeping on mats in the day hall.[36] If the Sailors' Home were full and he had no family locally, the man in need of accommodation had a choice between private or common lodging-houses, a room above a pub or bedding down with a prostitute.[37] He might, if he were lucky, be taken in by a shipmate's family, as witness numerous households' census entries listing a mariner 'visitor'. But not all married shipmates had the space to accommodate visitors, and unmarried seamen enjoying shipmates' hospitality were fewer in number than those whose shoreside accommodation comprised lodging-house, pub or prostitute's bed. It

[32] Ibid.
[33] Hardwicke, *Report*, p. 268 ss. 5078–81; p. 275 ss. 5274–6 (re: marine barracks), and pp. 2, 13, 62, 90, 118, 204, 265, *et al.* (re: hulks); White, *Victoria's Navy*, p. 68; Moon, '"Sailorhoods"', p. 96.
[34] Anthony Carew, *The Lower Deck of the Royal Navy 1900–1939: the Invergordon Mutiny in Perspective* (Manchester, 1981), p. 58.
[35] Sailors' Homes both preceded and differed from the 'Sailors' Rests' associated with the charitable work of Agnes Weston. First established in Devonport in 1876, with a Portsmouth branch opening in 1881, 'Rests' were intended as temperance houses for the promotion of the National Temperance League and its offshoot, the Royal Naval Temperance Society.
[36] Lewis, *Navy in Transition*, p. 181; Peter Kemp, *The British Sailor: a social history of the lower deck* (London, 1970), p. 209; White, *Victoria's Navy*, p. 77; Winton, *Hurrah!*, p. 217; Sarah Quail and John Stedman, *Images of Portsmouth* (Derby, 1993), p. 150; Montague Gore, *Sailors' Homes* (London, 1852), p. iii.
[37] Preston, 'Constructing Communities', p. 226; Woods, *Inner Life of the Navy*, p. 113; Kellow Chesney, *The Victorian Underworld* (London, 1970), p. 382.

follows that most unmarried seamen had limited experience of ordinary domestic life, which may explain some of the marital tensions described later, and naval wives' shouldering of greater domestic responsibility.

## THE REMITTANCE AND ALLOTMENT SYSTEMS

If things were tough for the seaman ashore, they were tougher still for his loved ones. On every lower deck it was common knowledge – had been so since at least the seventeenth century – that from port town to rural hamlet, naval dependants were turning to the parish for assistance.[38] The poor relief system, in turn, had in the eighteenth and early nineteenth centuries staggered under a dramatic increase in the poor population as a result of men's enlisting for military service, leaving dependants to fend for themselves or turn to the parish.[39] Even in peacetime, many naval dependants were struggling, some destitute.

The Navy's response was to establish a system by which ordinary seamen and warrant officers could make a portion of their pay available to approved dependants at home.[40] The creation in 1728 of the original remittance system, forerunner of the allotment scheme, came not out of admiralty altruism or corporate concern for dependants, nor out of parishes' protesting the cost of caring for poor naval families.[41] It came instead from the service's need to stem the loss of skilled, experienced, mature and steady seamen, and to ally itself with women in the hope they would both persuade men to enlist and dissuade them from desertion.[42] Given the scheme's political daring, and the bureaucratic and financial resources required for its operation, it is ironic that there was no equivalent of the modern-day post-implementation review to identify systemic weakness, inefficiency or areas for improvement. More than 130 years would pass before an admiralty clerk by the name of Pitcairn, working to a commission by Accountant General R.M. Bromley, produced the service's first report on the allotment system.[43] Handwritten, clearly intended for internal use only, the Pitcairn report

---

[38] Fury, 'Seamen's Wives and Widows', pp. 257–8; Lin, 'Caring for the Nation's Families', pp. 100–1; Winton, 'Life and Education in a Technologically Evolving Navy', p. 254.
[39] Patricia Lin, 'Citizenship, Military Families, and the Creation of a New Definition of "Deserving Poor" in Britain, 1793–1815', *Social Politics*, 7:1 (2000), 5–46, at p. 11.
[40] Hunt, 'Women and the Fiscal-imperial State', p. 34.
[41] *Navy Act*, 1 Geo. II, st. 2, c. 14 (1727).
[42] Lin, 'Caring for the Nation's Families', p. 101; Admiral Charles Knowles ('Philo Nauticus'), *A proposal for the encouragement of seamen to serve more readily in His Majesty's navy for preventing of desertion, supporting their wives and families, and for the easier and quieter government of His Majesty's ships* (London, 1758), *passim*.
[43] Pitcairn, *Report*.

provides a retrospective summary of the scheme's inception, development and scale of operation.

In bringing remittances into being, the 1728 Navy Act had laid the foundations of the later allotment system. Headed *An Act for encouraging seamen to enter into His Majesty's service*, it asserted the seaman's entitlement 'to empower and entitle any person or persons to receive pay, wages or allowances', this being achieved via letter of attorney from a third party, not necessarily a lawyer, who was empowered to act on behalf of the nominee by collecting the man's pay and forwarding it to the intended recipient.[44] Navy and dockyard clerks could in theory have filled the attorney role, but as agents for the corporate source of the money they were forbidden to act on behalf of its beneficiaries. For many families the attorney requirement was problematic, for 'apart from the difficulty in paying the ships as often as the Act required, it was difficult for the seamen to find honest and inexpensive attorneys.'[45] In addition to attorneys' charges (as much as eighteen or twenty shillings had been known to be levied for handling a bi-monthly pay packet of £2 5s 0d) there were logistical difficulties.[46] For example, the Act required wives receiving remittances to journey up to five miles from home to designated payment points, thus adding to the strain of naval family life and the burden of their poverty.[47] There was also a systemic rigidity which required men either to remit no money at all, or so small a sum as to be of little assistance.[48] Combined with irregular pay, these issues made the inaugural scheme less well-used than had been expected.[49] Indeed, within twenty years of the 1728 Act, naval administrators were advising seamen *against* remitting money via attorneys.[50] Seamen's families continued to be a charge upon their parishes, never more so than in port towns which in certain instances resorted to petitioning the House of Commons to provide some form of income for indigent naval dependants.[51]

The scheme's successor, introduced via the Navy Act of 1758, abolished remittance charges and the need for attorneys.[52] Now government officials such as customs and excise officers or receivers of land tax might be engaged

---

[44] Geo. II, st. 2, c. 14 (1727), s. X; Gradish, *Manning of the British Navy*, pp. 54–5.
[45] Rodger, *Wooden World*, p. 131.
[46] Margarette Lincoln, 'The Impact of Warfare on Naval Wives and Women', in Cheryl A. Fury (ed.), *The Social History of English Seamen, 1650–1815* (Woodbridge, 2017), 71–88, at p. 74.
[47] *Ibid.*
[48] Gradish, *Manning of the British Navy*, p. 56.
[49] Rodger, *Command of the Ocean*, p. 317.
[50] Gradish, *Manning of the British Navy*, p. 55.
[51] Lin, 'Citizenship, Military Families', p. 11; Gradish, *Manning of the British Navy*, p. 56.
[52] *Navy Act,* 31 Geo. II, c.10 (1758).

to disburse money free of charge, the threat of a heavy fine discouraging them from extracting fees for their services.[53] Despite these adjustments the remittance scheme remained unpopular, suggesting that wives' complaints continued to exert a negative influence upon participation levels. Stark ascribes the low take-up to the system's being intentionally complicated, its setting-up arrangements beyond the wit of most seamen.[54] It was complex, certainly, but only in order to prevent fraud and misuse; moreover, to devise and operate an 'intentionally' unwieldy and unpopular system would gain the Navy nothing but needless expense, political disapproval and mockery, while doing little to stem the dissatisfaction of serving men and their families. A more plausible explanation for the low take-up lies in the system's applying only to seagoing men, and benefitting only wives; for as Rodger points out, most deep-sea sailors were young single men, and married men were not common at sea.[55] Summary census information confirms that three-quarters of the Navy's lower-deck men were unmarried in 1851, the service's 23.9 per cent proportion of married men being over 10 per cent smaller than the civil equivalent.[56]

In 1795 and 1796, Acts of Parliament were introduced with a purpose of levying from English, Welsh and Scottish local authorities fixed numbers of men for service in the Navy, and fining those authorities which failed to meet their 'quotas'.[57] The Quota Acts duly raised up to 30,000 men, but scarcely one-sixth were seamen, the rest being from country trades.[58] Connected with the introduction of these Acts was the evolution, by 1795, of remittances into allotments, 'an improved mechanism by which men could "allot" a portion of their pay to be drawn once a month by a named relative, the intention being that men recruited under the Quota Acts did not leave their families destitute to become a charge on the parish poor rates'.[59] Permitted allottee relationships were at first limited to the seaman's

---

[53] Gradish, *Manning of the British Navy*, pp. 55–6.
[54] Lin, 'Citizenship, Military Families', p. 15; Suzanne J. Stark, *Female Tars: women aboard ship in the age of sail* (London, 1996), p. 23.
[55] Rodger, *Wooden World*, pp. 132, 134–5.
[56] Registrar General, Population Tables II, Vol. 1, England and Wales Divisions I–VI (1851), Registrar General <http://www.histpop.org/ohpr/servlet/PageBrowser2?ResourceType=Census&ResourceType=Registrar%20General&SearchTerms=portsmouth%20females%201851&simple=yes&path=Results&active=yes&treestate=expandnew&titlepos=0&mno=30&tocstate=expandnew&display=sections&display=tables&display=pagetitles&pageseq=212&zoom=4> [accessed 22 April 2024], pp. 47–8.
[57] *Manning of the Navy Act*, 35 Geo. III, c. 5 (1795); *Manning of the Army and Navy Act*, 37 Geo. III, c. 4 (1796).
[58] Rodger, *Command of the Ocean*, pp. 443–4.
[59] Ibid., p. 443.

wife and/or parent, but would in due course include grandparents, siblings and trustees for under-age children – a wider span than that of an equivalent system operated by the Dutch East India Company, which restricted payments to parents, wives and children.[60] Limitations notwithstanding, sailors continued to declare in favour of more distant relatives, and naval clerks continued to thwart their efforts. From HMS *Vernon* in 1841, AB Thomas Smith nominated his father-in-law.[61] The declaration was crossed out in red ink, with 'Cancelled not allowed' written across the entry. In 1851 Thomas Woods, a stoker later to survive the sinking of *Birkenhead*, named his aunt.[62] His declaration's more forbidding (and pompous) clerical superscript reads 'Cancelled not allowed by Act of Parliament – reported'. The range of permitted relationships did, however, make it possible for women to receive in more than one capacity, from more than one man. In 1850–51, for example, Christian[na] Nancarrow (*q.v.*) was named in three allotment declarations: as wife of William Nancarrow, captain of HMS *Cormorant*'s afterguard; as sister of AB Sampson Hooper, HMS *Hecate*; and as trustee for three-and-a-half-year-old William, son of Sampson's messmate AB John Appleby.[63] Multiple allotments to one recipient were entirely within the rules, but lamenting 'frequent instances of the same woman claiming the allotments of several seamen', one high-ranking witness to the 1859 Royal Commission on naval manning implied (wrongly) that rapacious allottees could impose their claims upon helpless sailors.[64] The opposite was true: choice and power to allot lay entirely in seamen's hands.

Other systemic changes followed, some benefiting allottees, others protecting men's interests. Stepmothers became eligible, and (via a trustee if they were under eighteen years old) half-brothers, half-sisters and illegitimate children.[65] Whereas remittances had been disbursed on a lunar-calendar basis, allotments became payable per calendar month, making life easier for pay office and recipient alike.[66] Places of payment, too, might be altered upon request, enabling wives and mothers to return to their home parishes rather than be restricted to the port where the allotting sailor's ship had been fitted out.

[60] Manon van der Heijden and Danielle ven den Heuvel, 'Sailors' Families and the Urban Institutional Framework in Early Modern Holland', *The History of the Family*, 12: 4 (2007), 296–309, at p. 301.
[61] ADM 27/74/186/285.
[62] ADM 27/113/387/23.
[63] ADM 27/111/284/76; ADM 27/112/180/68; ADM 27/111/359/67. Spellings of Christianna's forename vary.
[64] Hardwicke, *Report*, p. 73 s. 1067.
[65] Pitcairn, *Report*, p. 23.
[66] Ibid., p. 14; *Pay of the Navy Act*, 11 Geo. IV & 1 Will. IV, c. 20 (1830), s. XXXII.

Payments were capped at a moiety (half) of men's monthly wages, hence irrespective of the actual proportion of pay allotted, allotments were frequently referred to as 'half-pay', as witness one newspaper report of a servant, on trial for theft, 'going to the dockyard to take her half-pay'.[67] The moiety cap may reflect budgetary constraints on the part of a chronically underfunded Navy. It may also reflect political sensitivity, for there was potential for public disquiet should it be known that the greater part of men's earnings (which came, after all, from a public purse part-funded by tax receipts and managed by government) was being diverted into private hands, those hands almost exclusively female. Political and budgetary considerations aside, there may also be inferred an underlying principle that however needy his dependants on shore, the naval breadwinner should not be deprived of the lion's share of his earnings. If this principle obtained (nowhere is it articulated), it reflected a wider cultural assumption that notwithstanding his dependants' needs, the male breadwinner had a moral right to keep as much of his wages as he pleased. Whatever its rationale, the moiety cap frustrated the more generous family man; even more did it frustrate his wife at home, trying to make ends meet.

The cap was not entirely rigid. A measure of flexibility ensured that when sailors' wages increased, the amounts allotted rose likewise, in theory ensuring recipients never received less than half their men's earnings.[68] When a man was disrated, however, his pay shrank, his allotment likewise. There is evidence of this being ordered by naval authorities, but some men took what steps they could to manage their own adjustments. The 1850 declaration by AB Robert Shepherd, HMS *Excellent*, favouring his wife Sarah Ann, bears the red-inked legend 'Has an allotment in force as Gun[ner]'s Mate, but having been disrated, wishes it altered from £1 4s 0d to 18s.'[69]

No evidence has been found to suggest that men were routinely allotting to more than one person at a time. This is not unexpected: on a limited wage it was all but impossible for one man to award meaningful amounts to multiple recipients. Men could however stop payments to one nominee and transfer their money to another. The mechanism for doing so was clumsy, the requested change neither quickly processed nor guaranteed to be approved, which may explain why only three dozen of this study's 2,300 declarations feature successive allottees named by the same individual.[70] Transfers usually reflect a family event or change of civil status, for

---

[67] *H/Tel*, 14 October 1848, p. 7 col. E.
[68] *Navy Act*, 46 Geo. III, c. 127 (1806); Lin, 'Citizenship, Military Families', p. 16 n. 14.
[69] ADM 27/111/83/1525.
[70] Lin, 'Citizenship, Military Families', p. 116.

example a man's redirecting money from a now-deceased wife to the trustee caring for his motherless child; or his having acquired a wife to maintain, and wishing to stop his earlier allotment to a mother or sister. AB James Rowsell, HMS *Excellent*, had since 1847 allotted to his mother Susannah, but his 1851 declaration notes 'Has an allotment in favour of mother but wishes it transferred' [to Elizabeth Lowry Smith, his bride of two weeks].[71] Joshua Hussey, stoker HMS *Blenheim*, in January 1850 allotted to his sister Mary Kinsale; in August, following his marriage, a revised declaration from HMS *Niger* named his new wife Catherine Frances Thomas.[72] For sisters, mothers and trustees reliant on his support, a man's marrying meant financial loss. From 1843 to 1846 Ann Parker had received allotments from her brother AB Benjamin Martell, HMS *St Vincent*.[73] After marrying in January 1847, Benjamin named his bride, Mary Voller White.[74] Ann was fortunate in that Benjamin's money was extra to the allotment she received from her seaman-husband Philip following their marriage in 1834.[75] Without this, the redirection of Benjamin's support would have been a more severe blow to her domestic economy; and if that happened it would be natural were jealousy or resentment to colour in-law relationships.

Neither remittance nor allotment system eradicated the service's recruitment and retention problems.[76] Despite having better food, discipline, medical treatment and prospects than their merchant navy peers, in the 1840s Royal Navy men were still leaving at a rate of over a thousand per year, and not re-enlisting: speaking of the period 1840–52, Taylor notes 'some 1150 men … annually quitted the Navy after short periods of service; in 1848 alone over 6000 were discharged, many of whom left the country.'[77] Even so, the allotment system was not abandoned. Indeed, changes introduced in the fifty years 1795–1845 suggest the Navy was becoming more confident in the propriety and workability of its creation. The changes also bespeak an admixture of corporate self-interest, and – on paper at least – benign accommodation towards naval dependants. Developments such as procedural rules being relaxed and allottees' logistical difficulties

---

[71] ADM 27/100/412/3; England Marriages 1538–1973, parish marriages, Portsea, 21 April 1851; ADM 27/113/336/1528.
[72] ADM 27/109/423/410; E&W Marriages: Q3/1850, vol. 7, p. 248; ADM 27/111/126/24.
[73] ADM 27/81/364/97; ADM 27/89/4/702; ADM 27/94/15/38.
[74] CHU3/1D/45, p. 112 n. 224; ADM 27/107/231/292; ADM 27/112/411/65.
[75] ADM 27/37/19/72; ADM 27/38/130/72; ADM 27/56/232/28; ADM 27/76/122/49.
[76] Pitcairn, *Report*, p. 1; Lin, 'Caring for the Nation's Families', pp. 102, 116.
[77] Rodger, *Wooden World*, pp. 116–17; Winton, 'Life and Education in a Technologically Evolving Navy', p. 259; Walton, '"Great Improvement"', p. 41; R. Taylor, 'Manning the Royal Navy: the Reform of the Recruiting System, 1852–62' (Part 1), *Mariner's Mirror*, 44: 4 (1959), 302–13, at p. 303.

acknowledged were welcome to man and dependant alike; but the underlying concern of the Navy remained the retention and sailorly performance of its men, to which sailorly contentment was intimately linked.

Choice was a component part of that contentment.[78] It was for the Navy to determine the rules governing allotments; within those rules it was for the individual sailor to decide the amount his wife or other relative should receive. Having few unavoidable expenses at sea, a man could choose what he might allot to his family or keep for himself; what to save, or to spend on gambling, tobacco, soap, religious tracts, poll parrots, drinking or whoring. Measures were introduced to assert or retain on the one hand the Navy's corporate powers, on the other the individual sailor's control over his finances. All this made for an uneasy balancing act, the new regulations being 'found to work harshly as to the Families and Relatives of the men, prejudicially to morality and encouraging an immense amount of perjury and false assumption of Relationship … and imposed considerable trouble on the Paying Officers in satisfying themselves as to the Relationship of the Allottees.'[79]

## THE ALLOTMENT AS SYSTEM AND PROCESS

The allotment system was one in which the individual (usually female) nominee-recipient was dependent upon and subject to corporate and individual (entirely male) authority. Three senior officers were required to sign each ship's biannual record of declarations. Once the signed registers had found their way back to the Navy Office in London, three commissioners of the Navy Board were required to authorise each allotment.[80] A form authorising payment was then sent to the nominee's district, addressed to revenue officials representing central government; the nominee herself was sent a duplicate. These forms were standardised documents in which allottees' names were copied by hand on to pre-printed papers (Fig. 2). The use of standardised paperwork was historically remarkable, marking 'the first time that the state would use its efforts to document the identity of women and children who were not from the elite of society.'[81] Emblazoned with official crests, with inked swirls filling blank spaces to prevent the insertion of unauthorised wordage, and peppered with stern warnings as to the penalties for misuse, personation, etc., these pay bills (or vouchers) were daunting for individuals unused to handling official material. The

---

[78] Daniel Vickers and Vince Walsh, *Young Men and the Sea: Yankee seafarers in the age of sail* (New Haven, Conn., 2005), p. 179.
[79] Pitcairn, *Report*, p. 3.
[80] Rodger, *Wooden World*, pp. 33–4.
[81] Lin, 'Citizenship, Military Families', p. 20.

**Class C.**

All Letters relating to Navy Allotments are to be addressed to the "Secretary of the Admiralty, London," with the words "*Accountant General*" on the left corner.

## Party's Allotment Pay Bill.

No. 50436                                                   Ledger     Page

Wm Barrett, serving as *Able Seaman* on board Her Majesty's Ship Illustrious, having, according to the Provisions of the Act 11 Geo. IV, cap. 20, made an Allotment of his Wages for the Maintenance of his Wife, Hannah, living at 24 Chapel Row, Bottom, Middleton Street, Queenstown, Cork, Ireland in the County of Cork

You are hereby required to pay her the Sum of *Eighteen Shillings*, until further Notice, for every Calendar Month, from the First day of May 1849, on her producing a Duplicate hereof, with a Certificate under the Hands of the Minister and Churchwardens or Elders of the Parish where she resides, that, to the best of their knowledge, she is the Wife of the above-named Man.

N.B.—In Parishes which are divided into Districts, the Certificate of the Minister of the District alone will be admitted.

Signed by me at the Admiralty, this 7th day of June 1849.

Approved,

D'. Acc'. Gen'. of the Navy.

To the Paymaster General's Clerk Portsmouth

Collector of the Customs Cork

Collector of Excise

Before Payment is made, the Paying Officer will, in the case of a Wife, require the production of her Marriage Certificate.

If the Paying Officer shall, in any case, entertain any doubt as to the Identity of the Party, the authenticity of the Vouchers produced, or of his or her Title to receive Payment, such Paying Officer shall enquire into the same by the Declaration of the Party so applying, which Declaration such Officer is authorised by the Act of 11 Geo. IV. cap. 20, sect. 44, to administer for that purpose.

N.B. By Virtue of the Act 11 Geo. IV. the personating or falsely assuming the Name or Character of any Person, to obtain Payment of an Allotment, is made Felony. It is also enacted that any Person who shall be guilty of making a false Declaration or Affirmation, for the purpose of receiving an Allotment, shall be liable to the Penalty of Perjury.

*Examined,*

**Fig. 2** Allotment pay bill. Kew, The National Archives (TNA): ADM 27/109/542-3 (pay bill found between register pages). Reproduced under licence by kind permission of The National Archives, Kew.

use of pre-printed forms was nevertheless efficient, obviating the need for handwritten copies with their inherent costs, delays and risk of errors, and preventing the unentitled poor from availing themselves of a service-specific welfare system.

The named allottee would take her duplicate form to her church minister, churchwardens, elders of the parish or overseers of the poor. As local representatives of the Crown these men were responsible for verifying her identity. Verification was essential. Naval women wore no uniform, carried no identity card or badge and (as evidenced by marriage certificates in which brides made their mark) many could not sign their names. They were, in short, indistinguishable from their civilian peers. Photographic proof of identity was not yet a practice, and the logging of physical descriptions was a bureaucratic burden, as the Navy well knew from its practice of recording, in ships' description books, details of men's height, complexion, hair and eye colour, scars and distinguishing marks.[82] To every allottee, however, there was a parish minister and/or churchwarden, an overseer of parish relief. These authority figures were likely to have at least nodding acquaintance with her; and it was upon one of these worthies that the system rendered her dependent for written confirmation that she both existed, and was who she said she was.

As well as a local representative of the Crown, for every allottee there was also a central government representative, one with whom she would have had no previous dealings but who was trained to handle money and held to high standards of accountability. From their bases in rural land tax offices, merchant and fishing port customs houses and naval dockyard pay offices, these government officials coordinated with parish officials, forming 'a network of personnel geographically accessible to most residents of Britain.'[83] The men operating land tax offices and customs houses were not from allottees' own communities. Unlike parish ministers or overseers, they did not know the women or their circumstances. They were therefore in no position to ascertain eligibility.[84] Their role was to match their copy of the printed pay bill issued by the Navy Office with the duplicate issued to the allottee, her copy now annotated and signed by her parish representative. Once a match had been established and the allottee's identity confirmed either by letter from her parish officers or, where necessary, by oath (the Navy could assert its right to administer an oath as part of its inquiry into the veracity of the claim), and once the paperwork had been verified as 'genuine and authentick', payment could at last be made.[85]

---

[82] ADM 158.
[83] Lin, 'Caring for the Nation's Families', p. 17.
[84] Lin, 'Citizenship, Military Families', p. 20.
[85] *Navy Act,* 26 Geo. III, c. 63 (1786), s. IV; 11 Geo. IV & 1 Will. IV, c. 20 (1830), s. XXXIV; Gradish, *Manning of the British Navy*, pp. 55–6.

For the working-class woman who had never had to communicate with an agent of national government, the verification process was no small matter.[86] Something of the tensions involved, and the relative status of seamen's women and the officials with whom they must interact, may be discerned in Elizabeth Greenleaf's letters to Greenwich Hospital School. Wife of John Greenleaf (in naval service 1799–1829), Elizabeth was matriarch of the naval family depicted in Fig. 27, and mother of three daughters whose stories will be unfolded in due course. In 1829 she and John applied to Greenwich Hospital School for admission of their son Joseph as a pupil. The application being successful, they submitted another in respect of their daughter Phoebe. The now widowed Elizabeth knew the importance of documents submitted in support of the application, and was concerned they not be lost in the admission process. On 24 July 1831, from 'on board HMS *Venerable* at Portsmouth' (John Greenleaf had been *Venerable*'s boatswain), she wrote to ask for the return of her marriage certificate which more than two years earlier had been 'sent up for to enter my Son Joseph Greenleaf', explaining that 'They will not Enter me for my Annuity [widow's pension] till I can produce the Certificate of my Marrge thierfor I will Humbily thank you to send it me by the Return of Post'.[87]

Penned within days of her husband being 'Discharged Dead' at Haslar, Elizabeth's plea appears not to have had effect, since fifteen months later a follow-up letter was necessary.[88] The school approved Phoebe's admission, but Elizabeth's difficulties did not end there. Six years later still, she wrote to 'Mr Dean, the Clerk of the Cheque' at Greenwich:

> No. 41 Gloucester Street, Portsea
> 12 March 1837
>
> Sir,
>
> Pardon the Liberty I have taken to address you, but my daughters Phoebe and Joanna Greenleaf's Register of Birth and Affidavit and my own Marriage Certificate and my son Joseph's Affidavit (his Registry of Birth applied to you before) are now lying at your Offices, and being in want of them, should feel obliged if you would send them to me as soon as convenient.
>
> I am,
> Sir,
> Your very humble Servant
> Elizabeth Greenleaf[89]

---

[86] Lin, 'Caring for the Nation's Families', pp. 103–4.
[87] ADM 73/243/2.
[88] *Ibid.*
[89] *Ibid.*

In a different hand, the outer fold of this letter bears a laconic scrawl, '14 March 37, Return Documents'. Elizabeth's efforts had at last paid off.

From her long association with the Navy, Elizabeth was sensible of the comparative status of lower-deck men, warrant officers and commissioned officers. Clerks were another matter. Like her, they were non-uniformed civilians, but civilians in the employ of the Navy, civilians who interacted with senior officers, possessing the power to grant or withhold, to facilitate or delay. They were also, invariably, male. When dealing with remote authority figures, especially those on whom the seaman's wife was dependent for approval of benefits, a respectful and subservient tone was necessary. To demand or insist would cut little ice, might even delay matters or damage her chances of a positive response. The raucous, froward behaviour with which the naval woman was popularly associated would get her nowhere. Assertiveness and self-determination might be essential to the naval wife enduring her seaman-husband's long absences, but they were less effective when deployed in other arenas, to different ends. It is not impossible that, mindful of the ability of clerks and senior officers to affect their prospects of advancement, or simply not wanting to be embarrassed by their women's inappropriate behaviour, seamen urged this highly respectful manner upon their wives. If so, it was something Elizabeth maintained for years after her husband's death. As a woman supplicant in a man's world she knew when and how to be (outwardly) subservient.

Why did the Navy rely on local and central government agencies? Why not administer the allotment scheme itself, from on-board declaration to on-shore disbursement? Geography was one factor, expense another. Not all sailors' dependants lived in port towns where naval officials were located. Some lived in remote rural communities far from the sea, some in inland cities. A written return to the House of Commons showed that of 16,280 allotments in force in England and Wales in 1857–58, thirty related to dependants resident in or within collecting distance of Birmingham, forty-six in Manchester, fifty-two in or around rural Salisbury, eighteen apiece from Oxford and Cambridge, with Coventry, Halifax and Leicester having respectively twenty-three, twenty-six and twenty-four.[90] It was unrealistic to require poor women resident beyond the Hampshire border to travel to Portsmouth in order to have their identities verified by persons unacquainted with them. It was equally unrealistic on grounds of cost for the Navy to employ staff in every county to verify and vet men's wives, let alone men's parents, siblings or trustees.

There were other considerations. The Navy was concerned not to operate – or be perceived as operating – a monetary conduit benefitting undesirables. Reflecting a widespread belief that women were unsophisticated

---

[90] House of Commons Paper no. 295, XXXIX, 13, 1857–58, pp. 13–15.

and vulnerable to trickery, one statutory instrument expressed concern to prevent 'the unwary, the ignorant or the necessitous from being defrauded and injured by the extortion and usury of wicked and evil-designed persons'.[91] Fears of extortion and usury were detectable in successive legal instruments in which parish officers were variously required to: certify a woman's being a genuine naval widow and thus entitled to receive a bounty of her late husband's wages; approve as suitable to receive an allotment any person nominated by the seaman-father of a motherless child; report and certify misconduct disqualifying such a person from receiving payment; approve an individual as local substitute 'in the Room of [i.e. to replace] such a Person who may have abused the Trust reposed in him or them'; and certify the father of a seaman to be 'a widower and wholly unable to maintain himself' in order that he might qualify for a portion of his son's pay.[92] The word of the sailor alone, no matter how steady and respectable he be, was insufficient for a politically cautious Navy.

## STOPPAGES, SANCTIONS, SYSTEMIC GLITCHES

A man's word was not sufficient to confirm his relative's identity, relationship or qualification for an allotment, but until the late 1850s it was sufficient to initiate stoppage.[93] A letter dated March 1850 from HMS *Excellent* to the Accountant General of the Royal Navy requests the allotment of AB George Davis to his wife (Elizabeth née Williams, the former widow Thompson, whom he married in 1845) be stopped on the grounds of her living with another man.[94] Two months later, his request accepted, George declared an allotment favouring his sister Louisa Davis, resident of Little Newport Street, a narrow London thoroughfare between Charing Cross Road and Leicester Square.[95] It was months before Louisa received his money. Writing in September 1850 to the Board of Admiralty, she said she had just received a letter from her brother 'on board the *Excellent*, stating he had arranged for me to receive his half pay from the 3rd of May 1850, and [I] should be glad to know when I am to receive it.'[96] A repeat of George's declaration bears the red-inked superscript, 'This man made out an allotment ... from this ship on 2nd May 1850, but his Sister has not received any Allot.t Bill.'[97] The issue

[91] *Navy Act*, 31 Geo. II, c. 10 (1758), preamble and s. XIII.
[92] *Wages and Prize Money in the Navy Act*, 49 Geo. IV, c. 108 (1809), ss. XI, XII, XV.
[93] 46 Geo. III, c. 127 (1806), s. IV; 11 Geo. IV & 1 Will. IV, c. 20 (1830), s. XXXV; Pitcairn, *Report*, p. 9.
[94] ADM 27/110/225; ADM 27/108/151/1200; CHU3/1D/44, p. 35 n. 69.
[95] ADM 27/110/220/1200.
[96] ADM 27/110/224–5 (letter found between register pages).
[97] ADM 27/111/135/200.

here is not how long it took for Louisa's voucher to arrive, but the nature of George's relationship with her. Chapter Two explains the ambiguities associated with sisters' allotments, ambiguities to be borne in mind when we find no spinster Louisa Davis resident in Little Newport Street; instead, in Tavistock Row, Covent Garden, a few minutes' walk from where George's declaration located 'sister' Louisa, the census captured a George Davis, wife Louisa, and 1-year-old son George William.[98] If this 'Head of Family' were seaman George, his 'wife' Louisa the 'sister' named in his declarations (and if not, it is an extraordinary coincidence of namesakes and locations), in requesting that the allotment to his lawful wife Elizabeth be stopped on the grounds of her cohabiting with another man, George appears to have been a scheming and adulterous humbug.[99]

Husbandly hypocrisy aside, this example demonstrates women's vulnerability to seamen's fluctuating affections. Whether truth or confection, so long as men's stoppage requests were convincing, the result was wives being deprived of their allotments, thereby freeing the way for husbands' new nominees to receive the rerouted bounty. Indeed, until 1854 a husband could decide summarily to stop payments to his wife without having to account for his reasons.[100] As Pitcairn observed of the discretionary power of the British seaman,

> Only those engaged in the practical duty can be aware of the cases of hardship that occasion through Seamen, without assigning a reason, selfishly stopping their Allotments to their Wives for the purpose of getting increased Monthly Allowance [on board]. Perhaps it would only be an act of humanity if their Lordships were to insist on a reason being given for stopping Allotments in all instances, and in the case of Wives, to resume the exercise of the power they still hold of using a discretion in complying with the men's requests.[101]

It took more than verbal pleading for allottees to convince shoreside authorities. If she were ill or 'disabled by bodily Infirmity' from collecting her money, an allottee must not only obtain written confirmation of her ill-health from parish officials, or from a physician, surgeon or apothecary, but pay any fee charged for supplying such a letter. If she did not collect within six months of the allotment's inception, being prevented from doing so by illness, imprisonment or other circumstance, her money would be

---

[98] 1851 census: St Paul, Covent Garden, Westminster, HO107/1511, fol. 82, p. 8.
[99] ADM 27/110/225.
[100] *Navy Pay, Etc., Act,* 17 & 18 Vict., c. 19 (1854); National Archives (TNA) Kew, Admiralty Circulars ADM 7/890, no. 163 (30 September 1854); Pitcairn, *Report*, pp. 9–14.
[101] Pitcairn, *Report*, p. 9.

forfeit and added to the man's next regular pay.[102] Were she to return to her home from the port where her husband's ship had fitted out, a certificate was required from the ministers, churchwardens or elders of her home parish to confirm her residence there, otherwise her allotment payments would not be transferred to her local collection office.[103] These and other measures were not intentionally punitive. They reflected the Navy's proper concern to prevent embezzlement and personation, of which more in Chapter Eleven. Allottees were not only vulnerable to shoreside problems, however. Shipboard matters could affect their financial security. The mid-nineteenth century Navy's punishment for seamen's misconduct commonly took the form of fines or stoppage of pay.[104] If a man deserted, for example, his pay would stop pending his return or recapture; and with stoppage of pay went stoppage of allotment.[105] In short, aided by parish officers, both the Navy which had established the means to support sailors' wives, and/or those sailors who for richer, for poorer, had pledged themselves to their wives, could at any time abdicate their corporate and spousal responsibilities. The allottee's entitlement was predicated upon others' endorsement. She could not afford to be complacent.

Where in 1858 Pitcairn observed that 'It was … a great hardship on the Men that they should be kept often for months on board ship, without the power of doing anything to provide for their Families,' the view of the 1859 Hardwicke Royal Commission on naval manning was austere to the point of contemptuous, considering allotments ('the system has been much complained of') among many things negatively affecting recruitment and retention of seamen.[106] The Commission's conclusion is perverse. Only five years earlier several changes had been made to the allotment system, some inarguably for the better. For example, police inspectors were now required to vet and make recommendations as to the suitability of trustees, a move which helped reduce the risk of seamen's motherless children being cared for by dubious individuals.[107] The Commission, however, was more interested in problems than systemic improvements. Witnesses reported hardship caused by the Navy's prohibiting the making of declarations until

---

[102] Gradish, *Manning of the British Navy*, p. 56; 11 Geo. IV & 1 Will. IV, c. 20 (1830), s. XLV.
[103] 46 Geo. III, c. 127 (1806), s. IV.
[104] Walton, 'Social History', p. 213.
[105] Hardwicke, *Report*, p. 63 s. 830; Valerie Burton, 'The Myth of Bachelor Jack: masculinity, patriarchy and seafaring labour', in Colin D. Howell and Richard J. Twomey (eds), *Jack Tar in History: essays in the history of maritime life and labour* (Fredericton, N.B., 1991), 179–98, at p. 186.
[106] Pitcairn, *Report*, p. 18; Hardwicke, *Report*, p. ix s. 22.
[107] H/Tel, 2 September 1854, p. 7 col. E, citing Order in Council 11 August 1854.

a man were six months in a ship, until the ship were three months or more at sea.[108] Then there was the time taken to establish the allotment record, a month after which the first disbursement was supposed to occur; but two months was the more common waiting period, one witness averring to delays of five to six months before payments finally began.[109] Many a wife stranded without means had been known to sell or pawn her clothes in order to survive, or apply to the parish for relief, or (per the euphemism of the day) to 'get her living as best she can'.[110] One applicant for relief was Harriet Mould, wife of marine private James Mould. His 1851 allotment, declared on board *Prince Regent*, awarded the then childless Harriet twelve shillings per month.[111] The next six years saw three children born.[112] In 1859 James declared again, this time from *Illustrious*, but destruction of allotment records beyond 1852 means the sum awarded is unknown. What is known from the 1859 Royal Commission's minutes is that pending his money coming through, Harriet and her children had had to manage for eight weeks on out-relief of just two shillings per week, less than half the fifteen shillings per month allotted by most Royal Marine privates at the mid-century point.[113] According to one Rear Admiral's witness statement, however, the Navy could do nothing to make allotments more readily available 'without considerable risk of loss to the Crown', a remark neatly capturing the service's preoccupations and priorities.[114]

That wives and children were suffering periodic hardship was apparent from returns submitted to the Royal Commission by one parish's relieving officer, and from the sworn statements of several witnesses; yet the Commission only superficially explored the causative connection between, on the one hand, delays caused by the service's own restrictions and regulations and, on the other, families' mounting financial distress.[115] Instead, it probed witnesses upon the iniquity of rules which now allowed men to 'freely dispose their own money, by assigning it to any person whatsoever, rather than being restricted to allotting or remitting to relatives in a certain degree,

---

[108] *Navy Pay Act*, 4 & 5 Will. IV, c. 25 (1834); Hardwicke, *Report*, p. 266, s. 5030, pp. 267–8, ss. 5063–7.

[109] Hardwicke, *Report*, p. 266 ss. 5030, 5062–6.

[110] *Ibid.*, p. 118 s. 2070; p. 73 s. 1065; pp. 208–9 ss. 3582, 3643–4; p. 20 ss. 228–30; p. 271 ss. 5128–31; p. 274 s. 5224, *et al.*; p. 270 annex 1; Royal Navy, *The Queen's Regulations for the Government of Her Majesty's Naval Service* (Whitehall, 1844), pp. 181–2; Taylor, 'Manning the Royal Navy', (Part 1), at pp. 50–1.

[111] ADM 27/113/292/83.

[112] E&W Births: Q1/1853, vol. 2B, p. 402; Q3/1855, vol. 2B, p. 342; Q3/1857, vol. 2B, p. 389.

[113] Hardwicke, *Report*, p. 270 annex 1; p. 267 s. 5036.

[114] *Ibid.*, p. 20 s. 228.

[115] *Ibid.*, p. 268 s. 5102, appendix 1.

as prescribed.'[116] One witness averred that the power to allot to whomsoever men pleased 'is telling most injuriously; it lowers the moral, the social and the religious character of the seamen; it makes them entirely careless as to ... whom they allot.'[117] Another had come across instances of sailors allotting to 'other women', leaving their families destitute.[118] That seamen appreciated being allowed a greater choice of nominee, the Commission passed over without comment; it was clearly inconvenient news that men favoured non-relatives in only a minority (20 per cent) of all allotments.[119] In the report's summary, the sole issue raised under 'Allotments' was choice of nominee, it being stated that declarations 'are frequently made by seamen to very undeserving characters, to persons who have no natural claim whatsoever upon them'.[120] Troubling as this assertion must have been to those concerned with the Navy's reputation, it is notable that the Commission did not require further statistical evidence, or demand clarification as to the meaning of 'frequently' in this context, or challenge the definition of a 'deserving' character or 'natural' claim.

From the Commission's findings it would be easy to accept at face value Hurl-Eamon's description of the allotment system as 'highly inefficient'.[121] To support her judgement, however, on the tangential issue of paying sailors in arrears she cites Earle, whose focus is the merchant seaman, and Stark, who without evidence dismisses the allotment system as 'inefficient at best'.[122] None of these three commentators invokes original allotment data by way of support, and none acknowledges the achievement, in concept, construction, scale and operation, of a scheme which by 1853 saw some 14,600 allotments in force, by 1855 more than 23,800.[123] It was used, and arguably trusted, by significant numbers of seamen: on a notional basis of one allotment per man, the 13,212 allotments in force in 1850 related to 46 per cent of the 28,741 men borne on the Navy's books that year.[124] The exact number of dependants supported is incalculable, but may be estimated as a near-hundred thousand, if not more. In sum, while the Navy 'seemingly understood that to encourage men to enlist and keep them at sea

---

[116] *Ibid.*, p. 63 s. 827; p. 73 s. 1066; p. 74 ss. 1070–2; p. 209 ss. 3643–5, *et al.*; Order in Council 11 August 1854; *H/Tel*, 2 September 1854, p. 7 col. E.
[117] Hardwicke, *Report*, p. 269 s. 5092.
[118] *Ibid.*, p. 273 s. 5192.
[119] 173 *Ibid.*, p. 273 ss. 5193–6.
[120] *Ibid.*, p. ix s. 22.
[121] Hurl-Eamon, 'Fiction of Female Dependence', p. 482.
[122] Peter Earle, *Sailors: English Merchant Seamen 1650–1775* (London, 1998), p. 188; Stark, *Female Tars*, p. 21.
[123] Pitcairn, *Report*, p. 33.
[124] *Ibid.*, p. 1; Kemp, *British Sailor*, p. 193.

it was important to consider the material needs of seamen's wives', neither the Royal Commission's witnesses nor its Commissioners appear fully to have appreciated a system which for the most part must have worked.[125] Had it not, given the Navy's anxieties about misdirection of money, the abiding challenge of funding seamen's pay, the political and popular suspicion with which allotments were viewed, then the system would at least have been overhauled and adjusted, if not suspended or abandoned. And neither witnesses nor Commissioners considered the scenario that would have obtained had allotments never been introduced. Faulty as it may have been, from the naval dependant's point of view the system was better than no system at all; and from the Navy's point of view it was better than seeing their steadiest, most experienced seamen quit the service in order to support their dependants by other means.

## THE SEAMAN'S REPUTATION

Derived largely from his excessive behaviour on shore, the popular image and reputation of the naval seaman influenced public perception of naval women.[126] Combining 'carousing with comradeship, sexual prowess and bravery', Jack Tar was 'perceived to live outside of society', 'among the lowest order of society', his behaviour characterised by 'thoughtless prodigality when on shore'.[127] Ex-mariner Yexley claimed the bluejacket 'remains perennially light-hearted', an ambiguous term conveying both jollity and larkish irresponsibility.[128] Carelessness – of danger, future, health and money – was among those of his qualities most often remarked, but it was his drunkenness that was the stuff of legend, and his drunken reputation went before him.[129] 'When on leave it was assumed that men would drink too much', yet the 'run-ashore' in company with messmates was just one of many causes of drink-associated deaths from apoplexy, accidents,

---

[125] Lincoln, *Naval Wives*, p. 42.
[126] Walton, 'Social History', pp. 22, 169; Reibe, 'Public Perceptions of Sailors' Wives', pp. 50, 53–4.
[127] Joanne Begiato, 'Rough and Brave: What Can Soldiers Tell Us about 18th Century Masculinity?', in *Joanne Begiato Muses on History* (2019) <https://jbhist.wordpress.com/2019/08/02/rough-and-brave-what-can-soldiers-tell-us-about-18th-century-masculinity-part-ii/> [accessed 22 April 2024]; Andrew Gritt, 'Representations of Mariners and Maritime Communities, c.1750–1850', *History in Focus: The Sea* (2005), <http://www.history.ac.uk/ihr/Focus/Sea/articles/gritt.html> [accessed 22 April 2024]; J.D. Davies, *Gentlemen and Tarpaulins: the officers and men of the Restoration Navy* (Oxford, 1991), p. 78.
[128] Walton, 'Social History', p. 332.
[129] Padfield, *Rule Britannia*, pp. 22, 24.

delirium tremens and diseases acquired while under the influence.[130] As leave became more common, so drink became an even greater problem.[131] The Navy tried to reduce the hard-drinking culture. Halved in 1824, the grog ration was halved again in 1850, and steps were taken to support the teetotal man, including the provision of tea, soluble chocolate and sugar as alternatives to rum.[132] By the end of the century drunkenness would be much reduced, falling away as the seaman's public image improved; at the mid-century point, however, on shore or off, Jack sober remained a less common perception than Jack drunk, and the 'sailor's woman', in particular his wife, stood at risk of taint by association. Wives were expected to comply with Victorian ideas of subordination, modesty and sobriety. Seamen's wives were not recognised as qualifying for latitude in this regard, even though marriage to a sailor necessitated a woman's having to adopt an unusual level of independence and self-determination, qualities regarded as unseemly in the submissive Victorian wife. None of this justified her going so far as to be argumentative, uncompliant, immodest or drunk, yet it was precisely as argumentative, uncompliant, immodest and/or drunk that the naval woman was portrayed; and not just portrayed, but recognised, and stigmatised. In a paradox typical of Victorian morality her general behaviour was not exempted from societal norms, yet her bad behaviour was expected.

As with drink, so with sex. Sober or stocious, Jack was famously promiscuous, his sexual appetite the stuff of taproom ballad and cartoon.[133] His carnality placed him at high risk of infections which nineteenth-century society regarded as the (self-inflicted) result of 'immoral behaviour', a genteel euphemism for consorting with prostitutes.[134] There was a widely-held belief that the seaman was more likely to acquire a sexually-transmitted disease than was his land-based peer, a perception chiming with the fact that the annual death-rate from disease in the military was twice that of civilians.[135] Beyond men's fitness to serve their country, this had serious

---

[130] Preston, 'Constructing Communities', pp. 196–7; Jolly and Willson, *Jackspeak*, p. 373; Walton, 'Social History', pp. 165–7.

[131] Paula Bartley, *Prostitution: Prevention and Reform in England, 1860–1914* (London, 2000), pp. 84–5; Lloyd, *British Seaman 1200–1860*, p. 273.

[132] Walton, 'Social History', p. 311.

[133] 'Stocious: Angry, unreasonable, drunk, or all three at the same time': Jolly and Willson, *Jackspeak*, p. 429. The term is most commonly used to mean 'drunk', as in this instance.

[134] Hall, 'Poxy Sailor', pp. 113–14.

[135] Glen Petrie, *A Singular Iniquity: the campaigns of Josephine Butler* (London, 1971), p. 12; Hall, 'Poxy Sailor', pp. 115–16; R.E. Hooppell, *The statistical results of the Contagious Diseases Act as deduced from all the parliamentary papers which have been issued upon the subject, from the commencement of the Acts to the present time* (London, 1871), p. 2; E.M. Sigsworth and T.J. Wyke, 'A Study of Victorian Prostitution

health implications both for prostitutes serving the military community and for naval wives not engaged in the sex trade. But whether or not she were spared her husband's bringing contamination to the marital bed, the naval wife remained vulnerable to being suspected of complicity, tainted by her intimacy with a notoriously licentious breed.

Unsupervised in her friendships, amusements and movements during her husband's absence; her person, home and reputation unprotected by a resident spouse; left for years at a time to take on the unwomanly role of decision-maker in matters normally the province of males; her income limited by naval allotment policy and her husband's poor pay; her identity, status and character subject by law to (male) parochial validation in order that she receive her allotted due; viewed with an ambivalence which shifted with the tenor of public regard for her spouse: the nineteenth-century seaman's wife was inescapably connected to and affected by the naval context of the day. The next chapter looks beyond the context, to the woman herself.

---

and Venereal Disease', in Martha Vicinus (ed.), *Suffer and Be Still: women in the Victorian age* (Indiana, 1972), 77–99, at p. 86; Mary Jones, 'Towards a Hierarchy of Management: the Victorian and Edwardian Navy, 1860–1919', in Helen Doe and Richard Harding (eds), *Naval Leadership and Management, 1650–1950: essays in honour of Michael Duffy* (Woodbridge, Suffolk, 2012), 157–72, at p. 159.

## 2

## NAVAL WOMEN

Royal Navy ships' allotment registers for 1850–52 contain 2,300 declarations naming Portsea Island-resident allottees, all but 2 per cent of the 2,300 comprising seamen's wives, sisters, mothers and trustees of children under eighteen years of age, categories of relationship permitted under statute law.[1] This chapter examines these four permitted categories, and how sailors interpreted and used them.

Only forty-one of the 2,300 Portsea Island declarations named male recipients. At policy level, among its permitted allottee relationships the Navy included fathers, brothers and sons, and allowed allotments to male trustees. In operational terms, however, the scheme overwhelmingly involved women. Sailors directed their wages toward women, and women relied upon the sums allotted.

Table 2  Portsea Island allotments by category (n=2,300).

| Relationships cited in declarations favouring Portsea Island allottees, January 1850–July 1852 | Numbers of Portsea Island allotments declared January 1850–July 1852 |
| --- | --- |
| Aunt (disallowed: not permitted under law) | 1 |
| Brother | 5 |
| Daughter | 4 |
| Father | 26 |
| Grandmother | 6 |
| Mother | 412 |
| Mother-in-law | 7 |
| Sister | 342 |
| Son | 2 |

[1] Hardwicke, *Report*, p. 74 s. 1070; 4 & 5 Will. IV, c. 25 (1834), s. 4.

| | |
|---|---|
| Stepmother | 2 |
| Trustee (of which 8 male) | 150 |
| Wife | 1,343 |

These 2,300 are the Portsea Island *allotments* declared within the period January 1850 – July 1852. Several men declared repeatedly in favour of the same person, several to different individuals in turn, and not all nominees were locatable in the 1851 census. The 2,300 declarations thus yielded a nett of 1,581 located *allottees*, the individuals constituting the study's core cohort. Successive declarations naming the same allottee (156 were identified among the 2,300 total) might be prompted by a man's promotion and concomitant pay rise, or by a change in his nominee's circumstances, for example a wife's move to a new address, or a spinster sister's marriage resulting in a change of surname. From HM Ships *Fisgard*, *Excellent* and *Horatio*, gunner second class Charles Hicks made declarations naming his wife Margaret. Each gave a different home address, the third increasing her monthly payment from £2 8s 0d to £3 2s 0d.[2] In years 1834-51, George Lumb made multiple declarations favouring his wife Ellen (*q.v.*). They trace developments affecting both spouses: his progression from ordinary seaman, HMS *Portland*, to AB and captain of the foretop *Jaseur*, to AB *Excellent*, captain of the main top *Alert*, gunner third class, *Excellent* and *Sealark*, and gunner second class *Excellent* in January 1851; and Ellen's moves from Devonport to Portsea, and locally from Victoria Terrace to Cumberland Street and back again.[3] Repeat declarations from *Terrible*, *Illustrious* and *Blenheim* by boatswain George Martin show similar movements between rates, and his wife Catherine changing her home address three times in thirteen months.[4] James Wheeler's third allotment showed the benefit of his going from AB to stoker, HMS *Niger*, the monthly receipts of his wife Mary Ellen rising from nineteen shillings to £1 6s 0d.[5] Thomas Young's three allotments from HMS *Leander* track his progress from AB to sailmaker's crew to quartermaster, while his wife Mary Anne remained at her Surrey Street home.[6] These triple declarations were exceptions. All other sequential nominations involved two declarations, most of them naming wives.

Regardless of how many times a man declared in favour of the same individual, his nominee received from him just one payment per month.

---

[2] ADM 27/110/485/13; ADM 27/113/85/423; ADM 27/120/291/1.
[3] ADM 27/40/42/86; ADM 27/60/26/SB7; ADM 27/60/189/SB7; ADM 27/81/114/296; ADM 27/84/44A/28; ADM 27/110/229/35; ADM 27/102/133/1; ADM 27/110/493/320; ADM 27/112/100/SLWV320.
[4] ADM 27/109/481/1; ADM 27/110/362/7; ADM 27/113/263/4.
[5] ADM 27/111/127/46; ADM 27/120/391/36; ADM 27/120/397/46.
[6] ADM 27/109/265/177; ADM 27/120/361/177; ADM 27/110/392/177.

But as we have seen, an allottee could be named in multiple declarations by more than one sailor, and receive multiple payments each month. Of 112 individuals named in 238 such declarations, 90 per cent received in two different capacities, for example as mother of two allotting sons (as Fig. 3 shows, twenty-nine such women were found), or as both wife and sister of seamen (twenty-two found). Eleven individuals, among them Christianna Nancarrow (*q.v.*), had three allotments each. Elizabeth Hall received no fewer than four: as wife of bandsman James Hall, HMS *Victory*; as sister (allegedly) of James's bandsman-shipmate John Collins, notwithstanding that upon her marriage to James she had been not Elizabeth Collins but the widow Hillier, née Hogg; and twice as trustee, on behalf of George Hartman, another of James's musical shipmates, and of Charles Edwards, captain's cook, HMS *Superb*.[7] Married in 1831, Charles and his wife Mary Ann had been resident in Frederick Street at the time of their 9-year-old son Henry's baptism in the summer of 1849, so in January 1850 there was logic in Charles's choosing Frederick Street neighbour Elizabeth to stand trustee following Mary Ann's dying, or deserting her husband and son.[8] (In the absence of her name in death or burial records, that someone with Mary Ann's name is listed as resident 'prostitute' in a Warblington Street pub may explain Charles's needing to appoint a trustee.)[9]

The census found the now 11-year-old Henry Edwards in Elizabeth Hall's care, but listed as an orphan on parish relief; for six months after declaring his allotment Charles too had died, his payments to Elizabeth stopping with his demise.[10] Unfunded now, Elizabeth continued *in loco parentis*. Of her other entrusted child, little Henry Hartman, the census yielded no trace. His father George was one of four naval musicians – three of them German-born – enumerated as lodgers in the Hall household. His trustee allotment was declared a full year after that of Charles Edwards; it is therefore not impossible that George (out of sailorly sentiment, to contribute toward the care of a fellow seaman's orphan) invented a 7-year-old son baptised in Germany – the latter detail both fitting with his own birthplace, and making it harder for naval authorities to verify the child's existence.[11]

---

[7] Christianna Nancarrow: ADM 27/112/180/86, ADM 27/111/359/67, ADM 27/111/284/76; Elizabeth Hall: ADM 27/112/161/22, ADM 27/112/413/45, ADM 27/112/161/29, ADM 27/109/330/234 (CHU3/1D/45, p. 93 n. 185); ADM 27/112/161/29; ADM 29/084, p. 102.

[8] CHU2/1C/10, p. 122 n. 365; ADM 27/27/297/148; CHU3/1B/30, p. 34 n. 268.

[9] 1851 census: HO107/1658, fol. 666, p. 20.

[10] 1851 census: HO107/1658, fol. 433, p. 72; ADM 38/9120 (n.p.).

[11] Walton, 'Social History', p. 332; Lincoln, 'Impact of Warfare', p. 78; Joanne Begiato, 'The Tearful Sailor: Gendering Emotions', in *Joanne Begiato Muses on History* (2019) <https://jbhist.wordpress.com/2019/07/25/emotional-lives-intimacy-and-identity-in-18th-2/> [accessed 22 April 2024].

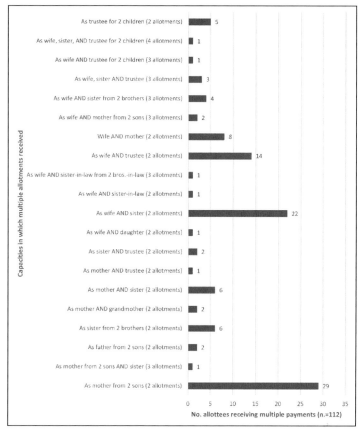

**Fig. 3** Number of allottees receiving multiple payments in different capacities (n=112). Total allotments per person shown in brackets.

These 'multi-allottees' are the visible evidence of a larger naval community. Collectively and individually they reveal shipmates' shared loyalties and affections, and dependants' naval interconnections, resourcefulness and mutual assistance. This was a shoreside community through which the Navy wove as warp and weft.

## WIVES

Marriage to a lower-deck Navy man set the seaman's wife apart from her civilian peers. She might, for example, enjoy an allotment for which the civilian's wife did not qualify ('might', because seamen could not be compelled to allot to their wives). Offsetting this benefit was the fact that civilian wives, among them sailors' sisters and mothers, had husbands to share the marital bed every night, whereas for much of her married life the naval wife slept alone. Furthermore, in lacking a husband to moderate her behaviour and satisfy her physical needs the naval wife was vulnerable to cynical conjecture; worse, to female suspicion, male opportunism. She was, in short, assumed to be sexually experienced, voracious and available. Like the wives of Trotter's émigré Cornishmen, she was for years on end a 'married widow', effectively husbandless, in consequence of choosing a sailor for a spouse.[12]

From its earliest eighteenth-century remittances, the Navy's chief intent had been to facilitate support of seamen's wives. Fifty-eight per cent of this study's original 2,300 declarations favoured 'wife', and wives formed 62 per cent of the 1,581 individuals located within the Portsea Island census. Over 90 per cent of located wives appear to have been receiving in no other capacity, though some may have been benefiting from allotments declared prior to this study period, from men other than their husbands. Additional allotments are most likely to have been declared by brothers to married sisters, or by bereaved fathers of motherless children entrusted to a fellow seaman's wife. Unless in these capacities, it was morally suspect for a wife to receive monies from a male non-relative.

To discern how seamen-husbands' trades and seniority may have affected their wives, four categories of naval rate were examined.[13] The most senior category comprised warrant officers – the boatswains, carpenters and gunners first, second and third class. Next came senior petty officers, who included gunners', carpenters' and boatswains' mates, captains of maintop, hold, forecastle and foretop, together with ropemakers, sailmakers, blacksmiths, quartermasters, leading stokers, ships' cooks, coxswains, captains' coxswains, masters at arms and ships' corporals. Petty officers, the third category, included armourers, coopers, coxswains of ships' cutters and captains of afterguard, mast and mizzen top. The lowest category, junior ratings comprised able and ordinary seamen, painters, sick berth attendants, stokers, carpenters' crews and stewards and cooks serving officers' various messes. The exercise focused on 1,328 individuals receiving one allotment each, in one of the four main categories of relationship, thus 273 mothers, 163 sisters, seventy-nine trustees and 813 wives. Wives' allotments amounted to 92.9 per cent of warrant officers' declarations, almost twice the 46.8 per cent of junior ratings' spousal payments. Echoing Rodger's observation, this confirms that older, more senior men were more likely to be married than were the younger, junior ratings; either that, or compared with their junior shipmates they were more sensible of their spousal responsibilities, and of the consequences of failing to support their women.[14]

---

[12] Trotter, *Married Widows*, passim.
[13] No RM or RMA allotments were included in this analysis.
[14] Rodger, *Wooden World*, pp. 132, 134–5.

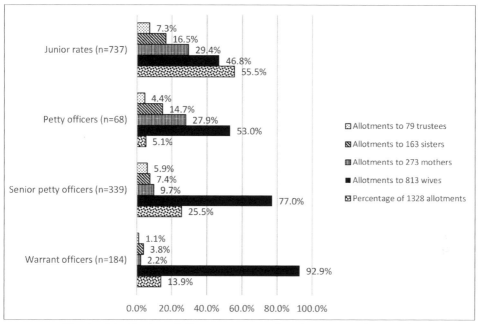

**Fig. 4** Distribution of allotments per men's rating category (n=1,328).

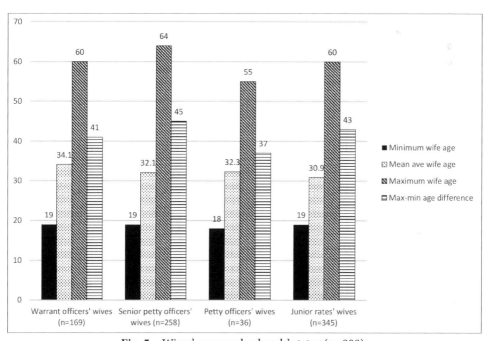

**Fig. 5** Wives' ages per husbands' status (n=808).

Wives' ages did not reflect husbands' seniority. Fig. 5 shows that when 808 wives were grouped according to husbands' status, their mean average age differed by a mere three years (30.9 / 34.1 years). Within each rate grouping, however, age-differences between the youngest and oldest wife ranged from thirty-seven to forty-five years, equivalent to well over a generation. For the husbands, this was of little significance. For the wives it had potential for bonding, division, even friction. Younger and older wives married to men of the same rate might find themselves living a few doors apart, the older woman of an age to be the younger's mother, or even (given Chapter Four's finding on naval brides' nuptial age) her grandmother. Such age differentials opened the possibility of empathetic older wives supporting, mentoring or 'mothering' their younger peers, of older and younger women finding common ground in their husbands' shared seniority. On a less positive note, they might lead to some older wives judging their younger peers' ability to cope, or being jealous of the younger women's husbands' having achieved promotion earlier in life than had theirs. There is potential, too, for the existence of a culture of seniority whereby wives internalised and adopted their men's service-inculcated consciousness of rank and seniority, warrant officers' spouses 'pulling rank' on wives of ordinary seamen, or the wives of lowly caulkers and privates deferring to wives of venerable boatswains. If the naval wife's identification with her husband's seniority afforded her a standing and dignity denied by the wider civilian community, it also determined her place within the naval community.

Grouping women according to their husbands' trades rather than their status has revealed a sixteen-year disparity between the average ages of youngest and oldest wives. Ordinary seamen's wives ranged in age from seventeen to thirty-eight years, with an average age of twenty-four; the average for carpenters' wives was forty years, their ages ranging twenty-four to fifty-eight. The former finding reflects the youthful strength, vigour and shorter active careers of seamen, the latter the carpenter's physical ability to pursue his trade over many years' service, and the Navy's valuing artisanship and skill. These were factors affecting the men's income prospects and their women's economic security during the men's naval service and beyond.

## PARENTS

A social norm has long required that grown children take responsibility for their elderly parents.[15] Most support was provided in the form of assistance, children helping with housework or taking a bereaved parent into

---

[15] Peter Laslett, 'The Family as a Knot of Individual Interests', in Robert McC. Netting, Richard R. Wilk and Eric J. Arnould (eds), *Households: comparative and historical studies of the domestic group* (Berkeley, 1984), 353–79, at p. 359.

their home. Unable to provide practical help while at sea, sons could instead support their ageing parents via allotments. Redirections of allotments from wives to parents or in-laws were not uncommon, and did not always indicate marital breakdown or parental need. The declaration by gunner's mate Henry William Messum, HMS *Excellent*, observes 'Has an allotment in favour of wife, but wishes it transferred to mother.'[16] In this instance the redirection signified not discord but tragedy, for at thirty-one years old, and a mere twelve days after their wedding, Henry's wife Elizabeth had died of 'Disease of Heart Effusion into Chest 10 Days Certified.'[17] In July 1850 Reuben Ferret, gunner's mate HMS *Excellent*, allotted to Eliza, his wife of five years.[18] Within a month of her death in December 1850 he altered his payments to benefit her 64-year-old widowed mother Ann Mason, at the same Hereford Street address.[19] In most instances, however, seamen's parents were on the losing end of allotment redirections, as newlywed sons re-routed their half-pay from mothers to brides. Sometimes redirection signified changes in family interrelationships and attitudes, sometimes changes in competence. In 1845 from HMS *Queen*, AB William Gimblet declared in favour of his father John in New Street, Plymouth.[20] In 1850, now carpenter's crew, HMS *Leander*, William rerouted the allotment to his mother Ellenor in nearby Love Lane. There the census found her, with five children aged four to twenty-one years, and husband John.[21] Yes, William's father was still living, fit enough to work as a horse porter, and still (or once again) co-resident with wife Ellenor; but he was no longer trusted with his sailor-son's money. If the family depended upon William's allotment to supplement the earnings of father John and William's apprentice ropemaker brother, they would soon feel its loss: nine months later William would remove the allotment from his mother (and thereby from the entire Plymouth-resident family), and award it to his Portsea-resident bride Harriet, of whom more is said in Chapter Fifteen.[22]

The transfer of an allotment from parent or sibling to new wife was the commonest alteration in payment arrangements, one which the Navy accepted without demur, ships' pussers justifying the fresh declaration via

---

[16] ADM 27/112/107/1563.
[17] ADM 27/111/381/1563; CHU42/1C/18, p. 243 n. 485; CHU42/1C/18, p. 243 n. 485; E&W Deaths: Q4/1850, vol. 7, p. 105 (certificate); Portsmouth History Centre (PHC) Portsmouth, Hampshire, Portsmouth Burials, Parish Burials, PHC G/PGC4/3 (1849), n.p., n. 8460.
[18] ADM 27/110/542/1427.
[19] E&W Deaths: Q4/1850, vol. 7, p. 105 ('Ferrett'); ADM 27/112/80/1427; 1851 census: HO107/1659, fol. 487, p. 18.
[20] ADM 27/92/310/421 ('Gimblet').
[21] ADM 27/92/310/421; ADM 27/109/266/193.
[22] ADM 27/110/156/193.

a red-inked superscript in the register. If a family had other seaman-sons allotting, cash flow could be maintained, the loss of income weathered; if not, the new arrangement could tip the deprived parent(s) into financial misery. A man's marrying might be a cause for joy, but for his financially dependent elders it was cause for understandable apprehension.

Mothers dominated allotments to parents. This goes in part to women's longevity, but there were other reasons for the trend, one of which was regulation. Whereas married or widowed mothers had only to navigate the usual bureaucratic hoops to qualify for their allotment, the rules said that fathers must not only be widowed but have church minister or elders confirm them as 'wholly unable to maintain [themselves]'.[23] Of the gross cohort of 2,300 declarations only twenty-six favoured fathers. Twenty were traced in the census, their ages ranging from forty-one to seventy-five years. Notwithstanding the 'wholly unable to maintain [themselves]' criterion, all were waged bar a half-dozen comprising a superannuated boatswain, two paupers (one 'afflicted'), and three Greenwich pensioners. That the majority were waged was not surprising, for former seamen were financially vulnerable. As a pamphlet handed to the 1859 Royal Commission on naval manning observed, 'Married pensioners experience considerable difficulty in finding a decent home for their wives and children … A miserable room in a wretched court or alley costs 18d or 2s 0d per week … at best, a most precarious existence is all that a pensioner's wife and child can hope for.'[24] A seaman-son's allotment was for some fathers more than merely welcome. It was a necessity.

In 412 declarations the allottee's relationship was described as 'mother', a further seven explicitly favouring mothers-in-law. Three hundred of the 412 were traced. There were twice as many mothers with husbands living as there were widows. That sons of living fathers *preferred* to allot to their mothers reflects the role-expectation captured in Humphries' concluding 'if a father's role was to earn, a mother's was to manage'.[25] To regard wives and mothers as managers was especially common where resources were modest. Men were notoriously poor shoppers, so by directing his money to the household manager rather than to his father, a son could with greater certainty benefit the domestic economy.[26] Besides, given the tendency for seafaring to run in families (see Chapter Four), a sailor's father might himself be away at sea, unable to collect the monthly sum; if a dockyard worker, he might be one of thousands who streamed past – and very

---

[23] 49 Geo. IV, c. 108 (1809), s. XII.
[24] Hardwicke, *Report*, p. 169 s. 2742. See Chapter Nine for Portsea Island rent figures.
[25] Jane Humphries, *Childhood and Child Labour in the British Industrial Revolution* (Cambridge, 2013), p. 109.
[26] Laslett, 'Family as Knot', p. 371; Perkin, *Women and Marriage*, pp. 175–6.

often through – the eighty-plus pubs lining walk-to-work routes between dockyard entrances and town gates, in which establishments many a wage packet was depleted.[27] As the longer-living parent subject to less narrow regulation than her spouse, as available recipient and budget manager, a seaman's mother was in all respects the better bet.

That said, twenty-one allottee-mothers appear in the census as paupers. Reflecting national patterns showing the greater financial vulnerability that followed a husband's abandonment or death, the proportion of our widowed pauper-mothers was six times that of still-married pauper-mothers.[28] The higher proportion reflects (on a small scale, even exceeds) a wider trend; for where Kidd quotes one-third of widows aged twenty to forty-five years being assisted under New Poor Law regulations in the 1850s and 1860s, here were found nine widowed allottee-mothers aged thirty-six to forty-five, of whom four (44 per cent) were paupers. Mothers receiving allotments from more than one son, or from a son and husband and/or brother, were better protected from extreme poverty, and not solely because of the amounts received. A mother with just one son would see her allotment stop once his ship returned. After that, the only form of financial help she could hope to receive from him was a share of his paying-off money, a portion she must eke out until the ship he (re)joined was repaired, resupplied, recommissioned, at sea again, and his allotment recommenced. If he were unwilling to share his paying-off money with her, or had been involuntarily relieved of it (as many a tipsy sailor was) between pay office and home, her only remaining options were to secure waged work, charitable doles or parish relief, none of which was guaranteeable.

The mother of multiple sailor-sons would be better protected against loss of income than would the mother of one, but only so long as her boys served in different ships.[29] She would lose one allotment with the return of one son's vessel, but her other sons' payments would continue until their ships' return, by which time – if she were lucky – the first son would have departed again, his allotment to her restarting once he were three months at sea. Thirty mothers were receiving two sons' allotments, all but six from sons serving in different ships. None was wholly reliant on her two sons for financial support, for in every case there was a husband working or pensioned, or both husband and wife were earning, or the widowed mother

---

[27] Hunt, *Directory of Hampshire and Dorsetshire, 1852* (Weymouth, 1852), p. 110; R.C. Riley and Philip Eley, *Public Houses and Beerhouses in Nineteenth Century Portsmouth* (Portsmouth, 1983), p. 11; Joy Harwood, *A Portrait of Portsea, 1840–1940* (Southampton, 1990), p. 17.

[28] Alan J. Kidd, *State, Society and the Poor in Nineteenth-century England* (Basingstoke, 1999), p. 37.

[29] Hunt, 'Women and the Fiscal-imperial State', p. 37.

herself had a trade. Given the low earnings associated with some mothers' occupations (laundress, charwoman, fishmonger, tailor, greengrocer), sons' allotments would have played an important part in avoiding maternal destitution. Even so, in four instances the mothers were receiving parish relief despite having a household income *and* their sons' support.

## SISTERS

Sisters had come within allotment regulations in 1834 when eligibility was extended beyond wives and parents.[30] Their inclusion was popular: by the mid-nineteenth century, after 'wife' and 'mother' the relationship most commonly cited in ships' registers was 'sister'. Inclusion was especially welcome among unmarried sisters. Poor remuneration (few single women could be self-supporting, the female wage barely providing a basic personal food ration), together with a lack of economically supportive children, left the parentless unmarried woman dependent on her brothers – if brothers she had.[31]

The large number of allottee-sisters owed in part to motives not envisaged by lawmakers, for if a sailor wished to allot to a woman neither his wife nor old enough to be his mother, and possessed of no affinal or kin-relationship recognised within the regulations, the easiest tactic was to name her his sister. He did not have to quote marriage details in order to pass her off as his spouse, or invent a child to justify a trustee allotment; she in turn did not have to provide proof of marriage, or produce the named infant. All she need do was convince minister or churchwarden of her sibling relationship to the absent brother, and have that same minister or churchwarden complete the certification on the back of her allotment form. As such, until 1854 when men could allot to whomever they thought fit, citing the 'sister' relationship was the simplest way to route money to any favoured female.[32] Given the 1859 Royal Commission's suspicions that men were allotting 'to very undeserving characters, to persons who have no natural claim whatsoever upon them', it was to be expected that some of our 'sister' allotments might prove questionable.[33]

Over 150 'sisters' had surnames different from those of their allotting sailor, but this did not necessarily indicate duplicity. Where these women

---

[30] 4 & 5 Will. IV, c. 25 (1834).
[31] Michael Anderson, 'The Social Position of Spinsters in mid-Victorian Britain', *Journal of Family History*, 9:4 (1984), 377–83, at p. 381; Olwen Hufton, 'Women without Men: widows and spinsters in Britain and France in the eighteenth century', ibid. 9: 4 (1984), 355–76, at p. 361.
[32] Hardwicke, *Report*, p. ix s. 22.
[33] *Ibid.*, pp. 273–4 ss. 5193–5208, 2521–5.

were also receiving allotments as wives of other seamen, the dates and places of their marriage were stated in their husbands' declarations, enabling name-differences to be verified via parish marriage registers' recording of maiden names which in turn could be correlated with those of the seafaring brothers. For the woman receiving solely as sister, however, for whom there was no spousal allotment to provide marriage data, a husband's appearance in the census went some way to explaining the name-difference, searches of parish and civil registers in some instances yielding verification of marriage.

Of 209 sister-allottees whose civil status the census legibly recorded, 11 per cent appeared as widowed, a quarter as unmarried. It was understandable that sailors might wish to support widowed or spinster sisters, but support for sisters who had living, co-resident breadwinner husbands warranted further consideration. The census provided the trades of 120 sisters' husbands. Occupations included cordwainer, farrier, provision merchant, tobacconist, waterman and labourer. Eighteen sisters' spouses worked in the dockyard. Fifty-eight husbands were naval, a dozen others Greenwich pensioners, so at least 58 per cent of the 120 sisters were, or had been, naval wives. As to those married sisters who, unaccompanied by spouse, were listed as 'visitor' or 'lodger' in others' households, their men's occupations could not be determined unless allotment declarations confirmed their absent spouses as seamen. Eight married sisters, heads of their own households, had no husband present. A husband's absence may signal his going on the tramp in search of work, or losing touch with his family or abandoning them.[34] In naval port town census returns, however, a married woman with no husband present has in many instances been identified as a naval wife. Eight allottee-sisters were enumerated as married household heads; if their absent husbands were seamen, it would bring to over 55 per cent the proportion of married sisters who were themselves naval wives, a finding to be borne in mind when, in Chapter Four, we examine the family backgrounds of seamen's brides.

Two-thirds of allottee-sisters had no occupation listed. When civil status is factored-in, signs of financial insecurity emerge. Economic need was driving unmarried and widowed sisters into the labour market: only 19 per cent of married sisters said they were in paid work, compared with 53 per cent of unmarried sisters and 63 per cent of widowed sisters. That the majority of married allottee-sisters had naval husbands may explain their lower tally of declared occupations; having allotment income from both husband and brother, sisters married to naval men may have felt less need to seek paid work. If so, seaman-brothers' additional contributions helped improve these women's domestic situations, health and welfare. An

---

[34] Humphries, *Childhood and Child Labour*, pp. 64, 184.

alternative explanation is that the seventy women's husbands were earning enough to keep wife and family without need of outside help, and that sailor-brothers were simply expressing fraternal affection by way of coin. It is possible too that the married sisters were acting as savings banks for their seagoing siblings, a service which less prudent mariners sought via dubious nominees such as publicans and beer-shop keepers.

Only three unmarried sisters were identified as household heads, the remainder being visitors, lodgers or sisters of civilian householders. Most, in short, were dependent on others for accommodation, on brothers for financial support. Their dependence was not a function of immaturity: with a mean average of twenty-eight years they ranged in age from eighteen to fifty-nine, only seven of them aged twenty or under. Widowed sisters had an average age of fifty-one years. The oldest was 79-year-old Ann Dawson, sister of AB John Holman, HMS *Blenheim*, the youngest 27-year-old Phoebe Saxton (*q.v.*), 'sister'[-in-law] of ordinary seaman Joseph Saxton, HMS *Phaeton*.[35] Five of the twenty-four widowed sisters – Phoebe among them – were clearly impoverished, listed in the census as paupers or receiving parish relief. Modest as their brothers' allotments were (they ranged from twelve shillings to £1 6s 0d per calendar month), the sums were enough to save them from the workhouse, and from complete destitution, but not from dependence on the parish.

Nine sisters proved to be under eighteen years old. By law they should have appeared in the allotment declarations alongside the names of adult trustees to whom payments were made on their behalf; but breaches of regulations do not always signal subterfuge or scams. Richard Mould, ordinary seaman, HMS *Excellent*, took a chance in allotting to his 12-year-old sister Martha. Named in his declaration as Martha Warner, on census day she was in Clarence and Forehouse Barracks, Portsmouth, with her 44-year-old mother, 39-year-old stepfather Private William Worner [*sic*], and three younger half-brothers.[36] Richard should have allotted to Martha via a trustee, in this case most logically their mother. His declaration may be interpreted as a token of the bond between full siblings, and/or a desire to prevent his money ending up in their stepfather's hands. Whatever the reasons behind the arrangement, Martha must either convince the pay office that she was old enough to qualify for Richard's monthly payments, or persuade a visibly older female to pose as his sister, passing the cash to Martha afterward.

---

[35] ADM 27/110/142/367; 1851 census: HO107/1658, fol. 383, p. 27; ADM 27/113/378/389 ('Saxton' mis-transcribed as 'Paxton'); 1851 census: HO107/1658, fol. 459, p. 28.
[36] ADM 27/111/134/1517; 1851 census: HO107/1658, fol. 762, p. 29.

Reflecting disquiet expressed in the 1859 Royal Commission report, some 'sister' relationships did indeed appear questionable. Licensed victualler and landlady Sophia Knell was in June 1851 named as 'sister' by bandsman William Woods, HMS *Phaeton*.[37] Given Sophia's occupation, her licensed premises, her (allegedly) unmarried state and the mismatch of seaman's and allottee's surnames, it is likely that William was less her brother than her customer.[38] Housekeeper to her brother John (who described himself as 'proprietor of houses', a term which if not meaning 'landlord' may be a grander way of saying 'brothel-owner'), 35-year-old unmarried Charlotte Constable was named 'sister' in declarations by both Archibald Boland and William Reilly, HM Ships *Cumberland* and *Amphitrite*.[39] The mismatch of her surname (confirmed via baptismal records) with those of Boland and Reilly suggests, but does not prove, that she was unrelated to them.[40] So-called 'sister' of AB James MacLaughlan, HMS *Encounter*, Sarah Newman was the 24-year-old unmarried daughter of alehouse keeper Charlotte Newman, a widow trading on the Common Hard and herself the recipient of at least two allotments, one of which appears spurious.[41] The census credits none of Charlotte's five daughters with an occupation, and it is more than possible that Sarah's residence – a drinking-place right outside the dockyard gates, on a pub-laden thoroughfare notorious for brothels – means she was working as a prostitute. If so, her 'sister' status is likely to be a euphemism for a different sort of relationship.

## TRUSTEES

Of all the categories of relationships permitted by allotment regulations, that of trustee was the only one neither denoting nor demanding kinship with the seaman. Its purpose was, very properly, to provide the means for men to ensure protection of minors via the funding of non-institutional care, whether those minors be a man's motherless children, or his orphaned siblings too young to fend for themselves. No proof of civil status was required: a trustee might be single, married, separated or widowed. No blood relationship was expected, so there need be no family or moral obligation or affective bond between trustee and sailor or child. Legislation

---

[37] ADM 27/113/378/388; 1851 census: HO107/1658, fol. 360, p. 37; 1841 census: HO107/415, fol. 77, p. 12.
[38] CHU3/1D/49, p. 204 n. 407.
[39] ADM 27/113/129/91; ADM 27/112/206/89; 1851 census: HO107/1659, fol. 244, p. 15.
[40] Thames & Medway Baptisms: Charlotte Constable, 27 November 1814, St. Mary's, Chatham.
[41] ADM 27/110/241/11; ADM 27/113/434/93; ADM 27/111/135/1510; 1851 census: HO107/1658, fol. 254, p. 7.

spoke of the need for trustees' suitability for their role, but set no criteria or mechanism by which suitability might be assessed or monitored. Trustees, in short, provided the equivalent of modern-day foster care, but without statutory vetting or supervision.

The 2,300 declarations named 147 trustees whose ages ranged from an improbable fifteen (Mary Scovell, co-resident daughter of a brick burner's wife), to a venerable sixty-four years (widowed Mary Baines, a schoolmistress on parish relief), with a mean average age of thirty-six.[42] Between them these individuals were caring for, or purportedly caring for, 144 children between the ages of five-and-a-half months and eighteen-and-a-half years.[43] One trusteeship began with an apparently straightforward declaration by a fresh-from-the-altar groom; future chapters will show it concealed a tangle of marital and parental relationships. In January 1847 William Wheadon (spellings vary) married Amelia Groom. He was the son of a boatswain RN, she a naval pensioner's daughter, aged fourteen.[44] From HMS *Excellent* quartermaster William duly declared an allotment naming his new bride.[45] In May and September 1848, from *Vesuvius* and *Excellent*, he made further declarations in her favour.[46] A superscript to his final declaration from *Phaeton* noted 'Former allotment from *Excellent* stopped, he having been DSQd'.[47] 'Discharged to sick quarters' meant all payments to Amelia ceased until *Phaeton* next put to sea, when William, his health recovered, might once more declare in her favour.[48] Having gone months without her regular cash-in-hand Amelia would have welcomed the resumption of income, for now she had a child to support. In October 1849, after two years of marriage, she had given birth to a boy whom gunner's mate William duly registered as his legitimate son and namesake.[49] In naval records William appears as 'Weedon', whereas in census, parish, civil and allotment records he also features as 'Weaden', 'Wheaden' and 'Wheden'. To avoid confusion with his namesake son, he is referred to hereafter as 'Weedon', the name by which he appears in his naval service record and his allotment declarations.

Thus far, this couple's marital story is unremarkable. It is curious, then, that baby William features in two declarations by another sailor entirely. An October 1850 declaration by AB George Wilkinson, HMS *Vengeance*,

---

[42] ADM 27/112/192/249; 1851 census: HO107/1659, fol. 683, p. 16; ADM 27/110/166/1343; 1851 census: HO107/1658, fol. 13, p. 18 ('Bayne').
[43] ADM 27/110/271/77; ADM 27/120/211/421.
[44] CHU3/1D/45, p. 110 n. 220 ('Wheadon').
[45] ADM 27/98/129/1471.
[46] ADM 27/103/220/190; ADM 27/105/195/929.
[47] ADM 27/110/34/290.
[48] ADM 29/046, p. 154.
[49] E&W Births: Q4/1849, vol. 7, p. 157 (certificate).

declared Amelia Wheden [*sic*] trustee for baby William Wheden.[50] Three months later George rerouted funding for little William's care to trustee Maria Balsh, her address 'Southsea, to be left at Mrs Jerome's, Cricketer's Public House', an establishment within walking distance of the dockyard pay office where allotments were disbursed.[51] Census day 1851 found 42-year-old Maria Balch [*sic*] living not in Southsea but in Alverstoke with her 12-year-old servant daughter and 10-year-old scholar son, but no little William.[52] He was in Trafalgar Street, Landport, with his original 'trustee' and *de facto* mother Amelia. The boy's 36-year-old father William was also present, his self-described occupation of 'seaman' at odds with his having been invalided from naval service.[53]

Why was George Wilkinson supporting little William? What lay behind his redirecting money from Amelia (clearly the child's mother) to Maria Balch (no relationship identified)? In light of what followed, the likeliest explanation is that George's allotment originated in his adulterous relationship with the married Amelia, and that seaman Weedon's unexpected return from sea raised the risk of his finding George's allotment voucher among Amelia's things. We may infer that to avoid this happening George recruited Maria Balch as his intermediary, her role being to keep safe the voucher naming her as allottee, and on Amelia's behalf to collect his money from the pay office, handing it over to her somewhere nearby. If this sounds improbable, later chapters' evidence of marital separation, questionable remarriage, desertion and disappearances add conviction. As it stands, however, it is the stuff of urban legend, echoing the dubious 'trustee' shenanigans reported by Royal Commission witnesses.

Consider also the April 1850 allotment of AB Joseph Dominy, HMS *Blenheim*, to 'trustee' Sarah Barfoot, address Gloucester Street, Portsea.[54] Sarah was a 48-year-old widow whose household included a teenage son, but not the entrusted 1-year-old Mary Dominy whom Joseph's declaration described as having been baptised in Blandford, Dorset.[55] Just as George Wilkinson appears to have used 'trustee' Maria Balch to act as courier for his allotment to Amelia Wheden, so Joseph seems to have used 'trustee' Sarah

---

[50] ADM 27/111/260/5.
[51] ADM 27/112/149/5.
[52] 1851 census: HO107/1660, fol. 49, p. 24.
[53] 1851 census: HO107/1657, fol. 52, p. 12; ADM 29/046/154.
[54] ADM 27/110/279/307.
[55] There did exist a Mary Dominy, the less-than-one-year-old daughter of unmarried button-maker Mary Dominy of Morden, Wareham (1851 census: Wareham, Dorset, HO107/1856, fol. 470, p. 16). Given the Dorset connection and comparative rarity of the surname, little Mary may have been a relative, possibly Joseph's niece, he borrowing her name to lend credibility to his declaration.

to collect his money and convey it elsewhere, in this case to his intended, Mary Ann Kennell, who as a non-relative and non-trustee did not qualify in her own right. The census located Sarah Barfoot not in Gloucester Street but in nearby Butcher Street, Portsea, a few hundred yards from the dockyard pay office where she could collect the cash, rendezvous with Mary Ann amid the usual throng of allottees, and covertly pass her the coin.[56] Within minutes of leaving her front door, Sarah could fulfil her intermediary mission and be home again, perhaps retaining a few pennies of Joseph's monthly one pound for her trouble.

If unprovable, the arrangement is feasible. A year after naming Sarah 'trustee' to his (invented) 1-year-old Mary Ann Dominy, Joseph declared an allotment favouring his (by then genuine) wife Mary Ann Dominy.[57] On 6 March 1851, by licence, he had married widow Mary Ann Kennell, née Carlisle, she having lost her naval pensioner husband John to phthisis eight months earlier.[58] The adult Mary Ann Dominy thus met allotment criteria, her now legitimate status as 'wife' obviating any need for a fictitious child and spurious trustee to act as courier.

Why did Joseph invent a trusteeship? Why not simply declare Mary Ann Kennell his 'sister' pending marriage? That she already had a seaman-brother (a real one, who had served alongside Joseph in *Excellent* 1847–48 and *Prince Regent* 1848–51, and with her late husband John Kennell in *Edinburgh* 1834–36) may have been a deterrent.[59] For Joseph to use the 'sister' ruse would have risked the pay office spotting that she was receiving money from brothers with different surnames, which would in turn necessitate her inventing and memorising a step-relationship to explain the difference. Besides, though it harked back to an incident some twenty years earlier, the name Kennell may have had an abiding notoriety in naval circles, enough to draw the attention of pay office and/or Whitehall staff; for Mary Ann's late husband John was one of four men discharged 'with disgrace' from HMS *Columbine* in the summer of 1830, he having served scarcely more than

---

[56] 1851 census: HO107/1658, fol. 73, p. 41.
[57] ADM 27/112/379/1680; ADM 27/113/84/1680.
[58] E&W Marriages: Poole, Dorset, 12 July 1842; E&W Deaths: Weymouth, Dorset, Q4/1844, vol. 8, p. 103 (certificate). On the marriage certificate Joseph declared himself widowed; his first wife, Mary Ann Brigham, whom he married in 1842, had died in 1844. Joseph's earliest allotment declarations, dated 1844–48, favour his pipemaker father James (ADM 27/85/288/24; ADM 27/100/433/368; ADM 27/102/262/621). ADM 27/85/288/24; ADM 27/100/433/368; ADM 27/102/262/621; ADM 27/81/156/SB201; CHU3/1D/49, p. 49 n. 97; CHU3/1D/33, p. 3 n. 9; ADM 27/51/159/SB121; E&W Deaths: Q3/1850, vol. 7, p. 89 (certificate); ADM 27/81/156/SB201; CHU3/1E/31, p. 23 n. 182.
[59] ADM 29/42/314, p. 318; ADM 139/112/11136; ADM 139/111/11136 (Joseph Dominy); ADM 29/52/366 (Frederick Carlisle); ADM 29/42/314 (John Kennell).

three weeks after entry.[60] As if to quell inevitable curiosity, across the foot of John Kennell's service record is written, 'No special notation in the Muster Book, nor in the Master's Log.' To be discharged within weeks of joining ship was bad enough. To be discharged 'with disgrace', as one of several men, reeked of scandal. Scandal there was, though not of a sexual nature. *Columbine* had returned to Portsmouth, bringing twelve convicts 'whose behaviour had been so refractory that for want of power to punish them, their longer stay in the settlement [of Bermuda] was considered dangerous'.[61] Transferred to the prison hulk *York* in Portsmouth Harbour, the twelve revealed that *Columbine*'s prisoners had caused an 'uproar' on board. Some had thrust knives through their prison bars, stabbing guards who immediately opened fire, killing two prisoners and wounding two others. So serious was the incident, a 'representation' was made to the Home Secretary 'of the circumstances under which they have been sent to England. These circumstances [the truth of which we cannot vouch] have only been divulged by the prisoners themselves'.[62] In the absence of a written report of the incident in naval records, it may be inferred that John Kennell was one of the guards responsible for the prisoners' deaths.

As well as her new husband's payments, Mary Ann Carlisle Kennell Dominy also had an allotment from a seaman-brother. In February 1851 Frederick Carlisle had rejoined *Excellent* on the same day as had Mary Ann's then sweetheart Joseph, promptly declaring an allotment in her favour. From husband and brother, Mary Ann was now receiving a total of £2 6s 0d per month. Former courier and 'trustee' Sarah Barfoot was getting nothing.

The Wheden and Dominy examples were unusual. Most trusteeships were unremarkable, most trustees genuine, named in respect of just one child. Seven trustees were named twice, in allotments involving fourteen different children. This suggests they were capable, experienced foster mothers willing to take on the care of multiple unrelated children at the same time, or in succession. In twenty instances the men making the declarations supplied no details of the children's age or place of baptism, and nine children went wholly unnamed, but it would be cynical to assume that untraced trustees and unnamed children signal specious allotments. For example, news might reach a father serving at sea, telling of the birth of a child whose conception was already known to him. He might learn of the newborn's sex, but not necessarily the name proposed by its mother, or the date and place of the christening (which might not occur until after the father were home from sea); and he would not foresee his wife's death in

---

[60] ADM 29/42/314.
[61] *H/Tel*, 24 May 1830, p. 4, col. 3.
[62] Ibid.

childbirth, or anticipate the need to find a foster carer for his motherless infant. Such a scenario would leave him with scant details to complete a trustee declaration.

Named or unnamed in the allotment registers, however, a startling ninety-four entrusted children could not be located, almost double the number found. Some may have been subsumed into other carers' families under the householder's surname; some may have died, though not one appears by its seaman-stated name in the death register. Some may have been jettisoned, placed with kin or in the workhouse to allow the trustees to undertake waged work or be freed of childcare responsibilities.[63] Some may have been fictitious, invented by sailors to facilitate allotments which would otherwise be deemed invalid. Less sensationally, some may simply have been retrieved by their fathers and taken home, as witness 15-year-old Catherine Walsh who, having left the care of Portsea allottee Ann Shaw, was located with her boatswain's mate father in a district close by Plymouth naval dockyard.[64]

The occasional questionable declaration aside, most sailors used the trustee facility for the admirable purpose of protecting their motherless offspring and underage siblings. Trusteeship also enabled men to support their illegitimate children: at least eight trustees featured in this study were identified, via parish and civil records, as mothers of the minors supposedly 'entrusted' to them. The Navy required no explanation for such declarations, or proof of identity or relationship, a feature making it easier for naval putative fathers to maintain financial responsibility for their bastards than could civilian putative fathers in the same communities. Given its misgivings about allotments in general (see Chapter One), this was not an aspect the 1859 Royal Commission would have found reassuring.

In numerous declarations there is no immediately discernible relationship between seaman and trustee or child. In these instances the declaration may indicate the man's belief, or hope, that a child was his; it may equally bespeak sailorly prudence, a ruse designed to forestall queries as to why one man was financially supporting another's offspring. In March 1850 and again in June 1851, George Ruggills, HMS *Blenheim*'s wardroom cook, named 45-year-old laundress Sarah Jennings as trustee to Albert 'Ruggills', the lad's surname hinting that George had acknowledged paternity.[65] In the census, however, 9-year-old Albert appears as Jennings, the name under

---

[63] David Vincent, *Bread, Knowledge, and Freedom: a study of nineteenth-century working class autobiography* (London, 1982), p. 65; William Acton, *Prostitution Considered in its Moral, Social, and Sanitary Aspects, in London and Other Large Cities and Garrison Towns: with Proposals for the Control and Prevention of its Attendant Evils* (London, 1972, reprint of 1870 edition), p. 281.

[64] ADM 27/113/272/13; 1851 census: East Stonehouse, Devon, HO107/1880, fol. 58, p. 58.

[65] ADM 27/110/279/354, ADM 27/113/255/161.

which his birth was registered; for he was Sarah's legitimate son, one of four children born of her marriage to mariner Cornelius Jennings.[66] The couple had been married for over twenty years when in 1849 Cornelius succumbed to a pulmonary abscess.[67] Why young Albert, and not his 5-year-old sister, 11-year-old brother or eldest sibling Cornelius, should be selected as object of George Ruggills's munificence is unknown. The choice may have been random, or deliberate and meaningful, or simply George's way of paying respect to his late friend Cornelius, keeping a promise that he would look after Sarah should anything untoward happen. Beyond sentiment of the brotherly/sailorly sort, however, the allotment may equally have been George's way of quietly supporting a woman for whom he had special affection. The easiest way to initiate this would have been to name Sarah his sister; instead, his declaration styled her trustee to her late husband's legitimate child, his declaration a hint that he was the lad's true father, which he may well have been.[68] Whatever the truth of the matter, the allotment was not his first supportive gesture, or his last. In 1848, a year before Cornelius Jennings's death, George's will had named Sarah his executrix and sole beneficiary.[69] Thirteen years later, her laundress days behind her, Sarah was keeping a shop; George, still a wardroom cook, was listed as her boarder.[70] Whether or not they were living as man and wife is irrelevant. Financially through his keep and physically through his presence, George supported Sarah and her family for years.

Other trustee arrangements were equally enduring, and suggestive of more than childcare alone. In April 1850 boatswain third class Swinfen Ball, HMS *Illustrious*, declared Mary Richards trustee for his son George.[71] This was a role Mary had borne for six months or more, caring for Swinfen's children by his late wife Elizabeth, to whom he had allotted from their marriage on Christmas Day 1840 to her death in 1849.[72] When towards the end of 1850 Swinfen married Mary, his subsequent allotment named her his wife.[73]

Male trustees featured in eight of the 150 declarations in this category. The arrangements did not last: five of the eight children are lost from view, and two were located not with their trustees but in institutional settings.

---

[66] 1851 census: HO107/1658, fol. 214, p. 41; E&W Births: Q1/1842, vol. 7, p. 156.
[67] CHU3/1D/28, p. 39 n. 116; E&W Deaths: Q1/1849, vol. 7, p. 146 (certificate).
[68] E&W Births: Q1/1842, vol. 7, p. 156 (certificate).
[69] ADM 48/82, image ref. 304.
[70] 1861 census: RG9/636, fol. 61, p. 25 ('Ruggels').
[71] ADM 27 110/271/77.
[72] ADM 27/109/59/1; ADM 27/73/112/461; ADM 27/85/69/60; ADM 27/103/99/31; E&W Deaths: Q4/1849, vol. 7, p. 96.
[73] E&W Marriages: Q3/1850, vol. 7, p. 241; ADM 27/111/374/10; ADM 27/120/299/14.

On census day 1851, 13-year-old Henry Wilson, 'born at sea', was one of seven scholars at a school above a wine merchant in Lion Terrace.[74] Three months later, in June 1851, bandsman John Wilson of HMS *Penelope* named his 10-year-old son Henry his allottee, giving an address in College Street, Portsea.[75] The College Street house was uninhabited on census day, and because John (and in this instance naval bureaucracy) ignored regulations requiring named trustees for children under eighteen it is impossible to identify the person John had in mind to serve as Henry's carer, if carer there were. We may hope that Henry's situation was better than that of 10-year-old James Smith. Featured in the 1850 allotment of his father, gunner's mate Thomas, HMS *Excellent*, naming trustee Mary Baskerville, James appears in the census as an 11-year-old pauper scholar in care of the Union.[76] At some point between declaration and census the trusteeship had broken down. A 'washing pauper', widow Mary was still alive (she lived until 1898), but James had simply 'run out of kin', and there was nowhere for him to go but the workhouse.[77]

Institutions of a very different kidney featured in twelve children's allotments, when sailors cited pubs as their trustees' addresses. Half these establishments were on the Common Hard, and two allotments favoured Ann and Louisa Wafer.[78] In all of Portsea Island there was only one woman called Wafer, and that was the redoubtable Louisa, so either leading stoker Alexander McCard gave the wrong forename for his trustee, or *Retribution*'s pusser's clerk wrote 'Ann' in error, perhaps because the allotment concerned Alexander's 6-year-old daughter Ann. Louisa Wafer was no ordinary woman, hers no ordinary pub. She and her husband ran the Earl St Vincent, and unique among Portsea publicans she had acquired a reputation as a one-woman naval recruiting dynamo.[79] One witness told the 1859 Royal Commission into naval manning of Louisa's role in securing, via her

---

[74] 1851 census: HO107/1658, fol. 5, p. 2.
[75] ADM 27/113/253/125.
[76] ADM 27/110/220/1411; 1851 census: HO107/1657, fol. 576, p. 46.
[77] 1851 census: HO107/1657, fol. 31, p. 8; E&W Deaths: Q3/1898, vol. 2B, p. 267; Portsmouth History Centre (PHC) Portsmouth, Hampshire, Portsmouth Burials, Parish Burials, PHC G/BBK4/10 (1898), p. 391 n. 67530; Jane Humphries, 'Care and Cruelty in the Workhouse: children's experiences of residential poor relief in eighteenth- and nineteenth-century England', in Nigel Goose and Katrina Honeyman (eds), *Childhood and Child Labour in Industrial England: diversity and agency, 1750–1914* (Farnham, Surrey, 2013), 115–34, at pp. 121–2.
[78] ADM 27/111/125/7; ADM 27/111/295/142.
[79] Slater, *Directory of Hampshire* (s.l., 1851), p. 61; Hunt, *Directory*, p. 110; Walton, 'Social History', p. 68, giving the Wafers' pub as the Hole in the Wall rather than the Earl St Vincent.

'respectable house', the staggering figure of 26,572 men for the Navy (for a fee per head, that is); another witness, a naval commander, was fulsome in praising her.[80]

In 1851 the Wafer household consisted of Louisa and husband James, their 2-year-old son, a visiting Irish widow, and a 19-year-old pot boy.[81] Of 6-year-old Ann McCard, likewise the 4-year-old Caroline Baxter supposedly entrusted by HMS *Niger*'s AB William Baxter, there was no sign.[82] Baxter and McCard were not the only seamen to allot to Louisa. In January 1849 Richard Saunders, gun room steward HMS *Driver*, named her trustee for a child on whom he supplied no detail whatsoever.[83] Coincidence of identical clerical error is improbable, so how to account for these seemingly void allotments? Expediency may have played a part. Well known within naval circles, Mrs Wafer's name was easily called to mind when the time came for men to make declarations which might not bear close scrutiny. Alternatively, in Royal Navy eyes her standing was such that any man naming her his trustee could expect his declaration to be processed without query or delay. Were she not actually fostering seamen's children (and given her commercial interests, her running of a thriving public house, her involvement in naval recruiting, it would not be unreasonable to suggest she was too busy to provide hands-on childcare), and were these allotments not a means by which men repaid monies owing on loans she had extended them or bar-room credit they had racked up, then might she have agreed to a different kind of deal? Did Louisa Wafer undertake to serve as go-between for unnamed women, women whose naming on allotment vouchers was prohibited under the regulations, or too risky or shaming? Louisa's pub was even nearer to the pay office than were the homes of Maria Balch or Sarah Barfoot (*q.v.*), so it was no great inconvenience for her to attend once a month to collect cash on behalf of unnamed others. It was easy, in turn, for the unnamed women to meet her on The Hard, or to slip discreetly into the Earl St Vincent, there to receive from 'trustee' Louisa their monthly cash sums, perhaps minus a few coins by way of commission. Louisa Wafer's regard for seamen was legendary, so the possibility remains that she was willing to facilitate certain seamen's support for their favoured women. Her

---

[80] Hardwicke, *Report*, p. 261 s. 4892, p. 265 ss. 5017–9; Walton, '"Great Improvement"', p. 30 n. 13, citing National Archives (TNA) Kew, Admiralty, and Ministry of Defence, Navy Department: Correspondence and Papers, ADM 1 (1660–1976), for ADM 1/6597, Louisa Wafer to Lord H.G. Lennox MP, 18 May 1867. With thanks to Jo Stanley for additional information.
[81] 1851 census: HO107/1658, fol. 256, p. 10.
[82] ADM 27/111/125/7.
[83] ADM 27/106/35/103.

standing, moreover, was such that few would have suspected her of subterfuge, or dared question the arrangement.

Trustee allotments, then, were used with sailorly ingenuity to get cash into non-relatives' hands. That some individuals cynically exploited the system, thereby fuelling political concerns about its encouraging immorality, should be set against the fact that without such a facility, over the decades hundreds of naval children would have been consigned to parish institutions or naval orphanages. As social benefit, the trustee role should not be underestimated; as altruistic device it should be approached with caution.

\*\*\*

These women, and these fewer men, were not the only members of the nineteenth-century naval community. There were other dependants still receiving their monthly payments on the basis of allotments declared years earlier; there were non-allottee dependants struggling to eke out their departing men's cash through the length of ships' commissions; there were dead seamen's widows and bereaved mothers and sisters whose allotments had stopped upon their men's demise; and there were others who, when their men went to sea, were left for months or years not only without allotment but with neither lump sum cash-in-hand nor income beyond anything they might earn for themselves.

*3*

# PLACE AND BIRTHPLACE

From allotment registers and census records we know these seamen's women lived in Portsea, Portsmouth, Kingston and Landport, the main built-up districts of mid-Victorian Portsea Island; but where did the women come from? Were they Portsmouth-born, or immigrants from other parts of the country, other port towns? Suggesting an influx from further afield, one writer asserts that Portsmouth was 'inundated' with naval wives and children, a claim at odds with the finding that of 970 Portsmouth-resident allottee-wives whose birthplaces are known, more than half (55.8 per cent) were Portsmouth-born natives.[1]

Townward migration tended to take place over relatively short distances, enabling migrants to flow through family and localised networks.[2] This does not seem to have applied to naval wives, only 11.4 per cent of whom came the relatively short distances from mainland Hampshire and the Isle of Wight. If to them we add immigrants from the Channel Islands, and the neighbouring counties of Sussex, Surrey, Berkshire, Wiltshire and Dorset, the proportion rises to 17.2 per cent, or 38.9 per cent of those born beyond Portsea Island. But most of the distances involved in this extended catchment area are greater than the ten- to twelve-mile 'short distances' proposed by Thompson.[3] To Portsmouth from the Reading birthplace of gunner's wife Linda Prindiville is seventy-five miles; forty-three miles separate Portsmouth from Guildford, birthplace of bandsman's wife Harriet Lockett; and Portsmouth is nearly one hundred miles from Lyme Regis, where gunner's wife Rachael Yealland was born.[4] If the net is cast to include

---

[1] Stark, *Female Tars*, p. 24.
[2] F.M.L. Thompson, *The Rise of Respectable Society: a social history of Victorian Britain, 1830–1900* (London, 1988), p. 178.
[3] Barry Stapleton and James H. Thomas, *The Portsmouth Region* (Gloucester, 1989), p. 115.
[4] ADM 27/111/175/3; 1851 census: HO107/1659, fol. 241, p. 9; ADM 27/113/254/127; 1851 census: HO107/1659, fol. 754, p. 12; ADM 27/112/235/299; 1851 census: HO107/1659, fol. 263, p. 13.

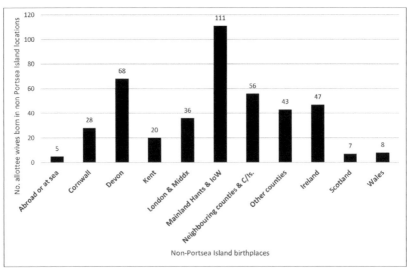

Fig. 6   Birthplaces of allottee wives born outside Portsea Island (n=429).

only Hampshire, the Channel Islands and Sussex, the distances involved still exceed the thirty-mile radius cited by Walkowitz.[5] In short, something approaching 70 per cent of non-Portsea born naval wives may be identified as 'long-distance' immigrants.

The January 1850 – July 1852 study period falls toward the end of Ireland's Great Famine, which saw at least a million emigrating to escape starvation, homelessness following eviction, and poverty. At no census date between 1841 and 1901 did the Irish-born population of England and Wales rise above 3 per cent of the total population, yet our forty-six Irish-born naval wives comprised a percentage three times that of the Hampshire tally (4.8 vs 1.6 per cent), and more than half as much again as the 3 per cent average for England and Wales.[6] In most instances the census gives these wives' origins only as 'Ireland', but it is not improbable that more came from Cork than the near-quarter of them recorded as such in the census, for it was off Cove of Cork, in the southernmost county of Ireland, that a Royal Navy guardship (in 1851, HMS *Ajax*) lay at anchor. Of the study cohort, twenty-one Irish wives had married in their birthplaces before emigrating; the rest left Ireland unmarried, their weddings taking place in

---

[5] Judith R. Walkowitz and Daniel J. Walkowitz, '"We Are Not Beasts of the Field": prostitution and the poor in Plymouth and Southampton under the Contagious Diseases Acts', *Feminist Studies*, 1:3–4 (1973), 73–106, at p. 78, referring to immigration from rural Devon to Plymouth.

[6] J.A. Banks, 'Population Change and the Victorian City', *Victorian Studies*, 11:3 (1968), 277–89, at p. 280.

Anglican churches within Portsmouth and Plymouth purlieus. Emigration brought isolation: by 1851 only three of the forty-six had Irish relatives living with them. Wife of HMS *Hogue*'s sick berth attendant, Cork-born and Cork-wed Margaret Bethell, was five years married, her 25-year-old unmarried sister sharing their Portsea sublet.[7] For safety and company the sisters may have left Ireland together; alternatively, finding herself alone after husband William's ship put to sea, Margaret wrote to ask Ann to join her. Born in Athlone in the west of Ireland, Elizabeth Hubbard had no Irish kin in her Landport household. She had made her move to England as a 20-year-old single woman, in 1833 marrying John Taw by licence in St Andrew's Church, Plymouth.[8] Eighteen years later she was living in Constitution Square, Landport, a warrant officer's wife with five children aged seven years to three weeks.[9]

Seamen's wives would frequently uproot to accompany husbands who had relocated to ports with better employment prospects.[10] The same applied when husbands relocated to join ships based in other Royal Navy ports. The potential for mobility was even greater when wives were the daughters of seamen. Nearly 12 per cent of the study's wives were born in Devon, Cornwall and Kent, traditional recruiting grounds of naval men. If this means (as it probably does) they were naval daughters, we may wonder whether it was their fathers' or their husbands' naval service that prompted the move from West Country birthplace to Portsea Island. Those immigrating as children, when their fathers joined Portsmouth-based ships, had had years in which to establish networks in their local communities before marriage opened up new kinship and social links; but immigrant wives moving from another naval port to join their husbands had to forge new networks from scratch, unsupported by their birth families.[11]

Of nineteen instances where the census showed a naval wife and both her parents as having the same or adjacent place(s) of birth, only three involved families from beyond Portsea Island. Like her parents, Sarah Hall, wife of captain of the afterguard Richard Hall, HMS *Arethusa*, was born on the Herefordshire–Wales border; the previously mentioned Hooper/Nancarrow family originated in Cornwall; and the parents of Fareham-born Ann, wife of gun room steward Charles Oddy, HMS *Contest*, came from Fareham and Botley, small Hampshire towns a mere eight miles apart, eight again

---

[7] ADM 27/112/178/362; 1851 census: HO107/1659, fol. 142, p. 38.
[8] ADM 27/113/39/52; Devon Marriages and Banns: St Andrews, Plymouth, 3 April 1833, p. 115 n. 344.
[9] 1851 census: HO107/1659, fol. 742, p. 43.
[10] Fury, 'Seamen's Wives and Widows', pp. 253–4.
[11] Walton, 'Social History', p. 79.

from the bridge to Portsea Island.[12] All other wives with co-resident parents were Portsmouth-born. None of their nineteen co-resident fathers was a serving seaman or Greenwich pensioner; eleven were dockyard workers or shipwrights, the rest comprising agricultural and general labourer, carpenter, bricklayer, plumber, greengrocer and shoe- or bootmaker. To infer that these were lifelong civilians ignores the possibility that some were former seamen who had quit sea service and taken up shoreside trades. It is also possible that unknown numbers of naval wives' fathers – some of them serving seamen – were simply absent on census night. What this small subset conveys is the comparative rarity of Portsea-resident fathers, mothers and naval-wife daughters sharing a *non*-Portsea birthplace.

One hundred and eleven mothers of allottee wives appear in the census as co-resident with their daughters. Maternal birthplaces include Ireland, Cornwall, Oxfordshire, Bedfordshire and Somerset, but the women of this older generation were local by birth to a greater extent than their daughters, nearly 60 per cent having been born on Portsea Island, the Isle of Wight, or in mainland Hampshire. In fifty-four instances both naval wife *and* mother were born in the same location, suggesting the mothers had either remained in their birthplace following the arrival of at least one child, or that having travelled beyond their community they had returned to the place of their birth and marriage, to give birth with kin close at hand. For thirty-eight of these mother–daughter pairs the shared place of birth was Portsea, for ten others Cornwall, Devon, Kent and Ireland. Forty-eight of the fifty-four involved places associated with the Navy, suggesting the mothers were naval wives or widows, an inference only strengthened in a dozen examples where mothers were born in Devonport, Ireland, Cornwall, their daughters in Chatham, Plymouth, Portsea. In seventy-one instances where birthplaces of wives and their widowed fathers were recorded, nearly one-third of the fathers were Portsea-born, their daughters likewise; and ten of eleven Hampshire-born men had daughters born on Portsea Island. In sum, that so many mothers and fathers of these naval wives were Portsea-born indicates a stratum of naval society deeply embedded in its local community; that many others were associated with seafaring communities elsewhere bespeaks a pattern of migration unique to naval families.

The Hooper/Nancarrow family's migration history merits closer scrutiny. As noted earlier, in 1851 Christianna Nancarrow was receiving allotments as wife, sister and trustee. She and her parents were born in Cornwall. Did she come to Portsea as a naval bride, or in childhood when

---

[12] ADM 27/110/179/138; 1851 census: HO107/1658, fol. 607, p. 23; ADM 27/112/180/68; 1851 census: HO107/1658, fol. 415, p. 33; ADM 27/109/476/58; 1851 census: HO107/1659, fol. 412, p. 8.

her father's work brought the family out of the West Country? Several clues suggest the latter. Her mother Christine Hooper appears in the 1841 census as a seaman's wife living in Hewlin's Court, Portsea.[13] Of Christine's six children, 8-year-old Elizabeth Maria was the youngest of four born outside Hampshire, 5-year-old Angelina the first of two born locally; in the three-year period between these girls' births the family had relocated to Portsea.[14] At twenty-two, in 1841 Christine's elder son Thomas was already a seaman, 11-year-old Sampson later following him to sea.[15] In 1837, eldest child Christianna had married the then AB William Nancarrow.[16] By 1841 she may have decamped to Newlyn, where a 'Christiane' appears in the household of (parents-in-law?) Elizabeth and William Nancarrow, he an agricultural labourer.[17] We do know that, at sea in *Crocodile*, in the summer of 1842 seaman William believed his wife Christianna to be living in Hawke Street, Portsea, and that by census day 1851 she was at her parents' Hewlin's Court address, a member of their household of ten.[18]

At home with her parents in 1841, Christine Hooper's second daughter Ann would five years later marry a William Sanford, and by 1851 establish a separate household with their two children in Bonfire Corner, Portsea, hard by the dockyard walls.[19] The marriage register shows that, like her brothers and brother-in law, and her father in years past (by 1846 Thomas Hooper senior was a 'convict guard'), Ann's husband was a sailor, as was his father. Another Hooper daughter, Elizabeth Maria, in 1855 married petty officer James Hewitt, one of their witnesses being her sister Angelina.[20] Two years later, Angelina married seaman William Gibbons; by census day 1861 she was a widow with sons aged two years and six months, the little family living as lodgers to a seaman and his wife.[21] Youngest sister Miranda was still in Portsea. Two years earlier she had married Samuel Mogg, a 26-year-old seaman, and on census night they and their 9-month-old daughter were in their Hawke Street sublet, barely five minutes' walk from elder sister Ann.[22]

---

[13] 1841 census: HO107/415/4, fol. 28, p. 12, Christine Hooper enumerated as 'Christian'.
[14] The child Elizabeth M[aria] listed in the 1841 census appears as Maria in the 1851 record (1851 census: HO107/1658, fol. 415, p. 33).
[15] ADM 27/112/180/68; ADM 139/258/25718.
[16] CHU23/1D/3, p. 1 n. 1.
[17] 1841 census: Newlyn, Cornwall: HO107/150, fol. 17, p. 1.
[18] ADM 27/79/308/40; 1851 census: HO107/1658, fol. 415, pp. 33–4.
[19] CHU3/1D/44, p. 165 n. 329; 1851 census: HO107/1658, fol. 447, p. 5.
[20] CHU3/1D/52, p. 125 n. 250.
[21] CHU36/1B/1, p. 66 n. 132; E&W Marriages: Q4/1857, vol. 2B, p. 673; 1861 census: RG09/632, fol. 72, p. 26 ('Angelina Gibens').
[22] CHU3/1D/57, p. 191 n. 382 ('Marinda Lucretia Hooper'); ADM 27/111/78/215/SB33; 1861 census: RG09/636, fol. 99, p. 7.

Intimately connected to the Navy, the Hoopers' migration created two layers within the same family. There were parents and older children born and brought up in Cornwall, for whom the move eastwards would cause a severing of West Country social and kinship connections; and there were younger members who, until marriage took them elsewhere, knew of no other place than the Portsea court where they were raised. Irrespective of birthplace, the lives of all seven Hooper children were affected by their parents' shift from Cornish hamlet to naval port town. Both sons served at sea, the likelihood of their doing so heightened not only by their father's being a seaman but by his moving the family into the heart of a populous naval community where recruitment was easy and immediate, seamen both role models and the norm. The Hooper daughters' clustering meanwhile reflects a mid-nineteenth century tendency for relatives to congregate together instead of dispersing across a wider area.[23] Incomers joining from outside could expect to find extended family enmeshed in the community, having enjoyed from birth the benefits of accessible kinship networks, geographical stability, peer-group support and local knowledge. In streets teeming with more people than they were used to, immigrants from market towns or remote hamlets may have been shocked by their new communities. The presence of kin – men to lend protection, women to advise, inform, support, reassure – would do much to make bearable these difficult transitions.

Locally-resident kin could also affirm incomers' identity. This was important for naval wives who often left immediate family behind in their birthplace, losing thereby the means to vouch for their identity.[24] Place of birth was a key criterion in determining eligibility for parish relief, and rules of settlement could disadvantage seamen's wives even more than soldiers' wives from 'foreign' parishes; for whereas army wives both arrived in port towns in large numbers and were eligible for army barrack accommodation with their menfolk, sailors' wives arrived alone and unaccompanied, and must find their own accommodation. To pay rent required an income; to qualify for income in the form of allotment or parish relief, wives must convince local authorities of their identities, which hinged in turn upon their proving their husbands' seagoing trade, entitlement or settlement – no easy task if documentation were lacking, their men absent at sea.[25] Here locally-resident relatives proved their worth, vouching for immigrants who

---

[23] Michael Anderson, 'The Study of Family Structure', in E.A. Wrigley (ed.), *Nineteenth-Century Society: essays in the use of quantitative methods for the study of social data* (Cambridge, 1972), 47–81, at p. 73.
[24] Fury, 'Seamen's Wives and Widows', p. 261.
[25] Lynn Hollen Lees, *The Solidarities of Strangers: the English poor laws and the people, 1700–1948* (Cambridge, 1998), p. 143.

lacked the means to confirm identity, status or relationship. Without this support the immigrant naval wife must convince her local church minister of her bona fides – a challenging prospect when she was a newcomer to a parish, a stranger in the congregation. For a woman arriving alone in a port town, her kin geographically inaccessible, the maritime community was important as a source of support. What it could not provide was the emotional sustenance obtainable only from family and loved ones.

# 4

# MARRIAGE

'Sailoring runs in families, even more than soldiering; and in Portsmouth, Chatham and Devonport there are families who have sent five or six generations to the lower deck.'[1] Lavery is quoting Gordon, whose 'chat' provides an admiring if schoolboy-simple picture of late nineteenth-century naval life.[2] What neither considers is whether, like sons following fathers into the Navy, naval daughters might tend to follow their naval mothers into naval marriage. Down the centuries this was a commonplace. Fury's study of Tudor seamen's women reveals one generation of seafarers producing another and marrying other seafarers' offspring. It identifies, apart from economic considerations, the key consideration of *compatibility* among naval couples, women who married seamen being 'prepared for the role they would assume as wives to often absent husbands and practitioners of a high-risk occupation'.[3]

McKee's sailors were speaking at a ninety-year remove from this study's mid-nineteenth century period, but their comments suggest little by way of attitudinal shift to differentiate them from their Tudor counterparts. Less preoccupied with factors such as compatibility, his twentieth-century interviewees polarised females as 'nice girls' (appropriate as wives and mothers of one's children, and committed to monogamy) and 'tarts', a self-defeating syllogism then asserting that those 'nice girls' of Portsmouth 'had seen too much drunken antisocial behaviour by sailors … to want these men as boyfriends or potential husbands.'[4] According to one chief petty officer, however, many a Portsmouth parent would take a more hard-nosed view, urging their daughters to 'go out and get a sailor' because when he went abroad 'you get your money whether he's there or whether he isn't.'[5] Old-fashioned love, it seems, did not come into it.

---

[1] Lavery, *Able Seamen*, p. 117.
[2] William John Gordon, *A Chat about the Navy* (London, 1891), p. 14.
[3] Fury, 'Seamen's Wives and Widows', p. 260.
[4] McKee, *Sober Men and True*, p. 183.
[5] Ibid., p. 185.

## NAVAL HUSBANDS, NAVAL DAUGHTERS

Consider the Greenleaf family. Born in 1791, John Greenleaf was a Navy man. Fig. 27 (p. 247) shows him and his wife Elizabeth (*q.v.*) having at least eight offspring, and numerous grandchildren. Within the younger generation of Greenleaf sons and daughters, by occupation and marriage there were eight direct naval connections, yet more among the next generation down. Chapter One showed Elizabeth's efforts to have her children admitted to the Royal Hospital School at Greenwich. Her eventual success was to have far-reaching effects upon the whole family. The school immersed all its pupils in naval culture, preparing for sea service the three Greenleaf sons who survived childhood, preparing the three surviving Greenleaf girls for a different kind of naval 'service'.[6] Eldest daughter Elizabeth married a seaman but died without issue; the youngest, Joanna (*q.v.*), clocked up three sailor-husbands within a decade. Middle daughter Phoebe (*q.v.*) was twice married to seamen, and produced three seamen-sons. From her brief marriage to gunner John Saxton, moreover, in addition to a sailor-son there was a daughter who had two seaman-husbands in succession; and Phoebe's subsequent marriage to Richard Page, of which more will be said in Chapter Thirteen, produced two sailor-sons and a daughter who married a sailor.[7] Remarkable as this family may look to twenty-first century eyes, it was then far from unique.

***

Lavery's assertion that sailoring 'ran in families' was tested here via a comparison of naval and civilian newlyweds.[8] The nett cohort of 1,581 allottees yielded nearly 1,000 marriages for analysis, 342 of them relating to wives whose dates of marriage featured in allotment declarations, and whose ages were established as firmly as possible via census and/or baptism registers. Their seamen-husbands' ages were similarly established via ships' books, census and parish records. It is upon these 342 naval unions that this chapter's initial analysis is based. From them a subset of newlyweds was extracted, comprising couples whose allotment details stated they had married in Portsea Island churches during the fifteen-month period preceding the mid-century census, January 1850 to March 1851. From the same parish records and fifteen-month period a comparator cohort of 'civilian' marriages was extracted, in each of which the groom's occupation

---

[6] ADM 73/243/2.
[7] E&W Marriages: Q1/1841, vol. 7, p. 169; Q4/1863, vol. 2B, p. 803.
[8] Lavery, *Able Seamen*, p. 117.

appeared to be non-naval. The two comparator groups comprised ninety-eight naval newlywed couples and 118 civilian.[9]

Brides' and grooms' fathers were then separated into four categories: those having a clear naval connection via current Royal Navy employment or as a Greenwich pensioner; those with a likely but unproven naval connection via 'crossover' trades such as shipwright, carpenter or rigger; civilians with no apparent naval association; and those whose occupations were illegible or left blank, or where a father was recorded as 'dead'. The categories cannot be regarded as watertight, since a late father with no occupation recorded might equally have been seaman or chimneysweep, while a father listed as 'chairmaker' might once have served as carpenter RN, a 'tailor' be about to return to sea as ordinary seaman. (One of Jack's more positive social attributes was his reputation as a 'handy man', for 'every sailor knows a little about his needle … and can cut clothes, especially trousers.')[10] Watertight or not, the categories allow broad comparisons to be drawn between naval and civilian marriage patterns.

In Fig. 7, the ninety-eight sailors' brides are grouped under 'newlywed RN couples', brides with non-naval husbands under 'newlywed civilian couples'. The chart shows that among fathers of naval brides, the 29.6 per cent proportion of serving or former seamen was almost three times the 10.3 per cent found among fathers of civilians' brides, suggesting that seamen's daughters were three times more likely to marry sailors than were the daughters of the paternal basket makers, brewers, thatchers and grocers of the civilian group. If we include those brides' fathers whose occupations fell within the ambiguous 'possibly ex-RN' category, the difference becomes even more acute, the 44.9 per cent of seamen's brides with naval or ex-naval fathers outnumbering 10.3 per cent of equivalent civilian brides by almost four-and-a-half to one.[11]

Less than one-third of naval couples had no discernible naval background on either side of the aisle, compared with 72.6 per cent of civilian couples; and whereas ten naval couples had serving or ex-naval fathers on both sides of the aisle, this could be said of none of the civilian pairs, among whom only ten brides and two grooms had any naval background

---

[9] These comparator groups of 118 civilian and ninety-eight naval newlyweds will feature at intervals in later chapters.

[10] Ellen Ross, *Love and Toil: motherhood in outcast London, 1870–1918* (Oxford, 1993), p. 69; Maya Wassell Smith, '"The Fancy Work What Sailors Make": material and emotional creative practice in masculine seafaring communities', *Nineteenth-Century Gender Studies* 14:2 (2018), n.p. <http://www.ncgsjournal.com/issue142/smith.html> [accessed 22 April 2024]; Conley, *Jack Tar to Union Jack*, p. 3; Rodger, *Command of the Ocean*, p. 504.

[11] 29.6% + 15.3% = 44.9%.

*Marriage*

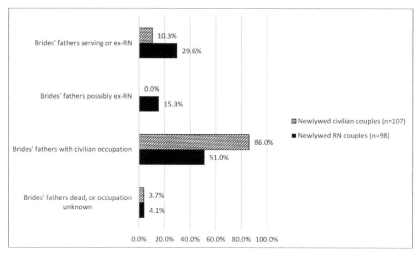

**Fig. 7** Brides' fathers' occupations per parish marriage records, 1850–51.

whatsoever. In sum, the civilian population produced fewer naval sons, and fewer daughters willing (or permitted) to marry sailors.

In a port town context, this finding is unremarkable and understandable. It was common knowledge among naval and civilian households alike that 'for many naval families, a comfortable domestic life enjoying the company of one's spouse and children remained a dream rather than the reality.'[12] That the very phrase 'sailor's wife' appears to have been in use nationally as a pejorative or supposedly comic term may also have played a part, as when local newspaper the *Hull Packet* quoted a rape victim's stating in court that when talking to builders in her place of work she had described herself as a sailor's wife, 'as usual, meaning the joke'.[13] 'Sailor's wife' signalled a husband's absence, a woman's availability and licentiousness. It invited speculation, if not cynical assumption.

The most important feature of this exercise, however, lies in its conveying the differing levels of understanding and support which naval brides could draw upon from either side of the family. Some 45 per cent of brides in the naval comparator group had fathers with current or past naval service; and since sailoring ran in families, it is safe to propose that a hefty proportion also had naval brothers, if not brothers-in-law. The Greenleaf sisters have already been mentioned, but consider also Amelia Wheden (*q.v.*),

---

[12] Ellen Gill, *Naval Families, War and Duty in Britain, 1740–1820* (Woodbridge, 2016), p. 7.
[13] *Hull Packett,* 4 August 1848, p. 6, col. B.

wife of boatswain's mate William Weedon, HMS *Phaeton*.[14] One of twelve children born to a seaman and his two successive wives, Amelia had four sailor brothers who were her senior by eight to twenty-four years; and, like her, at least three of her five sisters married seamen. Amelia's story will be unpacked more fully in due course.

The issue of naval parentage plays an important part in these women's childhoods and adult lives. Of our ninety-eight naval brides, those with seamen-fathers had since infancy known what it was like to have men go away for long periods, leaving households headed by women. Their still-living mothers were both role models and a source of empirical experience and practical advice on issues less familiar to the civilian household: how to cope with long separations; to raise a family without husbandly help; to effect domestic repairs unaided; to make decisions and undertake domestic tasks normally the province of husbands; to manage a household alone; to exercise authority over one's children; to budget on an allotment income that would never be more than half of a husband's already modest wage; and how to argue their corner when criticised for doing all that, and more. None of this, however, should be read as proposing that naval brides' choice of groom was based on calculation rather than love and affection (though parental connivance, as we shall see, may have played a part in some unions).

To the sailor's bride from a civilian background, unless he were an itinerant labourer, navvy or prone to deserting his family (many a family being fatherless at some stage), a father who disappeared for long periods was an alien concept.[15] There was less direct knowledge or understanding, perhaps less empathy too, to be had from mothers whose civilian husbands had never been away from home. Large numbers of men going out of town reduced women's prospects of marriage, and in Portsea Island no group of men was more likely to 'go out of town' than seamen.[16] Still, to marry into the naval community was not impossible for brides from civilian backgrounds: of our sample of newlyweds, just over 17 per cent of civilian daughters married sailors, some thereby acquiring naval or ex-naval in-laws as a source of the insight and support their civilian parents might struggle to provide. Those with least access to maternal practice-wisdom were the twenty-nine sailors' brides whose fathers *and* fathers-in-law were civilians.

On the other side of the aisle, half of the civilian grooms' fathers were themselves unambiguously civilian compared with 90 per cent of

---

[14] ADM 27/110/34/200. Spelling of the surname varies between naval and civil sources.
[15] Humphries, *Childhood and Child Labour*, pp. 66–9; Lewis, 'Married to the Navy', p. 37.
[16] Humphrey Southall and David Gilbert, 'A Good Time to Wed?: marriage and economic distress in England and Wales, 1839–1914', *Economic History Review*, 49:1 (1996), 35–57, at p. 47.

*Marriage*

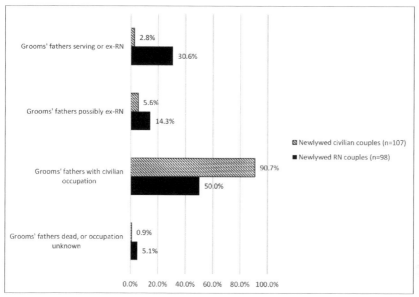

**Fig. 8** Grooms' fathers' occupations per parish marriage records, 1850–51.

sailor-grooms' fathers who were serving seamen. Moreover, fathers of naval grooms were two-and-a-half times as likely to hold one of the ambiguous occupations of carpenter, shipwright or rigger, which may imply that they were former seamen. Marriage of a civilian's daughter to a seaman was more likely to provide her with in-laws familiar with naval family life. If she were lucky, her groom's mother was still living, in a position to share wisdom gained from empirical experience of being, or having been, a seaman's wife.

In a period between Trafalgar and Crimea it is unlikely that these naval daughters were responding to what Gill conveys as a prevailing culture which regarded naval and military daughters as producers of future sailors and soldiers.[17] A safer assumption is that when it came to choice of spouse, paternal occupation played a part more practical than calculating and patriotic. After all, the seaman's daughter hoping to acquire a stay-at-home civilian husband was unlikely to meet one through a father who had spent more time at sea than in a community where he was a relative stranger. But were she willing to follow her mother into naval marriage, her seaman-papa was a useful conduit through which to meet prospective suitors. It was common for married men to bring shipmates ashore for home cooking and family time, a means by which many a bachelor would find himself meeting his host's unmarried daughter(s). Seaman-brothers, too, served as go-betweens, introducing a blushing bachelor-shipmate to an unmarried sister.

---

[17] Gill, *Naval Families*, p. 50.

If the introduction paid off, and mutual attraction bloomed, a factor likely to enhance prospects of parental approval was for the seaman-father of the would-be naval bride to have trade, rate or ship in common with her suitor, or even her suitor's father. The fathers of Henry William Messum and his twelve-day bride Elizabeth White (*q.v.*) were carpenters RN; compounding fatherly satisfaction in their shared trade was the fact that both were ex-*Victory* men who had served together in the mid-1840s.[18] In something of a self-fulfilling prophecy, these considerations may have made the naval daughter more attractive to the naval suitor. As Jack might reason, if her father were a seaman it surely followed that a naval daughter should know what she was letting herself in for when marrying a sailor; and not only know what she was in for, but be well prepared for it.

Distinct differences emerged in grooms' choice of bride. Sailors were equally likely to marry daughters of civilians or daughters of serving or former seamen, but the proportion of civilian men marrying civilians' daughters was eight times that of civilians marrying seamen's daughters. Within the port town community there was no lack of naval daughters of marriageable age, yet only one in ten civilian grooms chose a naval daughter as his bride. This may reflect civilian men's being more likely to mix in civilian circles (which itself suggests a clear social division between naval and civilian communities), thereby meeting more civilian daughters than naval. Beauty was not an issue: civilian brides were surely no more pleasing of face and form than their naval peers. Nepotism and/or hopes of occupational advancement played no apparent part either, for only sixteen of our 107 civilian grooms shared the same or similar occupation as their brides' civilian fathers, and then only in humble trades such as labourer, waterman, cordwainer and gardener.

How, then, to account for the disparity? Setting happenstance aside, might the figures be interpreted as suggesting civilian men found the very idea of the naval daughter unattractive? Did the civilian community regard naval daughters as socially suspect, a poor choice of bride, likely to lower a husband's standing? The naval daughter's language may have been deemed arcane, too obviously nautical (thereby betraying her origins), too salty, even unwomanly.[19] She may have been suspected of sharing her menfolk's legendary promiscuity; of sharing, too, her mother's unfeminine self-reliance and resourcefulness, thereby increasing the likelihood of her exhibiting a lack of submissiveness unbecoming the modest wife, and of expecting a married life offering independence and self-determination. Foreshadowing McKee's petty officer's recalling naval daughters being

---

[18] ADM 27/50/10/3; ADM 27/98/314/1730; ADM 29/4/221; ADM 29/23/275.
[19] Rodger, *Wooden World*, p. 118.

urged to 'go out and get a sailor' because 'you get your money whether he's there or whether he isn't,' nineteenth-century naval daughters may have been suspected of presuming that half of their (civilian) husbands' wages would be handed over, just as it was in naval circles, for was it not common knowledge that their mothers pocketed their sailor-fathers' 'half-pay'?[20] The association – apocryphal or otherwise – of the sailor's woman with drunkenness and prostitution may also have been a red flag, especially in light of local newspapers' coverage of police court proceedings against sailors' wives (see Chapter Eleven).[21] And in some men's minds there may have lurked the unutterable suspicion that a naval daughter would in time find her civilian husband dull, unadventurous, restrictive, too conventional, too often simply *there*.

## PLACE OF MARRIAGE

Almost two-thirds of over 900 of our naval wives were married in their place of birth or within five miles of it. Differences exist, however, between the wedding locations of West Country-born and Portsea Island-born brides. Whereas only 35.4 per cent of West Country women married in or near their place of birth, a hefty 83.1 per cent of Portsea-born wives were Portsea-married. Marriage close to birthplace does not mean these women never went elsewhere. Between wedding-day, husbands' allotment declaration and 1851 census, that some of the longer-married may have lived in Devonport, Chatham or other naval port communities is detectable when children's port town birthplaces reflect their parents' peregrinations.

There is little evidence of women marrying at intermediate distances of between five and twenty miles of their birthplace. A sizeable proportion of naval wives marrying at more than twenty miles from their birthplace will have had sailor-fathers whose work had required their families uproot to distant naval ports, where the daughters grew up and later married. For these women, a preparedness to move in connection with a husband's naval trade will have been inculcated from childhood, any social and kinship ties to their birthplace being stretched thin, if not broken. Some, however, will

---

[20] McKee, *Sober Men and True*, p. 185.
[21] The identification of defendants and/or victims as 'sailor's wife' was a journalistic habit not limited to the *Hampshire Telegraph*, or to court cases for theft, assault, etc. Reporting on three cases of attempted suicide (then a crime), a national newspaper identified one defendant as 'a sailor's wife', adding that she was 'in a state of drunkenness' when attempting to throw herself into a river. The other two defendants' marital status and husbands' occupations were not mentioned (*Express [London]*, 25 August 1852, p. 4 col. D).

have removed only in their late teens or twenties, the uprooting prompted by a husband-to-be joining a ship based in a different naval yard.

Marriage locations reveal strong naval associations, and all but one of the distant wedding locations had a coastal or seafaring connection. Regional patterns also emerge. Among the Portsea-born who married elsewhere, churches in the Devonian naval communities of Stoke Damerel, Stonehouse or Plymouth were where most made their vows, but Malta, Chatham, Woolwich, Bridport (on the main Portsmouth–Plymouth road), Cork (where a guardship was routinely stationed) and Cornwall also feature. The 58.3 per cent of West Country-born brides marrying far from their birthplace is almost nine times the 6.7 per cent of Portsea-born brides doing so. Of wives born in other counties than Hampshire, Devon or Cornwall who married far from their birthplace there was a seafaring element in the choice of wedding location, with 84.4 per cent marrying in Portsea or Alverstoke, a further 8.2 per cent in Woolwich, Chatham, the Channel Islands or London. They were primarily southerners: only sixteen originated in Midland counties or north of the Wash, but in their birthplaces there is a strong association with the sea: 76.9 per cent originated in coastal counties or London, with Woolwich, Deal, Bristol, Sheerness and Chatham featuring prominently. It is not fanciful to suspect that many had seafaring fathers, and that whether childhood or marriage-prompted, their move to Portsmouth was associated with the Navy.

Most of the aforementioned 342 marriages were sealed at the parish church of St Mary's, in the district of Kingston, Portsea Island. For a man simply to state 'Kingston' in his allotment declaration, as did 469 of over 900 husbands, was enough to satisfy naval bureaucracy. From Devonport to Whitehall, every sailor and admiralty clerk knew what 'Kingston' signified in the allotment register's 'Where and When Married' column. St Mary's was known locally as the sailors' church, but we should not infer that naval couples marrying there were regular attenders. Its choice as a wedding venue merely bespeaks sailorly culture, a local preference bordering on folk tradition. To St Mary's, then, our couples would repair between eight o'clock and noon (the Marriage Act of 1823 made it a felony for clergy to solemnise marriages outside those hours), often on a Sunday, sometimes on Christmas Day, on some occasions three, four or more pairs presenting at the altar within minutes of each other.[22] Just as banns may have been gabbled in great numbers at high speed, so marriage ceremonies were clearly brief, and briskly conducted.[23]

---

[22] *Marriage Act*, 4 Geo. IV, c. 76 (1823); Rebecca Probert, *Marriage Law for Genealogists* (Kenilworth, 2012), p. 132.

[23] Olive Anderson, 'The Incidence of Civil Marriage in Victorian England and Wales', *Past & Present*, 69 (1975), 50–87, at p. 65.

Marriage by civil registration and in nonconformist and Roman Catholic chapels had been possible since 1837, but there is little evidence of naval couples' hastening to take advantage of these options.[24] Of our subset of 342 marriages only three Portsea Island weddings (0.9 per cent) were declared as having taken place in register offices. The full cohort of 1,581 allottees yields a higher figure, its nineteen declared register office marriages equivalent to 1.9 per cent of wives, a figure chiming with Anderson's observation that until the 1880s civil marriage was comparatively uncommon south of the Thames.[25] The true figure may be higher, for sailors' willingness to play fast and loose with facts may mean that register office weddings were more numerous than allotment registers suggest; for just as men knew that 'Kingston' signified St Mary's, so they will have known that in addition to other church business, every month its minister and churchwardens must verify scores of allotment declarations, many relating to women who were not regular attenders. Just as these parish worthies may have been too busy to cross-check against their marriage records every declaration mentioning St Mary's, so too may Admiralty clerks have given only cursory attention to declarations referencing 'Kingston', focusing more closely upon those naming register offices or smaller, more obscure churches. If so, sailors cheerfully exploited a systemic weakness.

For proud husbands bent on respectability, that civil ceremonies were cheap, cost a few shillings, and thus appealed to the poor, were uncomfortable considerations; that civil marriage had connections to poor law machinery was a further taint. The equivalent of banns, notices of register office weddings were read at three successive meetings of the Board of Guardians, and vows taken 'at the Office and in the Presence of the Superintendent Registrar and some Registrar of the District', which usually meant the Guardians' clerk's room in the local workhouse.[26] In Portsea Island the superintendent registrar operated out of Lion Terrace, Portsea, in the building where the Board of Guardians met – a nicer location than the workhouse, but one still carrying a whiff of penury.[27] Class and respectability aside, civil marriage continued to be seen as unorthodox.[28] It broke with established law and practice, so much so that it was popularly considered 'not genuine marriage', 'fit only for infidels'.[29] And since the forces of tradition (one of which, we may posit, was the Navy) tend to uphold formal procedures such as the solemnization of marriage, rejection of

---

[24] *Act for Marriages in England*, 6 & 7 Will. IV, c. 85 (1836).
[25] Anderson, 'Incidence of Civil Marriage', p. 54.
[26] Probert, *Marriage Law*, pp. 91, 93; Anderson, 'Incidence of Civil Marriage', p. 65.
[27] Post Office, *Hampshire Trades Directory* (Portsmouth, 1847), pp. 1188, 1170; Hunt, *Directory*, p. 129.
[28] Anderson, 'Incidence of Civil Marriage', p. 54.
[29] *Ibid.*, p. 64.

church marriage signified 'estrangement from the established culture of the country', an attitude at odds with the hierarchical structure and discipline of shipboard life.[30]

Sixty-one of our 342 couples married in churches other than St Mary's. Had the religious orientation of these marriages reflected proportions for the numbers of sittings (available seats) per religious denomination in Portsmouth in 1851, we should expect to see 47 per cent of weddings taking place in Church of England locations, 18 per cent in Independent places of worship, 14 per cent in Baptist and 12 per cent in Methodist chapels, similar proportions arising from comparisons of attendance at public worship for the same denominations on census day.[31] Instead, the naval wedding tally is overwhelmingly Church of England, allotment declarations mentioning only three explicitly nonconformist chapels among 219 Portsea Island church unions. If a further seven unspecified churches are assumed to be nonconformist, the ten marriages amount to just 4.6 per cent of the total. This finding reflects the dominance of the Church of England in the conservative, impoverished, rural southern counties from which the Royal Navy recruited most of its men in the first half of the nineteenth century, for nonconformity was strongest in industrial districts, and among skilled workmen and the lower middle class – places and categories upon which the Navy did not yet draw.[32]

Most couples married after banns were read in their respective parish churches on three successive Sundays prior to the wedding. Some, however, preferred to circumvent this process by expending the cost of a bishop's licence. This was no small consideration, for the £3 fee in 1840 equated to nearly £250 in 2024.[33] In the years 1838–41, at national level there were nineteen to twenty marriages by licence for every hundred by banns, a ratio of approximately one to five.[34] From 175 Portsea Island naval marriages with legible record of legal process there emerges a ratio of one licence or certificate for every 3.9 banns, confirming licences' greater popularity among naval couples. Marriage by licence or certificate was an increasingly popular option for those who, reluctant to abandon religious ceremony for a civil union, wished to preserve privacy, or avoid inter-family ructions or teasing – potential consequences where the bride was middle-aged or older,

---

[30] Ibid., p. 52.
[31] Horace Mann, *Religious Worship in England and Wales* (London, 1854), p. 128. 'Baptist' here conflates figures for Baptist, Particular Baptist and Other Baptist, and 'Methodist' those for Wesleyan and Primitive Methodists.
[32] Walton, 'Social History', p. 341; Preston, 'Constructing Communities', pp. 66–7, 73, 74, 118, 128, 274, 280.
[33] Bank of England, 'Inflation Calculator' [accessed 30 March 2024].
[34] Perkin, *Women and Marriage*, pp. 21, 159.

or pregnant, where the age gap between bride and groom might trigger mockery, or where a couple were of different religions or faced parental opposition despite being of full age.[35] Neither licence nor certificate was significantly the choice of widowed naval spouses remarrying, and none of the seamen's brides marrying by these means appears to have been pregnant at the time, or by modern standards particularly advanced in years.[36] That said, when 43-year-old spinster Elizabeth Ford married by licence she was ten years the senior of bachelor Joseph Stephens, then of HMS *Rainbow*, while 41-year-old spinster Mary Clapshow was eight years older than 33-year-old AB Reuben Phippard.[37] Eschewing banns, certificate and licence, opting instead for the register office, Harriet Bettesworth (*q.v.*), was respectively ten and six years older than her second and third grooms, both of them seamen.[38] Most age differences, however, amounted to a year or two, which leaves ships' impending embarkation the most likely explanation for naval couples' greater usage of licences and certificates. If this were so, it supports Lavery's declaration that sailors had 'no time for conventional wooing'.[39]

## AGE AT MARRIAGE

A consistent message in demographic studies is that the norm was for first marriages to take place when bride and groom were able to create their own separate economic units. Whether via the couple's own efforts or with others' help, marriage had to be built on material foundations, a convention which 'denied marriage to those without material resources, and postponed it for those … able to accumulate them only slowly'.[40] Postponement was common among Victorian working-class couples. Long engagements allowed time for the bride's family to set aside money for the wedding, the groom-to-be to save for the first month's rent, the bride-to-be to accumulate

---

[35] Ibid., pp. 21, 162; P. Gaskell, *The Manufacturing Population of England* (London, 1833), p. 31; Peter Laslett, *Family Life and Illicit Love in Earlier Generations: essays in historical sociology* (Cambridge, 1980), p. 128.

[36] That is, no evidence has been found to show the survival of a child born within nine months of marriage.

[37] ADM 27/113/263/129 ('Joseph Stevens'); CHU2/1C/10, p. 257 n. 770 ('Joseph Stephens'); 1851 census: HO107/1657, fol. 166, p. 3; ADM 27/110/460/146 (Reuben Phippard); 1851 census: HO107/1659, fol. 13, p. 18; CHU2/1C/13, p. 204 n. 408.

[38] ADM 27/110/156/193; E&W Marriages: Q4/1849, vol. 7, p. 317 (certificate: Gimblet/Bettesworth); E&W Marriages: Q1/1851, vol. 7, p. 215 (certificate: Thomas/'Gimblett').

[39] Joan Chandler, *Women without Husbands: an Exploration of the Margins of Marriage* (London, 1991), p. 28; Lavery, *Able Seamen*, p. 87.

[40] Ralph A. Houlbrooke, *The English Family, 1450–1700* (London, 1984), p. 63.

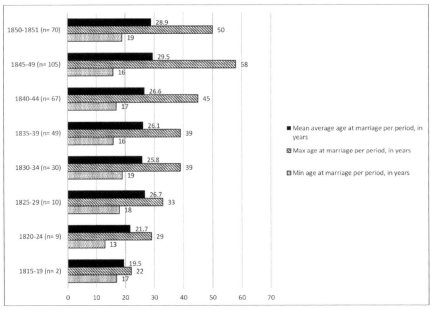

**Fig. 9** Naval grooms' age at marriage, 1815–51 (n= 342).

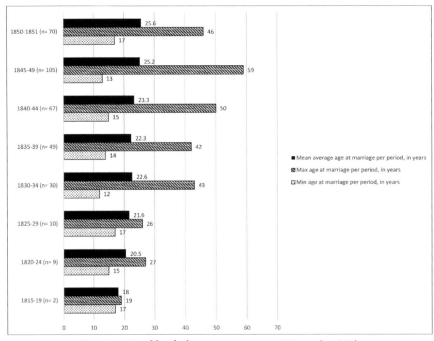

**Fig. 10** Naval brides' age at marriage, 1815–51 (n=342).

most of the household goods.[41] Even in the later Victorian period, when wages and standards of living improved, couples could still not be persuaded to marry younger. Padfield considers that it would have been impossible for ordinary seamen on a shilling a day or able seamen on 1s 2d to have supported wife and family 'in any conventional sense', arguing that of the 'few' sailors who were married, most were older men, petty officers or warrant officers.[42] Lavery declares that 'only a minority of lower-deck [men] were happily married' (raising not entirely frivolous questions as to whether the majority were unhappily married, or not married, and how relative happiness were measured).[43] Sailors interviewed by McKee agreed that prior to the 1914 introduction of a married man's allowance, (lack of) money was a major disincentive to early marriage, some going so far as to say that one could only be a married sailor despite the Royal Navy, not with its help.[44] Against this background, from our 342 naval marriages it emerged that the mean average age at which sailors married, as calculated for five-year periods from 1815, varied from 19.5 years in 1815–19 to 28.6 years in 1850–51, a 9.1-year increase over thirty-six years.[45]

Due to statistical outliers in the form of extremely young and markedly older grooms, variation in sample numbers of younger and older sailors, and caveats concerning parish registers' inconsistent recording of age at marriage, this upward trend must be viewed with caution. Similar caveats apply to the mean average age of our 342 naval brides, for which Fig. 10 shows an upward trend of 7.4 years, from eighteen years in 1815–19 to 25.4 years in 1850–51.

These polarisations, between 16-year-old and 58-year-old grooms, 14-year-old and 59-year-old brides, mask a trend towards marriage in couples' early twenties. In the wider population, by the mid-century point the proportion of females marrying at under twenty-one years was around 2.6 per cent.[46] Among our seventy naval brides marrying in 1850–51, however, a startling 30 per cent were under twenty-one. These figures, however, relate not to first marriages but to *all* marriages in the subset of 342 unions, some of

---

[41] Perkin, *Women and Marriage*, p. 120; Southall and Gilbert, 'A Good Time to Wed?', p. 39; Richard Wall, 'Beyond the Household: Marriage, Household Formation and the Role of Kin and Neighbours', *International Review of Social History*, 44:1 (1999), 55–67, at p. 58.
[42] Padfield, *Rule Britannia*, p. 24.
[43] Lavery, *Able Seamen*, p. 86.
[44] McKee, *Sober Men and True*, pp. 206–7; Carew, *Lower Deck of the Royal Navy*, pp. 58–9.
[45] The 1850–51 period covers the period January 1850 to April 1851, none of the 342 marriages having taken place beyond that date.
[46] Woods, *Demography*, p. 89.

which were second or subsequent marriages. To obtain first-marriage figures for comparison with previous research, widow-brides and widower-grooms were set aside. To eliminate the possibility of regional trends and traditions affecting statistics on age at marriage, weddings said to have taken place beyond Portsea Island were also set aside, as were those declared as having taken place at register offices. Counting only those marriages where both partners' marital status was recorded, a nett total of 176 records was obtained.[47] Table 3 shows how this sample of Portsea naval marriages compares with national averages for the half-century and mid-century point.

Table 3  Mean age at first marriages.

|  | Mean average age at first marriage (females) | Difference from Portsea Island naval first marriages (females) | Mean average age at first marriage (males) | Difference from Portsea Island naval first marriages (males) |
| --- | --- | --- | --- | --- |
| Portsea Island naval first marriages (n=176) | 22.5 years |  | 27 years |  |
| England and Wales at mid-century point[48] | 24.6 years | + 2.1 years | 25.8 years | - 1.2 years |
| England & Wales 1800–49[49] | 23.4 years | + 0.9 years | 25.3 years | - 1.7 years |

With a mean average age of twenty-seven years, these bachelor sailor-grooms were 1.2 years older at first marriage than the 25.8-year-old average for first-time grooms in England and Wales at the mid-century point, and 1.7 years

[47] Chapter Thirteen cites examples of already-married brides and grooms disguising their status by claiming to be bachelor or spinster, or declaring themselves widowed. None of those named individuals features among the 176 records in this analysis, but the possibility exists that the 176 may include other such examples.

[48] R.B. Outhwaite, 'Age at Marriage in England from the Late Seventeenth to the Nineteenth Century', *Transactions of the Royal Historical Society*, 23 (1973), 55–70, at p. 58, citing *Thirty-fourth Annual Report of the Registrar General* (H.C. 1873, xx, p. 1), p. xii; Woods, *Demography*, pp. 81–2. By 1861 the figure for females in Hampshire would drop fractionally to 24.3 years: N.F.R. Crafts, 'Average Age at First Marriage for Women in Mid-Nineteenth-Century England and Wales: a cross-section study', *Population Studies*, 21:1 (1978), 21–5, at p. 22.

[49] E.A. Wrigley and R.S. Schofield, *The Population History of England, 1541–1871: a reconstruction* (Cambridge, 1989), p. 255 table 7.26; Perkin, *Women and Marriage*, p. 125; Thompson, *Rise of Respectable Society*, p. 52.

older than the 25.3-year-old average for first-time grooms marrying in years 1800–49. This could be read as indicating that sailors' long absences, lack of local social connections (indeed, as a 'genuinely peculiar class', they were 'isolated by their profession from the bulk of their fellow-countrymen'), and limited courtship opportunities delayed their entry into matrimony.[50] Another factor to be acknowledged is the availability of port town prostitutes, tempering some men's physical urges and making prospects of marital fidelity less attractive to the fun-loving bachelor. Beyond carnal considerations, however, the more prudent will have marked time deliberately in the hope of saving enough money to support bride and marital home. Also having a delaying effect on matrimony were adult children's sense of filial duty, and parents' reliance on working children's wage contributions, either of which might keep courting couples waiting years. With delay came reward, however, for by adding an air of middle-class respectability and limiting the numbers of children to be supported, postponement might improve standards of living.[51] And just as there was a seasonality to country marriages, with workers postponing weddings until after the harvest when extra earnings had accumulated, so some sailors may have steered clear of hasty pre-embarkation unions, deliberately postponing marriage until their ship had returned and paid off. Postponement therefore had purpose, and benefits. It added lump-sum cash to savings, years to nuptial age, an air of respectability, and tested fiancées' emotional commitment before any legal commitment were made.[52]

Different inferences may be drawn about seamen's brides. Though 0.9 to 2.1 years younger at first marriage than those national averages for the 1800–49 period and mid-century point, sailors' sweethearts who had grown up in naval households may have considered themselves well-prepared for life as naval wives. Some may have been wise to the fact that in a district suffering chronic underemployment they were unlikely to achieve or maintain economic independence via their own earnings – if earnings they had.[53] Some naval daughters, too, may have intuited that, for reasons suggested earlier, as bridal candidates they possessed relatively low status locally. In the competitive marriage market of female-heavy Portsea Island, the naval daughter was simply happy to grab the opportunity for wifedom no matter how early in life it presented; and should the perils of sea-service

---

[50] Rodger, *Wooden World*, p. 118.
[51] Ross, *Love and Toil*, p. 67; Thompson, *Rise of Respectable Society*, pp. 55, 258.
[52] David Kent, 'Gone for a Soldier?: family breakdown and the demography of desertion in a London parish, 1750–1791', *Local Population Studies*, 45: Autumn (1990), 27–41, at p. 39.
[53] Kirsty McNay *et al.*, 'Excess Female Mortality in Nineteenth-Century England and Wales', *Social Science History*, 29:4 (2005), 649–81, *passim*.

leave her a young widow, and childless, she might still be young enough not only to marry again but to conceive.

The extreme youth of some brides, however, raises serious questions. Among twenty-two believed to be under sixteen at the altar, 12- and 13-year-olds have been found. These were children. Like the urban child-prostitutes whose plight concerned campaigners such as *Pall Mall Gazette* journalist W.T. Stead, and Catherine and Bramwell Booth of the Salvation Army, these girls were too young to menstruate, had not yet finished growing.[54] Their youth may have protected them from pre- and (for a while) post-marital pregnancy, but few will have been emotionally mature enough to deal with marriage in any other sense than 'playing house', and for many of them marriage meant little more than continuing to live with parents and siblings until husbands came home from sea. Physical damage due to underage sexual activity was not the only risk they faced. Hard for the most mature naval wife, prolonged husband-absence might strike the child-bride in ways she could not process intellectually or emotionally; and as teenage crushes evaporated, passions waxed and waned, the extremes of mood so often experienced in adolescence might trigger disillusionment and regrets when husband and wife were eventually reunited, if not before.

The story of Amelia Wheden (*q.v.*) shows how tangled life could become for a child bride when the nuptial gloss wore off. As noted earlier, Amelia was fourteen when in 1847 she married a man more than twice her age. Her 33-year-old groom William Wheden/Weedon later appeared in *Phaeton*'s description book, recorded as 5ft 5in tall, of dark complexion, with grey eyes, brown hair, no marks, wounds or scars, vaccinated, married, and – somehow, notwithstanding the three-hour trek from his Broadwindsor birthplace to the Dorset coast – 'brought up to sea'.[55] William was soon allotting to his teenaged bride; but as Chapter Two noted, in 1850 AB George Wilkinson, HMS *Vengeance*, also named Amelia his 'trustee'.[56] This could signify, as it did in numerous other examples, a widower's appointing a foster-mother for his motherless child. George, however, identified the entrusted child as William Wheden, none other than Amelia's own legitimate son.[57] We might interpret George's declaration as an act of simple

---

[54] W.T. Stead, 'The Maiden Tribute of Modern Babylon', *Pall Mall Gazette*, 6 and 8 July 1885, 2–4, *passim*; W.T. Stead and Antony E. Simpson (eds), *The Maiden Tribute of Modern Babylon: the report of the secret commission* (Lambertville, N.J., 2007), *passim*; Cathy Le Feuvre, *The Armstrong Girl: a child for sale: the battle against the Victorian sex trade* (Oxford, 2015); P.E. Brown, 'The Age at Menarche', *Journal of Epidemiology and Community Health*, 20:1 (1966), 9–14, at p. 10.

[55] ADM 38/8709/n.p./5 (entry 8 December 1849, as boatswain's mate).

[56] ADM 27/103/220/200; ADM 27/111/260/5.

[57] E&W Births: Q4/1849, vol. 7, p. 157 (certificate).

generosity towards a fellow seaman's family, a gesture akin to George Ruggill's allotment to Sarah Jennings (*q.v.*); but this charitable interpretation loses credibility when a chronology of events is constructed, and Amelia viewed in a wider context.

George Wilkinson had known Amelia since she was ten years old, their acquaintance arising from his serving alongside her brothers Thomas and Samuel Groom in HMS *Pique*; as fellow ABs, George and Samuel probably messed together.[58] In September 1846, four months before Amelia married William Weedon, George Wilkinson deserted, staying 'run' for nearly two years.[59] Returning (or returned) in July 1848, he spent a month in the house of correction before rejoining *Excellent*.[60] *Excellent*, it may be remembered, was the gunnery training school moored in Portsmouth Harbour. It was also the ship whence in September 1848 – just as George Wilkinson emerged from detention – gunner's mate William declared a fresh allotment to his bride of eighteen months.[61] The two men had served together for three days in September 1846, immediately before George deserted. In 1848–49 they served together again, this time for over a year. Whether his being three-day shipmates with William contributed to George's deserting; whether in 1848–49 William brought George ashore for a spot of home cooking, and to show off his bride; whether George and Amelia renewed their long acquaintanceship born of his being 'old ships' with her brothers Samuel and Thomas; and whether Amelia fell for the blue-eyed, fair-complexioned, 5ft 8in tall George and/or he for her, can only be guessed; but within four months of George's rejoining *Excellent*, Amelia was pregnant.[62]

The fact that Amelia conceived is unremarkable, she being two years a wife; but admiralty and parish records reveal a sequence of events which suggests she was enmeshed in an emotional tangle of far-reaching consequence. The baby, whom his parents named William Richard Weedon, was born in October 1849.[63] Two months later, William senior joined HMS *Phaeton* as boatswain's mate, and in March 1850, after three months at sea, he restarted his allotment to Amelia.[64] George Wilkinson meanwhile

---

[58] ADM 139/231/23014; ADM 27/80/237/141; ADM 27/81/253/68.
[59] ADM 38/9234, pp. 2–3, pay no. 5.
[60] ADM 139/231/23014.
[61] ADM 27/105/195/929.
[62] ADM 27/105/195/929; ADM 38/9234, pp. 2–3, pay no. 5. Further to *Victory*'s description, *Vengeance*'s muster book describes George as 5ft 10in, with fresh complexion, hazel eyes and brown hair, and missing the top of a finger on his right hand. 'Old ships: Abbreviation for *old shipmate*, someone you have served with before': Jolly and Willson, *Jackspeak*, p. 311.
[63] E&W Births: Q4/1849, vol. 7, p. 157.
[64] ADM 29/046, p. 154; ADM 27/110/34/290.

was still in *Excellent*. From when he joined ship in September 1846, as a trainee gunner George was entitled to leave five times per week. This meant he was able from early evening until the following morning to go ashore; and nearby was Landport, location of the Weedon household.[65] William will have been at home for many of George's visits, but in the six months from *Phaeton*'s departure in January 1850 to July 1850 when George joined *Vengeance* there was no paterfamilias to stand chaperone to 18-year-old Amelia, and every opportunity for adultery to flourish.

The two men were at sea in their respective ships when, in August 1850, in St John the Evangelist Roman Catholic cathedral, ten-month-old William was baptised alongside two cousins on his mother's side, Amelia's parents standing sponsor for all three grandchildren.[66] In October 1850, from *Vengeance* George Wilkinson declared his allotment, naming Amelia trustee to the now 1-year-old 'William Wheden'. George was supporting Amelia financially; so was her husband William.

Things took an unexpected turn when, in October 1850, William was DSQ'd from *Phaeton*, returning to England in *Hercules*. Arriving in December 1850, he spent his remaining weeks of naval service in *Excellent* (whence George had been discharged five months earlier), his allotment to Amelia finally stopping in March 1851 when he was invalided.[67] Weeks earlier, however, as noted in Chapter Two, little William had featured for a second time in *Vengeance*'s allotment register when, in an arguably specious declaration which may have been intended to disguise his financial support to Amelia, George named Maria Balch as the child's trustee.[68] This was curious enough, but events then took an even stranger turn; for in February 1851, six months after that triple baptism of the Groom sisters' babies, and in defiance of church precepts about once-for-all baptism for life, little William was baptised yet again, this time without his cousins. The ceremony took place at St John's Anglican chapel, Portsea, the child's father's name being given as 'George Wheden, mariner'.[69] Naval records have failed to yield a George Wheden whose age and service match, so unless the parish clerk inscribed the wrong forename in error we must consider the possibility that little William was George Wilkinson's child, a cuckoo in the Wheden marital nest, and that whether or not this were so, in reciting her

---

[65] ADM 139/231/23014; Holman, *Life in the Royal Navy*, p. 83; Woods, *Inner Life of the Navy*, p. 137.
[66] CHU71/1A/3, p. 89 nos 353–355 ('Weedon').
[67] William had been previously invalided n March 1846 due to 'rheumatism consequent on fever, N(orth) C(oast) of Africa', which may suggest a malaria-related condition (ADM 38/8709/n.p./5).
[68] ADM 27/112/149/5.
[69] CHU5/A/1/6, p. 24 n. 20.

son's details in the vestry, teenaged Amelia had scrambled the names of the two men in her young life, thereby expressing a private fantasy or hinting at a hidden actuality.

Why go through this second ceremony, let alone concoct a spurious name for the baby's father? In light of what is now known it may be inferred that Amelia requested the ceremony out of sentiment, adolescent romance or in an attempt nominally to attach George to the boy. Alternatively, believing little William to be his son but having been pipped to the post when William senior registered the boy as his own, George had persuaded Amelia to include him, somehow, in the paperwork of a second baptism, thus binding himself symbolically to mother and child.[70] Whatever the explanation, in going along with the ruse Amelia was playing with fire. What on the surface may look like the actions of an imaginative, headstrong and/or resourceful young woman might equally be viewed as a romantic and dangerous melodrama enacted by a girl too immature to accept the reality of her situation, or its potential consequences upon her security. How this marital triangle played out, and what it conveys about naval marriage more generally, will emerge in later chapters.

From teenage bride Amelia to naval brides' age at first marriage. Table 3 shows variances from national averages to be discernible but not necessarily significant. As noted earlier, the sample includes some very young brides indeed. Outwith the nobility and gentry, teenage marriage was unusual. That only 7.8 per cent of the seamen in this analysis married for the first time before they reached twenty years chimes with trends from fifty to one hundred years earlier, Wrigley and Schofield finding that of marriages taking place in 1750–99 not more than 7 per cent of men married for the first time before their twentieth birthday.[71] In short, like their civilian peers, our allotting seamen were still not inclined to marry young. Meanwhile, the percentage of teenage brides in England had risen from 11–13 per cent to 18 per cent in 1750–99, by 1851 the Registrar General reporting that 13.4 per cent of 51,141 spinsters – almost twice the percentage of grooms – were known to be under twenty years old at marriage.[72] In mid-nineteenth century Portsea Island, however, the proportion of naval brides marrying in their teens well exceeded those national figures. Of our 176 first-time

---

[70] E&W Births: Q4/1849, vol. 7, p. 157 ('Weeden'; certificate).
[71] E.A. Wrigley and R.S. Schofield, 'English Population History from Family Reconstitution: summary results 1600–1799', *Population Studies*, 37:2 (1983), 157–84, at p. 166.
[72] *Ibid.*; Registrar General, Fourteenth Annual Report: Ages of the Persons who were Married in 1851 <http://www.histpop.org/ohpr/servlet/PageBrowser?path=Browse/Registrar%20General%20(by%20geography)/England/1851-1860&active=yes&m-no=477&tocstate=expandnew&tocseq=400&display=sections&display=tables&display=pagetitles&pageseq=first-nonblank> [accessed 22 April 2024], p. 6.

## Naval Seamen's Women in Nineteenth-Century Britain

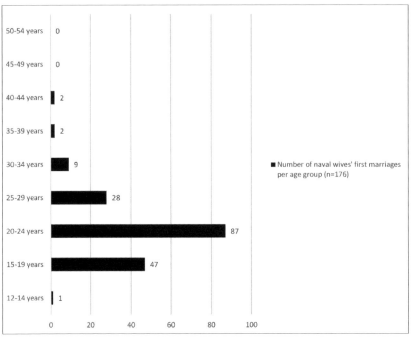

Fig. 11   Naval brides' age at first marriage (n=176).

brides, more than a quarter were not yet twenty on their wedding day. Yet more were found when the net was cast wider.

Laslett notes that working-class girls in 1830s Manchester could expect their first period at 15.6 years, while Brown finds the average age of menarche in 1845 Birmingham was 15.3 years.[73] Of 945 allottee-wives whose nuptial age has been calculated, 327 married before reaching twenty-one years, 93 per cent of them being 16- to 20-year-olds. Most of them had married in the three decades preceding the mid-century study-period, so Laslett and Brown's findings would suggest these women had been post-pubescent when they made their vows. One had been a bride of fifteen in the 1820s, while the 1830s had seen marriages of a 12-year-old, a 13-year-old, eight 15-year-olds and an 11-year-old. But in the late 1840s, toward the end of a half-century in which the mean age at first marriage in England and Wales had reached 23.4 years, we find that 14- and 15-year-old girls were still marrying sailors.[74]

---

[73] Peter Laslett, *The World We Have Lost: further explored* (London, 2000), p. 84; Wrigley and Schofield, *Population History*, p. 233 n. 66; Brown, 'The Age at Menarche', p. 10.
[74] Wrigley and Schofield, *Population History*, p. 255 table 7.26.

Couples who married young were more likely to have still-living parents, even grandparents.[75] This had particular significance for young naval brides who were the daughters of seamen, since their still-living mothers (many of them naval daughters themselves) were well placed to understand what it was like to have a husband at sea. And not just understand: through her husband's continuing absence on naval service, or through his having died, the naval mother might be available to help, even to co-reside during her son-in-law's absence, thus providing her young married daughter with companionship, childcare, understanding, on-site advice and support.

Fathers' occupations were not routinely recorded in parish registers of the 1820s and 1830s, so we cannot always determine whether women marrying in those decades were naval or civilian daughters. Of seven naval brides who married at fourteen and fifteen in the 1840s, the father of one was a gardener, another a mason, four were seamen and one a carpenter (a trade which may or may not signify former naval service). These examples raise questions. Given discernible differences between civilians' and seamen's daughters when it came to spousal occupation, might there also be discernible differences between civilians' and seamen's daughters when it came to bridal age? Did naval families condone a nuptial latitude eschewed by the rest of the community; and if such a latitude existed, what drove it? Was it a 'tribal' naval matter, alien to outsiders but familiar and unremarkable to its practitioners? Was it regarded as having practical benefits? Was it a function of parents' indulging their daughters, permitting them to do as they themselves had done? We have seen how Amelia Groom became gunner Weedon's wife at fourteen years old, her parents, seaman Samuel Groom and his bride Mary Ann Sebastian, having been minors when they married in 1807.[76] Did they take the view that 'Under-age marriage worked out all right for us, so why should we not let Amelia marry William'? Did they set aside reservations, caving into their daughter's pleading? Did fatherly indulgence play a part, or something else? Might it have been hard-nosed paternal calculation?

This last possibility goes to the allotment system, that economic and social benefit for which civilian brides were ineligible. Might seamen-fathers, with or without the endorsement of their wives, have connived in what amounted to a financial transaction, a bride-sale? At the lower end of the economic ladder it was not unknown for financial constraints to compromise parental consent. Naval pay was poor, naval pensions poorer,

---

[75] Steven Ruggles, 'Reconsidering the Northwest European Family System: Living arrangements of the aged in comparative historical perspective', *Population and Development Review*, 35:2 (2009), 249–73, at p. 253.
[76] CHU2/1C/7, p. 34 n. 135.

yet naval parents' rents and other essential outgoings remained the same whether the seaman-father were serving or retired, waged or pensioned. A deal between bride's parent and sailor-suitor made sense, for upon marriage a seaman's wife became eligible for an allotment in her own right; and her allotment, together with the wages she earned, could supplement her parents' household economy. Provided their newly-married daughter remain at home with them, naval papa and mama could thus profit from the union until their son-in-law returned from sea. Leaving money aside, such arrangements were not considered outrageous, as witness the number of young wives who, as Chapter Six shows, continued to live with their parents while their husbands were absent, in civil terms possessing wifely status but with little by way of wifely domestic responsibility. Pending her husband's return, for the stay-at-home child-bride little would change beyond her surname, the thrill of acquiring 'Mrs' as a title, and the enhanced status of 'wife'. Meanwhile, her groom's half-pay would boost parental household income, and she could keep the change.

Beyond financial considerations, however, there were issues of sailorly solidarity. These naval fathers had for years on end served alongside other seamen, spending more time in their company than with their own wives and daughters; and the male shipboard community exerted a very powerful influence. Men at sea were bound by 'neighbourhood norms and customs', peer-group trends powerful enough to shape a man's notion of the right amount of financial support to give a wife.[77] From there it is not too great a leap to the notion of a seaman-brother promising to introduce a shipmate to his unmarried sister, an act which, given the brother had neither authority over the sister nor financial investment in her marrying, constituted little more than fraternal matchmaking. If that notion is accepted, it is no greater a leap to the notion of a seaman-father promising to introduce his younger shipmate (or, given some bride/groom age-differences, his not-much-younger shipmate) to an underage daughter, permitting him to court her, and in due course marry her. Lavery's 'no time for conventional wooing' conveys the social challenges faced by young Jack pining for a sweetheart, and by older Jack anxious not to end up an elderly bachelor: how to meet the right sort of girl, obtain an introduction, gain her and her parents' trust, woo and persuade her to marry him, even effect the marriage itself, and all between paying-off and (re-)joining ship.[78] The naval father of a daughter would recognise the challenges facing his bachelor or widower fellows. He

---

[77] Andrew August, *Poor Women's Lives: Gender, Work, and Poverty in Late-Victorian London* (London, 1999), pp. 124–5.
[78] Lavery, *Able Seamen*, p. 87.

might relish the idea of a seaman son-in-law, especially if the suitor were his serving shipmate, a former messmate with credentials long established.

The shrewd papa would impose conditions: that after the ceremony, marriage proper (that is, consummation, and establishment of an independent household) not follow until the groom were home from his next long deployment, by which time the girl would be months if not years older, and better prepared; that his half-pay and his bride's earnings being his to dispose of, the groom declare an allotment favouring his bride; that as her lord and master he then require she hand it over to her parents as 'keep'; and that whatever was left be put toward the bride's purchase of household goods.[79] The parents would thus benefit both by their son-in-law's money and their daughter's continuing assistance around the house. Meanwhile the son-in-law had the happy prospect of a nubile young wife maturing nicely under her parents' supervision, training and chaperonage, with less chance of pre- or extra-marital conception to spoil his fun.

To the twenty-first-century eye this scenario is a cynical economic transaction. Privileging the shipmate bond above the daughter's physical and emotional needs and readiness, in exchange for cash it trades sexual access to an under-age girl. It is, in short, the commodification of a pubescent child. The arrangement acquires the even stronger whiff of barter where the bride was not only very young but the groom much older. At thirty-three to her fourteen, William Weedon was old enough to be Amelia Groom's father.[80] Mary Ann Saxey was just twelve when in 1834 she married, by licence and with her father's consent, 31-year-old boatswain's mate John Leary, of *Vernon, Victory* and *Victoria and Albert*, a later census return suggesting an age-gap even greater than this nineteen-year difference.[81] Among the marriages of more than twenty naval wives who married at eleven to fifteen years old, in ten instances there were bride/groom age-differences of seven to twenty-two years, with an average gap of 12.3 years. With their parents' permission (and sometimes not), some girls were marrying men more than twice their age. The examples found are not numerous, and motive – which must include anything from simple love and affection to older grooms' dubious predilection for prepubescent girls, by way of fathers privileging their shipmates' desires over their daughters' health and wellbeing – cannot

---

[79] Perkin, *Women and Marriage*, pp. 14, 120.
[80] ADM 38/2328, pp. 61–2 n. 47; CHU71/1A/2, p. 22 ('Catharina Amelia'); Dorset baptisms: St John the Baptist, Broadwindsor, 5 June 1814 ('Wheadon'); CHU3/1D/45, p. 110 n. 220; ADM 27/110/184/296; ADM 158/123/13, p. 1; ADM 27/113/59/9; CHU42/1C/13, p. 136 n. 408; 1851 census: HO107/ 1657, fol. 379, p. 9.
[81] CHU3/1B/9, p. 70 n. 559; CHU3/1D/33, p. 37 n. 260; ADM 27/41/134/230; ADM 27/75/316/48; ADM 27/89/253/11; ADM 27/105/423/85; 1851 census: HO107/1659, fol. 729, p. 16.

be proven; but we should not dismiss the possibility of money-motivated connivance on the brides' parents' part.

Feelings, intentions and collaboration being unprovable, the question of why naval parents consented to or connived at daughters' underage marriages must remain just that: a question. Fury's identification of couples' compatibility fits with the finding that many of our naval brides were seamen's daughters; but when it comes to under-age marriage, mere familiarity with naval family life is not enough to explain how a child bride might be deemed 'compatible' with an older husband who would inevitably be absent for years at a time. How could a child bride be expected to set up and run, without spousal support, a marital home? Why marry at all if marriage did not involve the assuming and exercising of adult responsibilities? Why not delay vows until the relationship were established, the bride mature enough to cope with intercourse and domestic management, and old enough to conceive? At a time when at national level there was a strong movement toward delaying matrimony, why allow (pre-)pubescent girls to marry? From the point of view of bride, groom and naval parents, *cui bono*?

5

# CHILDREN

Ships' long commissions limited naval couples' opportunities for conception. For this reason alone it would be easy to assume that naval families would prove smaller than their local civilian equivalents. It would be equally easy to assume that, knowing the window of fecundity might close before they had made as many babies as they hoped, naval couples tended to conceive their first child early, even before marriage.[1] Such assumptions ignore other factors impinging upon the individuals concerned, and the seaborne and shoreside communities in which they lived and worked. Locating its findings within that wider context, this chapter acknowledges the effects of social and political issues, weighing their impact upon couples whose marriages and fecundity were already subject to constraints rarely experienced by their civilian neighbours. Exploring evidence of premarital conception, age at first maternity and the size of naval families, it both challenges and extends the more obvious assumptions, and proposes explanations for some surprising findings.

A cautionary preface is necessary regarding civil, census and parish records, the chapter's main sources. Children hide within and from the census, which captures a point in time when some families might not yet be complete, others complete but depleted due to emigration, marriage or death. Children might be temporarily absent, young ones being cared for by extended family, older offspring ousted to make space for a lodger, or delegated to provide live-in care and company for a frail elderly relative.[2] Illegitimate children might be brought up by maternal grandmothers, presented to the wider world as years-younger siblings of daughters whose premarital pregnancy had been hidden.[3] This was the case with Harriet

---

[1] Southall and Gilbert, 'A Good Time to Wed?', p. 35.
[2] M.J. Daunton, *Progress and Poverty: an economic and social history of Britain, 1700–1850* (Oxford, 1995), p. 432.
[3] Dennis Mills *et al.*, 'Southern Historians and their Exploitation of Victorian Censuses', *Southern History,* 18 (1996), 61–86, at p. 69.

99

Betsworth, mother of AB George Betsworth, HMS *Retribution*. Her four-year-old 'daughter' Harriet, so described in the 1861 census, was in fact her granddaughter Harriet Sarah, illegitimate child and namesake of 44-year-old Harriet's wayward firstborn Harriet Sarah, George's allottee-sister.[4] Many an older child, too, was absent for occupational reasons or following the loss of a parent.[5] When childcare was unavailable some mothers resorted to the desperate measure of sending their children into the workhouse while they took on paid work, in evidential terms disconnecting child from parent(s).[6] A 'son' or 'daughter' might be a non-relative, as witness the way some sailors' children were enumerated in trustees' household schedules. And schedules might describe residents as 'son' or 'daughter' when they were another sort of kin entirely, or none, the use of one shared surname for the whole family merely cementing the error.

The naval community was particularly vulnerable to 'censual invisibility'. As Chapter Four noted, naval daughters were more likely than their civilian peers to marry young, some being absorbed into in-laws' households, some sharing accommodation with married siblings. Sons often followed fathers into the Navy, hence older boys of naval families were more likely than their civilian equivalents to be away from home. Enumerated offspring may therefore not be the only members of the naval family.

Children remain elusive in other sources. Baptismal records provide parents' names and other identifying details – occasionally the child's father's occupation, even an address; but baptismal dates might be detached from birth dates by many weeks, sometimes years.[7] The four daughters of private third class Robert Lewis, HMS *Illustrious*, were baptised on the same day in 1850, by which time eldest girl Rosina, product of her mother Amelia's premarital relationship, was six years old.[8] Nor can mid-nineteenth century birth registers be wholly relied upon, civil registration not being substantially complete until the 1870s.[9] Meanwhile, miscarriages left no documentary trace, and stillbirths went unrecorded until the 1920s.

---

[4] 1861 census: RG09/634, fol. 50, p. 4; E&W Births: Q1/1856, vol. 2B, p. 360 (certificate); ADM 27/111/292/21.

[5] Humphries, *Childhood and Child Labour*, p. 64; Richard Wall, 'Leaving Home and the Process of Household Formation in Pre-industrial England', *Continuity & Change*, 2:1 (1987), 77–101, at p. 91.

[6] Lincoln, 'Impact of Warfare', p. 74.

[7] E.A. Wrigley, 'Births and Baptisms: the use of Anglican baptism registers as a source of information about the numbers of births in England before the beginning of civil registration', *Population Studies*, 31:2 (1977), 281–312, at p. 311; Probert, *Marriage Law*, p. 128; Wrigley, 'Births and Baptisms', p. 281.

[8] CHU5/A/1/6, p. 18 nos 140–3; E&W Births: Q1/1844, vol. 7, p. 161 (certificate).

[9] Wrigley, 'Births and Baptisms', p. 281; Michael S. Teitelbaum, 'Birth Underregistration in the Constituent Counties of England and Wales: 1841–1910', *Population Studies* 28:2 (1974), 329–43, at pp. 329, 330.

Where children were born alive, their odds of survival were often poor. From the 1840s onward up to one-quarter of all recorded deaths had been of infants below one year of age, infant mortality being persistently high in towns, higher still among the poor and the offspring of working mothers.[10] Amelia Wheden (*q.v.*) was seventeen when she gave birth to her first surviving child, the son (according to his birth certificate) of her husband William. She was nineteen in 1851 when her second son, Louis, was born; he died at five weeks, a fortnight after his baptism.[11] Cause of death was marasmus: he died of malnutrition.[12] More grief followed when, at three years old, Amelia's firstborn succumbed to 'convulsions 36 hours'.[13] His was not an unusual death. Many Portsea children did not reach their second birthday, 'scarcely a week [passing] in Portsmouth without a child dying of convulsions'.[14] Fourteen when she married, Amelia had not reached her majority before she was a twice-bereaved mother. Her losses fit a known pattern, for studies of nineteenth-century communities' records show a higher risk of death for infants of under-20-year-old mothers than for infants of mothers aged twenty to twenty-four, a trend of particular relevance given Chapter Four's findings on naval brides' age at first marriage.[15]

Naval seamen were not their own masters. Just as world events governed their working lives, so their family lives were shaped by issues beyond their control. Big-picture issues impinged upon private life, taking men from their wives at a time when couples might be hoping to conceive. In examining naval couples' fecundity, that bigger picture must be borne in mind. How volatile or stable was the prevailing political-military situation

---

[10] James Walvin, *English Urban Life, 1776–1851* (London, 1984), p. 24; A.S. Wohl, *Endangered Lives: public health in Victorian Britain* (London, 1983), p. 11; Wrigley, 'Births and Baptisms', p. 304 table 15; Thompson, *Rise of Respectable Society*, p. 117; Margaret Hewitt, *Wives and Mothers in Victorian Industry* (London, 1958), pp. 102, 145; Carol Dyhouse, 'Working-Class Mothers and Infant Mortality in England, 1895–1914', *Journal of Social History*, 12:2 (1978), 248–67, at p. 251; Carl Chinn, *They Worked all their Lives: Women of the Urban Poor in England, 1880–1939* (Lancaster, 2006), p. 124; Annabel Venning, *Following the Drum: the lives of army wives and daughters, past and present* (London, 2005), p. 83.

[11] CHU71/1A/3, p. 120 n. 377.

[12] E&W Deaths: Q4/1851, vol. 7, p. 107 (certificate); CHU2/1D/4, p. 274 n. 2191 ('Lewis Weedon').

[13] E&W Deaths: Q2/1853, vol. 2B, p. 271 (certificate). (See p. 252.)

[14] Harwood, *Portrait of Portsea*, pp. 51, 20; J.D.A. Stanford, 'Working-Class Children in Mid-Nineteenth Century Portsmouth' (university unspecified, unpublished dissertation, 1971), p. 24, referencing *Hampshire Telegraph* reports 1845–60.

[15] S.L. Morrison *et al.*, 'Social and Biological Factors in Infant Mortality: mortality in the post-natal period', *Archives of Disease in Childhood*, 34:174 (1959), 101–14, at pp. 103, 102 fig. 1; Katherine A. Lynch and Joel B. Greenhouse, 'Risk Factors for Infant Mortality in Nineteenth-Century Sweden', *Population Studies*, 48:1 (1994), 117–33, at p. 121 table 2.

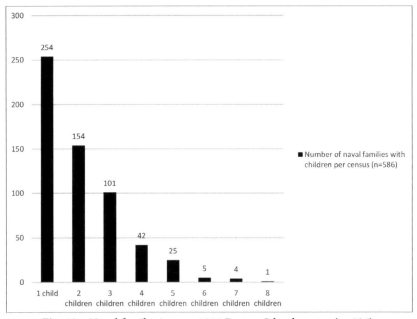

**Fig. 12**  Naval family size, per 1851 Portsea Island census (n=586).

during these wives' fertile years? How much longer than average were ships' commissions due to discovery service and expansion of empire, new maritime technology, the country's being on a war footing or reductions in the size of the fleet? It is against this shifting background, in which the Navy interrupted and delayed procreation, in which children could and did disappear from historical view, that the following should be viewed.

## FAMILY SIZE

At first glance the expectation that naval families would prove smaller than average appears to be met. Census records suggest that by 1851 at least 586 of our cohort of naval wives (59.8 per cent) had become mothers to a total of 1,224 children.[16] Subject to the usual caveats, the census tells us that their mean average family size was 2.1 children per couple, 70 per cent of the wives having only one or two offspring.

But those 1,224 comprise *all* located and enumerated children, some of them products of previous relationships. They include children of women who married at different ages, in different decades. Some had been married

---

[16] Not all sailors' trustees, sisters and mothers were naval wives, so their children are not included in this exercise.

*Children*

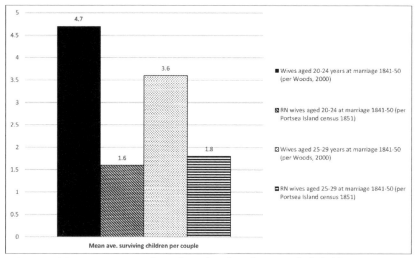

**Fig. 13** Mean average number of naval and civilian couples' children; per 1851 Portsea Island census, and Robert Woods, *The Demography of Victorian England and Wales* (2000), p. 116.

for over thirty years, some a few days. The figure takes no account of the unknown number of naval offspring who had perished in infancy, joined ship as boys, married early or slept elsewhere on census night.

Refining data by age at marriage and nuptial year enables the analysis to be better aligned with Woods's study of marital fertility. From the 1911 census Woods calculates numbers of surviving children of mothers who upon marriage in the period 1841–1901 were, respectively, aged twenty to twenty-four, twenty-five to twenty-nine, and thirty to thirty-four years old.[17] For example, among women marrying at age twenty to twenty-four years in the decade 1841–1850, Woods finds an average of approximately 4.7 surviving children.[18] By contrast, of 234 naval allottee brides who married aged twenty to twenty-four in the years 1841–50, 134 had between them 220 children, an average of just 1.6 per couple – approximately one-third Woods's figure. For women marrying at age twenty-five to twenty-nine in years 1841–50, Woods found c. 3.6 surviving children per couple, twice the mean average of 1.8 found among sixty-two of 120 naval brides marrying in the same age-range and period who between them had 110 children on census day.

Presented in chart form (Fig. 13), the differences are striking. Naval wives who married at age twenty to twenty-nine in years 1841–50 had an average

---

[17] Woods, *Demography*, p. 116.
[18] *Ibid.*, p. 177 fig. 4.1 (exact number not given in Woods' chart).

of 1.7 children by census day 1851. Woods's two groups yield a mean of 4.15 children per couple – more than double our naval families' average.

The chief difficulty with this exercise is that it rests upon women married in the years 1841–50, immediately preceding the study period. Naval or civilian, not all wives aged twenty to twenty-nine who married in this pre-census decade had completed their families by 1851, whereas those marrying in earlier decades were more likely to have finished childbearing. This is reflected in the finding that of naval wives who married in the years 1831–40, aged twenty to twenty-nine, by 1851 twenty had a mean average of three children each, a figure near-identical to the 2.9 children per couple found among a further twenty-nine naval wives of the same age-group who married in the years 1821–30.

Anderson approaches family size from a starting point of maternal age. Drawing on estimates produced by Wrigley and Schofield and by the Registrar General from the fertility census of 1911, for married women born 1771–1831 he finds a mean completed family size of between 5.7 and 6.2 children.[19] Of our 586 naval wives with children listed in the 1851 census, 571 had been born 1771–1831, their 1,204 children (per census data) yielding a mean average of just 2.1 per couple – an even greater differential than the one found in Woods's comparisons. The scale of the difference is such that in order for the mean average naval family size of 2.1 children to match a completed family comprising a notional mean of 5.9 children (the midway point between Anderson's two figures), our 571 naval wives would need to have produced (and by implication lost to illness, accident, naval service or emigration, since they do not appear in the census) some 2,193 more children than the 1,204 ascribed them. This works out at an average – *an average* – of 3.8 additional surviving children per woman, a figure to challenge any mid-nineteenth-century working-class couple, let alone the couple routinely separated by sea-service.

Year of marriage, nuptial age, maternal age: however the subject is approached, the figures bespeak a common fecundity issue. Naval families, it seems, had fewer children than the national average, a conclusion resonating with Humphries' finding that with a mean average of 4.91 children per family, seamen's families' sibling groups were the third-smallest of ten

---

[19] Michael Anderson, 'The social implications of demographic change', in F.M.L. Thompson (ed.), *The Cambridge Social History of Britain 1750–1950* (Cambridge, 1990), 1–70, at pp. 38–9 fig. 1.7. 'The [1911] census asked married women to state the years their marriage had lasted, the number of children born alive to the present marriage and how many had died': Unknown author, 'Census 1911: Fertility and Marriage' (UK Parliament, 2024) <https://www.parliament.uk/about/living-heritage/transformingsociety/private-lives/relationships/collections/1921-census> [accessed 22 April 2024].

*Children*

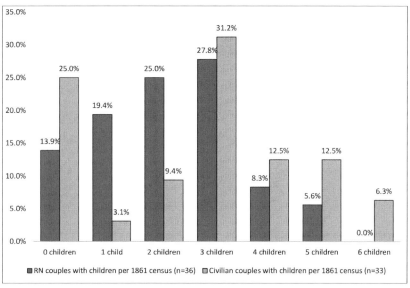

Fig. 14  Comparative size of naval and civilian families, per 1861 Portsea Island census.

occupational groupings, only soldiers' and factory workers' families having fewer offspring.[20]

Longitudinal comparison of naval and civilian family sizes became feasible when approximately one-third of the ninety-eight naval and 118 civilian newlyweds featured in Chapter Four were also located in the 1861 census. Thirty-six of the naval newlyweds appear to have had between them at least seventy-seven children, yielding a (minimal) mean average of 2.1 surviving children per naval couple. Their thirty-three civilian comparators had had ninety children, a mean of 2.7 surviving children per couple. Not only did the civilian couples produce more children; nearly a third had larger broods of four to six. Only 13.9 per cent of the naval couples had four or five children, none more than five. With 72.2 per cent of naval couples having one to three children, the trend was toward smaller broods.

An unexpected finding was that the proportion of apparently childless civilian couples was considerably greater (25 per cent vs 13.9 per cent) than that of their naval peers. It would be unsafe to ascribe the disparity to civilian wives' greater involvement in their husbands' trades increasing the possibility of miscarriage or necessitating the wife's avoiding pregnancy in order to remain active and available for work. Most of the trades associated with these seemingly childless civilian couples – stonemason, cabinet maker, brickmaker, labourer – hardly lent themselves to wifely participation; only

[20]  Humphries, *Childhood and Child Labour*, pp. 55–6 tables 3.2, 3.3.

boot-closing, printing and 'chymist' might be regarded as open to conjoint spousal effort. There is no common indication of poverty among these couples, and no occupational hazard or environmental oddity to account for the finding. Their apparent childlessness remains unexplained.

If the smaller size of naval families was not due to a greater tendency to infertility, miscarriage, stillbirth or infants' failure to thrive, alternative explanations may be posited. These include, most obviously, sailor-husbands' absences scuppering opportunity for sex; but there was also the comparative youth of naval brides which, for the very young, prevented conception for as many years as it took them to reach menarche. That said, in every generation there were naval families whose size defied these findings. Seaman Samuel Groom and his wife Mary Ann, parents of child-bride Amelia Wheden (*q.v.*), had twelve surviving children born at one- to five-year intervals in years the 1808–32, firstborn William old enough to be last-born Charlotte's father.

## CHILDREN OF PREVIOUS MARRIAGES

By April 1851 the proportion of our 118 civilian newlyweds with sons or daughters enumerated was two-and-a-half times that of their ninety-eight newlywed naval comparators marrying within the same fifteen-month period.[21] The children's ages ranged from one day to twenty-four years, yet no couple had been married more than fifteen months, so children older than fifteen months were either the product of previous unions or the illegitimate offspring of the now-married couple. Previous unions were identified via parish marriage registers' recording of couples' civil status. Of our ninety-eight naval brides, eleven (11.2 per cent) had stated themselves to be widows, as had twelve (10.2 per cent) of the 118 women marrying civilian grooms. The figure for naval widow-brides reflected the national picture: by the mid-nineteenth century, 11.3 per cent of those marrying in England and Wales were widowed.[22] Correlated with parish marriage data, census records indicated that the twelve widows marrying civilian grooms brought with them fifteen fatherless children; the eleven widows marrying sailors brought five. The threefold differential may be random; but it may indicate widows' perceiving that marriage to seamen would strand them for long periods with neither husbands for themselves nor father-figures for their own fatherless children, a burden made worse if they were also left with sole care and control of their seamen-spouses' motherless offspring. It

---

[21] 42.4 per cent vs 16.3 per cent.
[22] Perkin, *Women and Marriage*, p. 30; Wrigley and Schofield, *Population History*, pp. 258–9.

may equally signify a sailorly reluctance to take on step-parental roles and responsibilities for widows' children, with whom it might be hard to build or maintain relationships during limited periods of leave.

The 11.2 and 10.2 per cent proportions of civilian and naval widow-brides were not dissimilar; but at 7.6 per cent the proportion of civilian grooms who were widowers was more than twice the 3.1 per cent of naval widower-grooms. The ratio may partly be explained by the nine civilian widower-grooms' having eleven children aged two to seventeen years, any motherless children of the three naval widower-grooms having died, flown the nest, been left in the care of trustees or otherwise disappeared. The ratio may also express the different economic pressures to which widowers were subjected. To maintain his trade and income, a civilian widower must secure childcare via relatives, institutions or a new wife. Having access to the allotment system, and thus being able to use trusteeships, capitalising on a naval community in which there existed seamen's wives unable to conceive because of their husbands' absence (see Chapter Five), and seamen's wives needing to supplement their husbands' allotments (Chapter Nine), widowed naval fathers could the more easily maintain their seafaring trade without resorting to remarriage. Harder to tabulate, another factor contributing to the lower proportion of naval widower-grooms is the naval widower's being mindful that when he returned to sea, leaving his motherless offspring in his bride's hands, he could play little part in helping them bond with their new stepmother.

For widowed seamen-fathers seeking experienced long-term carers for their motherless children, widows had their attractions – never more so than when the widows' late husbands had been seamen. When in 1849 his wife Harriet died, Yorkshire-born AB Henry Scargill was left with motherless daughters aged six and two.[23] From *Blenheim* he named Jane Watt, a Hereford Street neighbour, as trustee.[24] So long as trustee and father were content with the arrangement, it could have continued until the children were old enough to fend for themselves; but two years after appointing Jane trustee, Henry married Mary Anne Clifford, and the trusteeship ceased.[25] A seaman's widow and mother of a 10-year-old boy, Mary Anne was well-placed to take on the roles of naval wife, allottee and stepmother to Henry's children.[26] The marriage was genuine, and should not be regarded as a substitute trusteeship. The 1851 census shows 'Seaman Wife' Mary Anne with four children: her late husband's son, the two Scargill girls, and a

[23] E&W Deaths: Q4/1849, vol. 7, p. 93; PHC: G/PGC4/3, n.p., n. 7853.
[24] ADM 27/109/49/266.
[25] CHU3/1D/48, p. 52 n. 104.
[26] CHU3/1B/27, n.p., n. 167; ADM 27/113/219/270.

three-month-old boy Henry. The household schedule obscures paternity: as head of household, Mary Anne listed her errand boy son and the two Scargill sisters under the surname 'Clifford', only little Henry being awarded the surname 'Scargill'.[27] A decade later the family was still together, seaman Henry by then a pensioner, and all six now listed as 'Scargill'.[28]

Not all widowed seamen's remarriages resulted in 'blended' families such as that of the Scargills. Five-year-old James, son of widower William Reece, gunner's mate, HMS *Excellent*, was in 1848 entrusted to Elizabeth Chambers.[29] In January 1851 from HMS *Hogue* William ('alias Wm. Rees') declared an allotment favouring his new wife Sarah (*q.v.*), widow of ordinary seaman John Gulliver; a Navy clerk added the red-inked note 'Allotment at present in force to his son James Reece', which suggests trustee Elizabeth was still receiving her monthly sum for fostering the now 8-year-old James.[30] Sarah's allotment as wife now superseded Elizabeth's trustee allotment, but Sarah did not succeed Elizabeth as James's carer. The census found Sarah at the address William quoted; of motherless James, likewise of trustee Elizabeth, there was no sign.[31] It would be natural for strong bonds to develop between trustees and their entrusted children; indeed, some carer-child relationships may have become stronger and more meaningful than children's relationships with their long-absent, seagoing fathers. In such circumstances a deal might be agreed, the trustee taking on parental status, relieving the father of financial responsibility and freeing him to enjoy remarried life. If this is what happened, Elizabeth not only retained parental care of James; she appears to have remarried, moved away and/or changed her (and his) surname, for no trace of her has been found.

## ILLEGITIMACY

Might there have been a practice for naval couples, knowing they were likely to be parted for long periods, to choose not to wait for matrimony before conceiving their first child? To conceive before marrying was not unusual.[32] Indeed, members of the 'rough working class' often married only when the arrival of a child looked certain; others embarked upon intercourse on the understanding that marriage would follow.[33] It is not in

---

[27] 1851 census: HO107/1657, fol. 404, p. 7 ('Scargoll').
[28] 1861 census: RG09/640, fol. 81, p. 15.
[29] ADM 27/104/342/873.
[30] ADM 27/78/185/452; ADM 27/112/178/2; CHU3/1D/48, p. 241 n. 482. (See pp. 214, 235.)
[31] 1851 census: HO107/1659, fol. 467, p. 29.
[32] Keith Thomas, 'The Double Standard', *Journal of the History of Ideas*, 20:2 (1959), 195–216, at p. 206.
[33] Perkin, *Women and Marriage*, p. 162; Gaskell, *Manufacturing Population of England*, p. 31; Laslett, *Family Life and Illicit Love*, p. 128.

itself a significant finding that more than a quarter of our 118 civilian brides appear to have been pregnant at marriage: the normative rule forbidding conception before marriage was broken far more often than were normative rules on household composition, some 5.3 per cent of all births in the years 1845–1921 being illegitimate.[34] The significant issue is that, on the basis of children listed in the census, their stated ages having been cross-checked against civil birth registers and parish baptisms, the 26.4 per cent proportion of our civilian brides likely to have been pregnant at the altar is over five times their naval counterparts' 5.1 per cent, a figure more nearly reflecting the 5.3 per cent national tally.

The higher civilian figure may reflect a wider demographic feature, for the mid-century point was at the tail-end of a one hundred-year period that had seen an enormous rise in illegitimacy and pre-marital pregnancy in Britain, Europe and North America.[35] Shorter argues that this was more likely a function of increased sexual activity than of factors such as improvements in female health and reproductive biology, adoption of systematic contraception or other social or economic processes.[36] If Shorter's argument is correct, a trend toward increased sexual activity will have had greater impact upon civilian couples' fertility than upon that of naval couples. Civilian brides' shore-based civilian partners were more consistently available, their opportunities for sexual congress greater. Gunnery school *Excellent*'s privileges apart (see p. 23), leave for lower-deck men was not granted as a right until 1890, even then the statutory minimum being just forty-eight hours every three months, with further limitations determined by commanding officers' preferences.[37] Officers' preferences, of course, took no account of wives' menstrual cycles; and whatever the near-legendary sexual activity of seamen during runs-ashore, their absences at sea reduced their chances of conception to a few months every two or three years, if that.

Early parenthood exposed couples to a double whammy of increased domestic outgoings (clothes, furniture, food, medicine) coupled with the new mother having to withdraw from the labour market – an especially unwelcome prospect when the naval husband was at sea, his wife stranded in a community suffering chronic female underemployment. If women wished to earn they must exercise agency, either by avoiding pregnancy or by ending it. To delay was not necessarily to tempt fate: conception

---

[34] Laslett, 'Family as Knot', p. 363; Laslett, *Family Life and Illicit Love*, pp. 105, 111.
[35] Edward Shorter, *The Making of the Modern Family* (London, 1976), pp. 82–3.
[36] Ibid., p. 88; R. Sauer, 'Infanticide and Abortion in Nineteenth-Century Britain', *Population Studies*, 32:1 (1978), 81–93, at p. 84, and n. 29, citing *Offences Against the Person Act*, 1 Vict., c. 85 (1837); Woods, *Demography*, p. 123; Perkin, *Women and Marriage*, p. 127.
[37] Walton, 'Social History', pp. 161–3.

occurring two or more years post-wedding did not take the naval bride beyond her fertile years, for having been younger at marriage than her civilian peers she had gained 'spare' years of fertility.

Mid-nineteenth century contraception was limited, and inconsistently effective. Only abstinence guaranteed protection. Ships' deployment imposed abstinence, but abstinence was difficult to maintain when long-absent husbands returned, or when desire flourished during their absence. For women who conceived an unwanted child within or outside marriage, help was available. Explicitly targeting 'females', local newspapers carried advertisements for pills 'truly excellent' and 'particularly efficacious' in removing 'obstructions'; and where pills alone did not work, there was a 'Professor Boaz' of Havant Street, Portsea, 'a few doors from Queen-street, near the Hard' (this detail a knowing wink to those with naval connections), whose advertisement assured readers of his expertise whereby 'Female Complaints, irregularities, obstruction, &c, from whatever cause, [are] successfully treated', 'the most obstinate cases cured within eight or ten days', with strictest secrecy observed.[38] And for the illiterate, or those too poor to purchase a newspaper, there was no shortage of advice, support and empirical experience to be obtained from older wives, women who in past decades had faced the same issue, the same hard choices.

For the woman unwilling to abort, options were limited. She might, like Harriet Sarah, daughter of Harriet Betsworth (q.v.), place her infant to be brought up by its maternal grandmother – if grandmother were still living, and available. Braving church minister's censure and neighbours' disapproval, she might keep the infant until (she hoped) her homecoming seaman acknowledged paternity, enfolded mother and child in lawful union and declared an allotment in her favour. With this option, however, nothing was guaranteed. Until 1873, no mother of an illegitimate child could impose financial responsibility upon a man serving in either of the armed forces.[39] The Navy's allotment scheme may have supported seamen's motherless children, but whether favouring wife or trustee, no allotment could be extracted against a man's will. This was something of particular relevance to Mary Roberts of Hobbs Court. A naval daughter (an allotment

---

[38] *H/Tel,* 9 July 1859, p. 3 col. D; *ibid.,* 2 October 1847, p. 6 col. E; *ibid.,* 2 April 1859, p. 3 col. A. No 'Boaz' features in the Portsea Island censuses for 1851 or 1861, and no medical practitioner is listed among the residents of Havant Street. No 'Boaz' is listed in the Calendar of Surgeons or Royal College of Physicians (per FindMyPast.com, Calendar of The Royal College of Surgeons in England and Members of The Royal College of Physicians [1830–1923], FindMyPast.com <https://search.findmypast.co.uk/search-world-records/britain-physicians-and-surgeons-1830-1923> [accessed 22 April 2024]).

[39] Sheila Rowbotham, *Hidden from History: 300 Years of Women's Oppression and the Fight Against It.* (London, 1983), p. 53.

declaration of 1837 confirms her mother Elizabeth as wife of Joseph Ford, master at arms, HMS *North Star*), Mary was the widow of captain of the main top William Roberts, HMS *Excellent*, who in August 1849, after just sixteen months of marriage, had died of cholera at Haslar Hospital.[40] By census day 1851 the Hobbs Court household consisted of mother-and-daughter naval widows, and a fatherless baby boy. All was not as it seemed, however. Despite Mary's having been William's lawful wife, and despite what it said on the birth certificate, Mary's infant son was not, could not possibly be, the posthumous child of 'William Roberts (deceased), seaman', for the six-week-old had been conceived after seaman William's demise.[41] Who, then, was the child's father? He may have been some unknown assailant who forced himself upon a defenceless widow; were that the case, however, the father's section of the birth certificate would have been left blank. The child's forenames, William Henry Holdaway, may provide a clue. In admiralty records for 1830–52 there are two naval ratings named Hold-away who would have been adult at the mid-century point, and two adult male Holdaways are listed in the Portsea Island census of 1851. Common to both sources was 28-year-old AB John Holdaway, HMS *Victory*, resident of Elm Lane, Kingston.[42] If he were little William's putative father (it is 'if', there being no proof either way), Mary could expect little by way of financial or other help, and not only because the aforementioned regulation prevented mothers of illegitimate children from imposing financial responsibility upon men serving in the armed forces; for AB Holdaway was recently married, and already supporting his new bride via an allotment.[43]

Without extended family to raise her child on her behalf, without a husband ready for fatherhood, the woman pregnant by a seaman did at least have another option particularly suited to a community in which naval service reduced couples' chances of conception. Arranged informally, often without any legal agreement, and bypassing church, poor law guardians and charities, private adoption both relieved unmarried women of their illegitimate infants, and fulfilled the hopes of naval couples unable to conceive during the brief interludes between one ship's commission and the next. All the adoptive couple need do was register the infant's birth under their surname, at which point his biological parentage vanished from the record. The extent of the practice may only be guessed; it was, after

---

[40] ADM 27/52/144/54; Medway Archives (Kent Marriages and Banns 1813–20), P153/1/23, p. 36; PHC: CHU2/1C/15, p. 51 n. 101; ADM 27/103/250/708; E&W Deaths: Alverstoke, Hampshire, Q3/1849, vol. 7, p. 26 (certificate).

[41] William Henry Holdaway Roberts, b. 16 February 1851, son of 'William Roberts (deceased)', per E&W Births: Q1/1851, vol. 7, p. 186 (certificate).

[42] ADM 27/112/412/SB75; 1851 census: HO107/1657, fol. 258, p. 29.

[43] Rowbotham, *Hidden from History*, p. 53; PHC: CHU9/1B/1, p. 116 n. 232; ADM 27/112/412/SB75.

all, private, covert and undocumented, the kind of thing to be spoken of neither by adoptive families fearful of disclosure or changes of heart, nor by birth mothers fearful of exposure or being stigmatised. It may be wondered whether private adoption were more common within the naval community than the civilian. For the childless couple frustrated in their attempts to conceive, for the adulterous wife conceiving during her husband's absence at sea, for the faithful wife unable to face motherhood without a husband's presence, it offered a solution.

## FIRST CHILDREN, AND WIVES' AGE AT MOTHERHOOD

If our naval newlyweds were younger at marriage than their civilian counterparts, does it follow that they were younger at the birth of their first child? Again, data sources bedevil analysis. Parish registers were more concerned to note whether a mother were married, hence her age at the birth of her child was not routinely recorded.[44] The following analysis therefore relies upon women's ages as stated in multiple censuses, correlated where possible with baptismal records for both mother and child.

By 1861 the naval and civilian newlyweds of our two comparator groups had been married for a decade or more: time enough to have started a family, for some even to have finished. Of couples recorded as spinsters marrying bachelors, 1851 and 1861 census schedules for thirty-seven naval and forty-nine civilian wives yielded sufficient data for analysis of age at first maternity. According to parish and civil registers, one-third of our naval brides gave birth to a surviving child within twelve months of their marrying, four-fifths before three years were up. Naval service notwithstanding, the average period between naval couples' marriage and first maternity emerges as 2.6 years. As far as may be established, naval wives' age at first maternity ranged from eighteen to thirty-seven years, civilian women's from seventeen to thirty-four. This modest weighting toward younger maternity among civilian wives, older among naval, is further emphasised when age-groups are aggregated, revealing that 71.4 per cent of civilian wives were mothers by age twenty-five, compared with 62.2 per cent of naval wives. Our naval brides may on average have been younger at marriage than their civilian peers, but over one-third of them were twenty-six or more at first maternity. They waited longer to become mothers, or at least to see a child survive infancy.

In terms of premarital pregnancy and numbers of surviving children the naval family was noticeably different from its civilian equivalent. It is unsafe, however, to assume that ships' absences alone account

---

[44] Woods, *Demography*, p. 111.

*Children*

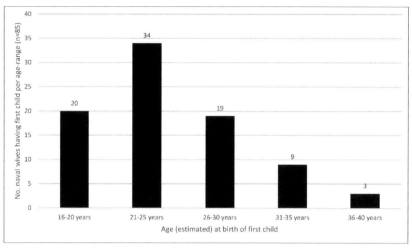

**Fig. 15** Naval wives' estimated age at birth of first surviving child (n=85).

for differences in family sizes. Individual choice will have played a part, as couples opted to postpone conception to maximise earning potential, consolidate affective relationships, and allow younger-than-average brides to mature. How far such decisions were taken jointly, how much imposed by husbands irrespective of wives' wishes, or left for wives to determine as they saw fit, are questions beyond answering here. As Pooley observes, 'the different motivations of, and power relations between, men and women … cannot be identified in quantitative data.'[45] It is possible, if unprovable, that a community-specific ethos obtained, an ethos which, recognising that lone parenthood could be especially tough for seamen's wives, esteemed and encouraged naval couples' postponing parenthood. If so, women choosing to postpone were aided by the fact that in street after street, court after court, there were older naval women with empirical experience of the pros and cons of early motherhood. Their knowledge of prophylactic methods, their availability to provide practical and emotional support to the wife wishing to prevent or terminate pregnancy, their empathy with the wife's situation, will have played a part. Central to all this, however, was naval women's agency, and the degree to which the individual wife determined and enacted her role as wife and mother.

---

[45] Siân Pooley, 'Parenthood, Child-rearing and Fertility in England, 1850–1914', *History of the Family* 18: 1 (2013), 83–106 <https://www.ncbi.nlm.nih.gov/pmc/articles/PMC3865739/> [accessed 22 April 2024], Introduction.

6

# HOUSEHOLD STRUCTURE

In their husbands' absence, seamen's wives were found in a range of household types: in households headed by relatives; in structures consisting of 'vertical' (older generation) or 'lateral' kin (same-generation relatives such as siblings and cousins); and heading households which included co-resident unmarried, married or widowed adult offspring. These arrangements were at odds with the prevalent 'simple family household' model consisting of parents and dependent children, likewise with Laslett's observation that 'parents did not live with their married children, nor bachelors or spinsters with their married brothers or sisters any more often than they do today'.[1] The notion of the 'domestic haven' of the nuclear family was something normalised during the nineteenth century, alongside a revised perception of participants' roles ('the father active in the world; the mother, isolated in the home'), an ideal which, as Moring and Wall observe, 'did not always fit the reality, but the image is triumphant, and lives with us still today'.[2] The image did not fit the reality of naval family life, even though few husbands and fathers could be said to be more 'active in the world' than the naval seaman, few mothers left more 'isolated in the home' than the naval wife.

To provide an overview of naval families' household structures, this chapter adapts Laslett's classifications into five broad models, here styled Types A to E.[3] Type A's 'small households' incorporate three variations: lone female allottees; two-person ménages comprising naval wife and

---

[1] Laslett, 'Introduction', pp. 60–2; Peter Laslett, 'The Comparative History of Household and Family', *Journal of Social History*, 4:1 (1970), 75–87, at p. 77.

[2] Beatrice Moring and Richard Wall, *Widows in European Economy and Society 1600–1920* (Woodbridge, 2017), p. 2.

[3] Laslett, 'Introduction', p. 42; Richard Wall, 'Economic Collaboration of Family Members Within and Beyond Households in English Society, 1600–2000', *Continuity & Change*, 25:1 (2010), 83–108, at p. 86; Richard Wall, 'Regional and Temporal Variations in the Structure of the British Household since 1851', in T.C. Barker and

co-resident adult who for obvious reasons was usually someone other than her absent, allotting husband; and naval wife with underage child. Type B consists of households headed by allottees (generally older married women such as seamen's mothers, or wives of mature and experienced warrant officers) accommodating adult offspring. Type C inverts this model, its non-allottee household heads accommodating daughters married to naval seamen (allottee-wives). Female householders accommodating non-relatives and/or relatives other than offspring are the subject of Type D. Finally, Type E examines laterally-extended households comprising co-resident adult siblings, one or more of them allottees; some Type E households had children present, but none contained members of the older generation. The analysis conformed to census conventions by which a household was held to constitute 'all the names listed in an enumerator's book from one entry "head" in the "relation to head of family" column to the last name preceding the next entry "head".'[4] All instances of co-residence were counted, whether or not the schedule indicated kinship between household members.

For clarity and certainty, this five-part analysis focuses primarily upon seamen's wives. Where seamen's mothers and sisters were married to civilians, their household income may have been significantly different from that of the naval household, with consequences in terms of size (capacity) and affordability of accommodation. There were other factors distinguishing seamen's wives from other permitted allottee relationships. These included breadwinners' or other occupants' working hours or shift patterns; proximity to a waged adult's place of work; the need for domestic space for outwork materials or labour; and the presence of kin able to contribute to a family's non-naval trade. Furthermore, where an allottee-sister or -mother was enumerated as 'married' but with no husband present, her spouse's absence might be due to his being a seaman, but might equally signify his having gone on the tramp in search of work, his being absent at work (for example, a navvy on an engineering project elsewhere in the country), in gaol, or his having abandoned wife and home. To focus solely upon seamen's allottee-wives reduced these variables, and with them the potential for skewed results.

---

Michael Drake (eds), *Population and Society in Britain 1850–1980* (London, 1982), 62–99, at p. 67.

[4] Wall, 'Economic Collaboration', p. 88; Wall, 'Regional and Temporal Variations', p. 67; Higgs, *Census Revisited*, p. 75.

## HOUSEHOLD TYPE A: 'SMALL HOUSEHOLDS', COMPRISING LONE WOMEN, AND TWO-PERSON MÉNAGES (NAVAL WIVES WITH CO-RESIDENT ADULT OR UNDERAGE CHILD)

There were sound reasons for the seaman's woman (indeed, for any lone individual) to avoid sole occupancy, whether of whole-house tenancy or one-room sublet. Simple economics argued against it. Co-residence reduced the cost per person of rent and poor rates, fuel and water, lamp oil, candles, food and drink, while the presence of co-resident adults or older teenagers meant domestic labour could be shared, loneliness ameliorated. The question of loneliness was perhaps less important to locally-born wives and/or those who had migrated into the island in childhood, they being more likely to have a network of kin and friends within reach. Of twenty-eight allottee-wives who were sole occupants of a whole house, half a dozen had been born at distance, in Devon, Dorset, Cornwall, Staffordshire, Leeds. For them, loneliness may have been a greater challenge, depending on how long they had lived in Portsmouth, whether any siblings had arrived with them and remained on the island, and the strength and extent of the social network they had developed. Regardless of birthplace, however, to women who had never lived alone or without male oversight the solitary life could be a severe shock.[5]

There was also the matter of protection, both physical and reputational. Women – young women especially – who lived alone were regarded as socially unorthodox, suspect, vulnerable, implicitly inviting approach or intrusion. In slum districts (of which Portsea Island had several) 'few women found it easy to survive ... without a male companion.'[6] Lacking husband or family to protect them or regulate their conduct, lone women were judged to be as degenerate as prostitutes; they were 'considered outcasts, and outcasts were regarded as defective women, so it followed that outcasts were also morally corrupt and sexually impure.'[7]

Thirty-two two-person households comprised allottee-wife and a co-resident adult other than her husband. Census terminology ('lodger', 'visitor') hid kinship. Using marriage details supplied in allotment registers, searches of parish and civil registers yielded wives' maiden names, which enabled some 'visitor' or 'lodger' co-residents to be identified as wives' sisters, their ages ranging from twelve to forty-five. Others proved to be extended family – niece, widowed aunt, sister-in-law. Few co-residents were male. In Hobbs Court, Portsea, within the two-person household of Martha Bone, wife

---

[5] Hallie Rubenhold, *The Five: the untold lives of the women killed by Jack the Ripper* (London, 2019), p. 51.
[6] *Ibid.*, p. 142.
[7] *Ibid.*, pp. 138, 70.

of AB Eli Bone (*q.v.*), HMS *Resolute*, nineteen-year-old labourer 'lodger' John Woodley proved to be Martha's half-brother by their father's second marriage.[8] Next door lived Eli Bone's labourer brother Daniel and his wife, their proximity affording young Martha a degree of security in her husband's absence. As Chapters Twelve and Thirteen will show, Eli was a difficult man. If he had taken on the Hobbs Court tenancy in order to fix Martha under Daniel's supervisory gaze, it may be that Martha's importing her kinsman as 'lodger' was as much a matter of disarming (or cocking a snook at) her watchful in-laws as it was a matter of economic prudence, company, familiarity, brotherly support, chaperonage, respectability and/or protection.

Prevailing culture awarded husbands the right to make decisions on important issues, one of which was choice of accommodation. Breadwinner-husbands' primary concern was affordability. Seamen's wives' criteria, too, will have been informed by affordability, but also by concerns such as the location of their workplace relative to the tenancy; the extent, strength and proximity of their kinship networks; the sublet's convenience, its domestic amenities, the number of stairs from yard to landing; its security and safety, which took into account the character of other residents; its proximity to the dockyard pay office (for collection of allotment monies); and its being of a size to accommodate, in due course, a sailor-husband home from sea. But just as 'neighbourhood norms and customs' varied from ship's mess to ship's mess, so the degree of agency ceded by husbands varied from couple to couple.[9] We have documentary evidence of a tendency toward sublet living (of seventy-five 'Type A' households comprising allottee-wife and seaman-husband, two-thirds occupied sublets in multi-occupancy buildings), but lack the means to discern whose was the decision to rent that tenancy, based on which criteria.

Another type of 'small household' reflected a popular sentimental image of 'naval wife'. Sixty-eight two-person households comprised allottee and underage offspring. These were the women whom Rodger described as 'bringing up small children, earning their living as best they might while their menfolk were at sea, enduring years of absence and uncertainty.'[10] Some will have chosen this arrangement out of preference for privacy and self-contained living; others, however, will have been disappointed in their attempts to find, or be accepted into, larger households affording company, mutual support and potential help with childcare.

---

[8] 1851 census: HO107/1658, fol. 47, p. 36; ADM 27/110/252/47; CHU42/1C/10, p. 139 n. 415 (father's first marriage); CHU3/1B/14, p. 77 n. 612 (Martha's baptism); CHU3/1E/14, p. 80 n. 633 (mother's burial); CHU3/1D/30, p. 72 n. 215 (father's second marriage); CHU5/A/1/5, p. 330, n. 35 (John's baptism).

[9] August, *Poor Women's Lives*, pp. 124–5.

[10] Rodger, *Command of the Ocean*, p. 407.

## HOUSEHOLD TYPE B: ALLOTTEE-HOUSEHOLDERS WITH CO-RESIDENT ADULT OFFSPRING

'Most people do not want to live with [their parents],' noted Young and Wilmott, 'they want to live near them.'[11] For adults not to live with parents or in-laws was one of what Laslett termed the noumenal normative rules of English society, neither proscribed by law nor referred to anywhere in English literary output, '[yet] here was a behavioural rule that seems to have been almost universally obeyed, from the earliest period in the thirteenth century … until the present day.'[12] Moring and Wall, however, observe that 'as age of marriage and mortality limit the time married children can co-reside with parents, and co-residence with more than one married child is difficult, the presence of a majority of households with only two generations … cannot be seen as proof of disinclination to cohabit.'[13] Among 5,843 households in 100 communities, Laslett found no more than 150 (2.6 per cent) containing married children living with their spouse within the households of married and widowed parents.[14] While bearing in mind Moring and Wall's caveat, for this exercise Laslett's figure provides a general comparator.

With 152 of 1,496 households (10.2 per cent) containing allottee-householders' co-resident adult offspring, our cohort appears at first glance to yield a proportion four times that of Laslett's. This is a false comparison, for Laslett's 2.6 per cent of parental households contained married children *with their spouse* – an arrangement less common within naval communities, where sons followed fathers into the Navy, daughters married seagoing men. Only twenty-one such structures were identified here, at 1.4 per cent of 1,496 households, the equivalent of little over half the proportion found by Laslett. It is likely that, captured by chance in the census, these were short-term living arrangements whereby, on leave or between ships' commissions, the seamen-husbands of householders' co-resident daughters were squeezed in temporarily. The default 'household' for these men was not their parents' or in-laws' shoreside residence; it was their ship.

Was married daughters' co-residence in parental households acceptable only when their seamen-husbands were present? It seems not. Of the 1,496

---

[11] Michael Dunlop Young et al., *Family and Kinship in East London* (London, 1957), p. 20.
[12] Laslett, 'Family as Knot', pp. 364–5.
[13] Beatrice Moring and Richard Wall, *Widows in European Economy and Society 1600–1920* (Woodbridge, 2017), p. 212.
[14] Peter Laslett, 'Mean Household Size in England from Printed Sources', in Peter Laslett and Richard Wall (eds), *Household and Family in Past Time* (Cambridge, 1972), 125–58, at p. 149.

households, 102 comprised wives co-residing in their parents' households *without* their husbands. The householder-parents comprised widowed mothers, widowed fathers, married mothers whose husbands were absent, and father and mother together. If to these 102 are added the twenty-one comprising co-resident married daughters *with* seamen-husbands present, the resultant 123 amount to 8.2 per cent of 1,496 households, a proportion more than three times Laslett's. To regard this as a norm, however, is to assume that when not at sea the seaman and his wife would together continue to co-reside with her parent(s), the arrangement being a flexible, long-term construct. This is debatable. Co-residence with parents or in-laws was an arrangement primarily benefiting wives in their husbands' absence. Space permitting, the couple might temporarily reunite under their parents' or in-laws' roof for such days or weeks as the husband was between ships, but couples' longer-term co-residence was likely to be regarded as undesirable.

It is arguable, then, that these co-residences were sustained and long-lasting for naval wives, intermittent and short-lived for their husbands; and that the arrangement was associated with, if not predicated upon, the husbands' occupation which, unlike that of civilians, routinely took them away for long periods. Parental age is another factor. A higher level of co-residence with parents connects to Chapter Four's finding that naval wives tended both to be younger at first marriage than their civilian peers, and to be the daughters of seamen. The younger the bride, the higher the chance of her having still-living parents or grandparents; and since many a naval bride's mother, if not widowed, was a naval wife living alone while her husband was at sea, she was more likely both to have the domestic space to accommodate a married daughter, and to be able to empathise with her daughter's circumstances. Twenty-four-year-old Henrietta, wife of carpenter's mate Alexander Edwards, HMS *Amphitrite*, lived with her 51-year-old mother Harriet Newman, herself a warrant officer's wife and allottee.[15] And 23-year-old Ann Lemmon, wife of captain of the foretop James Lemmon, HMS *Albion*, had within five months of his allotment declaration decamped from North Street to live with her mother in Wilton Street.[16] Ann's mother, 48-year-old household head Ann Layton, appears in the census as 'seaman's wife', a status duly confirmed via an allotment declared by her husband, Michael George Layton, quartermaster, HMS *Crocodile*.[17]

Domestic space determined household size and structure. Smaller housing, especially tenement flats, attracted 'lone women with or without

---

[15] ADM 27/112/202/20; ADM 27/49/191/SL19; 1851 census: HO107/1658, fol. 200, p. 13. Householder Harriet's census schedule recorded Henrietta under her maiden name.
[16] ADM 27/111/144/162; 1851 census: HO107/ 1659, fol. 311, p. 16.
[17] 1851 census: HO107/1659, fol. 311, p. 16; ADM 27/111/57/3.

families', while the smallness of working-class homes often made the accommodating of married daughters impossible, hence Chinn's finding that (in civilian communities at least) unmarried daughters were more likely than their married sisters to be found co-resident with their parent(s).[18] This premise is logistically sound: compared with her unmarried sister, the married daughter and her domestically present, occupationally static, civilian husband used twice the water, occupied twice the space in the home, ate twice the food, produced twice the waste, and required privacy for intimacy. It ignores, however, the married daughter whose husband's trade routinely sent him away for months or years at a stretch. The daughter married to an absent seaman could not expect to be granted the domestic space enjoyed by her married sister and civilian brother-in-law. She could, however, be expected to share a bed with, eat no more than, her unmarried sister(s), and comply with her householder-parent's regime. Things were not so straightforward when her husband returned. Domestic authority, responsibility and decision-making rested with the older (householder) generation, denying the younger marrieds agency and autonomy. Given the material shortcomings of Portsea Island housing, most homes offered limited space and little if any privacy, factors testing the younger couple's relationships with other occupants, and with each other. The naval wife was thus more easily accommodated than her sister and civilian brother-in-law, but only so long as her husband was at sea. His return significantly altered the household dynamic, and not necessarily for the better.

Chinn's statement about unmarried daughters being more likely to be found co-resident with their parent(s) resonates with the finding that sixty-two older allottees' households contained a total of seventy-seven co-resident unmarried daughters aged twenty years or more, plus half as many again below that age, most too young to marry. Previous studies show daughters within poor homes were retained far longer than sons, the girls contributing via childminding and housework, either earning their own wages or enabling the parent-householder(s) to do so, the parents in turn exercising their right of surveillance over their spinster-daughters' conduct.[19] Unmarried daughters were not expected to strike out on their own, it being unseemly (for reasons stated above) for a woman to live

---

[18] Eleanor Gordon and Gweneth Nair, 'The Myth of the Victorian Patriarchal Family', *The History of the Family*, 7:1 (2002), 125–38, at p. 133; Chinn, *They Worked all their Lives*, pp. 21–3.

[19] Rosemary O'Day, *The Family and Family Relationships, 1500–1900: England, France and the United States of America* (Basingstoke, 1994), p. 22; Bridget Hill, *Women Alone: spinsters in England, 1660–1850* (New Haven, Conn., 2001), p. 119; Hufton, 'Women without Men', p. 362.

unaccompanied.[20] For sons, the 'seemly' or 'unseemly' debate was irrelevant when wage insufficiency meant they could not afford to set up independently, or pay for bachelor lodgings; meanwhile, their householder-parent(s) could not afford to lose sons' keep, which because male wages were greater could be pitched higher than that expected of their sisters.[21] That our allottees' ninety-six co-resident unmarried adult sons outnumbered their seventy-seven co-resident unmarried adult daughters therefore runs counter to those earlier studies' findings. Whether this inverse proportion arose as a function of allottees' 'half-pay' household economies rendering them more dependent on sons' income than were their civilian equivalents; whether it was rooted in naval daughters' greater tendency to marry early (see Chapter Four); or whether these co-resident sons were paid-off seamen who, pending their (re-)joining ship, were working in civilian occupations and lodging with their parents, we cannot know. Whatever the reason for this inversion, the lower proportion of unmarried co-resident daughters yet again demonstrates the naval community's 'otherness'.

## HOUSEHOLD TYPE C: PARENT-HOUSEHOLDERS WITH CO-RESIDENT, MARRIED ALLOTTEE OFFSPRING

One hundred and ninety-six allottees were found accommodated in households headed by relatives. Chinn emphasises the part played by matrilocality (gravitation toward the mother's side of the family) in the mutual support and survival of women in poor urban communities, it being taken for granted that in order to access maternal help, comfort, childcare and wisdom, a married daughter's home would be established near her mother.[22] Here, matrilocality often took the extreme form of co-residence of married daughters (in this instance allottees) with their mothers. This was an arrangement common to many communities, for 'where a husband left town the wife might move in with one or other set of parents'.[23] Anderson having noted that of couples found living with parents, 57 per cent lived with the wife's parents rather than the husband's, it was expected that similar trends would emerge in this study.[24] Indeed, at 122 vs eleven, the number of allottee-sisters and -wives found co-resident with their own parent(s) proved to be more than eleven times the number found living with parents-in-law. Overall, 90 per cent of co-residents were seamen's wives living in

---

[20] See p. 116.
[21] Anderson, 'Study of Family Structure', p. 61.
[22] Chinn, *They Worked all their Lives*, pp. 21–9.
[23] Southall and Gilbert, 'A Good Time to Wed?', p. 47.
[24] Michael Anderson, *Family Structure in Nineteenth Century Lancashire* (Cambridge, 1971), p. 56.

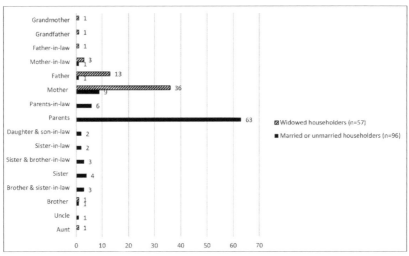

Fig. 16  Relationships of householders to co-resident (accommodated) married allottees (n=153).

households headed by their own kin (for example, with a brother and his wife) rather than in households headed by in-laws (for example, with a sister and brother-in-law, or daughter and son-in-law).

Household structure was shaped by the tendency for naval daughters to become naval wives. Lack of space often meant only one married daughter could be accommodated, leaving her married sisters facing the next best option of co-residence with in-laws, which usually meant parent(s)-in-law. Next best it may have been, but it was not popular. Some may have chosen (or been reduced to) co-residence with in-laws because their own parents were dead or living at a distance; others, as live-in carers, may have been helping their husbands' frail parents avoid dependence upon the parish.[25] It is not known whether ship's cook John Seager and his new bride Janet set up their own household after their marriage in 1849, or went straight away to live with John's father William, by then two years a widower.[26] Whatever the sequence of events, by 1851 Janet was living with her 73-year-old father-in-law.[27] The arrangement may have been prompted by Janet's need for accommodation, or by widower William's for assistance. Having neither

---

[25] Hanna Hagmark-Cooper, *To Be a Sailor's Wife* (Newcastle, 2012), p. 55; Jeremy Boulton, "'It Is Extreme Necessity That Makes Me Do This': some "survival strategies" of pauper households in London's West End during the early eighteenth century', *International Review of Social History*, 45:8 (2000), 47–69, at p. 62 table 4.

[26] ADM 27/111/130/96; CHU3/1D/49, p. 113 n. 225; E&W Deaths: Q1/1847, vol. 7, p. 143; O'Day, *Family and Family Relationships*, pp. 132, 173.

[27] 1851 census: HO107/1659, fol. 692, p. 35.

husband present nor waged work, childless daughter-in-law Janet, in return for bed and board, would have been regarded as not only available but the obvious provider of William's care. She also came with a monthly allotment.

Some of the seamen's wives found living with their parent(s) were very young, the majority not long married. These girls may never have left the parental home. As Laslett reflects, 'How could a child-bride have been expected to keep house for a mature, active man?'[28] Better, easier to stay put, retain a daughterly mien, and let Mother continue to run the household. But it should not be assumed that wives who had been married for ten to twenty years or more and who were still (or again) co-resident with their parents had never experienced independent married life. The 1851 census shows Charlotte Reeves, wife of sailmaker Henry, HMS *Victory*, and her sons living in a household headed by her widowed 82-year-old mother.[29] The 1841 census, however, had shown Charlotte as head of her own household; tacitly expressing their relative status, her children's names appeared above those of her elderly parents and younger and older sisters.[30] We do not know how long Charlotte and Henry maintained their own household, nor why Charlotte later resumed the subordinate position of co-resident daughter within her parent's home. To relinquish her own household may have caused pangs of regret and shame; alternatively, had she found household headship stressful, to retreat into co-residence may have been a relief.

It is inevitable that some wives had to give up their marital home when their husbands' departure reduced accessible family income to half-pay or less. Financial necessity apart, a combination of simple affection, available domestic space and the need for familiar and trustworthy company may have led others to be (re-)absorbed within their parents' households. Some may have hoped not to do so, but had no friends or same-generation relatives with whom to share accommodation. Rather than walk between dwellings several times a day, women physically caring for and supporting an ageing parent(-in-law) may have found it cheaper, less demanding and more convenient to provide live-in care. But whether living with parent(s) or in-law(s), co-resident wives and their transient seamen-husbands lacked the space, privacy and day-to-day self-determination enjoyed by couples occupying their own households. Given Chapter Five's findings on family size, it may be wondered how much a simple lack of privacy affected opportunities for intimacy.

---

[28] Laslett, 'Comparative History', p. 83.
[29] 1851 census: HO107/1659, fol. 13, p. 18.
[30] 1841 census: HO107/414, fol. 34, p. 21; ADM 27/112/154/44.

## HOUSEHOLD TYPE D: HOUSEHOLDER-ALLOTTEES ACCOMMODATING NON-RELATIVES AND/OR RELATIVES OTHER THAN OFFSPRING

Over a quarter of mid-century households contained at least one person unrelated to the household head.[31] In the poorer civilian community the sharing of accommodation by unrelated persons made sense. Women living in separate dwellings already exchanged services and household goods, so to co-reside lightened the financial load even further. Housework could be collaborative, freeing time for housemates to undertake paid work.[32] Outgoings could be split, domestic goods held in common, earnings pooled and used more economically.[33] One candle could light a room occupied by two or more, childcare be combined on a turn-and-turn-about basis or by one woman assuming the nanny-housekeeper role, the other the breadwinner. For these reasons, and because naval women's circumstances enabled them to adopt such arrangements flexibly, without reference to their husbands for approval, moderate to high rates of unrelated co-residence were expected. Few wives, however, were found to have chosen co-residence with non-relatives.

From a twenty-first century perspective, avoidance of what we call flat- or house-shares is baffling. Why reject an opportunity to reduce outgoings and loneliness by taking on a tenancy together? Why not capitalise upon a shared situation (the absence of a husband on naval service) and common culture (the naval community, with its traditions, celebrations, rituals, its arcane language) by setting up home with a fellow naval wife? The answer may lie not so much in missed opportunity as in preference for kinship-based arrangements. For those who had female relatives with whom to set up home, kinship-based co-residence had inarguable advantages. It needed no references, no establishing of bona fides, no explaining or defending. To live with family was natural, even admirable. Co-resident kin had a common network of concerned individuals on whom to call for practical help or financial support. They shared the same values and moral code, whereas co-residence by unrelated women was a leap in the dark, and open to misinterpretation. Suspicion attached to wives without husbands, to seamen's wives especially. At worst, the most innocent of living

---

[31] Michael Anderson, 'Households, Families and Individuals: some preliminary results from the national sample from the census of Great Britain 1851', *Continuity & Change*, 3:3 (1988), 421–38, at p. 425.

[32] Shani D'Cruze, 'Women and The Family', in June Purvis (ed.), *Women's History: Britain, 1850–1945: an introduction* (London, 1995), 51–83, at p. 64; Humphries, *Childhood and Child Labour*, p. 116.

[33] Hill, *Women Alone*, p. 118.

arrangements might be assumed to be brothels; at the very least they might attract cynical comment, casting doubt upon motive and character, undermining women's reputation, self-confidence, self-esteem and trust. If the arrangement foundered, within a tight-knit community the consequences could be severe: rumour, gossip, acrimony, fellow naval wives turning upon their own and absent husbands receiving worrying news of discord and domestic disruption. From every angle, co-residence with relatives was a safer bet.

Where allottees were household heads with co-resident adult children, apart from a handful of not unexpected sons- or daughters-in-law and their offspring, in only seven instances were other kin present: a brother, a grandmother, some nephews and nieces (most often children of the householder's co-resident sister). The rarity of such arrangements may bespeak lack of space; but it also suggests a collectively recognised pecking order which gave priority to householders' adult offspring, even the married ones who in wider society would be expected to have set up in homes of their own. For the seaman's wife to accommodate extended kin as well as her own offspring was asking too much.

## HOUSEHOLD TYPE E: CO-RESIDENT SIBLINGS (LATERALLY EXTENDED HOUSEHOLDS)

Thirty-seven (2.5 per cent) of the study's 1,496 households contained co-resident adult siblings with no older generation present, an arrangement Laslett described as 'household extended laterally'.[34] Each of the thirty-seven was depicted in genogram form, with conjugal units (married couples, with or without children) enclosed separately within their own circles.[35] Adjusting the model to reflect issues specific to this study, household members known to be naval allottees were identified by an asterisk; household heads were marked 'H'; and triangles (denoting male members of households) were shaded to denote seamen-spouses and -brothers absent on census day. Twenty-two (60 per cent) of the arrangements were found to hinge upon co-residence of two married sisters, some also accommodating a younger unmarried sister. All the host sisters were married, self-described either as household heads or as wives (of absent household heads). All co-resident brothers were unmarried, and most were seamen or marines, their sisters' hospitality enabling them to avoid being billeted in barracks or hulks.

---

[34] Laslett, 'Introduction', pp. 30, 31.
[35] Circling of conjugal units is omitted from genograms of the Greenleaf family (Fig. 27), and the Davey/Leese/Matthias/Plummer household (Fig. 19).

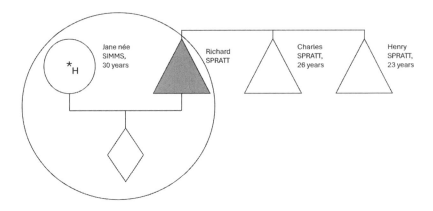

Fig. 17   Genogram of Spratt household. Genogram model based upon that used by Laslett (Laslett, 'Introduction', p. 42). Reproduced, with alterations as described in Chapter Six, by permission of the Licensor through PLSClear.

These 'households extended laterally' were socially acceptable living arrangements. Sibling co-residence did not raise neighbours' eyebrows, or cause absent husbands concern. Sisters shared a lifelong emotional bond. They were each other's moral guardians, confidantes and natural choice of fellow resident. Brothers too were natural co-residents: many nineteenth-century brother/sister relationships were intense and emotional, many a brother supporting his sister both financially and via fraternal compassion.[36] In this study, households founded upon brother/brother relationships were fewer in number than those built around relationships between sisters and their siblings. This makes sense, in that seamen-brothers were absent too often and too long to justify co-residence constructed around their fraternity. Another negative consideration was that fraternally-linked households juxtaposed a married, sexually experienced yet unaccompanied female (the absent seaman's wife) with a married man or bachelor (her husband's brother) unrelated to her by blood. This was an arrangement ripe for misinterpretation and speculation, which may explain why sailor-husbands are present in all but one of a half-dozen households accommodating their brothers. The exception (see Fig. 17) saw 30-year-old Jane Spratt, wife of stoker Richard, HMS *Comet*, heading a household comprising her 1-year-old daughter, and Richard's brothers Charles

---

[36] Leonore Davidoff, 'Kinship as a Categorical Concept: a case study of nineteenth-century English siblings', *Journal of Social History*, 39:2 (2005), 411–28, at p. 413; Humphries, *Childhood and Child Labour*, pp. 126–7.

(enumerated as 'brother' to Jane) and Henry (described as 'visitor').[37] Both Charles and Henry were born in rural Hampshire, and both were labourers, which may suggest that when migrating to Portsmouth in search of work they had sought accommodation with seaman brother Richard, or, in his absence, his wife.

In several households headed by allottee-wives there were co-resident sisters described as 'mariner's wife', 'sailor's wife' or similar. When one or both of their husbands returned, did the sisters dissolve their shared households and go their separate ways? Not always. Elizabeth Harwood and Mary Gough, nées Cook, lived together.[38] Census day 1851 found them at home in Kings Bench Alley with Elizabeth's husband, AB William Harwood, the two Harwood boys, and Mary Gough's 5-year-old son.[39] Since 1848 William had served in *Victory*, then *Blenheim*, latterly *Excellent*.[40] All three vessels were based in Portsmouth Harbour, so for the past three years William's presence in the household was probably intermittent, possibly frequent. As for Mary's husband, the absent George, since August 1850 he had served as AB in HMS *Britannia*, guard ship of vessels laid up in ordinary.[41] It is possible, therefore, that he too would from time to time be at home in Kings Bench Alley – just not on census night.

In an unknowable number of instances the census will have missed, by a few days or weeks, the presence of one co-resident sister's husband in the other sister's husband's absence. As much as it may be a function of limited domestic space, the dearth of households containing more than one sister's husband goes to those 'neighbourhood norms and customs' identified by August.[42] Lower-deck married men may have shared an opinion that co-residence of another couple, even one related via sibship, ran counter to the principle that whether present or absent, a man was master in his own home, and that in his absence another man's co-residence was unacceptable. From the sisters' point of view, however, a one-husband-present arrangement had its advantages, providing (if only via a brother-in-law, not her spouse) male company, protection and physical strength to help with the heavier chores. Yet something seems to have placed it beyond the pale, otherwise we should expect more than just five instances of a naval wife, her husband at sea, having both her sister *and* brother-in-law living with her. Some seamen, of course, had no brothers, or their brothers were also at sea. But beyond these practicalities simple jealousy may have played a part,

---

[37] ADM 27/111/31/5; 1851 census: HO107/1657, fol. 57, p. 23.
[38] CHU3/1D/42, p. 186 n. 372; CHU3/1D/37, p. 242 n. 484.
[39] ADM 27/112/216/1641; 1851 census: HO107/1658, fol. 135, p. 24.
[40] ADM 29/59/104.
[41] ADM 139/25/2449.
[42] August, *Poor Women's Lives*, pp. 124–5.

## Naval Seamen's Women in Nineteenth-Century Britain

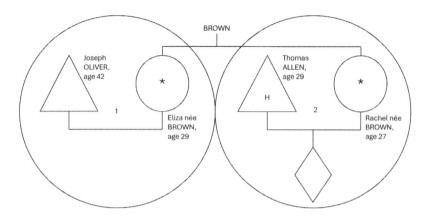

Fig. 18  Genogram of Oliver/Allen household. Genogram model based upon that used by Laslett (Laslett, 'Introduction', p. 42). Reproduced, with alterations as described in Chapter Six, by permission of the Licensor through PLSClear. See fn. 46 re: spelling of names.

the seaborne paterfamilias deeming it insufferable, even at the expense of his sister in-law's hurt feelings, for another man to be under his roof, his feet under his table. He might deem, but he could not determine: needing company and financial easement, his wife might yet accommodate, in return for keep, not only her sister but her sister's husband. In admitting them into her household she exercised a level of self-determination and independence unusual among working-class wives, and demonstrated by only five of our seamen's spouses.

As for two sisters' sailor-husbands both being present at once, naval service reduced the chances considerably. Among 1,496 households only two such arrangements were identified. Twenty-three-year-old Rebecca Lucas was married to Richard Lucas, gunner's mate, HMS *Excellent*, he describing himself as 'seaman in harbour' and household head.[43] Her senior by four years, Rebecca's sister Amelia was married to George Watson, formerly captain of the mast, HMS *Amphitrite*; householder Richard described him as 'seaman rigger'.[44] Meanwhile, in St George's Square, sisters Eliza and Rachael and their husbands Joseph Oliver (gunner third class, HMS *Excellent*) and Thomas Allen (steward, HMY *Victoria and Albert*) shared a house (see Fig. 18).[45] Household head Thomas described Joseph and Eliza as his

---

[43] ADM 27/111/54/1803; 1851 census: HO107/1657, fol. 352, p. 13.
[44] ADM 27/100/415/69.
[45] ADM 27/111/83/341; ADM 27/113/60/26 ('Rachael Allen'); 1851 census: HO107/1658, fol. 60, p. 15 ('Rachel Allen').

'lodger' and 'ditto [lodger's] wife', which suggests he regarded his relationship with them as more transactional than affinal or affectionate.

Thomas Allen was not alone in hiding kinship beneath neutral terminology. Household head Sarah Hinks and her 'lodger' Mary Ann Reeves, nées Groom, were sisters married to men serving in HMS *Blenheim*, Henry Hinks as captain of the foretop, William Rees (aka Reeves) as leading stoker.[46] *Blenheim* being moored in Portsmouth Harbour, it can hardly be said that Sarah and Mary Ann had set up home together the better to endure their men's long absences on far-reaching deployments. A more likely explanation is that the house they inhabited had been their home since childhood, the fact of Messrs Hinks and Rees/Reeves being shipmates tipping the balance toward the sisters' continued co-residence.

To the protagonists, and to neighbours, these laterally-extended, sibling-based co-residences would have seemed natural. There were inherent hazards, however, one of which was martial men vying for domestic supremacy, a competition which could easily be sustained by their wives when the men were at sea. Speaking of arrangements found in rural areas, O'Day captures the potential weaknesses of urban co-residences when he muses, 'When two or more couples and their children lived together, who had authority within the household? ... Who decided what was to be done, and by whom in the house itself ...?'[47] A key indicator of authority was the designation of household head. In three out of four cases this was the older sister or (where present) her husband. Where a younger sister used the census schedule to self-describe as household head, she may have been the one who secured the tenancy; alternatively, like Austen's Lydia Bennet, she may have assumed that her being married gave her precedence over an older spinster sibling, justifying her completing the census form and thereby ensuring her still-unmarried sisters, or those with absent husbands, were described relative to herself. Then again, something as simple as her husband's transient presence, or his being rated senior to her brother-in-law, may have been enough to justify (in her opinion at least) her superior status.

Some laterally-extended households were structurally highly complex, one especially so. Connected via sibling relationships and conjugal units, the Davey/Leese/Plummer/Matthias household had three adult members present on census day. In principle, however, it involved no fewer than seven living adults and five children.

Head of household was 31-year-old Elizabeth Davey, née Leese, wife of the second-eldest Davey sibling Joseph, a stoker in *Sprightly*, tender to

---

[46] ADM 27/110/279/274; ADM 27/110/280/496; 1851 census: HO107/1659, fol. 541, p. 31. Sarah and Mary Ann were the older sisters of Amelia Wheden (*q.v.*), née Groom.

[47] O'Day, *Family and Family Relationships*, p. 171.

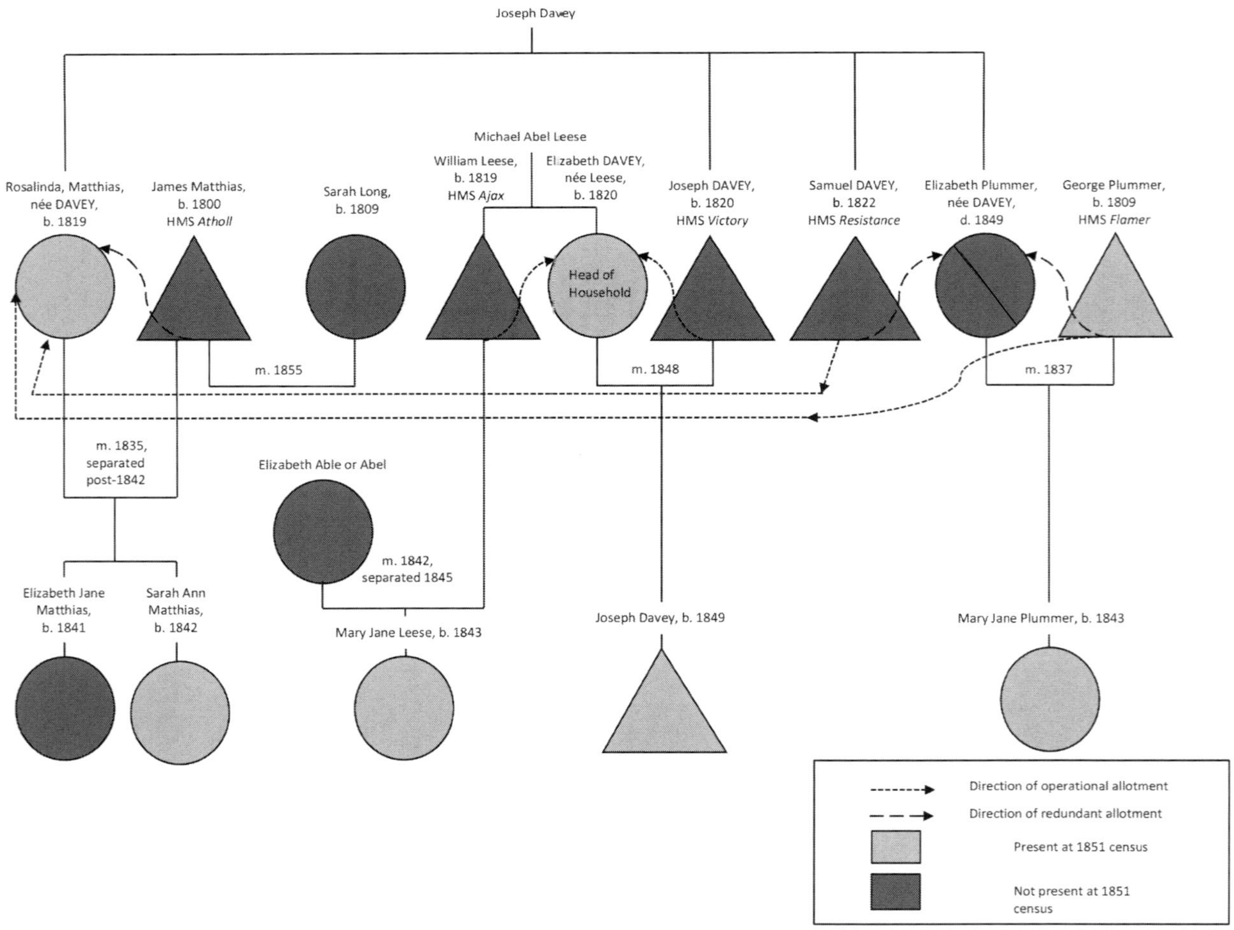

**Fig. 19** Genogram of Davey/Leese/Plummer/Matthias household. Genogram model based upon that used by Laslett (Laslett, 'Introduction', p. 42). Reproduced, with alterations as described in Chapter Six, by permission of the Licensor through PLSClear.

HMS *Victory*.[48] Elizabeth was not the eldest adult in the household, but her husband was the property's official tenant.[49] She was also the only one having a still-living spouse in a still-viable marriage. Three Davey siblings – Rosalinda Matthias, the said Joseph and Samuel – formed the household's lateral spine. Youngest Davey sibling Elizabeth had died in 1849, leaving her husband George Plummer (sailmaker, HMS *Flamer*) the widowed father of a 7-year-old daughter.[50]

Born within a twelvemonth of each other, two girl cousins were part of the household. Motherless Mary Jane Plummer was one; the other, a 'Mary J.L.' (Mary Jane Leese), appears in the census as 'ditto' below Elizabeth Davey's surname. As trustee to Mary Jane Leese, Elizabeth received an allotment from her brother AB William Leese, HMS *Ajax*.[51] Mary Jane was William's daughter, born of his marriage to Elizabeth Able or Abel.[52] William's need for a trustee arose not from widowerhood but from his being abandoned by the mother of his child: in 1845, just over a year after giving birth to Mary Jane, Elizabeth Abel Leese had abandoned husband and daughter, bigamously marrying Joseph Bragginton, a Royal Marine private who from HMS *St Vincent* duly declared an allotment in her favour, thus relieving William of financial responsibility for his still-lawful wife (resident in nearby St Mary Street), and enabling him to reroute his money to his sister-trustee.[53]

Home to this extended family, No. 2 Primrose Alley consisted of one ground floor room measuring 9ft 0in by 8ft 0in below a ceiling 7ft 0in high, and a first-floor room measuring 11ft 6in by 8ft 0in, its ceiling 6ft 9in high.[54] There was a cellar, a communal yard with wash-house, and two WCs for the use of the alley's twenty-one residents.[55]

There was scant chance of all four of the household's seamen being home at the same time. After departing Portsmouth in June 1850 and being anchored at Spithead in May–June 1851, William Leese's Cork guardship

---

[48] ADM 27/110/20/27.
[49] Portsmouth History Centre (PHC) Portsmouth, Portsea Island Poor Law Union, Rate Books, PHC DT/R/2/454-7 (1851), vol. 454, p. 57.
[50] ADM 27/99/462/345; ADM 27/102/90/6; E&W Deaths: Q2/1849, vol. 7, p. 130; E&W Births: Q3/1842, vol. 7, p. 143 (Mary Jane Plummer); CHU3/1B/27, p. 156 n. 1248.
[51] ADM 27/111/353/112.
[52] E&W Marriages: Q3/1842, Stoke Damerel, vol. 9, p. 482; E&W Births: Q4/1843, Falmouth, vol. 9, p. 84 (certificate).
[53] CHU3/1D/43, p. 99 n. 197; ADM 27/90/276/98; ADM 27/111/353/112.
[54] Portsmouth History Centre (PHC) Portsmouth, Ground Plan of Primrose Alley, Portsea, from Slum Inspection Reports, PHC PMRS/DV/9B/1, n. 145 (1929).
[55] Portsmouth History Centre (PHC) Portsmouth, Slum Inspection Report on Primrose Alley, Portsea, PMRS/DV/9B/1, n. 145 (1929); 1851 census: HO107/1658, fols 310–11, pp. 53–4.

*Ajax* was at station off Queenstown until September 1852.[56] As for AB Samuel Davey, from June 1850 to January 1852 his Sheerness-based troopship *Resistance* had been plying between Gibraltar, Malta, Corfu and Halifax, Nova Scotia, and sailmaker George Plummer's wooden paddle vessel *Flamer* had departed Portsmouth in September 1850.[57] It was likely therefore that the household had for ten months consisted solely of (married) Elizabeth and (separated) sister-in-law Rosalinda, plus the Matthias, Davey, Leese and Plummer children, augmented by the intermittent presence of Portsmouth-based Joseph Davey, and visits by, if not the consistent presence of, 10-year-old Jane Elizabeth Matthias.

From 1840 to 1851, multiple allotments name Elizabeth Plummer, Elizabeth Davey and Rosalinda Matthias, no fewer than four shared addresses suggesting that their sibling-based household was a mobile, recurrent, sustained arrangement designed to operate flexibly while the men were away. George Plummer's presence in the spring of 1851 was not part of the plan. Two months after departing, in November 1850 *Flamer* had been wrecked off West Africa, its surviving crew rescued and conveyed to Portsmouth; which is why, five months after his September 1850 departure, George had reappeared. However welcome his survival and homecoming, as affinal relative and sole adult male his presence changed the household's structure, sleeping arrangements and power balances. How long the arrangement lasted is unknown, but by 1861 the family had scattered. Samuel Davey had married, was living with his wife in Portsmouth; Elizabeth and Joseph Davey and their four (later to be five) children had decamped to a Landport sublet; George and his motherless daughter were 170 miles away in Stoke Damerel, Devon.[58] For years, however, as sisters and sisters-in-law these seamen's women had constructed and maintained an arrangement which, despite intense overcrowding, saw them and their children through bereavement, estrangement and spousal absence.

Time and again this study finds seamen's women making decisions normally the province of their husbands. As Chapter Nine will show, one kind of decision, made by many a naval wife after her husband's departure, was to remove self and family to a different address. Whereas removals were a logistical exercise, quickly completed, in adopting the laterally-extended model of household structure seamen's women took risks with long-term family relationships, challenging social mores which frowned upon co-residence of unrelated or affinally-related adults of the

---

[56] ADM 53/4239-43.
[57] ADM 53/5357B, 5358-9; ADM 53/1874.
[58] 1861 census: RG09/642, fol. 105, p. 23; 1861 census: RG09/641, fol. 170, p. 33; 1861 census: Stoke Damerel, Devon, RG09/1451, fol. 4, p. 2.

opposite sex. Some will have adopted the arrangement out of necessity (for company, domestic help, protection or financial easement); for others it was emotionally enriching, preferable to alternatives such as taking in lodgers, or co-residence with non-relatives. It was, in short, a construct intended to aid survival. In other countries and cultures, following death of the paterfamilias, the laterally-extended arrangement was a means by which strongly-bonded brothers could maintain a joint household, their sisters playing a 'marginal' role.[59] Within the naval community it reflected a woman's centrality in determining the arrangement best meeting her family's needs. If she were not in a position to accommodate others in her own accommodation, she might hope or expect others to welcome her into theirs. She possessed, after all, that most welcome of things, the naval allotment. Her monthly receipts were attributes positive enough to tip the balance, persuading a reluctant household head to take in his or her naval kin.

Certain features may have made the laterally-extended household less alien, less dubious; some may even have been prerequisite. The protagonists may have agreed the arrangement was to be impermanent, a shared expectation being that it would, upon ships' returns, dissolve into something more conventional. Childcare may have been a factor (there were young children in three-quarters of all laterally-extended households found), together with a belief that two or more naval (as distinct from civilian) wives should ideally be party to the arrangement, thereby guaranteeing a shared understanding of the strains of husband-absence.[60] Such criteria may have made the structure more acceptable. But even in a port town, in a society familiar with naval custom and culture, it is debatable how far the laterally-extended household was deemed respectable, how far viewed as 'abhorrent or different', signalling poverty and the inability of a husband to provide for his own household; as another symptom of the naval community's otherness.[61]

---

[59] Robert Wheaton, 'Family and Kinship in Western Europe: the problem of the joint family household', *Journal of Interdisciplinary History*, 5:4 (1975), 601–28, at pp. 620–1.
[60] O'Day, *Family and Family Relationships*, p. 172.
[61] Wall, 'Economic Collaboration', p. 87; Walton, 'Social History', p. 52.

7

## HOME ENVIRONMENT

Descriptions of mid-nineteenth century urban housing refer to congestive street layouts and 'little worlds' of working-class dwellings evolved in cellular patterns around shared facilities.[1] The bulk of working-class housing in early Victorian years comprised conjoined narrow buildings (one-up, one-down, or two-up, two-down, arranged vertically as in Christianna Nancarrow's Hewlin's Court dwelling, some taller dwellings having a third floor); other common types consisted of diminutive blocks, or rows with a footprint commonly of no more than twelve square feet.[2] Subletting, infilling and enclosing small areas into courts, a form of housing common in past centuries, were tactics favoured by an entirely private housing market.[3]

Those 'little worlds' of courts and congestive street layouts were familiar to seamen's women living in port towns. Courts were worst where they backed on to one another, forming dead ends, backwaters, introspective places seized on by the criminal classes; later additions such as a canal, railway line or new street – all features of the Portsea Island built landscape – often had a tourniquet effect 'below which gangrene sets in'.[4] Originally created for removal of night soil, the sunless back alleys became private spaces for courts' residents, the locus for women's collective activities or the exchange of gossip about bargains, neighbours' needs, work opportunities – things

---

[1] H.J. Dyos, 'The Slums of Victorian London', in David Cannadine and David Reeder (eds), *Exploring the Urban Past: essays in urban history* (Cambridge, 1982), 129–53, at pp. 140–1; M.J. Daunton, 'Public Place and Private Space: the Victorian city and the working-class household', in Derek Fraser and Anthony Sutcliffe (eds), *The Pursuit of Urban History* (London, 1983), 212–33, at pp. 214–15.

[2] Thompson, *Rise of Respectable Society*, p. 183.

[3] Simon Gunn, 'Urbanization', in Chris Williams (ed.), *A Companion to Nineteenth-Century Britain* (Oxford, 2004), 238–52, at p. 252; Thompson, *Rise of Respectable Society*, p. 186.

[4] Thompson, *Rise of Respectable Society*, p. 186; Dyos, 'The Slums of Victorian London, p. 141.

*Home Environment*

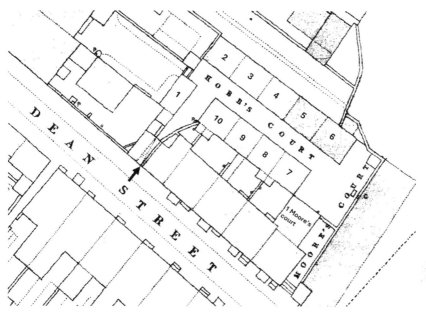

**Fig. 20** Hobbs Court, Portsea; covered alley entrance arrowed. Portsmouth History Centre (PHC), Portsmouth Ordnance Survey, 1:500 scale map of Portsea, showing Hobbs Court and Dean Street, PHC 114A/OS2/23, Hampshire Sheet LXXXIII.7.25 (C10) (1864). Detail; arrow and house numbers added. Reproduced, with these alterations, by kind permission of Portsmouth Library & Archive Service, Portsmouth City Council. All rights reserved.

which, for the urban poor, contributed to social and economic survival.[5] This haphazard development of odd, infilled dwellings, irregular in shape and size, runs counter to Muthesius's assertion that Portsmouth (by which he meant Portsea Island) was well organised in its town planning, its housing tending to be 'particularly regular'.[6] In Landport maybe, but not in the old townships.

Huddled between a barracks parade ground and the backyards of cul-de-sac Dean Street, Hobbs Court was typical of the many urban courts found in Portsea and Portsmouth. Accessed from Dean Street via an ungated, unlit covered alley scarcely a yard wide, its ten dwellings faced each other across a seven-foot-wide shared space, at the dead end of which

---

[5] Dyos, 'Slums of Victorian London', p. 140; Thompson, *Rise of Respectable Society*, p. 193; Ellen Ross, 'Survival Networks: women's neighbourhood sharing in London before World War I', *History Workshop*, 15:1 (Spring, 1983), 4–28, at pp. 9, 10, 17; Melanie Tebbutt, *Women's Talk?: a social history of "gossip" in working-class neighbourhoods, 1880–1960* (Aldershot, 1995), p. 75; Daunton, 'Public Place and Private Space', p. 222.

[6] Stefan Muthesius, *The English Terraced House* (Newhaven, 1982), pp. 19, 32.

lay one communal privy serving the needs of at least thirty-two residents.[7] None of the dwellings had rear access. In numbers 7–10, any rear-facing windows opened above the privies in Dean Street's backyards.

In the smallest Hobbs Court dwelling lived Amelia Lewis (*q.v.*), wife of Robert Lewis, HMS *Illustrious*, her four children, and a widowed charwoman 'lodger' named Elizabeth Flowers (Amelia's mother, *q.v.*), both women on parish relief. At the far end, a few feet from the privy, lived naval widow and pauper Elizabeth Ford, her daughter Mary Roberts (*q.v.*) who was the widow of seaman William Roberts, and Elizabeth's six-week-old grandson.[8] Across from them, at No. 7, lived 24-year-old Martha Bone (*q.v.*), wife of AB Eli Bone, HMS *Resolute*, and her 19-year-old half-brother 'lodger'. Like its covered alley entrance, the court was unlit, the nearest streetlight a wall-mounted gas lamp at the junction of Dean Street and Britain Street. Unless candle- or lamplight spilled through an uncurtained window, at night Hobbs Court's communal area would have been pitch dark.

Court living had positive and negative connotations. On the plus side, women deprived of their husbands' presence had immediate access to company, support and physical assistance from neighbours. Comforting though this was, the fact remained that infant mortality, deaths from tuberculosis and incidences of every category of disease were higher in courts and back-to-back housing.[9] Indeed, over one-third of our allottees were located in streets and courts named by the public health inspector as having epidemic, endemic, contagious disease present.[10] Other unwelcome attributes were noise levels, inadequate amenities and lack of security. It was bad enough that women had to share the use of the courtyard privy with male tenants unrelated to them, but via their wives or fellow males, these men could at least be prevailed upon to 'adjust their dress before leaving', to behave respectfully in the women's presence and not take advantage of the seaman's woman having no husband at home to protect her. Worse was the fact that, accessible from the street, courts' communal WCs were open to use by any passer-by. A female resident of any age could thus find herself

---

[7] Measurements calculated per PHC: 114A/OS2/23, Hampshire Sheet LXXXIII.7.25 (C10); 1851 census: HO107/ 1658, fol. 47, pp. 36–7.

[8] E&W Deaths: Alverstoke, Hampshire, Q3/1849, vol. 7, p. 26 (certificate).

[9] Wohl, *Endangered Lives*, p. 293; Robert Woods and John Woodward, 'Mortality, Poverty and the Environment', in Robert Woods and John Woodward (eds), *Urban Disease and Mortality in Nineteenth-Century England* (London, 1984), 19–36, at p. 25.

[10] Robert Rawlinson, *Report to the General Board of Health on a Preliminary Inquiry into the Sewerage, Drainage, and Supply of Water, and the Sanitary Condition of the Inhabitants of the Borough of Portsmouth in the County of Hampshire* (London, 1850), *passim*.

## Home Environment

Fig. 21  Havant Street, Portsea. Rogers, *Portsmouth & Southsea*, p. 32 (n.d.). Attempts to identify and locate the current copyright holder for this image have been unsuccessful.

face-to-face with a complete stranger exiting the privy with his fly unbuttoned or trousers at half-mast, or waiting for her to emerge, shaking out her skirts.

Lack of privacy was another issue. As noted earlier, next door to Martha Bone lived her brother-in-law and his wife. Through thin walls (a 1927 inspection of nearby housing found only sculleries and flues brick-built, everything else being lath and plaster, with rats occupying the partitions), every word Martha uttered was audible to her husband's kin.[11] And not just her in-laws: all the court's thirty-plus residents could overhear each other's business.

Overcrowding was something for which port towns were notorious. One hundred and thirty-five of our 1,581 allottees (8.5 per cent) lived in houses containing ten or more persons, their average occupation being thirteen persons per dwelling. These jam-packed houses were scattered across the island, most of them in Portsmouth and Portsea. The housing occupied by Portsmouth's subset of naval dependants included twenty-four large multi-occupancy dwellings, each containing an average of 16.4 persons; the same average was found in Portsea's equivalent which comprised no fewer than sixty-five large multi-occupancy dwellings.[12]

---

[11] Harwood, *Portrait of Portsea*, p. 16.
[12] The numbers of multi-occupancy houses and residents, and average occupancies per house, relate only to dwellings where the 1,581 allottees lived, and will vary from equivalent figures for *all* multi-occupancy housing in Portsea Island.

A closer examination of one Portsea street shows something of what high occupancy levels meant to naval families. We get an idea of Havant Street's houses from a description of Charles Dickens's childhood home in nearby Hawke Street as 'tiny ... without a front garden, on a squalid little street', and 'part of a terrace, having three floors and a basement'.[13] Havant Street's dwellings were much the same size and of a like design. In 1851 sixty-five of its seventy houses were inhabited, but occupancy levels varied considerably.

Where the 1851 census showed an average of 5.4 persons per house in England and Wales, Havant Street's 457 residents yielded an average of more than seven persons per occupied dwelling.[14] Thirty-seven of its seventy properties were undivided, variously accommodating between ten persons (a pub) and one. Undivided housing was less common than housing comprising discrete sublets. In houses of the size found in this street, the usual arrangement involved a couple of families occupying three to four rooms each, but it was not unknown for sublet tenants to rent out parts of their rooms, or for landlords to sublet a bed within a tenant's room (Dyos describes rooms' 'elastic shapes' changing with the addition of partitions and curtains) in return for threepence per night, water supply and amenities *non compris*.[15] Where properties were divided into ever smaller lettings, families faced having to split themselves between separate households, some older children going to live with a grandparent or aunt, little siblings remaining with parents.[16]

Twenty-nine allottees were scattered among twenty Havant Street houses. Naval mothers and sisters Mary Lee, Jemima Lang, Martha Symons, Ann Paul and their families occupied whole-house tenancies; the other twenty-five lived in properties subdivided into separate lettings.[17] Twenty of the street's twenty-seven sublet dwellings comprised two or three

---

[13] Claire Tomalin, *Charles Dickens: a life* (London, 2011), p. 8, quoting Gladys Storey, *Dickens and Daughter* (London, 1939), p. 40; Michael Allen, *Charles Dickens' Childhood* (Basingstoke, 1988), p. 22.

[14] Enid Gauldie, *Cruel Habitations: a history of working-class housing, 1780–1918* (London, 1974), p. 239 appendix 2.

[15] K. Theodore Hoppen, *The Mid-Victorian Generation, 1846–1886* (Oxford, 1998), p. 341; Jeremy Boulton, '"Turned into the street with my children destitute of everything": the payment of rent and the London poor, 1600–1850', in Joanne McEwan and Pamela Sharpe (eds), *Accommodating Poverty: the housing and living arrangements of the English poor, 1600–1850* (London, 2011), 25–49, at p. 34; Gauldie, *Cruel Habitations*, p. 159; Dyos, 'Slums of Victorian London', p. 152.

[16] Dyos, 'Slums of Victorian London', p. 152.

[17] ADM 27/111/249/88; 1851 census: HO107/1658, fol. 228, p. 7; ADM 27/112/335/213; 1851 census: HO107/1658, fol. 228, p. 7; ADM 27/110/541/1492; 1851 census: HO107/1658, fol. 232, p. 15; ADM 27/113/247/4; 1851 census: HO107/1658, fol. 233, p. 16.

tenancies; two properties comprised four sublets, two comprised five and one no fewer than six households, a veritable warren.

According to the census, the first of five sublets within No. 12 Havant Street contained allottee Mary Anne Bond, her husband Richard (captain's coxswain, HMS *Victory*) and two children, together with 16-year-old Jane Pooley, daughter of Charles Pooley, captain of the hold, HMY *Victoria and Albert*, and her 7-year-old brother, their allottee mother being listed as an unmarried nurse in nearby Sun Street.[18] Jane Wallbridge, wife of James Wallbridge, HMS *Contest*'s captain of the forecastle, occupied the third sub-tenancy together with her nine-month-old son.[19] In the fifth sublet, ordinary seaman John Burrough, HMS *Prince Regent*, was visiting a pilot and his wife; the whereabouts of his sister Esther, said in his declaration to be resident at this address, are unknown.[20] Twenty-one people inhabited the house, two sublets comprising two people each, one containing five, and two units holding six apiece. It bears repeating that the 1851 national average occupancy was 5.4 persons *per house*.[21]

Next door, fourteen people occupied six sublets. Among them, in separate tenancies, were allottees Ann Marshall and Elizabeth Goodger, respectively mother and wife of Benjamin and Richard, HMS *Excellent*.[22]

These women may have been attracted by their tenancies' cheapness and landlords' willingness to allow time to pay rent; but acceptance of poor conditions meant little incentive for exploitative landlords to make improvements, their cram-them-in tactics creating living conditions even worse than those found in institutions.[23] Nineteenth-century criminals were entitled to 1,000 cubic feet of space per person, healthy in-paupers 300 cubic feet, with 500 cubic feet per person allowed for the workhouse's sick.[24] The Army Sanitary Commission recommended not less than 600 cubic feet per man in barracks and guard rooms, an ambitious goal given that prevailing standards rarely achieved 450 cubic feet per man.[25] Where room sizes commonly measured eight feet by ten (per Gauldie's reckoning) with a ceiling height rarely more than seven-and-a-half feet (per

---

[18] ADM 27/112/152/7; ADM 27/113/59A/10; 1851 census: HO107/1658, fol. 227, p. 4; 1851 census: HO107/1658, fol. 43, p. 29; 1851 census: HO107/1658, fol. 43, p. 29 ('Jane Powley').
[19] ADM 27/120/64/101; 1851 census: HO107/1658, fol. 227, p. 4.
[20] ADM 27/113/279/252; 1851 census: HO107/1658, fol. 227, p. 5.
[21] Gauldie, *Cruel Habitations*, p. 239 appendix 2.
[22] ADM 27/111/60/1498; ADM 27/112/380/1709; 1851 census: HO107/1658, fol. 227, p. 5.
[23] Gauldie, *Cruel Habitations*, p. 154.
[24] *Ibid.*, p. 92.
[25] Skelley, *Victorian Army at Home*, p. 33; Edward M. Spiers, *The Army and Society, 1815–1914* (London, 1980), p. 56.

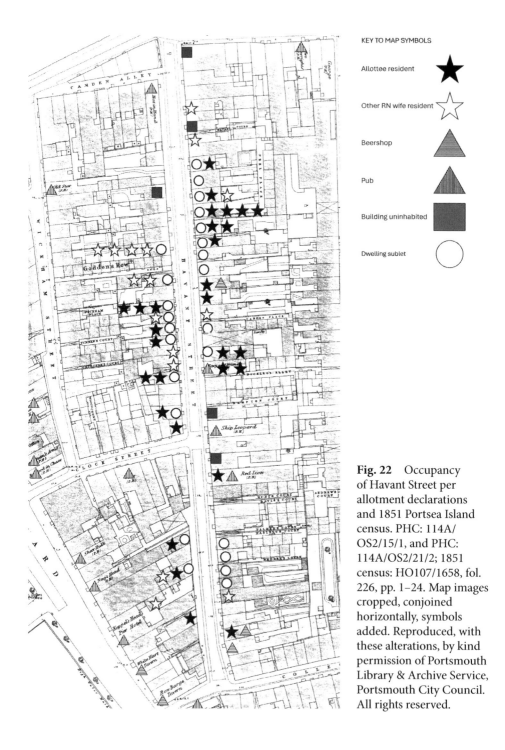

**Fig. 22** Occupancy of Havant Street per allotment declarations and 1851 Portsea Island census. PHC: 114A/OS2/15/1, and PHC: 114A/OS2/21/2; 1851 census: HO107/1658, fol. 226, pp. 1–24. Map images cropped, conjoined horizontally, symbols added. Reproduced, with these alterations, by kind permission of Portsmouth Library & Archive Service, Portsmouth City Council. All rights reserved.

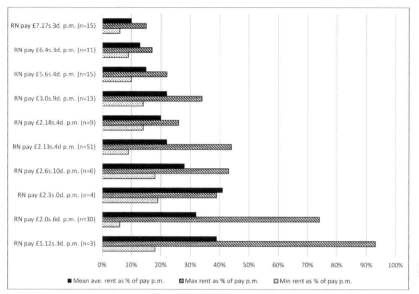

Fig. 23    Naval wives' monthly rent, as percentage of husbands' pay per *Navy List* 1851 (n=157). Allen, *Navy List* 1851, pp. 199–210 (selected text).

inspectors' measurements of some Portsmouth slums), and where the resultant 600-cubic-foot room might be occupied by a whole family, multi-occupancy houses such as these in Havant Street afforded less space per person than was allowed for criminals, paupers and soldiers.[26]

## HOUSING COSTS

A general principle held that rent as a household expenditure was inversely related to income: the lower the pay, the higher the proportion spent on accommodation.[27] To establish rent costs quoted in Portsea Island parish poor rate books (PRBs), a subset of 387 allottees was extracted from the main cohort. The 387 had two key characteristics in common: their monthly allotment income was known, and their names appeared in the PRBs for April 1851.[28] Completed quarterly, PRBs listed gross estimated rental (GER), parish rates and recoverable and non-recoverable arrears. Working class tenancies were usually weekly or monthly in nature, with rents collected weekly.[29] Naval allotments were disbursed on a monthly

[26]  Gauldie, *Cruel Habitations*, p. 93; PHC: PMRS/DV/9B/1, *passim*.
[27]  Richard Rodger, *Housing in Urban Britain 1780–1914* (Cambridge, 1995), p. 10.
[28]  PHC: DT/R/2/454-7.
[29]  Thompson, *Rise of Respectable Society*, pp. 169–70.

basis, so in order to allow comparisons the study divided GER figures for annual rent into notional calendar-monthly payments. Because PRBs' rent figures did not include additional charges levied by landlords (for example, for water supply or cesspit emptying), the results of the exercise are only broadly indicative. They nevertheless provide an overview of naval families' expenditure on accommodation.

From the PRBs it emerged that 88.5 per cent of our 387 allottees' weekly rents fell within the 1s 6d to 4s 8d range quoted by public health inspector Rawlinson.[30] How great a proportion of men's pay did such figures comprise? To enable pay and rent costs to be correlated, the sub-group of 387 allottees was modified to comprise only those 157 naval wives whose husbands' rates and pay scales were cited in the 1851 *Navy List*. Rent at this mid-century point accounted for 8 to 25 per cent of working income, the very poor spending up to 30 per cent or more on housing, almost 60 per cent by the end of the century.[31] The middle class spent proportionately less, considering it reasonable for rent to consume 10 per cent of earnings, anything more than 12.5 per cent being imprudent expenditure.[32] On the basis of these figures, it was expected that for our seamen's families a rent expenditure of 8 to 30 per cent would emerge. Aggregation of minimum and maximum rents for all seamen's pay bands revealed that rent for our naval wives' lettings accounted for 12 to 41 per cent of their husbands' pay, with a collective mean average of 24 per cent – figures spanning national averages. At 10 and 13 per cent of earnings, rent expenditure by allottee tenants in the top two (non-officer) naval pay bands chimed with those middle-class figures quoted by Thompson. In summary, when it came to the cost of accommodation, naval couples were no more or less thrifty or extravagant than the rest of the country. Their housing reflected local and national norms, nothing in the available evidence singularising their place within the built environment. Compared with their civilian neighbours they were no more overcrowded, no less inclined to inhabit streets previously ravaged by infectious disease, no more spared or subject to the effects of poor sanitation, substandard construction, crumbling building fabric and inadequate public health facilities. They spent no greater or smaller proportion of income on rent, and had broadly similar levels of poor rate debt.

[30] Rawlinson, *Report*, pp. 38–40.
[31] John Burnett, *A History of the Cost of Living* (Harmondsworth, 1969), p. 219; Rodger, *Housing*, p. 10; Boulton, '"Turned into the street"', pp. 33–4; Gauldie, *Cruel Habitations*, p. 157; Thompson, *Rise of Respectable Society*, p. 180; Dyos, 'Slums of Victorian London', p. 147; Wohl, *Endangered Lives*, p. 51.
[32] Thompson, *Rise of Respectable Society*, p. 172.

Unlike those civilian neighbours, however, naval couples faced economic challenges from two mutually conflicting and dependent conditions. The first was a form of monetary famine/glut whereby the pre-Continuous Service seaman remained unwaged from being paid off at the end of his ship's commission until being entered in another vessel's books; he was then paid much in arrears.[33] If he set aside enough paying-off money to cover several weeks of rent, and if he (re-)joined a ship promptly, declaring his allotment as soon as permitted, he might be able to keep a roof over his family's head; but if he dipped into that rent money, or were spendthrift, or robbed of his paying-off money on his way home, his tenancy would be jeopardised unless he earned some shoreside cash. The second economic challenge arose with his ship's departure, which triggered not famine/glut but slow monetary starvation. Before any ship could depart it must take on crew, establish internal order and take on stores for its commission – a process usually exceeding forty days.[34] On-board allotment declarations were not made until three months after departure, by which time more than four months had passed since men had taken leave of their dependants. After allotments were declared, there then followed the time taken for the completed register to reach Whitehall, and for each declaration to be processed per the routine described earlier. Only when disbursement at last took place would the recipient discover the sum on which she must thereafter subsist month to month until her man were home again; and unless her seaman were on discovery service, her allotment amounted to half his pay at best, in many instances less.

Given these challenges, and (as Chapter Eight explains) the relative underemployment of allottees, it is remarkable that naval dependants were not confined to the very poorest of alleys and courts or multi-occupancy buildings, or reduced to accommodating themselves in ways that placed them outside national patterns and norms, in greater numbers reduced to dependence on parish doles or in-relief. It is a finding to be borne in mind when considering economic survival strategies and the question of prostitution, aspects of naval women's life to be discussed in due course.

---

[33] Continuous Service would in due course maintain lower-deck income between ships' commissions.
[34] Preston, 'Constructing Communities', p. 44.

*8*

# WORK

The principle that it fell to husbands to serve as breadwinner was so embedded in Victorian culture, it is discernible in what Humphries describes as a 'slow retreat from the workforce' as women were ejected from the labour market in order to protect men's wages.[1] Given seamen's inadequate pay, and the capping of allotment monies, and the long history of poverty in the naval community, we might reasonably expect the census to show naval wives not retreating from but retaining their place in the labour market, supplementing their inadequate household income via paid work. Census officials' judgements were coloured, however, by a prevailing belief that married women had 'no occupation other than the care of their husbands and families', prompting them to ignore wives' describing themselves as waged workers in their household schedules, yet accepting self-descriptions which related them to their husbands' occupations.[2] Thus where the census might record a man's trade despite his being unemployed, many a waged, working woman was recorded as holding the 'trade' of housewife, or none at all.[3] Taking their editing role even further, in recording only those occupations held on census night some census officers ignored casual, seasonal, occasional or part-time labour, leading Higgs to conclude that '[the] treatment of women's work might depend to a considerable degree … on the outlooks and conventions

---

[1] Jane Humphries, 'Women and Paid Work', in June Purvis (ed.), *Women's History: Britain, 1850–1945: an introduction* (London, 1995), 85–105, at p. 90; Jane Humphries, *Tawney Lecture 2010: Childhood and Child Labour in the British Industrial Revolution* (2010) <https://ehs.org.uk/multimedia/tawney-lecture-2010-childhood-and-child-labour-in-the-british-industrial-revolution/> [accessed 10 April 2023].

[2] Humphries, 'Women and Paid Work', p. 91; Reibe, 'Public Perceptions of Sailors' Wives', pp. 16, 23.

[3] Sonya Rose, *Limited Livelihoods: gender and class in nineteenth-century England* (London, 1992), p. 80; Elizabeth Roberts, *Women's Work 1840–1940* (Basingstoke, 1988), p. 19; Mills *et al.*, 'Southern Historians and Victorian Censuses', p. 71.

employed by the enumerator'.[4] Such outlooks and conventions may explain why the 'rank, profession or occupation' columns of no less than 41.6 per cent of our naval wives aged twenty to fifty-nine, and 45.2 per cent of all female allottees, were blank.

The omission (or redaction) of occupational data skews evidence of women's efforts to keep family and home above the economic waterline. Parish guardians looked favourably upon applicants' waged employment, hence women anxious to qualify for poor relief often undertook casual work.[5] But naval women's efforts to obtain parish assistance are obscured not only by enumerators' under-recording of casual work, or any work at all, but by seamen's wives' describing themselves in relation to their husband's seagoing trade and rate, a habit clearly meeting with enumerator approval. The women's appearance as 'seaman's wife', 'stoker's wife', 'wife of gunner' or similar, should thus be viewed with caution, for such terms hide the true level of their waged employment.

Wives of male shopkeepers, publicans, butchers, farmers, shoemakers and certain others were 'supposed to take part immediately in their husband's business', hence the census instruction that they be described in relative terms per their husbands' trades, for example as 'shoemaker's wife'.[6] Terminology such as 'sailor's wife' was not required of Royal Navy sailors' wives, for they did not engage directly in their husbands' occupation.[7] Yet it was by their husbands' occupations that these shoreside women were often (self-)defined. The practice was widespread. Of 938 women aged twenty to fifty-nine and receiving allotments in the capacity of 'wife', 297 (31.7 per cent) appeared in the 1851 Portsea Island census with 'rank, profession or occupation' relative to their husband's work. This is more than three times the 9 per cent of married women aged twenty to fifty-nine who appeared in the National Sample with 'rank, profession or occupation' relating to their husband's principal economic activity.[8] And

---

[4] Humphries, 'Women and Paid Work', p. 91; Edward Higgs, 'Women, Occupations and Work in the Nineteenth-Century Censuses', *History Workshop Journal*, 23: 1 (1987), 59–80, at pp. 64, 68.
[5] Lincoln, *Naval Wives*, p. 148.
[6] Higgs, 'Women, Occupations, Work', p. 70; Roberts, *Women's Work*, p. 40 table 2:7; Humphries, 'Women and Paid Work', p. 91.
[7] Lincoln, 'Impact of Warfare', p. 86. Some wives who accompanied their husbands to sea in previous decades are known to have assisted ships' surgeons in battle. Their contributions are acknowledged, but do not represent the occupational efforts of the more numerous wives who did not go to sea.
[8] Michael Anderson, 'What can the mid-Victorian censuses tell us about variations in married women's employment?', *Local Population Studies*, 62 (1999), 9–30, at p. 11. The 9 per cent figure was distorted by enumeration inconsistencies. 'The National Sample is a systematic cluster transcript of one-fiftieth of the enumerators' books

whereas enumerators and census examiners edited certain self-descriptions (for example, by adding question marks, or scrawling through implausible terminology), they accepted self-descriptions such as 'Wife of Gunner RN'.

Why should so many wives describe themselves per their husbands' trades? If the habit were not urged upon them by enumerators, the most obvious explanation is that in 'seaman's wife', 'wife of gunner R.N.' or similar, we see how the women *wanted* to be perceived. Their asserting such 'occupations' tells us how they perceived themselves both as individuals and relative to their spouse, their community, their country. We may infer that they regarded being a seaman's wife as occupation in itself. We may also infer pride in their husbands' work and rate; a wish to associate themselves with patriotic service; identification with their man's rate or trade; an assertion of their 'seniority' relative to other naval wives; a childhood-ingrained belief (especially if expressed by naval daughters-turned-naval-wives) that they were part of a discrete community; and/or a way of giving definition and weight to an otherwise amorphous and low-status position in society. It appears not to have mattered that in describing themselves relative to their men's occupations they obscured their own waged labour and skills, and disobeyed the Registrar General's instruction that 'The occupations of women who are regularly employed from home, or at home, in any but domestic duties to be distinctly recorded'.[9]

Wives were not the only naval women to disobey the injunction. 'Rank, profession or occupation' entries left blank or referencing naval husbands' trades together comprise 68.8 per cent of census entries for all our female allottees – wives, mothers, sisters and trustees alike. If we include the forty-seven recorded neutrally in the 'occupation' column as visitors/lodgers, tradeless paupers and annuitants (individuals in receipt of an annuity), the proportion rises to 71.9 per cent, leaving just 28.1 per cent of female allottees declaring paid work in a recognisable trade.[10] After excluding females under eighteen years, and those whose ages are unclear or unknown, the proportion recorded as being in paid work emerges at 27.4 per cent, a figure little different from the 26.3 per cent of women designated at a national level in 1851 as 'occupied'.[11] When trustees, sisters and mothers are set aside, and naval wives alone considered, our 27.4 per cent of naval women

---

from the 1851 Census (except for institutions where every fiftieth family or person is sampled, and settlements with populations of less than 2,000 in England and Wales where one settlement in fifty is sampled).' *Ibid.*, p. 28 n. 12.

[9] RootsWeb, '1851 Census: Instructions for the completion of the Form' (Ancestry.com, 1997–2022) <https://sites.rootsweb.com/~pbtyc/1851_Census_Instr/1851_Census_Instr.html> [accessed 22 April 2024].

[10] Annuitant: one who receives an annuity, or fixed sum of money every year.

[11] Hoppen, *Mid-Victorian Generation*, p. 331; Humphries, 'Women and Paid Work', p. 93 table 4.1.

in paid work shrinks to 25.8 per cent. The difference appears negligible, but 25.8 is 6.3 per cent less than the 30 to 32.1 per cent of seafarers' wives whom Humphries selected for study as the mothers of working-class autobiographers, and whom she subsequently identified as participating in waged work; and 2.7 to 10.1 per cent less than the 28.5 to 35.9 per cent participation Humphries identified among autobiographers' mothers whose husbands were present.[12]

In short, presence or absence of a spouse affected wives' participation in work, Humphries finding that occupation levels among deserted wives outstripped those of wives whose husbands were present.[13] Naval husbands were absent for long periods, but they had not deserted their wives in the sense recognised by Humphries, nor had wives' domestic lives been dislocated by warfare, loss and grief in ways described by Lincoln.[14] Painful though it was, husband-absence was a normal part of naval seafaring, and seamen's wives are unlikely to have internalised it as spousal abandonment, which may explain why allottee-wives' 25.8 per cent participation in the workforce is less than half the 53.3 to 57.1 per cent participation rate of deserted or separated wives in Humphries' study. In all, on the basis of census data it appears these naval women were engaged in paid work to a lesser extent than deserted wives, seafarers' wives generally, soldiers' wives, and the married, unmarried and widowed female population nationally.[15] This is something of a paradox. 'The wives of soldiers and … some of the lowest-paid and least reliable male workers had to count more upon their own resources and exhibited relatively high participation rates,' observes Humphries; yet the participation of wives of poorly-paid, unreliably-paid Royal Navy sailor-breadwinners was markedly lower.[16] Their true participation rate was to an incalculable extent masked by their use of 'seaman's wife' and other self-descriptions. Compounding this is the possibility that seamen's women were particularly adroit participants in 'the economy of makeshift' discussed in later chapters, and/or that they had sources of income omitted from their census schedules.

***

[12] Humphries, *Childhood and Child Labour*, p. 105 table 4.5, p. 107. Since Humphries' figures for autobiographers are not age-related, allottee wives are included in this calculation irrespective of age.
[13] Ibid., pp. 107–8.
[14] Lincoln, 'Impact of Warfare', pp. 73–4.
[15] Humphries, *Childhood and Child Labour*, p. 107.
[16] Ibid., pp. 108–9.

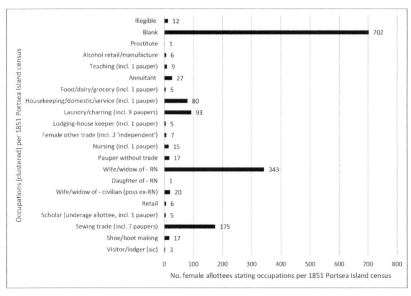

**Fig. 24** Occupations of female allottees, per 1851 Portsea Island census (n=1,549).

Lincoln describes eighteenth-century sailors' women as engaged in laundering, ballad-mongering and operating bumboats to supply ships near port; but the principal occupations for nineteenth-century Portsea Island women generally were stay-making, tailoring and dressmaking.[17] How far did these descriptions apply to seamen's women?

For coherence, in Fig. 24 allottees' occupations have been clustered. 'Alcohol', for example, encompasses both beer-shop keeper and licensed victualler. 'Education' includes schoolmistress and teacher of dancing. 'Miscellaneous' includes a painter, a sextoness [sic] and a blacking maker. In order of magnitude the largest groupings are the sewing trades and laundry, with charring and domestic labour close behind. This chapter considers what it meant for our allottees to be engaged in sewing and laundry, the two trades most often cited.

The average age of waged female allottees was 35.7 years.[18] Twenty-four were under twenty years old, all but one engaged in sewing, laundering or charring. The exception was Mary Ann Parnell, the 19-year-old Quebec-born 'painter/master' [sic] wife of carpenter's mate John Parnell, HMS

---

[17] Lincoln, *Naval Wives*, p. 147; J.L. Field, 'The Bourgeoisie of Portsmouth' (University of Warwick, unpublished PhD thesis, 1979), p. 76.

[18] Excluding scholars, paupers without trades, and women whose occupations were unrecorded, illegible or related solely to their husbands' occupation.

*Work*

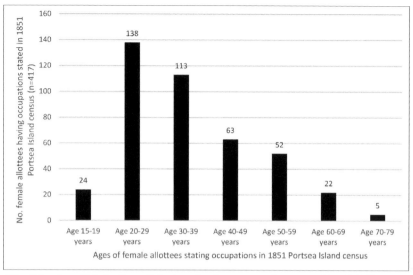

**Fig. 25** Age-distribution of allottees having occupations stated in 1851 Portsea Island census (n=417).

*Vengeance*.[19] Humphries quotes 34.5 per cent of the country's female population aged twenty to sixty-four years as being occupied in 1851.[20] Of our 1,425 female allottees known to be within those age brackets only 26.8 per cent were employed. The 7.7 per cent difference between this figure and Humphries' 34.5 per cent may be the product of one or more factors: of inconsistent enumerator practice; of naval women's regarding (and enumerators' approving) their 'occupation' as relative to their spouses; of their being disinclined (or denied the opportunity) to declare waged work in which they were not specifically engaged on census day. It is conceivable that, being in receipt of a monthly allotment income, the women had less need to take on paid work; however, given the economic constraints explored in Chapter Nine, only recipients of the most generous allotments might be in this happy position.

Hobbled by lack of evidence of women's wages in the mid-century decades, and by regional wage variations associated with surplus workforce or local demand for goods, exploration of naval women's earnings yields only provisional conclusions.[21] Different analysts quote different figures. Burnett has the mid-century semi-skilled worker earning fifteen shillings to one

---

[19] ADM 27/112/145/98; 1851 census: HO107/1657, fol. 7, p. 6.
[20] Humphries, 'Women and Paid Work', p. 93 table 4.1.
[21] E.H. Hunt, *Regional Wage Variations in Britain, 1850–1914* (Oxford, 1973), p. 114.

pound per week.[22] Benson suggests that in 1850 the normal weekly income of the average full-time worker (sex unspecified) was fourteen shillings, thirteen of which were from waged work and one from self-employment.[23] The 'self-employment' element was particularly significant for women who, in paid work or not, were adept at creating income by other means than formal employment, and in other forms than cash.[24] Commonly regarded as supplementary to male householders' earnings, female wages were pitched by employers at levels insufficient to support a whole family – a serious issue for wives whose seagoing husbands were engaged in high-risk work, or for naval widows who in most instances received no service pension.[25] In short, without supplementation via informal trading in services, goods and/or kind, few seamen's women could have maintained themselves and their dependants solely on their own earnings.

## THE SEWING TRADES

Of female allottees declaring waged work, more than a third (34.8 per cent) were engaged in sewing jobs of some kind, of which there were 2,800 in 1851 Portsea Island.[26] Here, 'sewing' includes allottee milliners, bonnet makers, needlewomen, stay-workers, shirtmakers, tailoresses and seam-stresses, one of the latter specifying that she was 'sempstress, dockyard', perhaps hinting at a position in the colour loft.[27] Harriet Aylward, wife of sailmaker George, HMS *Lily*, was, per her census entry, forewoman of a corset factory; a local trade directory lists her mother-in-law Charlotte Aylward as a stay-maker, and it is not impossible that Harriet was employed in Charlotte's Lion Gate manufactory, a short walk from Harriet's Voller Street address.[28] Sarah Jane Foreman, sister of William Hopkins, captain

---

[22] Burnett, *History of the Cost of Living*, p. 263.
[23] John Benson, *The Working Class in Britain, 1850–1939* (London, 2003), p. 53 table 5.
[24] Humphries, 'Women and Paid Work', p. 85; Mills *et al.*, 'Southern Historians and Victorian Censuses', p. 72.
[25] August, *Poor Women's Lives*, p. 68; Perkin, *Women and Marriage*, p. 164; Humphries, 'Women and Paid Work', p. 88; James H. Treble, *Urban Poverty in Britain, 1830–1914* (London, 1979), p. 23.
[26] Stapleton and Thomas, *Portsmouth Region*, p. 114. As they could not be assumed to be in receipt of earnings, the seven pauper-seamstress allottees were omitted from these calculations.
[27] Chatham Historic Dockyard, 'What Was the Sail and Colour Loft?' (Chatham Historic Dockyard Trust, 2019) <https://thedockyard.co.uk/news/what-was-the-sail-and-colour-loft/> [accessed 22 April 2024]
[28] ADM 27/110/110/13; 1851 census: HO107/1659, fol. 414, p. 13; PHC: CHU2/1C/13, p. 78 n. 155; 1851 census: HO107/1659, fol. 348, p. 15; Hunt, *Directory*, p. 77.

of the afterguard, HMS *Hecate*, was a maker of artificial flowers.[29] Dressmakers comprised nearly 68 per cent of our sewing-trade group, a figure likely to be distorted because the term 'dressmaker' had wider connotations, as Chapter Ten explains.

Dressmaking and millinery required long apprenticeships, hence our backstreet dress- and bonnet-makers were unlikely to be indentured.[30] Tailoring was dominated by men, and high class tailoring work was rare in Portsmouth, so it is heartening to find six tailoresses among our sewing trade allottees.[31] Less heartening is the fact that 'tailoress' was no female equivalent of the well-paid male artisan: women tailors were lower paid than their male peers, being restricted to the less important tasks such as oversewing of seams.[32] In Portsmouth they were primarily engaged by gentlemen's outfitters to do the gold lacework for officers' bespoke uniforms.[33]

Pre-Continuous Service sailors had to equip themselves with clothing at their own expense. Royal Navy ships being many, their crews often several hundred strong, there was a huge demand for shirts. One wholesale shirt-maker described the home-based shirt-making process as 'One stitches, another puts together, a third puts the buttons on and makes the holes; so they come into our hands and out again several times before they are finished.'[34] Outstripping shirt-making and other clothing manufacture, however, was the making of corsets, the trade for which Portsmouth was famous, it being 'an activity … more concentrated in Portsmouth than in any other town in Britain.'[35] By the start of the nineteenth century it was already 'a significant occupation' which for thirty years was carried out largely in domestic premises.[36] By 1841 it accounted for 4.5 per cent of the Portsea Island manufacturing population, the number of workers being fourteen times larger than the proportion of corset-makers in the total industrial population of England and Wales.[37] A decade later, the trade employed (or contracted via outwork) more than 500 individuals comprising 6.5 per cent

---

[29] ADM 27/111/357/40; 1851 census: HO107/1659, fol. 73, p. 15.
[30] Roberts, *Women's Work*, p. 39.
[31] *Ibid.*; Field, 'Bourgeoisie of Portsmouth', p. 76.
[32] Bartley, *Prostitution*, p. 7; Roberts, *Women's Work*, p. 39.
[33] Field, 'Bourgeoisie of Portsmouth', p. 81.
[34] *Ibid.*, p. 83.
[35] R.C. Riley, 'The Portsmouth Corset Industry in the Nineteenth Century', in John Webb, Nigel Yates, and Sarah Peacock (eds), *Hampshire Studies* (Portsmouth, 1981), 241–64, at p. 241.
[36] *Ibid.*, pp. 242, 244.
[37] *Ibid.*, p. 244.

of the island's industrial workers.[38] Mid-century trade directories list stay- and corset-manufacturers, proprietors of factories and workshops, their few numbers evidence of the trade's reliance on the 'putting out' system.[39] Here appears a trio of stay-makers in Queen Street, there a couple more in North Street, numerous others in Landport.[40] A high proportion of corset makers were naval wives and daughters. In the *Port of Portsmouth Chamber of Commerce Journal* for 1847, using the language of the day, a patronising Lasseter muses:

> There must be some reason for the Portsmouth corsets ... the n----- in the woodpile was the sailor's wife. See her in the 'good old days', lonely, in a little home in a mean street, her man gone 'foreign', her allowance by a grateful country barely enough to keep body and soul together, her children ragged and ill-fed – and she can, if she will, get all lit-up on three-penn'orth of gin. Here she is with her thousand sisters – cheap labour ripe for exploitation ... Observe, then, the beached women of the Service men, with so much energy, no means, and pitifully eager to better a miserable lot.[41]

Rather than seamen's mothers, trustees or sisters, most of our thirty-eight allottee stay-makers were wives. With an average of just over twenty-seven years they ranged in age from eighteen to forty five. Twenty of them lived in relatives' households or as lodgers, so unless they had their householders' permission to undertake outwork (with all this entailed by way of fuel and candle usage, and bulk materials taking up limited domestic space), they worked in one of the island's stay factories. Thirteen stay-makers headed their own households, able to work whatever hours they chose and bring home whatever materials they needed. In the early nineteenth century, to carry on a trade within the home had been considered respectable; by the 1850s it was regarded as sweated labour, but canny manufacturers exploited the view that home-based work did not contravene women's 'separate sphere', regardless of its impact on homeworkers' health, domestic space, peace and comfort.[42] These notions enabled manufacturers to disguise and distract attention from the fact that outwork pay was wretched, far lower than factory pay.[43] Productivity expectations were punishing, working

---

[38] *Ibid.*, p. 245.
[39] *Ibid.*, p. 246.
[40] Hunt, *Directory*, pp. 77, 114.
[41] Lasseter, 'Portsmouth Corset Industry', p. 23.
[42] Perkin, *Women and Marriage*, p. 137; Lucia Zedner, *Women, Crime, and Custody in Victorian England* (Oxford, 1994), p. 66.
[43] R.C. Riley, *The Industries of Portsmouth in the Nineteenth Century* (Portsmouth, 1976), p. 15.

hours long and earnings varied by place and manufacturer. In 1880s London a full-time clothing trade employee would still only bring in an average of eleven shillings per week.[44] Receiving sixpence, eightpence or tenpence per waistcoat at an average of three shillings per week, none of the fifty-one needlewomen Mayhew interviewed earned more than five shillings a week, some less than two.[45] Portsmouth outworkers worked ten to twelve hours daily, longer in summer months.[46] On Portsmouth's lower wages, with children to mind and houses to keep, our stay-maker-allottees would have struggled to achieve a gross income similar to that achieved elsewhere, especially if, like Anne Oddy (*q.v.*), wife of gun room steward Charles, HMS *Contest*, their allotment were a scant ten shillings per month, leaving a big difference to make up via earnings.[47] Ann Coles had it easier: wife of gunner's mate William, following *Resolute*'s departure to the Arctic she saw her allotment double to £2 8s 0d per month.[48] Despite her generous receipts, however, she maintained her occupation: no stay-maker could afford to reduce her workload lest the factory discard her as unproductive.

## LAUNDERING

The ease, flexibility and lack of upfront expense with which the laundry trade could be taken up may explain why, among our naval women, the washing of others' soiled garments and bedlinen came second only to the sewing trades. Conducted on an occasional basis as the need for extra cash arose, laundering could be carried out in a domestic setting, using easily-acquired equipment.[49] 'To take in washing' was a practical approach to adversity and a well-known way of supplementing out-relief; but doing other people's dirty laundry was not something every working woman wanted to admit to, and for that reason alone the number of laundresses listed in the census is likely to under-represent the actuality.[50] Like charring, it was traditionally a married woman's occupation.[51] This is reflected among our ninety-three laundresses and chars, more than two-thirds of whom were married.

---

[44] Field, 'Bourgeoisie of Portsmouth', p. 421; August, *Poor Women's Lives*, p. 96.
[45] Roberts, *Women's Work*, p. 40; Treble, *Urban Poverty*, p. 32.
[46] Jean Stanford and A. Temple Patterson, *The Condition of the Children of the Poor in mid-Victorian Portsmouth* (Portsmouth, 1974), p. 14.
[47] ADM 27/109/476/58.
[48] ADM 27/110/253/65.
[49] Patricia E. Malcolmson, *English Laundresses: a social history, 1850–1930* (Urbana, 1986), pp. xiii, 11–12.
[50] Ibid., p. 12; Kidd, *State, Society and the Poor*, p. 38; Rose, *Limited Livelihoods*, p. 78.
[51] Malcolmson, *English Laundresses*, pp. xiii, 7, 16.

With so many women taking in washing, and with customers hiring for one day at a time, laundresses had little chance of securing a run of three or more days' work.[52] At best, their gross earnings might range from £1 4s 0d to £1 8s 0d per month for a six-day week in the employer's home where costs of fuel, water, food and meal preparation were met, to £3 12s 0d to £4 4s 0d per month for full-time ironing at home, the cost of fuel, water and food being borne by the laundress. Our washerwomen's earnings supplemented allotments of very different sizes. The smallest allotments received by laundress-wives were the meagre twelve shillings declared by three Royal Marine privates to Ann Owen, Ann Trask and Elizabeth Betteridge – two shillings more per month than stay-maker Anne Oddy's receipts.[53] At the other end of the scale, two sailor-sons of 67-year-old widowed laundress Sarah Wheeler allotted her a total of £2 10s 0d per month, while gunner James Steward, HMS *Excellent*, allowed £1 18s 0d to his laundress wife Helena.[54] In theory, when combined with earnings these amounts would make for a monthly income of £1 16s 0d to £6 2s 0d. Whether allottees ever saw such sums is unknown.

Competition came not only from other laundresses but in the form of commercial laundries able to undertake larger loads, and complete the process more quickly and reliably than was possible at a domestic level.[55] Military establishments had their own wash houses, so army wives accommodated in Portsea Island's Anglesey, Cambridge and Colewort Barracks had access to barrack facilities for their laundering.[56] But non-resident naval dependants, and working laundresses in particular, were unlikely to have been allowed access to barrack facilities. As trade publication *The Builder* made clear, public wash houses would not become available locally until the mid-1870s.[57] Until these facilities were made available, the allottee-laundress therefore had to manage with the equipment and domestic space she had.[58] Within small, poorly-ventilated working-class dwellings it took days to complete the full process of soaking, boiling, blueing, dollying, wringing,

---

[52] Treble, *Urban Poverty*, p. 43.
[53] ADM 27/109/476/58; ADM 27/112/324/77; ADM 27/113/291/100; ADM 27/112/156/15.
[54] ADM 27/111/121/17; ADM 27/111/399/14; 1851 census: HO107/1658, fol. 233, p. 17.
[55] Alan King, *The Portsmouth Encyclopaedia: a history of places and people in Portsmouth, with an index to streets* (Portsmouth, 2011) <https://www.portsmouth.gov.uk/ext/documents-external/lib-portsmouthencyclopaedia-2011.pdf> [accessed 22 April 2024], p. 195.
[56] *Ibid.* pp. 12, 23–8, 127, 230, 232, 253, 286.
[57] *The Builder* (Wyman and Sons, London, 1853–1966).
[58] Unknown reporter, 'New Baths, Washhouses, and Laundry for Portsmouth', *The Builder*, 17 October 1874, p. 865, col. 1.

mangling, drying, ironing, airing and folding.[59] Physical strength was essential. To boil and rinse one load required nigh-on fifty gallons of water; and fifty gallons weighed 500lbs.[60] From communal tap or courtyard pump, water had to be lugged indoors and upstairs, the dirty sluicings carried back to the outdoor drain. It was a trade better suited to the young and vigorous, but the average age of our allottee-laundresses was forty, a third of them being that age or older. Grandmother of AB William Henry, HMS *Fox*, our oldest laundress was 72-year-old Sarah Savell, for whom Light's observation that 'at the bottom of the heap were elderly washerwomen' has particular resonance.[61] The younger the laundress, the stronger she might be; but the less likely she was to have children old enough to help her, whether by minding younger siblings while their mother laundered, or assisting with her heavy labour. Thirty-one of our married and unmarried laundresses had children of ten years or younger, too young to help with the heavier tasks, or to be left unsupervised while water boiled and smoothing-irons heated on stovetops. Almost one-fifth of our laundresses had a co-resident sister, mother or daughter in the same trade, one a laundress neighbour in an adjoining sublet. Others will have formed partnerships with friends, neighbours and fellow naval women to pool effort, borrow or lend equipment, and provide company while undertaking this physically demanding, physically debilitating, domestically disruptive work.

*\*\*\**

Seamen's long absences, low pay, 'erratic loyalties' and greater than usual risk of disablement and death were powerful incentives to their wives' developing independent sources of income.[62] Intermittently or regularly, as need compelled or seasons changed, many a naval wife contributed to the household economy.[63] Some ran their own enterprises, acquiring licences to keep beer-shops or sell alcohol. Some had education and talent enough to teach, as witness the schoolmistress, the teacher of dancing. There was artistic skill (the painter), and religious commitment (the sextoness), while the blacking maker was one of many prepared to get her hands dirty in order to earn. Missing, however, are the bakers, haberdashers, pawnbrokers, linen drapers, rag-pickers, confectioners, bookbinders, midwives, ladies' maids, hawkers and entertainers which, with other job titles, appear

---

[59] Malcolmson, *English Laundresses*, pp. xiii, 26.
[60] Ibid., p. 26.
[61] ADM 27/111/270/70; 1851 census: HO107/1657, fol. 231, p. 34; Light, *Common People*, p. 197.
[62] Hunt, 'Women and the Fiscal-imperial State', p. 31.
[63] Anderson, 'Mid-Victorian censuses', p. 25.

in the census alongside names of women not featured in this study. This absence is understandable: in requiring employees to clock in on time, open up a shop, be on stage when the curtain went up, run Madam's bath or lace her corset, fulfil customers' orders per quantity and deadline, or hasten to assist at a sudden onset of labour, such occupations did not easily accommodate lone parent responsibilities, or workers' absences necessitated by domestic problems. There being no shortage of women willing and available to replace unreliable employees, employers could afford to be unsympathetic and inflexible. Rigid terms – strict timekeeping, or availability expected during unsocial hours and/or at short notice – were unattractive to naval wives managing single-handed while their husbands were at sea. Earnings from self-employed sewing, laundering and charring were lower and less reliable, the working hours longer, but in these humble trades there was more choice and self-determination than could be had from a martinet employer unsympathetic to naval women's circumstances.

Some of those aforementioned bakers, haberdashers, pawnbrokers and other female workers found in the census may have been allottees whose husbands' declarations fell outside the study period, or naval wives who in completing their census returns chose not to identify themselves as such. If so, the range of waged work undertaken by naval women was wider than admitted by our allottees, who for the most part sewed or mended, laundered clothing and bedlinen, and cleaned. Theirs were ill-paid trades, benefiting the people who wore the clothes our seamen's women sewed, who soiled the linen they scrubbed and rinsed and ironed, who spilled crumbs and tramped mud across the tiles they swabbed. After their day's labour, and unhelped by seafaring husband, son or brother, weary naval women undertook the same work again for their own families, for themselves.

# 9

# MAKING ENDS MEET

Was the allotment enough to keep body and soul together? Beginning with an overview of the naval pay system on which seamen's women depended, this chapter compares income with outgoings, and considers economic survival strategies – pawning, borrowing, credit, debt, flitting from rent arrears, the taking in and living as lodgers – deployed by working-class people to make ends meet. The chapter's chief concern, however, is what these strategies implied for women whose men were habitually absent, and whose economic security was pegged to their moiety-capped allotment income, pegged in turn to seamen's pay.

Most allotments constituted between 49 and 52 per cent of men's monthly earnings, any minor variations being the result of administrative rounding-up or -down to avoid halfpenny and farthing sums. There was variation, however, in what men of different ships allotted. Consider HM Ships *Assistance* and *Resolute*. Despatched to the Arctic to search for the missing Franklin expedition, they shared the same mission, faced the same perilous and hostile environment. Within the study period four Portsea Island-related allotments were declared from *Assistance*, six from *Resolute*, all of them reflecting the double pay awarded by virtue of the ships being on discovery service; but whereas the average allotment by *Resolute*'s sailors was £1 18s 0d per month, at £2 4s 0d *Assistance*'s average was a hefty six shillings larger. The sum each man allotted may bespeak his nature (generous, mean, reckless, cautious), his relative financial security, his family size, the state of his marriage, his trust in his wife's ability to manage the domestic economy; but men were also influenced by on-board peer pressure and mess deck consensus. Earlier chapters have associated August's 'neighbourhood norms and customs' with shipmates' vouching for each other, or sharing views on acceptable household structures.[1] Generating intense loyalty and conventionality, these all-male communities had their own traditions and

---

[1] August, *Poor Women's Lives*, pp. 124–5.

codes of practice, generating in turn a self-belief and assurance which in the context of the wider naval family may be understood as capable of overriding individual moral codes or private commitments.[2] Each deck and mess thus had norms and customs capable of influencing the proportion of pay its members reserved for themselves and awarded their allottees.[3] The Navy did not require men to justify the amounts they chose to allot, but an individual seaman's resolve to allot the permitted maximum was vulnerable to pressure from his less generously-inclined shipboard peers. The reverse might equally apply, messmates urging the miserly husband to allot more, or shaming him into doing so.

Finite as these on-board communities were (each ended in paying-off upon completion of a commission), they engendered a strong sense of identity which varied from deck to deck, trade to trade.[4] Individual and collective norms reflected prevailing beliefs concerning men's determination of female-managed budgets, as witness Mrs Bosanquet's late nineteenth-century specification of 'the right amount of money a husband should give his wife', to which was added the warning 'she is to accept it without further enquiring as to actual earnings'.[5] The wifely subordination implicit in this remark is given added weight by Davidoff's conclusion that many husbands 'felt entitled to gratitude' for not spending their earnings on themselves, and D'Cruze's perception that men were often unaware of their wives' budget management skills – an ignorance surely afflicting the naval husband not at home to observe how his wife made ends meet, or incurious as to her methods.[6]

The capping of allotments meant the balance of a man's pay remained his own – a significant point, given that top-slicing (defined by Humphries as breadwinners' practice of keeping the first cut of wages for themselves) was one of the chief contributors to nineteenth-century male wage inadequacy.[7] Male wage inadequacy necessitated paid work by wives and children to make up the shortfall that had disappeared into the breadwinner's pocket, thereby reinforcing some parish guardians' belief that the primary duty of the working-class mother was to take paid work to support herself and her

---

[2] Walton, 'Social History', p. 349.
[3] Ann Coats, 'Foreword', in Helen Watt and Anne Hawkins (eds), *Letters of Seamen in the Wars with France, 1793–1815* (Woodbridge, 2016), x–xii, at p. xi; Hunt, 'Women and the Fiscal-imperial State', p. 39.
[4] Walton, 'Social History', pp. 136–8.
[5] August, *Poor Women's Lives*, p. 124; Helen Dendy Bosanquet, *Rich and Poor* (London, 1896), p. 88.
[6] Leonore Davidoff, *The Family Story: blood, contract and intimacy, 1830–1960* (London, 1999), p. 153; D'Cruze, 'Women and The Family', p. 62.
[7] Humphries, *Childhood and Child Labour*, p. 125.

family – a dogma not applied to middle-class mothers for whom the ideal role was that of homemaker.[8] In the naval community the moiety cap did the top-slicing, limiting the amount of money a seaman could allot. Beneficial as the allotment system was, it is arguable that naval family budgets were more severely top-sliced than those of most civilian households.

Those double-pay allotments declared from discovery ships *Assistance* and *Resolute* were not the largest in this study. Forty-eight warrant officers (first- and second-class gunners, carpenters and boatswains) each allotted monthly sums of more than three pounds, two second engineers over four pounds. Meanwhile, in the same pay bracket there were other second-class gunners, carpenters and boatswains who allotted little more than £2 6s 0d monthly. When the smallest sums allotted are set against the monthly wages of those fifty-two trades and rates whose pay grades feature in the *Navy List*, fourteen allotments individually comprise less than 40 per cent of the respective sailors' wages. If this seems meagre, consider the allotment James Johns declared in 1850. As gunner first class, HMS *Conflict*, Johns was receiving sea pay, a combination of factors making him one of the top earners in this cohort, yet the thirteen shillings per month he allotted to his wife Ann (a sum unchanged since 1843) amounted to just 8 per cent of his monthly wage.[9] In January 1851, Richard Kemp, carpenter first class, HMS *Victory*, on the same pay scale as Johns but without sea pay, awarded his wife Ann £3 18s 0d per month, a sum equivalent to 24 per cent of his wages.[10] Over the years the amount Ann actually received had fluctuated. As carpenter, HMS *Southampton*, in August 1830 Kemp had made a declaration which took an earlier allotment from £2 6s 8d to £2 19s 0d, a sum dropping to £2 6s 0d in his 1838 declaration as carpenter second class, *San Josef*.[11] As carpenter first class, in January 1841 he awarded Ann £3 3s 0d per month, a seventeen-shilling boost.[12] In February 1844, from HMS *Camperdown*, he awarded her £3 15s 0d per month, allotting £3 3s 0d (again) from *Wellington* in July 1848, and £3 18s 0d only upon Ann's removing from Plymouth to Portsmouth in 1849 following his joining *Victory*.[13] As her monthly receipts rose and fell, so Ann's domestic economy eased and tightened.

For women queuing at dockyard pay office, rural land tax office or harbour customs house, the proportion of pay allotted was of less significance than the

---

[8] Ibid.; Pat Thane, 'Women and the Poor Law in Victorian and Edwardian England', *History Workshop*, 6:1 (1978), 29–51, at p. 37.
[9] ADM 27/109/250/1; ADM 27/82/177/10.
[10] ADM 27/112/152/2.
[11] ADM 27/22/143/18; ADM 27/60/183/60.
[12] ADM 27/72/282/60.
[13] ADM 27/86/42/3; ADM 27/104/142/3; ADM 27/106/94/4.

amount actually received. Of 387 declarations detailing the sums awarded, the mean average sum was just £1 6s 6d per calendar month, equivalent to 6s 2d per week.[14] Seventeen per cent of the 387 allottees received this monthly average, twenty-one per cent a larger sum, but nearly two-thirds received smaller amounts. Four women (Matilda Backster, sister of Francis Henning, captain's cook; Mary Ann Allen, wife of Thomas Allen, gun room steward; and Elizabeth Fawkes, wife of Joseph Fawkes, sub-officers' steward, all three men serving in HMS *Sphinx*; and Anne Oddy (*q.v.*), wife of gun room steward Charles, HMS *Contest*) took home less than 38 per cent *of that £1 6s 6d monthly mean*, their ten shilling sums the most meagre receipts of all.[15] That three of the four men were of the same ship, three of them stewards and all four in domestic roles resonates with August's argument about 'neighbourhood norms and customs' influencing the amount of money a husband provided his wife.[16] At best modest, at worst miserable, their sums could not be enlarged by their allottees' securing a raise from the pay office; nor, if money ran out, could the next month's payment be released earlier than its due date. This had implications for even the thriftiest of wives. If she were not to resort to measures described in Chapter Ten, the seaman's wife must make her money last.

What did the allotment have to cover? Common to naval and civilian household economies alike were shelter, water, fuel and food. Only for a limited time could a household cut back on these necessities, anything more than brief reductions putting health and welfare at risk.

## WATER

Whether charged by the jugful or bucket, water commonly accounted for threepence per week of a working-class family's income.[17] At a halfpenny for two bucketsful (about four gallons), Portsea's water was cheaper than the penny-a-bucket quoted by Wohl, but it was still too costly for liberal use.[18] Too sparing a usage, however, meant grubbiness; and for a woman,

---

[14] Calculated as £1.6s.6d. x 12 ÷ 52, which yields a slightly smaller figure than the 31-day notional month tabulated in *Navy List* pay scales. Per 11 Geo. IV & 1 Will. IV, c. 20 (1830), allotments were declared on the first of the calendar month, and paid on the first of the following month. To align and compare pay and allotment receipts, in all subsequent analyses men's pay is calculated as 1/12 of the yearly rate quoted in Allen, *Navy List* 1851.

[15] ADM 27/110/310/3; ADM 27/110/311/26; ADM 27/110/314/56; ADM 27/109/476/58.

[16] August, *Poor Women's Lives*, pp. 124–5.

[17] Gauldie, *Cruel Habitations*, p. 75; Wohl, *Endangered Lives*, p. 62.

[18] Rawlinson, *Report*, pp. 23, 35, 52.

grubbiness – of face, neck, hands, hair, apron, collar, cuffs or other clothing – suggested slatternliness, if not immorality, sending the wrong message to prospective employers, and convincing outsiders that those prepared to appear in such a state must be irredeemably unrespectable.[19] These interpretations applied to all women, but they had particular significance for seamen's women. As allottees, they had to impress parish worthies whose imprimatur was required to confirm their identity, and whose judgements of a woman's character could result in her allotment being stopped. And were naval women to come before a court, not only would they be identified by their husbands' occupation (see Chapter Eleven), their character would be further judged by their appearance, thus affecting verdict and sentencing.

Visible cleanliness was one thing, health another. The risk of disease increased when poor families moved from one letting to another, for those going habitually unwashed could carry typhus and infect others in successive residences.[20] To economise on water was to jeopardise more than sanitary conditions and health. It also affected appearance, employability, continuing eligibility for the allotment, and ultimately one's respectability. Those halfpennies or pennies per bucket were core items in the household budget.

## HEATING AND LIGHTING

Open fires consuming coal in enormous quantities, fuel was a major expenditure. Our town-dwelling allottees could not gather wood to cook their food or heat their living space, so fuel had to be bought, for cash. Estimates vary as to the proportion of household budget spent on coal, kindling, candles and lamp oil. According to Burnett, in 1855 half a hundredweight of coal cost 2s 10d, equivalent to 7.7 per cent of a cutler's family's weekly expenditure of £1 16s 9d.[21] Wohl suggests fuel costs of a shilling a week, or up to one-third the cost of rent for a one-room tenancy.[22] Feinstein's calculations put fuel at 4 per cent of the weekly expenditure in years 1858–62, equivalent to 30.8 per cent of the amount allocated to rent; when to this is added the 1 per cent expenditure he allocates for lighting, the resultant 5 per cent total equates

---

[19] Zedner, *Women, Crime*, pp. 54–5.
[20] R.J. Morris and Richard Rodger, *The Victorian City: a reader in British urban history, 1820–1914* (London, 1993), pp. 214, 223; August, *Poor Women's Lives*, p. 70.
[21] Burnett, *History of the Cost of Living*, pp. 218, 263–4; John Burnett, *Plenty and Want: a Social History of Diet in England from 1815 to the Present Day* (London, 1966), p. 192.
[22] Wohl, *Endangered Lives*, p. 47.

to 38.5 per cent of rent expenditure, a higher proportion than Wohl's.[23] These figures show the inadequacy of that average monthly allotment of £1 6s 6d, with its notional weekly income of 6s 2d, of which a fuel expenditure of 5.3 to 7.7 per cent (per Burnett's analysis) would consume between four and six pence per week, one-third to a half of Wohl's suggested shilling.[24] For the lone allottee, four to six pence a week might be too small a sum on which to heat a room, boil kettles for tea, cook one-pan meals. A large family required more space, consumed even more fuel.

## FOOD AND DRINK

Food for Burnett's cutler family cost one pound per week, equivalent to 54.4 per cent of income.[25] A similar proportion (52.3 per cent) was found by Booth who noted a family's apportioning 13s 5d to food out of a weekly income of 25s 2d.[26] Feinstein pitches it higher, estimating food costs as accounting for 61 per cent of weekly expenditure.[27] At these levels we should estimate 3s 2½d to 3s 11d of that notional average 6s 2d per week allotment income being devoted to food. In all likelihood even more was expended, for the smaller the family income, the proportionately greater the food expenditure. Burnett's married couple's food, for example, accounted for 74 per cent of budget, equivalent to 4s 6½d of our notional 6s 2d per week.[28] This was bad enough, but substandard home conditions, as suffered by many in port towns' old districts, put up food costs even further. Lack of a larder or other cold storage meant perishables went off quickly; and where upper-floor sublets had a fireplace at all, it was at best an open grate with tiny hob, unsuited for anything but the smallest saucepan. Food therefore had to be bought ready-cooked or in small quantities, local shops making a comfortable mark-up selling goods that would have been cheaper bought in bulk.[29]

---

[23] Charles H. Feinstein, 'Pessimism Perpetuated: real wages and standard of living in Britain during and after the Industrial Revolution', *Journal of Economic History*, 58:3 (1998), 625–58, at p. 635 table 1.

[24] Mean average calculated from the subset of 387 individuals whose allotment rates are known.

[25] Burnett, *Plenty and Want*, p. 192.

[26] August, *Poor Women's Lives*, p. 66.

[27] Feinstein, 'Pessimism Perpetuated', p. 635 table 1.

[28] Malcolmson, *English Laundresses*, p. 7; Burnett, *History of the Cost of Living*, pp. 263–4.

[29] Gauldie, *Cruel Habitations*, p. 93; Peter Wood, *Poverty and the Workhouse in Victorian Britain* (Stroud, 1991), p. 15.

*Making Ends Meet*

Given the poor quality of water drawn from communal pumps, and the cost per bucketful levied by landlords, locally-brewed beer was a safer and cheaper option. To wash down what they ate, Burnett's married couple spent 1s 2d on seven pints of porter at 2d a pint, equivalent to 7.8 per cent of weekly income.[30] Feinstein estimates working-class outgoings on drink (he refers to beer) accounted for 12 per cent of total expenditure in 1858–62.[31] Twelve per cent was a modest amount: elsewhere, many working-class families spent between one-sixth and half their income on drink.[32] Tea was the woman's choice, but it came at cost: that 1s 2d expenditure on porter was fourpence less than the amount Burnett's couple spent on three ounces of tea and a pound of sugar; and boiling a kettle meant additional fuel consumption.[33] For allottees on an average weekly budget of 6s 2d, once food, rent and fuel had been covered and an amount set aside towards poor rate collections, it may be wondered how they had money left for tea, let alone anything stronger.

## BALANCING THE BOOKS

Was it possible to manage on the allotment alone? Table 4 compares income and essential expenditure for an individual receiving the notional average amount of £1 6s 6d per calendar month. Added to figures quoted above for water, fuel, food and drink are mean average weekly rents and poor rates, as extracted from the Portsea Island poor rate book (PRB) for April 1851.[34] Booth calculated that an income of eighteen to twenty-one shillings *per week* was necessary for a 'moderate' family to be considered poor or very poor.[35] Without income from waged work or other sources, allottees receiving payments of between ten shillings (the smallest receipt) to £1 6s 6d (the average receipt) *per calendar month* simply could not make ends meet. Here and elsewhere naval families were facing poverty.[36]

---

[30] Burnett, *History of the Cost of Living*, p. 263.
[31] Feinstein, 'Pessimism Perpetuated', pp. 633, 635 table I, 636, 642.
[32] Treble, *Urban Poverty*, p. 23; Burnett, *Plenty and Want*, p. 199; Hoppen, *Mid-Victorian Generation*, p. 355.
[33] Burnett, *History of the Cost of Living*, p. 263.
[34] PHC: DT/R/2/454-7.
[35] Hoppen, *Mid-Victorian Generation*, p. 61 (italics added).
[36] Hardwicke, *Report*, p. 267 ss. 5041, 5128–31.

**Table 4** Notional weekly budget for £1 6s 6d average monthly allotment.

| Income | Notional weekly allotment |
|---|---|
| Mean average allotment of £1 6s 6d per month | £0 6s 2d |
| **Outgoings** | **Estimated cost per week** |
| Water | £0 0s 3d |
| Fuel @ 6.5% of weekly income | £0 0s 5d |
| Food @ 54.4% of weekly income | £0 3s 4d |
| Porter/gin/tea/beer | £0 2s 0d |
| Rent – min. paid | £0 1s 2d |
| Rent A – mean average for allottees per PRB | £0 3s 3½d |
| Rent B – mean average for 88.5% of allottees per PRB* | £0 2s 10½d |
| Rent – max. paid | £0 12s 11d |
| Poor rates – min. paid | £0 0s 2d |
| Poor rates – mean average per PRB | £0 0s 5½d |
| Poor rates – max. paid | £0 1s 10½d |
| **Total weekly outgoings at Rent A** | **£0 9s 9d** |
| **Total weekly outgoings at Rent B** | **£0 9s 4d** |
| **Deficit** | |
| **Weekly budget deficit at Rent A** | **£0 3s 7d** |
| **Weekly budget deficit at Rent B** | **£0 3s 2d** |
| **Equivalent deficit per month, subject to rent level** | **£0 13s 8d to £0 15s 6d** |

*Note: 'Mean average rents' comprise (Rent A) the average for those allottees found in the PRB, and (Rent B) for the 88.5 per cent of them whose rents fell within the range quoted by public health inspector Rawlinson.

These are estimates. Some landlords charged more than threepence per week for water; some grates burned more fuel than others; some winters were colder; some rents were higher than average; and allotments were disbursed monthly, not weekly. Nevertheless, an allottee seeking to break even would require not the monthly average of £1 6s 6d, but £2 0s 2d to £2 2s 0d per month. This equates to one third as much again – more, were she a laundress needing quantities of water for washing, and coal to heat the water. Less than 10 per cent of allotments are known to have amounted to £2 0s 2d per month or more, most of them being time-limited because the men's ships were on discovery service, the men only temporarily on double pay. Were their next ships deployed on less hazardous sea service, both pay and allotments would revert to the usual, lower levels. In summary, as sole income the allotment was inadequate. Without additional income many allottees must have lived not just in fear of debt, but in a continual state of debt.

## DEBT TO THE PARISH

Every household was required to pay poor rates, and evidence of debt to the parish survives in poor rate books (PRBs). In many instances landlords, not tenants, paid parish rates; nevertheless, rate books reveal what some allottee-tenants owed. The following analysis draws on 339 PRB records relating to more than one-fifth of our 1,581 individuals. The 339 ratepayers met two criteria: their names appear in a Portsea Island PRB for 1851, and their allotting sailors' pay scales are known.

The poor rate book for April 1851 revealed exactly one-third of these allottee households (113 of the 339) owed money to the parish in the form of 'recoverable debts'; that is, their arrears from previous quarters' rate-days were considered by the collector (or promised by the debtor) to be payable together with the current quarter's rates due on the April 1851 collection day. Father of six children aged two to fourteen years, AB James Stallard was one such debtor. From HMS *Victory* in January 1851 he declared an allotment of one pound per month to his wife Elizabeth, a sum 6s 6d below the cohort's mean monthly average.[37] His rate arrears of 1s 4½d were the smallest owed by our debtors, but financial straits are signalled by the sum's being carried-over from the previous collection, and by nothing being paid on the April 1851 collection day.[38] The largest amount was owed by naval pensioner William Lee.[39] Lee paid the eleven shillings due for April 1851, but his 'recoverable' arrears of £1 10s 0d, carried over from the previous quarter, remained outstanding. In addition to husband William's naval pension, 59-year-old Elizabeth Lee's household budget included an allotment of one pound per month from son AB William Black, HMS *Excellent*.[40] William was at home on census day, as was Elizabeth's other naval son, engineer Henry Lee.[41] Had both sons awarded allotments the household would have had three income streams, all from naval sources; but whereas William was supporting his mother, there is no record of Henry's declaring in her favour. William was now at home, which may mean his ship had finished its commission, his allotment ended. If so, this may explain why the household

[37] ADM 27/112/158/15.
[38] 1851 census: HO107/1657, fol. 227, p. 27; PHC: DT/R/2/454-7, vol. 457, pp. 54, 62–4.
[39] *Ibid.*, vol. 456, pp. 74–6.
[40] ADM 27/102/106/393; ADM 27/113/84/1620.
[41] 1851 census: HO107/1659, fol. 81, p. 31.

had slid into arrears, for other than her husband's pension Elizabeth now had no regular source of income.

On the April 1851 collection day these 113 naval debtors owed a total of £27 6s 6d in recoverable arrears. All but four debtors were women, most of them seamen's wives rather than mothers, sisters or trustees. The combination of pre-existing arrears and new rates due that day raised the average debt owed by these 113 individuals to 9s 8d per person. The total actually paid was under two-thirds of the collective sum owed. Thirty-five of the 113 cleared their debts and paid the current amounts due; fifty-one had recoverable arrears averaging 7s 8d per head; twenty-seven owed non-recoverable sums averaging three shillings per head, five of them paying nothing off their arrears, and nothing towards April's rates. That the smaller sums were deemed non-recoverable suggests chronic financial problems from which no respite was envisaged.

Leah Goodfellow was one paying nothing off existing arrears and nothing towards April's rates. Amounting to 45 per cent of his pay, the allotment declared in October 1850 by her husband John (captain of the hold, HMS *Dragon*) was £1 4s 0d per month, a half-crown less than the notional average of £1 6s 6d.[42] From May 1850 Leah had been receiving an additional, unspecified sum from gunner's mate Thomas Smith, HMS *Excellent*, as trustee for 11-year-old John Smith.[43] The census shows her as 'pensioner's wife'. A red-inked note in *Dragon*'s muster book confirms John Goodfellow's pensioner status, he having been DSQ'd in 1844, joining *Plumper* five years later, *Dragon* in 1850.[44] Now he was at sea again, allotting again, and family income on shore was limited primarily to Leah's monthly receipts. It is of note that her PRB entry was one of three bearing the legend 'Abs.', meaning 'absent on collection day' – a common avoidance tactic.[45]

Worse-off than Leah was Elizabeth Lath. In April 1851 her husband William was at home, having four weeks earlier joined *Britannia* following his discharge from HMS *Powerful* five days previously.[46] He would eventually be paid, but pending that, or the disbursement of his allotment, the household's only source of income was a stayworker-daughter's wage. Of their poor rate arrears, 2s 3d was deemed recoverable, 1s 10½d

---

[42] ADM 27/111/245/5.
[43] ADM 27/110/364/142; 1851 census: HO107/1659, fol. 423, p. 30; PHC: DT/R/2/454-7, vol. 455, pp. 10–11; John Smith was neither located in Leah's household, nor found elsewhere. It is assumed, but not proven, that John was the elder brother of James Smith, entrusted to Mary Baskerville (see pp. 64, 267).
[44] ADM 38/7983/5; ADM 29/30/80–82.
[45] I am grateful to Dr John Stedman of Portsmouth History Centre for his clarification of PRB codings.
[46] 1851 census: HO107/1657, fol. 289, p. 36; ADM 38/2700/274.

irrecoverable.[47] Where Leah Goodfellow's entry was annotated 'Abs.', the letter 'V' was marked against the Laths' names. This signalled that their debt was to be voided (written off), an option where there was no prospect of settlement. Eviction for non-payment of arrears was the business of landlords, not rate-collectors, and distraint of debtors' goods, work tools or furniture would only create greater financial distress, might even necessitate in-relief via the workhouse, a far more expensive outcome for the parish. When it came to rate arrears, voiding a debt was the most pragmatic measure, to be applied only *in extremis*, and at the parish's discretion, not the debtor's request.

The irrecoverable arrears owed by these seamen's wives, mothers, sisters and grandmother ranged from eleven shillings to just sixpence. Half the sums amounted to less than one shilling per individual. None of the debtors was particularly shabbily maintained, for taken together their allotments yield an average of 48.4 per cent of each man's monthly wage – very nearly the maximum 'half-pay' allowed. Among the full cohort of 1,581 allottees, which included non-debtors, the average allotment of £1 6s 6d equated to 45.6 per cent of pay, so these women were on average receiving a fractionally larger portion of their men's wages than their non-debtor peers; but that is to cavil, for in cash terms the differences were minimal, mere pennies. Only seventy-nine (23.3 per cent of 339 ratepayers) made no payment whatsoever, a proportion not far above the 20 per cent of all rates going uncollected in Portsmouth.[48] The naval community was in difficulties with its poor rates, but to no significantly greater extent than the community as a whole.

## BORROWING AND CREDIT

Indebtedness to the parish was one way to juggle a budget, but when cash was needed the quickest solution was to borrow, a measure to which women often resorted. For some, however, to live thriftily within one's means was respectable, to borrow anathema.[49] When an RMA pensioner committed suicide, his widow was left with 'four helpless children quite destitute'; she was said to have struggled for years to gain an honest living by charring, being 'obliged ... to go without a dinner rather than run in debt'.[50] Borrowing from known and trusted individuals was easier and cheaper than extracting

---

[47] ADM 27/113/380/274; PHC: DT/R/2/454-7, vol. 457, p. 80.
[48] Elizabeth Edwards, 'The Poor of Portsmouth and their Relief, 1820–1850' (Portsmouth Polytechnic, unpublished dissertation, Diploma in English Local History, 1977), p. 36.
[49] Zedner, *Women, Crime*, p. 65.
[50] *H/Tel*, 19 June 1852, p. 5 col. E.

money from agencies. On the understanding that money would be repaid and goods safely returned, family, friends, even landladies charged no interest when extending what support, cash or material aid they could; but little is known about what was obtained through such networks.[51] Sometimes aid was substituted for coin. Mothers provided childcare in exchange for a share of a working daughter's wages; kin contributed commodities on the understanding that the recipient would help in turn when resources permitted.[52] Women loaned their mangles at cost to a neighbour so that she might make some small nett profit via laundering; daughters paid struggling mothers' rents; and 'small amounts of money ... were passed back and forth between households ... even on these cash-poor streets, women could launch collections toward such major expenses as funerals.'[53] In hiding the true extent of their borrowing, naval wives would have been no different from their civilian neighbours, for women's management of the family budget – drawing on 'a thriving subculture of credit activities' – was often achieved without their husbands' knowledge, direction or interference.[54] If that were true of poor women generally, it was especially true of naval women whose husbands were not present to direct, interfere or prohibit.

To have a network of kin, neighbours, shopkeepers and others willing to extend credit was essential.[55] This was a particular concern for the immigrant naval wife without local contacts, but messmates' wives and families often welcomed and helped the incomer, where practicable offering temporary accommodation, recommending trustworthy landlords and traders, and providing directions through unfamiliar streets. They might even, pending her first allotment via an unfamiliar pay office, help to secure credit on her behalf, their introductions and endorsements going some way to establish the incomer's identity and reputation. It was important for a poor woman to be known locally, to develop or tap into support networks, but in doing so she entered a 'widespread web of indebtedness' from which

---

[51] Fury, 'Seamen's Wives and Widows', p. 261; Hurl-Eamon, 'Fiction of Female Dependence', pp. 491–2; Leonore Davidoff, 'Mastered for Life: servant and wife in Victorian and Edwardian England', *Journal of Social History*, 7:4 (1974), 406–28, at p. 419.

[52] Wall, 'Economic Collaboration', p. 93; Humphries, *Childhood and Child Labour*, pp. 165–6; Anderson, 'Study of Family Structure', p. 50; Shani D'Cruze, *Crimes of Outrage: sex, violence and Victorian working women* (London, 1998), p. 47.

[53] Malcolmson, *English Laundresses*, pp. 19, xiii; Ross, 'Survival Networks', p. 6.

[54] Perkin, *Women and Marriage*, p. 153; Ross, *Love and Toil*, pp. 76, 78; Melanie Tebbutt, *Making Ends Meet: pawnbroking and working-class credit* (Leicester, 1983), p. 38.

[55] David R. Green and Alan G. Parton, 'Slums and Slum Life in Victorian England', in S. Martin Gaskell (ed.), *Slums* (Leicester, 1990), 17–91, at p. 32; Chinn, *They Worked all their Lives*, p. 65; D'Cruze, *Crimes of Outrage*, p. 48.

it was perilous to abscond – something to give pause to the tenant tempted to flee in lieu of settling rent arrears.[56]

Credit from commercial sources was costly. A ten-shilling loan racked up threepence per week in interest, so a month's debt for the naval dependant on an average allotment of £1 6s 6d per month would cost almost 4 per cent of income.[57] Whatever the going interest rate, the naval wife seeking credit faced a challenge, for just as traders regarded as uncreditworthy the deserted wife with no means, so the allottee on 'half-pay' (or less) might be deemed a bad risk. But in some lenders' eyes a regular monthly income was enough to justify a loan.[58] 'Regular' was the key word. The regular earner was a preferred customer, and once an allotment had come into effect the naval pay office was regular in its disbursements.

In extending credit, at interest, to low-income allottees, commercial lenders were forerunners to twenty-first-century payday loan sharks; and like twenty-first-century debtors, allottees borrowing from such sources would soon find themselves struggling to make repayments, and thereby avoid the bailiff.

## PAWNING

The pawning of goods was so common a debt-avoidance tactic, pawnshops were 'an urban institution ranking with the public house'.[59] Hunt's Directory for 1852 lists eleven pawnbrokers in Portsea township alone, their presence a clear sign of local need.[60]

The 1800 Pawnbrokers Act fixed the interest rate at 20 per cent on advances of less than two guineas, 15 per cent on anything in excess.[61] Until 1872, when regulation reduced loan-periods to a maximum of one year and a day, the longest period that goods could be pawned was fifteen months.[62] For naval families these time-limits had good and bad aspects, one advantage being that wives could pawn goods to the maximum, repeatedly,

---

[56] Green and Parton, 'Slums and Slum Life', p. 32; D'Cruze, *Crimes of Outrage*, p. 48; Fury, 'Seamen's Wives and Widows', p. 262.
[57] Tebbutt, *Making Ends Meet*, pp. 14–15.
[58] Alannah Tomkins, 'Pawnbroking and the Survival Strategies of the Urban Poor in 1770s York', in Alannah Tomkins and Steven King (eds), *The Poor in England, 1700–1850* (Manchester, 2003), 166–98, at p. 183.
[59] H.J. Dyos and Michael Wolff, *The Victorian City: Images and Realities* (London, 1973), vol. 1, plate 143; Tebbutt, *Making Ends Meet*, p. 22.
[60] Hunt, *Directory*, p. 112.
[61] Hoppen, *Mid-Victorian Generation*, p. 343; *Pawnbrokers Act*, 39 & 40 Geo. III, c. 99 (1800).
[62] Tebbutt, *Making Ends Meet*, p. 8.

during their husbands' absence. Women pledged handkerchiefs, bedding, tools, furniture, mangles, irons, blankets, aprons and gowns, some items being borrowed from other women with the express purpose of pawning.[63] The pawning of jewellery both raised cash and provided security from theft, but even among the very poor, whose lack of possessions cruelly reduced their ability to raise cash on a temporary basis, putting a wedding ring into hock was a desperate measure.[64] Desperation is evidenced, then, in a Landport mission's speaking of local women '[pawning] their wedding-rings each week, redeeming them on payday, pawning them again the next day.'[65] Given the number of seamen's women with no waged work, many will have used pawnbrokers as a source of cash between their monthly allotment days; and since they could choose for themselves which items to pawn, it is likely too that naval wives were among those using their wedding rings as collateral, without incurring husbandly wrath. If so, this was one aspect of seamen's absence which made budget management easier, though the emotional toll of pawning a ring always weighed heavy.

## FLITTING

Fleeing without paying rent arrears, or abruptly removing over short distances to secure cheaper accommodation, were features of working-class life.[66] Removals were easy for those whose few possessions were small enough to be bundled into a shawl or pushed on a handcart from street to street. But when many proprietors owned multiple dwellings in different districts, escape from an assiduous rent collector was not easy. Flitting might yet be worthwhile, however. When there was nothing left to pawn, when neighbourhood lending had reached its limits, a new location opened up fresh sources of credit from unsuspecting shops or lenders.[67]

Repeated removals were common. Between censuses, most working-class families occupied several houses in succession, but there is a dearth of

[63] Ibid., pp. 7, 13; Simon Fowler, *The Workhouse: the people, the places, the life behind doors* (Barnsley, South Yorkshire, 2014), p. 40; Tomkins, 'Pawnbroking', p. 181; Ross, 'Survival Networks', p. 6.
[64] Tebbutt, *Making Ends Meet*, p. 26; Gauldie, *Cruel Habitations*, p. 98.
[65] Roger Bryant, *Don't Touch the Holy Joe: Father Dolling's Battle for Landport and St. Agatha's Church* (Hampshire, 1995), p. 11.
[66] Thompson, *Rise of Respectable Society*, pp. 171–2; Green and Parton, 'Slums and Slum Life', p. 31; Hoppen, *Mid-Victorian Generation*, p. 339; Dyos and Wolff, *Victorian City*, p. 145; Dyos, 'Slums of Victorian London', p. 147; R.J. Dennis, 'Intercensal Mobility in a Victorian City', *Transactions of the Institute of British Geographers*, 2:3 (1977), 349–63, at p. 350; Davidoff, *Family Story*, p. 114; Boulton, '"Turned into the street"', p. 30.
[67] Perkin, *Women and Marriage*, p. 176; Dyos, 'Slums of Victorian London', p. 145.

material showing addresses occupied between successive enumerations.[68] Naval allotment records provide rare and valuable evidence of working-class mobility in years between censuses, adding documentary weight to the oral history evidence of Chinn *et al*.[69] They reveal, for example, that in the period January 1850 – July 1852, of 1,568 allottees whose data allow tracking of residential addresses, two-thirds were found not to have moved at all, or to have moved mere yards.[70] They were located either at the address given in the allotment register, or within the same street but (purportedly) at a differently-numbered house.[71] Seamen's carelessness with dates and numbers means that where we see successive allotment declarations citing different house numbers in the same street, we cannot be certain whether this indicates a house move or a misquoted number. Erring on the side of caution, same-street removals unconfirmed by census or other evidence are here counted as 'no change'.

If two-thirds of those 1,568 allottees were found not to have moved, or moved only a few doors along, the remaining one-third comprised those removing to different streets within the same district, or to different districts entirely. Some moved right across the island, others but yards from their former homes. Two-thirds having moved just a few doors away or not at all suggests a community at odds with the 'intrinsically itinerant' image of the sailor.[72] Evidence of mobility, however, is indisputable when multiple declarations name the same allottee(s). Twenty-one women had three addresses each. Nine of them had relocated between allotment declaration and subsequent census (a maximum of fifteen months), and were at a different address again according to allotments declared no more than fifteen months post-census. In fourteen instances prior to March 1851, two different addresses were declared by sailor-husbands, the enumerator later finding their wives at another address entirely. Eleven women appear to have returned to previously-cited locations. Elizabeth Davey, first met in

---

[68] Dennis, 'Intercensal Mobility', p. 351.
[69] Chinn, *They Worked all their Lives*, pp. 23, 25.
[70] 'Residential' excludes allottees whose seamen cited HM Ships in lieu of domestic addresses. Twenty allottees (1.3 per cent of 1,581) with allotment addresses either unrecognisable or per HM ships were set aside. Ships' addresses suggest either that the wives were living on board (a rare arrangement by this period), or that the citing of an HMS address was a means of initiating an allotment pending confirmation of a fixed address on shore.
[71] Higgs, *Census Revisited*, p. 62. 'Purportedly' because, as noted earlier, Portsea Island districts had differing house-numbering systems: WEA, *Queen Street*, p. 9; WEA, *Portsea*, p. 4.
[72] Davidoff, *Family Story*, p. 117.

Chapter Six, lived at four addresses within fourteen months.[73] As Chapter Two noted, 32-year-old Ellen Lumb, wife of gunner George, HMS *Excellent*, was according to his July 1850 declaration living with her parents in Victoria Terrace; four months later, his declaration from *Arrogant* placed her in Cumberland Street; a month later, another declaration (again from *Excellent*) revived the Victoria Terrace address, which was where, in March 1851, the census found her.[74] It is possible that Ellen had not moved at all, that she had simply, with George's knowledge, been visiting some Cumberland Street friends; then again, the Cumberland Street address may have been Ellen's short-lived attempt to establish herself independent of her parents. Whatever the explanation, in returning to their home she enjoyed a degree of economic easing, and (re)gained the social benefit of her parents' company.

Bartley's assertion that husbands had the right to decide when and how to live is belied by evidence that seamen's wives exercised choice of residence.[75] Resonating with this evidence are Moring and Wall's discerning that women saved money by renting smaller or cheaper flats in less desirable locations, and Chinn's placing the decision-making firmly in the hands of the wife.[76] D'Cruze goes further, concluding that wives' control of the budget meant they often decided where to live and when to remove, to the extent that a husband might come home from work to discover his family had moved house during the day, leaving neighbours to tell him where they had gone.[77] Given how long it took for mail to reach ships at sea, many a returning sailor will have been in exactly that position. Unaware of his family's having removed to a new address, he would find his home occupied by strangers, his wife and children gone; and unless he had been discharged and paid off, during limited leave he had little time in which to track them down.[78]

The evidence so far does not indicate an unduly high level of local mobility on the part of allottees, nor should it be assumed that allottee mobility was a function of poverty alone. Economic prudence played a part, certainly, but other things could tip the balance in favour of a move. A woman's social and emotional wellbeing, for example, might require that she live within easy reach of mother, grandmother or other member of her

---

[73] ADM 27/110/20/27; ADM 27/111/353/112; ADM 27/112/159/13; 1851 census: HO107/1658, fol. 311, p. 54.
[74] ADM 27/112/100/320; ADM 27/110/493/320; ADM 27/112/353/5; 1851 census: HO107/1659, fol. 727, p. 13.
[75] Paula Bartley, *The Changing Role of Women, 1815–1914* (London, 1996), p. 11.
[76] Moring and Wall, *Widows*, p. 65; Chinn, *They Worked all their Lives*, p. 23.
[77] D'Cruze, 'Women and The Family', p. 63.
[78] Holman, *Life in the Royal Navy*, pp. 109–10; Kemp, *British Sailor*, p. 205.

matrilocal survival network.[79] She might want to move closer to something or someone (an ailing parent, a sister and her newborn, a place of work, the dockyard pay office), or distance herself from something or someone (the abusive husband whom she had fled; the unwanted attentions of a rent collector or male neighbour; the fellow-tenant gossip curious as to the company she kept). Some moves were prompted by nothing more than a longing for home and family. When captain of the hold William Barrett, HMS *Phaeton*, declared an allotment to his wife Hannah in March 1850, he gave her address as Chapel Row, Portsea; a rare survival found within *Phaeton*'s register, her allotment voucher shows the Portsea address crossed out, and 'Middleton Street, Queenstown, Cork' superscribed.[80] Hannah had gone back to Ireland, Cove of Cork being where she and William had married.[81]

## LODGERS AND LANDLADIES

One of the simplest ways of reducing the cost of living was to lodge in another's household, enjoying bed, board and other domestic facilities without the formalities and complications of a tenancy; and one of the easiest ways to make money was to admit lodgers into one's domestic space. So popular a practice was lodging, particularly in cities, almost one in eight households nationally had lodgers, and many of those whom the census described as relative or 'visitor' would have been paying for their keep.[82] The taking-in of lodgers was a standard survival strategy for female-headed households, and in port towns 'even the smallest room could do as lodging for … sailors until their departure'.[83] But regardless of a property's size, facilities or condition, its being shared by multiple households signalled

---

[79] Chinn, *They Worked all their Lives*, pp. 23–9.
[80] ADM 27/109/543/309, pay bill no. 50436.
[81] Ireland Marriages 1619–1898: William Barrett to Hannah Whelton, 2 April 1846, Cove by Cloyne, Cork.
[82] Chesney, *Victorian Underworld*, p. 112; O'Day, *Family and Family Relationships*, p. 247; Anderson, 'Mid-Victorian censuses', p. 21; Anderson, 'Households, Families and Individuals', p. 428; Anderson, *Family Structure*, p. 46; W.A. Armstrong, 'A Note on the Household Structure of mid-Nineteenth Century York in Comparative Perspective', in Peter Laslett and Richard Wall (eds), *Household and Family in Past Time: comparative studies in the size and structure of the domestic group over the last three centuries* (Cambridge, 1972), 205–14, at p. 212; W.A. Armstrong, 'The Interpretation of the Census Enumerators' Books for Victorian Towns', in H.J. Dyos (ed.), *The Study of Urban History* (London, 1968), 67–85, at p. 72; Humphries, *Childhood and Child Labour*, pp. 73–4; Anderson, 'Study of Family Structure', p. 76.
[83] Humphries, 'Women and Paid Work', p. 91; van der Heijden and ven den Heuvel, 'Sailors' Families in Early Modern Holland', pp. 302–3.

diminished status.[84] To the respectable sort for whom it was important to 'possess' an entire house, the taking-in of lodgers implied straitened finances, a loss of gentility, the inability of the household head to preserve his family space uninvaded, and (of particular significance for the wife of an absent seaman-husband) a sexually ambiguous relationship between landlady and male lodger. It was the antithesis of keeping servants.[85]

Our allottees may have viewed lodging as something to be resorted to out of necessity, since those renting sublet accommodation outnumbered by more than four to one those enumerated as 'lodger'. Some 'lodger' scenarios were particularly humble. Of eighty-six dwellings inhabited by lodger-allottees, thirteen were already subdivided into multiple lettings, making these women lodgers-within-sublets. Joanna Greenleaf Fleming (*q.v.*) was enumerated as 'lodger' to a dockyard sawyer's family, yet a line drawn by the enumerator between their details and Joanna's suggests she comprised her own one-woman household.[86] Did she pay a sub-sublet rent to the sawyer, or to the absentee owner-landlord? Did she, as many lodgers did, provide her own food and cook for herself in a saucepan over her bedroom fireplace, or have access to a communal kitchen stove, or eat food prepared by the sawyer's wife, at table with the family?[87] Similarly blurred boundaries applied in the house occupied by Matilda Lawrence, wife of bandsman Pierre, HMS *Albion*. Matilda was lodger to a joiner and his wife in one sublet; in the other, a carpenter lodged with a corn meter and family.[88] The house would not have boasted two kitchens, so where each 'landlady' cooked, each 'lodger' slept and ate, can only be guessed. So long as rent was produced on time, absentee proprietors may have been unaware that their official tenants were acting as second-level landlords and landladies, subletting space within their already sublet rentals. Such double-layered subletting is strongly suggestive of straitened circumstances, of 'very poor and cramped families [finding] space for unofficial lodgers'.[89]

Apart from fourteen allottees whose 'lodgers' were ambiguously enumerated, there were 126 seamen's women letting space in their homes to 249 individuals. More than half of the 126 had just one lodger. Childless

---

[84] Leonore Davidoff, 'The Separation of Home and Work? Landladies and lodgers in nineteenth and twentieth century England', in Sandra Burman (ed.), *Fit Work for Women* (London, 1979), 64–97, at p. 69; Keith A. Cowlard, 'The Identification of Social (Class) Areas and Their Place in Nineteenth-Century Urban Development', *Transactions of the Institute of British Geographers*, 4:2 (1979), 239–57, at p. 242.

[85] O'Day, *Family and Family Relationships*, p. 247; Cowlard, 'Social (Class) Areas', p. 241; Davidoff, 'Separation of Home and Work', pp. 69, 76.

[86] 1851 census: HO107/1657, fol. 33, p. 12.

[87] Davidoff, 'Separation of Home and Work', p. 74.

[88] ADM 27/113/323/322; 1851 census: HO107/1658, fol. 206, p. 25.

[89] O'Day, *Family and Family Relationships*, p. 247.

Elizabeth Hall (she of the four allotments noted in Chapter Two) accommodated four 'musicians'.[90] Hers was a canny arrangement. Four adult lodgers, all earners, could each be charged keep; but a quadruple profit could not be wrung from the four lodgers accommodated by Maria Tipple and her quartermaster husband John, HMS *Excellent*, for the four comprised a seaman, his wife, their 2-year-old son and eight-month-old baby.[91] Only the seaman was waged, and he could not be charged fourfold. The arrangement was financially ineffective: Maria's parish rates were three shillings, and she owed almost the same amount in arrears.[92] The Tipples' lodging-house, however, may have been intended less as a money-making enterprise, more as an expression of sailorly comradeship. In numerous allottee households the lodgers were sailors or marines, which may suggest that where the householder or his spouse had naval connections, naval lodgers were more welcome than they might be elsewhere. Whether they were former shipmates or friends of the host, or shipmates of the host's absent sailor-son, -brother or -husband, seamen-lodgers were often regarded as part of the family.[93]

Amid these comradely arrangements were flintier commercial enterprises, such as those operated by three naval women who between them accommodated a total of twenty-seven lodgers. One of the three was Mary Davidge, mother of AB James Davidge, HMS *Enterprize* [*sic*]. Headed by her Greenwich pensioner-turned-victualler husband and located on the Common Hard, Mary's household contained eleven lodgers, all mariners.[94] Her younger daughter contributed to the family's income by working in-house as a barmaid; the older daughter, a 'dressmaker' (a term pregnant with ambiguity, as Chapter Ten explains) may also have contributed, albeit by means less decorous than needlework. Around the corner in Ordnance Row, three of seven lodgers accommodated by victualler's wife Amelia Rose were seamen; missing from the household, however, was 4-year-old Eliza Cameron, entrusted to Amelia by AB John Cameron, HMS *Excellent*.[95] Ordnance Row, the Hard, Queen Street: proximity to the dockyard was a major attraction for sailor-lodgers. Another popular feature was on-tap alcohol, its association with prostitution no doubt adding value.[96] Ten other allottees were taking in lodgers in ones, twos or threes. All ten were engaged in the alcohol trade, all but one of their dwellings lying close to the dockyard gates.

[90] ADM 27/109/330/234, *et al*; 1851 census: HO107/1658, fol. 433, p. 18.
[91] ADM 27/109/443/1285; 1851 census: HO107/1659, fol. 389, p. 8.
[92] PHC: DT/R/2/454-7, vol. 455, pp. 4–5.
[93] Anderson, *Family Structure*, p. 47.
[94] ADM 27/109/416/23; 1851 census: HO107/1658, fol. 253, p. 5.
[95] 1851 census: HO107/1658, fol. 54, p. 2; ADM 27/113/268/1683.
[96] Davidoff, 'Separation of Home and Work', p. 80.

At national level the 1851 census found 28 per cent of lodgers were sole lodgers.[97] In Portsea that proportion was almost doubled, which finding may be a function of the township's smaller living spaces. Twelve of our fifteen sublet-dwelling allottee-landladies had just one lodger. These women's rentals may have consisted of two rooms, of which they sub-sublet one. That was risky enough; but if theirs were a one-room sublet, to admit a lodger meant sharing bedroom and living space, a morally perilous arrangement. Louisa Street, sister of AB William Jenkins, HMS *Excellent*, had in her Church Road sublet five children aged one to sixteen years, and still managed to squeeze in a lodger.[98] Three other single-lodger sublets were home to three children apiece, the landlady-mothers and their children very likely sleeping together in order to make space for the person paying keep.

Seventeen naval 'landladies' were under thirty years old, and not necessarily what they seemed. They included Amelia Lewis (*q.v.*) of Hobbs Court, whose charwoman 'lodger' Elizabeth Flowers was her mother. Pauper Elizabeth could not have contributed much by way of keep, but helped with the care of Amelia's nine-month-old youngest, the crippled Louisa, with whom in later years she would live (see pp. 295–6).[99] Six other 'landladies' had lodgers on parish relief; and notwithstanding the keep their lodgers paid, three more 'landladies' were themselves on relief. Sixty-year-old Mary Ann Smith was one such. Mother of AB George, HMS *Albion*, she had no fewer than five lodgers: a 36-year-old widow and her two small children, a widowed 83-year-old annuitant, and a bachelor mariner in his thirties.[100] Both the younger widow and Mary Ann's 23-year-old daughter were recorded as dressmakers, as were the fellow residents of our youngest and most implausible 'landlady', 16-year-old head of household Harriet Sarah Bettsworth (*q.v.*), whose ménage was more mini-brothel than lodgings.[101] We first met Harriet Sarah in Chapter Five, along with her mother and namesake illegitimate daughter. In the 1851 census schedule her stated occupation of 'Household employ' was, like that of her 19-year-old co-resident cousin, briskly scrawled through by the examiner; her 24-year-old 'lodger', another unmarried woman, was marked 'no employ'.

\*\*\*

[97] Anderson, 'Households, Families and Individuals', p. 429.
[98] ADM 27/111/83/1469; 1851 census: HO107/1659, fol. 723, p. 5.
[99] ADM 27/110/106/22; 1851 census: HO107/1658, fol. 46, p. 35; 1871 census: RG10/1127, fol. 45, p. 3.
[100] ADM 27/110/220/1395; 1851 census: HO107/1658, fol. 215, p. 42.
[101] ADM 27/111/292/21; 1851 census: HO107/1658, fol. 92, p. 24 ('Harriett Bettsworth').

Poverty was a mutable condition, and not all counter-poverty stratagems were agreed between seaman and wife prior to his departure.[102] Each wife had her own hierarchy of resort, for the woman's role was ingeniously to 'confront the challenges of poverty'.[103] August conveys the idea of certain tactics being of last resort, but there is no evidence to suggest that naval women had a hierarchy of economic measures or survival strategies to which, in due order, they collectively subscribed.[104] Individual response varied according to the nature and urgency of the situation, the character and moral code of the woman herself. To fund the purchase of an essential item she might sell or pawn a household object, or approach the parish for a one-off handout, Portsea Guardians recording the giving of shoes, a coffin for a dead child.[105] Less urgent, longer-term need demanded different tactics. For one woman, the taking in of lodgers was anathema; for her neighbour, what a lodger brought in by way of company and keep was valued above personal pride and social standing; for a third, the prospect of huddling with her children in a lodger's bedroom was preferable to thieving. Beyond these, however, were worse options. Two of the most desperate are considered next.

---

[102] August, *Poor Women's Lives*, p. 65; O'Day, *Family and Family Relationships*, p. 233; Fury, 'Seamen's Wives and Widows', p. 262; Jane Long, *Conversations in Cold Rooms: women, work and poverty in nineteenth-century Northumberland* (London, 1999), p. 127.
[103] August, *Poor Women's Lives*, pp. 71–2.
[104] *Ibid.*, p. 72.
[105] Helen Bosanquet, 'Marriage in East London', in Ellen Ross (ed.), *Slum Travelers: ladies and London poverty, 1860–1920* (Berkeley, Calif., 2007), 64–71, at p. 68; Portsmouth History Centre (PHC) Portsmouth, Portsea Island Poor Law Union, Minute Books of Board of Guardians, BG/M/1/2, (1841–46), n.p., various.

## 10

# PARISH RELIEF AND PROSTITUTION

Beyond arrears, debt, pawning and flitting lay parish relief and prostitution. Beyond parish out-relief and prostitution lay subsistence crime, the workhouse and utter destitution. Given the limited income afforded through the allotment system, and what is now known about seamen's women's participation in the workforce, it would be reasonable to assume that a significant number of allottees were poor enough to qualify for out-relief. Given previous authors' assertions on prostitution it might equally be assumed that significant numbers of naval women were participating in the sex trade. This chapter suggests otherwise.

### PARISH RELIEF

The Portsea Island Union Board of Guardians' Minute Book for August 1851 – June 1855 makes no mention of numbers of people relieved by the Union.[1] For the same period the *Hampshire Telegraph* makes only broad and occasional reference to out-relief statistics. When correlated, however, summary information from these two sources suggests that at a mean average of 6.2 per cent of the civilian population, Portsea Island's proportion of out-relief paupers was lower than, or at the lower end of, the figures reported for the rest of Hampshire.[2] According to the census, fifty-three (3.6 per cent) of our 1,581 Portsea Island allottees were in receipt of out-relief, a ratio near-half the county average of 60–89 paupers per 1,000 total population in 1850, and just over half the Portsea Island estimated mean of 6.2 per cent.[3]

---

[1] PHC: BG/M/1/3, *passim*.
[2] *H/Tel*, 2 March 1850, p. 5 col. C; *ibid.*, 2 April 1853, p. 5 col. D; *ibid.*, 22 October 1853, p. 8 col. C; *ibid.*, 24 June 1854, p. 5 col. E; *ibid.*, 7 October 1854, p. 8 col. D; Barry Stapleton, 'Population', in Barry Stapleton and James H. Thomas (eds), *The Portsmouth Region* (Gloucester, 1989), 83–117, at p. 104 table 4.
[3] Mills *et al.*, 'Southern Historians and Victorian Censuses', p. 70; Lees, *Solidarities of Strangers*, p. 183.

Why this comparatively low figure? For a start it includes only allottees specifically listed in the census as receiving parish relief. Not counted were allottees who were co-resident with, and in many instances related to, a householder described in those terms, for example allottees listed as daughter or lodger of a seamstress on parish relief. Such households may have been poor, but the allottees were not counted here as paupers. Beyond this basic criterion it is possible (albeit remotely) that the cohort of 1,581 individuals is intrinsically skewed, the study's 1850–52 span having by chance captured a particularly small population of paupers. It is possible, too, that when asked in the census schedule forms whether they were in receipt of relief, some of the 1,581 lied by omission. It is worth reflecting, however, that to bring allottee pauper figures to a size where they match the county's, fifty or more allottees would not only have had to be paupers, but would have had to tell the enumerator otherwise, or persuaded their household heads to do so. Fifty additional 'hidden' paupers seems unlikely and would require a collective approach to schedule completion, so how to explain there being fewer allottee-paupers than expected? Were the women managing on their monthly receipts without parish assistance? Were poor law guardians refusing them relief? Or was it a matter of collective pride that in their census schedules seamen's women not identify themselves as paupers?

It was not that receipt of 'half-pay' made seamen's women ineligible for relief. The allotment was, after all, a portion of men's honest earnings, and parishes looked approvingly upon claimants' efforts to support themselves via paid work. Admittedly, the report which predated the 1834 Poor Law Amendment Act was 'even less interested [than earlier legislation] in the poverty of women without men, and had nothing to say about widows, deserted wives, *the wives of the absentee soldier or sailor ... with or without dependent children*' [italics added]; but the Poor Law Commission's 1844 Outdoor Relief Prohibitory Order allowed exceptions to the rule directing that every able-bodied person be relieved wholly within the workhouse, one exception relating specifically to wives of soldiers, sailors or marines in the service of the sovereign.[4] This was a development with special significance for poor law unions covering garrison and naval port towns, since it was they who were chiefly responsible for relieving servicemen's wives. Within these town boundaries, however, lay numerous government properties in

---

[4] Kidd, *State, Society and the Poor*, p. 37, citing S. and B. Webb, *English Poor Law Policy* (1910), p. 6; Lees, *Solidarities of Strangers*, pp. 199–200; K.D.M. Snell, *Parish and Belonging: community, identity and welfare in England and Wales, 1700–1950* (Cambridge, 2006), pp. 236–7; Myna Trustram, *Women of the Regiment: marriage and the Victorian army* (Cambridge, 1984), p. 143; Michael E. Rose, 'The Allowance System under the New Poor Law', *Economic History Review*, 19: 3 (1966), 607–20, at p. 617.

the form of dockyards, barracks, messes, workshops, storehouses, parade grounds and offices, none of them subject to the poor rate levies demanded of ordinary households and businesses. The Navy, through its servicemen, its dependants and its built estate, occupied Portsea Island, but did not pay its fair share of the poor rate. Compounding this burden, port town unions had to deal with high numbers of distressed wives of soldiers, incomers who accompanied their men to the dockside and, following troopships' departure, were left unsupported, jobless, without financial resources and far from their home parishes.[5] Portsmouth Overseers complained to the Admiralty, demanding additional money to provide for the many service wives 'destined to become, almost invariably, "fixed Burthens on the Parish".'[6] The Union even attempted to use its funds to despatch soldiers' dependants abroad to join their men, only to face problems when wives were sent back to England without their husbands, the War Office having assumed they would receive out-relief upon landing.[7]

Given these pressures, in a union like Portsea Island, squeezed between deficient income and excessive demand, with a relief system allowing autonomy and latitude in the regional operation of poor law policy, it would be reasonable to expect to find port town guardians seeking to restrict access to relief, or at least to prioritise applications, in which case the serviceman's spouse might find herself in a vulnerable position.[8] There were grounds for doing so. From 1834 'persons were deemed to be "settled" (i.e. possessing a right to relief from local funds) in the poor law union of their birth, or in the case of a married woman, in her husband's place of birth.'[9] Her man being at sea, in order to qualify for relief it would fall to the naval wife to convince the guardians that he was Portsmouth-born, this necessitating her knowing not only his age but his baptismal parish; but were her husband born elsewhere (as were those previously-noted seamen emigrating from Cornwall and Devon), she must hope not to be deemed a deserted wife, for some guardians 'argued that … deserted wives and children should not be a charge upon the rates', thus opening up the possibility of her being forcibly removed to her absent man's birth parish, a place which might be entirely

---

[5] Trustram, *Women of the Regiment*, pp. 143–4; H/Tel, 10 May 1851, p. 7 col. D; *ibid.*, 28 February 1852, p. 7, cols. E–F; Jennine Hurl-Eamon, *Marriage and the British Army in the Long Eighteenth Century: 'The girl I left behind me'* (Oxford, 2014), p. 42; Lin, 'Citizenship, Military Families', p. 11.

[6] Hurl-Eamon, 'Fiction of Female Dependence', p. 482.

[7] Trustram, *Women of the Regiment*, pp. 144–6.

[8] Kidd, *State, Society and the Poor*, p. 30; Snell, *Parish and Belonging*, pp. 236–7.

[9] Thane, 'Women and the Poor Law', p. 32, citing M.E. Rose, 'Settlement, Removal and the New Poor Law', in D. Fraser (ed.) *The New Poor Law in the Nineteenth Century* (London, 1976), 25–44.

alien to her.[10] Low numbers of allottee-paupers may therefore be a function of seamen-husbands having been born outwith Portsea Island, and/or allottee-wives being unable to verify that their men had been locally-born.

As for allottees who were relatives other than seamen's wives, any application for relief hinged upon their birthplace (or that of their spouses, in the case of married allottees), and how long they had been Portsea-resident. Applicants born outside the union's boundaries who had not been resident locally for anything up to five years could be deemed the responsibility of their place of origin and thus denied relief, some being incarcerated in the workhouse pending deportation to their home parishes.[11] Of our non-wife allottee-paupers, seven were born in mainland Hampshire or the Isle of Wight, twelve in other English counties or Ireland. That they had not been disqualified suggests they were adjudged entitled to relief.[12]

This apparent latitude should be set against the possibility that some guardians disagreed with the parish's supporting naval allottees who were not native Portsea Islanders, especially when locally-born paupers within the same community were in arguably greater need, not having a monthly allotment income.[13] However, much as budget-conscious guardians might have been tempted to deny relief to service dependants, it is doubtful they would have ventured into such politically dangerous waters. It is questionable, too, whether the Poor Law Commissioners would have condoned such deviations from national policy. Commissioners took a minute interest in union business, intervening to request information, sanction appointments, endorse proposals, take executive decisions. That the awarding of relief to naval dependants was problematic is evident only in fleeting references such as the observation, in an 1841 Guardians' Minute Book, that great expense was incurred by the wives and families of marines

> who are constantly drawing on parish funds. Many of the wives do not know their husbands' settlement, and the only information deliverable from [Marine] Head Quarters is the supposed place of birth. As no allotment is receivable by marines' wives until at least three months after the departure of a ship from port, and as, in the meantime, in doubtful or unknown settlements the Union has always to support them, it is submitted whether some provision could not be made ... for every Marine to have his examination taken on his enlistment or as soon as an order

---

[10] *Ibid.*, p. 32.
[11] Light, *Common People*, p. 224; Thane, 'Women and the Poor Law', pp. 32, 36; Lincoln, *Naval Wives*, p. 153.
[12] Poor Law Commissioners, *Order Prohibiting Outdoor Relief* (London, 1844), Article 1, clause 7.
[13] PHC: BG/AC 1/1; BG/AC 3/1; BG/AF 4/1; BG/FC 4/1, 2, 3, 6.

arrives for embarkation. Such a proceeding would be productive of great saving in every Sea Port, and produce no injury whatever to the family.[14]

No record of such a 'proceeding' (for verifying naval dependants' eligibility for relief prior to ships' departures) has been found. Without a policy framework the Union had to deal with each case individually, as witness minutes of the weekly Overseers' meetings for December 1845 – September 1846, which name individual applicants for out-relief, and the union's responses to each request.[15]

For the seaman convinced that allotting the bare minimum would qualify his dependant for assistance, to award a sub-moiety sum while his ship was on commission was a risky tactic, for should the parish deny relief there was no immediate remedy. It would take weeks for a wife's letter to reach her husband's ship, telling him of the parish's refusal to make up the difference. He in turn could not increase her portion until the ship's next declaration-day, anything up to six months later. Given the time taken to return ships' registers to Whitehall, and for Admiralty clerks to verify and process the paperwork, the naval dependant might thus be in financial distress for the better part of a year – indefinitely, were her spouse unmoved by her plea for more, his ship beyond contact with homeward-bound vessels. Not only were these drawbacks obvious to anyone familiar with the allotment system; on every seagoing vessel there was a messdeck lawyer, in every naval community on shore an allottee well versed in the workings of Admiralty and Union, with a fund of cautionary tales of administrative delays, of allottees reduced to begging, to 'going to the poor house for support' (or worse), while waiting in vain for an uplift in their monthly allowance.[16] Little wonder, then, that no evidence has emerged of widespread attempts by husbands to manipulate the system by forcing parishes' hands. None of the notably low-allotment wives has been found receiving supplements from other sailors, nor does waged work appear to have been relied upon as a fallback, for of sixty-five women identified as receiving 40 per cent or less of their husbands' pay, the census recorded only seven as having an occupation, and only one of the sixty-five (forty-year-old charwoman Henrietta Clack, mother of four and wife of gunner Henry, HMS *Gladiator*)

---

[14] Portsmouth History Centre (PHC) Portsmouth, Portsea Island Poor Law Union, Minute Books of Board of Guardians, BG/M/1/1 (1838–41), (n.p.), 19 March 1841.

[15] Portsmouth History Centre (PHC) Portsmouth, BG/FC4/2: Portsea Island Poor Law Union, Overseers and Collectors Summary Accounts for the Parish of Portsmouth (1836–48), *passim*.

[16] 'Messdeck lawyer: a Jack-me-tickler [someone who really believes he is omniscient] … always arguing the toss or quoting regulations and rules': Jolly and Willson, *Jackspeak*, pp. 238, 283; Hardwicke, *Report*, p. 20 s. 228.

was enumerated as a pauper.[17] Two other *Gladiator* gunners likewise allotted their wives just thirteen shillings per month, but neither of their allottees was on out-relief, and neither reported an occupation.[18]

Seamen's sub-par allotments cannot reliably be interpreted as a rational family strategy intended to improve dependants' prospects of obtaining out-relief. Another explanation may however be inferred from patterns detectable in sailors' rates, trades and ships. First, the finding that fully two-thirds of the sixty-five low-allotting husbands were gunners serving in fifteen different ships suggests the existence of a gunnery-trade culture that went beyond one ship's mess. August's 'neighbourhood norms and customs' have been detected (p. 160) among men occupying domestic roles, some of them serving in the same ship.[19] Across multiple shipboard communities, 'neighbourhood norms and customs' appear to have underpinned gunners' habitually awarding sub-moiety amounts, as witness the three *Gladiator* gunners noted above. Gunners, carpenters and boatswains were paid the same; yet instead of awarding the usual moiety, proportionally more gunners than bosuns and carpenters allotted just 40 per cent *or less* of their wages. Secondly, three-quarters of the sixty-five low-allotting men were serving in harbour-based ships *Excellent*, *Blenheim*, *Britannia* and *Victory*. For men on these vessels, cash-in-hand support of local dependants was feasible, in that a man might go ashore on overnight leave with coin to supplement his wife's allotment, or get money to her by hand of a trusted shipmate. Low allotments may therefore be less a rational family strategy, more a function of shipboard-, rate- or trade-specific culture, augmented by logistical opportunity in the case of harbour-based vessels.

At national level the average mid-century parish grant was 1s 6d per person per week, varying union to union and according to supplicants' civil status, age and condition.[20] Single parents were granted less than the elderly, and families' needs were aggregated, the allowance for a family with five children calculated at one shilling per head per week.[21] Paupers, in short, were 'subsisting on very small weekly allowances which often appear to have lacked any apparent rationale even within an individual union.'[22] When Portsea Island Guardians' Minute Book budgets are correlated with expenditure quoted at intervals in the *Hampshire Telegraph*, smaller sums appear to have been the norm. During years 1851–53 the average out-relief

---

[17] ADM 27/110/51/4; 1851 census: HO107/1659, fol. 83, p. 34.
[18] ADM 27/110/51/7; 1851 census: HO107/1658, fol. 646, p. 23; ADM 27/110/51/19; 1851 census: HO107/1659, fol. 181, p. 30.
[19] August, *Poor Women's Lives*, pp. 124–5.
[20] Lees, *Solidarities of Strangers*, p. 186.
[21] *Ibid.*, pp. 188–9.
[22] Wood, *Poverty and Workhouse*, p. 98.

per Portsea Island pauper fell somewhere between 9½d and 1s 6d per person per week.[23] These amounts reflect the Union's previously-mentioned budget difficulties. They also resonate with Boulton's opinion that parish relief was scarcely more than a housing subsidy, capable of covering rent costs and little else.[24]

To test this, the household poor-relief income of sixteen seamen's women was compared with monthly rent calculated from poor rate books. The sixteen received allotments ranging in size from twelve shillings per month (less than half the £1 6s 6d monthly average) to £1 18s 0d per month, with a mean of 19s 6d monthly. All but one were aged forty-two to sixty-five years, with fourteen dependent children between them. Poor law unions took children's ages into consideration, relief often being conditional upon older children's contributing to household income. Widowed Sarah Lee's 11-year-old would probably have been too young to work, her 4-year-old certainly so.[25] If Sarah and each individual in her Havant Street household qualified for out-relief, at 9½d per person per week it would have added 10s 5d to her monthly one pound allotment from her son, AB Frederick, HMS *Excellent*; at 1s 6d per person per week, it would have added 19s 6d, almost doubling what she received from Frederick.[26] Meanwhile, in Frett's Court, Portsea, where thirty-eight residents crowded into just five dwellings, Susan Kendall's family had a house to themselves.[27] Susan having four children to support, the Union would have awarded her out-relief of 13s 9d to £1 12s 6d per month, or 138 to 325 per cent of her ten-shilling monthly rent.[28] Her husband Joshua, gun room cook, HMS *Hecate*, allotted her a modest eighteen shillings per month.[29] To this she added her earnings as a laundress, and whatever her 14-year-old errand boy son brought home. Temple Street resident Sarah Quinnell was mother of 26-year-old AB Frederick Quinnell, HMS *Retribution*. Both Frederick and his shipmate George Grant, captain of the mast, named 68-year-old Sarah 'mother' in their allotment declarations of November 1850.[30] The poor rate book for April 1851 shows Sarah had recoverable debts of between 3s 9d and 6s 10½d, and irrecoverable arrears of ninepence to four shillings.[31] Next to the column for

---

[23] *H/Tel*, 7 October 1854, p. 8 col. D; *ibid*., 11 June 1853, p. 5 col. E; *ibid*., 4 June 1853, p. 5 col. D; PHC: BG/M/1/3, n.p., for 27 August – 22 October 1851.
[24] Boulton, "'Turned into the street'", p. 31.
[25] 1851 census: HO107/1658, fol. 226, p. 3.
[26] ADM 27/112/325/1689.
[27] 1851 census: HO107/1658, fol. 216, p. 44.
[28] PHC: DT/R/2/454-7, vol. 454, p. 19.
[29] ADM 27/109/257/1.
[30] ADM 27/111/292/35; ADM 27/111/292/3.
[31] PHC: DT/R/2/454-7, vol. 455, pp. 7–8.

non-recoverable debts, in the column marked 'Causes', the collector wrote 'No effects'. Despite the £1 2s 0d received each month from George Grant, and the unrecorded sum from son Frederick, and the 1s 6d to three shillings per week she received in relief, Sarah and her labourer-pauper husband had no coin, no goods to pawn, nothing worth distraining, a level of indigence making mockery of poor law unions' assumption that applicants for relief had hidden assets to fall back on.[32]

Poor law union policy and practice dictated which applicants' pleas for help were granted, which denied. Awareness of overseers' 'inquisitorial enquiry of painful, and very often, of a totally unnecessary character', of the 'helpless poor [being] put on the rack of explanation and rebukes', dissuaded all but the most distressed from applying.[33] Many a woman will have been repelled by the prospect of having her domestic arrangements, income sources, spending habits and earning potential scrutinised by a panel of male overseers, some of whom may have had cynical views as to seamen's women's morals. For seamen's women accustomed to exercising an unusual level of agency, it cannot have been pleasant to be subject to yet more institutional decision-making. Some of those who recoiled from applying may have been concerned not so much with loss of self-determination as convinced that resorting to poor relief meant loss of respectability.[34] But for those in desperate straits there remained another source of income, one even less respectable than out-relief; one capable, indeed, of irrevocably blighting a woman's reputation, safety and health. In earning power and immediacy of result it was, for some women, preferable to dependence upon the parish.

## PROSTITUTION

Admitting there being 'almost no data on prostitutes in … naval ports', and citing none, Stark nevertheless asserts that naval wives often resorted to prostitution during their husbands' absence, and that many a prostitute became a naval wife; noting, rightly, that details of their lives on shore can only be inferred 'from a few random records' and the passing impressions of a few individuals, she does not state which records, or whose impressions.[35] Drawing on Old Bailey records, Hurl-Eamon recognises that necessity drove military wives to theft, extortion and the sex trade, most prostituting themselves for basic subsistence.[36] Her examples paint a picture of large-

[32] Anthony Brundage, *The English Poor Laws, 1700–1930* (Basingstoke, 2002), p. 91.
[33] H/Tel, 19 July 1851, p. 5, cols. C–D.
[34] Thompson, *Rise of Respectable Society*, p. 353.
[35] Stark, *Female Tars*, pp. 27–31.
[36] Hurl-Eamon, 'Fiction of Female Dependence', p. 484.

scale desperation among soldiers' and sailors' wives; but the cases she cites are eighteenth-century, and, as she acknowledges, 'most of the women who resorted to the sex trade would never appear in [court], as prostitution itself was not a crime.'[37] For the same reasons, documentary evidence as to the extent of naval wives' involvement in Portsmouth prostitution is thin, generalised and often tangential, leading inevitably to the conclusion that what is visible in Victorian police and court records and newspaper reports of court proceedings is merely the tip of a prostitutional iceberg.

There is no escaping the fact that, rife as it was throughout Victorian England, prostitution was particularly associated with port and garrison towns, with sailors' and soldiers' women. Those 'hordes of profligate females … reeling in drunkenness, or plying upon the streets in open day with a broad immodesty which puts the great orb of noon to the blush' were famed for being of 'such peculiar figure and apparel, that it were, perhaps, difficult, in any other part of England, to find a correct resemblance of "sweet Poll of Portsmouth".'[38] Accounts of port town prostitution are numerous, ranging from clichés about sailors coming ashore with money to spend, via depictions of port town women as 'Amazonian…often the worse for drink but able to take care of themselves', to descriptions of pimps picking out the more toothsome of the 'poor unfortunates … taken to market [i.e. on board ships at anchor] like cattle'.[39] Paradoxically, port town prostitutes may have been portrayed more sympathetically than common prostitutes, the somewhat strained rationale being that by servicing sailors' sexual needs they were contributing to Britannia's war effort.[40] Such patriotic contribution required commitment: apart from paid-off sailors with lump sums to burn, most servicemen were so ill-paid that prostitutes went for quantity, their greater number of punters making up for lower individual receipts.[41]

If Mayhew is to be believed, the 1841 census listed not one prostitute; a decade later scarcely two score were explicitly identified in Portsea Island enumerators' books.[42] Ten years later still, the 1861 tally of Portsmouth prostitutes was 1,791.[43] In a paper entitled 'The Operations of the Contagious Diseases Acts', the Portsea Island Society for the Culture of Science

---

[37] Ibid., p. 485.
[38] George Pinckard, *Notes on the West Indies* (London, 1806), pp. 36–9.
[39] Lavery, *Able Seamen*, p. 87; Lincoln, *Naval Wives*, p. 144; Robinson, *Jack Nastyface*, p. 89.
[40] Lincoln, *Naval Wives*, p. 145.
[41] Petrie, *Singular Iniquity*, p. 13.
[42] P.S. Christie, 'Occupations in Portsmouth' (Portsmouth Polytechnic, unpublished MPhil dissertation, 1976), pp. 210, 343; R.C. Riley, *Old Portsmouth: a garrison town in the mid-19th century* (Portsmouth, 2010), p. 20.
[43] Walton, 'Social History', p. 168.

and Literature was informed that numbers of 'common women' had shrunk from 1,355 in 1865 to 590 by 1870, but these and other figures quoted are at odds with statistics cited by Hooppell.[44] Official statistics are part of a constantly shifting picture, for the number who under the CDAs would in due course be 'registered' with the police did not include large numbers of clandestine prostitutes, the 'factory or shop girls who supplemented their pay, young women or the wives of absent servicemen who supported their family'.[45] Little wonder that Pearsall talks of the 'incredible fatuity of some of the statistics relating to prostitution', leading to 'many experts' relying on data from hospitals for sexually transmitted diseases.[46] If evidence as to the size of port and garrison towns' populations of prostitutes is inconsistent, then missing altogether is evidence as to the proportion of prostitutes comprising naval seamen's women as distinct from civilian women.

Census under-recording of 'prostitute' as an occupation chiefly resulted from household schedules in which women ascribed themselves (or the household head ascribed them) more acceptable livelihoods, of which needlework was the most commonly cited. We have seen how among waged naval women the largest occupational group was the sewing trade. Sixty-eight per cent of sewing-trade allottees described themselves as 'dressmakers' or 'needlewomen', terms interpreted as representing the 'numerically significant occupation' of prostitute.[47] This is not to say that a woman styling herself 'dressmaker' had not practised that trade at some stage, and respectably so; for while some prostitutes chose less ambiguous titles in order to blend into the background, others wanted to suggest a former occupation to which they might return after quitting the street, or to disguise past necessitous resorts to it, or to mention only the more respectable of their trades.[48] Examples of dubious self-styling are to be found among our allottee cohort, some clearly arousing census officials' suspicions. As noted earlier, the enumerator scrawled through Harriet Sarah Bettsworth's self-description as 'household employ'; likewise, regardless of

---

[44] H/Tel, 30 March 1872, p. 8, cols. D–F; Hooppell, *Statistical Results of the Contagious Diseases Act*, p. 7.

[45] Patricia Pulham and Brad Beaven, *Dickens and the Victorian City* (Old Portsmouth, 2012), p. 31.

[46] Ronald Pearsall, *The Worm in the Bud: the world of Victorian sexuality* (Stroud, 2003), p. 276.

[47] Riley, *Old Portsmouth*, p. 20; Patrick Dunae, 'Sex, Charades, and Census Records: locating female sex trade workers in a Victorian city', *Histoire Sociale*, 42:84 (2009), 267–97, at p. 269; Petrie, *Singular Iniquity*, p. 77.

[48] Judith R. Walkowitz, 'The Making of an Outcast Group: prostitution and working women in nineteenth-century Plymouth and Southampton', in Martha Vicinus (ed.), *A Widening Sphere: changing roles of Victorian women* (London, 1977), 72–93, at p. 75; Lincoln, *Naval Wives*, p. 144.

how Emily Hood, 'sister' of ordinary seaman Thomas Hoar, HMS *Retribution*, and two other women described themselves in their Mitre Court household schedule, in the enumerators' book the householder's occupation was redacted, the others rendered as '? Dressmaker'.[49] Saucy baggage Ann Thomas made no bones about her trade. Named by AB William Hillyard, HMS *Resistance*, as trustee to a 3-year-old girl, Ann was one of five females inhabiting an Armoury Lane brothel.[50] She was, moreover, the only one of this study's more than 1,500 naval women whose (self-)description as 'prostitute' was accepted by the census. Perhaps unsurprisingly, of William Hillyard's entrusted child there was no sign.

Ann Thomas was an exception. Her more reticent allottee peers are camouflaged under 'respectable' occupations or none, discernible only by inference, with caution. The sharing of accommodation, for example, described earlier in terms of economic stratagem, was for some a temporary, virtuous measure adopted to ward off loneliness, secure mutual support and understanding, and protect reputation; and yet identical arrangements within the same street were brothels.

Prior to the 1860s, and statistics emerging from the implementation of the CDAs, local police records and newspaper reports of court proceedings constitute the main sources of information on women's involvement in the sex trade. Again, caution is required, for contemporary usage of the word 'prostitute' was inconsistent. Introduced under the 1824 Vagrancy Act, by the early 1850s the term 'common prostitute' had been available to police and courts for a quarter-century. The Act made it an offence to loiter or solicit in a street or public place for the purpose of prostitution; but as with soliciting, brothel-keeping or living off immoral earnings, the charge of 'common prostitute' was only selectively enforced under the 1824 Act or later legislation.[51] The Town Police Causes Act 1847 determined that 'every common prostitute or nightwalker loitering or importuning ... for the purposes of prostitution' be taken into custody by a police officer (no warrant required) and 'conveyed before a Justice'.[52] In many districts, however, the earlier Vagrancy Act was the preferred instrument, allowing police to arrest upon suspicion, and placing the onus on the arrested party to prove their good intent.[53] Prostitutes, unlicensed pedlars and beggars

---

[49] 1851 census: HO107/1658, fol. 92, p. 24; ADM 27/111/294/112; 1851 census: HO107/1658, fol. 134, p. 22.
[50] ADM 27/110/368/51; 1851 census: HO107/1657, fol. 311, p. 35.
[51] *Vagrancy Act*, 5 Geo. IV, c. 83 (1824), s. 1; Clive Emsley, *Crime and Society in England, 1750–1900* (London, 1996), p. 154; Zedner, *Women, Crime*, p. 35; *Vagrancy Act*, 1 & 2 Vict., c. 38 (1838).
[52] *Town Police Clauses Act,* 10 & 11 Vict., c. 89 (1847).
[53] 5 Geo. IV, c. 83 (1824).

could thus be deemed disorderly, swept up, and imprisoned for a month's hard labour upon conviction as idle and disorderly persons. Indeed, unless a prostitute were actually *being* disorderly, she was unlikely to be arrested simply for plying her trade.[54] The Metropolitan Police, for example, in 1848–50 took into custody an annual average of 2,336 disorderly prostitutes; by comparison, arrests for being a 'disorderly character' (a more general term not specifying sexual activity) averaged 4,822, vagrancy 5,308, drunk and disorderly 9,886, and drunkenness a whopping 10,579 annually.[55] Similar proportionality is reflected in the relative infrequency with which, in the years 1848–52, women appeared in Portsmouth courts on charges explicitly referencing prostitution. In Fig. 26, logged together under 'Prostitution' are 215 charges brought against women offenders, each referring to sundry sexualised behaviours associated with the trade. Eighteen include the word 'prostitute', eight of the eighteen referring to 'common prostitute', the rest to 'disorderly prostitute', 'common and disorderly prostitute', 'idle and disorderly prostitute' or simply 'prostitute'. The remaining 197 charges include twenty-six counts of disorderly conduct, 118 of riotous behaviour, and fifty-three of indecent behaviour (one 'exposing her person', the remainder embracing anything from a woman's lifting her skirts in order to pee in an alleyway, to sex acts committed in a public place).

Disorderly conduct, riotous behaviour, indecent behaviour: these were coded terms, rooted in legislation selectively enforced. In statute, disorderly behaviour was classified separately from prostitution.[56] Portsmouth police rarely made the distinction, frequently applying two or more discrete charges to cover all eventualities.[57] Women could thus be accused of being drunk and disorderly, or drunk and riotous, or riotous and indecent, or drunk, disorderly, riotous *and* indecent. It cannot be discerned which 'disorderly' charges were statute-specific and which were a matter of local prosecutorial practice. What is clear, however, is that while 'disorderly' had one meaning when coupled with 'drunk', it meant something different when coupled with 'riotous' or 'indecent'. 'Disorderly' and 'riotous' were legal terms linked with prostitution, while 'indecent' meant lewd, obscene or licentious conduct, behaviours not necessarily connected to the sex trade. In this exercise, charges relating to prostitution incorporate not only those mentioning the

---

[54] Stephen Inwood, 'Policing London's Morals: the Metropolitan Police and Popular Culture 1829–1850', in Paul Lawrence (ed.), *The New Police in the Nineteenth Century* (Farnham, 1997), 199–216, at pp. 209–10.
[55] *Ibid.*, p. 206 table 2.
[56] Chesney, *Victorian Underworld*, pp. 365–7; Emsley, *Crime and Society*, p. 140.
[57] Miles Jon Ogbourn, 'Discipline, Government and the Law: the response to crime, poverty and prostitution in nineteenth-century Portsmouth' (Cambridge, unpublished PhD thesis, 1990), p. 65.

word 'prostitute' but those referencing disorderly, riotous and/or indecent behaviour. These are relatively narrow criteria, for in a period when more than one-quarter of those termed 'drunkard' were female, charges such as 'drunk and disorderly' were often the means by which the police got 'immoral' women off the streets – a process the male inebriate escaped.[58] It being impossible to determine which 'drunk and disorderly' charges meant 'immoral' behaviour, the tally of 215 prostitution-related charges includes only those mentioning 'indecent' and/or 'riotous'.

The 215 figure is conservative. It does not, for example, include fifty-one cases of theft of a type known as 'trousering', only one of which related to a woman described in police record books as a prostitute. The commonest kind of theft, 'trousering' refers to a stealthy removal of pawnable items (coin, pocket watches, handkerchiefs, studs, watch chains, keys) from a postcoital punter's trousers, shirt collar or cuffs, waistcoat or jacket. So closely was it associated with prostitution, where witness or victim statements describe a theft typical of 'trousering' we may with reasonable confidence infer that it occurred as an adjunct to paid sex. Of the women charged with those 'trousering'-type offences, eighteen are recognisably allottees. One was Maria Stacey, also known as Harriet Maria Stacey. Named by AB John Robinson, HMS *Birkenhead*, as trustee of a 10-year-old girl, Maria was twice convicted of riotous behaviour, once of indecent behaviour and once explicitly stated to be a disorderly prostitute.[59] Among fifteen allegedly 'riotous' defendants was 25-year-old Caroline Capper, named trustee by Pte Isaac Phillips, HMS *Fox*.[60] Neither Caroline nor her entrusted child 'Sarah Jane' (surname and age not recorded in the allotment declaration) was found in the census, but Caroline made her presence known by other means. Appearing in court on at least ten occasions in the years 1849–52 on charges including drunkenness, indecent or riotous behaviour, vagrancy, theft, and the 'trousering' of an RMA gunner's silver watch, watch guard and two pounds cash, in local news coverage she features under the headline 'A Batch of Disorderlies', described as 'one of the pavé', 'a lady of the pavé', and bluntly as 'prostitute'.[61]

---

[58] Emsley, *Crime and Society*, p. 154; Zedner, *Women, Crime*, p. 22; Walkowitz and Walkowitz, '"We Are Not Beasts of the Field"', p. 87.

[59] ADM 27/113/387/18; *H/Tel*, 5 February 1848, p. 5 col. C; ibid., 18 March 1848, p. 5 col. D; ibid., 23 December 1848, p. 7 col. D; ibid., 27 April 1850, p. 7 col. F; ibid., 14 December 1850, p. 2 col. B.

[60] ADM 27/111/274/4.

[61] Portsmouth History Centre (PHC) Portsmouth, Borough of Portsmouth Police, Police Record Book, PHC SB/DF/P/1 (1843–49); Portsmouth History Centre (PHC) Portsmouth, Borough of Portsmouth, Calendar of Prisoners, general quarter sessions of the Peace, PHC S7/1 (1842–54), 6 January 1852; *H/Tel*, 24 June 1848, p. 7 col. D; ibid., 22 July 1848, p. 7 col. E; ibid., 28 October 1848, p. 7 col. D; ibid., 26 May

No other woman in this study was so many times brought to court, or so often depicted in those terms.

There is deliberate meaning in how Caroline's character and offences were described. Reporters' coded language conveyed to the reader that the charges implied something more than the theft or assault for which a woman stood in the dock. Coded language was also used when a female defendant was known to have been previously convicted of being a prostitute. To ensure readers were neither affronted by coarse language nor left in any doubt as to a woman's track record, coy terms such as 'one of the ladies of White's Row', or 'woman of questionable character' embellished the weekly articles. Even more coy a euphemism was 'a woman of a certain description'. Bland to the modern reader, the term was then gravid with disapproval. Elizabeth Allen was the wife of AB and later boatswain George Allen, HMS *Victory*, and allottee-sister – allegedly, and perplexingly, given their different surnames – both of Thomas Connell, AB *Victory*, and Henry Whitehead, AB *Excellent*.[62] A convicted Queen Street brawler whom the *Hampshire Telegraph* had previously depicted as a 'powerful-looking woman, and a singer in one of the Saloons in Portsea', when charged with riotous and indecent behaviour Elizabeth was said to be 'very indignant at being described as a woman of a certain description'.[63] Unmoved by her outrage, and convinced by the testimony of 'a witness who, instead of benefitting her case, clearly proved what character of person she was', the bench sentenced her to fourteen days' gaol with hard labour.

The youngest allottee prosecuted for prostitution-related offences was not yet twenty. Charged with being in a drunken state and using obscene language, Elizabeth Cummings and her co-defendant were described as 'two nymphs of the pavé parading the High Street at all hours'. Uttered in court, this phrase would have been sufficient to label her, even if the actual charge fell short of explicit reference to prostitution. Her youth may have helped when it came to sentencing: she was awarded just seven days' gaol with hard labour.[64] Elizabeth's husband was seamen's schoolmaster John Cummings, HMS *Excellent*, whose allotment brought her £1 8s 0d per month.[65] Her financial prospects should have been rosy when John

---

1849, p. 7 col. F; *ibid.*, 4 October 1851, p. 4 col. C; *ibid.*, 14 October 1851, p. 4 col. C; *ibid.*, 10 January 1852, p. 7 col. F; *ibid.*, 7 February 1852, p. 3 col. F; *ibid.*, 10 April 1852, p. 5 col. D, *et al.*

[62] ADM 27/110/20/30; ADM 27/112/159/11; ADM 27/112/159/19; ADM 27/111/134/1530. Elizabeth's maiden name was Watson, which throws into further doubt Connell and Whitehead's claims of fraternity.

[63] *H/Tel*, 9 August 1851, p. 8 col. E; *ibid.*, 16 August 1851, p. 7 col. F.

[64] *Ibid.*, 23 December 1848, p. 7 col. D.

[65] CHU3/1D/48, p. 27 n. 53; ADM 27/109/444/1299.

joined *Resolute* prior to its departure in search of the missing Franklin expedition. Reflecting his new status as gunner's mate, and boosted by discovery service, his double-pay allotment would have awarded Elizabeth a welcome £2 8s 0d per month, the maximum allowed.[66] His declaration was struck through, however, and 'Discharged' noted in the margin. Elizabeth being pregnant with their firstborn, John may have sought leave to return to shore; the muster book notes only his discharge ('D') on 29 April 1850 'to *Excellent* ... per Admiralty Order'.[67] A year later, while *Resolute* men were again braving Arctic cold, the census found John at home in West Street, Portsmouth Point, together with Elizabeth and their now five-month-old son, their co-residents including Elizabeth's sister Mary Purches, twice convicted of licensing offences.[68] Of Elizabeth's 'nymph of the pavé' activities there is no further trace. A combination of gaol time, marriage, an at-home husband and motherhood may have persuaded her to leave youthful roisterings behind.

Elizabeth's case demonstrates how drink-related behaviour was laden with significance for the female accused, a gendered bias visible in one Portsmouth magistrate's remarking that it was 'bad enough for a man to be in such a [drunken] state, but worse in a woman'.[69] Portsea's police record book for 1844–48 shows some 45 to 55 per cent of entries as 'drunk and disorderly' – an unsurprising figure.[70] Since police used 'drunk and disorderly' charges to get 'immoral' women off the streets, many of the entries involved women, a finding echoing that of Millbank prison's chaplain whose 1890 survey of more than 14,000 'fallen' women found most had been convicted of drunkenness offences.[71]

Prostitution was 'the foremost recreational activity associated with beerhouses'; and beerhouses being ubiquitous in port towns, it follows that prostitutes were to be found throughout Portsea Island.[72] By 1852 the Island boasted over 300 unlicensed beerhouses, the lowest class of which

---

[66] ADM 27/110/250/19.
[67] ADM 38/8862, n.p.
[68] ADM 27/111/226/69; 1851 census: HO107/1658, fol. 548, p. 24; *H/Tel*, 30 June 1849, p. 7 col. E; *ibid.*, 15 September 1849, p. 7 col. F.
[69] Judith Rowbotham, "Only When Drunk': the stereotyping of violence in England, c.1850–1900', in Shani d'Cruze (ed.), *Everyday Violence in Britain 1850–1950: Gender and Class* (Harlow, 2000), 155–69, at p. 165; *H/Tel*, 18 March 1848, p. 5 col. D.
[70] PHC: SB/DF/P/1, *passim*.
[71] F.H. Edwards, 'Crime, Law and Order in Portsmouth, 1835–1875' (Portsmouth Polytechnic, unpublished dissertation, 1987), p. 42; Riley and Eley, *Public Houses and Beerhouses*, p. 11; Philip Priestley, *Victorian Prison Lives: English prison biography, 1830–1914* (London, 1999), p. 72; Zedner, *Women, Crime*, p. 61.
[72] Riley and Eley, *Public Houses and Beerhouses*, p. 11.

served as 'the most prolific aids to prostitution and drunkenness'.[73] Often indistinguishable from neighbouring residential properties, like gin shops they served as places of assignation. In Warblington Street, Portsmouth, the public house at No. 31 accommodated four prostitutes, the youngest just ten years old; at No. 50, the Tap of One pub accommodated two prostitutes, a beerhouse at No. 39 held four, while in nearby St Mary Street a 'beershop and lodging-house' at No. 35 boasted three 'casual lodger' prostitutes.[74] Pub landlords rented adjacent buildings, allowing prostitutes to frequent their premises on condition the women encourage punters to buy alcohol before being led next door.[75] At No. 74 Hearns Court, in marine artilleryman Dowsett's brothel (described by the enumerator as '5 Tenements, Brothels, Doors opening into each'), thirteen prostitutes rented multiple sublets under the same roof.[76] Entering the court, residents and customers passed between a lodging-house and a spirit dealership. The landlord of the Fortune of War, Prospect Street, had four adjacent tenements, all functioning brothels.[77] In Sun Street and Smith's Court (mere yards from the Hobbs Court homes of Mary Roberts, Amelia Lewis and Martha Bone, *q.v.*) there were eight dwellings comprising nineteen separate households, sixteen of the twenty-two residents being young women, half of them recorded as in the sewing trades. Some of them shared rooms, but most inhabited one-room lettings.[78] In the moral climate of the time, such clusterings signalled sexual availability.[79]

Popular in the eighteenth and nineteenth centuries, those highly sexualised caricatures of seamen's women gloss over the fact that prostitution was dirty and dangerous, that women were driven to it by necessity born of poverty.[80] It offered 'a means to supplement inadequate wages, or a principal

---

[73] *Ibid.*, p. 3, table 1; *H/Tel*, 3 September 1864, p. 4 col. D.

[74] 1851 census: HO107/1658, fol. 666, p. 21; 1851 census: HO107/1658, fol. 670, p. 28; 1851 census: HO107/1658, fol. 668, p. 24; 1851 census: HO107/1658, fol. 664, p. 16.

[75] Patricia Haskell, 'Country and Town', in J. Webb *et al.* (eds), *The Spirit of Portsmouth: a history* (Chichester, 1989), 13–35, at p. 28; Riley and Eley, *Public Houses and Beerhouses*, pp. 7, 12–13; Berkeley Hill, 'Illustrations of the Working of the Contagious Diseases Act: Part I, Chatham and Portsmouth', *British Medical Journal*, 2:365 (1867), 583–5, at p. 584; Zedner, *Women, Crime*, p. 60; Lincoln, *Naval Wives*, p. 147.

[76] 1851 census: HO107/1658, fol. 669, p. 26.

[77] Riley and Eley, *Public Houses and Beerhouses*, p. 13.

[78] 1851 census: HO107/1658, fol. 689, p. 20, households 105–19, and p. 21, households 120, 121–9; Lincoln, *Naval Wives*, p. 148.

[79] Riley and Eley, *Public Houses and Beerhouses*, p. 12; Haskell, 'Spirit of Portsmouth', p. 28; Walkowitz, 'Making of an Outcast Group', pp. 79, 83.

[80] Zedner, *Women, Crime*, pp. 36, 155; Fraser Joyce, 'Prostitution and the Nineteenth Century: in search of the "Great Social Evil"', *Reinvention: a Journal of Undergraduate Research* 1:1 (2008), <https://warwick.ac.uk/fac/cross_fac/iatl/student-research/

occupation for women unemployed or unimpressed with the alternatives', a resort located somewhere between the failure of more reputable work, the non-payment of rent, and the pawning of clothes.[81] The poorly-paid trades associated with it – milliner, shop assistant, haberdasher, tailoress, laundress, servant and needleworker – were prime sources of recruits, offering a relative freedom for those caught in 'the semi-slavery of home-based work'.[82] We have seen that income from these banal occupations amounted to no more than six to ten shillings per week, earned by working a fourteen-hour day. By contrast 'a prostitute, *even a "sailor's woman"*, could earn that in one day, at a shilling a "shot"' [italics added], the implication being that sailors' women either charged less than prostitutes from other backgrounds, or were deemed by their customers as worth less.[83] Acton further reckoned the 'generous and prodigal son of Mars [i.e. common soldier] will perhaps pay 2s 6d, but usual payment is 1s', the woman's subsistence requiring she 'take home with her' eight to ten lovers every evening.[84] Benson suggests the 'successful prostitute' was capable of earning two pounds per week, which by Acton's reckoning required forty paid encounters.[85] But attractive as its earning potential may have seemed, for females of poverty-stricken families who considered themselves respectable, prostitution was not a viable means of earning.[86] Economic necessity it might be, and a survival tactic, but 'for the majority of girls it was unthinkable.'[87]

In Portsmouth police court hearings for 1848–52, of those women charged with prostitution-related offences who were identifiable as naval dependants, half were receiving their allotments in the capacity of seaman's wife, one as the sailor's widowed mother, the remainder comprising sisters

---

reinvention/archive/volume1issue1/joyce/> [accessed 22 April 2024]; John Tosh, *A Man's Place: masculinity and the middle-class home in Victorian England* (New Haven, Conn., 1999), p. 130; Bartley, *Prostitution*, p. 6; Judith R. Walkowitz, *Prostitution and Victorian Society: women, class, and the state* (Cambridge, 1980), p. 16, and n. 14; Anna Clark, *Women's Silence, Men's Violence: Sexual Assault in England, 1770–1845* (London, 1987), p. 22; Pearsall, *Worm in the Bud*, p. 274.

[81] Long, *Conversations in Cold Rooms*, p. 41.
[82] Walkowitz and Walkowitz, '"We Are Not Beasts of the Field"', pp. 83–4; Banks, 'Population Change', p. 288; Petrie, *Singular Iniquity*, pp. 71–7; Chesney, *Victorian Underworld*, pp. 375–6, 385; Walkowitz, 'Making of an Outcast Group', p. 76; Hill, *Women Alone*, p. 111; Zedner, *Women, Crime*, p. 65.
[83] Walkowitz and Walkowitz, '"We Are Not Beasts of the Field"', p. 83, quoting William Acton, *Prostitution* (New York, 1968, ed. Peter Fryer), p. 57.
[84] William Acton, *Prostitution Considered in its Moral, Social, and Sanitary Aspects*, pp. 24–5.
[85] Benson, *Working Class in Britain*, p. 44.
[86] Chinn, *They Worked all their Lives*, pp. 132–3.
[87] Ibid.

(two-thirds married, one-third unmarried) and three trustees: Maria Giles (pensioner's wife), the aforementioned Harriet Maria Stacey (married to a seaman) and recidivist Caroline Capper (civil status doubtful). The involvement of married women counters Perkin's assertion that women went through phases of prostitution, abandoning it upon marriage.[88] Allotment notwithstanding, for some seamen's women a husband's absence, with its corollary reduction to half-pay allotment income, both triggered the economic need to engage in paid sex, and provided opportunity and licence to do so.

These defendants' ages ranged from nineteen to fifty, with a mean average of thirty-two years. Seven were in their twenties, more than half over thirty, which nods toward King's view that the relative predominance of female criminals in the thirty- to forty-five-year age group is symptomatic of single or unsupported mothers trying to keep their families from starving at a time in life when prostitution as a source of income was closing or closed to them.[89] Allotments stopped with a seaman's death, so widowhood could bring about poverty regardless of the woman's age, necessitating the resumption of her former activity, or her venturing for the first time into the dangerous world of paid sex. Completing his survey of 'fallen women' prisoners, Millbank's chaplain concluded the trade was something to be turned to in hard times, abandoned in better when 'they gladly forsake the streets, and … "keep within doors".'[90] 'Hard times' could and did arise despite the monthly allotment, and husbands' survival. Of Portsea Island allottees charged with prostitution or its related offences, and whose allotment figures are known, all but one received less than the cohort average of £1 6s 6d per month, one receiving half *of that average*. That was bad enough. If resorting to prostitution brought her not solvency but arrest, the seaman's woman would find herself facing further hardship. Loitering for immoral purposes could result in a forty-shilling fine, a sum 13s 4d greater than that £1 6s 6d monthly average allotment.[91] Inadequate allotments could not stretch to such expenses, and to prevent women paying fines for prostitution-related offences with cash earned by servicing a few additional punters, magistrates usually imposed gaol sentences. Terms of three to twenty-one days were common, 'riotous' behaviour usually meriting the longer sentences, hard labour routinely added. These sentences were relatively light: those convicted of theft sometimes faced transportation.

---

[88] Perkin, *Women and Marriage*, p. 158.
[89] Peter King, 'Female Offenders, Work and Lifestyle Change in Late Eighteenth-century London', *Continuity & Change*, 11:1 (1996), 61–90, at pp. 82–3.
[90] Priestley, *Victorian Prison Lives*, pp. 72–3; Bartley, *Prostitution*, p. 8.
[91] Bartley, *Prostitution*, p. 31.

Husbands of our likely prostitute-allottees include fifer, stoker, bosun, able seaman, carpenter, gunner, Royal Marine private, and captains of the afterguard, forecastle and foretop. Some of these men's 'qualities' were highly respectable, achieved through long experience, good conduct and the acquisition of knowledge and skill. It would be natural to assume that their shoreside lives reflected those attributes, yet wives of senior lower-deck men have been found living in streets and courts notorious for prostitution. Thirty-three of the 1,581 allottees were variously located in Blossom Alley, the Hard, High Street, Southampton Row and White's Row, a finding which raises questions as to how far the respectability and seniority of husbands' ratings bore upon their wives' activities and choice of residence. For all their dubious addresses, these women may have been modest, law-abiding and respectable; but it must be allowed that some may have been prostitutes who simply avoided arrest.

Two lived up to their streets' reputation sufficiently to land them in court. Jane Harrison, wife of AB John Harrison, HMS *Blenheim*, together with a neighbour, assaulted 'one of the many unfortunate women' of notorious Southampton Row, for which attack she and the neighbour, a fellow naval wife were duly fined.[92] Whether Jane was an upright citizen meting out street justice to an importunate whore who had gone too far, or was herself a prostitute briskly seeing off a rival invading her patch, the evidence does not relate. Another infamous locale, White's Row, was home to 23-year-old Mary Ann Blake. In his declaration from HMS *Arethusa*, ordinary seaman William Blake named her his 'mother', an improbable relationship given her age.[93] Mary Ann was arrested for letting fly obscene language from her window, 'acting under the impression that the law could not take hold of her.' Unable to pay the 11s 6d fine and costs, she was imprisoned for five days.[94] Innocent though Jane Harrison may have been of any involvement in prostitution, she both lived in Southampton Row and had an implied association with a prostitute; meanwhile, Mary Ann Blake both lived in White's Row and let her obscene language and behaviour spill into the street. Both women were tainted by their own conduct, and by their residing in known haunts of pimps and prostitutes.

Of those hundreds of mid-century female defendants, just two dozen – a figure equivalent to 1.6 per cent of our 1,549 women – were so actively and imprudently associated with the sex trade as to come to the notice of police and magistrates. If defendants with generic names are set aside as namesakes, the number of allottees who may with confidence be said

---

[92] ADM 27/109/422/347; *H/Tel*, 31 August 1850, p. 7 col. F.
[93] 1851 census: HO107/1658, fol. 150, p. 16; ADM 27/110/184/290.
[94] *H/Tel*, 2 September 1848, p. 7 col. F.

to be involved in prostitution is even further reduced. Absence of proof, however, is not proof of absence from the trade. To argue that no seamen's women participated in the sex trade is to fly in the face of reason. For one thing, the qualities and behaviours that helped them survive their men's absence were the very ones most likely to propel them into the trade, and to protect them while active in it. As to the economic and social circumstances driving their involvement, conditional argument may provide an explanation. Thus if the allotment alone were not enough to live on; if only a minority of naval women were waged, and poorly so; if their dependence on the parish were half that of the wider Portsea Island community, then it follows that naval women, in order to survive, were supplementing their income by other means. And if the usual makeshift economy of barter and borrow were not supplement enough; if charitable and church doles could not be guaranteed; if subsistence theft risked incarceration or unmeetable fines; and if wages, pawning, debt and credit had their limits, it follows that the only reliable source of coin was from a punter's pocket.

Former seaman Yexley recognised the relationship between prostitution and poverty. Observing that port town women were 'part and parcel of naval life', he noted the precarity of their existence when ships were at sea.[95] That precarity is central to the place of seamen's women in the popular imagination. It underlies, in some instances explains, the saucy boldness, the roistering, the unseemly forwardness captured in image after image of the port town whore. Diffidence and restraint were counter-productive, did not attract custom, so if she were to take her domestic economy from precarity to security the seaman's woman must not merely exercise choice; she must adopt traits and behaviours alien to the respectable sort. In order to earn she must play the part. Lee concluded that an element of self-determination distinguished those who included prostitution in their makeshift economies from those who did not, and that a move into prostitution may reflect an element of agency.[96] Self-determination and agency were among the qualities enabling seamen's women to survive their men's long absences; they were also qualities likely to add notoriety, to set them apart from their civilian peers. It then required little imagination to regard (and portray) seamen's women as port-town doxies. Some, no doubt, were just that, habituated to the role, playing with gusto the role of roistering Nancy and saucy Sal, seeing the income it brought as fair exchange for the nastier aspects of the trade; but to assume that most if not all seamen's women

---

[95] Woods, *Our Fighting Seamen*, p. 59.
[96] Catherine Lee, *Policing Prostitution, 1856–1886: deviance, surveillance and morality* (Abingdon, 2015), pp. 47–9.

were prostitutes is to scapegoat an entire community, and to ignore the part played by civilian women in the same trade.

If we accept the inevitability of some seamen's women's involvement in prostitution, questions remain as to how they were able to operate 'under the radar' to the extent that they rarely appear among female defendants facing prostitution-related charges. Were they more discreet than their civilian peers, more adept at evading arrest? Had they developed networking tactics to help each other avoid being detained? Did local police, out of solidarity with their naval fellows, out of recognition of the women's straitened circumstances, or in return for sexual favours, turn a blind eye to seamen's women's activities? Did policemen trade leniency for unpaid sex, or blackmail the women with threats of exposure and arrest? Did they go so far as to provide a form of avuncular protection, alerting the women to raids and crackdowns? Did they regard seamen's women as canaries in the coalmine, protecting civilian women from the taint of prostitution? Were seamen's women controlled by pimps who, independently or in collusion with the police, ensured 'their' prostitutes kept working while civilian women were arrested? On the basis of what little evidence exists, all we can say in answer to these questions is that seamen's women did participate in the sex trade, but not to the extent of occupying a demonstrably dominant role in it, or so far as to explain their being singularised and vilified in contemporary literature and imagery, or to justify their characterisation and wholesale dismissal by later writers.

Let us complete the circle and return to the subject of parish relief, and consider how it related to the sex trade. We have seen that the proportion of allottees recorded as paupers on out-relief was near-half the county average for 1850, and just over half the Portsea Island estimated mean.[97] As the century wore on, poor law unions would increasingly enquire into out-relief applicants' moral character and way of life, guardians using a woman's conduct, 'unclean habits', cohabitation with a man or having male lodgers to justify a refusal to grant out-relief.[98] Could this practice have contributed to the unexpectedly small proportion of paupers found among our allottees? Might guardians have adopted a principle by which knowledge of or suspicion as to a woman's engagement in prostitution precluded her from parish support? No written policy to this effect has been found in the Portsea Island Union records, nor any record of an application being refused on the grounds of the applicant's being [believed to be] a prostitute;

---

[97] Mills *et al.*, 'Southern Historians and Victorian Censuses', p. 70; Lees, *Solidarities of Strangers*, p. 183.
[98] Thane, 'Women and the Poor Law', pp. 38–41.

but the possibility remains that, being based on prejudice and assumption rather than policy, such judgments went unminuted.

Equally feasible, and equally unprovable, is the obverse of this explanatory coin: that naval women's dependence upon the parish was reduced not because of poor law union discrimination, but because the women themselves were prepared to exploit local demand for paid sex. As explanation for the lower-than-average proportion of paupers among the study cohort this rests not on guardians' assumptions as to the women's morality and character but on the uncomfortable premise that prostitution was a near-inevitable component of naval wifedom, only the spouses of higher-paid senior ratings and/or most generous husbands being spared the hard moral choice. This is tricky, for it follows that seamen's brides knowingly signed on both for naval marriage *and* (if necessary, when hard times struck) for prostitution, and that sailor-grooms were complicit in the deal. Too cynical to be true? Lee notes a nineteenth-century Maidstone missionary stating he knew that married women who practised prostitution often did so with their husbands' knowledge, 'for the sake of obtaining dress'.[99] A boatswain RN, witness to the 1859 Royal Commission, confirms that seamen's wives were reduced to desperate measures in the 2–5 months that passed before ships were at Spithead and ready for sea, during which time 'the man has no means of furnishing his wife with a subsistence'.[100] Deploying the same meaningful phrase used 150 years later by Rodger, he states that 'a wife starves or sells her things, and tries to *get her living as best she can*' [italics added].[101] That this was reported to a Royal Commission – and by a serving warrant officer, no less – indicates that seamen's wives' resorting to prostitution was a practice both common and well-known in naval communities.

It is not impossible that some seamen trimmed their payments to measly levels in the knowledge, belief or expectation that their wives would – of necessity, by fair means or foul – make up the shortfall. In practical terms the argument is more viable than a man's gambling that pitching his allotment well below the moiety level would guarantee his dependants parish relief. It also recognises the uncomfortable, inarguable fact that women had greater agency and earning potential as prostitutes than as poor relief applicants, and seamen's women in particular had their own 'neighbourhood norms and customs'.[102] This is not to say that they enjoyed the trade or were proud of their involvement. It does, however, bespeak a sisterhood

---

[99] Lee, *Policing Prostitution*, pp. 47–8.
[100] Hardwicke, *Report*, p. 208 ss. 3585–6.
[101] Ibid., p. 208, s. 3587; Rodger, *Command of the Ocean*, p. 407.
[102] August, *Poor Women's Lives*, pp. 124–5.

that understood the economic pressures they all faced, and a pragmatism overriding social niceties and personal pride.

Consider Chapter Four's evidence that many naval daughters became naval brides, and the proximity, interconnectedness and social interaction of port town naval sisters, mothers and wives. It is not improbable that within the naval community it was understood that allotments alone were rarely enough to live on, and then only with hardship. From there it is not unreasonable to suggest that where all else failed – the borrowing, pawning, flitting and trading that made up the makeshift economy – a naval wife might at some point in her married life be reduced to taking the dangerous and unwelcome step of selling herself for cash, *and that her peers would not condemn her for doing so*. Outwith the naval community, for such an understanding to exist was regarded as proof that the popular image of the seaman's woman was spot-on: that she really was as promiscuous and mercenary as depicted, lacking the moral codes to which respectable people conformed. Within the female naval community this understanding was rooted in empathy, compassion, pragmatism and a shared belief that seamen's women must stick together, must do whatever it took in order to survive, if necessary in defiance of public opinion, if necessary at cost to naval women's collective reputation. It was that or starve.

*11*

# CRIME

This chapter looks at seamen's women's involvement in theft, assault and personation. These crimes were selected for consideration because the non-prostitution-related offences for which nineteenth-century women were most commonly charged and convicted include crimes involving property, crimes against people, and crimes arising from poverty, including vagrancy, begging and subsistence theft.[1]

Evidence of women's involvement in criminal activity begins with police records. Suspects' names first appear in the local force's logs of arrests and detentions, often within minutes of the events in question.[2] As well as names of the accused, and dates, places and reasons for arrest, the ledgers record time of arrival at the police station (a telling detail, usually confirming late-night or early-hours incidents, at a time when respectable people were abed), and how the matter was dealt with. There is an immediacy about the entries. Busy nights show successive detentions logged within minutes of each other, the duty officer's handwriting remaining steady amid detainees' drunken outbursts and disruptive behaviour. Locations – a street name, a courtyard, sometimes a specific public house – identify crime hot spots; but offenders' home addresses were not logged, suggesting that many of those who were brought to the police house were homeless or prone to frequent changes of residence, or that local police were familiar with repeat offenders' addresses to the point of not needing to record them. The records show some detainees being released without charge after a few hours in the cells; more often they appeared in court the following day.

Newspaper coverage of court proceedings was, like twenty-first-century 'true crime' television documentaries, hugely popular with mid-nineteenth-century readers.[3] Popular it may have been, but in the *Hampshire*

---

[1] Zedner, *Women, Crime*, pp. 34–6.
[2] PHC: SB/DF/P/1, *passim*.
[3] Kim Stevenson, 'Ingenuities of the Female Mind: legal and public perceptions of sexual violence in Victorian England 1850–1890', in Shani D'Cruze (ed.), *Everyday*

*Telegraph*, as in other publications, reporting was often subjective, judgemental and inconsistently detailed. Magistrates' pronouncements appear to have been transcribed verbatim, but were unlikely to have been reproduced in full. Headings, descriptions and additional comments were at reporters' or sub editors' discretion, tailored to incite moral indignation, arouse pity or amusement, or chime with readers' prejudices. Euphemisms such as 'outrage', 'the act' and 'had connexion' were commonly substituted for 'rape'; they disguised the nature and severity of events, while 'through sloppy note-taking, the mishearing of testimony or deliberate embellishment, journalists frequently twisted statements to cast a shadow over [a woman's] moral character.'[4] Language was coded, the full facts censored, but in a manner still capable of exciting readers' imaginations, as when *The Times* omitted details due to their being deemed 'unreportable' or 'too disgusting for publication'.[5]

The *Hampshire Telegraph* reported on proceedings of the quarterly assizes to which defendants were committed when charged with offences too serious to be dealt with by magistrates. Official record of this higher stage in the legal process took the form of printed calendars.[6] Concise, austere in style, court calendars frequently listed crimes under the umbrella term of 'felony', with no further explanation. 'Felony' usually meant theft, but sometimes enough detail was provided to indicate the nature and context of an offence other than larceny.[7]

In Victorian summary courts only one-fifth of those convicted were female.[8] Portsmouth courts in years 1848–52 saw more than 500 female defendants charged with nearly 900 offences. From the laughable ('continually annoying her sister') to the pitiable (attempted suicide by drowning; concealing the birth of a child and disposing of its body), charges are both familiar to the modern reader and evocative of a past age.[9] Criminal damage such as breaking pub windows is alleged alongside uttering false

---

*Violence in Britain, 1850–1950* (Harlow, 2000), 89–103, at p. 90.
[4] *Ibid.*, p. 94; Rubenhold, *The Five*, p. 82.
[5] Stevenson, 'Ingenuities', p. 94.
[6] PHC: S7/1.
[7] 'Simple larceny was a category created in 1827 following the abolition of the distinction between petty larceny and grand larceny. The offence covered all types of theft perpetrated without any other aggravating circumstance, such as assault or breaking and entering, theft from the person or from a specified place': Tim Hitchcock *et al.*, 'The Old Bailey Proceedings Online, 1674–1913' (University of Sheffield Digital Humanities Institute, 2012) <https://www.oldbaileyonline.org> [accessed 22 April 2024]. With the introduction of the *Criminal Justice Act* 18 & 19 Vict., c.126 (1855), many of these cases would be tried summarily by magistrates.
[8] Clive Emsley, *Crime and Society in England, 1750–1900* (London, 2010), p. 98.
[9] H/Tel, 24 March 1849, p. 7 col. D; *ibid.*, 22 April 1848, p. 8 col. E.

*Crime*

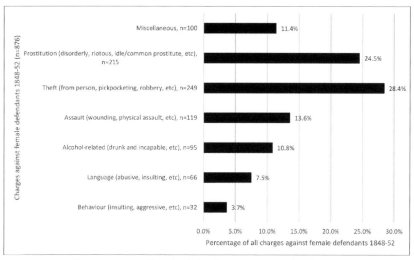

**Fig. 26**  Charges against female defendants, Portsea Island courts 1848–52 (n=876).

coin, an offence particularly associated with female offenders.[10] Serving alcohol during divine service is alleged alongside vagrancy and smuggling tobacco. There are women arraigned for begging, fraud, receiving stolen goods and failing to pay tax, and women accused of causing a chimney to catch fire, placing lines across the street and hanging clothes thereon, of being 'in want of sureties', or a wandering lunatic. Sailors' women appear as witnesses, co-defendants and victims. They both broke the law and turned to it for protection, justice and redress.

When those 876 women's offences are clustered by type, theft and prostitution-related incidents together account for half of all charges.

## THEFT

At 28.4 per cent of the 876 offences occurring in years 1848–52, theft was the single largest category. This finding chimes with the national picture. Across England and Wales, in urban and rural settings alike, larceny was the single largest category of crime for both sexes, in the period 1810–50 accounting for 75 to 83 per cent of Old Bailey cases.[11] Within those figures are gendered trends, men being more associated with violent offences, women with

---

[10] Uttering false coin: the crime of tendering a counterfeit coin with intent to defraud.
[11] George Rudé, *Criminal and Victim: crime and society in early nineteenth-century England* (Oxford, 1985), p. 61. Larceny: the theft of personal property.

non-violent property offences.[12] Theft required no special equipment or knowledge, and was likely to produce a quicker, more fruitful result than the usual economic tactics of taking in lodgers, flitting to cheaper digs or 'doing without'.[13] Contemporary social commentators blamed theft upon a greater female independence associated with urban living, a view having particular resonance for the arguably more 'independent' sailor's woman with spouse absent.[14] Old Bailey commentators have suggested that women thieves were more likely to steal clothes and household goods; they knew their value, were familiar with the barter process and local trading sites, and clothes were easy to sell, or pawn.[15] Moreover, because childcare, domestic duties and home-based outwork tended to restrict them to a limited geographical area, and because opportunities for theft occurred close to home, women were also more likely to steal from those they knew.[16] Regarded by some as morally preferable to debt or prostitution, in poor communities theft was a manifestation of need, a means of survival, and thus 'not always ruled out' – especially when it involved the stealing of food (an observation borne out in numerous *Hampshire Telegraph* court reports).[17] A debtor-thief might in mitigation plead poverty, might even sway magistrates or jury; but courts were less likely to appreciate a woman's reasons for resorting to prostitution to pay her debts or keep a roof over her head.

As noted previously, because of its association with the sex trade, the stealing of personal articles from male victims was known informally as 'trousering'. In this analysis, charges of 'trousering' are included among other thefts, but earmarked as a sub-category because of the nature of the stolen items and the circumstances of the theft. Sarah Wilson (receiving thirteen shillings per month from husband William, gunner HMS *Hecate*) appeared in court for thefts from the person of 'a man not her husband'.[18] Of Sarah's offence the court reporter observed, with unmistakable meaning, 'This was one of those cases where the woman accosts the man and importunes him to go to her home, and picks his pocket.'[19] At the subsequent quarter sessions Sarah was imprisoned for three weeks with hard labour, which for

---

[12] M.M. Feeley and D.L. Little, 'The Vanishing Female: The Decline of Women in the Criminal Process, 1687–1912', *Law & Society Review*, 25:4 (1991), 719–58, at p. 735.
[13] Chinn, *They Worked all their Lives*, pp. 63–4.
[14] Emsley, *Crime and Society*, p. 97.
[15] L. Mackay, 'Why They Stole: Women in the Old Bailey, 1779–1789', *Journal of Social History*, 32:3 (1999), 623–39, at pp. 625–6.
[16] Zedner, *Women, Crime*, pp. 36, 629.
[17] Chinn, *They Worked all their Lives*, pp. 63–4; Ross, 'Survival Networks', p. 7.
[18] ADM 27/109/257/5; ADM 27/110/316/5; *H/Tel*, 14 July 1849, p. 5 col. D; *ibid.*, 7 April 1849, p. 7 col. D.
[19] *Ibid.*, 3 June 1848, p. 8 col. E.

female felons in the non-debtor wards of Portsmouth's gaol usually meant needlework, picking oakum or domestic duties.[20] Described in the *Telegraph* as 'one of the pavé', Mary Smith, wife of captain of the mizzen top Thomas Smith, HMS *Excellent*, was arraigned for 'easing a gentleman upwards of 14L [*sic*], but as the gentleman was not present [the court] discharged her with an intimation not to be brought there again.'[21]

That 'trousering' appears so frequently in Portsmouth police court reports supports the argument that it comprised the most prevalent form of larceny from the person, this despite its going under-reported due to clients' reluctance to face the consequences of their complaint.[22] 'Encouraged perhaps by the feeling that these men had brought their troubles on themselves', judges and magistrates 'often took a hard line with the [male] prosecutor', while defence lawyers '[had] a field day with the morals and sullied respectability of such victims'.[23] The prospect of being named in a newspaper and rebuked by a contemptuous bench deterred many a sex trade punter from taking his accusation into court. Should he fail to bear witness to his loss he did not escape censure, and things did not always end well for him when he did appear. Describing one case dismissed for lack of evidence, the journalist smirked, 'One would have supposed that under the circumstances … Mr Wise would have been *wise* enough to have stopped away in the first place.'[24]

The case against gunner's wife Eliza Langford, charged by a Joseph Moss with relieving him of three shillings, was dismissed when her prosecutor failed to appear.[25] Jane Brooks (receiving £3 11s 0d per month via allotments from two Royal Marine brothers) was not so lucky: for stealing four shillings and three sixpences from a James Harvey she got six months' gaol with hard labour, the first and last weeks solitary.[26] Jane was employed in her husband's shop, had daughters aged three and two, and a son of three months who was probably still breastfeeding. Given her husband's business preoccupations, day-to-day care of the little ones during their mother's

---

[20] Ibid., 8 July 1848, p. 5 col. D; Pat Thompson, *Portsmouth Borough Gaol in the Nineteenth Century* (Portsmouth, 1980), p. 8.
[21] ADM 27/112/41/1498; H/Tel, 23 September 1848, p. 7 col. D. '14L': £14 0s 0d.
[22] Mackay, 'Why They Stole', p. 626; Frances Finnegan, *Poverty and Prostitution: a study of Victorian prostitutes in York* (Cambridge, 1979), p. 118; Emsley, *Crime and Society*, p. 100; Lincoln, *Naval Wives*, p. 165.
[23] John M. Beattie, 'The Criminality of Women in Eighteenth-Century England', *Journal of Social History*, 8:4 (1975), 80–116, at p. 95; Emsley, *Crime and Society*, p. 100.
[24] H/Tel, 22 July 1848, p. 7 col. D.
[25] ADM 27/120/100/2; PHC: SB/DF/P/1, p. 364.
[26] ADM 27/112/208/11; ADM 27/113/430/4; H/Tel, 14 July 1849, p. 5 col. D.

incarceration would very likely have fallen to 12-year-old Charlotte, Jane's daughter by her previous marriage to a Royal Marine, a wet nurse being employed for the infant.[27] The consequences of even the pettiest of thefts were felt by the entire family.

Given the inadequacy of sailors' pay and the smallness of some allotments, it was expected that evidence would emerge to show seamen's women committing subsistence-related theft. Twenty-seven allottees are known to have faced charges of theft, some on multiple occasions and under circumstances other than 'trousering'. One was Kate Godfrey, wife of private third class Henry, HMS *Leander*.[28] In the 1851 census she described herself as 'sempstress'. The amount Henry allotted her is unknown, but she appears to qualify as one who stole out of necessity after pawning her raw materials, a common outworker tactic. By the time of her offending, in 1853, she was no longer a sempstress but a servant, stealing from her master a shawl, silver tablespoons and pillowcase which she sold to a Southsea broker, and a gold locket which she pawned for a shilling. 'She begged her master to forgive her, saying she was in debt at Gosport.'[29] Under the Pawnbroker's Act, 'unlawfully pledging or disposing' (which usually involved servants' attempts to pawn their employers' goods with a view to redeeming them on pay-day) was the only summary offence for which the number of women convicted was consistently higher than the number of men.[30] Few employers would retain a servant found guilty of such an offence, and few would be inclined to vouch for the (now ex-)worker's employability. Dismissal without a 'character' from an employer usually spelled disaster.[31] Due to the greater stigma attached to the female criminal it was far harder for the woman ex-offender to secure employment, especially in menial posts requiring trust.[32] Domestic service in particular relied upon householders' ability to trust servants with their material goods, personal papers and private concerns, and employers relied upon workers' honesty in handling goods, tools, jewellery, keys and cash. Convicted of theft, Kate would be unlikely to get domestic work again.

The goods which Mary Ann Morley stole from her milliner employer – collars, neckerchiefs, a veil, silk stockings and other haberdashery – were less valuable than Kate Godfrey's haul. Taking place over four months, however, Mary Ann's thefts appeared more calculated than impulsive, earning her a

---

[27] 1851 census: HO107/1658, fol. 17, p. 27; CHU14/A/2/1/1, p. 60 n. 476; CHU3/1D/31, p. 69 n. 205.
[28] ADM 27/109/273/45.
[29] 1851 census: HO107/1659, fol. 14, p. 20; PHC: S7/1; *H/Tel*, 19 February 1853, p. 5 col. E, and p. 7 col. F.
[30] Emsley, *Crime and Society*, p. 102.
[31] Petrie, *Singular Iniquity*, p. 77.
[32] Emsley, *Crime and Society*, pp. 98–9; Zedner, *Women, Crime*, p. 43.

sentence of five months' imprisonment, the last week solitary.[33] Mary Ann had been due to receive £1 16s 0d per month from her brother, AB Richard Binstead, HMS *Resolute*.[34] Regulations decreed that uncollected payments stopped after two months, the allotment not restarting until a fresh declaration were made. Assuming Richard's May 1850 declaration were promptly processed, it is likely that Mary Ann was in gaol when her monies first became available, and was still there when payments were stopped due to non-collection. This unfortunate timing meant she missed out on the doubling of pay that went with *Resolute*'s commission on discovery service in search of the Franklin expedition.

Being married to or otherwise dependent upon seamen did not dissuade allottees from robbing seamen. When stoker's sister Eliza Day ('a denizen of White's Row') stole eleven pounds from mariner Ambrose Funnell, she pocketed more than many an allottee received in a year.[35] Seaman Timothy Allen was robbed of a serge frock by Mary Ryan, trustee for the daughter of quartermaster Joseph Marshall, HMS *Victory*.[36] Named trustee by private third class William Northover, HMS *Blenheim*, Maria Giles was described in court as a prostitute who stole five pounds from the master of a vessel. Declining the bench's invitation to plead guilty, she said the master 'gave her the note to sleep with him', an explanation unlikely to have helped her case; she was committed for trial.[37] Mary Webb stole a silk kerchief from the neck of a seaman asleep on a Common Hard doorstep.[38] Wife of quartermaster John Webb, HMY *Victoria and Albert*, she was aided and abetted by a sailor, the offence earning the partners in crime six weeks' hard labour.

Items stolen were for the most part small and pawnable – shirts from a washing line, a book, yards of cloth from a merchant. Walkowitz notes newspaper reports' frequent mention of women stealing blankets, sheets and other moveables, items taken from lodgings in order to be pawned.[39] It is a finding replicated here. Two women steal a bundle of clothes from 'a sailor belonging to the *Victoria and Albert* yacht'; one woman steals a gown from another's room; a nurse takes a scarf from the family of a sick child she

---

[33] 1851 census: HO107/1659, fol. 373, p. 14; *H/Tel*, 15 July 1848, p. 7 col. E; *ibid.*, 8 October 1848, p. 7 col. E.

[34] ADM 27/110/250/17.

[35] ADM 27/113/249/31; 1851 census: HO107/1658, fol. 151, p. 19; *H/Tel*, 21 June 1856, p. 5 col. C.

[36] ADM 27/112/158/8; 1851 census: HO107/1658, fol. 132, p. 19; *H/Tel*, 24 September 1853, p. 5 col. D.

[37] ADM 27/110/280/92; 1851 census: HO107/1658, fol. 71, p. 36; 2 October 1858, p. 8 col. C.

[38] ADM 27/113/59/8; *H/Tel*, 16 August 1856, p. 5 col. D.

[39] Walkowitz and Walkowitz, '"We Are Not Beasts of the Field"', p. 86.

had been tending, and sells it to a friend.[40] Allottees appear as victims and perpetrators. Caroline Payne, named 'trustee' in *Birkenhead* stoker John Darkenman's allotment, was robbed of two blankets worth 9s 6d from the room she let at 3s 6d per week, alleged thief Ann Laxton having told her she was the wife of a sailor gone to sea; 'wife of a sailor' was true, AB George Laxton, HMS *Leander*, having earlier that year declared an allotment in Ann's favour.[41] Trustee Maria Giles, she who stole five pounds from the master of a vessel, discovered her lodging house in White's Row had been relieved of a blanket by two sailors.[42] Fifty-three-year-old Elizabeth Fry's theft was of another variety, her spoils a bracelet and parasol belonging to the wife of a brazier.[43] She may have intended to sell them on, boosting the one-pound-per-month allotment she received from her son Edward Donnelly, HMS *Penelope*.[44] Elizabeth's husband was an East Street publican, a fact affording her no shortage of contacts to fence her stolen goods in exchange for cash.[45]

Where Elizabeth's offending has the hallmarks of cupidity, other women's thefts – of cabbages from a field, a loaf of bread, an enticing meal of bread, butter and cheese – speak more of hunger and poverty.[46] That said, thefts from employers, and of food, and the seemingly impulsive stealing of pawnable clothing, are associated less often with identifiable allottees than are thefts bearing the hallmarks of 'trousering'. The theft committed by Matilda White, wife of captain of the foretop Richard, HMS *Thetis*, was altogether different.[47] With two male and two female accomplices she stole sixteen jackets, property of Her Majesty – very likely from military stores in local barracks or the dockyard. The two men were gaoled for eight months with hard labour, the women receiving sentences half as long.[48] Consider, by contrast, the sentences dealt three women not known to be allottees, at quarter sessions during the same period. For thefts of a shawl and a sheet, two were transported for seven years; the third stole a pewter measure and a glass, and was transported for ten years.[49] Tried between 1849 and 1851,

[40] *H/Tel*, 22 July 1848, p. 7 col. D; *ibid*. 2 June 1849, p. 7 col. C; *ibid*. 3 November 1849, p. 7 col. D.
[41] ADM 27/113/430/60; *H/Tel*, 18 May 1850, p. 5 col. F; ADM 27/109/262/81.
[42] ADM 27/110/280/92; *H/Tel*, 31 December 1859, p. 5 col. C.
[43] *H/Tel*, 1 November 1856, p. 5 col. E.
[44] ADM 27/113/251/73.
[45] 1851 census: HO107/1658, fol. 521, p. 20.
[46] *H/Tel*, 22 July 1848, p. 7 col. D; *ibid.*, 6 January 1849, p. 7 col. D; *ibid.*, 23 June 1849, p. 7 col. E.
[47] ADM 27/111/180/104.
[48] *H/Tel*, 30 October 1852, p. 7 col. F.
[49] *Ibid.*, 26 July 1851, p. 8 col. F; *ibid*, 2 November 1850, p. 7 col. F; *ibid.*, 14 July 1849, p. 5 col. D.

these cases narrowly predated implementation of legislative changes which would substitute imprisonment for transportation.[50] The Portsmouth judiciary, however, took a dim view of women felons, and had no hesitation in imposing the severe sentences allowed under prevailing law.

## ASSAULT

Of those 876 offences clustered by type, assault comprised the third largest cluster. Twenty-one of the 119 alleged assailants were either allottees or a curiously large number of allottee namesakes.

Female-on-female attacks were three times the number of female-on-male attacks. This was partly a function of men's greater strength, but there was a social element to the ratio. Men tended to be away most of the day, leaving women in a largely female environment where jealousies, resentments over unpaid debts, inferred insult, unresolved disputes, gossip and criticisms could quickly spill into physical expression by way of a hurled chamber pot, pulled hair, a slap. Reporters often depicted woman-on-woman incidents as catfights, their victims as morally responsible or guilty by association. The Cork-born wife of boatswain third class Thomas Van Studer, HMS *Blenheim*, was wounded by another woman.[51] How and why this happened is lost amid the reporter's gleeful account of the court hearing in which 'Mistress Vanstuder' [*sic*] and 'Mistress Murphy' are mocked for their Irish accents, fast-paced speech, garrulity and wandering off the point. Mary Van Studer's being bitten on the breast – an acutely painful and shocking wound – is rendered in cod 'Oirish' as 'Mistress Murphy *bate* her on the breast'. As well as failing to recognise the hurt suffered, such reporting hardened the prevailing belief that Irish women had a particular reputation for violence.[52] Like the other half-dozen allottee-victims of assault, Mary had no husband at home to comfort her after her attack. Humiliation in court and mockery in print can only have added to her distress.

We have heard how 50-year-old Jane Harrison, wife of AB John Harrison, HMS *Blenheim*, joined forces with a 47-year-old unmarried woman cordwainer from three doors down in Southampton Row to assault Elizabeth Smith, 'one of the many unfortunate women of that place'.[53] They laid into her with a will, for she appeared in court with a black eye. 'As is usual in these cases,' lamented the *Telegraph*, 'witnesses brought forward by the different parties gave different versions of the affair, which taken altogether

[50] *Convict Prisons Act,* 16 & 17 Vict., c. 121 (1853), *Penal Servitude Act,* 16 & 17 Vict., c. 99 (1853); *Penal Servitude Act,* 20 & 21 Vict., c. 3 (1857).
[51] ADM 27/110/401/515, ADM 27/113/39/55; *H/Tel*, 4 May 1850, p. 7 col. F.
[52] Emsley, *Crime and Society*, p. 103.
[53] ADM 27/109/422/347; *H/Tel*, 31 August 1850, p. 7 col. F.

was a very disgraceful one; but as an assault had been committed, the Court could not do otherwise than commit the parties.' Two women against one was bad enough, but Matilda Wright, wife of leading stoker Robert Wright, HMY *Victoria and Albert*, was said to have gone further, joining forces with three men to attack another woman.[54] She was lucky. Witnesses attested that she had been sitting up with her landlady at the time of the alleged incident, and had been 'called upon by the complainant's husband to assist him in getting her indoors.' When one of Matilda's co-accused requested their prosecutrix be punished, the bench assured him that the press would 'do away with any stigma' attaching to their characters. The reporter duly obliged, his sub-heading 'An Unfounded Charge of Assault Against Four Respectable Persons' going some way to restore Matilda's reputation.

In many instances a defendant's language triggered her arrest for verbal assault. 'Indecent' and 'obscene' were the commonest descriptions, distinguishing the generally offensive utterance from the explicitly threatening and abusive. We glimpse tensions between women as they denounced each other, fought, hurled insults, jeered. Deeming their language 'beastly', 'not fit for publication', the *Telegraph* made it clear these were not respectable people. That their arrests had taken place late at night or in the small hours, on the Common Hard and Queen Street (at the junction of which lay the main dockyard gate), in White's Row and other notorious alleys completed the moral indictment, for no respectable woman would be abroad at that time of night, let alone in such places. To be the object of another woman's indecent language or abuse was to be tarred with the same brush, details of timing, location and preceding events casting doubt upon all concerned. Hannah Cox, named trustee by stoker Joseph Brown, HMS *Retribution*, was on the street at night when a woman used foul language against her.[55] Hannah may have been a modest and respectable matron going about her lawful business, but the time and place of the incident, the very fact that her name was reported in an unsavoury context, combined to cast doubt on her character.

Apart from sly nudges as to the parties concerned ('two of a trade', 'both of [the women] are light characters', 'a squabble between two neighbours arising out of what one had said about the other'), court reporting was socially myopic, rarely mentioning the circumstances surrounding victim-prosecutrix and assailant.[56] Small but telling details are occasionally captured. Private third class Robert Lewis's wife Amelia (*q.v.*) was insulted

---

[54] ADM 27/113/59A/16; *H/Tel*, 14 October 1848, p. 7 col. E.
[55] ADM 27/111/293/69; *H/Tel*, 3 June 1848, p. 8 col. E.
[56] *H/Tel*, 20 January 1849, p. 7 col. D; *ibid.*, 12 May 1849, p. 7 col. D.

and verbally abused by an Elizabeth Dyer.[57] Minutes before hearing Amelia's accusations, the court had tried Elizabeth for stabbing her husband in retaliation for his throwing a kettle of water over her; the case was dismissed 'the charge not being pressed'. Evidence of Elizabeth's attack bore upon Amelia's credibility, for what respectable woman would be acquainted with such a virago, such a violent and unsubmissive wife? To Amelia's further detriment it was stated that before Elizabeth used the language attributed to her (the offence having been prompted by Amelia's muttering 'There she goes', as Elizabeth passed her door), Amelia had told Elizabeth's son to go and tell his mother to stab her husband again. The case was dismissed, but not before doubt had been cast upon the prosecutrix: Amelia knew the woman, was her neighbour, had made a goading remark, had encouraged further violence. Neither victim nor assailant emerged untainted.

Sailors' women were not above fighting. Sometimes they fought each other, but at a cost to both purse and reputation.[58] Needlewoman and able seaman's wife Elizabeth Pinhorn charged Ann Marshall, mother of a gunner's mate, with assaulting her.[59] For what was described as a dispute between two neighbours about what one said of the other, Ann was fined five shillings with nine shillings costs, or seven days' imprisonment, the fine amounting to over half her son's monthly allotment. Thirty-nine-year-old Elizabeth Marks was convicted of assaulting a Jane Hoare. Not in court to hear the verdict, she was fined ten shillings or fourteen days' imprisonment, and a warrant of committal issued.[60] She was better placed than many to pay the fine, which amounted to one-fifth the monthly total of £2 10s 0d she received as wife of ship's corporal Thomas Marks, HMS *Victory*, and trustee for the child of stoker George Banyer, HMS *Blenheim*.[61] Elizabeth Guithard received £1 4s 0d monthly from her husband Henry, gunner's mate HMS *Blenheim*; this was less than half the amount enjoyed by Elizabeth Marks via her two allotments, so the 2s 6d fine and nine shillings costs imposed on Guithard for assaulting her neighbour would have cut deep into her monthly budget.[62] Her alleged crime? To throw mud over a yard wall, soiling the neighbour's bonnet and shawl. Considering the case not clearly established, the magistrates 'recommended an amicable adjustment'. This might have given the defendant an 'out' had she and her alleged victim been prepared to set their grievances aside; but the recommendation went

---

[57] ADM 27/110/106/22; *H/Tel*, 16 June 1849, p. 7 col. E.
[58] Emsley, *Crime and Society*, p. 103.
[59] ADM 27/111/134/1531; ADM 27/111/60/1489; *H/Tel*, 12 May 1849, p. 7 col. D.
[60] *Ibid.*, 20 February 1858, p. 8 col. E.
[61] ADM 27/112/60/7; ADM 27/110/142/362.
[62] ADM 27/111/382/1539; *H/Tel*, 12 February 1848, p. 8 col. E.

unheeded, hence the monetary sentence with its alternative of five days' imprisonment.

Unlike Elizabeth Guithard, Mary Anne Kate Harding was unmarried. Like Elizabeth, however, Mary Anne Kate's inflexibility led to her court appearance. Later named by ordinary seaman Richard Fleming, HMS *Leander*, as trustee for a 1-year-old girl, she was seventeen when charged with assaulting and dragging by the hair a young woman she believed had laughed at her.[63] 'I can't pay,' she announced when fined 2s 6d with seven shillings costs. Sentenced to seven days' imprisonment, she 'kissed her hand to several weeping friends in the gallery, who appeared much afflicted by their temporary bereavement,' noted the *Telegraph*, 'and retired below to become acquainted with the internal arrangements of the asylum for many an unhappy wanderer.' At the time of her gaoling Mary Anne Kate had yet to become a mother (the 1-year-old in Fleming's later declarations was hers, and more will be said of her in Chapter Fifteen). In this respect her timing was fortunate. For the naval woman with husband at sea and dependent children at home, inability to pay a fine meant dependence on others for childcare during the days or weeks of her incarceration.

## SCAMS

Some individuals – in seamen's memoirs invariably female – successfully operated scams, most commonly depicted as naval women exploiting seamen's gullibility and trust. Pretending to be seamen's relatives, the scammers are described as collecting multiple allotments to which they were not entitled. To pretend to be a seaman's sister, trustee, mother or grandmother (or as the wording on allotment vouchers put it, to '[make] a false Declaration or Affirmation for the purpose of receiving an Allotment') amounted to perjury.[64] Where a scammer went further, persuading one seaman after another to marry her, to perjury must be added the crime of bigamy. As found in this study, evidence of bigamy (see Chapter Thirteen) is primarily suggestive of complex family relationships rather than greed and calculation. By contrast, Clayton asserts that there were 'plenty of women who would marry a sailor ... for the convenience of relieving him of some of his pay ... in some cases marrying again when convenient.'[65] Portsea residents, too, describe tactics adopted by women taking on 'shorter-term sailors' while their long-term partners were at sea, until a total of four or five allotments had been acquired.

---

[63] ADM 27/110/156/184; ADM 27/112/313/184; *H/Tel*, 1 April 1848, p. 3 col. E.
[64] See Fig. 2.
[65] Tim Clayton, *Tars: the Men who Made Britain Rule the Waves* (London, 2007), p. 89.

She's worked it all out so that when one's home the other's away. So she's getting three or four pounds a week coming in ... But if she's unfortunate enough for one to come home earlier and find her in the pub with a different man, he goes over and slits her throat.[66]

No case of punitive throat-slitting has been found in police or court records or local newspaper reports, suggesting the remark was mere oral swagger on the part of the interviewee. However, the gendered mix of condemnation and approval is likely to reflect lower-deck thinking, an expression of seamen's sense of entitlement in return for their monetary support. Unless as another man's sister or trustee, a woman discovered by her husband to be covertly accepting coin from an unrelated sailor could expect recrimination, even stoppage of her allotment; and as her benefactor-spouse turned oppressor, for her perceived perfidy she might face physical danger, as Chapter Twelve observes.

Defined as the assuming of another person's identity with intent to deceive, personation was an act of fraud constituting felony. As a means of acquiring an allotment it was more serious than contriving a spurious relationship with a seaman, for it necessitated the appropriating of a genuine allottee's papers. Simple envy of an allottee's financial benefit was something felt by many, whether the unentitled civilian, or the naval wife resentful of the comparative meanness of her own allotment sum; stealing and misusing a fellow allottee's documents, however, was something else entirely, for it disadvantaged a financially vulnerable person who might struggle to re-establish her entitlement. Little wonder, then, that personation could and did result in neighbour peaching on neighbour, ensuring the perpetrator was punished for her crime. 'Navy sources do not support facile notions of "sisterhood" ... They contain far too much evidence of women defrauding and exploiting each other, denouncing friends and even relatives to the Navy Board, and pursuing their own or their immediate families' interest at everyone else's expense.'[67] It was not always necessary for neighbours to inform on suspected personators. Pay office staff were adept at spotting unfamiliar faces and dubious presentations, and unafraid to report their suspicions. As one witness told the Royal Commission on naval manning, personation 'has been done and people tried for it'.[68] Of the true scale of the problem, however, the Commission was not advised. Few incidents have been found. A sailor's wife from Gosport, receiving half-pay from her husband, attempted personation of another seaman's wife, on

---

[66] Kevin Haines and Claire Shilton, *Hard Times, Good Times: Tales of Portsea People* (Horndean, 1987), p. 63.
[67] Hunt, 'Women and the Fiscal-imperial State', p. 43.
[68] Hardwicke, *Report*, p. 275 s. 5237.

the same day endeavouring to obtain yet another's half-pay by the same means.[69] A stern headline 'Attempted Fraud on the Admiralty' proclaimed the seriousness of another such offence.[70] Newspaper coverage described Landport Street neighbours Sarah Rees and Elizabeth Jane Payne as 'two respectable-looking females', which if not an example of journalistic irony may simply have involved their making themselves look clean and neat, for sensible women knew that 'a lady's dress, or even that of a respectable working-woman, was a *protection*'.[71] The two fraudsters were not civilians jealous of naval women's monthly monies. Sarah (*q.v.*) was wife to William Reece alias Rees, gunner's mate, HMS *Hogue*, Elizabeth the pub-dwelling mother of William Payne, carpenter's crew, HMS *Leander*.[72] Each in turn had attempted to pass herself off to pay office staff as an allottee entitled to two pounds per month. They were remanded, but discharged the following week, a surprising outcome given the pay office staff's evidence, the seriousness of the charge and the warning printed on every allotment bill. Their apparent willingness to cause loss and distress to a fellow allottee illustrates only too clearly that unreliable sisterhood to which Hunt refers.

Personation was a complicated crime requiring careful planning, access to documents likely to be kept in a safe place, knowledge of how the disbursement system worked, confidence sufficient to convince pay office staff, and preparedness to face legal consequences. This, however, is to ignore the fact that, like their civilian neighbours, most naval women will have been brought up to honour the Commandments and obey the law. To the majority, personation was unthinkable, a branch of theft which, as every allotment voucher warned, 'By Virtue of the Act 11 Geo. IV, the personating or falsely assuming the Name or Character of any Person, to obtain Payment of an Allotment, is … a Felony'.[73] Moral and judicial jeopardy aside, it remains likely that within a community where seamen's women were surviving in straitened circumstances, personation was a particular anathema. Of financial necessity you might approach the parish for relief, but so did many a respectable person in reduced circumstances. You might even enter the sex trade, but the safety and reputation you risked was yours alone. What you did not do was rob a fellow allottee of what might be her only means of support.

---

[69] *H/Tel*, 31 October 1857, p. 5 col. D.
[70] *Ibid.*, 10 May 1862, p. 5 col. C.
[71] *Ibid.*, p. 6 col. F; Rubenhold, *The Five*, p. 70, citing Mary Higgs, who went undercover as a female tramp.
[72] ADM 27/112/178/2; 1851 census: HO107/1659, fol. 467, p. 29; ADM 27/109/265/170; 1851 census: HO107/1659, fol. 304, p. 2. (See pp. 108, 235.)
[73] 11 Geo. IV & 1 Will. IV, c. 20 (1830).

At corporate level, the Navy's fear of fraud underpinned every aspect of the allotment system, was written into its many precepts. Whether because those systemic measures worked, whether because seamen's women obeyed a moral code prohibiting their usurping another woman's allotment, or because they were simply adept at avoiding prosecution for doing so, personation posed little real threat to public funds and/or public morals.

## SINGULARISATION OF THE SEAMAN'S WIFE

Sailors' women's criminality appears little different from that of women in the wider community. In one respect, however, the naval wife stands apart, in that she was frequently identified as such. In article after article female offenders were described as 'a sailor's wife' or 'the wife of a seaman'. This had meaning, for 'A woman who was "drunk and disorderly", who embarrassed herself in public ... *who did not have a respectable home or a husband and family to regulate her conduct*, was judged to be as much a degenerate as a prostitute' [italics added].[74] If her husband were not at home to regulate her conduct, the seaman's wife was open to being judged as degenerate; if her husband were home, she was open to being judged by his character, his legendary promiscuity, drunkenness and irresponsibility.

The singularising of seamen's women was not a feature of all court proceedings or reportage, but only sailors' wives receive such frequent identification in print. The trades of other offenders' husbands were rarely noted. Even as victims, sailors' wives were made conspicuous where others were not.[75] It was court practice to establish women's civil status: reports frequently note female defendants as widow, married or 'singlewoman'. Some magistrates, when considering the size of fine to impose, enquired as to the trade of married women's spouses. This goes to coverture, which was still a feature, for '*feme covert* worked with traditional ideas of patriarchy to give considerable benefit to women, especially in magistrates' courts, well into the nineteenth century', in that any woman who committed felony in company with her husband could argue that she acted under his direction, and thus gain an acquittal.[76] Benefit to women? Not when husbands were routinely absent at sea and thus unable to accompany their wives in the committing of felonies. And *feme covert* did not always play in the woman-defendant's favour. Fined twelve shillings for assaulting a police constable, one defendant claimed only to possess ten. The magistrate

---

[74] Rubenhold, *The Five*, pp. 137–8.
[75] For example, *H/Tel*, 23 August 1856, p. 5 col. F.
[76] Emsley, *Crime and Society*, p. 98. As Emsley notes, there was no excusing serious felonies such as murder.

replied, 'You are a married woman, your goods are your husband's; in default of payment you are to be imprisoned and kept in hard labour for ten days.'[77]

Searches of Portsmouth police court reports for references to wives of butchers, watermen, pensioners, shipwrights, carpenters, smiths, painters, fishermen and bakers in the years 1850–59 yielded just two results, yet in the same period the number of references to 'sailor's wife' was more than ten times greater. Did the prosecution volunteer the information, believing it strengthened the case against her, and/or diminished her credibility as victim or witness? Was her spousal relationship considered to be of greater relevance to her crime or victimhood than was that of her civilian peer, or simply more likely to chime with the preconceptions of *Telegraph* readers? Whatever the explanation, in the reader's mind a connection was generated between 'sailor's wife' and crime. She was repeatedly identified as violent drunkard, thief and prostitute, by implication likelier than her civilian equivalent to commit offences both moral and criminal, or to consort in unrespectable places with the unrespectable sort who made her their unrespectable victim. Used selectively, the term 'sailor's wife' endorsed a stereotype portraying military families as prone to drunken, immoral behaviour, making it harder for the naval wife to be viewed as respectable, even when modest, law-abiding, patient and thrifty.[78]

---

[77] *H/Tel*, 13 May 1848, p. 7 col. E.
[78] Hurl-Eamon, 'Fiction of Female Dependence', p. 482; Chinn, *They Worked all their Lives*, pp. 132–3.

*12*

# MARITAL VIOLENCE

Beyond neighbourly fisticuffs, beyond even a woman's being bitten on the breast and mocked instead of pitied, a more serious form of assault involved domestic abuse. One analysis of Portsmouth quarter session papers found sailors comprising the largest group of wife-beater assailants, and domestic abuse tending to peak when men came home from war.[1] Warner and Lunny's focus was on an earlier period (1653–1781), yet viewed against a background of mid-nineteenth century domestic violence in Portsea Island, their findings – that assaults on wives were more severe than assaults on strangers and acquaintances, involving a greater tendency to use potentially lethal weapons and often resulting in greater injury – appear far from anachronistic. Their type of study, based firmly on statistics, is less sensational and more balanced than the 'extremely bizarre' episodes of domestic life which made it into print.[2] But local sources depict not so much the bizarre as the appalling severity of husbands' attacks on wives, supporting Warner and Lunny's conclusion that 'Portsmouth's women lived in what was by all accounts an exceptionally violent town' – this at a time when sentimental commentators upheld domestic tranquillity as an ideal.[3]

Just as bad news makes headlines more often than good, so the historical record will always contain more conflict than marital tranquillity, care and support.[4] Unrecorded (though not necessarily unremarkable, given the challenges of naval family life) are the long and contented marriages

---

[1] Jessica Warner and Allyson Lunny, 'Marital Violence in a Martial Town', *Journal of Family History,* 28:2 (2003), 258–76, at pp. 263, 268–9.
[2] Lincoln, *Naval Wives,* p. 136.
[3] Elizabeth A. Foyster, *Marital Violence: an English family history, 1660–1857* (Cambridge, 2005), p. 22; Light, *Common People,* p. 196; Warner and Lunny, 'Marital Violence', p. 268; Gill, *Naval Families,* p. 39.
[4] Tanya Evans, 'Review: Ginger Frost, *Living in Sin: Cohabiting as Husband and Wife in Nineteenth-Century England*', *Reviews in History* (Institute of Historical Research, 2009) <https://reviews.history.ac.uk/review/830> [accessed 22 April 2024].

in which tenderness was expressed, disagreement amicably resolved, and home-from-sea sailor-husbands both appreciated and helped with wives' domestic toil. In volume and severity, the visible domestic violence should not be assumed to be representative of the whole. Nevertheless, in years 1848–51 more than eighty men – on average, one every eighteen days – appeared in Portsmouth magistrates' court, the charges they faced representing a fraction of the domestic abuse inflicted in households across Portsea Island.

Except in cases of rape, the law required that the injured person bear the financial cost of prosecution.[5] Noting that poor women could not afford to take their husbands to court, Tomes observes that wives, out of stoicism or fear, bore extraordinary levels of injury without going to the police; that working-class neighbours would often intervene, reproaching a violent husband, checking upon or sheltering a vulnerable wife; that local police would monitor abusive relationships, when necessary threatening gaol.[6] But even where not incapacitated by fear, or discouraged by police and judicial indifference to domestic conflict, many women lacked the social skill and economic resources to seek redress via the courts.[7] When they did, their suffering was often trivialised by reporters describing them in belittling or disparaging terms.[8] Editorial style and subjectivity in court reporting have already been noted; but journalists' versions must be treated with particular caution in cases of domestic assault, for 'gothic, grotesque and melodramatic imagery' often distorted factual accounts, and when it came to sexual assault, 'discretion of language screened from public view the shocking realities of the physical and emotional harm [done] to women'.[9] Remarks about a couple's living a 'cat and dog life' or there being 'recrimination on both sides' are of unknown provenance: are they word-for-word transcriptions of magistrates' comments, a witness's interpretation of his neighbours' relationship, the verbal flummery of a defendant's solicitor, or the opinions of a local hack?[10] In a piece entitled 'Wife Against Husband', a Greenwich pensioner's wife accusing her spouse of violence is dismissed as 'very flighty', the journalist's jibe 'her ladyship' hinting that she was so full of her own importance, it was beyond her husband's bearing *not* to strike

---

[5] Stevenson, 'Ingenuities', p. 91.
[6] Nancy Tomes, '"A Torrent of Abuse": crimes of violence between working-class men and women in London 1840–1875', *Journal of Social History,* II:3 (1978), 328–45, at pp. 333–4, 336.
[7] J. Carter Wood, *Violence and Crime in Nineteenth-century England: the shadow of our refinement* (London, 2004), p. 61.
[8] Warner and Lunny, 'Marital Violence', p. 264.
[9] D'Cruze, *Crimes of Outrage*, p. 173; Stevenson, 'Ingenuities', p. 95.
[10] H/Tel, 5 February 1848, p. 5 col. D; *ibid.*, 14 October 1848, p. 7 col. E.

her.[11] A piece sardonically headed 'A Kind Husband' does not describe the wounds suffered by a Portsea woman, yet her husband's words ('I did not strike her, I merely chucked her in the mouth') are quoted verbatim, resonating with Gill's observation that the rank and sex of witnesses in marital abuse trials meant husbands' testimony was valued above that of wives.[12] A petty officer's wife deposed that he violently beat her, held her by her hair, put a razor to her throat and threatened to kill her; the journalist opined that the accused 'by his defence appeared to be a *leetle* jealous of her' [*sic*].[13]

Attitudes had changed since the seventeenth and eighteenth centuries when it was generally accepted that a man might physically chastise his wife, but any sexual dimension to assaults on wives continued to be ignored, for 'husbands' sexual access to their wives was unlimited and incontestable'.[14] Mid-nineteenth-century newspapers were seldom critical of husbands' behaviour, not even when quoting a police constable who both witnessed one man's attack upon his wife and was himself attacked by the same violent husband. Sub-headed 'Assault on a Constable' (and neatly conveying the *Telegraph*'s opinion as to the relative importance of the injured parties), the article reported that '[The defendant] said [the victim] was his wife and he had a right to do what he liked with her ... "I merely gave her a smack in the face and she fell down to prevent my striking her again."'[15] Descriptions of male perpetrators' violence and threats may be verbatim reporting of witness statements, but the pally ambiguity of ironic subheadings such as 'An Affectionate Husband' undermines the seriousness of the cases in question. To this must be added the frequent impugning of assaulted wives' innocence ('By the evidence [the accused husband] was more sinned-against than sinning'), references to wives' drinking, to their visiting beerhouses (establishments 'suspected of being run by a lower class, more venal and disreputable'), of their being assertive ('She was always aggravating him'), suggestions that a victim was of doubtful character due to the husband's having 'a suspicion which appeared ... well grounded, that another man was favourably received by her'; even her 'keeping company with a lot of women she had made her companions', this last hinting darkly at her indulging in (female) gossip and rowdyism while neglecting her domestic duties.[16] Newspaper reporting of domestic violence cases was patronising, condescending or played for humour, and – as with coverage of the Ripper

---

[11] *Ibid.*, 8 July 1848, p. 7 col. D.
[12] *Ibid.*, 3 February 1849, p. 7 col. D; Gill, *Naval Families*, pp. 166–7.
[13] H/Tel, 6 January 1849, p. 7 col. D.
[14] Emsley, *Crime and Society*, p. 106; Stevenson, 'Ingenuities', p. 98.
[15] H/Tel, 9 December 1848, p. 7 col. D.
[16] *Ibid.*, 5 January 1850, p. 7 col. D; *ibid.*, 7 January 1854, p. 8 col. D; *ibid.*, 29 September 1860, p. 6 col. F; *ibid.*, 20 January 1849, p. 7 col. D; *ibid.*, 21 July 1849, p. 7 col. E; *ibid.*,

murders – rather than her attacker it was the woman victim whose reputation and personal integrity were put on trial.[17] Reading such coverage, or hearing it read to her, an abused wife would get a foretaste of what she would be subjected to in the witness box were she to bring a prosecution against her husband.

Were naval wives more likely to suffer spousal abuse than their civilian counterparts? Of those eighty-one men appearing in Portsmouth magistrates' court in 1848–51 on charges of assaults upon women, the occupations of sixty are mentioned. Their civilian trades include waterman, labourer, excavator, cowkeeper, fish dealer, stonemason, blacksmith and oyster seller. Beyond a half-dozen beerhouse-keepers, landlords and publicans, no one civilian trade appears significantly more often than the others. Dockyard employees, the island's single largest category of worker, are not absent – a boilermaker here, a shipwright there – but they far from make up the single largest category of domestic abuser. That dubious title goes to serving or retired Navy men who together comprise 48.3 per cent of defendants whose occupations were stated in court. This figure is particularly startling given that serving seamen enjoyed only limited time ashore on leave or between ships ('Statistically it appears that a high percentage of wife beaters were sailors even though, as a rule, they did not live with their wives all year round'), and that marital abuse by men of all backgrounds went largely unreported.[18] The number of naval husbands appearing in court might suggest a greater willingness by police to intervene when seamen (as distinct from civilians) lashed out; if so, it is unlikely to have been officially endorsed as constabulary policy. A corporate approach specifically targeting naval abusers would have created tensions between military and civil powers, raising the risk of retaliatory attacks by resentful seamen on local coppers – an unwise scenario in Portsea, where in 1850 there occurred a major riot involving seamen.[19]

There is another factor which may account for Navy men's comprising nearly half of defendants charged with spousal abuse. As Lincoln observes, naval wives may simply have been more likely than their civilian equivalents to experience domestic violence, a conclusion challenging the popular image of 'perennially light-hearted' Jack Tar as sentimental, benevolent and

---

23 August 1851, p. 7 col. F; *ibid.*, 12 August 1848, p. 7 col. F, *et al.*; Thompson, *Rise of Respectable Society*, p. 311.

[17] D'Cruze, *Crimes of Outrage*, pp. 1, 77; Rubenhold, *The Five*, pp. 7–8, 14–15.
[18] Lincoln, *Naval Wives*, pp. 137, 145.
[19] *H/Tel*, 30 November 1850, p. 7 col. F; Moon, "Sailorhoods", p. 167; Brad Beaven, 'The Resilience of Sailortown Culture in English Naval Ports, c.1820–1900', *Urban History* 43:1 (2015), 1–24 <http://journals.cambridge.org/abstract_S0963926815000140> [accessed 22 April 2024], at p. 23; *H/Tel*, 31 August 1850, pp. 5 col. E, and 7 col. F.

kinder toward his woman than was his soldier peer.[20] Many if not most naval men would indeed have been light-hearted, benevolent and kind, only too content to be home from sea. For some, however, the transition was difficult, especially for those brutalised by floggings and hard-horse discipline exercised by the officer cadre, or traumatised by warfare or tragedy, or who were by nature given to hot temper, impatience, aggression.[21] Unlike their eighteenth- and early nineteenth-century predecessors, however, the men arraigned here had not returned from battle, so for this generation of naval husband it cannot be said that their marital discord arose from 'the enormous impact of near-constant war upon military families' intimate concerns'.[22]

Setting aside personality differences and the effects of war, every naval man experienced a culture shock upon returning home. His shipboard world was a hyper-masculine one in which physical strength, courage and brotherhood were valued. At home, these qualities were only intermittently appreciated. His income was suspended, too, likewise his roles of fighting man and breadwinner. The Victorian working-class ideal of happy domesticity was hard to exhibit when the male earner simply did not earn.[23]

There were other causes of friction. The self-sufficient sailor was used to making and mending, at sea undertaking 'domestic' tasks which on shore were the province of women, for 'Jack had to be his own washerwoman, tailor and cook, besides being housemaid in general.'[24] At home, there was no need for him to demonstrate his dexterity with needle and thread, but if his wife's efforts at sewing, laundering and cleaning did not meet with his approval, was not her self-sufficient sailor-husband entitled to critique her, demonstrate how to do it, even outdo her (or claim he could, since to be bested by a woman would impugn his natural superiority)?[25] If after a few days or weeks the novelty of the homecomer's sharing domestic duties began to wither, the naval wife would once again find herself unaided, for in the 'natural patriarchy' of the nineteenth century, did not the husband occupy a position of authority equivalent to that of captain?[26] On board he had been subject both to formal naval discipline and to messdeck discipline, the latter an unwritten code by which shipmates dealt collectively with men who did not respect the etiquette required of all those sharing a confined space. On board he enjoyed the status of his rate, the respect it

---

[20] Walton, 'Social History', p. 332; Lincoln, 'Impact of Warfare', p. 78; Begiato, 'Tearful Sailor'.
[21] Humphries, *Childhood and Child Labour*, p. 131.
[22] Gill, *Naval Families*, p. 48.
[23] D'Cruze, *Crimes of Outrage*, p. 16.
[24] Holman, *Life in the Royal Navy*, p. 80.
[25] Walton, 'Social History', p. 228.
[26] *Ibid.*, pp. 217–24.

required of those above and below him, and whatever authority went with it. At home he was unsupervised, his behaviour no longer subject to naval regulation or messdeck etiquette. His woman, however, was used to heading her own household, making decisions usually the province of men, being responsible for disciplining their children and determining how money was spent. Faced with conflicting expectations, no longer enjoying the social heft he exercised on board, our lower-deck, lower-class man might well find himself regarding his physical strength as his most significant resource.[27]

Environment was another stressor. Used to fresh air, open horizons and regulated society, to cleanliness and order, decks being scrubbed, heads (ships' latrines) sluiced clean of filth, brass polished and food provided at fixed intervals, some men found the dirt, disorder, overcrowding and untidiness of urban life beyond bearing.[28] Gone was the shipboard respect for personal space, however small it be, and for the limiting of noise levels, the maintaining of standards of cleanliness. Crowded hugger-mugger in noisome and noisy Portsea courts, with no bosun's call to 'pipe down' during night hours, no messmates to intervene when tempers frayed, the sailor at home might have difficulty adjusting to conditions tolerated by his wife and children. If he pictured himself – worse, behaved – as commander of the metaphorical vessel that was his household, he might well encounter resistance from a wife reluctant to cede her authority, and from children who habitually deferred to their mother and sought her approval before deferring to him. He was used to responding to officers' orders with unquestioning obedience; as paterfamilias he expected no less from his family. If a child baulked at his command, if a wife stepped in to shield son or daughter from his raised fist, or herself answered back, the scene was set for friction.

The seaman unable to express his frustrations might find himself preferring the company of those who would appreciate his point of view. Sailors tended to go ashore in groups, congregating in the same places, hence during leave it would be natural for him to seek shipmates' company.[29] Lower-deck messes fostered both strong emotional ties and a resilient male bonding born of several things: identification with the ship and its name; same-trade labour (gunnery, carpentry and the like); collective physical work; agreed parameters of emotional expression; the sharing of risks and living space; and recreation during runs-ashore.[30] Deprived of the peer group with whom for years they had messed and worked and faced danger and had fun; facing a wageless period until they could join ship again; given

[27] Wood, *Violence, Crime*, p. 25.
[28] *Ibid.*, pp. 98–105; Jolly and Willson, *Jackspeak*, p. 219; Walton, 'Social History', p. 79.
[29] Walton, 'Social History', p. 165.
[30] Wassell Smith, '"The Fancy Work What Sailors Make"', n.p.

to hard drinking; suffering distress caused by shipwreck, by witnessing shipmates' accidental injuries and death, or the terrible danger of terrible seas, it was easy for some men to feel that no-one at home appreciated what they had been through. In port towns there was no shortage of places for shipmates to meet, drink, revive relationships, rehearse 'dits' familiar from previous tellings and share grievances.[31] This last had consequences for a man's home life, for if collectively his mess companions took a negative view of their women's behaviour, paid work or participation in prostitution, they would 'follow the communal system of feeling in how they respond to stimulus, engage in emotional relationships and express emotions'.[32] Thus a man might ponder what his shipmates would think or do upon meeting wifely opposition or independence. Messdeck groupthink might provide an answer, but it was unlikely to recognise the woman's individuality, her home circumstances, the necessity driving her decisions.

The mention of pub reunions is far from fanciful. Alcohol was a common denominator in marital violence generally, as contributing factor, catalyst and as rationale for the qualifying of condemnation. Moderate chastisement of a disobedient wife was considered acceptable, whereas a man's inflicting physical assault in anger, exceeding reasonable boundaries, was very likely to incur punishment.[33] It was a common tactic to cite alcohol as explanation or defence for what might otherwise be regarded as inexcusable violence, thereby deflecting the court's attention from the possibility that, sober or drunk, the man in the dock was a thug.[34] Husbands appearing in mid-nineteenth century magistrates' courts are described as repeatedly 'ill-using' their wives when drunk, one having indulged in alcohol 'to such excess as to become a madman'.[35] Referring to the effects of drink, 'madness' in domestic abuse cases was a common theme, used with deliberation: 'The abused wives, and their supporting witnesses, ensured that they used the language of anger when describing the men's actions to the authorities, with words such as "passion", "fury", and "rage"'.[36]

To interpret this within the context of the naval community requires caution. Like many working-class husbands and sons, sailors drank; but sailors' drinking – usually a group activity, crammed into the limited

---

[31] 'Dit: Any written (or spoken) account of an incident or event in a sailor's life': Jolly and Willson, *Jackspeak*, p. 137.
[32] Wassell Smith, '"The Fancy Work What Sailors Make"', n.p.
[33] Joanne Begiato, 'Angry Husbands: Emotional Objects and Wife-beating', in Joanne Begiato Muses on History (2019) <https://jbhist.wordpress.com/2019/07/25/emotional-lives-intimacy-and-identity-in-18th-2/> [accessed 22 April 2024].
[34] Rowbotham, "Only When Drunk", pp. 164–5.
[35] H/Tel, 15 April 1848, p. 8 col. F; *ibid.*, 12 January 1850, p. 7 col. F.
[36] Begiato, 'Angry Husbands'.

timeframe of a run-ashore, involving legendary quantities of alcohol and often associated with fights, riotous behaviour or damage to property – was in a different league. Some of their women might drink with them, and in a port town community both sexes had easy access to alcohol; but it was never acceptable for women to indulge freely in drink.[37] Gender bias and stereotypes operated not only in pub, street and home, but in the courtroom where women victims' ingenuity in defending themselves was frequently interpreted as fabrication.[38] Sober or fuelled by alcohol, wives who lashed out at their husbands were demonised as debauched, abnormal, lacking femininity, so bad as to be subnormal, the inciters of their own suffering.[39] Trustee Jane Elliott (whom we shall meet in different circumstances in Chapter Fourteen) complained that her boatswain husband William had ill-used her; both appeared in court 'with faces disgraceful to them, but it appeared the wife began the attack'.[40] This latter detail may have tipped the balance in her husband's favour. Both were cautioned; he was acquitted. The *Telegraph*'s reporter considered Mary Phillips 'brutally used' [by her husband Joseph, ship's cook, HMS *Excellent*], but in adding that 'it appeared she was a drunken dissipated character' the article slyly invited readers to blame the victim.[41] Appearing on a charge of violence towards her husband John, Ann Thomas, mother of fifer William Thomas, HMS *Fox*, was mocked for speaking up for herself, 'Her tongue [being] in perpetual motion all the time she was before the court.'[42] For the naval wife used to being in charge of her own household, effectively asserting herself in dealings with tradespeople and bureaucrats, managing her limited monthly income and thriftily denying herself the indulgence of drink, to restrain herself in the face of her husband's wastrel behaviour may have been asking too much. Court and public opinion, however, saw no excuse for her behaviour.

When stoker George Richards attacked his wife Ann, he was between ships, selling beer in Portsmouth; 'far gone in pregnancy', she appeared in court with two black eyes.[43] Richards, later of HMS *Dragon*, stated he was very well when sober, but 'always spit his spite upon her if anything went wrong', on this occasion knocking her to the ground and kicking her there, 'she at the time expecting to be confined every day'. He argued that it only happened when he had been drinking. Devonshire-born David Doward, formerly HMS *Penelope*'s carpenter's crew, was charged with violent assault

[37] *H/Tel*, 18 March 1848, p. 5 col. D.
[38] Stevenson, 'Ingenuities', p. 90.
[39] Rowbotham, '"Only When Drunk"', pp. 163–5.
[40] ADM 27/112/154/51; *H/Tel*, 20 May 1848, p. 1 col. B.
[41] ADM 27/112/216/1645; *H/Tel*, 15 July 1848, p. 7 col. D.
[42] ADM 27/111/274/3; *H/Tel*, 4 August 1849, p. 7 col. E.
[43] ADM 27/111/247/68; *H/Tel*, 13 April 1850, p. 7 col. E.

upon his wife Elizabeth.[44] It was not his first time in court, he having 'on several occasions ... [been] remanded in consequence of his wife being unable to attend through the violence he had made use of toward her'.[45] On this occasion Elizabeth did attend. Unable to support herself, she was led into court by two women, 'her face [bearing] the marks of great violence ... her head bound round with a white cloth which covered the marks of a most severe blow'.[46] The court heard that having told her, 'I'm glad to meet you here [in our home], for I'll now butcher you', Doward had punched her down on to a fender, causing her to pass out; he then hit her repeatedly, and threw her downstairs. She struck her head violently, and again passed into unconsciousness. Deflecting blame on to his victim (a tactic known today as DARVO, acronym for 'Deny, Attack, and Reverse Victim and Offender', a common manipulation strategy deployed by abusers), Doward said she was intoxicated, 'must have fallen downstairs'.[47] All this took place on 21 April 1854, and it is notable that across Doward's name in HMS *Powerful*'s muster book, a red-inked superscript reads 'R April 1854'.[48] Fined ten shillings for straggling in August 1849 and again in November 1850, now he had deserted proper and may according to his wife have been 'going amongst loose characters'.[49] On the run from the Navy, mixing in bad company, facing further fines for desertion and with a wife suspicious of his activities (despite his threatening her, she had followed him when he went out of the house), Doward was in a hole of his own making; his reaction: to lash out with his fists.

Portsmouth police record books for 1850 onward have not survived, so we cannot know when these two violent men were arrested, or whether prosecution was pursued by the police or by the abused wives at their own expense. Taken as a whole, the record book for 1843–49 suggests that following their arrest Doward and Richards would have been detained overnight in police cells, as is recorded in other instances of men being detained for assaulting their wives.[50] What happened next was decided by individuals named in the record book as 'Wm. James, esq.' and 'Wm. Jones, esq.', the 'esq.' suffix indicating that these were gentleman-civilians, in all

---

[44] HO107/1659, fol. 357, p. 33; ADM 38/8763, n/p.
[45] *H/Tel*, 20 May 1854, p. 5 col. C.
[46] ADM 27/113/255/149; *H/Tel*, 20 May 1854, p. 5 col. C.
[47] Narcissistic Abuse Rehab, 'How Narcissists Use DARVO to Escape Responsibility' (Narcissistic Abuse Rehab, 2020) <https://www.narcissisticabuserehab.com/darvo/> [accessed 22 April 2024].
[48] ADM 38/4495, n.p.
[49] ADM 38/4494, n.p.; *H/Tel*, 20 May 1854, p. 5 col. C.
[50] PHC: SB/DF/P/1, pp. 250, 355, 356, 374, *et al.*

likelihood lawyers from the public prosecutor's office.[51] There are instances of their discharging accused persons without further action, and instances where the decision to prosecute appears to have been taken by the victim, only for the court to dismiss the charge on account of 'the Prosecutrix not appearing'.[52] Elsewhere we read of 'the Prosecutor [sic] not pressing the charge', which suggests proceedings were brought by someone other than the victim; in this instance the accused was said to have stabbed her, she being saved from serious injury by 'the bone of her stays'.[53] We read also of 'the charge not being pressed' (the accused being 36-year-old Elizabeth Dyer, who – as we saw earlier – was said to have stabbed her husband with a knife, and who subsequently insulted and verbally abused Amelia Lewis).[54] In this latter case it is tempting to infer that the public prosecutor withdrew the charges, he perhaps having concluded that Elizabeth had been punished enough by his having 'committed [her] to gaol' prior to her court appearance.[55] The *Hampshire Telegraph*, however, presents a different picture:

> [The] husband appeared, and on being sworn, deposed that he and his wife had a quarrel about one of the children; that he threw a kettle of water at her, and then knocked her down, and that she then took up the knife … and stabbed him; that it was done in consequence of his conduct towards his wife, and that he brought it entirely on himself, and he had no desire that the charge should be proceeded with.[56]

From this and other examples it would appear that while Messrs James and Jones had the power to decide whether to discharge the accused after a night in the cells, it was primarily left to the victims of domestic abuse – male or female – to initiate (and, on occasion, withdraw) prosecution.

We may conclude, albeit without hard evidence, that Elizabeth Doward and Ann Richards took their abusive husbands to court. Doward's sentence was a five-pound fine (equivalent to five months' worth of his allotment to Elizabeth) or imprisonment for two months. Unable to pay, or opting for the cheaper alternative, 'He went below'. As for Richards, the bench did reprimand him for his 'unmanly and brutal conduct' but his sentence – a fine of fifty-two shillings plus costs, or one calendar month's imprisonment – was half the punishment imposed upon Doward; and like Doward, rather than fork out his cash he too went below. This pattern, whereby the convicted man was fined only to be gaoled in lieu of paying, recurs in

---

[51] *Ibid.*, pp. 212, 229, 250, 338, 343, 367, 368, *et al.*
[52] *Ibid.*, pp. 250, 356, *et al.*
[53] *H/Tel*, 7 April 1849, p. 7 col. D.
[54] PHC: SB/DF/P/1, pp. 355, 367, *et al*; *H/Tel*, 16 June 1849, p. 7 col. E; see pp. 210–11.
[55] PHC: SB/DF/P/1, p. 367.
[56] *H/Tel*, 16 June 1849, p. 7 col. E.

numerous reports. Most fines were accompanied by a default alternative of gaol, though for these male defendants imprisonment came with notably fewer prescriptions of hard labour than did the same court's sentencing of women for far less serious offences.

Male assailants' fines varied, from as little as one shilling with nine shillings costs, to the five-pound sentence imposed on David Doward. A common sentencing device was to require the guilty man enter into recognizance in the sum of twenty pounds, consisting of two sureties of ten pounds each. For most working-class men such sums would have been hard if not impossible to raise, hence those convicted often opted for the alternative of a few days' or weeks' imprisonment. As well as signalling lack of funds, however, their choosing gaol may also suggest a reluctance to part with coin for something they neither regretted nor regarded as wrong; a recognition that they would be only too likely to breach the peace by losing their temper again, thereby forfeiting their sureties; and preference for a sentence that could be quickly completed without the necessity of changing behaviour in the longer term. True, a man such as Richards might end up out of pocket, due to loss of wages while in gaol, but any resultant hardship could always be laid at the injured woman's door: 'If you hadn't gone to the police, we wouldn't be in this fix.' It could even be used to justify another beating.

Richards' selling of beer no doubt involved the occasional testing for quality, but that is not to say he was an alcoholic. No cause of Doward's or Richards' behaviour is posited here, for their backgrounds could not be established via naval records.[57] HMS *Illustrious*'s description book, however, tells us that Dorset-born RMA private Robert Lewis, husband of Amelia Lewis (*q.v.*), was blue-eyed, dark haired, swarthy, pockmarked, tattooed, at five feet eight inches outstripping messmates of only five feet two.[58] As private third class, HMS *Victory*, he had allotted to Amelia since 1845, his first declaration falsely naming her his sister.[59] Only when he joined *Illustrious* in 1848, by which time they were two years married, did he identify her as his wife, declaring for a third time when *Illustrious* put to sea in the spring of 1850.[60] Later that year he was admitted to Haslar Royal Naval Hospital where, after being invalided in January 1851 for 'Tremor and Debility contracted in the Service' (terminology making him eligible for a

---

[57] It is known, however, that Doward died within three years of being convicted of abusing his wife (TNA: BT153, Box 0003, p. 110, British Armed Forces And Overseas Deaths And Burials, died 21 September 1857, at sea).
[58] ADM 38/8326, muster no. 2.
[59] ADM 27/92/422/164.
[60] ADM 38/8326/2, 21, 22; CHU3/1D/44, p. 103 n. 206; ADM 27/102/167/2; ADM 27/110/106/22.

pension), he was for several months an in-patient.[61] His conduct had been indifferent, his career undistinguished. He had no craft or trade (a labourer prior to joining up, he claimed he had been 'brought up to sea'), and being invalided he was now probably unfit for physical work. In June 1851 he was discharged, becoming a Greenwich out-pensioner.[62] Three months later, Amelia deposed that he had inflicted repeated violence upon her.[63]

On census day 1851 Amelia's household included her four daughters aged nine months (the crippled Louisa) to eight years, and an ageing pauper mother.[64] Amelia herself was in marital limbo. On parish relief, with no occupation entered in her census schedule, she was dependent upon Robert's pension, one of 'the many cases of desperate women seeking to retain links to unstable men [underlining] the vital need for a male breadwinner.'[65] That she had not taken the children and fled the marital home when first attacked reflects one or more of several factors: economic and psychological dependence; lack of opportunity; belief that he was truly sorry and would never hit her again; fear that he would find and injure her further; lack of protective accommodation within the local community (few neighbours would have had space to take in a whole family, and many might have jibbed at the prospect of Lewis's arriving at their door, outraged at their involvement in his private business, and demanding access to his frightened dependants); a belief that things would simply get better. For Amelia alone to flee would leave her mother and children unprotected; to stay risked further injury, for neighbours were reluctant to get involved in what was perceived as a 'family matter'.[66] Naval wives may have been sensible of an additional cultural barrier, in that the aforementioned mess-deck bond, forged during months and years at sea together, might dampen a steadier naval husband's willingness to intervene in a shipmate's domestic conflict, no matter how much the steadier man's spouse might plead on behalf of her abused friend and fellow naval wife.

Robert Lewis's repeated assaults culminated in his beating and kicking Amelia so savagely 'she was compelled to leave the house, almost in a

---

[61] ADM 157/384, item 66; 1851 census: HO107/1660, fol. 474, p. 21.
[62] ADM 157/384, item 65.
[63] *H/Tel*, 13 September 1851, p. 8 col. E.
[64] 1851 census: HO107/1658, fol. 46, p. 35.
[65] Humphries, *Childhood and Child Labour*, p. 101.
[66] Joanne Bailey, "'I Dye by Inches': locating wife beating in the concept of the privatisation of marriage and violence in eighteenth-century England', *Social History*, 31:3 (2006), 273–94, at p. 285. Cf. Emsley's assertion that in urban working-class districts, neighbours might intervene when a husband exceeded the boundaries that a community recognised (Emsley, *Crime and Society*, p. 107).

state of nudity'.[67] His stripping her has significance, for just as husbands' practice of progressively abusing their wives through kitchen, living and bedroom spaces of the home signifies 'their attempts to take back control of space that was both a source of feminine power and identity, and a symbol of feminine subordination,' so their tearing wives' clothing from them in public space, in full view of onlookers known or unknown to attacker or victim, signifies a performative controlling of the feminine body as much as it does a deliberate shaming.[68]

For many ex-servicemen, discharge from military service was often internalised as a form of unmanning. Robert Lewis's violence erupted just weeks after his being discharged from the Marines. Whether or not he felt himself unmanned, in light of Frost's observation that jealousy underpinned most domestic violence there may have been another cause for his behaviour.[69] Given Amelia's poverty (the census has her receiving parish relief) and the stoppage of her allotment upon Robert's being invalided, to ensure her family's survival she may have resorted to prostitution. If so, as much as by his physiological condition or loss of military status, Robert's violence may have been triggered by jealousy of Amelia's clients, of the cash she earned through servicing them, and by humiliation at his effectively being cuckolded by more able and monied men.

Robert's attack took place when he returned home at one o'clock in the morning.[70] This suggests he had been drinking for some hours. The unbuttoning effect of alcohol could bring domestic tensions to the surface. It could also unleash darker urges. Leaving aside rancour over household labour, money or the presence of Amelia's mother, did Robert try to force himself upon his unwilling wife?[71] Was he trying to re-establish himself as master in his own house by having her service his sexual demands? Did he rape her? D'Cruze observes that in extracting a woman's 'consent' to sex a good measure of physical violence was regarded as acceptable.[72] In this instance the combination of Robert's beating *and* stripping Amelia may have had an additional significance. He may have been seeking to punish and shame her for some sexual affront to his dignity – an infidelity, perhaps, or her involvement in prostitution. Adjunct to this possibility is the fact that to turn wives and children into the street at night, thus exerting complete

---

[67] *H/Tel*, 13 September 1851, p. 8 col. E.
[68] Bailey, "I Dye by Inches", p. 293.
[69] Ginger Suzanne Frost, '"He could not hold his passions": domestic violence and cohabitation in England, 1850–1905', *Crime, History and Societies* 12:1 (2008), 45–63 <http://journals.openedition.org/chs/64> [accessed 22 Apr. 2024], at p. 2 [sic], para. 4.
[70] *H/Tel*, 13 September 1851, p. 8 col. E.
[71] D'Cruze, *Crimes of Outrage*, p. 66.
[72] *Ibid.*, p. 19.

dominance over the family's (predominantly female) domestic space and overriding the woman's household status, was a strategy common to violent men.[73] Common it may have been, but this was the first time that Robert Lewis faced the consequences of his violence in civil court. Coverage of the hearing does not say how the incident came to the court's attention, but most cases were brought by women themselves, only a minority being initiated by police called in to deal with a disturbance. It is of note, therefore, that where d'Cruze found numerous instances of women fleeing to or calling for neighbours when attacked or injured, in Amelia's case those neighbours included – mere feet away, at the entrance to Hobbs Court passage – the stolid personage of Frederick Charters, 50-year-old dockyard policeman.[74] Ex-marine Lewis was a daunting prospect even for male neighbours; but Charters, a figure of authority and likely to be Robert's height or taller (the Portsmouth police force had a minimum height requirement of 5ft 8in), may have had fewer qualms about restraining such a man, more experience of doing so, and handcuffs.[75]

His health ruined, his service career over, his pension inadequate to support a family of six, his home a cramped slum rental in a sunless Portsea court, Robert Lewis made no defence against the charge. Unable to pay a ten-shilling fine and nine-shilling costs, he was committed to fourteen days' imprisonment. Of his seventeen years in the Marines, between leaving one ship and joining another he had spent only four years ashore in total, and prior to admission to Haslar he had spent a month in Portsmouth's house of correction.[76] He was institutionalised, acutely militarised, used to all-male company since joining up at just eighteen, with little adult experience of civilian life. This neither explains nor excuses his violence, for there were men with similar backgrounds and conditioning, experiencing similar home environments and likewise suffering culture shock from loss of status, loss of income, and severance from the acutely masculine world they had known since boyhood, who did not beat their wives.

These seamen's women had been hopeful of husbandly tenderness, of appreciation for the effort required to keep family together, unaided and in difficult conditions, during their men's absence. They had been hopeful of their men's help with the backbreaking work of keeping a clean house despite the introdden mud, the endless coal dust, the filth of the shared privies; hopeful, too, of husbandly understanding and forgiveness should

---

[73] *Ibid.*, p. 68.
[74] *Ibid.*, pp. 69, 49; 1851 census: HO107/1658, fol. 46, p. 35.
[75] James Cramer, *A History of the Police of Portsmouth: the Story of the Constables, Tythingmen, Watchmen and Other Peace Officers of the Portsmouth Area, from c.1271 to 1967* (Portsmouth, 1967), p. 12.
[76] ADM 38/8326, muster no. 22.

they have had to resort to prostitution to supplement the little allotted them; fearful that their men might discover this, and punish them for it; hopeful of attaining a quiet heart and quiet home. To set these tender yearnings against the contempt, self-justification and swagger of defendants' utterances in court is to see how, for some women, a seaman-husband's presence was far from the happy 'Sailor's Return' captured in print and pottery figurine.[77] Wives and partners of such men had to learn not only how to manage household and family unaided in their absence, but how to survive their ambiguous presence.

It is here, acknowledging naval women's survival skills, that another explanation should be considered for the finding that, of defendants with stated occupations appearing in Portsmouth courts in the period 1848–51 on charges of violence towards women, 48.3 per cent were naval men. That occupational and gendered factors contributed to seamen's marital violence is credible; but seamen's women were, as we have seen, more assertive, self-reliant, independent and resourceful than was expected of wives within the prevailing culture. As wives and mothers they had coped alone for years on half or less than half of an already inadequate income, supporting their partners as best they could via letter, prayer and good domestic management, 'earning their living as best they might while their menfolk were at sea, enduring years of absence and uncertainty.'[78] Where a sailor returned and assaulted his wife, repaying her loyalty and hard work with harsh words, threats and hard blows, she may have been quicker to protest, readier than her civilian neighbour to prosecute, her peers more supportive of her doing so. They may even have encouraged her, for which wife could be certain that she herself would not one day fall victim to a husband's abuse, and need the support of sympathetic peers? The 48.3 per cent figure may not only signify seamen's greater propensity for marital violence; it may signal seamen's women being less inclined than their civilian equivalents to tolerate it.

---

[77] Begiato, 'Tearful Sailor'; J. Welles Henderson and Rodney P. Carlisle, *Marine Art & Antiques: Jack Tar: a Sailor's Life, 1750–1910* (Woodbridge, 1999), pp. 159–65.
[78] Rodger, *Command of the Ocean*, p. 407.

*13*

# MARITAL COMPLEXITIES

Former seaman Henry Capper recalls that 'taking advantage of the long commissions … women of the town (the "Polls" and "Sues" …) would contract marriage with two, or in some cases even four, men with whom successively they had been associated, and from all of these they would be in receipt of half-pay.'[1] The picture Capper painted would have amused his readers, and no doubt helped boost sales. However, much as contemporary perceptions and prejudices were fed by the notion of the naval wife whose 'line abreast' marriages raked in as many allotments as husbands, this notion ignored the more likely scenario of the naval wife whose marriage was unexceptional, unfulfilling, violent or simply unhappy.[2] Looking beyond the yarns recounted by Capper *et al*, this chapter reveals stories every bit as extraordinary as his; unlike his, however, these are supported by documentary evidence.

The nineteenth century being 'a period of energetic marital non-conformity amongst couples of all social classes', in marital circumstance and stratagem naval wives were far from exceptional.[3] Three marital non-conformities are explored here: cohabitation, affinal marriage and bigamy. Cohabitation was common in the nineteenth century, especially among the working classes. Cohabiting women, however, were locked in moral and legal jeopardy. Considered to be 'living in sin', unable to claim the status of wife, they bore from birth to thirteen years full financial responsibility for any *filius nullius* ('child of no-one', or illegitimate offspring) born of the union.[4] Although restrictive and tainting, cohabitation was at least legal. Affinal marriage – of a widow to her late husband's brother, a widower to

---

[1] Capper, *Aft – from the Hawsehole*, pp. 13–14.
[2] Line abreast: in nautical terms, ships arranged or proceeding side-by-side rather than in single file ('line astern').
[3] Evans, 'Review: Living in Sin' [accessed 22 April 2024], n.p.
[4] Ginger Suzanne Frost, *Living in Sin: Cohabiting as Husband and Wife in Nineteenth-Century England* (Manchester, 2008), pp. 11–12.

his late wife's sister – was not. The law regarded the wives of affinal unions as not married, ergo children of such unions were bastards. The husbands of affinal marriages could deny financial responsibility, and when cornered for support could plead 'nullity of marriage'; yet despite the inherent risks and weaknesses in affinal unions, 'working-class couples ignored the law, or at least assumed it did not apply to their particular cases'.[5] Also illegal (it had been a felony since 1828) was bigamy, which on a national basis in the years 1857–1904 resulted in an annual average of ninety-eight trials – an unrepresentative figure, since more bigamy went unprosecuted than ever reached court.[6] As well as attracting prurient mockery, the private prosecutrix (more often the second wife than the first) had to endure her case being passed from magistrates' court to quarter sessions to assizes, and then risked being judicially, if briefly, deprived of her spouse. Public prosecutions were rare, more often initiated as a result of bigamist husbands leaving their wives chargeable to an indignant parish.[7]

Despite these known pitfalls, and the Navy's subjecting allottees to more institutional oversight and vetting than most women endured, seamen's wives were no less energetic in their marital non-conformity than the rest of a society in which cohabitation, bigamy, adultery and other unlawful unions were practised to a greater degree than judicial statistics suggest. To determine the extent of seamen's women's unorthodoxy is of less concern here than to illustrate the painful situations some faced, to consider the ramifications of the decisions some took, and the consequences of their and their seamen-husbands' actions.

For most seamen's wives, marriage was bearable because sad partings were followed by happy returns. We find couples still together across decades, their families increasing at intervals between ships' commissions. For some women, however, wedding-day vows became hollow in the wake of husbandly infidelity, of physical abuse such as described in the previous chapter, of unrequited need for physical comfort and pleasure, or estrangement grown during prolonged separations. This last is particularly significant, Bailey noting that in marriages in which the wife was unfaithful, nearly one-fifth of couples had experienced lengthy or regular separations due to the husband's occupation.[8]

---

[5] *Ibid.*, pp. 52–5.
[6] *Ibid.*, pp. 72–4.
[7] *Ibid.*, pp. 75–7; David J. Cox, '"Trying to Get a Good One": bigamy offences in England and Wales, 1850–1950', *Plymouth Law and Criminal Justice Review*, 4 (2012), 1–32, at pp. 4, 12, 21.
[8] Joanne Bailey, *Unquiet Lives: Marriage and Marriage Breakdown in England, 1660–1800* (Cambridge, 2003), p. 154.

An unhappy wife's options were few, and each came with its own risks. Marital breakdown being more likely to cause poverty among women than among men, it was perilous for a woman deliberately to step outside marriage.[9] Parish officials subjected deserted or separated wives to particular scrutiny and challenge. This applied even to deserted naval wives, who under Section 7 of the 1844 Outdoor Relief Prohibitory Order were supposed to qualify for support from their poor law union. Among husbandless married women, however, there was one category that did not incur additional parish scrutiny, for widows with legitimate children qualified for aid. In light of this, some separated wives regarded a spurious bereavement as an economically better bet than admitting to having left or been abandoned by their husbands.[10] Then again, civil status was also a matter of self-respect, separated couples describing themselves as widowed simply in order to hide feelings of shame.[11] But as we shall see, a false 'widow' status was sometimes adopted for reasons other than masking wounded pride, duping the parish guardians or maintaining respectability.[12]

For the working class, escape from unhappy marriage came only via separation, or the death of a spouse. Not until the Matrimonial Causes Act of 1857 would there be a divorce law of general application, available to rich and poor alike.[13] Where previous divorce pleas had had to be set before Parliament, the 1857 Act introduced divorce through the court. Men were able to petition on the basis of their wife's proven adultery. Women could cite their husbands' adultery, but had to prove an additional, aggravating factor such as rape or incest. Given this legal hurdle, and the logistical difficulties (no local procedures; only the High Court in London could hear divorce cases), and the publicity and costs incurred, working-class women made little use of the new legislation. It was easier and cheaper for a couple simply to part ways. That too had its drawbacks. Robbed of their sexual partner and household manager, their male pride wounded, some men tracked down their estranged wives and violently attacked them.[14] Marital assaults ending in the Portsmouth police court bear the hallmarks of such stalk-and-punish violence, as witness the menace with which David Doward (p. 225) greeted his wife: 'I'm glad to meet you here [in our home], for I'll now butcher you.'[15]

---

[9] Thane, 'Women and the Poor Law', p. 33.
[10] Poor Law Commissioners, *Order Prohibiting Outdoor Relief*, ss. 6, 7.
[11] Humphries, *Childhood and Child Labour*, pp. 68–9; Higgs, *Census Revisited*, p. 83.
[12] Pamela Sharpe, 'Marital Separation in Eighteenth and early Nineteenth Centuries', *Local Population Studies,* 45 (1990), 66–70, at p. 66.
[13] *Matrimonial Causes Act,* 20 Vict., c. 85 (1857).
[14] D'Cruze, *Crimes of Outrage*, p. 73.
[15] *H/Tel*, 20 May 1854, p. 5, col. C.

The disillusioned sailor-husband was tied by more than marriage vows. An allotment to a wife was irrevocable unless the minister or churchwardens of her parish provided a certificate stating the reasons for the cancellation, the Commissioners of the Navy until 1854 retaining discretion to approve or reject men's requests.[16] A seaman therefore had to wax cunning if he were both to shrug off his spouse and retrieve his full monthly wage; which may explain why disaffected married sailors might, on joining ship, say they were single, or adopt an alias. In this respect they were little different from men who joined the army to escape family responsibilities, enlisting as 'bachelor' or changing their names.[17]

Recorded in ships' description books, most seamen's aliases appear to have been openly declared, and do not necessarily signal subterfuge. Some simply acknowledged alternative spellings, as with William Reece ('alias Wm. Rees'), HMS *Hogue*.[18] Alternatively, a man might join under his birth or baptismal name but prefer to be known by his stepfather's surname – an innocent and laudable arrangement. Deserter AB William Menhinnick, HMS *Dauntless*, was one whose alias was adopted for duplicitous purposes. His switches of name and civil status involve no fewer than four, possibly five, women, their story showing how a man given to impulse and fabrication might engage trusting females in what they believed were lawful, long-term relationships, thereby robbing them of any prospect of security or married respectability.

Menhinnick had joined *Dauntless* in August 1850, logged as a Mevagissey-born 26-year-old.[19] His record describes a tall man (5ft 8in), ruddy-complexioned, with hazel eyes and brown hair; despite being 'first entry', on his right arm he already sported an anchor tattoo.[20] He was married (he said), and had been brought up to no trade. These unremarkable details contained untruths. William Menhinnick was no first-entry novice. As 21-year-old Thomas Jenkins, on Christmas Eve 1847 he had joined HMS *Prince Regent* with (so his service record says) nine years' previous service in merchant vessels.[21] In February 1848 he had been invalided to Haslar. Returning to *Prince Regent* three weeks later he immediately declared an allotment naming his sister Susan Jenkins, address: Haslar.[22] In September 1848 he

---

[16] Pitcairn, *Report*, p. 9.
[17] *Mutiny Act*, 7 Will. IV and 1 Vict., c. 7 (1837), s. 3; Trustram, *Women of the Regiment*, pp. 50, 141.
[18] ADM 27/112/178/2. (See pp. 108, 214.)
[19] ADM 38/3147/22.
[20] ADM 38/7940.
[21] ADM 38/8771/93; ADM 139/32/3171.
[22] ADM 27/103/179/93.

declared another allotment, again naming a Susan Jenkins, this time as his wife of two years, address: Guernsey.[23]

It is not impossible that Jenkins had both a sister and a wife named Susan; but in light of what has and has not been found it is reasonable to propose that he had taken up with a nurse during his time in Haslar, initially concocting a sibling relationship in order to send money to her; that the same woman was the subject of his subsequent 'wife' declaration; and that his invention of a marriage was part of a plan by which the pair would set up home together, she supported via his half-pay. Whatever the rationale, everything changed when he deserted, at which point his wages were forfeit, his allotment(s) null. His whereabouts for the next two years are unknown, but the 1851 census shows a 26-year-old Susan Jenkins resident in Guernsey, working as a live-in cook in a judge's household a few hundred yards from the address her 'husband' had declared.[24] What it does not show, in that household or anywhere else on Guernsey, is a Thomas Jenkins, seaman, or a William Menhinnick, ditto.

Two years after being marked 'Run' from *Prince Regent*, 'Jenkins' joined HMS *Dauntless* under his birth name of Menhinnick.[25] It is not improbable that in dropping his alias he wished not only to escape punishment for desertion but also to shrug off financial responsibility for his abandoned lover Susan, and as 'Menhinnick' (re-)acquire a naval income in order to support a new amour; for in November 1850, within three months of joining *Dauntless*, he declared an allotment favouring naval carpenter's daughter Harriett Carstairs.[26] In her parish baptism record and in William's allotment declaration, 'Harriett' is the given spelling; however, in their parish marriage record and the 1851 census 'Harriet' is used. To avoid confusion, 'Harriett' is how she will be described from here onward. The declaration named Harriett trustee for a fourteen-month-old Harriett Menhinnick, by implication his daughter.[27] His plan came to nothing. The following day he was returned from *Dauntless* to *Prince Regent*, 'per order being a deserter from that ship'.[28] How his alter ego was unmasked remains a mystery. Perhaps a sharp-eyed pusser's clerk queried the naming of a trustee when only weeks earlier new entrant 'Menhinnick' had stated himself to be married; perhaps a former shipmate greeted him as Jenkins, and the

---

[23] ADM 27/105/90/544.
[24] 1851 census: Guernsey and Adjacent Islands, Channel Islands, HO107/2531, fol. 477, p. 2.
[25] ADM 38/3147; ADM 139/32/3171.
[26] Birth, Marriage and Death (Parish Registers), Parish Baptisms, Cornwall Baptisms, Saltash, 4 October 1835, 'Harriett Bill [*sic*: mistranscription of 'Bell'] Carstairs'; ADM 27/111/227/90; CHU3/1D/49, p. 57, no 113; 1851 census: HO107/1658, fol. 200, p. 12.
[27] ADM 27/111/227/90; CHU3/1D/46, p. 3 n. 6.
[28] ADM 38/3147.

deception unravelled. Either way, *Prince Regent*'s description book recorded the return of one Thomas Jenkins 'alias Menhinnick', a fine of three pounds for 'Desertion, straggling, etc.' against his name.[29] Why he had deserted one ship only to join another under a different name was not recorded. The Navy was uninterested in motive.

That 'trustee' declaration was not a total fabrication. There does appear to have been a baby girl, but whose child she was is unclear. Neither as Carstairs or Menhinnick was any civil registration of birth completed, but in November 1850, the same month that Menhinnick named 'trustee' Harriett, at St John's Anglican chapel, Portsea, Harriott [*sic*] Menhinnick was baptised, her father's name recorded as William Menhinnick, seaman.[30] The child's mother was given not as Harriett but Eliza, a detail at odds both with Menhinnick's trustee declaration and the fact that four months later, in March 1851, 'bachelor' William Menhinnick married spinster Harriett Bell Carstairs.[31] When a week later the census was taken, William and Harriett Menhinnick were enumerated as visitors to the Hawke Street household of a marine sergeant's wife.[32]

Witness to the marriage was Harriett's sister, Eliza Rachel Tyler, allottee-wife of boatswain William Tyler; and the census shows that around the corner from Hawke Street, Eliza's Havant Street ménage included her 1-year-old daughter Elizabeth.[33] It cannot be said with certainty that little Elizabeth was the infant 'Harriett' of Menhinnick's allotment declaration, or the 'Harriott' baptised later that month; but if not an error by the parish clerk, the naming of Eliza as 'mother' in the baptismal register suggests some sort of collusion between the sisters. Was William party to a ruse? The baptism, after all, went some way to providing proof of his purported fatherhood, enough to justify his allotment in the event of a query. Alternatively, it may have been the unmarried Harriet's entrapment device, designed to lure her sailor to the altar by pretending to have had his child – a child in reality borne by her sister, and loaned (or furtively borrowed) to justify a shotgun marriage.

---

[29] ADM 38/3147/23-5; ADM 38/4515.
[30] CHU5/A/1/6, p. 20 n. 159. In light of this apparent subterfuge, it is of note that the same Anglican chapel saw baby William Wheden jr. baptised for a second time, contrary to church tenets (see p. 92).
[31] CHU3/1D/49, p. 57 n. 113.
[32] 1851 census: HO107/1658, fol. 200, p. 12. ('Murinick' per Findmypast.co.uk, 'Muennink' per Ancestry.com.)
[33] E&W Marriages: Q4/1845, vol. 9, p. 586; ADM 27/94/209/51; ADM 27/109/61/50; ADM 27/120/599/4; 1851 census: HO107/1658, fol. 234, p. 18; 1861 census: RG09/641, fol. 4, p. 4.

Menhinnick's matrimonial commitment(s) were shorter-lived than his naval career, which thanks to Continuous Service lasted until 1858. In 1856, toward the end of the Crimean War, on the Greek island of Proti he deserted again, and yet again was absent for two years.[34] Upon his return he added another marriage to his tally when in May 1858, stating himself a bachelor, he took 28-year-old Sarah McRoy as his bride.[35] Previously married to a naval pensioner, Sarah gave her civil status as widow, which if not true might explain why the couple married by licence. Alternatively (or additionally), with William's wife Harriet still alive (in 1864 she would have a daughter by one Robert Winton; in 1865, as 'widow' she would marry again, becoming Mrs Henry Johnston, seaman's wife), and with Carstairs relatives scattered around the Portsea/Portsmouth community, the still-married William may have been reluctant to have banns call attention to his latest union.[36] Then again, he and Sarah may have been in haste, for HMS *Marlborough* – given as William's address in the marriage register, but which he had yet to join – was about to depart on commission.

William served just five months in *Marlborough* before being invalided, at which point his naval service came to an end.[37] Sarah already had a four-year-old son and 2-year-old daughter by her former husband, so William now found himself both husband and stepfather.[38] We do not know how well he fulfilled those roles, but a combination of invalidity, loss of income and the death of his stepdaughter at just two-and-a-half would test any husband's character, especially one given to deception and dodging of responsibility.[39] What, then, should we read into the fact that on census day 1861 the now 33-year-old Sarah described herself as widow McRoy, 'Pensioner on Patriotic Fund'?[40] If by the latter she meant Menhinnick's naval pension, she was over-egging it somewhat: applying within days of being invalided from *Marlborough*, William had been awarded a gratuity of just five pounds, the sum limited because all service prior to his desertion from *Prince Regent* was forfeit.[41] 'Patriotic Fund' is more likely to have meant a pension awarded on the basis of the late McRoy's service, the use of her late husband's surname suggesting that by April 1861 Sarah had distanced herself from her sailor-husband of four years (had she discovered

---

[34] ADM 139/32/3171.
[35] CHU2/1C/17, p. 172 n. 343.
[36] E&W Births: Q1/1864, vol. 2B, p. 495 (Harriet Mary Winton); E&W Marriages: Q4/1865, vol. 2B, p. 800 (certificate); CHU3/1D/65, p. 28 n. 55.
[37] ADM 139/32/3171.
[38] CHU2/1B/5, p. 122 nos 972–3.
[39] PHC: G/PGC4/3, n.p., n. 14604 (Alice McRoy).
[40] 1861 census: RG09/636, fol. 148, p. 9.
[41] ADM 6/319; ADM 139/32/3171, p. 6.

William's earlier, still valid marriage to Harriet Carstairs?), and wanted no longer to be associated with him. Alternatively, after marrying Menhinnick she may have retained her widow-surname for financial purposes. Naval widows awarded a pension had 'to make an affidavit each quarter on collecting [it]', and lost it entirely upon remarriage.[42] To maintain entitlement to her pension, Sarah must cover up the fact that she had remarried; must continue to make her quarterly affidavits; and as part of the charade must continue to be known by her late husband's name.

William Menhinnick did not die in service (his being invalided in November 1858 was the final entry in his service record), and no conclusive evidence has been found of death occurring between then and the 1861 census when Sarah described herself as widow McRoy. In 1862, still 'widow', Sarah McRoy married, by certificate, a widowed sergeant in the Royal Marines Artillery, thereby becoming Mrs Coley, and stepmother to two motherless children aged eight and five.[43] Of her union with William Menhinnick there is no further trace.

Menhinnick's story shows how feckless, duplicitous seamen could take advantage of a range of naval and civil factors: the allotment system, the act of desertion, obedience to orders, the Navy's pre-Continuous Service ship-specific recruitment process, ships' long absences, and clerics' reliance on couples' self-affirmation of civil status, any and all of them providing 'cover' for men bent on deceit. Sarah McRoy, Harriet Carstairs and her sister Eliza, and one if not two Susan Jenkins: as many as five women came within William Menhinnick's orbit, at least two entering into short-lived marriages with him. There may even have been a third wife, for whereas no civil or parish records have been found to verify marriage details ('Gosport, June 1846') supplied in the 'Jenkins' declaration favouring Guernsey-resident Susan, records do exist for the marriage of a Thomas Jenkins, bachelor seaman, to Maria Laura Johnson, a minor, in September 1847 in Portsmouth.[44] If this were 'our' seaman Jenkins, it means that within fifteen months of one unverifiable marriage he contracted another (verifiable) with a child-bride, a year later allotting not to her but to his previous 'wife' Susan.

Sister and/or wife, Susan Jenkins's background is unknown; but the Carstairs girls were naval daughters.[45] That Harriet Carstairs succumbed to Menhinnick's charms, was persuaded by his lies, trusted his vows and was abandoned by him; that her sister Eliza appears to have been persuaded to allow her infant daughter's name (if not the infant herself, at a baptism) to

---

[42] Doe, 'Those They Left Behind', pp. 8–9.
[43] CHU3/1D/61, p. 75 n. 149; E&W Marriages: Q4/1851, vol. 7, p. 268.
[44] E&W Marriages: Q3/1847, vol. 7, p. 125; CHU3/1D/46, p. 3 n. 6.
[45] CHU3/1D/49, p. 57 n. 113; E&W Marriages: Q4/1845, vol. 9, p. 586.

be used in a scam: these show that for all their familiarity with the Jack Tar/ Rambling Sailor persona of legend, women from naval backgrounds were not immune to seductive charms, and were open to taking nuptial chances which placed them, as women, in greater jeopardy than their naval paramours.

***

Could the nineteenth-century naval wife escape a dysfunctional marriage more easily than her civilian peer? Possibly. Her husband's absence at sea afforded time, safety and emotional space to contemplate her options and make good her escape. Unlike her civilian peer she still had her monthly half-pay, and she could (at a pinch, with supplementation) live on this while making whatever arrangements were needed. But upon her husband's return – earlier, should he report her as having left him, as unfit to receive his support – the allotment's cash-in-hand income would cease. Her options thereafter were limited. Were she not an immigrant wife who had left family far away she might be able to return to her parental home nearby, or beg a bed from relatives; indeed, it is not impossible that some of the married daughters found co-resident at their parents' addresses, or making up later-ally-extended households with sisters, were not so much wives patiently sitting out their husbands' absence at sea as wives whose marriages were over, who had given up their marital homes and were marking time pending longer-term living arrangements.

Rosalinda Matthias may have been one such. The oldest of the Davey siblings whose complex Primrose Alley household features in Chapter Six, she appears variously as Elinda, Elinday, Rosa Linda, Linday and Rose Almida. Her husband James's naval service, begun in 1822, had seen him as ordinary seaman, master at arms, second master, captain of the forecastle, quartermaster and, finally and briefly, ship's cook, the latter earning him more than his previous roles (see Table 1).[46] He had allotted to Rosalinda at successive junctures from their marriage in 1835 until 1846 when, in what may be the first documented sign of their marital difficulties, he switched payments from her to his mother.[47] Discharged for the last time in March 1850, by 1851 he was living in a Havant Street pub.[48] Rosalinda meanwhile was in Primrose Alley with her sister-in-law, brother-in-law, a nephew, and

---

[46] ADM 38/7587/18.
[47] ADM 27/59/47/517; ADM 27/75/74/388; ADM 27/89/52/54; ADM 27/92/264/18; ADM 27/97/157/716.
[48] 1851 census: HO107/1658, fol. 229, p. 9.

two nieces under ten.[49] Her 9-year-old daughter Sarah Ann was with her; the elder daughter, 12-year-old Jane Elizabeth, was a visitor in King Street.[50]

We do not know when Rosalinda joined the Primrose Alley household, but we do know that she was in a better financial position than many other wives in marital difficulties. As Fig. 19 shows, she was receiving allotments from her unmarried brother Samuel Davey, AB HMS *Resistance*, and from widowed brother-in-law George Plummer, sailmaker HMS *Flamer*, whose 1850 allotment recognised her role as trustee for his daughter Mary Jane.[51] Within a matter of months, however, these remaining sources of Rosalinda's income dried up. George's allotment ceased upon his return to England in February 1851 following *Flamer*'s wrecking; Samuel's would end in September 1852, twenty-one days after he was marked 'R' at Woolwich.[52] There had been two other sources of household income, both directed to Rosalinda's sister-in-law Elizabeth Davey. The first was from Elizabeth's husband Joseph, HMS *Victory*, the second from her brother William Leese, HMS *Ajax*; but William's payments had ended in February 1851 when, disrated AB to ordinary, at Queenstown he too deserted.[53] Unless Samuel and George continued to serve, and made fresh declarations from their next ships, of the seven spousal and fraternal allotments shown in Fig. 19, by the end of 1852 there remained only Joseph's to Elizabeth, and this only so long as Joseph continued to serve. Rosalinda, previously the recipient of three men's half-pay, was by then without financial support.

Did Rosalinda even know where husband James was living? She probably did. Within crowded Portsea streets, on an island in which every district was within walking distance, as much as naval wives shared news of ships' movements and safety they shared gossip about individuals' activities, whereabouts and fidelity; and James's Havant Street pub lodgings were less than a half-mile from Primrose Alley.[54] Whether or not the couple ever met, they never reconciled. Falsely declaring himself widower, in 1856 James married a Sarah Long, and passing themselves off as husband and wife the pair set up home in Landport, well away from the extended Davey family.[55] The whereabouts in the 1860s of the still-living Rosalinda are

---

[49] 1851 census: HO107/1658, fol. 311, p. 54.
[50] 1851 census: HO107/1658, fol. 371, p. 2.
[51] ADM 27/110/371/52; ADM 27/111/121/11; E&W Births: Q3/1842, vol. 7, p. 143; CHU3/1B/27, p. 156 n. 1248.
[52] ADM 38/8857/52.
[53] ADM 27/110/20/27; ADM 27/112/159/13; ADM 27/111/535/112; ADM 38/7474/112.
[54] Fury, 'Seamen's Wives and Widows', p. 258; Tebbutt, *Women's Talk?*, *passim*; Ross, 'Survival Networks', p. 10.
[55] CHU3/1D/53, p. 77 n. 153; 1861 census: RG09/637, fol. 115, p. 34; Bailey, *Unquiet Lives*, p. 150.

unknown, but she eventually made a home with daughter Sarah, Sarah's labourer-husband and their growing family.[56] Like James Matthias on his second appearance at the altar, in the 1871 census Rosalinda adopted a fictitious widowhood, a status both justifying her lack of spouse and conferring respectability. The pair had achieved the poor person's divorce.[57]

The wife who abandoned her naval husband risked penury, for she forfeited his allotment. A civilian man, shore-based, with occupation and income, made a satisfactory replacement spouse. Top-slicing aside, his regular wage was at her disposal once she were installed as household manager. This was the prospect awaiting Amelia Cavander.[58] Married in 1844 to AB James Cavander, HMS *Firebrand*, Amelia had given birth on Christmas Eve 1848.[59] This second child, a boy to follow her 4-year-old daughter, she named Esau.[60] The name was no biblical nod, but a link to the child's father; for in the three years and nine months that James Cavander was at sea, his friend Esau Barrett had, in the words of a *Hampshire Telegraph* hack, 'extended his friendship to [James's] wife, the fruits of which was a little one.'[61] Nailing both the infant's paternity and her adultery, on the birth certificate Amelia named Esau senior as father.[62] The *Telegraph* reported that James showed forbearance, 'took to his partner again and joined the *Victory*, and left his wife his half-pay.'[63] From *Victory*'s anchorage in Portsmouth Harbour he declared an allotment favouring Amelia, but in his absence she 'took away the goods' from the marital home in Moore's Square. Coming ashore in early 1849, James 'kicked up a shindy' on finding his wife had taken up with her lover. Esau Barrett then assaulted him, in court having the gall to claim that 'what he had done was in kindness to [James].' The affair featured in the *Hampshire Telegraph*'s weekly police court report, its headline 'The Husband's Friend' rubbing salt in the cuckold's wound.

Amelia lost no time in setting up home with her lover. With her went Esau junior, the cuckoo whose conception James had been prepared to forgive, and Amelia Elizabeth, her daughter by James. The little girl, like

---

[56] 1871 census: RG10/1128, fol. 140, p. 21.
[57] Perkin, *Women and Marriage*, p. 117; Ginger Suzanne Frost, '"As if she was my own child": cohabitation, community, and the English criminal courts, 1855–1900', *The History of the Family*, 20:4 (2015), 546–62, at p. 559.
[58] Both 'Cavander' and 'Cavender' appear in naval and civil records; spellings are as documented.
[59] CHU3/1D/42, p. 219 n. 441. (Amelia Hussey m. James Cavander.)
[60] E&W Births: Q2/1845, vol. 7, p. 123; CHU3/1B/28, p. 154 n. 1226 (Amelia Elizabeth).
[61] *H/Tel*, 10 Feb. 1849, p. 7 col. D. Subsequent quotes also from this source.
[62] E&W Births: Q1/1849, vol. 7, p. 138 (certificate). Née Hussey, Amelia gave her maiden name as 'Cavander'.
[63] ADM 27/101/16/45. *Victory*'s muster book (ADM 38/9263/n.p./79) shows AB James Cavander joining ship in July 1848, declaring an allotment to Amelia (ADM 27/104/272/79) in August, four months before baby Esau's birth.

her mother, would now experience something unfamiliar: the presence of a man about the house.

For James to sever financial ties required only that he point to the child conceived in his absence, this being evidence enough to persuade a church minister to support his wish to stop his allotment, and the Navy to grant it. He then declared an allotment naming one Frances Childs trustee to a 12-year-old Eliza Cavander.[64] In the census 51-year-old Frances Childs appears alongside her carpenter husband and two younger members of the household: 12-year-old Eliza Childs ('Daughter'), and 23-year-old Emma Cavander, a married visitor.[65] Emma was James's sister-in-law, she having married Charles Cavender, seaman, in September 1850, Frances Childs witnessing the wedding.[66] James's 1849 declaration thus routed support (deviously, via proxy Mrs Childs) to his newlywed sister-in-law pending her husband's declaring his own allotment from HMY *Victoria and Albert*; to James's undoubted satisfaction, it also denied Amelia his money.[67]

Still married to James, Amelia was now dependent upon Esau Barrett's income from bricklaying. This may have fluctuated with the seasons, but it was more regular than seamen's pay, more substantial than any half-pay. Once Esau had top-sliced for himself, Amelia had his nett wage with which to manage their household. As Mr and Mrs Barrett they set up home in Diamond Street, had three further children, quit Portsea Island, and lived out the rest of their days in the Hampshire hamlet of Bitterne.[68]

Amelia's affair was far from unique, its association with husband-absence having implications for many another naval marriage. Leaving adverse publicity behind she made a new life for herself, albeit on the basis of spurious matrimony. It helped that her estranged husband transferred his affections elsewhere, thereby loosening his jealous attachment to her. In January 1851, two years after Esau's assault, James Cavander declared yet another allotment, to yet another trustee. This trustee was Jane Elliott, she who in court was alleged to have initiated a brawl with her abusive husband (see p. 224).[69] James named the entrusted child as 2-year-old Maria, surname not supplied. Weeks later the census found little Maria listed as daughter to James and Jane, they purporting to be man and wife.[70] In 1856, James (still married to Amelia) and Jane (still married to William) tied the knot, she reverting to spinsterhood and maiden name to avoid

---

[64] ADM 27/107/235/SB79.
[65] 1851 census: HO107/1659, fol. 287, p. 22.
[66] CHU3/1D/48, p. 188 n. 375.
[67] ADM 27/113/62/54.
[68] 1861 census: RG09/681, fol. 44, p. 32; 1871 census: RG10/1197, fol. 52, p. 46.
[69] ADM 27/112/154/51; *H/Tel*, 20 May 1848, p. 1 col. B.
[70] 1851 census: HO/107/1659, fol. 131, p. 17.

being unmasked as Mrs Elliott.[71] It had taken six years, but the original Mr and Mrs Cavander had finally resolved their differences – via two bigamous marriages.

Like Jane Elliott, Martha Bone (*q.v.*) appears to fit the image of 'serial naval bride', discarding one living sailor-husband for another. We met Martha as wife of AB Eli Bone, HMS *Resolute*; but as spinster Martha Woodley, resident of the Common Hard, in January 1847 she had first married seaman Charles Job Lewis.[72] He was thirty-six, she nineteen. Had she hoped for his allotment she was to be disappointed, the last in his name being an 1840 declaration favouring his mother.[73] His Chalton Street address, however, would have life-changing implications for Martha, for witnesses to the wedding – Charles's sister Emma and her husband – were Chalton Street residents too, as was another of his sisters, naval wife Harriet Lock; and *their* near-neighbours included Rebecca Heath, half-sister of sailor Eli Bone. And in due course, via the avunculate marriage of Rebecca's teenage daughter, the neighbours would also include Eli's older brother, AB Thomas Bone, HMS *Excellent*.[74] Her groom's home address, therefore, brought Martha within the orbit of a large and complex family.

Three years after her marriage to Charles Job Lewis, from a shared address in Nile Street, on New Year's Day 1850 Martha and Eli Bone were married, their union witnessed by Martha's sister Clara. Two things arouse suspicion. First, the bride presented herself as Martha Woodley (again), spinster (again).[75] Were she widowed it would have been natural for her to describe herself as such, and to use her late husband's surname. To declare herself never-married therefore suggests deceit. Secondly, theirs was a register office wedding. Opting for a civil ceremony avoided the calling of banns, a prudent move in a naval community where names were known and news travelled fast. To infer subterfuge is not cynical: the marriage was bigamous. Husband No. 1 was still living, though under circumstances which enable us to view Martha not as one of Gillray's rapacious Portsea Polls, or Capper's cynical serial brides '[contracting] marriage with two,

---

[71] E&W Marriages: Q3/1856, vol. 2B, p. 621 (certificate).
[72] CHU3/1D/45, p. 106 n. 212.
[73] ADM 27/70/247/132.
[74] 1851 census: HO107/1657, fol. 89, p. 41 (cf. Harriet Lock, John and Emma Stroud), and fol. 88, p. 39 (cf. Rebecca Heath, née Bone); ADM 27/95/109/159; 1861 census: RG09/632, fol. 93, p. 30; ADM 27/100/263/334; CHU3/1D/55, p. 34 n. 68. In the marriage certificate of Ann Heath and Thomas Bone, to cover their consanguinity both bride and groom gave false forenames for their fathers; other details confirm their identities.
[75] 1851 census: HO107/1657, fol. 88, p. 39; E&W Marriages: Q1/1850, v. 7, p. 207 (certificate).

*Marital Complexities*

or in some cases even four, men … from all of [whom] they would be in receipt of half-pay', but as a 22-year-old fleeing a union in which she could see no happy ending.[76]

For Charles Job Lewis had neither died nor abandoned his bride, but had fallen victim to a depression that had dogged him for years. In October 1848, just eighteen months after marrying Martha, from the Portsea Island workhouse he had been admitted to Camberwell House lunatic asylum. This facility had opened two years previously, accommodating twelve private and 150 pauper patients.[77] Charles was a pauper patient. Admission records described him as 'Suffering from melancholia, having been two years insane, of quick temper, with his general mental powers much impaired.'[78] The 'two years insane' included, even exceeded, his time married to Martha. References to his being 'extremely obstinate, and occasionally very violent', together with repeated reports of no improvement in his mental condition, further explain Martha's decision to put her first marriage behind her. It may also, along with loss of Charles's naval pay, have informed her decision to set up home with Eli Bone, she having little prospect of improving her situation via other means. Widowhood would bring release, but the Camberwell institute would no doubt do its utmost to prolong Charles's life, delivering better care than could be provided on out-relief in a Portsea rental.

Now in effect the 'married widow' of an ailing, estranged husband, Martha determined (or was persuaded) to create a new life for herself, with Eli. From her perspective, matrimony would bring security, respectability, an allotment. From Eli's point of view, cohabitation had advantages over marriage, for whereas Martha might be the object of sharp remarks for 'living in sin', he (being a man) was less likely to be reviled. More to the point, under the New Poor Law of 1834 he could not be forced to support Martha or any children of their cohabitation; he could refuse even to acknowledge paternity.[79] And from Eli's perspective, bigamous marriage to Martha was no more scandalous than his brother's avunculate union with their elder half-sister's teenage daughter. Complex interrelationships were nothing new to the Bone family.

Whether and how news of Martha's remarriage ever reached Camberwell is unknown, as is when she ceased writing to Charles, or visiting (if she ever had). Two years after Martha took Eli as her husband, in January 1852 Charles Job Lewis was recorded as displaying symptoms of 'tubercular

---

[76] Capper, *Aft – from the Hawsehole*, pp. 13–14.
[77] London, Wellcome Collection, Camberwell House Asylum catalogue, Vol. 2: male and female patients admitted March 1847 – May 1850, MS. 6220 (1847–50).
[78] *Ibid.*, p. 647.
[79] Frost, *Living in Sin*, p. 17.

disease of the lungs'.[80] In February he was 'hectic, emaciated … feeble' and coughing blood.[81] In March, at just forty years old, he died of '*phthisis pulmonalis* certified'.[82] Martha Woodley Lewis Bone was now officially widowed, but her status as Eli's bigamous wife gained no post-mortem, post-matrimonium legality. And as Chapter Fourteen will show, like Jane Elliott Cavander she would find that remarriage to another seaman brought little comfort or security.

Cavander, Matthias, Bone: these wives' stories feature the chopping and changing of declared civil status, a tactic commonly deployed in bigamous marriages. At the altar bachelors became widowers, married men reverted to bachelorhood, wives revived maiden names and spinster status. The previously mentioned Greenleaf family includes a still-married sailor passing himself off as 'bachelor'; but there were further complications to the Greenleaf women's matrimonial arrangements, as we shall now see.

Joanna Greenleaf Barrow Fleming was twice widowed when, a respectable three-plus years after the death of her second husband James George Fleming, seaman James Charlo made her his bride.[83] Allotment declarations in 1839, 1844, 1846 and 1848 provide the way into Charlo's past.[84] The earlier three named his first wife Sarah, their 1836 marriage confirmed via parish registers.[85] The fourth named his 19-year-old sister Louisa Charlo. There was indeed a sister, but she was thirty-three years old and twelve years a married woman when James, giving her maiden name, declared his allotment to her.[86] Upon marriage in 1836 she would have taken the surname of her seaman husband John Whitehead, something which in 1848 her brother forgot, did not know, or tactically ignored. The errors do not appear accidental, but nothing has been found to account for James's stating Louisa to be nineteen, or using her maiden name.[87] His wife of fifteen years, Mrs Sarah Charlo, meanwhile, was still alive, a 36-year-old visitor in a Portsea carpenter's household, her civil state given as 'married'.[88]

It is unlikely that the Greenleaf family knew nothing of Charlo prior to his marriage to Joanna. Like Joanna's late husbands and brother-in-law he was a gunner who had served several times in *Excellent*, and his natal family,

---

[80] Camberwell House Asylum catalogue, MS.6220: Vol. 2, p. 647.
[81] *Ibid*.
[82] E&W Deaths: Q1/1852, Camberwell, London, vol. 1D, p. 311 (certificate).
[83] CHU3/1D/53, p. 163 n. 326.
[84] ADM 27/64/30/30; ADM 27/86/185/878; ADM 27/95/442/27; ADM 27/104/56/755.
[85] CHU42/1C/13, p. 143 n. 427 ('Charlow').
[86] CHU23/1B/1, p. 88, n. 699 ('Charlow'); CHU2/1C/11, p. 68 n. 202 ('Charlow').
[87] CHU2/1C/11, p. 68 n. 202.
[88] 1851 census: HO107/1658, fol. 208, p. 28.

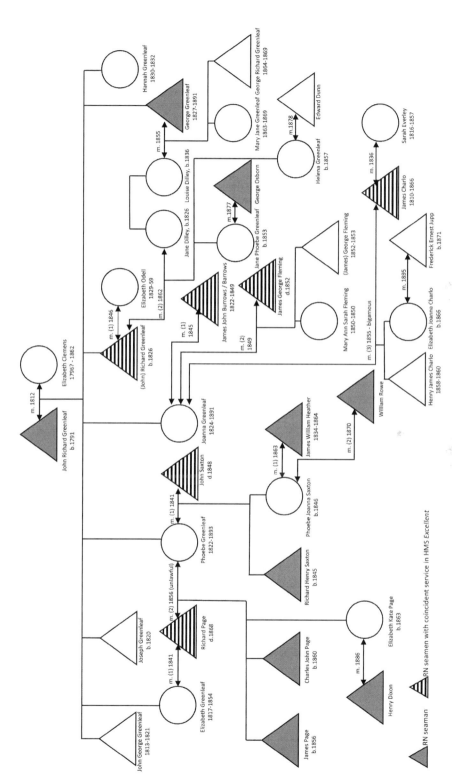

**Fig. 27** Genogram of Greenleaf family. Genogram model based upon that used by Laslett (Laslett, 'Introduction', p. 42). Reproduced, with alterations as described in Chapter Six, by permission of the Licensor through PLSClear.

in-laws and still-living wife were local.[89] The wedding went ahead, which may suggest that, believing Charlo would bring Joanna belated happiness after her many losses, Greenleaf kin were willing to condone the bigamy. The marriage ceremony was conducted by licence, thus removing any risk of banns alerting the true, extant and lawful Mrs Charlo who, having no husband to support her, would die two years later in the workhouse, a pauper.[90] Her surviving husband may have considered her death a release, but – as with Charles Job Lewis's demise, and Martha Lewis's marriage to Eli Bone – it did not legalise a previously bigamous union.

It was one thing for twice-widowed Joanna in 1855 to marry her late husband's shipmate, the still-married Charlo; that union was merely bigamous. The 1856 remarriage of her widowed sister Phoebe was another thing entirely.[91] In 1841 newlywed Phoebe Greenleaf Saxton and her seaman brother George Greenleaf had witnessed their elder sister Elizabeth's marriage to gunner Richard Page.[92] The marriage was not Page's only connection to the family. He had been shipmates with Phoebe's husband, gunner John Saxton, they in the 1840s serving at least five years together in HMS *Excellent*; another old *Excellent* hand was brother-in-law James George Fleming, Joanna's second husband.[93] In matrimony and in shared naval service, therefore, Richard Page's credentials were sound – sounder certainly than James Charlo's. Unlike Charlo's faked bachelorhood, Page's widower status was indisputable following Elizabeth's death in 1854.[94] Family approval aside, however, his marriage to the now-widowed Phoebe was unlawful. He was marrying his deceased wife's sister.

Neither bride nor groom can have been unaware of their union's invalidity. Not only did the law prohibit it, but the issue of marriage with a dead wife's sister was a hot topic reported upon locally at intervals through 1847–48.[95] A *Hampshire Telegraph* article noted that nationwide some 33,000 such marriages had taken place in the twelve years following the 1835 Act; that children of such marriages were illegitimate; and that 'many

---

[89] ADM 139/12/1113.
[90] E&W Deaths: Q1/1857, vol. 2B, p. 238 ('Charlow'; certificate); Portsmouth History Centre (PHC) Portsmouth, Hampshire, Portsmouth Burials, Parish Burials, PHC G/BBK4/1 (1857), p. 79 n. 1093.
[91] CHU3/1D/54, p. 30 n. 59.
[92] CHU3/1D/40, p. 151 n. 301.
[93] Richard Page: ADM 27/77/42/1510; ADM 27/79/334/118; ADM 27/80/127/243; ADM 27/97/236/1622. John Saxton: ADM 27/73/114/1182; ADM 27/73/174/1182; ADM 27/83/42/575; ADM 27/89/273/575; ADM 27/90/130/575; ADM 27/94/255/575; James Fleming: ADM 27/81/362/422.
[94] E&W Deaths: Q3/1854, vol. 2B, p. 235; CHU3/1E/32, p. 117 n. 931.
[95] *Marriage Act,* 5 & 6 Will. IV, c. 54 (1835).

women who, in ignorance of the statute, have married the husbands of their deceased sisters have been subject to the most harsh and contumelious treatment, being taunted as concubines'.[96] A commoner form of incest than marriage between blood-kin, affinal marriage of in-laws remained one the most controversial of Victorian prohibitions.[97] A popular novel trumpeted its perils, and between April and July 1855 a Bill to amend marriage laws had been repeatedly debated in both Houses of Parliament, Gladstone himself opining that to amend the law would be to 'open floodgates' and 'establish an anarchy'.[98] So notorious was the issue, it would even feature in operetta, Gilbert and Sullivan's *Iolanthe* referring to 'that annual blister / Marriage with a dead wife's sister'; but that is to jump ahead.[99] Marriage with a dead wife's sister remained unlawful for a further half-century.[100] Ignoring this, in March 1856 Phoebe Saxton and Richard Page married, both parties truthfully declaring themselves widowed, their different surnames giving no clue as to their kinship.[101] In marrying by licence they avoided any voicing of just cause or impediment during the calling of banns; they also protected Phoebe's modesty, she being by then five months pregnant. Anglican clergy being more disapproving of affinal marriage than were local communities, there was also a risk that if the couple were regular church attenders and known to him, the minister might decline to officiate.[102] Phoebe and Richard were lucky. The service went ahead; but as with James Charlo's wedding to Joanna Fleming, no Greenleaf kin stood witness. Perhaps they were unavailable. Perhaps they disapproved of the breach of law, or of the groom's having bedded his late wife's sister within scant months of his being bereaved, if not sooner.

Family disapproval may similarly have played a part in young Amelia Wheden's fleeing Portsmouth. Previous chapters have described how, married at fourteen to a man more than twice her age, by twenty she had suffered the loss of two children, one of whom may have been fathered by AB George Wilkinson. Census day 1851 found Amelia with husband

---

[96] *H/Tel*, 3 July 1847, p. 2 col. C; *ibid.*, 5 August 1848, p. 6 col. C; *ibid.*, 14 October 1848, p. 2 col. D.
[97] Frost, *Living in Sin*, pp. 52–3.
[98] Felicia Mary F. Skene, *The Inheritance of Evil; or, the consequences of marrying a deceased wife's sister* (London, 1849); *H/Tel*, 21 April 1855, p. 3 col. C; *ibid.*, 28 April 1855, p. 3 col. F; *ibid.* 12 May 1855, p. 3 col. D; *ibid.*, 28 July 1855, p. 3 col. D.
[99] Chris Angelico and Adam Cuerden, 'The Gilbert and Sullivan Archive' <https://gsarchive.net/iolanthe/html/> [accessed 30 March 2024]. With thanks to Dick Hobbs for the reminder.
[100] *Deceased Wife's Sister's Marriage Act*, 7 Edw. VII, c. 47 (1907).
[101] CHU3/1D/54, p. 30 n. 59.
[102] Frost, *Living in Sin*, p. 55.

William and elder son (the suspected cuckoo) in a Trafalgar Street sublet.[103] DSQ'd from *Phaeton* in February 1850 and subsequently invalided, William was now unemployed, not yet pensioned, and unwaged.[104] In his census schedule he nonetheless said he was a seaman. Homeward bound in *Hercules* in August 1850 he would have been happy to learn of little William's baptism at St John the Evangelist Roman Catholic church, alongside infant cousins on Amelia's side.[105] In February 1851, serving his final weeks in *Excellent* amid the mudflats of Portsmouth Harbour, he was unlikely to have known of the boy's second baptism at a different church, for that ceremony was clandestine.[106] As noted previously, on that occasion little William's father was recorded as 'George Wheden', and only days earlier from HMS *Vengeance* George Wilkinson had declared an allotment in the boy's name, identifying a Maria Balch as trustee, by inference to act as courier of his money to Amelia.[107]

Amelia was now nineteen, and pregnant with her second child. She was living in a Landport sublet with an out-of-work husband of uncertain health, an eighteen-month-old likely conceived by her lover, and a covert allotment from the child's putative father. It was a situation even the most mature of naval wives would have found difficult to navigate. William's being several years Amelia's senior only added to the likelihood of breakdown.[108]

In April 1851 William was granted a naval pension of £9 4s 0d, but for two years only.[109] In June 1852 a correspondence began between the Navy pensions department and the Portsea Island Union poor law guardians. It concerned money, but reveals a marriage breakdown. Pieced together, surviving Admiralty correspondence suggests the following sequence: that William and Amelia had separated; that William had ceased to support his wife; that Amelia had been reduced to applying to the parish for relief for herself and her child, and had been deemed chargeable to the Union at a rate of two shillings per week; that parish guardians wanted to offset their outgoings by having her husband's pension recompense them the same amount; that William demurred; and the guardians, believing it might swing the discussion in their favour, demanded the smaller sum of 1s 6d per week.[110] The Navy agreed. William did not. There being no legal obligation

---

[103] 1851 census: HO107/1657, fol. 52, p. 12 ('Weaden').
[104] ADM 29/046, p. 154.
[105] CHU71/1A/3, p. 89 nos 353, 354, 355.
[106] CHU5/A/1/6, p. 24 n. 20. See p. 92.
[107] ADM 27/112/149/5; see p. 59.
[108] Bailey, *Unquiet Lives*, p. 154.
[109] ADM 6/312, n.p.
[110] National Archives (TNA) Kew, War Office: Secretary-at-War, Out-Letters, Greenwich Pensions, WO 4/890 (1851–53), p. 213.

for husbands to maintain their wives, he may have objected to maintaining a woman for whom he felt no further responsibility; as a ratepayer he may have regarded it as the parish's duty to support his wife. If so, he was deluding himself: the prevailing view held that living husbands should not be allowed to escape responsibility for the care of their families, and that deserted wives and children should not become a charge upon the rates; hence should a wife apply for poor relief, her husband's support could be enforced.[111]

On 1 October 1852 the Navy pensions department wrote to a pensions sub-section known as S.O.2 East London: 'Unless [Weedon] can give a satisfactory reason for refusing to support his wife, [you should] arrange for the payment of 1/6 a week to the Portsea Island Union for the maintenance of herself and child'.[112] The correspondence log confirms a copy was sent to the Portsea Island Union, but the Guardians' Minute Books make no mention of their response. On 13 October 1852 the pensions department wrote again to S.O.2 East London, 'requesting to make a note of the parish's claim in order that it may be settled on Wm Weedon's … return, when he is to apply to this office for instructions.'[113] Those instructions may be inferred from evidence that on the following day, six months before his two-year pension expired, William Weedon returned to naval service.[114] On 20 October, via the following brisk diktat to the pensions department, the matter was closed:

> This man having joined HMS *Agamemnon* on the 14 Inst is entitled to his Arrears to the preceding day only, which may be paid to him after deducting the 1/6 a week claimed by the Portsea Island Union for the support of his wife and child. You will discontinue his name on your List [of out-pensioners]; noting the cause and annexing this letter as your authority. The [pension] Certificate is herewith returned. You are requested to make the necessary communication … with a view to settlement of the parish claim.[115]

If William saw re-enlistment as an escape, he was to be disappointed, seeing that same amount docked not from his naval pension but his naval pay.[116] And Amelia? Now a lone mother with no income other than the parish's 1s 6d per week and George Wilkinson's allotment of October 1850 (which hinged upon Maria Balch's handing over the cash), her son Louis

---

[111] Thane, 'Women and the Poor Law', pp. 32–3.
[112] TNA: WO 4/890, p. 282.
[113] *Ibid.*, p. 295.
[114] ADM 38/2328, pp. 61–2 n. 47.
[115] TNA: WO 4/890, pp. 298–9.
[116] Lincoln, 'Impact of Warfare', p. 86.

dead within days of birth, Amelia turned to her sisters for support.[117] Two of them still lived in their childhood home in Marylebone Street, and it was there in May 1853, in the house where he was born, that Amelia's firstborn died. He was three years old. Cause of death, as we have seen, was 'convulsions 36 hours'. His aunt reported the death.[118]

As for William senior, his service in *Agamemnon* was brief. Joining ship on 14 October 1852 as boatswain's mate, he deserted eight weeks later at Sheerness.[119] No record has been found of his being apprehended and returned, and what became of him thereafter is unknown. He may have joined another ship under a different name, as did that other deserter Menhinnick/Jenkins (*q.v.*). He may have lain low in Kent after *Agamemnon*'s departure, or returned to Dorset, the county of his birth, where there were numerous branches of the Weedon family. He may equally have returned to Portsea Island where he had contacts, and where under normal circumstances his Greenwich out-pension would have been disbursed. But that benefit had been suspended with his being entered on *Agamemnon*'s books as 'R', and to seek monies from naval sources would risk a sharp-eyed clerk's identifying him, his being arrested, charged and facing the usual proceedings for deserters. In Portsea Island there may also have been people who took Amelia's side, and were willing to inform the authorities of his presence. Thus William Weedon, naval gunner, husband, cuckold, deserter, drops from sight.

George Wilkinson meanwhile was serving in *Vengeance*. The ship being for nigh-on five years part of the Mediterranean fleet, it is possible that he and Amelia did not see each other from July 1850 to April 1855. Her feelings for him, and his for her, were undimmed. Following his return, during his month-long service in *Excellent*, in May 1855 they married. The ceremony took place not in Amelia's home parish on Portsea Island but in South Bersted, Sussex, which the 23-year-old bride, citing herself a widow, gave as her place of residence.[120] Reducing Amelia's residential requirement from twenty-one to seven days, their purchase of a three-pound licence (nearly £270 in 2024) suggests haste or urgent need.[121] As to why they chose this village, a mile north of Bognor and twenty-five from Portsea, we can only speculate. If their adulterous relationship had attracted comment within the Portsea gunnery community they may have felt it prudent to marry somewhere secluded, a Portsea wedding having potential to trigger objections from William's former shipmates. Alternatively, they may have wished

[117] ADM 27/112/144/5; 1851 census: HO107/1660, fol. 49, p. 24.
[118] E&W Deaths: Q2/1853, vol. 2B, p. 271 (certificate). (See p. 101.)
[119] ADM 38/2328, pp. 61–2 n. 47.
[120] E&W Marriages: South Bersted, Sussex, Q2/1855, vol. 2B, p. 407 [487] (certificate).
[121] Bank of England, 'Inflation Calculator' [accessed 30 March 2024].

to make their vows in a place of private emotional significance. Or perhaps bride or groom had kin there, willing to accommodate Amelia during her pre-nuptial residency; in South Bersted's North Street there were unmarried Wilkinson sisters.[122] Whether these were George's relatives is irrelevant, for the ceremony had family endorsement. One of the witnesses was 'S. Hinks': Sarah Hinks, née Groom, Amelia's sister, eleven years Amelia's senior and herself a naval wife and allottee.[123]

\*\*\*

The true extent to which seamen and their wives flouted marital law may never be known, and in the absence of personal testimony it remains unclear whether the women acted out of passion, cupidity, desperation to escape misery, emotional estrangement and/or marital violence. In seamen's memoirs, and in the urban legends and imagery of the day, naval women are depicted as unfaithful, disorderly, promiscuous, serially bigamous and mercenary. Some will have deserved those labels; but in suggesting a collective tendency toward such conduct these depictions ignore both cruel necessity, and the fact that other sections of society were inclined to the same sort of behaviours. Affinal marriage of in-laws, for example, was not the province of the working classes alone, or of lower-deck naval men and their women. It was entered into by mayors, magistrates, barristers, physicians, naval and military officers, merchants and manufacturers, any one of which occupational groups contained serial adulterers and fathers of illegitimate offspring.[124] These other men's wives would likewise have conceived lovers' children, sought refuge in relatives' households, passing themselves off as widowed or never-married to avoid the shame and publicity of divorce, or the loneliness and vulnerability of remaining separated. In choosing to escape unhappy marriages, naval women took the same risks, the same bold steps as many a civilian.

---

[122] 1851 census: South Bersted, St Peter the Less, Chichester, HO107/1653, fol. 334, p. 11.
[123] ADM 27/110/279/274.
[124] H/Tel, 3 July 1847, p. 2 col. C.

## 14

## FAREWELLS, RETURNS, AND BETWEEN

Naval family life was waymarked by departures and homecomings.[1] So polarised were these events, so extreme the emotions they aroused both directly and vicariously, as 'The Sailor's Farewell' and 'The Sailor's Return' they were commodified, depicted in popular prints, popular songs, on the sides of teapots and by the thousand in Staffordshire figurines. 'The woman's tears are central to these depictions, represented by her holding a handkerchief to her eye … representations of the emotionally expressive Jack Tar [being] used to promote an ideal of masculinity in a time of war and national crisis.'[2]

### FAREWELLS

The popularity of the image of the sailor taking leave of his weeping woman was not merely sentimental. Emphasising both martial masculinity and sentimental male self-sacrifice, it was intended to touch the viewer's patriotic nerve; in doing so, however, it vaunted the male experience over that of the female.[3] On board, as ships prepared to leave port, each parting involving the same shipboard routines. There was for each man a 'thread of continuity', the immediate distraction of involvement in duties being itself a form of relief.[4] This is not to dismiss men's deep sense of connection with home: Walton observes that men at sea felt intimately involved with life on shore, their relationship with family being more permanent than with ship and shipmates.[5] More permanent, certainly; but those shipboard 'neighbourhood norms and customs', that messdeck etiquette, the intensity and

---

[1] Rodger, *Command of the Ocean*, p. 400.
[2] Begiato, 'Tearful Sailor'.
[3] Begiato, 'Rough and Brave'.
[4] Begiato, 'Tearful Sailor'; Hagmark-Cooper, *To Be a Sailor's Wife*, p. 26; Janet Finch, *Married to the Job: wives' incorporation in men's work* (London, 1983), p. 53.
[5] Walton, 'Social History', p. 173.

commonality of seafaring experiences and privations, and the accumulation of years spent at sea combined to create between men and their ships, men and their shipmates, bonds which could prove every bit as strong as those with wives and children seen for a few weeks every few years.

As for the female experience, there was realism in images of 'the toddler with face buried in its mother's skirt, and the grumpy boy with clenched fists,' but in depicting women primarily in passive, dependent roles, it omitted the bleak reality, the 'black despair' of departure, which in some seafarers' wives could develop into depression.[6] It did not show parents' readying children for goodbyes, or children's misery being expressed in clinging, bedwetting and other behaviour problems, or their dawning realisation that mama's weeping or irritability might be rooted in fear that papa might never return.[7] These emotions were instead given a sentimental gloss, emphasising undying love, steadfast hope of reunion, an emotional bond spanning oceans to connect sailor and lover.[8] Tokens such as pre-printed Valentine's letters (one version bearing the promise of 'Cupid's recreations' to follow a happy homecoming) were popular in the wider community; among naval women and families they possessed special meaning, for along with the ensigns, jolly sailors and patriotic doggerel that decorated tea-sets, figurines, lustre-glazed wall plaques and jugs, they signalled owners' connections to the country's brave and fighting seamen.[9]

Ships' departure dates had a monetary significance that went beyond the emotion of farewells. Vessels might spend weeks in harbour, undergoing repairs, taking on stores and ammunition, with crew embarked but unable to allot until the ship had sailed, the statutory three months' sea-time elapsed. Eliza Riley and Sophia Ann Jones, married to gunners third class William Riley and John Jones, saw their previous allotment levels rise by thirteen shillings and fourteen shillings respectively when the deployment of *Ferret* and *Simoom* at last took their men from harbour pay to sea-pay.[10] These were planned departures, and the experienced naval wife would have known to expect a boost to her monthly income once the ships were at sea.

---

[6] Lincoln, 'Impact of Warfare', p. 83; Chandler, *Women without Husbands*, p. 66; Finch, *Married to the Job*, p. 115.

[7] Begiato, 'Rough and Brave'; Lincoln, 'Impact of Warfare', p. 86; Hagmark-Cooper, *To Be a Sailor's Wife*, pp. 19–20.

[8] Karl Bell, 'Civic Spirits? Ghost Lore and Civic Narratives in Nineteenth Century Portsmouth', *Cultural and Social History*, 11:1 (2014), 51–68, at p. 55.

[9] Henderson and Carlisle, *Marine Art & Antiques*, pp. 159–65; for example, Portsmouth, Portsmouth History Centre (PHC), Valentine Letter, PHC 181A/1 (1841); Lincoln, 'Impact of Warfare', p. 84.

[10] ADM 27/113/267/1702; ADM 27/120/221/1; ADM 27/113/84/416; ADM 27/120/550/3.

## BRIDGING THE GAP

Whether she busied herself with housework or waved him off from Point, the Hoe, Round Tower or Hot Walls, the seaman's woman faced abrupt and enormous changes when his ship departed. No spouse to talk to, or to help with the heavier tasks, or discipline the children. No body to provide warmth at night, or sexual release. No sound of his tread on the stair, or whistling in the yard; his clothes and boots gone, his familiar scent lingering for a few days only. For some women the silence of home aroused mixed emotions, 'longing, peace, the enjoyment of time alone.'[11] Some experienced loneliness and frustration, others quiet relief at no longer being expected to engage in intercourse, or risk unwanted pregnancy. Those hoping to conceive faced months or years of involuntary infecundity; those allowing themselves physical leeway risked conceiving another man's child, or acquiring a sexually transmitted disease.[12]

For the woman who took her chances, only to conceive by someone other than her husband, the options were few, and grim. She might choose to omit from her letters any mention of her condition, go to full term, and find some other woman willing to adopt the ill-timed baby. To keep this high-risk strategy from her husband, however, relied upon the collective discretion of the naval community and the woman's civilian neighbours, neither of which could be guaranteed. Alternatively, if her husband were of a forgiving nature and their marital relationship robust, the compromised wife might risk keeping the child. This meant confessing all, either by letter (which if the addressee were illiterate must be read aloud by a shipmate) or orally upon his homecoming, and hoping that her husband would reconcile to the cuckoo in the marital nest, and to her. We have seen how the marriage of James and Amelia Cavander (*q.v.*) initially survived just such a challenge. James was reportedly willing to forgive Amelia's infidelity, and accept the child fathered by their neighbour Esau Barrett.[13] Their marriage could not however survive the humiliating beating that Esau inflicted on James.

Their men at sea, naval women had no choice but to take decisions, keep house, protect resources, and manage money, children and the household's other residents. Heavy enough with a husband present, heavier still in a poor household, domestic responsibilities put abnormal stress on the unsupported and servantless wife; but joint effort with washing dolly or mangle could see two women complete their laundering more swiftly, and two women's sewing could be completed by the light of one woman's lamp,

---

[11] Chandler, *Women without Husbands*, p. 66; Finch, *Married to the Job*, p. 115. Hagmark-Cooper, *To Be a Sailor's Wife*, p. 26.
[12] Lincoln, 'Impact of Warfare', p. 86.
[13] ADM 27/112/154/51; *H/Tel*, 10 February 1849, p. 7 col. D.

gossip and shared confidences helping to pass the time. Beyond the daily grind of housework, however, there were pleasures to be taken. Tea could be drunk with neighbours, with same-ship or old-ship naval wives, with family. To venture out to the seafront was to enjoy the tang of air fresher than that of a mould-ridden rental or the dank and smoky atmosphere of an enclosed court. Even the monthly trip to the pay office could be a source of enjoyment, as women caught up with each other before heading home, their pockets heavy with coin. For some, church provided comfort and company. Money permitting, funfairs and music halls provided excitement and colour; military bands marched and played; and if warmth, light and company were needed, a beershop or pub was never far away. Between these releases, however, there were long hours of loneliness and longing.

Communication between ship and shore was relatively efficient, and affordable. A cheap subsidised postal service for officers and men had been introduced in 1795, lower-deck men paying just 1d per single-sheet letter (countersigned by their commanding officer to confirm the sender was employed on HM's service), with free delivery of mail brought to the United Kingdom by one of HM ships, or at a 2d charge if via private vessel.[14] In Bath Square, Portsmouth, Arnoldus Vanden Bergh and Son operated as Navy Post Office agents, proclaiming that 'Ship letters, stamped and unpaid, are received and forwarded from this office to all parts of the Kingdom.'[15] Letters between London and Malta took at most a week, a month between London and China, Peru or west Africa, six weeks to Valparaiso.[16] For men serving in steamships, frequent re-coaling made the exchange of letters between ship and home both speedier and more reliable, Royal Navy ships being able to transfer mail bags to British packet agents on carrying vessels; but the process was slower for mid-century seamen on passage to distant stations, and especially slow for those on discovery service.[17] For the naval wife, then, the type of ship her husband served in and the nature of its commission were as relevant to their communication as either partner's ability to write.

In the few items of correspondence to survive, exploration of emotional aspects of naval family life is frustrated by phraseology so formulaic and conventional as to appear encoded. 'The conventional beginning of all

---

[14] Walton, '"Great Improvement"', p. 36; Walton, 'Social History', p. 175; Lincoln, *Naval Wives*, p. 34; Osborn, *Naval Officers' Letters*, p. 5; Watt and Hawkins, *Letters of Seamen*, pp. 10–11; Lincoln, 'Impact of Warfare', p. 74.

[15] Post Office, *Directory*, p. 1169.

[16] Lewis, 'Married to the Navy', p. 38; Walton, 'Social History', p. 176.

[17] Osborn, *Naval Officers' Letters*, p. 1; Peter Boyden, *Tommy Atkins' Letters: the History of the British Army Postal Service from 1795* (London, 1990), pp. 7, 10; Walton, 'Social History', p. 175.

letters home … hoping their correspondent is as well as they are, "thank God for it", reflects the real uncertainty [the men] must have felt, not only about their own lives, but those of their families at home as well.'[18] But if some remarks were expected, and conventionally expressed, some things also went unsaid. It was pointless for a woman to describe her grief, worry or despair when the events in question, and the emotions they aroused, were long past by the time her letter describing them reached its seaborne addressee. Self-censorship not only demonstrated women's concern not to arouse distress in a spouse helpless to do anything by way of support.[19] It also spared the writer embarrassment of admitting she had made a mess of things, and enabled her to maintain a reassuring, competent façade. No naval wife, especially not the naval daughter married to a seaman, wanted to be thought of as 'not coping', as failing in her duty.

Self-censorship of another kind coloured men's letters. A prevailing culture discouraged their articulating emotion, whether verbally or in letter form.[20] Ford's correspondence – stoic, measured in its expression of affect, its opening and closing sentences especially formulaic – suggests he had memorised suitable phrases, or that a literary shipmate supplied front and end remarks *pro forma*, writing the middle sections at Ford's dictation. Between these ritual toppings and tailings the letters feature courteous enquiries after family, friends and neighbours, the expressing of kind regards. Their style supports Gill's discerning, from officers' letters, that men were keen to hear of 'the domestic realities of life at home', asking to be kept informed of everyday events and in particular of the health of their spouses.[21] Whether lower-deck men were as keen to hear of the 'domestic realities' of life in a sunless Portsea court or Blossom Alley sublet is debatable; nevertheless, by showing continuing interest men could sustain their connection with home.[22] Since letters were often passed around or read aloud, individuals other than addressees could be acknowledged, thus maintaining intimate involvement with life on shore.[23] This, of course, could mean private news becoming common knowledge among a husband's messmates. Writers' awareness of these practices affected tone and content;

---

[18] Preston, 'Constructing Communities', p. 232, citing National Museum of the Royal Navy (NMRN) Portsmouth, John Ford, letter to Sarah Evans, NMRN 353/85/13 (13 July 1845).
[19] Gill, *Naval Families*, p. 8.
[20] Bruce Hindmarsh, '"Wherever I go I whill right to you"', in Hamish Maxwell-Stewart and Lucy Frost (eds), *Chain Letters: narrating convict lives* (Carlton South, Vic., 2001), 165–76, at p. 174.
[21] Gill, *Naval Families*, pp. 25, 145, 151.
[22] Walton, 'Social History', p. 178.
[23] *Ibid.*, p. 173.

so did awareness of addressees' likely response to certain disclosures.[24] Letters to husbands could be tailored to hide mounting disenchantment with the lot of a naval wife. Infidelity could be concealed, illness made light of, debts go unmentioned, chronic anxiety refashioned as serenity. Friends, neighbours and family members, however, might be less guarded in what they disclosed. The man at sea might from his wife's letters get one impression of her activities, health and welfare, quite another via a shipmate whose wife's correspondence painted a different picture. Time and distance might separate husband and wife, but the porosity of separation meant news could and did leak through, in either direction.

## DISEASE AND DISABLEMENT AT SEA

Ships departed, women worried – about shipboard illness and accident, drownings and injuries. Above all they worried about the weather, that common denominator of all seafaring which for many women posed concerns greater than drink and infidelity.[25] Even 'unexceptional' weather conditions could cause a ship to capsize, as witness HMS *Captain* which foundered off Finisterre in 1870 with the loss of nearly 500 men.[26] Maritime tragedy was a Victorian trope. Wilkie Collins, assisted by Dickens, wrote a stage play inspired by the missing Franklin expedition, while Holl's 'No Tidings from the Sea' and Bramley's 'A Hopeless Dawn' were among numerous popular images dwelling upon, even relishing, the plight of mariners' ageing parents awaiting news, of seamen's wives facing destitution from widowhood by drowning.[27] Exploitative though they were, the images capture something genuine and enduring: a generational difference in response. As Hagmark-Cooper observed of a twentieth-century seafaring community, older women were more likely to repress and reason through their anxieties; for the younger, less experienced wife, to know (or be told) that it was useless to worry did not lessen the worry.[28]

---

[24] Begiato, 'Tearful Sailor'.
[25] Hagmark-Cooper, *To Be a Sailor's Wife*, p. 35; Lincoln, 'Impact of Warfare', p. 74.
[26] Unknown author, 'The turret ship HMS "Captain"' National Maritime Museum, Greenwich, London <https://www.rmg.co.uk/collections/objects/rmgc-object-15244> [accessed 22 April 2024].
[27] John Kofron, 'Dickens, Collins, and the Influence of the Arctic', *Dickens Studies Annual*, 40 (2009), 81–93, *passim*; Frank Holl, 'No Tidings from the Sea' (Royal Collections Trust, 1870) <https://www.rct.uk/collection/405161/no-tidings-from-the-sea> [accessed 22 April 2024]; Frank Bramley, 'A Hopeless Dawn', Tate Gallery (tate.org.uk, 1888) <https://www.tate.org.uk/art/artworks/bramley-a-hopeless-dawn-n01627> [accessed 22 April 2024].
[28] Hagmark-Cooper, *To Be a Sailor's Wife*, pp. 25, 34.

To worry was understandable. In the years 1829–47, of a sample of Royal Navy ships' crews some 12.4 per cent of men were discharged sick or dead.[29] A seaman's trade, rate and role, his ship and/or its commission: all had a bearing upon his earning capacity, his risk of injury, ill-health, disablement or death; and all had inevitable consequences for his dependants. Even tedious and routine tasks had hidden dangers. Involving the entire crew, the periodic coaling of steam ships was loathed by all for its invasive black dust. A sudden uprush of coal dust was dangerous, as witness AB Angeley, HMS *Erebus*, who in 1840 'died by suffocation from charcoal'.[30] Stokers had to work with coal every day, and for them the dangers were not limited to daily tending of boilers.[31] Toiling in immense heat, around moving machinery, they faced hazards such as explosions and steam leaks, and 'as steam pressures increased so did the chances of a stoker being injured or killed'.[32]

Seamen working sails and masts in all weathers risked falls to the deck or into the sea. If hitting the water did not kill them, drowning usually did. Forty-five per cent of deaths on board Royal Navy ships for which cause is known were due to falls or drowning, for until the 1850s the Navy's fear of desertion meant that boys and ships' crews were not taught to swim.[33] *Vengeance*'s medical journal speaks of a man who 'whilst going aloft fell from the main futtock rigging to the quarter deck (60 feet) whereby he received fracture of the base of the skull'.[34] Even the drop of a few feet from hammock to deck could be fatal.[35] Gun crews might suffer ruptures and crush injuries or the devastating effects of explosion. Seamen letting go anchor could be caught and mangled as hurtling cables dragged them into the bitts.[36] Marine John Chitty, allotting to his sister Mary Whealan, was 'taken ill at Gibraltar' after suffering 'severe contusion of left leg and foot, whilst employed on lower deck in bringing the ship to an anchor, a hook rope caught his left leg and dragging him violently along the deck'.[37]

---

[29] Preston, 'Constructing Communities', p. 174 table 6.2.
[30] John Fabb, *The Victorian and Edwardian Navy, from old photographs* (London, 1976), images 44, 46, 47 (n.p.).
[31] Walton, 'Social History', p. 335.
[32] Tony Chamberlain, '"Stokers – the Lowest of the Low?" A Social History of Royal Navy Stokers 1850–1950' (University of Exeter, unpublished PhD thesis, 2013), p. 45.
[33] Preston, 'Constructing Communities', p. 232.
[34] National Archives (TNA) Kew, 'Medical journal of HMS *Vengeance*, from 1 July 1852 to 30 July 1853, by William Graham, Surgeon, during which time the said ship was employed in the Mediterranean Station', ADM 101/124/3 (1851–52), fols 29–30, case no. 31.
[35] Preston, 'Constructing Communities', p. 186; ADM 101/124/3, fol. 50, case no. 53.
[36] Preston, 'Constructing Communities', p. 188.
[37] ADM 27/109/178/13.

Cooks might be scalded, while any man might miss his footing and drop through a hatch to the deck below; and all were at risk of disease in tropical climates.[38] One bout of malaria could leave a man with persistent episodic illness, weakening his ability to work, and thereby to maintain his family. Lack of protection from sunlight could allow skin cancer to take hold, while tainted food, water or poor hygiene might infect an entire messdeck with dysentery, which if chronic might be passed to wife and family at home. Accidents – a tool dropped from aloft, a fall from rigging or down hatchway – might cost a man an eye, a limb, or impair mobility, sending him home disfigured or crippled.

Bad weather and prolonged exposure to cold and damp had insidious effects: over 12 per cent of HMS *Thetis*'s ship's company died during a four-year commission begun in 1850, seven of them perishing within the same five-day period during a transatlantic passage, the pusser's clerk adding to the 'DD' entries only a laconic 'At Sea' by way of explanation.[39] Twenty-five were DSQ'd, and of seven whose deaths were recorded in one muster book, one was 'Killed by a fall from aloft'.[40] One man drowned at Plymouth, another at Valparaiso, three more at Vancouver.[41] *Thetis* spent months surveying off Vancouver, its surgeon's log recording case after case of bronchitis, pneumonia, chronic catarrh and other respiratory ailments, conditions which might ruin a man's long-term health.[42] The medical journal of HMS *Vengeance* records

> concern about the health of the men, namely the ventilation of the ship … 196 people sleep in the orlop deck which included the after and fore cockpits and store room and when the ship was at sea all scuttles were closed generally in the day and always at night, in which the atmosphere became densely vitiated.[43]

Similar concerns were recorded by *Resolute*'s surgeon during one commission to the Arctic. His journal lists ten men with catarrh, one with a fractured rib, another a fractured radius, four suffering ophthalmia, five with rheumatism, three with syphilis of which two were at the secondary stage, one case of frostbite, and two men whose frostbite had turned

---

[38] Winton, *Hurrah!*, p. 14.
[39] ADM 38/9173 (n.p.); ADM 38/9174 (n.p.), ADM 38/1974 *passim*.
[40] ADM 38/9173 (n.p.).
[41] ADM 38/9174 (n.p.).
[42] National Archives (TNA) Kew, 'Medical journal of HMS *Thetis* for 1 July 1851 to 30 September 1852 by John Douglas, Surgeon, during which time the said ship was employed in the Pacific Station', ADM 101/123/4 (1851–52), fols 31, 34.
[43] ADM 101/124/3/3, fols 54–7.

gangrenous.[44] Psychological damage and behavioural changes also arose, not only among crews of discovery service vessels. Seventy-seven unhappy observations recorded in HMS *Dauntless*'s muster books include: two men despatched to prison; two discharged to *Retribution* as 'given to liquor' and 'with disgrace, v. bad', the conduct of one described as 'V. Good as a steward, but not sober'; another ('an objectionable character, perfectly useless') dismissed following his first entry; and thirty-seven invalided to Haslar Hospital, one being William Angus, quartermaster and three-badge diver, the allotment to his wife Henrietta promptly stopping.[45] Fever is discernible. Forty-six *Dauntless* men were 'DD' at the military hospital in Barbados between February 1851 and January 1853, the dead including carpenters, seamen's schoolmaster, stoker, captain of the mizzen top and foretop, sailmaker's mate, caulker, pusser's steward's mate, master at arms and numerous ordinary and able seamen.[46] The psychological impact upon surviving shipmates may be imagined. So much fear of contamination; so many deaths; so many funerals in the humidity and heat of a foreign land, and burials at sea of men who never made it to shore. And after the deaths, the traditional auctioning- and re-auctioning-off of dead shipmates' kit (proceeds went to the widows and orphans), the letters to be written to dead friends' widows, the prospect of calling upon a dead friend's bereaved family, of trying to find the right words.[47]

Men's physical safety and health were not their women's only concerns. Might husbands have grown cold, formed other attachments while in foreign ports? Might their characters be affected by the events they had lived through, the sights they had seen? Would they recoil from the damp and overcrowded Portsea sublet, the stink of malthouse and communal privy, the noise of children playing, a wife's hands made coarse by lye soap, her eyesight damaged by sewing in poor light, her looks impaired by drudgery, inadequate diet and anxiety? Less easily shared was the more intimate worry that men might have visited brothels while they were away, have picked up disease. Prostitution and sexual infection were serious problems

---

[44] National Archives (TNA) Kew, 'Medical and surgical journal of HMS *Resolute* for 28 February 1850 to 9 October 1851 by R A Bradford, Surgeon, during which time the said ship was employed in a searching expedition to the Arctic Regions', ADM 101/117/3 (1850–51), pp. 11, 12–14.

[45] ADM 38/7940 (n.p.); ADM 38/3146 (n.p.), *passim*; ADM 27/111/227/76.

[46] ADM 38/7940 (n.p.).

[47] 'Auction of kit: The sale, by open bidding as at an auction, of the personal kit of some deceased member of a ship's company ... Outrageous sums of money can then be offered for the most useless items, with the article often returned to the pool for re-auction': Jolly and Willson, *Jackspeak*, p. 15.

in the Royal Navy, not only as a result of far-flung deployments.[48] Sure, Portsmouth had its share of brothels, prostitutes and venereal disease, but Plymouth was considered particularly noxious.[49]

For a woman to struggle on, nursing troubled thoughts, was to live a life of unremitting stress. For some the strain proved overwhelming. Anne Clarke was one who may have succumbed. Since the mid-1830s the allotment declarations of her husband Charles, HMS *Encounter*, had marked his transfers from ship to ship, his promotion to boatswain second class, and her move from Abercrombie Street to Arundel Place.[50] In 1850, however, a fresh declaration redirected Charles's money from 39-year-old household head Anne to their 18-year-old son Francis Henry, a National School teacher.[51] 'Has an allotment in force to his wife', noted the pusser's clerk, adding the bracketed aside '(become of unsound mind)'.[52] Anne was fortunate. Whatever mental calamity had engulfed her, within four months she was sufficiently recovered that Charles could once again declare in her favour, at three shillings more per month.[53]

The period between Trafalgar and Crimea was not without international conflict, but few of the women in this mid-century cohort had had to fear losing their men to war. Among its more than 400 mothers, mothers-in-law and grandmothers, however, were some whose husbands had seen active service in earlier decades. Ten mothers were in their seventies, fifty aged sixty-one to sixty-nine. At the time of Trafalgar the oldest would have been in her early thirties, the youngest fifteen and old enough to be a naval bride. By 1851, thirty of them were widows. We do not know whether the others' still-living husbands – ropemakers, shipwrights, carpenters, brushmakers, sawyers, smiths and servants – were former Navy men or civilians who had married naval widows, but the fact that all these older women were mothers of serving seamen strongly suggests they had once been naval wives. If so, they were some of 'the numberless women whose lives were blighted by naval warfare', and whose experiences passed unrecorded into history.[54] What they had learned via those experiences would pass to a younger generation, some of whom retained childhood memories of scenes of grief in relatives' or neighbours' houses; of their fathers' eventual homecoming from war; of seeing injured and disabled men hobbling down the street; of

---

[48] Preston, 'Constructing Communities', pp. 227–8.
[49] Ibid., p. 230; Acton, *Prostitution Considered in its Moral, Social, and Sanitary Aspects*, p. 65.
[50] ADM 27/72/174/47; ADM 27/77/114/1; ADM 27/100/9/132; ADM 27/101/297/16; ADM 27/106/333/14; ADM 27/120/201/421.
[51] 1851 census: HO107/1659, fol. 371; p. 10.
[52] ADM 27/120/211/421.
[53] ADM 27/120/181/421.
[54] Lincoln, 'Impact of Warfare', pp. 71, 86.

experiencing, by proxy, the mental and emotional stress of fathers suffering what nowadays would be recognised as survivor-guilt, as PTSD. They may also have witnessed the emotional damage wrought upon their mothers by years of loneliness, economic hardship, lone parenting and worry, all compounded by a prevailing fear of invasion.[55] For some, that damage was short-term, receding with the passage of time and the return of the victorious sailor. For others, the mental scars lasted longer, leaving chronic anxiety, bitterness that their wifely sufferings went unrecognised, or were dismissed as no worse than what every naval woman must bear.

## DESERTION

One worry unlikely to have been uppermost in a woman's mind was that her man might desert his ship, yet desertion was devastating for those at home. Its immediate impact was economic, as pay and allotment stopped. Longer-term consequences were even more serious. While on the run the deserter was without means, shelter, nourishment or protection, the combined effects of which could wreck a man's physique. HMS *Vengeance*'s medical journal describes deserters found in the street in Mediterranean port towns; suffering cholera and typhus, they were taken to sick quarters only to die a few hours later.[56] Even if he survived, the deserter's health might be compromised, and with it his ability to work and earn. Beyond these practicalities there was another, more intimate consequence, as the deserter's wife realised that until and unless he were found, her husband was not only abandoning his naval service. He was in effect abandoning her.

Desertion was a significant problem. Its causes and scale are hard to determine, but men's motives included tyrannical officers and harsh punishment regimes, lack of leave, economic opportunism, homesickness, a romantic liaison formed during time ashore, and ships' less frequent entry into port.[57] Here sailmaker Bill Simpson, son-in-law of Robert Mackenzie, in the hope of being granted compassionate leave to visit his ailing father, begs his wife to endorse his reasons for requesting leave. The desperate tone of his letter suggests he was close to an emotional crisis of the kind which could drive a man to desert, if only until the crisis had passed.

> My Dear Wife and child I was determined to come up To see Father as he was Bad i only had leaf Till sunday morning But i was determend to com and see you the master dont belive That father was bad I told him that father Was dangelsy ill and Thay wrote for me to Come up to see him So

---

[55] *Ibid.*, p. 73.
[56] ADM 101/83/2/6.
[57] Walton, 'Social History', pp. 157–60; Rodger, *Wooden World*, pp. 196–7, 203; Watt and Hawkins, *Letters of Seamen*, p. 57.

you must rite a Letter to me a[s] though Mother rote it so i can Show it so thay know that I have not told A Fallshood for if I had not have come up you wold have though[t] I did not try to Come My dear Wife you must date the Letter May 28 So It corspond With what i Say And then thay will Belive me [wr]ite it As ergain [urgent] as you Can God bless you Boath I must now conclude With my kindest Love to you bothe As the Lord can Afford god bless you

xxxxxx
xxxxx
xxxx

Kepp this to your
Own hart do Bless you both[58]

'R' (deserted) features in many if not most ships' muster books. A muster book for HMS *Thetis* shows thirty-one men listed as 'Rq' (yet to return within the twenty-one day deadline, which is to say stragglers yet to be deemed deserter), fifteen others as 'R'.[59] The subsequent book shows sixteen of the ship's company marked 'R'.[60] Desertion was not limited to foreign ports or long voyages. In early 1852, within the same ten-day period, eight *Dauntless* men deserted in Devonport.[61] When men 'ran' in their home ports, ships would send an armed detachment to retrieve them from their marital or family homes. Brothers Henry and Frederick Winsor, stokers aged twenty and twenty-one, joined *Dauntless* on 27 August 1850, and ran in Portsmouth six days later.[62] Where men had previously been members of a settled shipboard community on one vessel, it was a known pattern for some to desert within the first few months aboard a new ship. These brothers, however, were particularly quick to quit. Their alacrity, and the numbers of *Dauntless* men deserting elsewhere, may signal that it was an 'unhappy ship', to the extent that men were prepared to throw away accumulated unpaid wages by deserting.[63] The brothers' family may have been sympathetic, dismissing their desertion as 'tried it, didn't like it', and questioning why the Navy should pursue them; others may have inferred character weakness or cowardice. Differing reactions could easily arouse hostility between neighbours, even between family members.

Muster books hint at the pull exercised by some foreign locations, drawing men to gold rushes, wide open spaces and a belief that merchant marine service would be better paid.[64] Whatever the pay, they were certainly

---

[58] National Museum of the Royal Navy (NMRN) Portsmouth, William Simpson, letter to wife, NMRN 627/86/11 (1 June 1857).
[59] ADM 38/9173 (n.p.).
[60] ADM 38/9174 (n.p.).
[61] ADM 38/3148 (n.p.).
[62] ADM 38/3146 (n.p.).
[63] Rodger, *Command of the Ocean*, p. 316.
[64] Walton, 'Social History', pp. 158–9.

employable. Seamen rated able had portable skills highly valued in any sailing vessel, hence their good prospects of re-employment outside the Royal Navy. Some desertions were acts of impulse, some carefully planned. By allotting to friends acting as his bankers at home, a man might safeguard his wages in anticipation, '[putting] his money to one side, and [taking] away the whole of it so that he has nothing to lose if he runs away'.[65] Many desertions were a joint enterprise. In 1851 three men of HMS *Thetis*'s crew ran at Montevideo.[66] On one day in 1852 a further five ran, perhaps sticking together for company and safety, perhaps scattering to avoid detection.[67] Twenty-one of the ship's company, equivalent to 8 per cent of the crew, deserted during its four-year commission, their chosen points of departure including Valparaiso, San Francisco, Vancouver Island.[68] Some may simply have sought adventure, others an escape not only from shipboard life but from the prospects of returning to an unhappy home. For them, desertion effected a form of divorce, their wives and families never hearing from them again.[69]

In this study, only five of a dozen sailors who deserted are known to have been husbands. One was William Weedon, whose complex marital situation has been described. Another was AB Charles Bull, *Prince Regent*. Married only a year when discharged under the 1847 Naval Deserters Act to Winchester gaol, he left his Wiltshire-born wife Emma without allotment.[70] The remaining three were AB George Scott of HMS *Fox*, steward Robert Lee of HMS *Fantome*, and AB William Menhinnick (*q.v.*) of *Dauntless*.[71] The 'R' against their names obscures three very different back-stories. George Scott had entered sea service as a boy in 1830, his conduct thereafter noted as 'Good', 'Very Good' and 'Very Good Indeed'.[72] In March 1851 he was on the sick list for 'intermittent fever' (probably malaria, his ship being on commission in the East Indies at the time); within a month he was invalided.[73] In April 1854, Scott 'ran' at Capel Sound in south Australia, thereby stopping his 1851 allotment to his pregnant wife

---

[65] Hardwicke, *Report*, p. 63, s. 827.
[66] ADM 38/9174, n.p.
[67] Ibid.
[68] Ibid.
[69] Lincoln, *Naval Wives*, p. 141.
[70] CHU3/1D/49, p. 65 n. 129; ADM 38/8772; *Naval Deserters Act*, 10 & 11 Vict., c. 62 (1847); ADM 27/113/289/505.
[71] ADM 27/111/275/4; ADM 27/112/318/19; ADM 27/111/227/90.
[72] ADM 38/8155/n.p./4.
[73] National Archives (TNA) Kew, 'Medical and surgical Journal of Her Majesty's Ship *Fox* for 19 July 1850 and the 31 July 1851 by Mr John M Minter, Surgeon, during which time the said ship was employed in the East Indies', ADM 101/101/2 (1850–51).

Harriet.[74] The remoteness of the location, a shore about fifty miles from Melbourne, together with his solidly commendable service record, suggest that rather than desert, George was simply left behind by mistake when the ship departed. Those on board would have known only that he had failed to return, not why, and after twenty-one days as a straggler he would have been logged a deserter.[75] He did in fact return, and redeemed himself with the Navy: his warrant officer register of service has him joining HMS *Furious* in January 1855, thereafter serving in ten ships' eighteen commissions before being pensioned in 1868.[76] He also redeemed himself with Harriet: the 1861 census shows the pair reunited, and two more children added to the family.[77]

For allottee-sisters with breadwinner-husbands, and for naval mothers reliant on multiple sons' support, stoppage of an allotment due to a brother's or son's desertion was not necessarily catastrophic. The consequences were far worse for a deserter's wife. She lost not only her allotment, but would in later years also suffer the effects of his naval pension being reduced. More immediately, she lost all prospect of her husband's paying-off money, his accumulated arrears being forfeit to Greenwich Hospital.[78] Economic loss was one consequence. Harder to evidence are the emotional effects of desertion, which might include a wife's anxiety, grief, shame, bewilderment, anger; the strain of what to tell the children; the whispers as she passed by; the credit being refused; the head-shakings and finger-pointings; the loss of allotment income forcing hard choices upon her. Even if he survived the swim ashore, even if he somehow managed to inform his family of his survival, unless the deserter funded her joining him in a new life she would find herself in 'the anomalous state of a wife without a husband', which in turn affected her prospects of qualifying for parish relief, of remarrying.[79] Like the wives of Trotter's émigré Cornishmen, she would become a 'married widow'.[80] As well as financial security and marital status, she also lost standing within her community, for 'the position of naval wives

---

[74] ADM 38/8156; E&W Births 1837–2006 Q4/1852, vol. 2B, p. 392; CHU 3/1B/30, p. 284 n. 2268.
[75] Hardwicke, *Report*, p. 63, s. 830; QRs 1844, p. 103, s. 5.
[76] National Archives (TNA) Kew, Admiralty: Officers' Service Records (Series III), ADM 196 (1798–1870), for ADM 196/29/222.
[77] ADM 38/8155-6, July 1850–April 1854; 1861 census: RG09/644, fol. 48, p. 12.
[78] 11 Geo. IV & 1 Will. IV, c. 20 (1830), s. XXII.
[79] Chandler, *Women without Husbands*, p. 26.
[80] Trotter, *Married Widows*, passim. The term 'married widows' has not been found applied to naval wives; it is, however, apt when applied to wives of men on discovery service, and deserters' wives.

worsened the lower they were down the social scale', deserted wives being among the lowest of the low.[81]

If a man could (albeit unlawfully) quit a Navy he no longer liked, so too could the Navy with impunity expel a man whose performance or conduct fell short. In muster books' Conduct columns, entry after entry reads 'Excellent', 'VG' (Very Good), 'Good', with here and there a 'Fair'. Occasionally, however, there appears a different grade. The conduct of AB Robert Benson, HMS *Vengeance*, not only earned him a 'Bad' rating but discharge direct to Portsmouth's borough gaol, depriving his sister Hannah Bishop of her money.[82] Sick berth attendant George Davis, HMS *Fox*, was marked 'V. Bad', a rare judgement; after a spell on two-thirds pay he ended his service by being invalided, which stopped his allotment.[83] His wife Ann, living with three sisters in her parents' house, was fortunate in having another source of cash, carpenter's mate William Gill, HMS *Illustrious*, allotting her £1 8s 0d per month for fostering his 9-year-old daughter Fanny.[84] The conduct of AB Eli Bone (*q.v.*), bigamous husband of Martha Bone, was so egregious, his shipmates may have come close to throwing him overboard, or down a hatch. Despatched to the Arctic in search of the missing Franklin expedition, in the winter of 1850–51 HMS *Resolute* had been 'nipped' (frozen in ice) between Cornwallis and Griffiths islands. If vessel and crew were to survive it was essential that good order, discipline and respectful working relationships be maintained. An incident occurred. Eli was involved, suffering what the ship's surgeon called a 'vulnus' (wound). That same day, AB Alexander Thompson also suffered a 'vulnus'. This coincidence, the surgeon's terse terminology, and the omission of his usual medical description and explanation, combine to suggest the two men had been fighting, or set upon by others.[85] Thompson was discharged as fit to work, Eli listed as a supernumerary for wages and victuals (SLWV), forfeiting the double pay enjoyed by the rest of the ship's company.[86] Released by seasonal thaw, *Resolute* returned to home waters, destination Woolwich, where in October 1851 the ship's company was paid off. Two days earlier, however, alone of the crew, his conduct recorded as 'V. Bad', Eli Bone was discharged at Greenhithe; Captain Horatio Austin could not wait to get rid of him. In light of this, and of Eli's 'vulnus', it is worth noting Rodger's observation

---

[81] Lincoln, *Naval Wives*, p. 16.
[82] ADM 38/2043; 10 & 11 Vict., c. 62 (1847); ADM 27/112/149/91; 1851 census: HO107/1659, fol. 427, p. 39.
[83] ADM 38/8156; ADM 27/111/273/175. This George Davis should not be confused with adulterous humbug AB George Davis, HMS *Excellent* (see pp. 36–7).
[84] 1851 census: HO107/1657, fol. 470, p. 36; ADM 27/109/396/437.
[85] ADM 101/117/3, p. 11.
[86] ADM 38/8862 (n.p.).

that '[nothing] more quickly destroyed the mutual trust of a happy ship's company than the presence of a thief among them, and it was the one crime for which a prime seaman might be discharged without hesitation.'[87]

*Resolute* crew members will have found themselves facing a barrage of questions, a curious and admiring public who wanted to shake their hands, to glean behind-the-scene details of Arctic danger and heroism. As a *Resolute* survivor arriving in Portsmouth ahead of his shipmates, Eli will have aroused especial curiosity. Family, friends and neighbours will have wanted to know why he, alone of all his shipmates, enjoyed a premature homecoming. In due course Martha would be concerned to know why his paying-off money did not reflect the accumulated double pay every other man enjoyed, her enhanced allotment having been deemed an overpayment from the day Eli was reduced to SLWV status, the excess deducted from his cash-in-hand.

Ignominious discharge to shore was less common – or at least, less explicitly stated – than discharge by virtue of ill health, injury or desertion. As with the 'V. Bad' sick berth attendant George Davis of *Fox*, in muster books some dismissals for bad behaviour are obscured by clerical use of 'DSQ', 'Inv', or a blandly ambiguous 'D'. But whether her man were hospitalised, invalided or discharged with disgrace, for the dependent wife the economic impact was identical: the household economy she had managed so carefully over many months was jeopardised. The now ex-seaman must either find entry into another vessel (no easy feat when his conduct was recorded as bad, or worse), or employment on shore (no easier, if he lacked transferable skills); and his wife must further tighten the domestic economy, and/or find other sources of income. And since it was the breadwinner's own misbehaviour that had brought the family to such a pitch, marital rancour and recrimination were natural followers.

## THE SAILOR'S RETURN

Who shall estimate the joy and delight of such a meeting after dangers passed through by those who had been away, and the dreary time of anxious waiting which had been experienced by those left behind? What pleasure, what beatitude to know that the dear ones were once more 'home again!'[88]

In articles and illustrations filling four pages, weekly newspaper *The Graphic* celebrated the return to Portsmouth of HM Ships *Alert* and *Discovery* after

---

[87] Rodger, *Wooden World*, p. 170.
[88] *The Graphic*, 11 November 1876, p. 469 col. C.

Fig. 28 '"Home Again": a Sketch on the Deck of the *Discovery* at Portsmouth', Godefroy Durand. Image © Illustrated London News/Mary Evans Picture Library. Reproduced by kind permission of the Mary Evans Picture Library.

eighteen months on Arctic service, observing 'Here a young wife rushing to her husband's arms; there a mother gazing joyously into the face of her darling son.'[89]

From start to finish, the consequences of men's absences required careful management. Ships' commissions might change with political developments, disrupting mail deliveries, delaying men's return and thereby protracting allottees' dependence upon half-pay. HMS *Superb*'s tour was extended, causing John Ford, frustrated at lack of contact with his sweetheart Sarah Evans, to explain: 'at present the squadron is still Lying in The tagus the reason is that we are Laying here so long that the rebells is expected to Walk into Lisbon and take the Place.'[90] Three months later, his prospects of an early homecoming were still dim:

> I did say in my Last Letter of Coming to england But The case is altered we are going to Malta for a Change. I dare say you would be very happy

[89] Ibid.
[90] National Museum of the Royal Navy (NMRN) Portsmouth, John Ford, letter to Sarah Evans, NMRN 353/85/17 (18 January 1847).

of the Ship Coming home I should Be the Sa'me myself – But I expect it will Be some time first.[91]

Where time at home was limited (Holman speaks of six weeks' leave after three years away), friction and disillusion might be avoided because the initial post-homecoming period could, for the wife at least, feel 'like falling in love again'.[92] But after years of looking forward to the ship's return, after days of baking, cleaning and 'preparing the house as if for visitors', scenes of rejoicing – the women in their best bonnets, the men kissing children they were seeing for the first time – were often followed by a sense of anti-climax and emotional conflict.[93] A wife accustomed to being in charge might soon find herself hoping her husband would not stay home long enough to arouse regret; worse, she might begin to wish him gone.[94] If in his absence she had shared a tenancy with a fellow naval wife, her man's return would end the co-residence. He might even try to disrupt the friendship, for after years at sea some men resented their women's mutual solidarity, objected to being shut out of their society, while others were jealous at not being the centre of attention.[95]

Short-term homecomings were less damaging than long ones, there being less time for couples to have arguments (but less opportunity, too, to make up before re-embarkation).[96] Short-term absences, on the other hand, were the most difficult. A woman would scarcely have time to assert her role as household head before finding herself either relinquishing it upon her man's return or fighting his expectations that she do so, having in the meantime not been deprived of him long enough to cause too great a pang.[97]

If naval women had to adjust to their men's unaccustomed presence, their returning men equally had to adjust to being back, for after years away 'fathers could adopt bad habits and forget their responsibilities'.[98] Disappointed with the home his spouse had created in his absence, a husband might find fault with her appearance, her housekeeping, the nature or quantity of the food she served (for he was used to good and plentiful food on board ship), or

---

[91] National Museum of the Royal Navy (NMRN) Portsmouth, John Ford, letter to Sarah Evans, NMRN 353/85/18 (28 April 1847).
[92] Holman, *Life in the Royal Navy*, pp. 109–10; Hagmark-Cooper, *To Be a Sailor's Wife*, p. 70.
[93] Chandler, *Women without Husbands*, pp. 66–7; Hagmark-Cooper, *To Be a Sailor's Wife*, p. 63; Finch, *Married to the Job*, p. 115.
[94] Light, *Common People*, p. 214; Burton, 'The Myth of Bachelor Jack', p. 193.
[95] D'Cruze, *Crimes of Outrage*, p. 71.
[96] Hagmark-Cooper, *To Be a Sailor's Wife*, p. 86.
[97] Chandler, *Women without Husbands*, p. 69.
[98] Humphries, *Childhood and Child Labour*, p. 130.

the children's behaviour; or he might 'do rounds', even lose his temper.[99] He was used to the masculine environment of the ship, to accepting discipline as necessary for good order within the confines of a naval vessel. At home he would drill the children, take command of the household as if it were a part of ship and he the divisional officer, only to discover that this made for friction within the feminine sphere of home.[100] Some of his wife's domestic changes might be admired, others cause consternation. Those knick-knacks, that mantel runner, how nice she had made everything look! How long had she been pinning her hair like that? (No, he wasn't saying he disliked it; well, not exactly 'dislike'.) Did this new piece of furniture mean he had been giving her too much money? If not, how had she got the cash to purchase it? Where was the teapot, the framed picture he remembered from his last time at home? What had she done with the ornament he had bought her on his last deployment, in that foreign port town? Where was the macramé he himself had fashioned, and the brooch, rolling pin, the shell-covered box he had made and sent her?[101] If the answer to the latter two questions was 'lost, broken, stolen, pawned', it could cause hurt feelings, or worse, since from the husband's point of view the object brought back memories of a happy run-ashore with messmates, an exotic bazaar, his triumphant bartering. It may have taken him hours in make-and-mend at sea, cross-legged under an awning or hunched in his hammock, patiently carving or sewing while thinking of home. Bought or crafted, souvenirs would for years retain meaning for the sailor who wanted to remember his travels; moreover, for men used to having little space on board in which to keep personal items, possessions were to be treated with respect.[102] From the wife's point of view, a pretty but unsought-for souvenir was treasured, but it also required dusting and protecting, must be kept out of reach of children, took up space in a cramped rental; and when money ran short, it was of more use at the pawnshop. But woe betide her if she did not redeem in time, for the pawning of men's goods was a particular trigger for male rage.[103]

There was potential for friction, too, in how the reunited couple disported themselves. The same wife who out of modesty or thrift had for months avoided beerhouse, pub or music hall, now wanted to step out with her

---

[99] Hagmark-Cooper, *To Be a Sailor's Wife*, p. 63; Rodger, *Wooden World*, pp. 116–17. 'Rounds: formal tour of inspection through some designated area of a warship or establishment': Jolly and Willson, *Jackspeak*, p. 371.

[100] D. Lewis, 'Married to the Navy', p. 50; McKee, *Sober Men and True*, p. 210; Walton, 'Social History', p. 344.

[101] Walton, 'Social History', p. 142; Wassell Smith, '"The Fancy Work What Sailors Make"', *passim*.

[102] Walton, 'Social History', pp. 177, 230–1.

[103] Frost, '"He could not hold his passions"', p. 4.

husband, enjoy promenading with him, basking proudly in his presence. By contrast, after so long away, her man enjoyed being home, quiet at his own fireside, it little occurring to him that this was where his wife had spent hundreds of lonely evenings. If they went to the pub together, rather than talk with her did he seek others' company, regale listeners with his 'dits'?[104] Sailors were famous for talking about their lives at sea, sharing stories, poems, songs about heroism and spectacular sights. In peacetime, with no war stories to recount, they would cheerfully describe participating in British representation abroad, the splendour of official receptions, the twenty-one gun salutes on entering harbour, the pride in marching through towns with drums beating and flags flying – experiences no civilian owned, but other seamen shared.[105] Walton notes one seaman defending his holding forth as having but 'seven weeks' leave to talk about our three years and four months in the *Linnet* to our friends at home and relate all our hair breadth escapes and adventures'.[106] Hearing her husband's 'dits' repeated, the naval wife might wonder when he would ask about her life on shore; but given the hardship and tedium of home life, what was there to tell him that did not sound like a complaint? And in any case, were she to express her disappointment or bottled-up resentment she was more likely to be met with silence than reciprocal candour, for the intimacy of shipboard life taught men that friendship was 'more about tolerance than emotional openness'.[107]

It was in the region of domestic authority that friction was most likely to arise. Never mind that women's work in and beyond the home had enabled the Navy to keep men at sea for long periods; at domestic level, when couples were reunited there was sometimes more tension than appreciation.[108] Adjustments had to be made, roles and authority ceded. With experience, some seafarers' wives grew used to exercising greater, more 'masculine' responsibility while alone, making the shift between lives together and apart.[109] It is a shift experienced to this day: 'We took care of everything and then, when he came home, we were just supposed to let go and let him take over. He was used to being in command at sea, so he wanted to be in command at home as well.'[110]

---

[104] 'Dit: Any written (or spoken) account of an incident or event in a sailor's life': Jolly and Willson, *Jackspeak*, p. 137.
[105] Walton, 'Social History', pp. 179–86.
[106] *Ibid.*, p. 152.
[107] *Ibid.*, p. 344.
[108] Lincoln, 'Impact of Warfare', p. 86.
[109] Chandler, *Women without Husbands*, pp. 27–8, 69; McKee, *Sober Men and True*, p. 210; Hagmark-Cooper, *To Be a Sailor's Wife*, p. 15.
[110] Hagmark-Cooper, *To Be a Sailor's Wife*, p. 1.

It was harder for some than for others. Wives who were themselves naval daughters had more realistic expectations; but whether naval daughter or no, upon her husband's return a naval wife must to some degree switch from a dominant, independent and authoritative role as head of household and family, to subservient, dutiful, obedient spouse, in the process relinquishing authority over her children.[111] This last concession caused particular ambivalence, especially when, as often happened, a child neither recognised his homecoming father nor bonded with him.[112] Prolonged absence, however, was not the only cause of friction. Money, or the lack of it, played a part. Poor men tended to abandon wives and children at times of greatest economic stress, a pattern easily applying where a seaman returned to find his wife in debt, living in more wretched conditions than when he went to sea. The fact that she had survived his absence on half (or less) of his wage, by washing others' soiled linen or sewing shirts by lamplight, by turning to prostitution for a necessary supplement, or imposing upon herself the strictest of domestic economies allowing not the simplest of small pleasures – this was, in the naval community, a feat so commonplace as to be taken for granted.

---

[111] Reibe, 'Public Perceptions of Sailors' Wives', p. 57; D. Lewis, 'Married to the Navy', pp. 37, 50.

[112] Richard A. Isay, 'The Submariners' Wives' Syndrome', *Psychiatric Quarterly*, 42:4 (1968), 647–52, at p. 650; Hagmark-Cooper, *To Be a Sailor's Wife*, p. 69; Humphries, *Childhood and Child Labour*, p. 130.

# 15

# DEATH

Divorce being unobtainable at the mid-century point, in legal terms each and every working class marriage ended only in the death of husband or wife. This chapter considers how naval wives' lives changed when their men died, and how their own lives came to a close.

## SEAMEN-HUSBANDS' DEATHS

The death rate for Royal Navy sailors was higher than the national average, to the extent that sailors should be counted among those whose life expectancy was adversely affected by occupation. Indeed, it was unusual for a ship's muster book not to include, by the end of a commission, at least one 'DD'.[1] Whether the country were at peace or war, seamen's wives were among those more likely to be widowed during their husbands' working lives, at a time when their children (if children they had) were too young to support themselves, or to marry and establish independent households. The heightened risk of widowhood was not battle-related. Even in wartime, half the Navy's deaths were caused by disease, while deaths from individual accident were almost four times those caused by enemy action. The commonest causes of death were typhus, influenza and dysentery.[2] Between August 1850 and May 1853 HMS *Dauntless* lost over 10 per cent of its crew to yellow fever; in addition to this death toll, and the behavioural issues described in Chapter Fourteen, four *Dauntless* crew members drowned, one died at Portsmouth, one at Devonport, two at Lisbon, one at the Haulbowline Hospital to which three additional men had been

---

[1] Preston, 'Constructing Communities', pp. 173, 175–6, 178; Winton, *Hurrah!*, p. 14; Clayton, *Tars*, p. 293.
[2] Rodger, *Command of the Ocean*, p. 399; men's deaths, as recorded in muster books, 'may be assumed to be from illness unless otherwise indicated', Rodger, *Naval Records*, p. 51.

discharged in need of medical care, three others perished at sea and one was killed on board on Christmas Eve.[3] Of *Dauntless* wives who socialised and supported each other during their men's absence, many were widows by the time the ship returned.

Women's awareness of being bereaved or spared was felt most acutely in times of mass loss. Newspapers routinely reported arrivals and departures of naval and merchant vessels, ships' movements filling entire paragraphs in publications such as the *Hampshire Telegraph*; but when disaster occurred, the routine jostled for space alongside the tragic. Little thought was given to the placement of naval announcements, as witness the *Telegraph*'s 10 April 1852 edition in which wives of men serving in *Persian*, *Driver*, *Amphitrite*, etc., found welcome news of those ships' arrivals and departures from foreign ports. In the next street, a few doors away, across the landing from each other, wives of men serving in Portsmouth-based troopship HMS *Birkenhead* were reading, in the same newspaper, on the same page, of the total loss of the ship, and of 'Englishmen having come to so lamentable an end'.[4]

*Birkenhead*'s sinking cost the lives of sixty Navy men and eight boy seamen.[5] The disaster saw blindfolded horses led overboard, and terrified women and children – relatives of troops being transported – set adrift in lifeboats in pitch darkness on heaving seas. Soldiers, sailors and marines drowned, or were eaten by sharks. All told, 450 perished. Forty of this study's 2,300 allotments were declared by *Birkenhead* men, fifteen of them leaving seven widows and at least eleven fatherless children. Two mothers lost sons, and four allottee-sisters their brothers.

Most Portsmouth-resident *Birkenhead* dependants lived within a few hundred yards of each other. As news trickled in, and lists of dead and survivors were posted on doors of post offices and shops, so *Birkenhead* wives, mothers, sisters and former shipmates found themselves standing side by side on the pavement, scanning the notices for familiar names. One poor woman was seen 'looking down the list of drowned which was displayed in a shop window, and pointing out the name of a brother in one place, a friend in another.'[6]

The loss of any ship was most severely felt in its home port, for there the greatest number of wives were widowed – with serious social consequences,

---

[3] ADM 38/7940, *passim*. Haulbowline Hospital: when men on foreign stations were unfit for service they were sent home as invalids, on arrival being admitted to the naval hospital at their home port: Hardwicke, *Report*, p. 27 s. 241.
[4] *H/Tel*, 10 April 1852, p. 5, cols. A and B.
[5] ADM 38/2621.
[6] *H/Tel*, 10 April 1852, p. 5 col. D.

given the Admiralty's lack of provision for the bereaved.[7] Reverend gentlemen sermonised, appealing to the country's conscience. 'How often must come tidings of shipwreck, which tell the wife that she is a widow; that one whom she best loved has gone down with the waves for his winding-sheet, and that her children must henceforth be destitute. Oh! Not so; English benevolence – your benevolence – will forbid this'; yet public interest fluctuated.[8] There were reports of meetings at which officials and local worthies at one minute intoned solemn sentiments, at the next expressed indignation about being inconveniently assembled on a Saturday.[9] Donations raised over £6,500 'for the relief of widows, orphans and relatives of the victims', one admiral proposing that crews of Portsmouth-based ships subscribe a day's pay to the relief of windows and orphans; large numbers of men asked to donate double that amount.[10] For added pomp, distribution of the £6,500 to *Birkenhead*'s bereaved dependants took place within the dockyard, at the Royal Naval College. It appears not to have occurred to those organising the disbursement that to reach the College, scores of shocked and still-grieving women must walk past the pay office where for years their allotments had been paid, and would be paid no more. Four years later, the *Hampshire Telegraph* reported that some £518 of the monies donated (a sum equivalent to £46,450 in 2024) remained undisbursed, and that steps were being taken 'to ascertain if further claimants on the fund existed', noting that 'as time went on … the applicants diminished in number.'[11] It further emerged that the fund had not been 'put out at interest', and that complaints had been made 'of the committee holding in its hands so large a balance'.[12] The committee argued that 'the fact was that a larger sum had been subscribed than was needed. This arose from the fact that many of the earlier applicants were widows of newly-married men, and had since remarried.'[13] None of this took into account the continuing material needs of *Birkenhead*'s bereaved, irrespective of civil status.

---

[7] Stapleton, 'Population', p. 112; Barry Stapleton, 'The Admiralty Connection: port development and demographic change in Portsmouth, 1650–1810', in Richard Lawton and Robert Lee (eds), *Population and Society in Western European Port-Cities, 1650–1939* (Liverpool, 2002), 212–51, at pp. 242–4; Conley, *Jack Tar to Union Jack*, p. 73; Light, *Common People*, p. 216.
[8] Gore, *Sailors' Homes*, pp. 31–2, quoting Revd Melville's sermon on behalf of the Merchant Seamen's Orphan Asylum (n.d.).
[9] H/Tel, 17 April 1852, p. 8 col. E.
[10] Ibid., 10 April 1852, p. 5 col. A.
[11] Bank of England, 'Inflation Calculator' [accessed 30 March 2024]; H/Tel, 23 August 1856, p. 5, col. D.
[12] H/Tel, 23 August 1856, p. 5, col. D.
[13] Ibid.

*Birkenhead* widows learned of their men's fate via official announcements in the press, and by word of mouth as news spread through the streets. A wife whose husband died in less extraordinary circumstances would more likely hear of her bereavement via fellow crew members, who were not only valued communicators but providers of support to new widows.[14] In rare instances, as in the case of George Ruggills's declaration naming Sarah Jennings (*q.v.*), a shipmate might go so far as to support the widow via a contrived allotment, an act especially welcome to those ineligible for a pension.[15]

Wives were not the only recipients of bad news. Mothers lost sons, sisters their brothers. Consider AB William Nancarrow, HMS *Arrogant* (not the husband of Christianna [*q.v.*], but a namesake). William was twenty-five years old when in March 1852 he died, at work, after swallowing chloride of zinc, a highly corrosive, ulcerative chemical.[16] With other sailors he had been sent to remove stores from below deck. Spotting a two-gallon jar, with typical Jack Tar glee he assumed it contained beer; pulled the cork; drank. His messmates 'disrelished it, spat it out, and ran up the ladder, when emetics were given them and they felt no ill effects.'[17] William was not found until a quarter-hour later, and died at Haslar the next day. As the inquest heard, the jar was marked 'Poison', but in the gloom of the ship's hold the warning was invisible. In those few impetuous gulps, William lost his life. His 59-year-old mother Sarah, whom he had been supporting since 1845, lost both son and allotment.[18]

## WIDOWS' REMARRIAGE

Some widows were quick to remarry, their need for material support (and, if childless, their hopes of motherhood) overriding expectations as to a 'proper' period of mourning. Others were more measured, or simply less fortunate in finding a new spouse. Ann Tapscott and her stoker-husband James had been married eleven years when he perished in the loss of HMS *Birkenhead*; it was twelve years before she married again, this time to seaman Benjamin Grace.[19] Three years passed before Caroline Aldridge, widow of *Birkenhead* boatswain's mate Francis, married seaman Benjamin Donald.[20] Joanna Fleming, née Greenleaf (*q.v.*), was another who took her

---

[14] Doe, 'Those They Left Behind', p. 10.
[15] ADM 27/110/279/354; Walton, 'Social History', pp. 145–8.
[16] PHC: G/PGC4/3 n. 9165.
[17] *H/Tel*, 20 March 1852, p. 5 col. F.
[18] ADM 27/89/122/712; ADM 27/107/157/7.
[19] CHU2/1C/19, p. 23 n. 48.
[20] CHU3/1D/52, p. 211 n. 421.

time remarrying. Her husband James was on board *Birkenhead* for its final voyage. Joanna had married him within weeks of her first sailor-husband's death from bone cancer and exhaustion.[21] That earlier union had produced no children, and hopes of a family from her three years with Fleming ended in grief: her daughter died at ten months; her son, born a half-year after his father's drowning, died at eight months.[22] To lose both husband and children, and within so short a time, was especially cruel; some women, however, had never so much as conceived when widowhood left them childless. For women longing for a family this was cause for additional sorrow; and yet, facing a future with neither husband nor means, other widows may have experienced a private, barely expressible relief that there was no fatherless child to bring up unsupported.

Some widows' grief was not so much assuaged by new love as swiftly superseded by pragmatism. 'There were plenty of women who would marry a sailor ... for the convenience of relieving him of some of his pay, and would then go on with their normal course of life, in some cases marrying again when convenient.'[23] The post-bereavement decisions of Harriet Gimblet (*q.v.*), née Trim, formerly Bettesworth, suggest that 'convenience' meant a hard-nosed pecuniary interest which swiftly trumped sentiment. Harriet's 1834 marriage to Edward Bettesworth ended in August 1849 when he succumbed to an abscess on the lung, the result of his employment in one of Portsea Island's five grain mills.[24] Twelve weeks later, at Portsea Island register office, Harriet married Devon-born bachelor William Gimblet, carpenter's crew, HMS *Leander*.[25] Ten days later, *Leander* sailed for Lisbon.[26] William was twenty-five, widowed Harriet ten years older with at least five children. As noted in Chapter Two, William had been allotting for years, first to his father, then to his mother.[27] In May 1850 he diverted his payments from mother to bride, giving Harriet's address as Meeting House Alley, Portsea, a narrow defile just yards from her former marital home.[28] Within six months of that declaration, however, William was sick

---

[21] CHU3/1D/47, p. 77 n. 154 ('Barrows'); E&W Deaths: Q1/1849, vol. 7, p. 102 (James Burrows; certificate).
[22] CHU3/1B/30, p. 75 n. 597; CHU3/1E/31, p. 30 n. 234; CHU3/1B/30, p. 263 n. 2100; E&W Deaths: Q2/1853, vol. 2B, p. 265 (James George Fleming).
[23] Clayton, *Tars*, p. 89.
[24] CHU3/1D/33, p. 29 n. 87; 1841 census: HO107/415/1, fol. 68, p. 18; E&W Deaths: Westbourne, Sussex, Q3/1849, vol. 7, p. 548 (certificate, 'Betsworth'); King, *Portsmouth Encyclopaedia*, p. 225.
[25] E&W Marriages: Q4/1849, vol. 7, p. 317 (certificate); ADM 38/8432/193.
[26] ADM 27/110/156/193.
[27] ADM 27/92/310/421; ADM 27/109/221/193.
[28] ADM 27/110/156/193.

or hurt badly enough to be hospitalised abroad. Left behind when *Leander* departed Lisbon, he died four days later. Logging him as 'DD', the pusser's clerk noted, 'Allotment dated 1 May 1850 Transferred to wife Stopped'.[29]

In the 1851 census, widow Gimblet's elusiveness proved not to be due to death or migration but another naval union, another change of name. Just four months after William's death, at Portsea Island register office (again), Harriet Trim Bettesworth Gimblet had married seaman Hugh Thomas, a 29-year-old just six years her junior.[30] The happy couple gave Meeting House Alley as their home address; before tying the knot, the sailor-groom was already installed in his dead predecessor's marital home. Leaving her four youngest there to fend for themselves, within a fortnight our thrice-married Victorian cougar had set up home in Albion Street, a lodger supplementing her groom's naval pay.[31]

The union appears to have failed. Without declaring an allotment in Harriet's favour, Hugh Thomas dropped from sight. By 1861, still describing herself as 'seaman's wife', 44-year-old Harriet was once again going by the surname Betsworth [sic].[32] This, however, was no mark of nostalgia for her first late spouse, miller Edward. In 1852 she had married his brother William, HMS *Angel*.[33]

William Betsworth had played an important part in Harriet's life. A source of financial support since 1843, he had allotted initially to Harriet but soon rerouted his money to brother Edward.[34] In August 1849, however, purportedly for the benefit of a namesake son whose existence is debatable, he named 'trustee' Louisa Callaway; three weeks later he married her.[35] The union was bigamous. Appearing in St Mary's marriage register as 'Hughes', Louisa Callaway declared herself a spinster, an unnecessary subterfuge were she genuinely the widow of the David Hughes she had married two years previously.[36] Witness to the charade was groom William's sister-in-law, the newly widowed Harriet, relict of the groom's brother, miller Edward.

Three years and two seamen-husbands later, Harriet became Mrs William Betsworth, her groom stating himself a widower.[37] On several

---

[29] ADM 38/8432/193.
[30] E&W Marriages: Q1/1851, vol. 7, p. 215 (certificate; 'Gimblett').
[31] 1851 census: HO107/1658, fol. 92, p. 24; 1851 census: HO107/1658, fol. 161, p. 39.
[32] 1861 census: RG09/634, fol. 50, p. 4.
[33] CHU2/1C/16, p. 93 n. 186.
[34] ADM 27/81/365/233 ('sister' signifying 'sister -in-law'); ADM 27/83/35/233.
[35] ADM 27/107/179/293; ADM 27/108/172/293; E&W Marriages: Q4/1848, vol. 7, p. 289; CHU3/1D/47, p. 191 n. 382.
[36] England Marriages 1538–1973: parish marriages, Portsea, 25 December 1847.
[37] CHU2/1C/16, p. 93 n. 186; Hampshire Marriages: parish marriages, Portsmouth, 25 October 1852.

points their marriage was questionable. For one thing, William Betsworth was no widower, being still married to the former Louisa Callaway Hughes whose spouse was likewise extant. For another, Harriet's eighteen-month marriage to seaman Hugh Thomas was probably still in force; 'probably', because no pre-1852 record of Thomas's death has been found. And irrespective of Hugh Thomas's being alive or dead, and of David Hughes's being alive, Harriet was the widow of William's late brother Edward, and it would not be until 1921 that the law allowed a deceased man's widow and brother to wed.[38] On three counts, then, the marriage was unlawful. Nothing daunted, at St Thomas's church in Portsmouth, declaring themselves widowed, Harriet and William tied the knot.

Their wedding post-dates by mere weeks the last allotments surviving in Admiralty records, so we do not know whether William Betsworth ever declared an allotment in Harriet's favour. However, with one bigamous wife still living, another equally bigamous recently acquired, and matrimonial proscriptions well and truly breached, William may have been reluctant to attract attention by attempting to redirect his allotment from Louisa to Harriet – a discretion running counter to his having married Harriet by banns rather than licence or register office.

For the next few years the record is silent as to their whereabouts or affiliations. Then in 1861, in Duke Street, again enumerated as 'seaman's wife', the now 44-year-old Harriet Betsworth reappears.[39] With her were two children: 13-year-old apprentice Samuel (her youngest by late miller Edward), and 4-year-old 'daughter' Harriet, who was in fact a grandchild, the offspring of Harriet's firstborn Harriet Sarah.[40] Where, meanwhile, was William Betsworth? Not with his bigamous and unlawful wedded wife Louisa, who in 1862, across the harbour mouth in Forton, describing herself yet again as 'spinster', would marry her third mariner-husband, one William Johns.[41] Marriage of convenience? Opportunism, economic exploitation, love match? Whatever the nature of that union, it did not last. Ten years later, Louisa Callaway Hughes Betsworth Johns and William Betsworth were together again; if they had ever separated; if William's marriage to sister-in-law Harriet and Louisa's to seaman Johns had not been scams, or misbegotten flings hastily regretted.[42]

These matrimonial excuse-me's were unusual but far from unique. They illustrate the brisk pragmatism underpinning widows' decisions to remarry, and the attractions, for some the necessity, of securing another

---

[38] *Deceased Brother's Widow's Marriage Act*, 11 & 12 Geo. V, c. 24 (1921).
[39] 1861 census: RG09/634, fol. 50, p. 4.
[40] E&W Births: Q1/1856, vol. 2B, p. 360 (certificate).
[41] CHU52/1C/1, p. 99 n. 198.
[42] 1871 census: RG10/1140, fol. 141, p. 33.

cash-in-hand allotment when left financially high and dry after a naval husband's demise. Most seamen's widows' spouses came and went in customary 'line astern' formation, the living decorously following the late lamented by periods ranging from mere weeks to long and patiently endured years.[43] Endorsing port town legend, however, evidence now confirms that certain naval wives preferred their spouses 'line abreast', not waiting for the death of one before adding another to their tally. Some husbands were outraged at being cuckolded or displaced. Some shrugged off the implied insult, spotted an opportunity, and took other partners themselves, their own 'line abreast' unions muddying the legal waters even further. It is worth reflecting that of all the actors in Harriet and Louisa's complicated narrative, the only ones of unambiguous civil status were Harriet's first husband, miller Edward Bettesworth, and his immediate successor, seaman William Gimblet, both dead.

## SEAMEN'S WOMEN'S DEATHS

Data on deaths attributable to men's naval service – drownings, falls, diseases and battle injuries – are obtainable via ships' muster books. There is no equivalent ledger from which to extract information upon the mortality of seamen's wives. For that we must turn to death certificates and parish burial records. These reveal commonalities, since naval port towns exposed not just seamen's women but working-class women generally to a range of social, environmental and health hazards. Civilian and naval wife alike suffered accidents, the physical strain of drudgery, and long-term effects of environmental poverty manifest in inadequate sanitation, polluted air, vermin, damp, mould and impure water supply. Like their poor civilian peers, naval wives were vulnerable to infectious disease. They suffered hereditary conditions, diets deficient in quantity and nutritional quality, their resultant debility exacerbated by pregnancy and childbearing. Whether the mortality of civilian and naval female populations differed significantly is a question requiring examination of variables such as upbringing, childhood disease and poverty, domestic and wider environment, age at marriage and at birth of first child, number of children, age at death and certified cause of death. Pending such a specialist study we can only see how some naval women died, and reflect upon what their deaths convey about the lives they lived, and the lives of seamen's women generally.

A sample of 190 allottee-wives born between the 1790s and early 1830s yields a mean average age at death of sixty-two years. Most lived into what

---

[43] Line astern: in nautical terms, a formation in which ships follow one another single-file, in a line.

*Death*

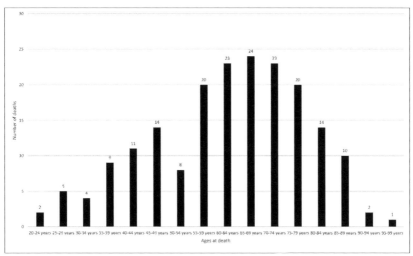

**Fig. 29** Allottee wives' age at death (n=190).

would then have been regarded as old age, 47.4 per cent dying at sixty to seventy-nine years, a further 14.2 per cent surviving into their eighties and nineties. More than a quarter perished in what would now be regarded as middle age (forty to fifty-nine years), but over 10 per cent did not reach forty.

Sussex-born Martha Kelsey died at the advanced age of ninety-seven. She had married in 1839, between 1842 and 1853 producing at least six offspring by husband George.[44] Originally a labourer, he served for six years as a stoker, surviving the loss of HMS *Birkenhead*. His death in 1863, only three years after quitting naval service, left Martha with four dependent children.[45] She had maintained strong links with her birth family. Seven years after George's death, taking her youngest daughter, she went to live with her widowed brother-in-law in Aldingbourne, Sussex, later decades finding her in her eldest son's Portsea household together with her widowed brother and great-nephew.[46] She died in 1907, having outlived a petty officer son, and seen one daughter marry a labourer, another a stoker RN, both of which occupations had been held by their late father.[47]

Amelia Wheden (*q.v.*) was another to live to great old age. Just fourteen when in 1847 she married William Wheden/Weedon, she suffered the deaths of two young sons before reaching her majority, and was still

---

[44] ADM 27/102/269/182; ADM 27/111/167/223; ADM 27/111/356/13; ADM 27/113/386/11.
[45] E&W Deaths: Q2/1863, vol. 2B, p. 252.
[46] 1871 census: RG10/1115, fol. 20, p. 5; 1881 census: RG11/1155, fol. 80, p. 4; 1891 census: RG12/869, fol. 50, p. 15; 1901 census: RG13/1003, fol. 48, p. 16.
[47] E&W Deaths: Q4/1907, vol. 2B, p. 319; CHU3/1E/57, p. 357; CHU3/1D/73, p. 51 n. 102; CHU3/1D/62, p. 2 n. 4.

only twenty-three when in 1855 she married AB George Wilkinson. Thereafter Amelia's life took her well beyond her Portsea Island birthplace, her upbringing and first marriage. This sets her apart from most other naval wives, for in the latter half of the mid-century only a minority of the study cohort lived anywhere other than their home district. Their seamen-husbands may have seen the world, but these wives' world was Portsea Island.

George Wilkinson was in *Cornwallis* when it departed for Hull to begin an eight-year association with the city, and it was in Hull that the 1861 census found Amelia with two-month-old Yorkshire-born Henry.[48] Two years later, a second son of the marriage was named George.[49] When seaman George's naval service ended in 1864 he moved his family to Luton, where he worked as a labourer and fathered four more children.[50] The family remained in Luton for more than twenty years until, in 1897, in a move prompted by widowhood, Amelia returned to Portsmouth.[51] There she was enumerated in 1901, living with son George (by now a tailor) and youngest daughter Emily.[52] Her return did not last. When Emily married and moved to Newmarket, and George followed, Amelia upped sticks to Hove, to live with her petty officer son Alfred and his family.[53] How long the arrangement lasted is unknown. At some point she was accommodated again by Emily, for it was in Emily's Newmarket home that in 1922 Amelia Groom Wheden Wilkinson died, aged ninety, her son-in-law present at her end.[54] A sailor's daughter, with her father's consent (possibly at his connivance with her groom) Amelia had been child bride to a man twice her age. She had fallen in love with a shipmate of her sailor-brothers; still a minor, she had mourned the death of two little sons; experienced marriage breakdown; endured poverty caused by her husband's refusal to support her; quietly married the sailor she had known since childhood; given birth to at least eight children; buried three; and lived to see one son attain petty officer rank in the same Navy that had shaped her long life.

Amelia was unusual in reaching such advanced years. Numerous wives died before reaching middle age, but of this sample group only one death refers to childbirth. Elizabeth Anne Giddy, wife of AB Nicholas Giddy,

---

[48] E&W Births: Hull, Yorkshire, Q1/1861, vol. 9D, p. 207; 1861 census: RG9/3594, fol. 104, p. 7.
[49] E&W Births: Sculcoates, Yorkshire, Q2/1863, vol. 9D, p. 167.
[50] ADM 139/231/23014; 1871 census: Luton, Bedfordshire, RG10/1659, fol. 33, p. 11; 1881 census: Luton, Bedfordshire, RG11/1648, fol. 31, p. 9; 1891 census: Luton, Bedfordshire, RG12/12712, fol. 4, p. 1.
[51] E&W Deaths: Q4/1879, vol. 3B, p. 263.
[52] 1901 census: RG13/979, fol. 120, p. 4.
[53] 1911 census: Hove, Steyning, Sussex, RG14/5196, Sch 385.
[54] E&W Deaths: Newmarket, Suffolk, Q4/1922, vol. 3B, p. 494 (certificate).

HMS *Excellent*, died in 1853 of 'Convulsions from Labor 3 Days', leaving Nicholas the widowed father of a newborn.[55] Her death post-dates the last surviving allotment records, so we do not know whether widower Nicholas nominated a trustee to raise his infant daughter. It is more likely he took her to Devonport where lived his father, a former dockyard sawyer now Greenwich pensioner, and his mother, to whom he had allotted prior to marrying Elizabeth Anne; and in Stoke Damerel, five years after Elizabeth Anne's death, Nicholas married again.[56] The 1861 census shows his new wife Emma, 8-year-old motherless Elizabeth, and a ten-month-old baby girl, the little family resident just a few doors down from Nicholas's ageing parents.[57] Before their deaths in 1867, the senior Giddys enjoyed a decade or more of proximity to their son and grandchildren.[58]

Emma Giddy's mother-in-law's long experience of naval married life and motherhood may have provided both support and consolation to the new naval wife. Emma's own mother, the splendidly-named Britannia Keast, was of little practical help: having remarried shortly before Nicholas Giddy married her daughter, she lived more than twenty miles away in Lanreath, Cornwall.[59] But a different situation obtained for the family of Nicholas's late wife Elizabeth Anne. For them, Nicholas's removal of little motherless Elizabeth from Landport to Devonport compounded the loss of a beloved daughter and sister.[60] Contact between maternal grandparents and grandchild will have amounted thereafter to no more than letters, perhaps an occasional visit. Following a parent's death, attenuated contact with grandparents was not unusual, many bereaved grandparents struggling to sustain relations with their widowed sons-in-law and motherless grandchildren. Given seamen's periodic change of ship, and the distances between naval port towns, parents of dead naval wives may have faced a more complex loss and greater logistical challenges than did the parents of deceased civilian wives.

---

[55] E&W Deaths: Q3/1853, vol. 2B, p. 241 (certificate).
[56] CHU3/1D/49, p. 23 n. 45; ADM 27/101/157/102; ADM 27/109/200/1256; E&W Marriages: St Germans, Cornwall, Q3/1858, vol. 5C, p. 67 (Nicholas Giddy and Emma Keast).
[57] 1861 census: Stoke Damerel, Devon, RG09/1449, fol. 32, p. 2, and fol. 34, p. 6.
[58] Plymouth and West Devon Record office: Devon burials: Nicholas Giddy and Rebecca Giddy, 1015/3.
[59] E&W Marriages: Q1/1858, vol. 5C, p. 96 (Britannia Keast and James Bray); 1861 census: Lanreath, Cornwall, RG09/1532, fol. 27, p. 10; 1871 census: Lanreath, Cornwall, RG10/2244, fol. 32, p. 14; 1881 census: Lanreath, Cornwall, RG11/2288, fol. 40, p. 12.
[60] 1851 census: HO107/1657, fol. 9, p. 10 (Carter family).

Of this sample group, Elizabeth Anne Giddy's was the only death directly attributed to childbirth. Among our other young wives, however, one cause accounts for at least 40 per cent of deaths. Usually defined as respiratory tuberculosis, phthisis was common in the nineteenth century. Taking rich and poor alike, it was particularly associated with poverty and overcrowding, conditions certainly found in Hobbs Court where lived Martha Bone (*q.v.*), who died of the disease. In its original Greek meaning, phthisis implies malnutrition and starvation, Brooks proposing that coroners and registrars deployed the term as shorthand for pulmonary diseases exacerbated by poverty and hunger.[61] In describing the emaciated state of female victims of 'pulmonary consumption', *Hampshire Telegraph* reportage on coroners' inquests echoes Brooks's observations.[62] A naval surgeon's note that a patient was of 'delicate constitution & phthisical tendency, marked by clear skin and large lips with blue eyes & dilated pupils – narrow and long neck, also long delicate fingers with bent nails' has particular resonance when we see Jane Purcell's life ending at just twenty-seven.[63] A minor when she married James Purcell, Jane Tate was one of three daughters of a Shetland-born Royal Navy seaman.[64] Her sisters had married Navy men, and one of her three brothers was a seaman who dutifully allotted to their mother.[65] The family was close-knit: the 1851 census shows Jane's parents and their youngest son sharing a house with the two older married sisters and their children.[66] Jane was elsewhere, visiting a fellow naval wife (their husbands were old *President* hands).[67] After seven years of marriage she had given birth to a daughter.[68] Motherhood would be short lived, for at fifteen months little Jane Amelia died of 'eruptive disease of the skin since birth, irritative fever certified', tended by her Shetlander grandfather.[69] Jane Purcell followed sixteen months later, succumbing to the same *phthisis pulmonaris* that would within a half-year take her husband James.[70] Pensioner James was house-servant to naval officers accommodated in the elegant Georgian

[61] Kate Brooks, 'Death in the Archives', *Social History Society*: (2020), <https://social-history.org.uk/shs_exchange/death-in-the-archives/> [accessed 22 April 2024].
[62] For example, *H/Tel*, 19 October 1850, p. 5 col. C.
[63] ADM 101/124/3, fol. 41.
[64] CHU9/1B/1, p. 72 n. 144; CHU3/1B/17, p. 6 n. 41.
[65] CHU3/1D/34, p. 113 n. 331; CHU3/1D/39, p. 221 n. 442; ADM 27/72/257/607; ADM 27/86/219/141; ADM 27/91/193/85.
[66] 1851 census: HO107/1659, fol. 496, pp. 35–6.
[67] 1851 census: HO107/1659, fol. 434, p. 2; ADM 139/34/3312; ADM 27/111/167/223; ADM 27/99/221/301 (William 'Grunsell' to wife Martha)
[68] E&W Births: Q4/1854, vol. 2B, p. 372 (Jane Amelia Purcell); CHU3/1B/31, p. 124 n. 987.
[69] E&W Deaths: Q1/1856, vol. 2B, p. 265 (certificate).
[70] E&W Deaths: Q3/1857, vol. 2B, p. 238 (certificate).

terrace of Short Row, behind St Ann's church in Portsmouth dockyard. He died at his place of work, his death certificate confirming he had been tubercular for two years.[71] This raises the possibility that he had infected Jane, the disease's impact upon her being aggravated by the rigours of childbirth followed by her baby's chronic illness and pitifully young death.

Among the 190 wives examined, another common cause of death was recorded in certification as 'dropsy' (oedema), then synonymous with heart failure. One to die of this condition was 24-year-old Sarah Jane Harvey, who after five years of marriage to sailmaker Francis, HMS *Flying Fish*, succumbed to heart disease and lung congestion.[72] Other certified causes of death included 'epilepsia [x] weeks', 'ulceration of the palate 4 years, of the windpipe 4 months', 'fever, ulceration of bowels 1 month', and 'chronic gastritis 4 months, sloughing of inside of mouth 3 weeks'.[73] Most of them died at home, tended by husband or other close relatives. Witness to Elizabeth Page's death from gastritis was her sister Phoebe Greenleaf Saxton, who within twenty months would marry Elizabeth's widower Richard (see Chapter Thirteen).

One third of these young wives died in the workhouse, of phthisis, syphilis, and 'insanity from brain disease'.[74] These women were not necessarily poor. They may have required a level of nursing beyond the capability of family and neighbours, or had no-one to provide even basic personal care during their final decline. Like little James Smith, whom gunner's mate Thomas entrusted to the care of Mary Baskerville, and who was located as a pauper scholar in the workhouse (p. 64), these women had simply 'run out of kin'.[75] Within a matter of months – weeks, in some instances – they had gone from widowhood to a workhouse death.

None of them fits the popular image of port-town prostitute, Pompey Brute or hard-nosed exploiter of gullible seamen. Of those whose opportunist or unsocial behaviour most nearly matched that trope, the majority vanished into obscurity. Some, like recidivist Caroline Capper (*q.v.*), reappear only to fade again. Since of all the women mentioned in this study, Caroline most nearly reflects the judgemental nineteenth-century image of the sailor's woman as drunken brawling prostitute, it would have been

---

[71] E&W Deaths: Q1/1858, vol. 2B, p. 307 (certificate).
[72] ADM 27/110/263/39; E&W Deaths: Q3/1852, vol. 2B, p. 210 (certificate).
[73] E&W Deaths: Q1/1867, vol. 2B, p. 294 (Elizabeth Huggett; certificate); E&W Deaths: Q2/1868, vol. 2B, p. 248 (Rosabella Archbold; certificate); E&W Deaths: Q1/1866, vol. 2B, p. 297 (Mary Ann Adshead; certificate); E&W Deaths: Q3/1856, vol. 2B, p. 208 (Elizabeth Northover; certificate); E&W Deaths: Q3/1854, vol. 2B, p. 235 (Elizabeth Page; certificate).
[74] E&W Deaths: Q2/1865, vol. 2B, p. 242 (Mary Ellen Wheeler; certificate).
[75] ADM 27/110/220/1411; Humphries, 'Care and Cruelty', pp. 121–2.

unsurprising to find that she ended her days choked on her own vomit in a Portsea alley, or dying of cirrhosis or tertiary syphilis in lock ward or workhouse. Yet in 1853, within a year of receiving seven days' hard labour for the theft of a silver watch, watch guard and cash from a drunken soldier, she moved in with and married William Linney, a Greenwich pensioner whose 26-year-old wife had died eight months earlier.[76] Was this a love match, or was Caroline just after his pension? Had she tired of the streets and/or the tedium of picking oakum, and was seeking some calm and warmth? Nothing further has been found to throw light upon her later years. We cannot know whether she abandoned her marriage to Linney, moved away, changed her name, emigrated, remarried or ended as one of the unidentified female corpses from time to time found floating in a Portsea moat.

Some of Caroline's fellow miscreants proved more traceable. Twice gaoled as a 17-year-old for indecent behaviour and assault on another young woman (see p. 212), Mary Anne Kate Harding thereafter led a long and largely unremarkable life. From HMS *Leander* AB Richard Fleming had in 1850 and 1851 named her trustee to his daughter Mary Anne, surname not stated but acknowledged as his when in 1854 the then 4-year-old's baptismal name was given as Mary Anne Fleming.[77] Her legal surname was Harding, however, and in the parish register only her mother was recorded as parent. Baptised on the same day, little Mary Anne's younger sister Maria enjoyed two parents' names on the register, and her father's surname. Richard and Mary Anne Kate were by then two years married. They would have two decades and at least four children together, all at the same Berkeley Street address, before Richard's death at forty-five, six years after his naval service ended.[78]

Mary Anne Kate was forty-five years a widow – the greater part of her life. As naval wife she had been a stay-maker. As widow she did laundry work to supplement the pension to which she was entitled due to Richard's time in Continuous Service, in later years being aided in her laundry labours by her youngest daughter, Laura.[79] Their seemingly innocuous mother-

---

[76] See p. 190. CHU3/1D/51, p. 42 n. 84 (William Linney m. Caroline Capper); CHU3/1D/44, p. 87 n. 174 (William Linney m. Mary Ann Martin); E&W Deaths: Q2/1852, vol. 2B, p. 259 (Mary Ann Linney); CHU3/1E/31, p. 204 n. 1627 (Mary Ann Linney).

[77] ADM 27/110/156/184; ADM 27/112/313/184; CHU3/1B/31 p. 79 nos 625–6.

[78] CHU3/1D/50, p. 44 n. 88; 1861 census: RG09/644, fol. 13, p. 21; 1871 census: RG10/1145, fol. 16, p. 26; E&W Deaths: Q4/1872, vol. 2B, p. 301; Portsmouth, Portsmouth History Centre (PHC), Hampshire, Portsmouth Burials, Parish Burials, PHC G/BBK4/3 (1869), p. 649 n. 2148; ADM 29/71/453; ADM 139/18/1785.

[79] 1861 census: RG09/644, fol. 13, p. 21; 1871 census: RG10/1145, fol. 16, p. 26; 1881 census: RG11/1158, fol. 134, p. 33; 1891 census: RG12/857, fol. 141, p. 21.

*Death*

and-daughter household was not what it appeared, for Laura's parentage is mysterious. On her birth certificate her mother was named as Mary Anne Kate Fleming 'formerly Harding'; her father, Richard Fleming, was recorded as a naval pensioner of Berkeley Street.[80] The Berkeley Street address chimes with the family's previous places of residence, and though she would have been forty-four years old at the time it is not impossible that Mary Anne Kate was indeed the infant's mother. But little Laura Brooks was born in May 1875, and Richard Fleming, her purported papa, had died in December 1872.[81] The most likely explanation is that our Mary Anne Kate agreed to assume parental responsibility for the illegitimate child of one of her older daughters, by then in their twenties – an arrangement seen elsewhere in this study. In doing so she camouflaged the infant's bastardy by pretending she was the mother, still married to the sailor-husband whose death two years earlier she omitted to mention when registering the child's birth. An alternative interpretation proposes that widowed Mary Anne Kate had allowed herself some late intimacy, or conceived as the result of an assault, naming her late husband as the child's father in order to spare herself the shame of middle-aged, husbandless parenthood. Whatever their true relationship, she provided nineteen years of mothering before Laura married in 1894.[82] Born in the reign of William IV, Mary Anne Kate died in 1917 of acute bronchitis and heart failure; she was eighty-five.[83] The death certificate described her as 'Patriotic Fund annuitant', and widow of Richard Fleming, naval pensioner. It made no mention of the occupations by which she had contributed to the family economy and supported herself through decades of widowhood.

For good or bad, their marriages played a pivotal part in naval women's health and longevity, and in marital complexities the innocent party was not always the longest-lived. We have seen how, to escape marriage to her mentally ill and violent husband, Martha Woodley Lewis had opted for bigamy, and how her unlawful husband Eli Bone ('Conduct: v. bad') had been discharged early – alone of all the crew – upon *Resolute*'s completing its first Arctic commission. Within weeks of his return Martha was pregnant, and a son was born in the summer of 1852.[84] A daughter followed in May 1854, by which time the little family had moved from Hobbs Court

---

[80] E&W Births: Q2/1875, vol. 2B, p. 176 (Laura Brooks Harding).
[81] E&W Deaths: Q4/1872, vol. 2B, p. 301 (Richard Fleming); PHC: G/BBK4/3, p. 649 n. 21498.
[82] E&W Marriages: Q2/1894, vol. 2B, p. 885 (Laura Brooks Fleming and James Edgar Olding).
[83] 1901 census: RG13/982, fol. 50, p. 5; E&W Deaths: Q1/1917, vol. 2B, p. 725 (Mary Ann [*sic*] Kate Fleming; certificate).
[84] E&W Births: Q3/1852, vol. 2B, p. 330 (Cornelius Bone).

to Beeston Street, Landport.[85] Eli registered his daughter's birth, declaring himself a seaman RN – another falsehood to follow his several muster book lies, there being no service record for him following his abrupt discharge at Greenhithe in October 1851.[86]

Just over a fortnight after giving birth, Martha died of phthisis.[87] She was twenty-seven. Her death was registered not by husband Eli, but by a family member present at her death: Elizabeth Bone, the Hobbs Court-resident wife of Eli's brother Daniel. Eli was now the widowed father of two small children, and still clinging to his seagoing past: when his daughter was baptised at St Mary's Church in October 1854 he again gave his occupation as 'seaman'.[88] The baby's mother's name was given as Martha, but with no mention of her being six months dead. Within a year of baptism the little one too was dead. Cause of death was 'dentitional diarrhoea': she had been teething, and from 'diarrhoea' we may infer that she suffered dehydration, wasting and seizures.[89] Present at the death, and reporting it to the registrar, was Martha's sister Clara Woodley, who gave her address as Beeston Street. Clara, however, was not merely visiting Eli as nursemaid to his children. At the time of her niece's death the unmarried aunt was six months pregnant, by her widowed brother-in-law. A daughter, whom she named Clara Martha Eliza Woodley, was born in January 1856.[90] If conception occurred in May 1855, it means that within a year of Martha Bone dying of consumption, her husband Eli was bedding her sister, and vice versa. Reprehensible as this may seem, it is not impossible that the dying Martha condoned the relationship. After all, were it to flourish, it would bind Clara to Eli, by extension securing a beloved and trusted stepmother for Martha's about-to-be-motherless children.

No father was named on baby Clara Martha Eliza's birth certificate, but at her baptism in September that year her parents gave their names as Eli and Clara Bone, neatly (if falsely) suggesting they were married.[91] By 1861 they were living together in Basin Street, Landport, Eli describing Clara as his wife, and giving her surname as Bone.[92] The pair were still unwed.

---

[85] E&W Births: Q2/1854, vol. 2B, p. 355 (Martha Clara Woodley Bone); CHU3/1B/31, p. 7 n. 53 (Martha Clare [sic] Woodley Bone).
[86] ADM 38/8862 (n.p.).
[87] E&W Deaths: Q2/1854, vol. 2B, p. 217 (Martha Bone; certificate); CHU3/1E/32, p. 132 n. 1053.
[88] CHU3/1B/31, p. 7 n. 53.
[89] E&W Deaths: Q3/1855, vol. 2B, p. 208 (Martha Clara Woodley Bone; certificate); CHU3/1E/33, p. 29 n. 226.
[90] E&W Births: Q1/1856, vol. 2B, p. 367 (Clara Martha Eliza Woodley; certificate).
[91] CHU3/1B/32, p. 87 n. 689.
[92] 1861 census: RG09/635, fol. 28, p. 8.

*Death*

The 1835 Marriage Act still prohibited a widower's marrying his late wife's sister, but whereas the likes of Phoebe Saxton and Richard Page (*q.v.*) were prepared to break the law, Eli and Clara opted to cohabit.[93] Whether by mutual agreement, or at Eli's insistence, for three decades they avoided unlawful union, maintaining instead a façade of respectable matrimony. Their 'married' life may have been a charade, but it was longer – and, one may surmise, more comfortable – than the few years of slum-court wedlock in which Martha Bone had lived her last. At her death she was just twenty-seven, less than half the age her husband and sister would attain.[94]

Echoes and inversions of Martha's story may be found in that of Amelia Cavander, last seen in Chapter Thirteen. Fleeing her marital home, Amelia had moved to Diamond Street with her lover Esau Barrett, her 6-year-old daughter by sailor husband James and 2-year-old Esau junior. She was pregnant, a second Barrett son being born in late 1851.[95] By 1861 the family had moved to South Stoneham, near Bitterne, where two more sons were born.[96] But while Amelia would have five children and enjoy a relatively long life with her partner, it was different for the woman who replaced her. As we have seen (p. 243), within two years of his humiliating beating at the hands of bricklayer Esau, cuckolded AB James Cavander was financially supporting a Jane Elliott, whom he identified as 'trustee' to a 2-year-old Maria, surname undisclosed.[97] Twelve weeks later, the three of them were living in Grigg Street.[98] Though enumerated as 'Cavender', Jane was still the wife of mariner William Elliott; at their wedding in 1840 he had been a 30-year-old widower, she a child bride.[99] Now forty, and three years on from the court hearing at which he was acquitted of ill-using Jane (see p. 224), Elliott was in West Street, lodging with fellow mariner John Cummings and his allottee wife Elizabeth (*q.v.*) whom the *Hampshire Telegraph* described as one of 'two nymphs of the pavé'.[100]

That his lawful wife Amelia was still alive did not prevent James Cavander marrying the equally still-married Jane Elliott, a move we may surmise was prompted by pregnancy. Whether out of sentiment, keenness to lose the surname Elliott or to avoid being outed as intent upon bigamy,

---

[93] *Marriage Act*, 5 & 6 Will. IV, c. 54 (1835).
[94] Clara died at sixty-five (E&W Deaths: Q1/1890, vol. 2B, p. 334), Eli at sixty-eight (E&W Deaths: Q2/1892, vol. 2B, p. 225).
[95] E&W Births: Q3/1851, vol. 7, p. 166.
[96] 1861 census: RG09/681, fol. 44, p. 32 ('Barritt').
[97] ADM 27/112/154/51.
[98] 1851 census: HO107/1659, fol. 131, p. 17.
[99] CHU2/1C/12, p. 203 n. 405.
[100] *H/Tel*, 20 May 1848, p. 1 col. B; *ibid.*, 23 December 1848, p. 7 col. D; see p. 191.

at the register office Jane reverted to her maiden name.[101] Daughter Martha arrived in 1857, but the family's happiness was already blighted.[102] In early 1860, in Grigg Street, Southsea, seaman James died of 'chronic bronchitis – many years'.[103] He was thirty-seven. Within weeks of his death, daughter Martha and the heavily pregnant Jane were admitted to the workhouse; and it was there, in June 1860, that Edward was born.[104] The 1861 census shows 3-year-old Martha as a workhouse resident still; of Jane and posthumous Edward it bears no trace.[105] It is possible that mother and baby had been discharged, but a widow with a 1-year-old and no means of support would have been hard put to secure accommodation in the community, let alone support herself; besides, to leave the Union house with Edward meant leaving behind the still very young Martha, a choice no mother would want to make. Other than search engine insufficiency, the next least fanciful, if unlikely explanation is accidental omission from the workhouse's census schedule; but wherever Jane was on census night, she and her baby evaded enumeration. We do know, however, that it was in the workhouse (still, or again) that in 1863 Jane Crosby Elliott Cavender died, age forty, of phthisis.[106] Recorded as a pauper, she was buried in consecrated ground.[107] Daughter Martha remained an in-pauper for a further seven years before succumbing to consumption; just twelve years old, she was buried in unconsecrated ground.[108] Posthumous Edward, by then a labourer, followed ten years later, dying of chronic phthisis in the workhouse where he too was buried, but in consecrated ground, unlike his sister.[109] Meanwhile, in Bitterne, ex-naval wife Amelia outlived them all, in 1880 dying of oedema and heart disease, age sixty-one.[110]

Which workhouse inmate merited burial in consecrated or unconsecrated ground was determined according to their known (or presumed) faith. In the parish burials register, on the page in which Jane Cavender's

---

[101] E&W Marriages: Q3/1856, vol. 2B, p. 621 (James Cavender and Jane Crosbey [sic]).
[102] E&W Births: Q2/1857, vol. 2B, p. 357 (Martha Elizabeth Cavender).
[103] E&W Deaths: Q2/1860, vol. 2B, p. 275 (certificate); PHC: G/BBK4/1, p. 319 n. 4454.
[104] E&W Births: Q2/1860, vol. 2B, p. 341 (certificate).
[105] 1861 census: RG09/635, fol. 118, p. 3 (Martha Cavender, three years old).
[106] E&W Deaths: Q3/1863, vol. 2B, p. 236 (certificate).
[107] Portsmouth History Centre (PHC) Portsmouth, Hampshire, Portsmouth Burials, Parish Burials, PHC G/BBK4/2 (1863), p. 143, n. 8120.
[108] PHC: G/BBK4/3, p. 372 n. 17604; E&W Deaths: Q2/1870, vol. 2B, p. 273 (Martha Cavander [sic], certificate).
[109] E&W Deaths: Q3/1880, vol. 2B, p. 283 (Edward Cavender, certificate); CHU3/1E/42, p. 90 n. 716; Portsmouth History Centre (PHC) Portsmouth, Hampshire, Portsmouth Burials, Parish Burials, PHC G/BBK4/5 (1880), p. 118 n. 33377.
[110] E&W Deaths: South Stoneham, Hampshire, Q3/1880, vol. 2C, p. 41, (certificate, 'Barratt').

burial is recorded, 'Consecrated' appears nine times, 'Unconsecrated' five. In seven of the 'Consecrated' instances, the 'Ceremony Performed By' column bears the name of the local curate, the remaining two giving the name of the curate of St John's. In all five 'Unconsecrated' instances, the ceremony was performed by a dissenting minister, implying the deceased had not been of Anglican persuasion. Née Crosby, Jane Cavender had been baptised a Wesleyan.[111] Following her register office marriage to James she may have brought up her children in the same faith, though no baptismal record – Anglican or nonconformist – has been found in Martha's name, or in the posthumous Edward's. Given Jane's Wesleyan origins, and Martha and Edward's apparently unbaptised state, it would be reasonable to expect to find all three being consigned to unconsecrated ground; but unlike his mother and sister, Edward somehow escaped that fate.

A fortnight's imprisonment for marital violence in September 1851 did not lead to long-term rapprochement between former marine private third class Robert Lewis and his wife Amelia (*q.v.*), of Hobbs Court. They appear to have remained together for a few months after Robert's release from gaol, for whether through affection or forced intercourse Amelia conceived her fifth and last child the following March, their only son, named after his father, being born in December 1852.[112] Of their circumstances during the next eight years no record survives. By 1861, separated by age and sex, Amelia and the five children were in the workhouse.[113] Their admission robbed them of the live-in support of Amelia's mother, widowed charwoman Elizabeth Flowers. Listed as 'unmarried', but no longer on out-relief, Elizabeth was now lodging with a French polisher's family in Albion Street, close enough to the workhouse to enable her to supplement the children's institutional diet, if she could afford to do so.[114] As for paterfamilias Robert, he had been discharged from the Marines due to 'Tremor and Debility', for which symptoms from January 1851 he had been treated as an in-patient in Haslar Hospital.[115] Nothing further is known of him until Christmas

---

[111] National Archives (TNA) Kew, Hampshire: Gosport, Middle Street Chapel (Wesleyan): Births & Baptisms, England & Wales Non-Conformist Births And Baptisms, Parish Baptisms, TNA/RG/4/1081, (1823), p. 21 n. 168.

[112] E&W Births: Q1/1853, vol. 2B, p. 367.

[113] 1861 census: Portsea Island Union Workhouse, No. 1/635, fol. 107, pp. 30, 15, 38, 36; Peter Higginbotham, 'The Workhouse: the story of an institution' (workhouses.org.uk, 2016) <http://www.workhouses.org.uk/life/classification.shtml> [accessed 22 April 2024].

[114] 1861 census: RG09/636, fol. 162, p. 38; Fowler, *Workhouse*, p. 104; Humphries, 'Care and Cruelty', pp. 123, 130–1.

[115] ADM 157/384, item 66 (proceedings of Divisional Board, 23 January 1851).

Day 1861 when he died, age forty-four.[116] His death reopens the issue of his violent marital conduct. The certificate refers to 'Disease of the Brain – Certified', a phrase with multiple meanings; but where other contemporary death certificates explicitly mention tumours and cancers, his does not. Instead, medical euphemism suggests that Robert was suffering from advanced syphilis. The evidence is circumstantial, but taken together his 'tremor and debility', admission to Haslar (locus of specialist treatment for venereal diseases), repeated episodes of violence and certified 'disease of the brain' make syphilis a reasonable inference.

By the time Robert died he was no longer an in-patient: in the 1861 census his initials do not feature among inmates of the Haslar lock ward where sexually transmitted conditions were treated by the ingestion of mercury.[117] No trace of him has been found elsewhere. He may have been living rough, or under an assumed name in some flophouse lodgings. He died on a Gosport slipway, his death reported by a Landport woman of unknown relationship to him, or none, but possessing enough information to satisfy the registrar. In proposing his true cause of death, however, what tips the balance is Amelia's death in the workhouse, in 1864, of 'natural decay from Syphilis, certified'.[118] By then, as well as dementing she may have become disfigured.

If Robert Lewis's 'Disease of the Brain – Certified' were the same condition that later killed his wife, it may be wondered which of them first contracted it, from what sort of liaison, and when. Sexually transmitted disease being rife within the armed forces, it would not be surprising if Robert had become infected through some shoreside dalliance abroad, or sex with a Devonport prostitute. If so, on his return he had seeded his wife with the disease that would eventually kill her. But just as circumstantial evidence points to his suffering syphilis, so other circumstantial evidence raises the possibility that Amelia had resorted to prostitution, another possible source of disease. She had been poor enough to depend on parish relief, Robert's allotment notwithstanding. His discharge from the RMA then reduced his income to a pension, further straining the household budget, and increasing the need for a supplementary source of income. Finally, their subsequent separation left Amelia without financial support; and parish records show that in previous years she had resided in Blossom Alley, a location notorious for prostitutes.[119] The pieces do not comprise one aggregate evidential whole, and to label Amelia a prostitute is to speculate. There remains only

---

[116] E&W Deaths: Alverstoke, Hampshire Q4/1861, vol. 2B, p. 286 (certificate).
[117] Preston, 'Constructing Communities', pp. 225–31.
[118] E&W Deaths: Q4/1864, vol. 2B, p. 261 (certificate).
[119] CHU5/A/1/6, p. 18 nos 140–3.

the certified cause of her death, and the poignant possibility that she died unaware of her widowed status, for her death certificate styles her 'wife' (not widow) of Robert Lewis, 'a Sergeant Rl. Marines'; but then, as witness the death certificate of Joanna Greenleaf Page (see p. 298, and n.150), workhouse staff were ignorant of inmates' key details and circumstances.

If Amelia had resorted to selling herself it may have been on her own initiative, a decision taken either without her husband's knowledge or despite his forbidding her to do so, despite his pleading. Alternatively, she may have been forced into the sex trade by a husband who, possessing neither trade nor skill to bring in a wage, saw his wife's prostitution as a quick and easy solution to their money problems. The injuries Robert then inflicted upon her may have been intended as punishment for her activities, or for her being slow to do his bidding and bring home cash; his stripping her near-naked may similarly have been intended as punishment for her servicing other men, or to advertise her trade. If the decision to prostitute herself had been Amelia's alone, Robert's beating her only attracted attention to the very thing of which he was ashamed; but if he had forced her into selling herself for sex, to punish her for doing so was rank hypocrisy.

What of Amelia's children? Aged twenty-one, eighteen, sixteen, fourteen and twelve at the time of her death, they survived their workhouse incarceration. Youngest of the five, namesake Robert followed his father into the Royal Marine Artillery; he appears in the 1871 census as a bugler.[120] Amelia's eldest, Rosina, married seaman Henry Tallon and had three children.[121] Middle child Maria married seaman William Garland; the 1881 census locates her just four doors down from Rosina, by 1891 her brood comprising seven sons and a daughter.[122] 'Cripple from birth', Louisa found a home in Lower Charlotte Street with maternal grandmother Elizabeth Flowers, and made a living as a governess.[123] Elizabeth's only recorded trade was charwoman, an occupation she maintained while receiving out-relief in the 1850s. She was still charring two decades later. Age seventy-five, in 1872 she died in the workhouse of 'decay of Nature, Certified', her 'Rank or Profession' given as 'Widow of James Flowers, a Seaman'.[124] Listed in the burial register as 'pauper', she was laid to rest in unconsecrated ground.[125] Now alone, Louisa never married, but despite her disability lived to eighty-four years, dying in 1934 of heart failure and liver cancer, a 'spinster

---

[120] 1871 census: RG10/1148, fol. 75, p. 36.
[121] CHU3/1D/64, p. 64 n. 127; 1871 census: RG10/1127, fol. 45, p. 3.
[122] CHU3/1D/70, p. 8 n. 16; 1881 census: RG11/1152, fol. 35, p. 20; 1891 census: RG12/866, fol. 134, p. 25.
[123] 1871 census: RG10/1127, fol. 45, p. 3.
[124] E&W Deaths: Q1/1872, vol. 2B, p. 286 (certificate).
[125] PHC: G/BBK4/3, p. 551 n. 20116.

housekeeper'.¹²⁶ From her first recorded appearance in that job-lot baptism of Lewis daughters, Louisa reaches into the living memory of twenty-first century readers.¹²⁷

It is debatable whether Harriet Trim Bettesworth Gimblet Thomas Betsworth enjoyed much happiness during her four marriages. She was fortunate that her children survived to adulthood, all four sons becoming sailors and marrying.¹²⁸ Their sister Harriet Sarah, however, came before the courts on more than one occasion, first for assaulting another young woman, then for theft.¹²⁹ In 1856 she gave birth to an illegitimate child, the namesake later enumerated as 'daughter' to grandmother Harriet.¹³⁰ Disapproving her unmarried motherhood, the Union may have refused her outdoor relief; if so, it left her with no alternative but the workhouse, there 'to be left in no doubt of [her] shameful condition'.¹³¹ In 1869 she died of consumption in the workhouse, and was buried in the paupers' plot; despite her having been baptised an Anglican, in St Mary's, she was laid in unconsecrated ground.¹³² It may have been beyond grandmother Harriet's ability or home circumstances to nurse 30-year-old Harriet Sarah through her advancing consumption; likewise, judging by census data, Harriet's four sons were unable to accommodate their mother, their lack of domestic space leaving her with no alternative other than institutional accommodation.¹³³ It is also possible that her health was beyond any daughter-in-law's nursing ability. In the Portsea Island workhouse, within weeks of the 1871 census she died of dropsy. Her death certificate proclaimed her 'Widow of William Bettesworth, A Seaman', terminology neatly obscuring her much-married past.¹³⁴ Like her daughter, she was

---

[126] E&W Deaths: Q2/1934, vol. 2B, p. 581 (certificate).

[127] CHU5/A/1/6, p. 18 nos 140–3. See p. 100,

[128] E&W Marriages: Q3/1862, vol. 2B, p. 674 (George Gilbert Betsworth and Emma Eliza Kennett); CHU2/1C/18, p. 175 n. 350; E&W Marriages: Q1/1864, vol. 2B, p. 593 (Edward Charles Betsworth and Mercy Anna Walker); CHU2/1C/19, p. 4 n. 8; E&W Marriages: Q2/1869, vol. 2B, p. 703 (Samuel Benjamin Wade Bettsworth [sic] and Elizabeth Horton); CHU3/1D/68, p. 236 n. 472; E&W Marriages: Q4/1870, vol. 2B, p. 843 (William Betsworth and Mary Ann Henrietta Chipp); CHU2/1C/20, p. 133 n. 266.

[129] H/Tel, 9 October 1852, p. 7 col. F; ibid., 16 April 1864, p. 7 col. A.

[130] E&W Births: Q2/1856, vol. 2B, p. 360 (Harriet Sarah Betsworth; certificate); see pp. 110, 281.

[131] Thane, 'Women and the Poor Law', p. 32.

[132] E&W Deaths: Q3/1869, vol. 2B, p. 247 (Harriet Bettesworth; certificate); PHC: G/BBK4/3, p. 286 n. 16406; CHU3/1B/22, p. 29 n. 229 ('Harriet Sarah Betworth').

[133] 1871 census: RG10/1791, fol. 19, p. 34; 1871 census: G10/1138, fol. 91, p. 29; 1871 census: RG10/1128, fol. 168, p. 32; 1871 census: RG10/1128, fol. 143, p. 28.

[134] E&W Deaths: Q2/1871, vol. 2B, p. 263 (certificate).

interred in the paupers' plot, but in consecrated ground.[135] Her estranged brother-in-law-cum-husband William Betsworth died in 1878 of a head injury suffered when falling from a ladder.[136] He was fifty-eight. Louisa Hughes (*q.v.*) – she who had married William despite having at least one living husband, and to whom William had returned following his marriage to Harriet and Louisa's to seaman Johns – outlived both William and Harriet. To make ends meet, and perhaps for company, she took in a boarder; and like Harriet, she ended her days in the workhouse, dying there in 1890 of senile dementia, aged sixty.[137]

Styling herself 'widow', Rosalinda Matthias (*q.v.*) outlived her bigamous husband James and his unlawful wife. Her younger daughter Sarah married a dockyard fitter by whom she had at least six children. For over a decade grandmother Rosalinda lived with the growing family, listed in the census as 'laundress' but no doubt providing childcare support within the home.[138] In 1889, aged seventy-five, she died of 'moribus cordis' (heart disease), a reference to 'hemiplegia' suggesting she had at some stage suffered a stroke.[139]

Phthisis, typhoid, heart disease and exhaustion are recurrent themes, but accident too played a part. Warrant officer's widow Abigail Patterson, mother of AB John Patterson, HMS *Excellent*, met her end by domestic fire.[140] Just short of her sixtieth birthday she was found 'dead and severely burnt' in the back parlour of her Guildford Street house, the inquest returning a finding of death by suffocation.[141] A similar end awaited Phoebe Greenleaf Saxton Page (*q.v.*), but not until her offspring had extended the family's naval connections. At her childhood home in Gloucester Street, where two children of her first marriage were born, Phoebe had three more children and twenty-two years of unlawful married life with her late sister's husband. Of the children of her first marriage, Richard Saxton became a gunner; his sister Phoebe Joanna married first a boatswain RN, then a seaman. Elizabeth Kate Page, Phoebe's daughter by Richard Page, married a private in the Marines; and both James and Charles John Page served in

---

[135] PHC: G/BBK4/3, p. 477 n. 19084.
[136] E&W Deaths: Q1/1879, vol. 2B, p. 310 (certificate).
[137] 1881 census: RG11/1141, fol. 107, p. 50; E&W Deaths: Q2/1890, vol. 2B, p. 313 (Louisa 'Betsworth', certificate); Portsmouth History Centre (PHC) Portsmouth, Hampshire, Portsmouth Burials, Parish Burials, PHC G/BBK4/8 (1891), p. 192 n. 52128.
[138] 1871 census: RG10/1128, fol. 140, p. 21.
[139] E&W Deaths: Q2/1889, vol. 2B, p. 257 (certificate).
[140] ADM 27/110/166/1397.
[141] *H/Tel*, 4 November 1854, p. 5 col. A; E&W Deaths: Q4/1854, vol. 2B, p. 286; CHU3/1E/32, p. 106 n. 847.

the Navy.¹⁴² Richard Page's death in 1868 may have forced a downshifting, for by 1871 the widowed Phoebe was living in Cross Street; in telling the enumerator she was a 'seaman's wife' she revealed how she continued to define herself.¹⁴³ By 1881 she had moved house, admitted to widowhood, taken in lodgers, and of her children only Charles and his sister Elizabeth were still at home.¹⁴⁴ Ten years later still she was 'living on [a] government annuity' (naval pension), aided by a 20-year-old 'domestic companion'; in 1893 she was once more in Gloucester Street, and dead.¹⁴⁵ The coroner gave cause of death as 'exhaustion and pneumonia following burns accidentally sustained.'¹⁴⁶

Phoebe was the last of our Greenleaf women to die, but not the only one to meet a sad end. Thrice-married Joanna Charlo, formerly Barrow, formerly Fleming, was forty-two when her third (and bigamous) husband, 56-year-old James Charlo, succumbed in Haslar Hospital to 'dropsy of long duration'.¹⁴⁷ Five years later the 1871 census found Joanna, occupation 'House Keeper', listed as 'visitor' to a Cross Street bootmaker a few doors down from Phoebe.¹⁴⁸ She may have acquired something of the craft, for the 1891 census recorded her as a (pauper) shoemaker in the workhouse, to which institution she had been admitted two years earlier.¹⁴⁹ Described as 'the widow of ____ [sic] Charlo whose rank or occupation is unknown to the informant' [workhouse matron], in 1891 Joanna died of 'paralysis, certified.'¹⁵⁰ She was seventy-four, and had spent her final four years a pauper inmate.¹⁵¹ She outlived by more than thirty years her husband's

---

[142] ADM 29/104/8/14619a; CHU6/1B/1, p. 181 n. 362; CHU6, 1B/1, p. 224 n. 447 ('Phebe Johanna'); CHU3/1D/84, p. 184 n. 367; National Archives (TNA) Kew, Admiralty: Royal Navy Register of Seamen's Services, ADM 188 (1853–1924), for ADM 188/273/167557.

[143] E&W Deaths: Q2/1868, vol. 2B, p. 264 (certificate); 1871 census: RG10/1133, fol. 17, p. 27.

[144] 1881 census: RG11/1147, fol. 84, p. 26.

[145] 1891 census: RG12/862, fol. 90, p. 23; ADM 6/316; ADM 6/320.

[146] E&W Deaths: Q2/1893, vol. 2B, p. 276 (certificate).

[147] E&W Deaths: Q4/1866, vol. 2B, p. 284 (certificate); Portsmouth History Centre (PHC) Portsmouth, Hampshire, Portsmouth Burials, Parish Burials, PHC G/BBK/4/2 (1866), p. 441 n. 12283; CHU3/1E/38, p. 165 n. 1305.

[148] 1871 census: RG10/1133, fol. 14, p. 22.

[149] 1891 census: RG12/860, fol. 96, p. 14; Portsmouth History Centre (PHC) Portsmouth, Portsea Island Poor Law Union, Portsmouth Board of Guardians Workhouse Register, PHC BG/W2/2 (1892–5).

[150] E&W Deaths: Q3/1891, vol. 2B, p. 235 (certificate); PHC: G/BBK4/8, p. 297 n. 53492; CHU3/1E/46, p. 170 n. 1360. Joanna was baptised in May 1824 (CHU3/1B/11, p. 145 n. 353).

[151] The workhouse misinformed the registrar that Joanna was sixty-nine years old, this age appearing on her death certificate.

lawful wife Sarah, who in 1857 had expired of phthisis, age forty. Like Joanna, Sarah died in the workhouse. Making no reference to her still-living husband James, her death certificate described her as 'Almswoman and domestic servant'.[152]

In union house records, Joanna's 'shoemaker' description may simply have captured her last paid work prior to admission. It was not necessarily a full-time occupation, and she was clearly not earning enough to support herself. If as a naval widow she were receiving a pension, that too was inadequate to her needs. Her latter years stand testament to the vulnerability of seamen's widows having neither trade nor occupation of their own, and the economic insecurity which often followed their husbands' deaths. Their careful budgeting, practised over years when dependent upon an allotment amounting to no more than a moiety of their men's already low pay, was in widowhood insufficient to protect them from dependence upon the parish, and being laid to rest in a pauper's plot.

---

[152] E&W Deaths: Q1/1857, vol. 2B, p. 238 (certificate); CHU3/1E/33, p. 167 n. 1356 ('Charlord').

# CONCLUSION

Years have passed since Nicholas Rodger highlighted the lack of attention paid to 'the female half of the naval community as a whole … the wives and mothers who stayed at home'.[1] Since then, a few articles and books have considered naval women as part of composite studies of English seamen, as seamen's women who went to sea, as wives of naval officers. This book, however, is concerned solely with the female dependants of lower-deck Royal Navy seamen, their individual stories, living conditions and lives on shore.

We think we already know who (or what) these women were, for captured over the centuries in cartoons, etchings, ballads and jokes, their prevailing image, widely disseminated via a variety of media, has been that of porttown whore. Little has been done to dim or deconstruct that image. Some writers have endorsed it, one declaring that seamen's wives 'often resorted to prostitution during their husbands' absence', yet presenting no statistical evidence or individual case study to substantiate that claim.[2] This follows a recognised pattern. To borrow from Hughes, 'women aren't allowed to be characters in history, they have to be stereotypes.'[3] The stereotyping of seamen's women as prostitutes ignores both the women's individuality, and the less sensational but fundamental aspects of their condition. Theirs were lives in which there were children to be fed and educated, loaves to be baked, floors to be washed, hems mended, households and budgets managed, relatives to care for and bury, and all without the support of their menfolk. That wider day-to-day actuality emerges here; and yes, part of it involves prostitution. To say so is not a cop-out, or to collude with the caricaturists; to say otherwise is to ignore grim actuality. From correlation of admiralty and parish evidence this book concludes that many naval women will have had no choice but to derive income from the sex trade. Going further, it proposes that the naval community's collective experience may

---

[1] Rodger, *Command of the Ocean*, p. 407.
[2] Stark, *Female Tars*, pp. 27–31.
[3] Bettany Hughes, 'Why Were Women Written Out of History? An Interview with Bettany Hughes' History In-Depth (English Heritage, 2016) <https://www.english-heritage.org.uk/visit/inspire-me/blog/blog-posts/why-were-women-written-out-of-history-an-interview-with-bettany-hughes/> [accessed 22 April 2024].

have been dire enough to reshape moral codes governing naval women's survival strategies. Recognising – often sharing – the enormous challenge of managing on their men's 'half-pay' (a misnomer, since many received but a fraction of that fraction), naval women could not afford to ostracise those among them who turned to prostitution, for such was the precarity of their condition, any one of them might find herself facing exactly that necessity, in which case she would need – or at least hope for – the understanding and support of her peers. That the naval community did not ostracise or expel its moral transgressors was enough to brand seamen's women generally as fellow travellers on the road to ruin. In a damn-one, damn-all approach the wider community condemned them, depicting them as poxed and drunken whores, in court singularising them as 'a sailor's wife', 'a seaman's woman', thereby cementing their association with criminality. Yes, there were seamen's women who, in return for money, slept with men other than their husbands; and there were seamen willing to pay for sex; yet it was the wider, civilian community – land-based, waged, striving for respectability – which, via the coin it slipped into a port town prostitute's palm, was the income-source of the very women it condemned. Herein lay the great hypocrisy. The sex trade was not exclusive to one section of society. Its punters and purveyors were both civilian and naval. For society to focus only on the naval purveyors, and then to depict seamen's women generally as prostitutes, was to exploit an easy target, deflecting attention from non-naval participants in a reviled exchange. Seamen's women 'took the heat', leaving other participants in the shadows.

They may have – must have – participated in the sex trade; but the key feature of their wider day-to-day actuality is not prostitution. It is that they were ordinary women living among ordinary women, alongside other ordinary members of the community. To augment their household incomes they held down ordinary jobs – laundress, sempstress, char – which required no special training or expensive equipment, but which equally left hidden their talents and business potential.[4] They did ordinary things, going into debt, getting drunk, arguing with their neighbours, moving house, taking in lodgers. Other writers have shown how women were responsible for budget management, for supporting their children and relatives, and for contributing to the care and protection of other women and their families.[5] The survival strategies of naval women show them shouldering the same responsibilities; but even the modestly-comported naval wife, whose household, choices and conduct were unremarkable by contemporary

---

[4] Humphries, *Childhood and Child Labour*, p. 110.
[5] For example, Tebbutt, *Making Ends Meet*; Ross, 'Survival Networks'; Chinn, *They Worked all their Lives*.

standards, stood apart from other women. She did so by virtue of choosing a sailor-husband. This decision was life-changing. Until that point she may have been a naval daughter, well used to a father-breadwinner going away for months at a time; but whereas she was not responsible for her father's occupation and absences, in agreeing to become a naval wife she herself chose a form of married life which mid-Victorian society regarded as abnormal. The respectable wife's role was to tend her spouse, not live apart from him, and to accept his authority within the home, not assume that authority for herself. Even if her man were home, she did not escape censure. A wife's character reflected that of her husband, hence at worst the naval wife took on by proxy the sailor's reputation as promiscuous drunkard, brawler and spendthrift; at best she appeared to condone it. And all this was due to her choosing a seaman for a husband. She brought it on herself, must have wanted it.

If our understanding of the seaman's woman goes no further than this, we join her contemporaries in judging her solely by her choice of husband. To do so is myopic and exclusionary. It ignores the fact that, like seamen's women in other port towns and of other generations, the women of this study were more than wives, mothers, sisters. More than relatives, they were absolutes. Each had her own personality, background, challenges, lived experience. Apart from their womanhood, the common denominator defining and uniting them was their extraordinary resilience. They lived in the same streets, inhabited the same crumbling houses as their civilian peers; but whereas those peers had husbands on hand to take decisions and share the burden, seamen's wives managed unaided. They took decisions normally the province of husbands. They cared for their families, managed their households, and sometimes made mistakes, got careless or took risks. They did everything their civilian neighbours did, but without a husband to help, direct, protect or rescue them. From a position somewhere between deserted wife and widow they survived and coped, their husbands' financial support consisting of less than half an already poor wage.[6] They survived in a judgemental, sometimes hostile society, a society in which 'sailor's wife' was a term laden with ambiguity, both synonym for sexual availability and licentiousness, and a joke. It is not their sexual activity but their ordinariness which makes these seamen's women exceptional. They were extraordinary for being, despite everything, so ordinary.

That ordinariness was far from uniform. We see some moving house while others stayed put. Some adopted living arrangements unusual for the time. They fostered seamen's motherless children, brawled in the

---

[6] Valerie Burton, 'Fish/Wives: gender, representation and agency in coastal communities', *Journal of Women in Culture and Society*, 37:3 (2012), 528–36, at p. 532.

street, sewed in dim rooms, stole from their employers, undertook church work. Their chances of having children of their own were reduced by their husbands' repeated and lengthy absences; and when conception led to a birth, and the survival of a living child, they faced the challenge of raising it largely unaided. Little wonder that many are found living with parents, especially with their still-married or widowed mothers who in numerous instances were themselves seamen's wives, or had been until their husbands quit sea service, or died. This marked tendency for seamen's daughters to marry seamen, for seamen's sons to become seamen and marry seamen's daughters, suggests a near-tribal cohesion within a wider community possessed of an ambivalent attitude to its naval component. Whereas the naval community sometimes drew on the civilian community for its marital partners, the civilian community emphatically preferred its own kind. Young civilian men distanced themselves from the naval community with its younger-than-average brides, its questionable morals and legendary love of drink. It is far from frivolous to wonder whether civilian grooms suspected marriageable naval daughters of being likely to exhibit a lack of submissiveness unbecoming the modest mid-Victorian wife. Submissiveness and dependence were of little use to the seaman's woman. As Light said of her forebears, 'These nineteenth-century women had to wear the trousers. Without their men they got on or they went under.'[7]

Got on they did. With no more education than any other working-class urban woman, and on half a pay packet at most, they 'stayed at home, bringing up small children, earning their living as best they might while their menfolk were at sea, enduring years of absence and uncertainty.'[8] For some, the absence and uncertainty corroded the affection that had bound them to their husbands in the first place. Couples parted, remarried without waiting for a spouse to die. Presenting to the world as 'Mr and Mrs', they cohabited in order to appear respectable, or because the risk and shame of arrest for bigamy were too great.

In a society which prized respectability, the seaman's wife was hobbled by her association with Jack Tar's reputation of past centuries. When positive recognition finally came her way, it too came by association with her hero husband; the recognition and admiration were still not hers alone.[9] Toward the end of the nineteenth century she would see her husband's trademark sailor collar adopted as a mark of status by affluent women enjoying no connection to naval life, and sons of pork butchers and bank

---

[7] Light, *Common People*, p. 188.
[8] Rodger, *Command of the Ocean*, p. 407.
[9] Margarette Lincoln, *Representing the Royal Navy: British sea power, 1750–1815* (Aldershot, 2002), p. 32.

clerks wearing sailor-suits as if being 'brought up to sea'.[10] If pork butchers and bank clerks blenched at the prospect of their sons joining the Navy, or marrying a seaman's daughter, it only added to the irony.

This book's preface observed that 'it is the business of the historian to plunge into the deep waters of the past and to bring up vanished lives.'[11] Fresh evidence obtained from original source material has answered the 'What?' question, so that in bricks and mortar, bread and water, rent, rates and living arrangements, these women's lives are now revealed. The 'So what?' question, too, has in many respects been answered, in that we see how these women's lives contrast and compare with those of their civilian neighbours, and with other women of nineteenth-century Britain. In one respect the question remains unanswered. We cannot know the toll that naval family life took on these women, for almost nothing survives to tell their experiences in their own words. Without their voices, their words, we can only part-fill what Rodger termed the 'enormous void of ignorance' blighting our perception of 'the female half of the naval community as a whole'.[12] From the evidence available we nevertheless see enough to know that these were ordinary women doing extraordinary things. On this basis we may assert that whatever their backgrounds, living arrangements or means of making ends meet, in sustaining self and family and home, seamen's women did indeed embody a 'remarkable naval effort'.[13]

---

[10] Unknown author, 'The Origins of Nautical Fashion in Britain' (Royal Museums Greenwich, n.d.) <https://www.rmg.co.uk/stories/topics/origins-nautical-fashion-britain> [accessed 22 April 2024].
[11] Rodger, 'I want to be an Admiral'.
[12] Rodger, *Command of the Ocean*, p. 407.
[13] Lincoln, *Naval Wives*, p. 15.

# BIBLIOGRAPHY

### PRIMARY SOURCES:
### MANUSCRIPT AND ARCHIVAL COLLECTIONS

Kew, National Archives (TNA), Admiralty and Predecessors: Office of the Director General of the Medical Department of the Navy and Predecessors: Medical Journals, ADM 101, 1785–1963

——, Admiralty, and Ministry of Defence, Navy Department: Correspondence and Papers, ADM 1, 1660–1976

——, Admiralty: Circulars 1844–57, ADM 7/890

——, Admiralty: Miscellanea: History of the Allotment System in the Navy ('Pitcairn Report'), ADM 7/719, 1858

——, Admiralty: Officers' Service Records (Series III), ADM 196, 1798–1870

——, Admiralty: Royal Marines: Description Books, Woolwich Division, ADM 158, 1750–1940

——, Admiralty: Royal Navy Continuous Service Engagement Books, ADM 139, 1853–72

——, Admiralty: Royal Navy Register of Seamen's Services, ADM 188, 1853–1924

——, Admiralty: Royal Navy, Royal Marines, Coastguard and Related Services: Officers' and Ratings' Service Records (Series II), ADM 29, 1802–1919

——, Admiralty: Ships' Musters (Series III), ADM 38, 1793–1878

——, Admiralty: Supplementary Logs and Journals of Ships on Exploration, ADM 55, 1757–1904

——, Hampshire: Gosport, Middle Street Chapel (Wesleyan): Births & Baptisms, England & Wales Non-Conformist Births And Baptisms, Parish Baptisms, TNA/RG/4/1081, 1823

——, 'Medical and surgical Journal of Her Majesty's Ship *Fox* for 19 July 1850 and the 31 July 1851 by Mr John M Minter, Surgeon, during which time the said ship was employed in the East Indies', ADM 101/101/2, 1850–51

——, 'Medical and surgical journal of HMS *Resolute* for 28 February 1850 to 9 October 1851 by R A Bradford, Surgeon, during which time the said ship was employed in a searching expedition to the Arctic Regions', ADM 101/117/3, 1850–51

——, 'Medical journal of HMS *Thetis* for 1 July 1851 to 30 September 1852 by John Douglas, Surgeon, during which time the said ship was employed in the Pacific Station', ADM 101/123/4, 1851–52

——, 'Medical journal of HMS *Vengeance*, from 1 July 1852 to 30 July 1853, by William Graham, Surgeon, during which time the said ship was employed in the Mediterranean Station', ADM 101/124/3, 1851–52

——, Navy Board, and Admiralty, Accountant General's Department: Registers of Allotments and Allotment Declarations, ADM 27, 1792–1852

*Bibliography*

—, Navy Board, Navy Pay Office and Admiralty, Accountant General's Department: Seamen's Wills, ADM 48, 1786–1882

—, Navy Board: Navy Pay Office: Ships' Pay Books (Series III), ADM 35, 1777–1832

—, War Office: Secretary-at-War, Out-Letters, Greenwich Pensions, WO 4/890, 1851–53

London, Wellcome Collection, Camberwell House Asylum catalogue, Vol. 2: male and female patients admitted March 1847 – May 1850, MS. 6220, 1847–50

Portsmouth, National Museum of the Royal Navy (NMRN), John Ford, letter to Sarah Evans, NMRN 353/85/13, 13 July 1845

—, John Ford, letter to Sarah Evans, NMRN 353/85/17, 18 January 1847

—, John Ford, letter to Sarah Evans, NMRN 353/85/18, 28 April 1847

—, William Simpson, letter to wife, NMRN 627/86/11, 1 June 1857

—, William Simpson, letter to wife, NMRN 627/86/9, 19 December 1856

Portsmouth, Portsmouth History Centre (PHC), Portsea Island Poor Law Union, Rate Books, PHC DT/R/2/454-7, 1851

Portsmouth, Portsmouth History Centre (PHC), BG/FC4/2: Portsea Island Poor Law Union, Overseers and Collectors Summary Accounts for the Parish of Portsmouth, 1836–48

—, Borough of Portsmouth Police, Police Record Book, PHC SB/DF/P/1, 1843–49

—, Borough of Portsmouth, Calendar of Prisoners, general quarter sessions of the Peace, PHC S7/1, 1842–54

—, Ground Plan of Primrose Alley, Portsea, from Slum Inspection Reports, PHC PMRS/DV/9B/1, n. 145, 1929

—, Hampshire, Portsmouth Burials, Parish Burials, PHC G/PGC4/3, 1849

—, Hampshire, Portsmouth Burials, Parish Burials, PHC G/BBK4/1, 1857

—, Hampshire, Portsmouth Burials, Parish Burials, PHC G/BBK4/2, 1863

—, Hampshire, Portsmouth Burials, Parish Burials, PHC G/BBK4/2, 1866

—, Hampshire, Portsmouth Burials, Parish Burials, PHC G/BBK4/3, 1869

—, Hampshire, Portsmouth Burials, Parish Burials, PHC G/BBK4/5, 1880

—, Hampshire, Portsmouth Burials, Parish Burials, PHC G/BBK4/8, 1891

—, Hampshire, Portsmouth Burials, Parish Burials, PHC G/BBK4/10, 1898

—, Ordnance Survey, 1:500 scale map of Portsea, showing Havant Street (upper part), PHC 114A/OS2/15/1, Hampshire Sheet LXXXIII.7.19 (B9), 1864

—, Ordnance Survey, 1:500 scale map of Portsea, showing Havant Street (lower part), PHC 114A/OS2/21/2, Hampshire Sheet LXXXIII.7.24 (B10), 1864

—, Ordnance Survey, 1:500 scale map of Portsea, showing Hobbs Court and Dean Street, PHC 114A/OS2/23, Hampshire Sheet LXXXIII.7.25 (C10), 1864

—, Portsea Island Poor Law Union, Minute Books of Board of Guardians, BG/M/1/1, 1838–41

—, Portsea Island Poor Law Union, Minute Books of Board of Guardians, BG/M/1/2, 1841–46

—, Portsea Island Poor Law Union, Minute Books of Board of Guardians, BG/M/1/3, 1851–55

—, Portsea Island Poor Law Union, Portsmouth Board of Guardians Workhouse Register, PHC BG/W2/2, 1892–95

—, Slum Inspection Report on Primrose Alley, Portsea, PMRS/DV/9B/1, n. 145, 1929

—, Slum Inspection Reports, PHC PMRS/DV/9B/1, 1929

—, Valentine Letter, PHC 181A/1, 1841

## PRINTED PRIMARY SOURCES: CONTEMPORARY BOOKS AND ARTICLES

Bosanquet, Helen Dendy, *Rich and Poor* (London: Macmillan and Co., 1896)
Durand, Godefroy, '"Home Again": a Sketch on Board the Discovery at Portsmouth', *The Graphic* (London, 11 November 1876), p. 469
Gaskell, P., *The Manufacturing Population of England* (London: Baldwin and Cradock, 1833)
Gordon, William John, *A Chat about the Navy* (London: Simpkin, 1891)
Gore, Montague, *Sailors' Homes* (London: G. Norman, 1852)
Holman, Thomas, *Life in the Royal Navy, by 'a ranker'* (Portsmouth: publisher unknown, 1891)
Hooppell, R.E., *The statistical results of the Contagious Diseases Act as deduced from all the parliamentary papers which have been issued upon the subject, from the commencement of the Acts to the present time* (London: Tweedie & Co., 1871)
Hunt, *Directory of Hampshire and Dorsetshire, 1852* (Weymouth: Benson and Barling, 1852)
Admiral Charles Knowles ('Philo Nauticus'), 'A proposal for the encouragement of seamen to serve more readily in His Majesty's navy for preventing of desertion, supporting their wives and families, and for the easier and quieter government of His Majesty's ships' (London, 1758)
Pinckard, George, *Notes on the West Indies* (London: Longman, Hurst, Rees, and Orme, 1806)
Post Office, *Hampshire Trades Directory* (Portsmouth: publisher unknown, 1847)
Skene, Felicia Mary F., *The Inheritance of Evil; or, the consequences of marrying a deceased wife's sister* (London: Joseph Masters, 1849)
Slater, *Directory of Hampshire* (s.l.: publisher unknown, 1851)
Stead, W.T., 'The Maiden Tribute of Modern Babylon', *Pall Mall Gazette* (6 and 8 July 1885), pp 2–4
Unknown reporter, 'Bow-Street', *Express (London)* (London, 25 August 1852), p. 4
—, 'New Baths, Washhouses, and Laundry for Portsmouth', *The Builder* (London, 17 October 1874), p. 865
—, 'Serious Charge Against a Clergyman', *Hull Packet* (Hull, 4 August 1848), p. 6

## PRINTED PRIMARY SOURCES: OFFICIAL DOCUMENTS AND PUBLICATIONS

*Act for Marriages in England*, 6 & 7 Will. IV, c. 85 (1836)
*Convict Prisons Act*, 16 & 17 Vict., c. 121 (1853)
*Deceased Brother's Widow's Marriage Act*, 11 & 12 Geo. V, c. 24 (1921)
*Deceased Wife's Sister's Marriage Act*, 7 Edw. VII, c. 47 (1907)
*Manning of the Army and Navy Act*, 37 Geo. III, c. 4 (1796)
*Manning of the Navy Act*, 35 Geo. III, c. 5 (1795)
*Marriage Act*, 4 Geo. IV, c. 76 (1823)
*Marriage Act*, 5 & 6 Will. IV, c. 54 (1835)
*Matrimonial Causes Act*, 20 Vict., c. 85 (1857)
*Mutiny Act*, 7 Will. IV and 1 Vict., c. 7 (1837)
*Naval Deserters Act*, 10 & 11 Vict., c. 62 (1847)
*Naval Enlistment Act*, 16 & 17 Vict., c. 69 (1853)

*Navy Act*, 1 Geo. II, st. 2, c. 14 (1727)
*Navy Act*, 31 Geo. II, c. 10 (1758)
*Navy Act*, 26 Geo. III, c. 63 (1786)
*Navy Act*, 46 Geo. III, c. 127 (1806)
*Navy Pay Act*, 4 & 5 Will. IV, c. 25 (1834)
*Navy Pay, Etc., Act*, 17 & 18 Vict., c. 19 (1854)
*Offences Against the Person Act*, 1 Vict., c. 85 (1837)
*Pawnbrokers Act*, 39 & 40, Geo. III, c. 99 (1800)
*Pay of the Navy Act*, 11 Geo. IV & 1 Will. IV, c. 20 (1830)
*Penal Servitude Act*, 16 & 17 Vict., c. 99 (1853)
*Penal Servitude Act*, 20 & 21 Vict., c. 3 (1857)
*Town Police Clauses Act*, 10 & 11 Vict., c. 89 (1847)
*Vagrancy Act*, 5 Geo. IV, c. 83 (1824)
*Vagrancy Act*, 1 & 2 Vict., c. 38 (1838)
*Wages and Prize Money in the Navy Act*, 49 Geo. IV, c. 108 (1809)
Allen, Joseph, *The New Navy List* (Whitehall: Parker, Furnivall and Parker, 1850)
—, *The New Navy List* (Whitehall: Parker, Furnivall and Parker, 1851)
Hardwicke, Earl, *et al.*, *Report of the Commissioners appointed to Inquire into the Best Means of Manning the Navy* (London: HMSO, 1859)
House of Commons Debate, Ministry of Defence: Royal Navy Ratings (Allotments), 13, cc311-2W (23 November 1981)
House of Commons Paper no. 295, Navy: 'Return of the Number of Seamen, and Petty Officers of the Royal Navy and Marines, who allot a Portion of their Pay for the Support of their Families and Others; and showing the Place of Residence of such Persons', XXXIX, 13 (1857–58)
House of Commons: Report of the Commissioners appointed to Inquire into the Best Means of Manning the Navy, 1859, [Command Paper] 2469
Mann, Horace, *Religious Worship in England and Wales* (London, 1854)
Poor Law Commissioners, *Order Prohibiting Outdoor Relief* (London, 1844)
Rawlinson, Robert, *Report to the General Board of Health on a Preliminary Inquiry into the Sewerage, Drainage, and Supply of Water, and the Sanitary Condition of the Inhabitants or the Borough of Portsmouth in the County of Hampshire* (London, 1850)
Royal Navy, *The Queen's Regulations for the Government of Her Majesty's Naval Service* (Whitehall, 1844)

## PRINTED PRIMARY SOURCES: NEWSPAPERS AND PERIODICALS

*Express (London)* (London: William King Hales, 1846–69), 25 August 1852
*Hampshire Telegraph, and Sussex Chronicle* (Portsmouth: publisher unknown, 1799–1961), multiple issues
*Hull Packett* (Hull: George Prince, 1799–1886), 4 August 1848
*Pall Mall Gazette* (London: Smith, Elder & Co., 1865–1923), 6 and 8 July 1885
*The Builder* (London: Wyman and Sons, 1853–1966), 17 October 1874
*The Graphic* (London: Illustrated Newspapers Ltd., 1869–1932), 11 November 1876

## SECONDARY SOURCES

Acton, William, *Prostitution* (New York: Praeger, 1968, ed. Peter Fryer)
—, *Prostitution Considered in its Moral, Social, and Sanitary Aspects, in London and Other Large Cities and Garrison Towns: with Proposals for the Control and Prevention of its Attendant Evils* (London: Frank Cass, 1972, reprint of 1870 edition)
Allen, Michael, *Charles Dickens' Childhood* (Basingstoke: Macmillan, 1988)
Anderson, Michael, *Family Structure in Nineteenth Century Lancashire* (Cambridge: Cambridge University Press, 1971)
—, 'Households, Families and Individuals: some preliminary results from the national sample from the census of Great Britain 1851', *Continuity & Change*, 3:3 (1988), 421–38
—, 'The Social Implications of Demographic Change', in F.M.L. Thompson (ed.), *The Cambridge Social History of Britain 1750–1950* (Cambridge: Cambridge University Press, 1990), pp. 1–70
—, 'The Social Position of Spinsters in mid-Victorian Britain', *Journal of Family History*, 9:4 (1984), 377–83
—, 'The Study of Family Structure', in E.A. Wrigley (ed.), *Nineteenth-Century Society: essays in the use of quantitative methods for the study of social data* (Cambridge: Cambridge University Press, 1972), pp. 47–81
—, 'What Can the Mid-Victorian Censuses Tell Us About Variations in Married Women's Employment?', *Local Population Studies*, 62 (1999), 9–30
Anderson, Olive, 'The Incidence of Civil Marriage in Victorian England and Wales', *Past & Present*, 69 (1975), 50–87
Armstrong, W.A., 'The Interpretation of the Census Enumerators' Books for Victorian Towns', in H.J. Dyos (ed.), *The Study of Urban History* (London: Arnold, 1968), pp. 67–85
—, 'A Note on the Household Structure of mid-Nineteenth Century York in Comparative Perspective', in Peter Laslett and Richard Wall (eds), *Household and Family in Past Time: comparative studies in the size and structure of the domestic group over the last three centuries* (Cambridge: Cambridge University Press, 1972), pp. 205–14
August, Andrew, *Poor Women's Lives: Gender, Work, and Poverty in Late-Victorian London* (London: Fairleigh Dickinson University Press, 1999)
Bailey, Joanne, '"I Dye by Inches": locating wife beating in the concept of the privatisation of marriage and violence in eighteenth-century England', *Social History*, 31:3 (2006), 273–94
—, *Unquiet Lives: Marriage and Marriage Breakdown in England, 1660–1800* (Cambridge: Cambridge University Press, 2003)
Banks, J.A., 'Population Change and the Victorian City', *Victorian Studies*, 11:3 (1968), 277–89
Bartley, Paula, *The Changing Role of Women, 1815–1914* (London: Hodder & Stoughton, 1996)
—, *Prostitution: Prevention and Reform in England, 1860–1914* (London: Routledge, 2000)

Baugh, Daniel A., 'The Eighteenth-Century Navy as a National Institution, 1690–1815', in J.R. Hill (ed.), *The Oxford Illustrated History of the Royal Navy* (Oxford: Oxford University Press, 1995), pp. 120–60

Baynham, Henry *Before the Mast: Naval Ratings of the Nineteenth Century* (London: Hutchinson, 1971)

—, *From the Lower Deck: The Old Navy, 1780–1840* (London: Hutchinson, 1969)

Beattie, John M., 'The Criminality of Women in Eighteenth-Century England', *Journal of Social History*, 8:4 (1975), 80–116

Bell, Karl, 'Civic Spirits? Ghost Lore and Civic Narratives in Nineteenth Century Portsmouth', *Cultural and Social History*, 11:1 (2014), 51–68

Benson, John, *The Working Class in Britain, 1850–1939* (London: I.B. Tauris, 2003)

Bosanquet, Helen, 'Marriage in East London', in Ellen Ross (ed.), *Slum Travelers: ladies and London poverty, 1860–1920* (Berkeley, Calif.: University of California Press, 2007), pp. 64–71

Boulton, Jeremy, '"It Is Extreme Necessity That Makes Me Do This": some "survival strategies" of pauper households in London's West End during the early eighteenth century', *International Review of Social History*, 45:8 (2000), 47–69

—, '"Turned into the street with my children destitute of everything": the payment of rent and the London poor, 1600–1850', in Joanne McEwan and Pamela Sharpe (eds), *Accommodating Poverty: the housing and living arrangements of the English poor, 1600–1850* (London: Palgrave Macmillan, 2011), pp. 25–49

Boyden, Peter, *Tommy Atkins' Letters: the History of the British Army Postal Service from 1795* (London: National Army Museum, 1990)

Brown, P.E., 'The Age at Menarche', *Journal of Epidemiology and Community Health*, 20:1 (1966), 9–14

Brundage, Anthony, *The English Poor Laws, 1700–1930* (Basingstoke: Palgrave, 2002)

Bryant, Roger, *Don't Touch the Holy Joe: Father Dolling's Battle for Landport and St. Agatha's Church* (Hampshire: Ragged Right, 1995)

Burnett, John, *A History of the Cost of Living* (Harmondsworth: Penguin, 1969)

—, *Plenty and Want: a Social History of Diet in England from 1815 to the Present Day* (London: Nelson, 1966)

Burton, Valerie, 'Fish/Wives: gender, representation and agency in coastal communities', *Journal of Women in Culture and Society*, 37:3 (2012), 528–36

—, 'The Myth of Bachelor Jack: masculinity, patriarchy and seafaring labour', in Colin D. Howell and Richard J. Twomey (eds), *Jack Tar in History: essays in the history of maritime life and labour* (Fredericton, N.B.: Acadiensis Press, 1991), pp. 179–98

Capper, Henry D., *Aft - from the Hawsehole: Sixty-two Years of Sailors' Evolution* (London: Faber & Gwyer, 1927)

Carew, Anthony, *The Lower Deck of the Royal Navy 1900–1939: the Invergordon Mutiny in Perspective* (Manchester: Manchester University Press, 1981)

Chandler, Joan, *Women without Husbands: an Exploration of the Margins of Marriage* (London: Macmillan, 1991)

Chesney, Kellow, *The Victorian Underworld* (London: Maurice Temple Smith Ltd, 1970)

Chinn, Carl, *They Worked all their Lives: Women of the Urban Poor in England, 1880–1939* (Lancaster: Carnegie Publishing, 2006)

Clark, Anna, *Women's Silence, Men's Violence: Sexual Assault in England, 1770–1845* (London: Pandora, 1987)

Clayton, Tim, *Tars: the Men who Made Britain Rule the Waves* (London: Hodder & Stoughton, 2007)

Coats, Ann, 'Foreword', in Helen; Watt and Anne Hawkins (eds), *Letters of Seamen in the Wars with France, 1793–1815* (Woodbridge: Boydell Press, 2016), pp. x–xii

Cock, Randolph and N.A.M. Rodger, *A Guide to the Naval Records in the National Archives of the UK* (London: University of London, 2008)

Colledge, J.J., *Ships of the Royal Navy: an Historical Index* (Newton Abbot: David & Charles, 1969)

—, *Ships of the Royal Navy: the Complete Record of all Fighting Ships of the Royal Navy from the Fifteenth Century to the Present* (London: Greenhill, 1987)

Conley, Mary A., *From Jack Tar to Union Jack: Representing Naval Manhood in the British Empire, 1870–1918* (Manchester: Manchester University Press, 2009)

Cowlard, Keith A., 'The Identification of Social (Class) Areas and Their Place in Nineteenth-Century Urban Development', *Transactions of the Institute of British Geographers*, 4:2 (1979), 239–57

Cox, David J., '"Trying to Get a Good One": bigamy offences in England and Wales, 1850–1950', *Plymouth Law and Criminal Justice Review*, 1 (2012), 1–32

Crafts, N.F.R., 'Average Age at First Marriage for Women in Mid-Nineteenth-Century England and Wales: a cross-section study', *Population Studies*, 21:1 (1978), 21–5

Cramer, James, *A History of the Police of Portsmouth: the Story of the Constables, Tythingmen, Watchmen and Other Peace Officers of the Portsmouth Area, from c.1271 to 1967* (Portsmouth: Portsmouth City Council, 1967)

D'Cruze, Shani, *Crimes of Outrage: sex, violence and Victorian working women* (London: UCL Press, 1998)

—, 'Women and The Family', in June Purvis (ed.), *Women's History: Britain, 1850–1945: an introduction* (London: UCL Press, 1995), pp. 51–83

Daunton, M.J., *Progress and Poverty: an economic and social history of Britain, 1700–1850* (Oxford: Oxford University Press, 1995)

—, 'Public Place and Private Space: the Victorian city and the working-class household', in Derek Fraser and Anthony Sutcliffe (eds), *The Pursuit of Urban History* (London: Edward Arnold, 1983), pp. 212–33

Davidoff, Leonore, *The Family Story: blood, contract and intimacy, 1830–1960* (London: Longman, 1999)

—, 'Kinship as a Categorical Concept: a case study of nineteenth-century English siblings', *Journal of Social History*, 39:2 (2005), 411–28

—, 'Mastered for Life: servant and wife in Victorian and Edwardian England', *Journal of Social History*, 7:4 (1974), 406–28

—, 'The Separation of Home and Work? Landladies and lodgers in nineteenth and twentieth century England', in Sandra Burman (ed.), *Fit Work for Women* (London: Croom Helm, in association with Oxford University Women's Studies Committee, 1979), pp. 64–97

Davies, J.D., *Gentlemen and Tarpaulins: the officers and men of the Restoration Navy* (Oxford: Clarendon Press, 1991)

—, 'A Permanent National Maritime Fighting Force, 1642–1869', in J.R. Hill (ed.), *The Oxford Illustrated History of the Royal Navy* (Oxford: Oxford University Press, 1995), pp. 56–79

Dennis, R.J., 'Intercensal Mobility in a Victorian City', *Transactions of the Institute of British Geographers*, 2:3 (1977), 349–63

Dixon, Conrad, *Ships of the Victorian Navy* (Southampton: Ashford Press in association with the Society for Nautical Research, 1987)

Doe, Helen, 'Those They Left Behind: navy wives and widows during the French wars', *Trafalgar Chronicle* (2015), 188–200

Dunae, Patrick, 'Sex, Charades, and Census Records: locating female sex trade workers in a Victorian city', *Histoire Sociale*, 42:84 (2009), 267–97

Dyhouse, Carol, 'Working-Class Mothers and Infant Mortality in England, 1895–1914', *Journal of Social History*, 12:2 (1978), 248–67

Dyos, H.J., 'The Slums of Victorian London', in David Cannadine and David Reeder (eds), *Exploring the Urban Past: essays in urban history* (Cambridge, 1982), pp. 129–53

Dyos, H.J. and Michael Wolff, *The Victorian City: Images and Realities* (London: Routledge & Kegan Paul, 1973)

Earle, Peter, *Sailors: English Merchant Seamen 1650–1775* (London: Methuen, 1998)

Emsley, Clive, *Crime and Society in England, 1750–1900* (London: Longman, 1996)

—, *Crime and Society in England, 1750–1900* (London: Longman, 2010)

Fabb, John, *The Victorian and Edwardian Navy, from old photographs* (London: Batsford, 1976)

Feeley, M.M. and D.L. Little, 'The Vanishing Female: The Decline of Women in the Criminal Process, 1687–1912', *Law & Society Review*, 25:4 (1991), 719–58

Feinstein, Charles H., 'Pessimism Perpetuated: real wages and standard of living in Britain during and after the Industrial Revolution', *Journal of Economic History*, 58:3 (1998), 625–58

Finch, Janet, *Married to the Job: wives' incorporation in men's work* (London: Allen & Unwin, 1983)

Finnegan, Frances, *Poverty and Prostitution: a study of Victorian prostitutes in York* (Cambridge: Cambridge University Press, 1979)

Fowler, Simon, *The Workhouse: the people, the places, the life behind doors* (Barnsley, South Yorkshire: Pen & Sword History, 2014)

Foyster, Elizabeth A., *Marital Violence: an English family history, 1660–1857* (Cambridge: Cambridge University Press, 2005)

Frost, Ginger Suzanne, '"As if she was my own child": cohabitation, community, and the English criminal courts, 1855–1900', *The History of the Family*, 20:4 (2015), 546–62

—, *Living in Sin: Cohabiting as Husband and Wife in Nineteenth-Century England* (Manchester: Manchester University Press, 2008)

Fury, Cheryl A., 'Seamen's Wives and Widows', in Cheryl A. Fury (ed.), *The Social History of English Seamen, 1485–1649* (Woodbridge: Boydell Press, 2012), pp. 253–76

Gauldie, Enid, *Cruel Habitations: a history of working-class housing, 1780–1918* (London: George Allen & Unwin, 1974)

Gill, Ellen, *Naval Families, War and Duty in Britain, 1740–1820* (Woodbridge: Boydell Press, 2016)

Gordon, Eleanor and Gweneth Nair, 'The Myth of the Victorian Patriarchal Family', *The History of the Family*, 7:1 (2002), 125–38

Gradish, Stephen F., *The Manning of the British Navy during the Seven Years' War* (London: Royal Historical Society, 1980)

Green, David R. and Alan G. Parton, 'Slums and Slum Life in Victorian England', in S. Martin Gaskell (ed.), *Slums* (Leicester: Leicester University Press, 1990), pp. 17–91

Gunn, Simon, 'Urbanization', in Chris Williams (ed.), *A Companion to Nineteenth-Century Britain* (Oxford: Blackwell, Historical Association (Great Britain), 2004), pp. 238–52

Hagmark-Cooper, Hanna, *To Be a Sailor's Wife* (Newcastle: Cambridge Scholars, 2012)

Haines, Kevin and Claire Shilton, *Hard Times, Good Times: Tales of Portsea People* (Horndean: Milestone, 1987)

Hall, Lesley A., 'What Shall We Do with the Poxy Sailor? The problem of venereal diseases in the British mercantile marine, 1860–1950', *Journal of Maritime Research*, 6:1 (2004), 113–44

Harwood, Joy, *A Portrait of Portsea, 1840–1940* (Southampton: Ensign, 1990)

Haskell, Patricia, 'Country and Town', in J. Webb, *et al.* (eds), *The Spirit of Portsmouth: a history* (Chichester: Phillimore, 1989), pp. 13–35

Henderson, J. Welles and Rodney P. Carlisle, *Marine Art & Antiques: Jack Tar: a Sailor's Life, 1750–1910* (Woodbridge: Antique Collectors' Club, 1999)

Hewitt, Margaret, *Wives and Mothers in Victorian Industry* (London: Rockliff, 1958)

Higgs, Edward, *Making Sense of the Census Revisited: census records for England and Wales 1801–1901, a handbook for historical researchers* (London: Institute of Historical Research, 2005)

—, 'Women, Occupations and Work in the Nineteenth-Century Censuses', *History Workshop Journal*, 23:1 (1987), 59–80

Hill, Berkeley, 'Illustrations of the Working of the Contagious Diseases Act: Part I, Chatham and Portsmouth', *British Medical Journal*, 2:365 (1867), 583–85

Hill, Bridget, *Women Alone: spinsters in England, 1660–1850* (New Haven, Conn.: Yale University Press, 2001)

Hindmarsh, Bruce, '"Wherever I go I whill right to you"', in Hamish Maxwell-Stewart and Lucy Frost (eds), *Chain Letters: narrating convict lives* (Carlton South, Vic.: Melbourne University Press, 2001), pp. 165–76

Hoppen, K. Theodore, *The Mid-Victorian Generation, 1846–1886* (Oxford: Clarendon Press, 1998)

Houlbrooke, Ralph A., *The English Family, 1450–1700* (London: Longman, 1984)

Hufton, Olwen, 'Women without Men: widows and spinsters in Britain and France in the eighteenth century', *Journal of Family History*, 9:4 (1984), 355–76

Humphries, Jane, 'Care and Cruelty in the Workhouse: children's experiences of residential poor relief in eighteenth- and nineteenth-century England', in Nigel Goose and Katrina Honeyman (eds), *Childhood and Child Labour in Industrial England: diversity and agency, 1750–1914* (Farnham, Surrey: Ashgate Publishing, 2013), pp. 115–34

—, *Childhood and Child Labour in the British Industrial Revolution* (Cambridge: Cambridge University Press, 2013)

—, 'Women and Paid Work', in June Purvis (ed.), *Women's History: Britain, 1850–1945: an introduction* (London: UCL Press, 1995), pp. 85–105

Hunt, E.H., *Regional Wage Variations in Britain, 1850–1914* (Oxford: Clarendon Press, 1973)

Hunt, Margaret, 'Women and the Fiscal-imperial State in the late Seventeenth and early Eighteenth Centuries', in Kathleen Wilson (ed.), *A New Imperial History: culture, identity, and modernity in Britain and the Empire, 1660–1840* (Cambridge, 2004), pp. 29–47

Hurl-Eamon, Jennine, 'The Fiction of Female Dependence and the Makeshift Economy of Soldiers, Sailors and their Wives in Eighteenth-century London', *Labor History*, 49:4 (2008), 481–501

—, *Marriage and the British Army in the Long Eighteenth Century: 'The girl I left behind me'* (Oxford: Oxford University Press, 2014)

Inwood, Stephen, 'Policing London's Morals: the Metropolitan Police and Popular Culture 1829–1850', in Paul Lawrence (ed.), *The New Police in the Nineteenth Century* (Farnham: Routledge, 1997), pp. 199–216

Isay, Richard A., 'The Submariners' Wives' Syndrome', *Psychiatric Quarterly*, 42:4 (1968), 647–52

Jolly, Rick and Tugg Willson, *Jackspeak: a guide to British naval slang and usage* (Torpoint: Palamando, 2000)

Jones, Mary, 'Towards a Hierarchy of Management: the Victorian and Edwardian Navy, 1860–1919', in Helen Doe and Richard Harding (eds), *Naval Leadership and Management, 1650–1950: essays in honour of Michael Duffy* (Woodbridge: Boydell Press, 2012), pp. 157–72

Kemp, Peter, *The British Sailor: a social history of the lower deck* (London: Dent, 1970)

Kent, David, 'Gone for a Soldier?: family breakdown and the demography of desertion in a London parish, 1750–1791', *Local Population Studies*, 45 (1990), 27–41

Kidd, Alan J., *State, Society and the Poor in Nineteenth-century England* (Basingstoke: Macmillan, 1999)

King, Peter, 'Female Offenders, Work and Lifestyle Change in Late Eighteenth-century London', *Continuity & Change*, 11:1 (1996), 61–90

Kofron, John, 'Dickens, Collins, and the Influence of the Arctic', *Dickens Studies Annual*, 40 (2009), 81–93

Lambert, Andrew, 'The Shield of Empire, 1815–1895', in J.R. Hill (ed.), *The Oxford Illustrated History of the Royal Navy* (Oxford: Oxford University Press, 1995), pp. 161–99

Laslett, Peter, 'The Comparative History of Household and Family', *Journal of Social History*, 4:1 (1970), 75–87

—, 'The Family as a Knot of Individual Interests', in Robert McC. Netting, Richard R. Wilk, and Eric J. Arnould (eds), *Households: comparative and historical studies of the domestic group* (Berkeley: University of California Press, 1984), pp. 353–79

—, *Family Life and Illicit Love in Earlier Generations: essays in historical sociology* (Cambridge: Cambridge University Press, 1980)

—, 'Introduction', in Peter Laslett and Richard Wall (eds), *Household and Family in Past Time* (Cambridge: Cambridge University Press, 1972), pp. 1–89

—, 'Mean Household Size in England from Printed Sources', in Peter Laslett and Richard Wall (eds), *Household and Family in Past Time* (Cambridge: Cambridge University Press, 1972), pp. 125–58

—, *The World We Have Lost: further explored* (London: Routledge, 2000)

Lasseter, W.L., 'The Portsmouth Corset Industry: its origins and growth', *Port of Portsmouth Chamber of Commerce Journal*, 1:12 (1947), 23–9

Lavery, Brian, *Able Seamen: the lower deck of the Royal Navy from 1850 to the present day* (London: Conway, 2011)

—, *Royal Tars: the lower deck of the Royal Navy, 875–1850* (London: Conway Maritime, 2010)

Le Feuvre, Cathy, *The Armstrong Girl: a child for sale: the battle against the Victorian sex trade* (Oxford: Lion, 2015)

Lee, Catherine, *Policing Prostitution, 1856–1886: deviance, surveillance and morality* (Abingdon: Routledge, 2015)

Lees, Lynn Hollen, *The Solidarities of Strangers: the English poor laws and the people, 1700–1948* (Cambridge: Cambridge University Press, 1998)

Lewis, Michael, *The Navy in Transition, 1814–1864: a social history* (London: Hodder & Stoughton, 1965)

Light, Alison, *Common People: the history of an English family* (London: Fig Tree, Penguin Group, 2014)

Lin, Patricia, 'Caring for the Nation's Families: British Soldiers' and Sailors' Families and the State, 1793–1815', in Alan I. Forrest, Karen Hagemann and Jane Rendall (eds), *Soldiers, Citizens and Civilians: experiences and perceptions of the revolutionary and Napoleonic Wars, 1790–1820* (Basingstoke: Palgrave Macmillan, 2009), pp. 99–136

—, 'Citizenship, Military Families, and the Creation of a New Definition of "Deserving Poor" in Britain, 1793–1815', *Social Politics*, 7:1 (2000), 5–46

Lincoln, Margarette, 'The Impact of Warfare on Naval Wives and Women', in Cheryl A. Fury (ed.), *The Social History of English Seamen, 1650–1815* (Woodbridge: Boydell Press, 2017), pp. 71–88

—, *Naval Wives and Mistresses* (Stroud: History, 2011)

—, *Representing the Royal Navy: British sea power, 1750–1815* (Aldershot: Ashgate, 2002)

Lloyd, Christopher, *The British Seaman 1200–1860: a social survey* (London: Collins, 1968)

Long, Jane, *Conversations in Cold Rooms: women, work and poverty in nineteenth-century Northumberland* (London: Royal Historical Society, published by Boydell Press, 1999)

Lynch, Katherine A. and Joel B. Greenhouse, 'Risk Factors for Infant Mortality in Nineteenth-Century Sweden', *Population Studies*, 48:1 (1994), 117–33

Mackay, L., 'Why They Stole: Women in the Old Bailey, 1779–1789', *Journal of Social History*, 32:3 (1999), 623–39

Malcolmson, Patricia E., *English Laundresses: a social history, 1850–1930* (Urbana: University of Illinois Press, 1986)

McKee, Christopher, *Sober Men and True: sailor lives in the Royal Navy, 1900–1945* (London: Harvard University Press, 2002)

McNay, Kirsty, Jane Humphries, and Stephan Klasen, 'Excess Female Mortality in Nineteenth-Century England and Wales', *Social Science History*, 29:4 (2005), 649–81

Mills, Dennis, Michael Edgar and Andrew Hinde, 'Southern Historians and their Exploitation of Victorian Censuses', *Southern History*, 18 (1996), 61–86

Mitchell, Sally, 'The Forgotten Women of the Period: penny weekly family magazines of the 1840s and 1850s', in Martha Vicinus (ed.), *A Widening Sphere: changing roles of Victorian women* (Indiana, 1977), pp. 29–51

Moring, Beatrice and Richard Wall, *Widows in European Economy and Society 1600–1920* (Woodbridge: Boydell Press, 2017)

Morris, R.J. and Richard Rodger, *The Victorian City: a reader in British urban history, 1820–1914* (London: Longman, 1993)

Morrison, S.L., J.A. Heady and J.N. Morris, 'Social and Biological Factors in Infant Mortality: mortality in the post-natal period', *Archives of Disease in Childhood*, 34:174 (1959), 101–14

Muthesius, Stefan, *The English Terraced House* (Newhaven: Yale University Press, 1982)

O'Day, Rosemary, *The Family and Family Relationships, 1500–1900: England, France and the United States of America* (Basingstoke: Macmillan, 1994)

Osborn, Geoffrey, *Naval Officers' Letters: a study of letters sent to and from British Royal Navy officers serving abroad in the Victorian era* (Bristol: Stuart Rossiter Trust Fund, 1995)

Outhwaite, R.B., 'Age at Marriage in England from the Late Seventeenth to the Nineteenth Century', *Transactions of the Royal Historical Society*, 23 (1973), 55–70

Padfield, Peter, *Rule Britannia: the Victorian and Edwardian Navy* (London: Pimlico, 2002)

Pappalardo, Bruno, *Tracing Your Naval Ancestors* (Kew Record Office, 2002)

Payton, Philip, 'Foreword', in Lesley Trotter (ed.), *The Married Widows of Cornwall: the Story of the Wives Left Behind by Emigration* (Cornwall: Humble History Press, 2018), pp. i–vii

Pearsall, Ronald, *The Worm in the Bud: the world of Victorian sexuality* (Stroud: Sutton, 2003)

Perkin, Joan, *Women and Marriage in Nineteenth-century England* (London: Routledge, 1989)

Petrie, Glen, *A Singular Iniquity: the campaigns of Josephine Butler* (London: Macmillan, 1971)

Priestley, Philip, *Victorian Prison Lives: English prison biography, 1830–1914* (London: Pimlico, 1999)

Probert, Rebecca, *Marriage Law for Genealogists* (Kenilworth: Takeaway Publishing, 2012)

Pulham, Patricia and Brad Beaven, *Dickens and the Victorian City* (Old Portsmouth: Tricorn Books, 2012)

Quail, Sarah and John Stedman, *Images of Portsmouth* (Derby: Breedon Books, 1993)

Rasor, Eugene L., *Reform in the Royal Navy: a social history of the lower deck, 1850 to 1880* (Hamden, Conn.: Archon Books, 1976)

Riley, R.C., *The Industries of Portsmouth in the Nineteenth Century* (Portsmouth: Portsmouth City Council, 1976)

—, *Old Portsmouth: a garrison town in the mid-19th century* (Portsmouth: Portsmouth City Council, 2010)

—, 'The Portsmouth Corset Industry in the Nineteenth Century', in John Webb, Nigel Yates and Sarah Peacock (eds), *Hampshire Studies* (Portsmouth: Portsmouth City Record Office, 1981), pp. 241–64

Riley, R.C. and Philip Eley, *Public Houses and Beerhouses in Nineteenth Century Portsmouth* (Portsmouth: Portsmouth City Council, 1983)

Roberts, Elizabeth, *Women's Work 1840–1940* (Basingstoke: Macmillan, 1988)

Robinson, William, *Jack Nastyface: memoirs of an English seaman* (London: Chatham, 2002)

Rodger, N.A.M., *The Command of the Ocean: a naval history of Britain, 1649–1815* (London: Allen Lane in association with the National Maritime Museum, 2004)

—, *Naval Records for Genealogists* (Richmond: PRO Publications, 1998)

—, *The Wooden World: an anatomy of the Georgian Navy* (Annapolis, Md.: Naval Institute Press, 1986)

Rodger, Richard, *Housing in Urban Britain 1780–1914* (Cambridge: Cambridge University Press, 1995)

Rogers, Peter N., *Portsmouth & Southsea* (Stroud: Sutton, 1996)

Rose, Michael E., 'The Allowance System under the New Poor Law', *Economic History Review*, 19:3 (1966), 607–20

—, 'Settlement, Removal and the New Poor Law', in D. Fraser (ed.), *The New Poor Law in the Nineteenth Century* (London: Macmillan, 1976), pp. 25–44

Rose, Sonya *Limited Livelihoods: gender and class in nineteenth-century England* (London: Routledge, 1992)

Ross, Ellen, *Love and Toil: motherhood in outcast London, 1870–1918* (Oxford: Oxford University Press, 1993)

—, 'Survival Networks: women's neighbourhood sharing in London before World War I', *History Workshop*, 15:1 (Spring, 1983), 4–27

Rowbotham, Judith, '"Only When Drunk": the stereotyping of violence in England, c.1850–1900', in Shani D'Cruze (ed.), *Everyday Violence in Britain 1850–1950: Gender and Class* (Harlow: Pearson, 2000), pp. 155–69

Rowbotham, Sheila, *Hidden from History: 300 Years of Women's Oppression and the Fight Against It* (London: Pluto Press, 1983)

Rowbotham, W.B., 'Soldiers' and Seamen's Wives and Children in HM Ships', *The Mariner's Mirror*, 47:1 (1961), 42–8

Rubenhold, Hallie, *The Five: the untold lives of the women killed by Jack the Ripper* (London: Doubleday, 2019)

Rudé, George, *Criminal and Victim: crime and society in early nineteenth-century England* (Oxford: Clarendon Press, 1985)

Ruggles, Steven, 'Reconsidering the Northwest European Family System: Living Arrangements of the Aged in Comparative Historical Perspective', *Population and Development Review*, 35:2 (2009), 249–73

Sauer, R., 'Infanticide and Abortion in Nineteenth-Century Britain', *Population Studies*, 32:1 (1978), 81–93

Sharpe, Pamela, 'Marital Separation in Eighteenth and early Nineteenth Centuries', *Local Population Studies*, 45 (1990), 66–70

Shorter, Edward, *The Making of the Modern Family* (London: Collins, 1976)
Sigsworth, E.M. and T.J. Wyke, 'A Study of Victorian Prostitution and Venereal Disease', in Martha Vicinus (ed.), *Suffer and Be Still: women in the Victorian age* (Indiana: Indiana University Press, 1972), pp. 77–99
Skelley, Alan Ramsay, *The Victorian Army at Home: the recruitment and terms and conditions of the British Regular, 1859–1899* (London: Croom Helm, 1977)
Snell, K.D.M., *Parish and Belonging: community, identity and welfare in England and Wales, 1700–1950* (Cambridge: Cambridge University Press, 2006)
Southall, Humphrey and David Gilbert, 'A Good Time to Wed?: marriage and economic distress in England and Wales, 1839–1914', *Economic History Review*, 49:1 (1996), 35–57
Spiers, Edward M., *The Army and Society, 1815–1914* (London: Longman, 1980)
Stanford, Jean and A. Temple Patterson, *The Condition of the Children of the Poor in mid-Victorian Portsmouth* (Portsmouth: Portsmouth City Council, 1974)
Stapleton, Barry, 'The Admiralty Connection: port development and demographic change in Portsmouth, 1650–1810', in Richard Lawton and Robert Lee (eds), *Population and Society in Western European Port-Cities, 1650–1939* (Liverpool: Liverpool University Press, 2002), pp. 212–51
——, 'Population', in Barry Stapleton and James H. Thomas (eds), *The Portsmouth Region* (Gloucester: Alan Sutton, 1989), pp. 83–117
Stapleton, Barry and James H. Thomas, *The Portsmouth Region* (Gloucester: Alan Sutton, 1989)
Stark, Suzanne J., *Female Tars: women aboard ship in the age of sail* (London: Constable, 1996)
Stead, W.T. and Antony E. Simpson (eds), *The Maiden Tribute of Modern Babylon: the report of the secret commission* (Lambertville, N.J.: True Bill Press, 2007)
Stevenson, Kim, 'Ingenuities of the Female Mind: legal and public perceptions of sexual violence in Victorian England 1850–1890', in Shani D'Cruze (ed.), *Everyday Violence in Britain, 1850–1950* (Harlow: Longman, 2000), pp. 89–103
Taylor, R., 'Manning the Royal Navy: the Reform of the Recruiting System, 1852–62' (Part 1), *The Mariner's Mirror*, 44:4 (1958), 302–13
——, 'Manning the Royal Navy: the Reform of the Recruiting System, 1852–62' (Part 2), *The Mariner's Mirror*, 45:1 (1959), 46–58
Tebbutt, Melanie, *Making Ends Meet: pawnbroking and working-class credit* (Leicester: Leicester University Press, 1983)
——, *Women's Talk?: a social history of "gossip" in working-class neighbourhoods, 1880–1960* (Aldershot: Scolar, 1995)
Teitelbaum, Michael S., 'Birth Underregistration in the Constituent Counties of England and Wales: 1841–1910', *Population Studies*, 28:2 (1974), 329–43
Thane, Pat, 'Women and the Poor Law in Victorian and Edwardian England', *History Workshop*, 6:1 (1978), 29–51
Thomas, Keith, 'The Double Standard', *Journal of the History of Ideas*, 20:2 (1959), 195–216
Thompson, F.M.L., *The Rise of Respectable Society: a social history of Victorian Britain, 1830–1900* (London: Fontana, 1988)
Thompson, Pat, *Portsmouth Borough Gaol in the Nineteenth Century* (Portsmouth, 1980)
Tomalin, Claire, *Charles Dickens: a life* (London: Viking, 2011)

Tomes, Nancy, '"A Torrent of Abuse": crimes of violence between working-class men and women in London 1840–1875', *Journal of Social History*, II:3 (1978), 328–45

Tomkins, Alannah, 'Pawnbroking and the Survival Strategies of the Urban Poor in 1770s York', in Alannah Tomkins and Steven King (eds), *The Poor in England, 1700–1850* (Manchester: Manchester University Press, 2003), pp. 166–98

Tosh, John, *A Man's Place: masculinity and the middle-class home in Victorian England* (New Haven, Conn.: Yale University Press, 1999)

Treble, James H., *Urban Poverty in Britain, 1830–1914* (London: Batsford, 1979)

Trotter, Lesley, *The Married Widows of Cornwall: the story of the wives left behind by emigration* (Cornwall: Humble History Press, 2018)

Trustram, Myna, *Women of the Regiment: marriage and the Victorian army* (Cambridge: Cambridge University Press, 1984)

van der Heijden, Manon and Danielle ven den Heuvel, 'Sailors' Families and the Urban Institutional Framework in Early Modern Holland', *The History of the Family*, 12:4 (2007), 296–309

Venning, Annabel, *Following the Drum: the lives of army wives and daughters, past and present* (London: Headline, 2005)

Vickers, Daniel and Vince Walsh, *Young Men and the Sea: Yankee seafarers in the age of sail* (New Haven, Conn.: Yale University Press, 2005)

Vincent, David, *Bread, Knowledge, and Freedom: a study of nineteenth-century working class autobiography* (London: Methuen, 1982)

Walkowitz, Judith R., 'The Making of an Outcast Group: prostitution and working women in nineteenth-century Plymouth and Southampton', in Martha Vicinus (ed.), *A Widening Sphere: changing roles of Victorian women* (London: Indiana University Press, 1977), pp. 72–93

——, *Prostitution and Victorian Society: women, class, and the state* (Cambridge: Cambridge University Press, 1980)

Walkowitz, Judith R. and Daniel J. Walkowitz, '"We Are Not Beasts of the Field": prostitution and the poor in Plymouth and Southampton under the Contagious Diseases Acts', *Feminist Studies*, 1:3/4 (1973), 73–106

Wall, Richard, 'Beyond the Household: Marriage, Household Formation and the Role of Kin and Neighbours', *International Review of Social History*, 44 (1999), 55–67

——, 'Economic Collaboration of Family Members Within and Beyond Households in English Society, 1600–2000', *Continuity & Change*, 25:1 (2010), 83–108

——, 'Leaving Home and the Process of Household Formation in Pre-industrial England', *Continuity & Change*, 2:1 (1987), 77–101

——, 'Regional and Temporal Variations in the Structure of the British Household since 1851', in T.C. Barker and Michael Drake (eds), *Population and Society in Britain 1850–1980* (London: Batsford Academic and Educational, 1982), pp. 62–99

Walton, Oliver, '"A Great Improvement in the Sailor's Feeling towards the Naval Service": recruiting seamen for the Royal Navy, 1815–1853', *Journal for Maritime Research*, 12 (2010), 27–57

——, 'New Kinds of Discipline: the Royal Navy in the second half of the nineteenth century', in Richard Harding, Helen Doe and Michael Duffy (eds), *Naval*

*Leadership and Management, 1650–1950: essays in honour of Michael Duffy* (Woodbridge: Boydell Press, 2012), pp. 143–55

Walvin, James, *English Urban Life, 1776–1851* (London: Hutchinson, 1984)

Warner, Jessica and Allyson Lunny, 'Marital Violence in a Martial Town', *Journal of Family History*, 28 (2003), 258–76

Watt, Helen and Anne Hawkins, *Letters of Seamen in the Wars with France, 1793–1815* (Woodbridge: Boydell Press, 2016)

WEA, *Gateway to Queen Street* (Portsmouth: WEA, 1982)

—, *Memories of Portsea* (Portsmouth: WEA, 2007)

Wheaton, Robert, 'Family and Kinship in Western Europe: the problem of the joint family household', *Journal of Interdisciplinary History*, 5:4 (1975), 601–28

White, Colin, *Victoria's Navy: the end of the sailing Navy* (Havant, 1981)

Williams, David M., 'Henry Mayhew and the British Seaman', in Stephen Fisher (ed.), *Lisbon as a Port Town, the British Seaman and Other Maritime Themes* (Exeter Maritime Studies No. 2, Exeter: Exeter University Publications, 1988), pp. 111–27

Winton, John, *Hurrah for the Life of a Sailor!: life on the lower-deck of the Victorian Navy* (London: Joseph, 1977)

—, 'Life and Education in a Technologically Evolving Navy, 1815–1925', in J.R. Hill (ed.), *The Oxford Illustrated History of the Royal Navy* (Oxford: Oxford University Press, 1995), pp. 250–79

Wohl, A.S., *Endangered Lives: public health in Victorian Britain* (London: J.M. Dent, 1983)

Wood, J. Carter, *Violence and Crime in Nineteenth-century England: the shadow of our refinement* (London: Routledge, 2004)

Wood, Peter, *Poverty and the Workhouse in Victorian Britain* (Stroud: Alan Sutton, 1991)

Woods, James, *The Inner Life of the Navy, by Lionel Yexley* (London, 1908)

—, *Our Fighting Seamen, by Lionel Yexley* (London, 1911)

Woods, Robert, *The Demography of Victorian England and Wales* (Cambridge: Cambridge University Press, 2000)

Woods, Robert and John Woodward, 'Mortality, Poverty and the Environment', in Robert Woods and John Woodward (eds), *Urban Disease and Mortality in Nineteenth-Century England* (London: Batsford Academic and Educational, 1984), pp. 19–36

Wrigley, E.A., 'Births and Baptisms: the use of Anglican baptism registers as a source of information about the numbers of births in England before the beginning of civil registration', *Population Studies*, 31:2 (1977), 281–312

Wrigley, E.A. and R.S. Schofield, 'English Population History from Family Reconstitution: summary results 1600–1799', *Population Studies*, 37:2 (1983), 157–84

—, *The Population History of England, 1541–1871: a reconstruction* (Cambridge: Cambridge University Press, 1989)

Young, Michael Dunlop, Peter Willmott and Richard Morris Titmuss, *Family and Kinship in East London* (London: Routledge & Kegan Paul, 1957)

Zedner, Lucia, *Women, Crime, and Custody in Victorian England* (Oxford: Clarendon Press, 1994)

*Bibliography*

## UNPUBLISHED THESES

Chamberlain, Tony, '"Stokers - the Lowest of the Low?" A Social History of Royal Navy Stokers 1850–1950' (unpublished PhD thesis, University of Exeter, 2013)

Christie, P.S., 'Occupations in Portsmouth' (unpublished MPhil dissertation, Portsmouth Polytechnic, 1976)

Edwards, Elizabeth, 'The Poor of Portsmouth and their Relief, 1820–1850' (unpublished dissertation, Diploma in English Local History, Portsmouth Polytechnic, 1977)

Edwards, F.H., 'Crime, Law and Order in Portsmouth, 1835–1875' (unpublished dissertation, degree unknown, Portsmouth Polytechnic, 1987)

Field, J.L., 'The Bourgeoisie of Portsmouth' (unpublished PhD thesis, University of Warwick, 1979)

Holihead, Melanie, 'Portsea Poll, Poor Poll? The social condition of wives and families receiving allotments of pay from Royal Navy sailors in mid-nineteenth century Portsea Town' (unpublished MSc dissertation, University of Oxford, 2011)

Lewis, David, 'Married to the Navy: the lives of naval officers' wives, 1870–1914' (unpublished master's degree dissertation, Thames Polytechnic, 1988)

Moon, Louise, '"Sailorhoods": sailortown and sailors in the port of Portsmouth circa 1850–1900' (unpublished PhD thesis, University of Portsmouth, 2015)

Ogbourn, Miles Jon, 'Discipline, Government and the Law: the response to crime, poverty and prostitution in nineteenth-century Portsmouth' (unpublished PhD thesis, Cambridge, 1990)

Preston, Virginia, 'Constructing Communities: living and working in the Royal Navy, c.1830–1860' (unpublished PhD thesis, University of Greenwich, 2008)

Reibe, Melissa, 'Public Perceptions of Sailors' Wives in Eighteenth-Century England' (unpublished MA thesis, University of Missouri-Kansas City, 2011)

Stanford, J.D.A., 'Working-Class Children in Mid-Nineteenth Century Portsmouth' (unpublished dissertation, degree unknown, university unspecified, 1971)

Walton, Oliver, 'Social History of the Royal Navy, c.1856–1900: corporation and community' (unpublished PhD thesis, University of Exeter, 2004)

## WEB-BASED SOURCES

Angelico, Chris and Adam Cuerden, 'The Gilbert and Sullivan Archive' <https://gsarchive.net/iolanthe/html/> [accessed 30 March 2024]

Bank of England, 'Inflation Calculator' (Bank of England, 1209–2024) <https://www.bankofengland.co.uk/monetary-policy/inflation/inflation-calculator> [accessed 30 March 2024]

Beaven, Brad, 'The Resilience of Sailortown Culture in English Naval Ports, c.1820–1900', *Urban History / FirstView Article*: 1 (2015) <http://journals.cambridge.org/abstract_S0963926815000140> [accessed 22 April 2024]

Begiato, Joanne, 'Angry Husbands: Emotional Objects and Wife-beating' in Joanne Begiato Muses on History (WordPress.com, 2019) <https://jbhist.wordpress.com/2019/07/25/emotional-lives-intimacy-and-identity-in-18th-2/> [accessed 22 April 2024]

—, 'Rough and Brave: What Can Soldiers Tell Us about 18th Century Masculinity?' in Joanne Begiato Muses on History (WordPress.com, 2019) <https://jbhist.wordpress.com/2019/08/02/rough-and-brave-what-can-soldiers-tell-us-about-18th-century-masculinity-part-ii/> [accessed 22 April 2024]

—, 'The Tearful Sailor: Gendering Emotions' in Joanne Begiato Muses on History (WordPress.com, 2019) <https://jbhist.wordpress.com/2019/07/25/emotional-lives-intimacy-and-identity-in-18th-2/> [accessed 22 April 2024]

Bramley, Frank, 'A Hopeless Dawn' (tate.org.uk, 1888) <https://www.tate.org.uk/art/artworks/bramley-a-hopeless-dawn-n01627> [accessed 22 April 2024]

Brooks, Kate, 'Death in the Archives', *Social History Society* (2020) <https://social-history.org.uk/shs_exchange/death-in-the-archives/> [accessed 22 April 2024]

Evans, Tanya, 'Review: Ginger Frost, *Living in Sin: Cohabiting as Husband and Wife in Nineteenth-Century* England' (Institute of Historical Research, 2009) <https://reviews.history.ac.uk/review/830> [accessed 22 April 2024]

FindMyPast.com, 'British Royal Navy Allotment Declarations, 1795–1852' (FindMyPast.com in association with The National Archives (TNA), Kew), <https://search.findmypast.com/search-world-records/british-royal-navy-allotment-declarations-1795-1852> [accessed 22 April 2024]

—, Calendar of The Royal College of Surgeons in England and Members of The Royal College of Physicians (1830–1923), FindMyPast.com <https://search.findmypast.co.uk/search-world-records/britain-physicians-and-surgeons-1830-1923> [accessed 22 April 2024]

Frost, Ginger Suzanne, '"He could not hold his passions": domestic violence and cohabitation in England, 1850–1905', *Crime, History and Societies*, 12:1 (2008) <http://journals.openedition.org/chs/64> [accessed 22 April 2024]

Gritt, Andrew, 'Representations of Mariners and Maritime Communities, c.1750–1850', *History in Focus: The Sea* (2005) <http://www.history.ac.uk/ihr/Focus/Sea/articles/gritt.html> [accessed 22 April 2024]

Higginbotham, Peter, 'The Workhouse: the story of an institution' (workhouses.org.uk, 2016) <http://www.workhouses.org.uk/life/classification.shtml> [accessed 22 April 2024]

Historic Dockyard, Chatham, 'What Was the Sail and Colour Loft?' (Chatham Historic Dockyard Trust, 2019) <https://thedockyard.co.uk/news/what-was-the-sail-and-colour-loft/> [accessed 22 April 2024]

Hitchcock, Tim, *et al.*, 'The Old Bailey Proceedings Online, 1674–1913' (University of Sheffield Digital Humanities Institute, 2012) <https://www.oldbaileyonline.org> [accessed 22 April 2024]

Holl, Frank, 'No Tidings from the Sea' (Royal Collections Trust, 1870) <https://www.rct.uk/collection/405161/no-tidings-from-the-sea> [accessed 22 April 2024]

Hughes, Bettany, 'Why Were Women Written Out of History? An Interview with Bettany Hughes' (English Heritage, 2016) <https://www.english-heritage.org.uk/visit/inspire-me/blog/blog-posts/why-were-women-written-out-of-history-an-interview-with-bettany-hughes/> [accessed 22 April 2024]

Humphries, Jane, *Tawney Lecture 2010: Childhood and Child Labour in the British Industrial Revolution,* Economic History Society <https://ehs.org.uk/multimedia/tawney-lecture-2010-childhood-and-child-labour-in-the-british-industrial-revolution/> [accessed 10 April 2023]

# Bibliography

Joyce, Fraser, 'Prostitution and the Nineteenth Century: in search of the "Great Social Evil"', *Reinvention: a Journal of Undergraduate Research*, 1:1 (2008) <https://warwick.ac.uk/fac/cross_fac/iatl/student-research/reinvention/archive/volume1issue1/joyce/> [accessed 22 April 2024]

King, Alan, *The Portsmouth Encyclopaedia: a history of places and people in Portsmouth, with an index to streets*, (Portsmouth City Council, 2011) <https://www.portsmouth.gov.uk/ext/documents-external/lib-portsmouthencyclopaedia-2011.pdf> [accessed 22 April 2024]

Lee, John Ingle, 'Sweethearts and Wives' (Walker Art Gallery, Liverpool, 1860) <https://www.liverpoolmuseums.org.uk/artifact/sweethearts-and-wives> [accessed 22 April 2024]

Narcissistic Abuse Rehab, 'How Narcissists Use DARVO to Escape Responsibility' (Narcissistic Abuse Rehab, 2020) <https://www.narcissisticabuserehab.com/darvo/> [accessed 22 April 2024]

Pappalardo, Bruno, 'A Lot to be Excited About - Admiralty Allotment Registers' (The National Archives, 2019) <https://blog.nationalarchives.gov.uk/lot-excited-admiralty-allotment-registers/> [accessed 22 April 2024]

Pooley, Siân, 'Parenthood, Child-rearing and Fertility in England, 1850–1914', *History of the Family*, 18:1 (2013), <https://www.ncbi.nlm.nih.gov/pmc/articles/PMC3865739/> [accessed 22 April 2024]

Registrar General, Fourteenth Annual Report: Ages of the Persons who were Married in 1851 <http://www.histpop.org/ohpr/servlet/PageBrowser?path=Browse/Registrar%20General%20(by%20geography)/England/1851-1860&active=yes&mno=477&tocstate=expandnew&tocseq=400&display=sections&display=tables&display=pagetitles&pageseq=first-nonblank> [accessed 22 April 2024]

—, Population Tables II, Vol. 1, England and Wales Divisions I-VI (1851), Registrar General <http://www.histpop.org/ohpr/servlet/PageBrowser2?ResourceType=Census&ResourceType=Registrar%20General&SearchTerms=portsmouth%20females%201851&simple=yes&path=Results&active=yes&treestate=expandnew&titlepos=0&mno=30&tocstate=expandnew&display=sections&display=tables&display=pagetitles&pageseq=212&zoom=4> [accessed 22 April 2024]

Rodger, N.A.M., 'I want to be an Admiral', *London Review of Books*: 15 (2020) <https://www.lrb.co.uk/the-paper/v42/n15/n.a.m.-rodger/i-want-to-be-an-admiral> [accessed 22 April 2024]

RootsWeb, '1851 Census: Instructions for the completion of the Form' (Ancestry.com, 1997–2022) <https://sites.rootsweb.com/~pbtyc/1851_Census_Instr/1851_Census_Instr.html> [accessed 22 April 2024]

Unknown author, 'Census 1911: Fertility and Marriage' (UK Parliament, 2024) <https://www.parliament.uk/about/living-heritage/transformingsociety/private-lives/relationships/collections/1921-census> [accessed 22 April 2024]

—, 'The Origins of Nautical Fashion in Britain' (Royal Museums Greenwich, n.d.) <https://www.rmg.co.uk/stories/topics/origins-nautical-fashion-britain> [accessed 22 April 2024]

—, 'The turret ship HMS 'Captain' <https://www.rmg.co.uk/collections/objects/rmgc-object-15244> [accessed 22 April 2024]

*Bibliography*

Wassell Smith, Maya, '"The Fancy Work What Sailors Make": material and emotional creative practice in masculine seafaring communities', *Nineteenth-Century Gender Studies*, 14:2 (2018), <http://www.ncgsjournal.com/issue142/smith.html> [accessed 22 April 2024]

www.gov.uk, 'Order a Birth, Death, Marriage or Civil Partnership Certificate' (HM Government, 2023) <https://www.gov.uk/order-copy-birth-death-marriage-certificate> [accessed 22 April 2024]

# INDEX

Page numbers in **bold** type refer to illustrations and their captions. Married surnames refer back to women's maiden names, where known.

Abortion, abortionist (implied)   110
Adoption, private   111–12
Affinal relationships   54, 129, 132, 232–3, 248–9, 253, 280–2
Allotment declarations   xxii, 6–8, 15, 16, 28–30, 31, 35, 36–7, 38, 40, 44–6, 48, 51–2, 55, 56, 57, 58–9, 60 n. 58, 61, 62–3, 64, 65, 66, 75, 82, 83, 84, 90, 92, 108, 111, 119, 131, 139, **140**, 143, 154, 156, 157, 159, 160 n. 14, 165, 166, 171, 172, 173, 182, 184, 190, 192, 196, 207, 208, 212, 227, 235–6, 237, 239, 241, 242, 243, 244, 246, 250, 263, 276, 278, 279, 280, 281
Allotment system: history
   as successor to remittance system   26–8
   central government, role of   26–7, 29, 33, 34, 35
   development of system   25–31
   House of Commons return, 'Number of allotments in England and Wales'   3, 35
Allotment system: overview   31–6
   Allotment system, process, regulations
   amounts allotted and received   8, 29, 31, 53, 143, 153, 154, 157, 158, 159–60, 162, 163, 164, 165, 166, 167, 169, 182, 183, 184, 195, 206, 211
   as percentage of seaman's pay   157–60, 167
   average payments   157, 160, 162–7, 169, 184, 195
   disbursements
     at customs house   33, 160
     at HM Dockyard pay office   28, 33, 53, 56, 60, 65, 117, 159, 160, 168, 169, 173, 213, 214, 277

     at land tax office   26, 33, 159
   forfeiture of allotment   37–8, 242
   frequency and location of payments   28
   illness or disability preventing collection   37–8, 207
   irrevocability   235
   moiety, 'moiety cap', sub-moiety amounts   29, 157, 159, 182, 183, 199, 299
   oaths   33
   pay bill, or voucher   31, **32**, 33, 36, 37, 59, 65, 173, 212, 214
   permitted relationships   27–8, 31, 36, 44–5, 54, 57, 62, 115
   pre-printed forms   31, **32**, 33
   relocation of allottee (changing place of payment)   28, 38, 69
   stoppage of payments   29–30, 36–8, 46, 53, 58, 66, 92, 161, 195, 207, 213, 229, 243, 262, 264, 266, 267, 268, 280
   ships' registers   6, **7**, 8, 9, 18 n. 14, 31, **32**, 44, 52, 54, 62, 67, 82, 92, 116, 143, 171, 173, 182
   time taken to process declarations   38–40, 53–4, 143, 181–2, 255
   transfer payments to different allottee   29–30, 51–2, 280
   variations between ships   157–60
   variations per men's rates and trades   157–60, 183
   verification process   **32**–6
Allotment system: roles
   churchwarden   33, 38, 54, 83, 235
   customs officer   26, 33
   parish minister   33, 38, 52, 73, 83, 110, 235, 243
   parish overseer   33

325

pay office staff   60, 213, 214
receivers of land tax   26, 33
Allotments as 'half-pay'   29, 51, 81, 96, 97, 121, 123, 167, 169, 179, 195, 213–14, 232, 236, 240, 241, 242, 243, 245, 270, 301
Allottees: relationships
 aunts   28, **44**, 116
 brothers   28, **44**, **47**
 daughters   15, 34, **44**, 57, 64, 69–72, 74–7, 79–81, 89, 95–8, 99–100, 106–7, 110–11, 118–**22**, 136, 146, 152, 179, 200, 236, 239, 240, 258, 274, 286, 302–4
 entrusted children   8, 46, 48, 59, 62, 65, 90, 108, 166 n. 43, 175, 188, 190, 243, 287
 fathers   **44**, **47**, 52
 grandparents   28, **44**, 50, 155, 212, 263, 285, 296, 297
 half-siblings   28, 56, 117, 136
 in-laws   28, 30, **44**, 51, 52, 56, 71, 77, 78, 79, 95–7, 100, 116–17, 119, 120, 121, **122**, 123, 125, 127, 128, 132
 mothers   15, 28, 30, 34, **44**, 46, **47**, 48, 51–4, 62, 66, 70, 74, 78, 79, 80, 81, 95, 100, 101, **102** and n. 16–103, 110, 111, 112–**13**, 114–15, 119, 121, 138, 139, 146–7, 152, 155, 166, 167, 168, 172, 176, 194, 195, 196, 200, 211, 212, 222, 231, 240, 243, 244, 255, 263–4, 267, **270**, 276, 278, 279, 285, 289, 300, 302, 303
 parents   50–4
 sisters   15, 28, 30, 37, **44**–5, **47**, 48, 54–7, 60, 63, 66, 69, 70, **77**–8, 79, 96, 102 n. 16, 114, 115, 116, 120, 121–**2**, 125, **126**–7, **128**–9, 132, 133, 138, 146, 152, 155, 166, 167, 194–5, 200, 212, 213, 237, 239, 240, 248–9, 267, 268, 276, 278, 286, 302
 sons   **44**, 46, 51, 52, 53–4, 64, 72, 74–5, 77, 100, 108, 118, 120–1, 263
 step-relatives   28, **45**, 56, 60, 107, 235, 238, 239, 290
 trustees   8, 28, 30, 38, **44**–5, 46, **47**, 48, 54, 56, 57–66, 70, 90, 92, 100, 102 n. 16, 107 ,108, 110, 131, 146, 152, 166, 188, 190, 195, 207, 208,
210, 211, 212, 213, 224, 236–7, 241, 243, 250, 280, 285, 288, 291
 wives   2, 11, 12, 14, 15, 16, 26–8, 35, 37, 38, 39, 41, 42, 43, 44–**5**, **47**, 48, **49**, 50, 51, 54, 55, 67, **68**, 69–70, 72, 74, 75, 81–2, 83, 89, **94**, 95–7, 101–4, 107, 109, 110, 112–**13**, 114–15, 116–17, 119, 121–3, 124–5, 127–**8**, 129, 133, **141**, 142, 144–5, 146, 150, 152, 154, 155–6, 160, 166, 167, 168, 169, 170, 171 and n. 70, 172, 179–82, 183, 185–6, 196, 199, 200, 215–16, 220, 228–30, 231, 232, 233, 240, 241, 246, 250–1, 253, 255, 257, 259, 263, 266, 267 and n. 80–268, 274, 275–6, 282–**3**, 284–5, 286, 287, 300, 302–3
Allottee-wives
 accompanying husbands to sea   12, 145 n. 7
 age at motherhood   112–13
 ages per husbands' rates and seniority   **49**–50
 as 'married widows'   48, 245, 267
 born or married in Ireland   **68**–9, 173, 181
 longevity, and cause of death   282, **283**–99
 migration   13, 67, **68**–9, 70, 72, 99, 104, 116, 180, 280, 288
 moving house (local relocation)   45, 64, 69, 71–2, 81–2, 108, 121, 132, 159, 161, 170–3, 180, 201, 263, 280, 284, 288, 289, 290, 291, 298
 'nice girls and tarts'   74
 place of birth   67–70, 71, 72, 81–2, 116, 181, 284
 singularisation of   142, 198, 215–16, 301
Allottees: general
 as defendants   81 n. 21, 190, 191, 195, 196, 198, 202–3, 210, 211, 215
 as landladies   57, 173–7
 as lodgers   55, 56, 71, 116, 129, 136, 146, 152, 173–7, 179
 locations within England and Wales   35
 male allottees   44–5
 male trustees   44–5, 63–4
 'multi-allottees'   28, 46, 53–4, 212

## Index

paupers 53–4, 56, 64, 136, 146, 176, 179, 181, 183, 185, 198, 248, 287, 292, 295, 296–7, 298, 299

Allottees: named individuals
Aldridge, Caroline 278
Allen, Elizabeth 191
Allen, Mary Ann 160
Allen, Rachael **128**
Angus, Henrietta 262
Aylward, Harriet 150
Backster, Matilda 160
Baines, Mary 58
Balch, Maria 59, 65, 92, 250, 251
Ball, Elizabeth 63
Ball, Mary *see* Richards, Mary
Balsh, Maria *see* Balch, Maria
Barfoot, Sarah 59–61, 65
Barrett, Amelia *see* Hursey, Amelia
Barrett, Hannah 173
Barrow, Joanna *see* Greenleaf, Joanna
Baskerville, Mary 64, 287
Bethell, Margaret 69
Betteridge, Elizabeth 154
Bettesworth otherwise Bettsworth, Betsworth, Harriet *see* Trim, Harriet
Bettesworth, Louisa *see* Callaway, Louisa
Bishop, Hannah 268
Blake, Mary Ann 196
Bond, Mary Anne 139
Bone, Martha *see* Woodley, Martha
Brown, Eliza **128**–9
Bull, Emma 266
Burrough, Esther 139
Callaway, Louisa 280–1
Capper, Caroline 190–1, 195, 287–8
Carlisle, Mary Ann 60–1
Carstairs, Eliza Rachel 237, 239–10
Carstairs, Harriett Bell 236–8, 239
Cavander, Amelia *see* Hursey, Amelia
Cavander, Jane *see* Crosby, Jane
Chambers, Elizabeth 108
Charlo, Joanna *see* Greenleaf, Joanna
Charlo, Louisa 246
Charlo, Sarah 246–8
Childs, Frances 243
Clack, Henrietta 182–3
Clapshow, Mary 85
Clarke, Anne 263
Clifford, Mary Anne 107–8
Coles, Ann 153
Constable, Charlotte 57

Cook, Elizabeth 127
Cook, Mary 127
Cox, Hannah 210
Crosby, Jane 224, 243–4, 246, 291, 292–3
Cummings, Elizabeth 191, 291
Davey, Elizabeth 129–32, 171–2
Davey, Elizabeth *see* Leese, Elizabeth
Davey, Rosalinda 18, **130**–2, 240–2, 297
Davidge, Mary 175
Davis, Ann 268
Davis, Elizabeth *see* Williams, Elizabeth
Davis, Louisa 36–7
Dawson, Ann 56
Dominy, Mary Ann *see* Carlisle, Mary Ann
Doward, Elizabeth 225–6, 234
Edwards, Henrietta 119
Elliott, Jane *see* Crosby, Jane
Fawkes, Elizabeth 160
Ferret, Eliza 51
Fleming, Joanna *see* Greenleaf, Joanna
Fleming, Mary Ann Kate *see* Harding, Mary Ann Kate
Ford, Elizabeth (mother of Mary Roberts) 111, 136
Ford, Elizabeth (later Stephens) 85
Ford, Mary 110–1, 136, 193
Foreman, Sarah Jane 150–1
Giddy, Elizabeth Anne 284–6
Giles, Maria 195, 207, 208
Gimblett, Harriet *see* Trim, Harriet
Goodfellow, Leah 166–7
Goodger, Elizabeth 139
Gough, Mary *see* Cook, Mary
Greenleaf, Joanna 34, 75, 174, 246–9, 278–9, 295, 298–9
Greenleaf, Phoebe 34, 56, 75, 248–9, 287, 291, 297–8
Groom, Amelia 58–9, 77–8, 90–3, 95, 97, 101, 106, 129 n. 46, 249–50, 251–3, 283–4
Groom, Sarah 129, 235
Guithard, Elizabeth 211–12
Gulliver, Sarah 108
Hall, Elizabeth *see* Hogg, Elizabeth
Hall, Sarah 69
Harding, Mary Anne Kate 212, 288–9
Harrison, Jane 196
Harvey, Sarah Jane 287

327

## Index

Harwood, Elizabeth *see* Cook, Elizabeth
Hicks, Margaret   45
Hillier, Elizabeth *see* Hogg, Elizabeth
Hinks, Sarah *see* Groom, Sarah
Hogg, Elizabeth   46, 175
Hood, Emily   188
Hooper, Christian[na]   46, 70–1, 134, 278
Hooper, Miranda   71
Hughes, Louisa *see* Callaway, Louisa
Hursey, Amelia   242–4, 256, 291–2
Hussey, Catherine Frances *see* Thomas, Catherine Frances
Jenkins, Susan   235, 236, 239
Jennings, Sarah   62–3, 91, 278
Johns, Ann   159
Johns, Louisa *see* Callaway, Louisa
Johnson, Harriett *see* Carstairs, Harriett Bell
Jones, Sophia Ann   255
Kelsey, Martha   283
Kemp, Ann   159
Kendall, Susan   184
Kennell, Mary Ann *see* Carlisle, Mary Ann
Kinsale, Mary   30
Knell, Sophia   57
Lang, Jemima   138
Lath, Elizabeth   166–7
Lawrence, Matilda   174
Leary, Mary Ann *see* Saxey, Mary Ann
Lee, Elizabeth   165–6
Lee, Mary   138
Lee, Sarah   184
Leese, Elizabeth   129–32, 171–2, 241
Lemmon, Ann   119
Lewis, Amelia   8, 100, 136, 176, 193, 210–11, 226, 227–30, 293–5
Lewis, Martha *see* Woodley, Martha
Lucas, Rebecca   128
Lumb, Ellen   45, 172
Rowsell, Elizabeth Lowry *see* Smith, Elizabeth Lowry
Marks, Elizabeth   211
Marshall, Ann   139, 211
Martell, Mary Voller *see* White, Mary Voller
Martin, Catherine   45
Mason, Ann   51
Matthias, Rosalinda *see* Davey, Rosalinda

Menhinnick, Harriett otherwise Harriott *see* Carstairs, Harriett Bell
Messum, Elizabeth (mother)   51
Messum, Elizabeth, *see* White, Elizabeth
Mogg, Miranda *see* Hooper, Miranda
Mould, Harriet   39
Mould, Martha   56
Nancarrow, Christian[na] *see* Hooper, Christian[na]
Nancarrow, Sarah   278
Newman, Charlotte   57
Newman, Sarah   57
Oddy, Ann   69, 153–4, 160
Oliver, Eliza *see* Brown, Eliza
Owen, Ann   154
Page, Phoebe *see* Greenleaf, Phoebe
Parker, Ann   30
Parnell, Mary Ann   148–9
Patterson, Abigail   297
Paul, Ann   138
Payne, Elizabeth Jane   214
Phippard, Mary *see* Clapshow, Mary
Pinhorn, Elizabeth   211
Plummer, Elizabeth *see* Davey, Elizabeth
Purcell, Jane *see* Tate, Jane
Quinnell, Sarah   184–5
Reece otherwise Rees, Sarah *see* Gulliver, Sarah
Rees otherwise Reece, Sarah, *see* Gulliver, Sarah
Reeves, Charlotte   123
Richards, Ann   224, 226
Richards, Mary *see* Ball, Mary
Riley, Eliza   255
Roberts, Mary *see* Ford, Mary
Rose, Amelia   175
Rowsell, Elizabeth Lowry *see* Magee, Elizabeth Lowry
Rowsell, Susannah   30
Savell, Sarah   155
Saxey, Mary Ann   97
Saxton, Phoebe *see* Greenleaf, Phoebe
Scargill, Mary Anne *see* Clifford, Mary Anne
Scott, Harriet   266–7
Scovell, Mary   58
Seager, Janet   122–3
Shaw, Ann   62
Shepherd, Sarah Ann   29
Smith, Elizabeth Lowry   30

## Index

Smith, Mary Ann   176
Spratt, Jane   **126**-7
Stacey, [Harriet] Maria   190, 195
Stallard, Elizabeth   165
Stephens, Elizabeth *see* Ford, Elizabeth
Steward, Helena   154
Street, Louisa   176
Symons, Martha   138
Tapscott, Ann   278
Tate, Jane   286-7
Thomas, Ann   224
Thomas, Ann ('prostitute')   188
Thomas, Catherine Frances   30
Thomas, Harriet *see* Trim, Harriet
Tipple, Maria   175
Trask, Ann   154
Trim, Harriet   51, 85, 99-100, 176, 279-82, 296-7
Tyler, Eliza Rachel *see* Carstairs, Eliza Rachel
Van Studer, Mary   209
Wafer, 'Ann'   64
Wafer, Louisa   64-6
Wallbridge, Jane   139
Warner, Martha, *see* Mould, Martha
Watson, Amelia   128
Watt, Jane   107
Whealan, Mary   260
Wheden otherwise Wheaden, Amelia *see* Groom, Amelia
Wheeler, Mary Ellen   45
Wheeler, Sarah   154
White, Elizabeth   51, 80
White, Mary Voller   30
Whitehead, Louisa *see* Charlo, Louisa
Wilkinson, Amelia *see* Groom, Amelia
Williams, Elizabeth   36-7
Woodley, Martha   116-17, 136, 137, 193, 244-6, 248, 268, 269, 286, 289-91
Wright, Matilda   210
Yealland, Rachael   67
Young, Mary Anne   45

Allottees' relatives
  Able otherwise Abel, Elizabeth   **130**, 131
  Aylward, Charlotte   150
  Barrett, Esau (sr.)   242-3, 256, 291
  Barret, Esau (jr.)   242, 256, 291
  Betsworth, Harriet Sarah   100, 110, 176, 187, 281, 296
  Betsworth, Harriet Sarah (jr.)   100, 110, 281, 296
  Betsworth, Samuel   281, 296 n. 127
  Bettesworth, Edward   279, 280, 281, 282, 296 n. 127
  Bone, Clara, *see* Woodley, Clara
  Bone, Daniel   117, 290
  Bone, Thomas   240
  Bragginton, Elizabeth, *see* Abel otherwise Able, Elizabeth
  Cavander, Amelia Elizabeth   242-3
  Cavander, Edward   292
  Cavander, Martha   292-3
  Clarke, Francis Henry   263
  Constable, John   57
  Fleming, Laura Brooks   289
  Fleming, Maria   288
  Fleming, Mary Ann Kate, *see* Harding, Mary Ann Kate
  Flowers, Elizabeth   136, 176, 293, 295
  Flowers, James   295
  Ford, Elizabeth (later Stephens)   85
  Ford, Elizabeth (mother of Mary Roberts)   111, 136
  Garland, William   295
  Garland, Maria *see* Lewis, Maria
  Gibbons, Angelina *see* Hooper, Angelina
  Giddy, Elizabeth   285
  Gimblett, Ellenor   51
  Gimblett, John   51
  Greenleaf, Elizabeth (sr.)   34-5, 75, **247**
  Greenleaf, Elizabeth (jr.)   75, **247**, 248, 287
  Greenleaf, Joseph   34, **247**
  Groom, Charlotte   106
  Groom, Mary Ann (jr.)   129
  Groom, Mary Ann (sr.), *see* Sebastian, Mary Ann
  Groom, Samuel (jr)   91
  Groom, Samuel (sr.)   95, 106
  Groom, Sarah   129, 253
  Groom, Thomas   91
  Groom, William   106
  Harding, Mary Ann Kate   212, 288-9
  Heath, Rebecca   244
  Hewitt, Elizabeth Maria *see* Hooper, Elizabeth Maria
  Hinks, Sarah *see* Groom, Sarah
  Hooper, Angelina   71
  Hooper, Ann   71
  Hooper, Christine   71
  Hooper, Elizabeth Maria   71
  Hughes, David   280, 281

## Index

Layton, Ann   119
Leese, Elizabeth *see* Abel otherwise Able, Elizabeth
Leese, Mary Jane ('Mary J.L.')   **130**, 131
Lewis, Louisa   176, 228, 295–6
Lewis, Maria   295
Lewis, Robert (jr.)   293, 295
Lewis, Rosina   100, 295
Linney, William   288
Lock, Harriet   244
Matthias, Jane Elizabeth   **130**, 132, 241
Matthias, Sarah Ann   **130**, 241
Newman, Harriet   119
Page, Charles John   **247**, 297–8
Page, Elizabeth *see* Greenleaf, Elizabeth (jr.)
Page, Elizabeth Kate   **247**, 297
Page, James   **247**, 297–8
Purcell, Jane Amelia   286
Purches, Mary   192
Rees otherwise Reeves, Mary Ann *see* Groom, Mary Ann
Reeves otherwise Rees, Mary Ann *see* Groom, Mary Ann
Roberts, William Henry Holdaway   111
Sanford, Ann *see* Hooper, Ann
Saxton, Phoebe Joanna   **247**, 297
Seager, William   122–3
Sebastian, Mary Ann   95, 106
Spratt, Charles   **126–7**
Spratt, Henry   **126–7**
Stroud, Emma   244
Stroud, John   244
Tallon, Rosina *see* Lewis, Rosina
Tallon, Henry   295
Thomas, John   224
Tyler, Elizabeth   237
Wafer, James   64–5
Weedon, Louis (Lewis)   101, 251–2
Wilkinson, Alfred   284
Wilkinson, Emily   284
Wilkinson, George (jr.)   284
Wilkinson, Henry   284
Woodley, Clara Martha Eliza   290
Woodley, Clara   244, 290–1
Woodley, John   117, 136

Baptism   xxiii, 8, 10, 46, 57, 59, 61, 75, 92, 93, 100, 101, 109, 112, 180, 235, 292
Barracks   10, 24, 56, 72, 125, 135, 139, 154, 180, 208
Beerhouses, beershops   4, 192, 193, 219, 220, 257, 272
Bigamy, and bigamous unions   18, 131, 212, 232, 233, 244, 245, 246, 248, 253, 268, 280, 281, 289, 291, 298, 303
Birthplace, brides and parents with same   70
'Boaz, Professor' *see* Abortion, abortionist
Booth, Bramwell   90
Booth, Catherine   90
Brothels, *see* Prostitution
Budget, *see* Making ends meet
Burial
  consecrated / unconsecrated ground   292–3, 295, 296–7
  pauper's plot   296–7, 299

Childcare   38, 46, 57, 58, 59–61, 62, 65, 95, 100, 106, 107, 108, 117, 121, 124, 133, 168, 176, 204, 205, 212, 297, 302
Child maintenance, entitlement to   110, 111
Children
  causes of death   101, 251–2
  family size   **102, 103**–6
  in laterally-extended households   133
Churches
  St Ann's, Portsmouth dockyard   287
  St John the Evangelist Roman Catholic cathedral   92, 250
  St John, Anglican chapel of   92, 237 and n. 30
  St Mary's, Fratton   82, 83, 84, 280, 290, 296
  St Thomas's, Portsmouth   281
'Civilian'
  civilian brides   76, 80, 95, 109
  civilian grooms   78–9, 80, 106–7, 303
  civilian grooms' preference for civilian brides   80–1, 303
  civilian husbands   78
  use of term   xxii
Cohabitation   37, 118, 198, 232, 233, 245, 291, 303
Contraception   109, 110
Correspondence
  communication between ship and shore   257–9

*Index*

literacy (of seamen and relatives)   2, 6, 11, 110, 256, 257, 258
postal / mail services   11, 16, 172, 257–9
self-censorship   257–8
survival of correspondence   1, 11, 257–8
Court sentences   191–2, 195–7, 205, 207, 208, 211–12, 215, 218, 226–7, 230, 237, 266, 268
Courting: introductions, wooing   79–80, 85, 89, 96
Courts
　assizes   202, 233
　cost of prosecution   218
　gendered value of witness statements   218–20, 223
　magistrates, magistrates' courts ('police courts')   192, 195, 196, 202, 204, 205, 211, 215, 218, 223, 233
　non-appearance of prosecutor/prosecutrix   205, 226
　quarter sessions   204, 208, 233
Coverture   215
Crimean War   79, 238, 263
Criminal offences
　assault   14, 81 n. 20, 191, 196, 201, 202 n. 7, **203**, 209–12, 215
　disorderly conduct   189–90, **203**
　fighting   **203**, 211
　fraud, and attempted fraud   27, 36, **203**, 213, 214, 215
　indecent behaviour   189, 191, **203**, 210, 288
　marital violence   217–31, 234, 253, 293, 294
　offensive language   **203**, 210
　personation   31, 38, 201, 213, 214, 215
　riotous behaviour   189–91, 195, **203**, 224
　scams   56, 212–15, 240, 281
　theft   14, 29, 81 n. 21, 170, 185, 190, 191, 195, 197, 201, 202 and n. 7, **203** and n. 11, 204–9
　'trousering'   190, 204–8

DARVO ('Deny, Attack, Reverse Victim and Offender')   225
Davey/Leese/Plummer/Matthias household   125 n. 35, 129–32, 171, 240–2

Deaths (children)
　convulsions   101, 252
　dentitional diarrhoea   290
　malnutrition   101
　marasmus   101
　skin disease and fever   286
Deaths (seamen)
　accident   8, 41, 223, 261, 275
　battle injuries   4, 275, 28
　bone cancer   279
　cholera   111, 264
　chronic bronchitis   261, 292
　disease of the brain   294
　dropsy   298
　drowning   259, 260, 261, 275, 276, 279, 282
　exhaustion   279
　explosion   260
　falls   260, 261, 282, 297
　influenza   275
　phthisis pulmonaris (tubercular disease of the lung)   60, 246
　poison   278
　skin cancer   261
　steam leakage   260
　suffocation   260
　syphilis   261, 294
　tropical disease   261
　typhus   264, 275
　yellow fever   275
Deaths (seamen's women)
　ages at death   **282–4**
　accident   282, 297, 298
　bronchitis   289
　burns   298
　childbirth   284–5, 286
　chronic gastritis   287
　'epilepsia'   287
　exhaustion   297, 298
　'moribus cordis' (heart disease)   51, 287, 292, 297
　hemiplegia   297
　'insanity from brain disease'   287
　lung congestion   287
　'dropsy' (oedema due to heart failure)   287
　paralysis   298
　phthisis pulmonaris (tubercular disease of the lung, consumption)   286, 287, 290, 292, 297, 299
　pneumonia   298
　senile dementia   297

331

## Index

sloughing of inside of mouth   287
syphilis   288, 294
typhoid   297
ulceration of bowels   287
ulceration of palate and windpipe   287
Desertion, social consequences of   265–8
Disease and disablement (seamen's)
  bronchitis   261
  catarrh   261
  dysentery   261
  fall injuries   260–1
  fracture(s)   260–1
  frostbite   261
  loss of limb(s), eye(s), etc   261
  malaria   92 n. 67, 261, 266
  ophthalmia   261
  pneumonia   261
  psychological damage   262
  scalds   261
  syphilis   261
Disease, sexually transmitted
  association with prostitution   42, 187, 261, 262–3, 287–8, 294–5
  in armed forces   4, 42–3, 187, 294
  mercury treatment   294
  syphilis   261, 288, 294
Dissenting, non-conforming churches   293
Divorce   234, 242, 253, 266, 275
'Divorce' by naval desertion   266
Domestic abuse   *see* Marital violence
Drink, drinking, drunkenness   14, 31, 41–2, 74, 81 and n. 21, 175, 186, 189–90, 191, 192–3, 201, 215, 216, 219, 223–4, 227, 229, 259, 287, 301, 302, 303
Dutch East India Company   28

Emotional impact of naval family life   254–5, 257–8, 258–9, 267, 271–4
Entrusted children   8, 48, 57–8, 62, 108
  illegitimate children   62
Entrusted children: named individuals
  Maria [surname not stated]   243
  Sarah Jane [surname not stated]   190
  Ball, George   63
  Banyer, Mary Elizabeth   211 n. 61
  Baxter, Caroline   65
  Cameron, Eliza   175
  Cavander, Eliza   243
  Dominy, Mary Ann   59, 60
  Edwards, Henry   46
  Gill, Fanny   268
  Hartman, Henry   46
  Jennings, Albert   62–3
  McCard, Ann   64
  Menhinnick, Harriett otherwise Harriott   236–7
  Plummer, Mary Jane   **130**, 131, 241
  Pooley, Jane   139
  Reece, James   108
  Ruggills, Albert *see* Jennings, Albert
  Smith, James   64, 287
  Walsh, Catherine   62
  Weedon otherwise Wheden, William Richard (William jr.)   58–9, 148–53, 249–50
  Wilson, Henry   64
Environment
  air pollution   282
  communal facilities   131, **135**–7, 155, 163, 174, 262
  comparative space per person   139, 141
  construction materials   137, 142
  court accommodation   52, 72, 113, 134–7, 143, 155, 193, 196, 201, 222, 230, 257, 258, 291
  damp   11, 262, 282
  mould   11, 257, 282
  multi-occupancy dwellings   117, 137, 138–41, 143
  overcrowding   4, 132, 137, 138–40, 142, 184, 222, 241, 262, 286
  street lighting   10, 136
  stress caused by   222
  vermin   11, 282
  water supply   4, 10, 138, 142, 160–1, 163, 164, 282
  WCs and privies   10, 131, 136, 137, 262

Farewells   254–5
Franklin expedition   5, 157, 192, 207, 259, 268

Garrison towns   4, 179, 186, 187
Genograms   **10, 126, 128, 130, 247**
Gold lacework, and sewing of   4, 151
Greenwich Hospital   267
Greenwich, Royal Hospital School   34, 75

# Index

*Hampshire Telegraph*   178, 183, 191, 201–2, 204, 205, 209, 210, 212, 216, 219, 224, 226, 242, 248, 276, 286, 291
Hardwicke Report *see* Royal Commission into the Best Means of Manning the Navy, 1859
Haslar Hospital, Gosport   34, 111, 227, 230, 235, 236, 262, 278, 293, 294, 298
Haulbowline Hospital   275, 276 n. 3
Health
   dietary deficiency, malnutrition   101, 282
   hereditary conditions   282
   poverty as contributing factor   286
   pregnancy and childbearing   61–2, 282, 284, 286
HM Dockyard: occupations   17, 70, 150, 174, 220, 230, 285, 297
HM Ships
   *Agamemnon*   251, 252
   *Ajax*   68, 131, 132, 241
   *Albion*   119, 174, 176
   *Alert*   45, 269
   *Amphitrite*   57, 119, 128, 276
   *Angel*   280
   *Arethusa*   69, 196
   *Arrogant*   172, 278
   *Assistance*   157, 159
   *Birkenhead*   28, 190, 208, 276–9, 283
   *Blenheim*   18, 30, 45, 56, 59, 62, 107, 127, 129, 183, 196, 207, 209, 211
   *Britannia*   16, 127, 166, 183
   *Camperdown*   159
   *Captain*   259
   *Columbine*   60–1
   *Comet*   126
   *Conflict*   159
   *Contest*   69, 139, 153, 160
   *Cormorant*   28
   *Cornwallis*   284
   *Crocodile*   71, 119
   *Dauntless*   235–6, 262, 265, 266, 275–6
   *Discovery*   269–**70**
   *Dragon*   166, 224
   *Driver*   65, 276
   *Edinburgh*   60
   *Encounter*   57, 263
   *Enterprize*   175
   *Erebus*   260
   *Excellent*   16, 23, 29, 30, 36, 45, 51, 56, 58, 60, 61, 64, 91, 92, 108, 109, 111, 127, 128, 139, 154, 165, 166, 172, 175, 176, 183, 184, 191, 192, 205, 224, 244, 246, 248, 250, 252, 268, 285, 297
   *Fantome*   266
   *Ferret*   255
   *Firebrand*   242
   *Fisgard*   45
   *Flamer*   131–2, 241
   *Flying Fish*   87
   *Fox*   155, 190, 224, 266, 268, 269
   *Furious*   267
   *Gladiator*   182, 183
   *Goliath*   12
   *Hecate*   28, 151, 184, 204
   *Hercules*   92, 250
   *Hogue*   69, 108, 214, 235
   *Horatio*   45
   *Illustrious*   8, 39, 45, 63, 100, 136, 227, 268
   *Jaseur*   45
   *Leander*   45, 51, 206, 208, 212, 214, 279, 280, 288
   *Lily*   150
   *Linnet*   273
   *Marlborough*   238
   *Niger*   30, 45, 65
   *North Star*   111
   *Penelope*   64, 208, 224
   *Persian*   276
   *Phaeton*   56, 57, 58, 78, 91, 92, 173, 250
   *Pique*   91
   *Plumper*   166
   *Portland*   45
   *Powerful*   166, 225
   *Prince Regent*   39, 60, 139, 235–8, 266
   *Queen*   51
   *Rainbow*   85
   *Resistance*   132, 188, 231
   *Resolute*   8, 117, 138, 153, 157, 159, 192, 207, 244, 261, 268, 269, 289
   *Retribution*   100, 184, 210, 262
   *San Josef*   159
   *Sealark*   45
   *Simoom*   255
   *Southampton*   159
   *Sphinx*   160
   *Sprightly*   129
   *St Vincent*   30, 131
   *Superb*   46, 270

*Terrible*   45
*Thetis*   208, 261, 265, 266
*Venerable*   34
*Vengeance*   58, 90, 92, 149, 250, 252, 260, 261, 268
*Vernon*   28, 97
*Vesuvius*   58
*Victory*   16, 46, 80, 97, 111, 123, 127, 131, 139, 159, 165, 183, 191, 207, 211, 227, 241, 242
*Wellington*   159
HM Yacht *Victoria and Albert*   22, 97, 128, 139, 207, 210, 243
Home environment   4, 5, 134–43
Household structure
   co-resident adult offspring   114–15, 116–17
   co-resident extended kin   116, 125
   co-resident relatives other than offspring   115, 124–5
   co-resident unmarried daughters   120–1
   co-resident unmarried sons   120–1
   'flat-share' and 'house-share'   124–5
   'household heads', per census convention   115, 144–5
   seamen's women living in households of parents or parents-in-law   90, 96–7, 118–19, 120–1, **122**, 172, 240, 303
   Type A: 'small households' (lone woman, or two-person households)   114–15, 116–17
   Type B: households headed by allottees, with co-resident adult offspring   115, 118–21
   Type C: households with co-resident married allottee offspring   115, 121–3
   Type D: households accommodating co-resident non-relatives   115, 124–5
   Type E: laterally-extended (co-resident siblings)   115, 125–33
Housing costs   **141**–3

Illegitimacy, illegitimate children   28, 62, 99, 100, 106, 108–12, 176, 232, 248, 253, 289, 296
Incest see Affinal relationships
*Iolanthe*   249

Journalists, journalism   81 n. 21, 90, 191, 202, 204, 205, 209, 210, 214, 218, 219, 224

Kin, kinship   xiv, 8, 10, 57, 69, 72, 81, 115, 116, 117, 124, 129, 249
   extended   72, 99, 111, 116, 125, 131, 241
   'lateral' kin   114, 115, 125–33
   'vertical' kin   114

Locations (non-Portsea Island)
   Aldingbourne (Sussex)   283
   Alverstoke (Hampshire)   59, 82
   Athlone (Ireland)   69
   Arctic, the   16, 53, 157, 192, 261, 268, 269, **270**, 289
   Australia   16, 266
   Barbados   262
   Bedfordshire   70
   Berkshire   67
   Birmingham   35, 94
   Bitterne (Hampshire)   243, 291, 292
   Bognor (Sussex)   252
   Botley (Hampshire)   69
   Bridport (Dorset)   82
   Bristol   82
   Broadwindsor (Dorset)   90
   Camberwell (Surrey)   245
   Capel Sound, Australia   266
   Channel Islands   67, **68**, 82
   Chatham (Kent)   1, 3, 13, 70, 74, 81, 82
   China   257
   Corfu   132
   Cork, and Cove of Cork (Ireland)   15, **68**, 69, 82, 131, 173, 209
   Cornwall   69, 70, 72, 82, 116, 180, 285
   Cornwallis Island (Arctic Archipelago)   268
   Deal (Kent)   82
   Devon(shire)   **68** and n. 5, 69, 70, 82, 116, 132, 180, 224, 279
   Devonport (Devon)   3, 24 n. 35, 45, 70, 74, 81, 82, 265, 275, 285, 294
   Dorset   59, 67, 90, 116, 227, 252
   East Indies   266
   Fareham (Hampshire)   69
   Finisterre (Spain)   259
   Gibraltar   132, 260
   Gosport   206, 213, 239, 294
   Greenhithe (Kent)   268, 290

*Index*

Griffiths Island (Arctic Archipelago)   268
Guernsey (Channel Islands)   236, 239
Guildford (Surrey)   67
Halifax (Nova Scotia)   132
Halifax (Yorkshire)   35
Hampshire   35, 67–8, 69, 70, 71, 82, 88 n. 48, 127, 178, 181, 243
Hull (Yorkshire)   77, 284
Ireland   **68**–9, 70, 173, 181
Isle of Wight   **68**–70, 173, 181
Kent   69, 70, 252
Lanreath (Cornwall)   285
Leeds (Yorkshire)   116
Lisbon (Portugal)   270, 275, 279–80
London   31, 36, 82, 153, 234, 251, 257
Luton (Bedfordshire)   284
Lyme Regis (Dorset)   67
Malta   82, 132, 257, 270
Manchester (Lancashire)   35, 94
Mediterranean Sea   16, 252, 264
Melbourne (Australia)   267
Mevagissey (Cornwall)   235
Midland counties   82
Montevideo (Uruguay)   266
Newmarket (Suffolk)   284
North America   109
Oxfordshire   70
Pacific Ocean   16
Peru   257
Plymouth (Devon)   4, 51, 62, 69, 70, 82, 159, 261, 263
[Plymouth] Hoe (Devon)   256
Proti (Greece)   238
Queenstown (Ireland)   132, 173, 241
Reading (Berkshire)   67
San Francisco   266
Sheerness (Kent)   3, 82, 132, 252
Shetland Islands (Scotland)   286
Somerset   70
South America   16
South Bersted (Sussex)   252–3
South Stoneham (Hampshire)   291
Staffordshire   116
Stoke Damerel (Devon)   82, 132, 285
Stonehouse (Devon)   82
Surrey   67
Sussex   67, **68**, 252, 283
Tagus, River (Portugal)   270
Wash, The (East Anglia)   82
Valparaiso (Chile)   257, 261, 266
Vancouver   261
Vancouver Island   266

Wales   xxiii, 5, 35, **68**, 69, 88, 94, 106, 138, 151, 203
West Africa   16, 132, 257
West Country   69, 71, 72, 81, 82
West Indies   16
Whitehall (London)   6, 8, 60, 82, 143, 182
Wiltshire   67, 266
Winchester (Hampshire)   266
Woolwich (Kent)   82, 241, 268
Locations (Portsea Island)
  Abercrombie Street   263
  Albion Street   280, 293
  Armoury Lane   188
  Arundel Place   263
  Basin Street   290
  Bath Square   257
  Beeston Street   290
  Berkeley Street   288–9
  Blossom Alley   156, 258, 294
  Britain Street   136
  Butcher Street   60
  Chalton Street   244
  Chapel Row   173
  Church Road   176
  Clarence and Forehouse Barracks, Portsea   56
  College Street   64
  Common Hard ('The Hard')   57, 64, 65, 110, 175, 196, 207, 210, 244
  Constitution Square   69
  Cross Street   298
  Cumberland Street   45, 172
  Dean Street   **135**–6
  Diamond Street   243, 291
  Duke Street   281
  Frederick Street   46
  Frett's Court   184
  Gloucester Street   34, 59, 60, 297, 298
  Grigg Street   291–2
  Guildford Street   297
  Havant Street   **137**–41, 184, 237, 240, 241
  Hawke Street   71, 138, 237
  Hearns Court   193
  Hereford Street   51, 107
  Hewlin's Court   71, 134
  High Street   191, 196
  Hobbs Court   110–11, 116–17, **135**–6, 176, 193, 230, 286, 289, 290, 293
  Hot Walls, the   256
  King Street   241

335

*Index*

Kings Bench Alley   127
Kingston district   67, 82, 111
Landport district   59, 67, 69, 92, 132, 135, 152, 214, 241, 250, 285, 290, 294
Lion Gate   150
Lion Terrace   64, 83
Marylebone Street   252
Meeting House Alley   279, 280
Mitre Court   188
Moore's Square   242
Nile Street   244
North Street   119, 152
Ordnance Row   175
Portsea township   24, 34, 45, 51, 59, 60, 62, 64, 67, 69, 70, 71, 72, 81, 83, 92, 101, 110, 116, 135, 137, 138, **140**, 160, 169, 173, 176, 184, 191, 212, 219, 220, 222, 230, 237, 238, 241, 245, 246, 258, 262, 279, 283, 288
Portsmouth Harbour   16, 23, 61, 91, 127, 129, 242, 250
[Portsmouth] Point   256
Portsmouth township   136, 137, 141, 193, 224, 238, 257, 281, 287
Primrose Alley   131, 240–1
Prospect Street   193
Queen Street   24, 110, 152, 175, 191, 210
Round Tower, the   256
Short Row   287
Smith's Court   193
Southampton Row   196, 209
Southsea   59, 206, 292
St George's Square   128
St Mary Street   131
Sun Street   139, 193
Surrey Street   45
Temple Street   184
Trafalgar Street   59, 250
Victoria Terrace   45, 172
Voller Street   150
Warblington Street   46, 193
West Street   192, 291
White's Row   191, 196, 207, 208, 210
Wilton Street   119
Lock ward(s)   288, 294

Making ends meet
  borrowing and lending of goods   155, 157, 170, 197, 200
  borrowing money, obtaining credit   65, 157, 167–9, 170, 197, 267
  debt   13, 157, 167, 168–9, 178, 197, 204, 205, 206, 209, 259, 274, 301
  debt to parish   142, 165–7, 184–5
  distraint of goods   167
  eviction   68, 167
  flitting, removals   11, 157, 170–3, 178, 200, 204
  food and drink   23, 54, 109, 116, 120, 154, 160, 161, 162–3, 164, 174, 204, 208, 271
  heating and lighting   116, 124, 152, 161–2
  'hierarchy of resort'   177
  lodgers, living as and taking in of   55, 56, 71, 99, 116, 117, 129, 133, 136, 146, 152, 157, 173–7, 179, 193, 198, 204, 280, 298, 301
  makeshift economy   147, 197, 200
  parish poor rates   27, 116, 141, 163, **164**, 165–7, 175, 180, 251, 304
  pawning, pawnbrokers   10, 39, 155, 156, 157, 169–70, 177, 178, 185, 190, 194, 197, 200, 204, 206, 207, 208, 272
  rational family strategy   183
  shortfall, deficit   158, 164, 199
  water   4, 116, 138, 142, 154, 160–1, 163, 164
Mariner 'visitors' or lodgers   24, 175
Marriage
  adultery   37, 59, 92, 112, 233, 234, 242, 252, 253, 268 n. 83
  affinal (unlawful) in-law unions see Affinal relationships
  age at first marriage   87–90, 93–5
  age-difference of bride and groom   84–5, 96
  avunculate marriage   244, 245
  benefits of postponement   89–90
  brides' age at marriage   85–98
  brides' fathers' occupations   75–8, 80–1, 95
  brides' seamen-fathers and -fathers-in-law   80
  by banns   82, 83, 84, 85, 238, 244, 248, 249, 281
  by bishop's licence or certificate   60, 69, 84–5, 97, 238, 248, 249, 252, 281

*Index*

by civil registration 83–4, 85, 244, 279, 280, 281, 291–2, 293
child brides 90, 93–8, 101
compatibility of bride and groom 74, 98
connection of civil marriage to Poor Law 83
cost of marriage licence 84, 252
deserted wives 234, 267
early marriage condoned in the naval community 95–8
friction 221, 222, 271–4
infidelity 229, 233, 253, 256, 259
'Kingston' (euphemism for St Mary's parish church as place of marriage) 82–3
'line abreast' 232 and n. 2, 282
'line astern' 232 and n. 2, 282
marital violence 217–32, 253
non-conformist and Roman Catholic churches, rites, etc 83, 84, 92, 232, 250
place of marriage 81–5
separation, separated 14, 57, 59, 78, 104, 132, 147, 233, 234, 250, 253, 259, 281, 294
wedding notices 83
'Married widows' 48, 267
Matrilocality 121, 173
Menarche, age of 94, 106
Menstruation 90, 109
Mental illness or crisis 245, 263–4, 289
Merchant navy
conditions, food, medical treatment 2, 30
pay, prospects 2, 30, 265
reporting of ships' movements 276
sea areas frequented by 5
seamen's service in 235
Millbank prison chaplain's report 192, 195
Motherhood
adoption, private 111–12
age at birth of first surviving child 112, **113**
conception outside marriage 13, 97, 99, 109, 242, 290
contraception 109, 110
Maternal grandmothers raising grandchildren 99–100, 110, 288–9

Motherless children 30, 36, 38, 48, 57, 62, 90, 106, 107, 108, 110, 131, 132, 239, 285, 290, 302

Naval dependants charged with prostitution-related offences
ages of 195
civil status 215
fines imposed 195, 196, 215
gaol sentences 191, 192, 195
seamen-husbands' trades 216
Naval outfitters and tailors 4, 17, 151
'Neighbourhood norms and customs' 96, 117, 127, 157, 158, 160, 183, 199, 254

Occupation (paid work)
ages of waged allottees 148–**9**
as declared in census 145–6
as specified in census directives 144–6
charring **148**, 153, 156, 167, 295
corset (stay) factories 150, 152, 153, 187
corset- or stay-making 151, 152, 166
dressmaking **148**, 151, 175, 176, 187, 188
estimated wages 149–50
husbands' trades cited in census 144–6, **148**
laundering **148**, 153–5, 156, 168, 221, 256
laundresses' access to wash-houses 154
outwork 115, 151, 152, 153, 204, 206
participation in workforce 146–7
self-employment and enterprises 155, 156, 175
sewing, needlework, millinery, tailoring, shirtmaking **148**, 150–3, 194
Old Bailey records 185, 203, 204
Original sources
census schedules, enumerators' books 100, 108, 112, 115, 129, 144, 145 and n. 8, 146, 147, 149, 171, 174, 179, 186, 187, 188, 193, 228, 250, 292, 298
civil registers of births, marriages and deaths xxiii, 10, 55, 62, 83, 84, 99, 100, 109, 112, 116, 237, 239, 244
maps, town plans 10

*Index*

parish guardians' minute books   10, 178, 181, 182, 183, 251
parish registers of baptisms, marriages and burials   xxiii, 55, 58, 62, 63, 71, 75, 87, 93, 95, 100, 106, 109, 111, 112, 116, 237, 238, 280, 288, 289, 290, 292, 295
Pitcairn Report   25–6, 37, 38
seamen's correspondence   1, 11, 36, 257–8, 259, 262, 264–5, 270–1
seamen's service records   9, 11, 18, 58, 61, 235, 267, 290
seamen's wills   9, 63
ships' allotment registers   xxiii, 6, 7, 8, 9, 18 n. 4, 31, 44, 52, 54, 62, 67, 82, 92, 116, 143, 171, 173, 182
ships' muster and description books   xxii, 8, 12, 18 n. 14, 19, 61, 91 n. 62, 166, 192, 225, 242 n. 63, 261, 262, 265, 268, 269, 275 and n. 2, 282, 290
slum inspection reports   10, 137
surgeons' logs   9, 261, 268, 286
Orphaned siblings   57, 62
Other named individuals
　Austin, Captain Horatio   268
　Bennet, Lydia (Jane Austen character)   129
　Bramley, Frank   259
　Bromley, R.M.   25
　Cavander, Charles   243
　Cavander, Emma   243
　Collins, Wilkie   259
　Dickens, Charles   138, 259
　Giddy, Emma   285
　Gilbert and Sullivan   249
　Gillray, [James]   244
　Gladstone, W.E.   249
　Holl, Frank   259
　Johnson, Maria Laura   239
　Keast, Britannia   285
　Long, Sarah, later Matthias   241
　McRoy, Sarah, later Menhinnick, later Coley   238–9
　Stead, W.T.   90
　Vanden Bergh, Arnoldus   257
　Winton, Robert   238
　Winton, John   13

Parish guardians (Poor Law guardians)   10, 83, 145, 158, 177, 178, 179–82, 183, 198, 199, 234, 250–1

Parish minster(s)   33, 38, 52, 54, 73, 83, 110, 235, 243, 249, 293
Parish overseers   33, 180, 182, 185
Parish in-relief *see* Workhouse
Parish out-relief   14, 25, 33, 39, 46, 53–4, 56, 58, 72, 136, 143, 145, 153, 176, 178–85, 198, 199, 214, 228, 229, 234, 245, 250, 251, 267, 293, 294, 295, 296
　allottee-paupers   52, 53, 56, 146, 179, 181, 198, 199, 296
　amount granted   177, 183–5
　children's contribution to paupers' household income   184
　moral judgement as disqualification   185, 198–9
　as housing subsidy   184
　for single parents   183
Parish poor rate
　arrears, non-recoverable   141, 166, 167, 185
　arrears, recoverable   141, 165, 166, 184
　gross estimated rent (GER)   141
　poor rate books (PRBs)   141–2, 163, 164, 165, 166
　voiding of debt   167
　weekly rate payable   163–4
Paupers (Hampshire and Portsea Island)   178, 198
Pawning *see under* Making ends meet
Police, Metropolitan   189
Police, Portsea Island   189, 192, 194, 205, 216, 225, 227, 234
Police   38, 81, 186, 189, 190, 192, 196, 198, 201, 213, 215, 218, 219, 220, 225, 227, 242
Poor Law Commissioners   181
Port towns
　hazards (social, environmental, health)   134, 137, 162, 179–80, 186, 282
　port town prostitutes   89, 186, 192–3, 197, 301
　port town women   vii, 4, 39, 42, 55, 72–3, 77, 80, 134, 180, 186, 223–4, 282, 302
Portsea Island
　house numbering systems   10, 171 n. 71
　Board of Guardians   83, 178
　[Poor Law] Union   10, 178, 198, 250, 251

338

# Index

Post office agents, Navy  257
Pregnancy, premarital  99, 100, 108–12
Prison hulk *York*  61
Privies, WCs  4, 10, 131, 136, 137, 230, 262
Prostitution: overview  4, 14, 81, 178, 185–200, 204, 223, 230–1, 262–3, 300, 301
Prostitution
   as income source  194, 295
   associated trades  194
   association with port and garrison towns  4, 186, 187
   association with seamen's women  185–6, 197–8
   association with shared accommodation  188, 192–3
   brothels  4, 57, 125, 176, 188, 193, 262, 263
   census recording of  186, 187–8
   'clandestine' prostitutes  187
   'common prostitute'  186–9
   defendants appearing in Portsmouth courts  188–90
   'disorderly prostitute'  189, 190, 235
   'dressmaker' self-description  151, 175, 187, 188
   'idle and disorderly prostitute'  189
   naval community's attitude to  14, 199, 200, 300–1
   'nymph[s] of the pavé'  191, 192, 291
   parish relief, refusal of  181, 182
   payments, earnings  194
   pimps  4, 186, 196, 198
   Portsmouth, numbers of prostitutes  186–7
   relationship with local police  198
   Royal Commission witness statement  199
   sex trade, paid sex  14, 43, 178, 185, 186, 188, 189, 190, 195–9, 204, 205, 214, 295, 300, 301
   statistics  186–8
   'trousering' as an associated offence  190, 204–8
Pubs  4, 10, 24, 46, 57, 59, 64, 65, 138, 169, 193, 201, 202, 213, 214, 223, 224, 240, 241, 257, 272, 273
Pubs, named
   Earl St Vincent  64, 65
   Fortune of War  193
   Hole in the Wall  64, n. 79
   Tap of One  193

The Cricketers  59

Rent
   arrears  157, 170, 178
   as percentage of working income  **141**–2
   minimum, mean average, maximum  164
Report, Hardwicke *see* Royal Commission into the Best Means of Manning the Navy, 1859
Report, Pitcairn *see under* Royal Navy
Reporters *see* Journalists, journalism
Reputation of seamen's women
   alcohol, drinking  42, 301
   as prostitutes  287–8, 300, 301
   in song, caricatures, cartoons, imagery  35, 41, 42, 193, 197, 200, 254, 287, 300
   prejudice  199, 202, 232
   seamen's reputation, applied by proxy  42, 302, 303
   seamen's daughters as prospective brides  80–1
   'sailor's wife' as pejorative term  77, 302
   'the joke'  77, 300, 302
Respectability  1, 14, 36, 65, 83, 89, 117, 133, 152, 161, 167, 174, 185, 187, 188, 194, 196, 197, 200, 201, 205, 210, 211, 214, 215, 216, 234, 235, 242, 245, 291, 302, 303
Returns from sea  4, 5, 38, 53, 59, 61, 89, 91, 92, 96, 110, 120, 127, 133, 170, 192, 221, 231, 233, 238, 240, 252, 254, 255, 264, 269, **270**–5, 276, 289, 294
Riot, Portsea (1850)  220
Riotous behaviour  189–90, 191, 195, 224
Royal Commission into the Best Means of Manning the Navy, 1859
   on allotments  38–40
   on imposing allotment claims on sailors  28
   on Louisa Wafer as recruiting agent  64–5
   on men's freedom to allot  40, 54
   on naval pensioners' income  52
   on occupations open to seamen  17
   witness statement re: prostitution  199
Royal Marines

## Index

dependants' eligibility for parish relief   181–2
Royal Marines Artillery (RMA)   18, 167, 190, 227
Royal Marines Light Infantry (RMLI)   18
Royal Marines – named individuals
  Boland, Archibald, bandsman   57
  Bragginton, Joseph, private   131
  Chitty, John, private third class   260
  Collins, John, bandsman   46
  Dowsett, John, marine artilleryman (and brothel-keeper)   193
  Hall, James, bandsman   46
  Hartman, George, bandsman   46
  Lawrence, Pierre, bandsman   174
  Lewis, Robert, private third class   8, 100, 136, 210, 227, 228–30, 293–5
  Mould, James, marine private   39
  Reilly, William, musician   57
  Thomas, William, fifer   224
  Wilson, John, bandsman   64
  Woods, William, bandsman   57
  'Worner' [Warner], William, private   56
Royal Marines rates and trades, general and individual
  bandsman   18, 22, 46, 57, 64, 67
  corporal   18
  fifer   196, 224
  gunner   190
  musician   17, 21, 46, 175
  private   18, 39, 50, 56, 100, 131, 154, 196, 206, 207, 210, 227, 293, 297
  sergeant   18, 237, 239, 295
Royal Naval College, Portsmouth   277
Royal Navy
  Accountant General   9, 25, 36
  alcohol consumption, attempts to reduce   42
  auctioning-off of dead seamen's effects   262
  burials at sea   262
  clerks (civilian), role of   26, 34, 35, 83, 92, 237, 303–4
  'compensation' for victuals purchased on shore   23
  condition of naval families on shore   25, 39, 182
  Continuous Service   3, 4, 9, 15, 19, 143 and n. 33, 151, 238, 239, 288

desertion   8, 19, 25, 38, 59, 91, 225, 234, 235–8, 239, 241, 252, 260, 264–9
discovery service   5, 16, 102, 143, 157, 159, 164, 192, 207, 257
  communication with shore   16, 257
  double pay   16, 153, 157, 159, 164, 192, 268, 269
  impact on health   262
  risks and dangers   16
disrating   29, 241
fictitious individuals entered on books   17
fines   8, 38
fleet size   15–16
flogging   221
forfeiture of pay and/or pension   19, 236, 238, 265, 267, 268
funerals   262
harbour duty, harbour-based ships   16, 20, 23, 24, 91, 127, 128, 129, 183, 242, 255
hulk accommodation   24, 61, 125
impact of warfare   4–5, 102, 147, 186, 217, 221, 254, 263, 275
invalided from service, or to hospital   8, 9, 19, 59, 62, 92 and n. 67, 227, 228, 229, 235, 238, 239, 262, 266, 268, 269, 276 n. 3
language   80, 124
leave   16, 23–6, 41, 42, 92, 107, 109, 118, 172, 183, 192, 220, 222, 264, 271, 273
manning   2, 17, 28, 38, 52, 64, 213
navy and naval trade-associated culture   42, 75, 82, 124, 133, 183, 221, 230, 258
quitting naval service   2, 25, 30, 41, 70, 283, 303
married man's allowance   87
married quarters   24
men's conduct   9, 20, 38, 196, 226, 228, 262, 266, 268, 269, 289
'old ships' (former shipmates)   91
'paid off', paying-off money   8, 19, 53, 89, 96, 121, 143, 158, 172, 186, 267, 268, 269
Patriotic Fund   238, 289
pay   xxii, 1, 3, 6, 15, 16, 17, 19–23, 29, 36, 38, 40, 41, 43, 45, 142–3, 144, 155, 157, 158–9, 164–5, 182, 206,

# Index

207, 212, 243, 245, 251, 255, 264, 268, 269, 277, 279, 280, 299
pension, pensioners 3, 11, 17, 34, 52, 53, 55, 58, 60, 70, 76, 95, 96, 108, 150, 165-6, 167, 175, 195, 216, 218, 228, 230, 238-9, 250-1, 252, 267, 278, 285, 286, 288, 289, 294, 298, 299
pensions department 250-1
Pitcairn Report 14, 40, 60, 62
prize money 11
proportion of married seamen 27
recruitment and retention 27, 30, 38, 64, 65, 69, 72, 84, 194, 239
remittance system 3, 6, 25-7, 28, 30, 39, 48
'run-ashore' 4, 41, 109, 222, 224, 272
seamen's aliases 108, 214, 235-7
steamships, steam power 16, 20, 22, 257, 260
stoppage of pay (as punishment, upon desertion, or due to death or being invalided) 38, 46, 66, 229, 262, 264, 266, 267, 268, 280
straggling, straggler xxiii, 8, 225, 237, 265, 267
Supplementary List for Wages and Victuals (SLWV) 12, 268, 269
technological progress 12, 15, 16, 102
troopships 12, 132, 180, 276
'unhappy ship' 8, 265
widows' pension 17, 34, 146, 150, 166, 198, 238-9, 278, 288, 298, 299
'wives at sea', women on board RN ships xxii, 12, 34, 171 n. 70
Royal Navy rates and trades, general and individual
    able seaman (AB) 8, 18, 22, 28, 29, 30, 36, 45, 51, 56, 57, 58, 59, 65, 71, 85, 87, 90, 91, 107, 111, 117, 127, 132, 136, 155, 165, 175, 176, 184, 188, 190, 191, 196, 207, 208, 211, 235, 241, 242, 244, 249, 260, 262, 266, 268, 278, 284, 288, 291, 297
    armourer 21, 48
    blacksmith 21, 48
    boatswain (bosun) 11, 17, 18, 20, 23, 34, 45, 48, 50, 52, 58, 63, 159, 183, 191, 199, 209, 234, 237, 263, 297

boatswains' mate 21, 48, 62, 78, 90 n. 55, 91, 97, 252, 278
captain of', e.g. hold, forecastle, mizzen top 18-19, 21, 28, 45, 48, 69, 111, 119, 128, 129, 139, 150-1, 166, 173, 184, 196, 205, 208, 240, 262
captain's coxswain 18, 21, 48, 139
carpenter 18, 20, 23, 48, 50, 76, **79**, 80, 95, 159, 183, 196, 216, 236, 243, 262, 263
carpenter's crew 18, 22, 48, 51, 214, 224, 279
carpenter's mate 18, 21, 48, 119, 148, 268
caulker 18, 21-2, 50, 262
caulker's mate 21-2
cook (captain's, wardroom, etc) 17, 18, 22, 46, 48, 62, 63, 160, 184, 221, 261
cook, ship's 1, 18, 21, 48, 122, 224, 240
cooper 17, 21, 48
cooper's crew 22
coxswain 17, 18, 21, 48
gunner 17, 18, 20, 23, 45, 48, 67, 75, 95, 128, 145, 146, 154, 172, 182, 183, 196, 204, 205, 246, 248, 252, 255, 297
gunner's mate 21, 48, 51, 58, 64, 91, 108, 128, 153, 166, 192, 211, 214
gunner, trainee 23, 92
junior ratings 48-9
keeper of apartments 22
master at arms 21, 48, 111, 240, 262
ordinary seaman 11, 18, 22, 23, 25, 45, 48, 50, 56, 76, 108, 139, 188, 196, 212, 240, 241, 262
painter 17, 22, 48
petty officers 18, 23, 48, 71, 80, 87, 219, 283, 284
quartermaster 21, 45, 48, 58, 119, 175, 207, 240, 262
ropemaker 21, 48, 51, 263
sailmaker 21, 48, 123, 131, 132, 150, 241, 264, 287
sailmaker's crew 22, 45
sailmaker's mate 21, 262
senior petty officers 48, 74
ship's corporal ('crusher') 18, 21, 48, 211
shipwright 18, 70, 76, **79**, 216, 220, 263

341

sick berth attendant   22, 48, 69, 268, 269
steward (gun room, pusser's, etc)   17, 21–2, 23, 48, 65, 69, 128, 153, 160, 262, 266
stoker   17, 20, 21, 22, 28, 30, 45, 48, 126, 129, 145, 196, 207, 208, 210, 211, 224, 260, 262, 265, 278, 283
stoker, leading   18, 21, 48, 64, 129, 210
substantive and non-substantive roles   6, 18, 23
trimmer of lamps   22
warrant officers   17–18, 19, 23, 25, 35, 50, 69, 87, 115, 119, 159, 199, 267, 297

'Sailor', 'seaman': use of terms   xxii
Sailors' Homes   24
Sailors' Rests   24 n. 35
Scams   56, 212–15, 239–40, 281
Seamen-brothers   4, 30, 36, 44, 48, 51, 53, 54, 55, 56, 57, 60, 61, 77, 78, 79, 91, 96, 127, 131, 156, 175, 205, 207, 241, 246, 248, 265, 267, 276, 278, 280, 284, 286
Seamen-grooms
  age at marriage   85–9
  fathers' occupations   75–81
Seamen-husbands
  general   48, 75, 115, 117, 118–19, 123, 174, 181, 183, 231, 233, 275–8, 280–1
  absence due to ships' commissions   xxii, 3, 4, 5, 13, 14, 15, 35, 43, 77, 88–9, 90, 95, 97, 99, 106, 107, 109, 110, 111, 112, 114, 117, 119, 124, 127, 129, 132, 133, 147, 155, 170, 185, 195, 197, 230, 231, 232, 239, 240, 242–3, 261, **270**, 271, 274, 276, 300, 303
Seamen-sons   51–2, 53–4, 75, 123, 154, 175
Seamen – named individuals
  Aldridge, Francis, boatswain's mate   278
  Allen, George, able seaman and boatswain   191
  Allen, Thomas, gun room steward   **128**, 129
  Angeley, James, able seaman   260
  Angus, William, quartermaster   262

Appleby, John, able seaman   28
Aylward, George, sailmaker   150
Ball, Swinfen, boatswain third class   63
Banyer, George, stoker   211
Barrett, William, captain of the hold   173
Baxter, William, able seaman   65
Benson, Robert, able seaman   268
Betsworth otherwise Bettesworth, William   85 n. 38, 280–1, 297
Black, William, able seaman   165
Blake, William, ordinary seaman   196
Bond, Richard, captain's coxswain   139
Bone, Eli, able seaman   8, 117, 244–6, 268–9, 289–91
Brown, Joseph   210
Bull, Charles   266
Burrough, John, ordinary seaman   139
Cameron, John, able seaman   175
Carlisle, Frederick, gunner's mate   61
Cavander, James, able seaman   242–4, 256, 291–2
Charlo, James, able seaman   246–9, 298
Clack, Henry, gunner   182
Clarke, Charles, boatswain second class   263
Coles, William, gunner's mate   153
Connell, Thomas, able seaman   191
Cummings, John, seaman's schoolmaster   191–2, 291
Davey, Joseph, stoker   129–32
Davey, Samuel, able seaman   **130**–2, 241
Davidge, James, able seaman   175
Davis, George, able seaman   36–7
Davis, George, sick berth attendant   268, 269
Dominy, Joseph, able seaman   59–61
Donald, Benjamin   278
Doward, David, carpenter's crew   224–5, 226–7, 234
Edwards, Alexander, carpenter's mate   119
Edwards, Charles, captain's cook   46
Elliott, William, boatswain   224, 243, 291
Fawkes, Joseph, sub-officers' steward   160
Ferret, Reuben, gunner's mate   51

## Index

Fleming, James George, able seaman and quartermaster   246–8, 279
Fleming, Richard, ordinary seaman   212, 288–9
Ford, John, ordinary seaman and chief boatswain   11, 270–1
Ford, Joseph, master at arms   111
Gibbons, William, rate unspecified   71
Gill, William, carpenter's mate   268
Gimblet otherwise Gimblett, William, able seaman and carpenter's crew   51, 85, 279, 280, 282
Goodfellow, John, captain of the hold   166
Goodger, Richard, able seaman   139
Gough, George, able seaman   127
Grace, Benjamin   278
Grant, George, captain of the mast   184–5
Greenleaf, George, able seaman   **247**, 248
Greenleaf, John, boatswain   34, 75, **247**
Guithard, Henry, gunner's mate   211
Hall, Richard, captain of the afterguard   69
Harrison, John, able seaman   196, 209
Harvey, Francis, sailmaker   287
Harwood, William, able seaman   129
Henning, Francis, captain's cook   160
Henry, William, able seaman   155
Hewitt, James, petty officer   71
Hicks, Charles, gunner second class   45
Hillyard, William, able seaman   188
Hinks, Henry, captain of the foretop   129
Hoar, Thomas, ordinary seaman   188
Holdaway, John, able seaman   111
Holman, John, able seaman   56
Hooper, Sampson, able seaman   28, 71
Hooper, Thomas, able seaman   71
Hopkins, William, captain of the afterguard   150–1
Hussey, Joshua, stoker   30
Jenkins, Thomas, alias William Menhinnick, able seaman   235–9, 252
Jenkins, William, able seaman   176
Jennings, Cornelius (jr.), rate unknown   63
Jennings, Cornelius (sr.), 'mariner', rate unknown   63
Johns, James, gunner first class   159
Johns, William, 'mariner', rate unknown   281
Jones, John, gunner third class   255
Kelsey, George, stoker   283
Kemp, Richard, carpenter first class   159
Kendall, Joshua, gun room cook   184
Kennell, John, able seaman   60–1
Lath, William, able seaman   166–7
Layton, Michael George, quartermaster   119
Leary, John, boatswain's mate   97
Lee, Frederick, able seaman   184
Lee, Henry, engineer   165
Lee, William, naval pensioner   165–6
Leese, William, able seaman   **130**, 131, 241
Lemmon, James, captain of the foretop   119
Lewis, Charles Job, able seaman   244–5, 24
Lucas, Richard, gunner's mate   128
Lumb, George, ordinary seaman, gunner second class, et al   45, 172
Mackenzie, Robert   11, 264
MacLaughlan, James, able seaman   57
Marks, Thomas, ship's corporal   211
Marshall, Benjamin, gunner's mate   139
Martell, Benjamin, able seaman   30
Martin, George, boatswain   45
Matthias, James, ship's cook   18, **130**, 240, 241, 242
McCard, Alexander, leading stoker   64, 65
Menhinnick, William, able seaman, alias Thomas Jenkins   235–9, 252, 266
Messum, Henry William, gunner's mate   51, 80
Mogg, Samuel, rate unspecified   71
Mould, Richard, ordinary seaman   56
Nancarrow, William, able seaman   278
Nancarrow, William, captain of the afterguard   28, 71

343

*Index*

Oddy, Charles, gun room steward   69, 154, 160
Oliver, Joseph, gunner third class   **128**–9
Page, Richard, gunner   75, 248–9, 287, 291, 297, 298
Parker, Philip, able seaman   30
Parnell, John, carpenter's mate   148–9
Patterson, John, able seaman   297
Phillips, Isaac, private   190
Phippard, Reuben, quarter master, gunner's mate and able seaman   85
Plummer, George, sailmaker   **130**, 131, 132, 241
Pooley, Charles, captain of the hold   139
Purcell, James   286–7
Quinnell, Frederick, able seaman   184
Reece otherwise Rees, William, gunner's mate   108, 214, 235
Reeves, Henry, sailmaker   123
Reeves otherwise Rees, William, leading stoker   129
Richards, George, stoker   224
Riley, William, gunner third class   255
Roberts, William, captain of the main top   111, 136
Robinson, John, able seaman   190
Rowsell, James, able seaman   30
Ruggills otherwise Ruggles, George   62–3, 91, 278
Sanford, William, able seaman and boatswain's mate   71
Saunders, Richard, gun room steward   65
Saxton, John, gunner   75, 248
Saxton, Joseph, ordinary seaman   56
Scargill, Henry, able seaman   107–8
Scott, George, boatswain second class   166–7
Seager, John, ship's cook   122
Shepherd, Robert, able seaman   29
Simpson, Bill (William)   1, 11, 264–5
Smith, George, able seaman   176
Smith, Thomas, able seaman   28
Smith, Thomas, captain of the mizzen top   205
Smith, Thomas, gunner's mate   64, 166, 287
Spratt, Richard, stoker   **126**–7
Stallard, James, able seaman   165

Stevens otherwise Stephens, Joseph, gun room steward, sub(ordinate) officers' steward   85
Steward, James, gunner   154
Tapscott, James, stoker   278
Thomas, Hugh   280–1
Thompson, Alexander, able seaman   268
Tipple, John, quartermaster   175
Tyler, William, boatswain   237
Van Studer, Thomas, boatswain third class   209
Wallbridge, James, captain of the forecastle   139
Walsh, [John], boatswain's mate   62
Watson, George, captain of the mast and 'seaman rigger'   129
Weedon otherwise Wheadon, William, quartermaster and gunner's mate   58–9, 78, 90–3, 95, 97, 101, 251–2, 266, 283
'Wheden, George, mariner' (false name)   92, 250
Wheeler, James, able seaman and stoker   45
Whitehead, Henry, able seaman   191
Whitehead, John   246
Wilkinson, George, able seaman   58–9, 90–3, 249–53, 284
Winsor, Frederick, stoker   265
Winsor, Henry, stoker   265
Woods, Thomas, stoker   28
Wright, Robert, leading stoker   210
Young, Thomas, able seaman, sailmaker's crew and quartermaster   45
Seamen's memoires, autobiographies, recollections   12, 13, 212, 253
Settlement (parish entitlement per place of birth)   72–3, 180–2
Shipwreck
 donations for relief of the bereaved   277
 HMS *Birkenhead*   28, 276, 277, 278, 279, 283
 HMS *Captain*   259
 HMS *Flamer*   132, 241
 impact upon survivors and relatives   223, 132, 277
Soldier(s), soldiers' dependants, soldiering   12, 17, 72, 74, 79,

344

*Index*

105, 139, 141, 147, 154, 179, 180, 220–1, 235, 276, 288
Statutes
  *Act for Marriages in England* 1836  83
  *Contagious Diseases Acts* (CDAs), 1860s  4, 186, 187, 188
  *Convict Prisons Act* 1853  209
  *Deceased Brother's Widow's Marriage Act* 1921  281
  *Deceased Wife's Sister's Marriage Act* 1907  249
  *Manning of the Army and Navy Act* 1796  27
  *Manning of the Navy Act* 1795  27
  *Marriage Act* 1823  82
  *Marriage Act* 1835  96, 248, 291
  *Matrimonial Causes Act* 1857  234
  *Mutiny Act* 1837  235
  *Naval Deserters Act* 1847  266
  *Naval Enlistment Act* 1853  3
  *Navy Act* 1727  25, 26
  *Navy Act* 1758  26, 36
  *Navy Act* 1786  33
  *Navy Act* 1806  29, 36, 38
  *Navy Pay, Etc, Act* 1854  37
  *Offences Against the Person Act* 1837  109
  *Outdoor Relief Prohibitory Order* 1844  179, 234
  *Pawnbrokers Act* 1800  169
  *Pay of the Navy Act* 1830  28, 33, 36, 38, 214, 267
  *Penal Servitude Act* 1853  209
  *Penal Servitude Act* 1857  209
  *Poor Law Amendment Act* ['New Poor Law'] 1834  179
  'Quota Acts' *see Manning of the Navy Act* 1795
  *Town Police Causes Act* 1847  188
  *Vagrancy Act* 1824  188
  *Vagrancy Act* 1838  188
  *Wages and Prize Money in the Navy Act* 1809  92
Suicide  81 n. 21, 167, 202

'The Sailor's Farewell' (trope)  254
'The Sailor's Return' (trope)  254
'Top-slicing' of male wage  158–9, 242
Trafalgar, Battle of  4, 79, 263
Tudor seamen's women  74

Visitors  24, 55, 56, 116, 127, 146, 173, 237, 241, 243, 246, 271, 298

Waterloo, Battle of  4
Widowers
  as stepfathers  106–7
  option of trusteeship  107–8
  remarriage  107, 108
  widowed fathers, eligibility for allotment  36, 52
Widows
  poverty  53–4, 179, 234, 239, 281–2, 299
  as stepmothers  106–7, 239
  remarriage  85, 108, 239, 248, 267, 277, 278–82, 303
Women living alone  116, 119–20
Workhouse  10, 13, 56, 62, 64, 83, 101, 139, 143, 167, 178, 179, 181, 245, 248, 287, 292, 293, 294, 295, 296, 297, 298, 299

Printed and bound by CPI Group (UK) Ltd, Croydon, CR0 4YY
03/12/2024
14603884-0001